FOUNDATIONS OF AMERICAN EDUCATION

Fifth Edition

L. Dean Webb
Arizona State University

Arlene Metha
Arizona State University

K. Forbis Jordan
Arizona State University

PEARSON

Merrill
Prentice Hall

Upper Saddle River, New Jersey
Columbus, Ohio

Library of Congress Cataloging-in-Publication Data

Webb, L. Dean.
   Foundations of American education / L. Dean Webb, Arlene Metha, K. Forbis Jordan.–5th ed.
      p. cm.
   Includes bibliographical references and index.
   ISBN 0-13-171670-0
1. Education–United States. I. Metha, Arlene. II. Jordan, K. Forbis (Kenneth Forbis), III.
Title
LA217.2.W43 2007

370.93–dc22
2006000634

Vice President and Executive Publisher: Jeffery W. Johnston
Executive Editor: Debra A. Stollenwerk
Senior Editorial Assistant: Mary Morrill
Development Editor: Amy Nelson
Assistant Development Editor: Elisa Rogers
Production Editor: Kris Roach
Design Coordinator: Diane C. Lorenzo
Photo Coordinator: Valerie Schultz
Cover Designer: Ali Mohrman
Cover Image: Getty One
Production Manager: Pamela D. Bennett
Director of Marketing: David Gesell
Senior Marketing Manager: Darcy Betts Prybella
Marketing Coordinator: Brian Mounts

This book was set in Garamond Book by Carlisle Publishers Services. It was printed and bound by
R.R. Donnelley & Sons Company. The cover was printed by Phoenix Color Corp.

Photo Credits: Please see photo credits on page viii.

Pearson Education Ltd.
Pearson Education Singapore Pte. Ltd.
Pearson Education Canada, Ltd.
Pearson Education Japan

Pearson Education Australia Pty. Limited
Pearson Education North Asia Ltd.
Pearson Educación de Mexico, S.A. de C.V.
Pearson Education Malaysia Pte. Ltd.

10 9 8 7 6 5 4 3 2 1
ISBN: 0-13-171670-0

PREFACE

W hy is the understanding of the fundamentals of American education important to today's teachers? Explore this text for answers to this fundamental question and gain an understanding of how the evolution of education affects today's teaching and learning. Become a highly qualified teacher by connecting theory and practice, and by examining the philosophical and historical roots of education, its current structures, and the future of the field.

ABOUT THE FIFTH EDITION

In the fifth edition, the authors emphasize how learning about the past and its impact on education today leads readers to become highly qualified, professional teachers through reflection and active engagement.

This Fifth Edition Invites You to:

Reflect on educational issues through...

Ask Yourself feature
Encourages readers to think critically about and make the connection between the historical content being discussed and their future teaching practice. A great tool for readers as they develop their personal educational philosophy. (Chapters 1, 3, 4, 5, and 9).

 ASK YOURSELF

Do I Want to Be a Teacher?

Historical Note feature
Familiarizes readers with key individuals and hallmark educational developments in the history of education. Located in every chapter, the feature encourages readers to reflect on, research, and explore this topic further by going to this text's Companion Website at **http://www.prenhall.com/webb**.

 HISTORICAL NOTE

The Columbian School: The First Formal
Teacher Training Institution

Professional Reflection **feature**

Presents readers with practical advice and reflections from national board certified teachers across the nation and teachers of the year in some of the major issues facing education regarding classrooms, students, parents, colleagues, and administrators. Located in every chapter, the feature invites readers to analyze the reflections by going to this text's Companion Website at **http://www.prenhall.com/webb**.

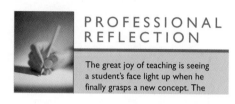

PROFESSIONAL REFLECTION

The great joy of teaching is seeing a student's face light up when he finally grasps a new concept. The

For Your Reflection and Analysis **margin notes**

Encourage readers to stop, think critically, and reflect on chapter content, connect it to their own thinking and beliefs, and then consider their responses. Located in every chapter, these questions help readers learn and practice reflection now and throughout their teaching careers. Readers are encouraged to answer the questions online via the Companion Website to promote reflection and group discussion.

For Your Reflection and Analysis

Should schools concern themselves with questions regarding the origin of the universe? Why or why not? *To submit your response online, go to http://www.prenhall.com/webb.*

CW

Actively engage in current educational issues...

Video Insight DVD **and** *Video Insight* **feature**

- Dynamic ABC News video clips now available to readers on the DVD *(Contemporary Perspectives in American Education, Volume II)* in the back of this text bring to life current and controversial issues in education today. In this edition, three new videos have been added for a total of 9. See pages xxiii–xxiv for a complete description of the ABC News videos.
- Each of the 9 videos is integrated into Chapters 1 and 7–14 through a text feature titled *Video Insight*. This feature includes a synopsis of the video segment along with thought-provoking questions that challenge readers to explore and consider the real-life experiences presented and their impact on their future teaching practices. Readers are invited to submit their responses online via the Companion Website.

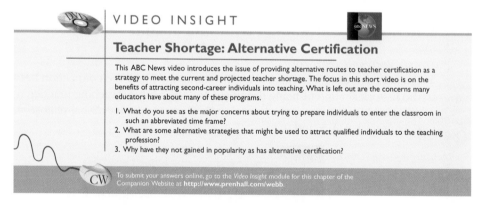

VIDEO INSIGHT

Teacher Shortage: Alternative Certification

This ABC News video introduces the issue of providing alternative routes to teacher certification as a strategy to meet the current and projected teacher shortage. The focus in this short video is on the benefits of attracting second-career individuals into teaching. What is left out are the concerns many educators have about many of these programs.

1. What do you see as the major concerns about trying to prepare individuals to enter the classroom in such an abbreviated time frame?
2. What are some alternative strategies that might be used to attract qualified individuals to the teaching profession?
3. Why have they not gained in popularity as has alternative certification?

CW To submit your answers online, go to the *Video Insight* module for this chapter of the Companion Website at **http://www.prenhall.com/webb**.

Controversial Issue **feature**

Presents controversial school issues with *for* and *against* statements for readers to consider. Questions guide them to consider their values and beliefs and to critically analyze both sides of the issue. Readers are encouraged to take a side by posting their responses via the Companion Website (Chapters 1, 2, 3, 6, 7, 8, and 10–16).

CONTROVERSIAL ISSUE

Individual Performance-based Pay

Become a professional...

NEW! Professional Development Workshop
Begin your journey to become a professional, highly qualified teacher through the
workshop activities at the end of each chapter.

PROFESSIONAL DEVELOPMENT WORKSHOP

- *NEW! Prepare for the Praxis™ Examination*—This case-based feature
  provides opportunities to assess reader knowledge of chapter content in realistic
  case studies similar to those found in the *Praxis® II Principles of Learning and
  Teaching* examination. Readers are encouraged to practice answering these case-
  based scenarios and receive immediate feedback on the Companion Website.
- *Build Your Knowledge Base*—Questions provide opportunities for readers to
  integrate and personalize the chapter content as they interact with their peers in
  discussion formats.
- *Develop Your Portfolio*—Incorporating the INTASC standards, these activities
  serve as a guide as readers begin to develop materials to include in their
  professional portfolio. These activities involve readers in a range of activities,
  including visiting websites of professional organizations and beginning to work on
  their own philosophy of education.
- *Explore Teaching and Learning: Field Experiences*—Invite readers to apply
  chapter content to themselves and school settings through opportunities for
  interviews with educators and classroom observation.
- *Professional Development Online*—Directs readers to the Companion Website
  at **http://www.prenhall.com/webb** to gain access to a variety of questions,
  activities, and exercises to help build their knowledge of chapter content. Below are
  just a few items on this text's Companion Website.
  - *NEW! Classroom Video*—Located on the textbook's home page, link to other
    Websites that give readers the opportunity to view quality classroom video
    footage.
  - *Teaching Tolerance*—To go to this organization's website and complete
    activities to explore issues and topics dealing with how to teach tolerance to
    readers, click on the *Teaching Tolerance* module for this chapter.
  - *Self-Test*—Readers can review terms and concepts presented in this chapter by
    clicking on the *Self-Test* module for this chapter.
  - *Internet Resources*—Websites related to topics in this chapter are located on
    the *Internet Resources* module for this chapter of the Companion Website.
- *NEW! INTASC Correlation Grid*—This guide, found on the inside front and back
  covers, connects chapter content to the INTASC standards for easy reference.

Integrated Supplements for Students

Video Insight DVD—These videos, packaged on DVD in the back of this text, allow
students to view the videos outside of class.

Companion Website: at **http://www.prenhall.com/webb**
The Companion Website provides students with resources and immediate feedback on exercises and other activities linked to the text. These activities, projects, and resources enhance and extend chapter content to real-world issues and concepts. The Companion
Website contains the following modules or sections:

- Professional Development Workshop
  - Prepare for the Praxis™ Examination
  - Develop Your Portfolio
  - Professional Development Online
    - NEW! *Classroom Video*—links to websites give students the opportunity to view quality classroom video footage.
    - *Teaching Tolerance*—Activities to guide students to explore issues and topics relating to diversity in the classroom and beyond.
    - *Self-Test*—includes multiple choice, true/false, and essay questions with automatic grading to provide immediate feedback to students
    - *Internet Resources*—links to websites that relate to and enhance chapter content
- Chapter Objectives—outlines key topics and concepts in the chapter.
- NEW! *Historical Note feature*—focuses on key individuals and educational developments in the history of education. Readers are able to research and explore the topic further online.
- NEW! *For Your Reflection and Analysis*—chapter margin note questions help readers learn and practice reflection now and throughout their teaching career. Readers are encouraged to answer the questions online to promote reflection and group discussion.
- *NEW! Professional Reflection feature*—connected to the chapter feature, this module is based on advice and experiences with students, parents, their colleagues, and administrators from teachers around the nation, including board certified teachers and teachers of the year, students are able to analyze and respond to the advice online.
- *NEW! Controversial Issue feature*—presents controversial school issues with *for* and *against* statements for readers to consider. Questions guide them to consider their values and beliefs and to critically analyze both sides of the issue. Readers are encouraged to take a side by posting their responses online.
- *Video Insight feature*—thought-provoking questions challenge readers to explore and consider the real-life experiences presented and their impact on their future teaching practices and submit their responses online.
- NEW! *Annotated Key Terms*—provide students with chapter key terms, allowing them to visit websites for additional information.
- Web Extension Activities—Include meaningful activities that connect to chapter content and provide Web-based resources for students to use when completing the activities.
- PowerPoints—*PowerPoint* presentations for each chapter can be used as a study guide.

OneKey Course Management Content

OneKey is Prentice Hall's exclusive new resource for students and instructors. OneKey is an integrated online course management resource featuring everything students and instructors need for work in or outside of the classroom, available in the nationally hosted CourseCompass platform, as well as WebCT and Blackboard.

VangoNotes

Study on the go with VangoNotes. Just visit **VangoNotes.com** website and download chapter reviews from your text and listen to them on any mp3 player. Now whenever you are—whatever you're doing—you can study by listening to the following for each chapter of your textbook:

- Big Ideas: Your "need to know" for each chapter
- Practice Test: A gut check for the Big Ideas—tells you if you need to keep studying
- Key Terms: Audio "flashcards" to help you review key concepts and terms
- Rapid Review: A quick drill session—use it right before your test

VangoNotes are **flexible;** download all the material directly to your player, or only the chapters you need. And they're **efficient.** Use them in your car, at the gym, walking to class, wherever. So get yours today. And get studying.

SafariX

SafariX is Prentice Hall's exciting new digital platform where students can subscribe to textbooks at savings of up to 50% over the suggested list of print editions. SafariX will help meet the needs of students who are looking for lower cost alternatives to print editions.

For more information about OneKey, VangoNotes, or SafariX, please contact your local Merrill representative prior to placing your textbook order.

Supplemental Materials for the Instructor

Instructor's DVD

Instructor's Manual/Media Guide and Test Bank. This manual provides concrete suggestions to actively involve students in learning and to promote interactive teaching using the *PowerPoints*, Companion Website, and the ABC News videos. Each chapter contains chapter outlines, student objectives, lecture and discussion guides, extended projects and assignments, and an instructional media guide. The test bank includes multiple-choice, true/false, and essay questions.

Computerized Test Bank Software. This software gives instructors electronic access to the test questions printed in the Instructor's Manual, and allows them to create and customize exams on their computer. Available on a dual platform CD for Macintosh and PC/Windows users.

PowerPoint Slides. Designed as an instructional tool, the *PowerPoint* presentations for each chapter can be used to present and elaborate on chapter content.

Companion Website

Located at **http://www.prenhall.com/webb**, the Companion Website for this text is organized by chapter and includes a wealth of resources for both students and instructors.

Instructor Resource Center

Instructor supplements can also be accessed at our Instructor Resource Center located at **http://www.prenhall.com**. The Instructor Resource Center opens the door to a variety of print and media resources in downloadable, digital format. Resources available for instructors include:

- Instructor Manual/Media Guide and Test Bank
- Computerized Test Bank
- *PowerPoint* slides
- Request and/or review Webb's OneKey WebCT and Blackboard course content
- Obtain instructions for downloading a Blackboard or WebCT e-pack

Your one-time registration opens the door to Prentice Hall's premium digital resources. You will not have additional forms to fill out or multiple user names and passwords to remember to access new titles and/or editions. Register today and maximize your time at every stage of course preparation.

For instructors who have adopted this text and would like to receive book-specific supplements, please contact your Prentice Hall sales representative, call Faculty Services at 1-800-526-0485, or e-mail us at merrillmarketing@prenhall.com. We look forward to hearing from you.

Acknowledgments

The authors wish to recognize the many persons who have contributed to the preparation of this edition and the previous editions of this text. First, we give special recognition to the teachers and other educators who work each day to provide learning opportunities for the youth of America. Second, we wish to acknowledge the diverse scholars who have provided the past and present record of the development of elementary and secondary education and the researchers and policy analysts who are charting the future. Third, we express our appreciation to our students and professional colleagues for their critical comments and suggestions about ways to improve the fifth edition. We extend a special thanks to the many National Board Certified Teachers who responded to our request for professional reflections.

We extend our sincere appreciation to Executive Editor Debbie Stollenwerk and her most valuable assistant, Mary Morrill, and to Development Editors Amy Nelson and Elisa Rogers and Production Editor Kris Roach. We also want to thank Lorretta Palagi for her thorough copyediting. To the various reviewers of the fourth edition, we extend our sincere thanks for their constructive comments. Their efforts helped us improve the text in this fifth edition. For their participation, we extend our thanks to Morris L. Anderson, Wayne State College; Paul D. Bland, Emporia State University; Donna Adair Breault, Illinois State University; Kerry Holmes, University of Mississippi; and JoAnn H. Hohenbrink, Ohio Dominican University.

Special recognition and appreciation is extended to Teresa Jordan for her assistance and contributions to the manuscript.

Photo Credits

Scott Cunningham/Merrill, pp. 2, 11, 13, 192, 235, 332; Getty Images, Inc., p. 18; Bill Bachmann/PhotoEdit Inc., p. 23; Larry Hamill/Merrill, p. 30; Kathy Kirtland/Merrill, p. 38; Anthony Magnacca/Merrill, pp. 39, 316, 377, 400; Patrick White/Merrill, p. 42; Russ Curtis/courtesy of AFT, p. 45; Stockbyte, pp. 52, 203; courtesy of L. Dean Webb, pp. 59, 340; Corbis, p. 61 (left); Erin Hogan/Getty Images, Inc. – Photodisc, p. 61 (right); Tony Freeman/PhotoEdit Inc., pp. 63 (left), 201; courtesy of the Library of Congress, p. 63 (right); © Bettmann/Corbis, pp. 65 (left), 128; Joe Sohm/Chromosohm/The Stock Connection, p. 65 (right); EyeWire Collection/Getty Images – Photodisc, p. 72; AP Wide World Photos, pp. 77 (left), 283; University of Chicago Archives, p. 77 (right); Bettmann/Corbis, pp. 80 (left), 87 (left); courtesy of Ted Sizer, p. 80 (right); National Library of Medicine, p. 82; courtesy of Miller Photography, p. 87 (right); Bob Daemmrich/The Image Works, p. 89; courtesy of Michael Apple, p. 93; © Alinari Archives/Corbis, p. 100; © Scala/Art Resource, p. 104; Dagli Orti/Picture Desk, Inc./Kobal Collection, p. 106; The Granger Collection, pp. 110, 132; Getty Images Inc. – Hulton Archive Photos, p. 115; Corbis/Bettmann, pp. 118, 139, 146, 149, 160, 167; Library of Congress, p. 153; John F. Kennedy Library, p. 173; Ed Clark/Getty Images/Time Life Pictures, p. 174; Diana Walker/Time Life Pictures/Getty Images, p. 180; Arthur Tilley/Getty Images, Inc. – Taxi, p. 196; Leslye Borden/PhotoEdit Inc., p. 213; Tom Watson/Merrill, pp. 220, 393, 396 (right); © Ed Kashi/Corbis, p. 224; Michael Newman/PhotoEdit Inc., pp. 228, 326, 362; Shelly Katz/Shelly Katz Photographer, p. 231; Richard Hutchings/PhotoEdit Inc., p. 244; Dennis MacDonald/PhotoEdit Inc., p. 248; Mary Kate Denny/PhotoEdit Inc., p. 252; © Jim Erickson/Corbis, p. 255; Frank Siteman/Stock Boston, p. 263; Ron Chapple/Getty Images, Inc. – Taxi, p. 272; Jeff Atteberry, Indianapolis Star/SIPA Press, p. 276; Rob Crandall/The Stock Connection, p. 286; Andersen Ross/Getty Images, Inc. – Photodisc; p. 294; David Young-Wolff/PhotoEdit Inc., p. 300; Elena Rooraid/PhotoEdit Inc., p. 304; Shelley Boyd/PhotoEdit Inc., p. 311; Stephen Ferry/Getty Images, Inc. – Liaison, p. 349; courtesy of Scottsdale Unified School District, p. 350; Arthur Tilley/Getty Images Inc. – Stone Allstock, p. 353; Nancy P. Alexander/PhotoEdit Inc., p. 365; Jacksonville-Courier/Clayton Statler/The Image Works, p. 368; courtesy of Elliot W. Eisner, photographed by Eric Hausman, p. 372; KS Studios/Merrill, p. 384; A. Ramey/PhotoEdit Inc., p. 388; Valerie Schultz/Merrill, p. 396 (left); NASA/Johnson Space Center, p. 410; Michal Heron/PH College, p. 415 (left); Krista Greco/Merrill, p. 415 (right); courtesy of Florida Virtual School; p. 420; © Kim Kyung-Hoon/Reuters/Corbis, p. 421.

Teacher Preparation Classroom

TEACHER PREP

MERRILL
PRENTICE HALL

See a demo at
www.prenhall.com/teacherprep/demo

Your Class. Their Careers. Our Future. Will your students be prepared?

We invite you to explore our new, innovative and engaging website and all that it has to offer you, your course, and tomorrow's educators! Organized around the major courses pre-service teachers take, the Teacher Preparation site provides media, student/teacher artifacts, strategies, research articles, and other resources to equip your students with the quality tools needed to excel in their courses and prepare them for their first classroom.

This ultimate on-line education resource is available at no cost, when packaged with a Merrill text, and will provide you and your students access to:

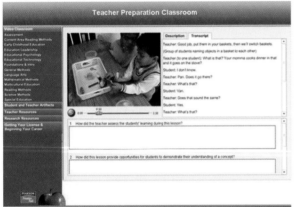

Online Video Library. More than 150 video clips—each tied to a course topic and framed by learning goals and Praxis-type questions—capture real teachers and students working in real classrooms, as well as in-depth interviews with both students and educators.

Student and Teacher Artifacts. More than 200 student and teacher classroom artifacts—each tied to a course topic and framed by learning goals and application questions—provide a wealth of materials and experiences to help make your study to become a professional teacher more concrete and hands-on.

Research Articles. Over 500 articles from ASCD's renowned journal *Educational Leadership*. The site also includes Research Navigator, a searchable database of additional educational journals.

Teaching Strategies. Over 500 strategies and lesson plans for you to use when you become a practicing professional.

Licensure and Career Tools. Resources devoted to helping you pass your licensure exam; learn standards, law, and public policies; plan a teaching portfolio; and succeed in your first year of teaching.

How to ORDER Teacher Prep for you and your students:
For students to receive a Teacher Prep Access Code with this text, instructors must provide a special value pack ISBN number on their textbook order form. To receive this special ISBN, please email **Merrill.marketing@pearsoned.com** and provide the following information:
- Name and Affiliation
- Author/Title/Edition of Merrill text

Upon ordering Teacher Prep for their students, instructors will be given a lifetime Teacher Prep Access Code.

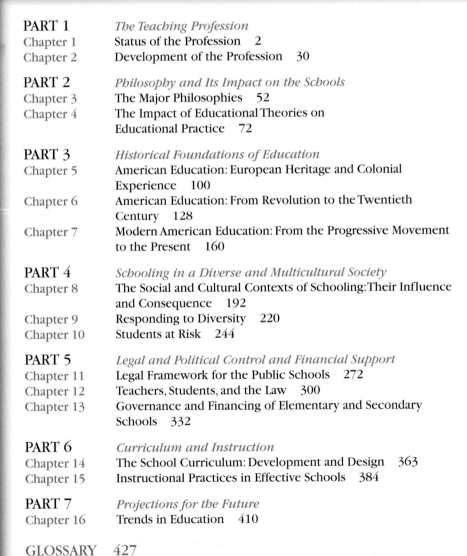

BRIEF CONTENTS

CONTENTS

Note: Every effort has been made to provide accurate and current Internet information in this book. However, the Internet and information posted on it are constantly changing, so it is inevitable that some of the Internet addresses listed in this textbook will change.

VIDEO INSIGHT DVD AND
VIDEO INSIGHT FEATURE

VIDEO INSIGHT   abc NEWS

Teacher Shortage: Alternative Certification

This ABC News video introduces the issue of providing alternative routes to teacher certification as a strategy to meet the current and projected teacher shortage. The focus in this short video is on the benefits of attracting second-career individuals into teaching. What is left out are the concerns many educators have about many of these programs.

1. What do you see as the major concerns about trying to prepare individuals to enter the classroom in such an abbreviated time frame?
2. What are some alternative strategies that might be used to attract qualified individuals to the teaching profession?
3. Why have they not gained in popularity as has alternative certification?

CW To submit your answers online, go to the *Video Insight* module for this chapter of the Companion Website at **http://www.prenhall.com/webb**.

CONTEMPORARY PERSPECTIVES
IN AMERICAN EDUCATION

Now available on DVD in the back of every copy of *Foundations of American Education*, Fifth Edition!

Engage your readers through ABC News video segments, available on DVD in the back of their book, focusing on controversial educational issues that illustrate chapter content relevancy and bring chapter content to life. Video Insight sections within the text indicate when a video is available and offer a short summary of each episode.

TOPICS INCLUDE

TEACHER SHORTAGE: ALTERNATIVE CERTIFICATION

This ABC News video introduces the issue of providing alternative routes to teacher certification as a strategy to meet the current and projected teacher shortage. The focus in this short video is on the benefits of attracting second-career individuals to teaching. What is left out are the concerns many educators have about many of these programs.

Chapter 1
Running time 2:10

THE REUNION

This ABC News video segment examines the lasting effects of school integration that began during the 1960s civil rights struggle. *The Reunion* celebrates the reuniting of classmates who participated in a controversial social experiment on school integration that took place in one of America's wealthiest suburbs, Shaker Heights, Ohio. Each of the former students had the opportunity to live and attend school in a racially mixed community starting in kindergarten through high school.

Chapter 7
Running time 38:22

FAMILY LOST, FAMILY FOUND: CHILDREN RAISED BY THEIR GRANDPARENTS

This ABC News video segment explores the lives of children from four families whose parents abandoned them because of drug abuse, incarceration, mental illness, or other social problems. Besides being deserted by their parents, the children have one other experience in common. They are all being raised by their grandparents. Plagued with insurmountable challenges, these children survive. The video depicts the true meaning of love, compassion, and devotion on the part of grandparents and great-grandparents, one of whom is 85 years old.

Chapter 8
Running time: 57:59

CONTROVERSY OVER BILINGUAL EDUCATION

This ABC News segment follows up with California students and teachers two years after the passage of Proposition 227, which ended California's 22-year program of bilingual education in public schools.

Chapter 9
Running time: 3:10

ACTION, REACTION, AND ZERO TOLERANCE: HOW FAR IS TOO FAR?

This ABC News segment focuses on the effect of zero-tolerance policies being adopted in school districts across the United States. Featured are discussions with students, families, and school and law enforcement representatives regarding the cases of two students, eight-year-old Hamadi Alstead of Irvington, New Jersey, who was suspended after playing cowboys and Indians using a gun made of paper, and high school sophomore Ryan Scofield, of Loudon County, Virginia, who was refused in his request to carry a cardboard sword as part of his school mascot costume, both due to zero-tolerance policies adopted by their schools.

Chapter 10
Running time: 19:32

RELIGION VERSUS SCIENCE

The ongoing debate over "science versus faith" is alive and well in Kansas, where the state board of education is debating whether Darwin's theory of evolution—the scientific standard around the country—should be criticized and challenged in schools. At the heart of the debate is the "origin of man." This ABC News segment goes right to the heart of the debate by asking two questions: "Should the origin of man be taught in science or religion class? And is the current political climate pressing the issue to challenge American standards?"

Chapter 11
Running time: 29:35

TRANSGENDER TEACHER

This ABC News segment features David Warfield, a California transgender high school teacher undergoing gender reassignment surgery. David lost his job at Center High School in Sacramento after requesting to return as a woman after the summer break. The segment presents some of the major educational and legal issues associated with the employment of a teacher who undergoes a medical transformation from male to female.

Chapter 12
Running time: 16:00

VOUCHERS

This ABC News video includes interviews with individuals who both support and oppose the use of vouchers to pay the tuition of K–12 students to attend private, including church-related, schools. Supporting arguments include the value of choice and competition in bringing about reform in education. Opponents question the effectiveness of competition in education and the consequences of taking money from already financially challenged schools to support vouchers.

Chapter 13
Running time: 9:40

CHEATING 101: PRESSURES TO BOOST STANDARDIZED TEXT SCORES

This ABC News video segment explores recent allegations levied at school districts across the country of cheating on state-mandated standardized tests.

Chapter 14
Running time: 20:02

SPECIAL FEATURES

PART

1 THE TEACHING PROFESSION

CHAPTER 1

What most determines whether students learn is not family background or even dollars spent per pupil, but the talent, the ability, and the dedication of their teachers.
—President Bill Clinton, January 21, 1999

STATUS OF THE PROFESSION

Dr. Flynn enters the room of a patient who was recently admitted to University Hospital complaining of severe abdominal pain. Several interns follow Dr. Flynn to the patient's bedside. Dr. Flynn begins to ask the patient a series of questions. After the patient responds, Dr. Flynn turns to one of the interns and asks for a diagnosis. The intern gives a diagnosis. Dr. Flynn follows with a series of questions related to the basis for the diagnosis and possible treatment.

The ABC Corporation has just initiated a new data management plan. All middle managers have been told to report to the conference room at 8:30 A.M. on Monday. Upon arrival, the director of human resources introduces Ms. Dominguez from Data Resources, the retailer of the software supporting the new data management plan. Ms. Dominguez distributes a packet of materials and spends the remainder of the day with the managers, reviewing the materials in the packet, presenting additional information using a computer presentation platform, and showing a video related to the data management plan.

Mr. Pell stops at Amy Black's desk and answers a question. He moves to the desk of another student, observes the student writing in a workbook, points to something the student has written, and then, in a low voice, tells the student that the response is not correct and explains why. He continues around the room, stopping at almost every desk to make some remark. After about 10 minutes he goes to the front of the room and says, "Class, it appears that several people are having problems with this assignment. Let's review how to divide one fraction by another fraction." Mr. Pell walks to the blackboard and begins to speak.

Which of these individuals—Dr. Flynn, Ms. Dominguez, or Mr. Pell—is a teacher? Why? What defines the act of teaching?

Teaching has been considered by some to be the most noble of professions. H. G. Wells went so far as to say, "The teacher, whether mother, priest, or schoolmaster, is the real maker of history." Perhaps you are asking yourself "What is a teacher?" "What is this profession of teaching all about?" And, perhaps most important, "Should I become a teacher?" This chapter presents an overview of the teaching profession. After studying the chapter, you should be able to:

- Provide a demographic overview of America's teaching force.
- Evaluate your motives for becoming a teacher.
- Identify the most commonly cited satisfactions and dissatisfactions of teaching.
- Describe a typical teacher preparation program.
- Identify the most common strategies being used to recruit minorities into teaching.
- Discuss current issues related to teacher certification, including testing for certification, emergency certification, and interstate certification.
- Discuss the advantages and disadvantages of providing alternative routes for teacher certification.
- Compare projected data related to teacher supply with that projected for demand, and explore the factors contributing to supply and demand for teachers.
- Identify the major elements of teacher compensation, including supplemental pay and performance-based pay.
- Discuss the public's views of the schools and students' ratings of teachers.

The Teacher and Teaching: Definitions

Put most simply, a teacher is one who instructs another. A more formal definition from Good's *Dictionary of Education* (1973) defines a teacher as "a person employed in an official capacity for the purpose of guiding and directing the learning experiences of pupils or students in an educational institution, whether public or private" (p. 586). Teaching is defined in another work as "the process of helping pupils acquire knowledge, skills, attitudes, and/or appreciations by means of a systematic method of instruction" (Shafritz, Koeppe, & Soper, 1988, p. 468). B. O. Smith (1987), a well-known educator and writer in the field of education, provides five definitions of teaching:

1. *The descriptive definition of teaching:*   Defines teaching as imparting knowledge or skill.
2. *Teaching as success:*   Defines teaching as an activity such that X learns what Y teaches. If X does not learn, then Y has not taught.
3. *Teaching as intentional activity:*   Defines teaching as intended behavior (i.e., paying attention to what is going on, making diagnoses, changing one's behavior) for which the aim is to induce learning.
4. *Teaching as normative behavior:*   Defines teaching as a family of activities, including training, instructing, indoctrinating, and conditioning.
5. *Scientific or technical definition of teaching:*   Defines teaching by the coordinating propositions; teaching is not explicitly defined, but its meaning is implicated in the sentences where it occurs (e.g., "The teacher gives feedback").

Perhaps the most provocative definition defines the teacher as an artist and teaching as an art. According to Eisner (2002), teaching can be considered an art from at least four perspectives:

> First, it is an art in that teaching can be performed with such skill and grace that, for the student as well as for the teacher, the experience can be justifiably characterized as aesthetic. . . .
>
> Second, teaching is an art in that teachers, like painters, composers, actresses, and dancers, make judgments based largely on qualities that unfold during the course of action. . . . The teacher must "read" the emerging qualities and respond with qualities appropriate to the ends sought. . . .
>
> Third, teaching is an art in that the teacher's activity is not dominated by prescriptions or routines but is influenced by qualities and contingencies that are unpredicted. The teacher must function in an innovative way in order to cope with these contingencies. . . . Fourth, teaching is an art in that the ends it achieves are often created in the process . . . teaching is a form of human action in which many of the ends achieved are emergent—that is to say, found in the course of interaction with students rather than preconceived and efficiently attained. (pp. 154–155)

To consider teaching an art does not negate the necessity of establishing a scientific basis for the art of teaching and for developing a theoretical framework for teaching that addresses what we know and believe about intelligence, the conditions of learning, and what defines an effective teacher. The stronger the scientific basis, the greater the potential to improve teaching.

Profile of the Teaching Profession

Whatever definition is used, there is little argument that the teacher is the central element in the educational system. It is of interest to review what we know about the teacher in American society today. Table 1.1 presents some characteristics of public school teachers.

As indicated in the table, the teaching force is predominantly, and increasingly, female and white. While only 15.6% of the teaching force is minority, this is actually an increase from the 13.5% of 10 years earlier. The data also reflect a trend toward greater numbers of teachers attaining advanced degrees and, continuing a trend that began in the 1980s, the average class size of secondary teachers was larger than that of elementary teachers. However, in a reversal of what has been reported for several decades, elementary teachers reported spending more hours per week on their teaching duties than did secondary teachers.

For Your Reflection and Analysis

Do you believe that teachers are "born not made"? In your experience as a student have you been exposed to teachers who were "artists" in the classroom?
To submit your response online, go to http://www. prenhall.com/webb.

Table 1.1 — Selected Characteristics of Public School Teachers

Teacher Characteristics	1991	2001
Sex (percent)		
Male	27.9	21.0
Female	72.1	79.0
Race/ethnicity (percent)		
White, non-Hispanic	86.5	84.3
Black, non-Hispanic	8.3	7.6
Hispanic	3.4	5.6
Asian or Pacific Islander	1.0	1.6
American Indian or Alaskan Native	0.8	0.8
Average age (years)	41.6	46.0
Highest degree (percent)		
Bachelor's	46.3	43.1
Master's or specialist	52.6	56.0
Doctorate	0.6	0.8
Average years teaching experience	15.0	14.0
Average number of students per full-time classroom teacher		
Elementary	23.0	21.0
Secondary	26.0	28.0
Average number of hours per week spent on all teaching duties		
Elementary teachers	44.0	50.0
Secondary teachers	50.0	49.0

Source: U.S. Department of Education, National Center for Education Statistics. (2005). *Digest of education statistics, 2004.* Washington, DC: U.S. Department of Education.

The number of teachers and other instructional personnel employed in the public school systems of the United States has grown over the years as enrollments have increased. Table 1.2 gives a historical summary of public elementary and secondary school enrollments; number of instructional staff; and number of teachers, librarians, and other nonsupervisory staff. As can be seen, in the years since 1960 the total number of teachers, librarians, and other nonsupervisory staff more than doubled. The growth in staff reflects not only enrollment increases, but the steady reduction in pupil–teacher ratios, the enactment of legislation requiring increased services and specialized personnel, and the increased utilization of teacher aides, librarians, guidance counselors, and other instructional support personnel.

Why Become a Teacher?

There are many reasons why an individual might choose a career in teaching. Very few teachers would be able to identify a single reason for entering the profession. Many were positively influenced by former teachers. For others an important reason might be a practical consideration such as job security, or something as forthright as the fact that their first career choices were blocked (i.e., they didn't make it into medical school or into professional sports). Others may be attracted by the long summer vacations or a schedule that allows them to spend more time with their families. A less positive reason might be that teaching is a good temporary job while waiting to prepare for or be accepted into another career.

All of the preceding reasons are indeed motives for becoming a teacher, but they are not the primary motives. Over the years, numerous researchers have asked teachers what attracted them to the profession. The three reasons given most consistently are (1) a caring

Table 1.2 — Historical Summary of Public Elementary and Secondary School Statistics: United States, 1869–70 to 2001–02

	1869–70	1879–80	1889–90	1899–1900	1909–10	1919–20
Total enrollment (in thousands)	7562	9867	12,723	15,503	17,814	21,578
Total instructional staff (in thousands)	—	—	—	—	—	678
Total teachers, librarians, and other nonsupervisory staff (in thousands)	201	287	364	423	523	657
Men	78	123	126	127	110	93
Women	123	164	238	296	413	585

Source: U.S. Department of Education, National Center for Education Statistics. (2005). *Digest of education statistics, 2004* (Table 36). Washington, DC: U.S. Government Printing Office.

for and desire to work with young people, (2) a desire to make a contribution to society, and (3) an interest in a certain field and an excitement in sharing it with others.

The reasons one has for becoming a teacher have a significant effect on the ultimate satisfaction one finds in the job. For this reason, Herbert Kohl (1976), elementary school teacher and well-known educator, suggests that prospective teachers question themselves about what they expect to gain from or give to teaching. Several sets of questions suggested by Kohl to guide you in this inquiry are found in the *Ask Yourself* Feature on page **7.**

Satisfactions and Dissatisfactions With Teaching

Just as each individual has personal motives for becoming a teacher, each individual will find certain aspects of the position satisfying and certain aspects dissatisfying. In fact, it is possible that a particular aspect may be both satisfying and dissatisfying. Long summer vacations are satisfiers, but the reduced salary is a dissatisfier. Working with children can be both satisfying and frustrating. Although each individual will find personal satisfactions and dissatisfactions with teaching, it is of interest to look at what practicing teachers have identified as the satisfactions or attractions of teaching, as well as the dissatisfactions or challenges of teaching. Prospective teachers in particular need to know and prepare themselves for what they will encounter when they enter the classroom.

Understanding the satisfactions and dissatisfactions of teaching is also important for those making policies that affect teachers, because teacher satisfaction has been found to be associated with teacher effectiveness which, in turn, affects student achievement (U.S. Department of Education, 1997). The good news for those considering entering the teaching profession is that two-thirds of teachers with 5 years or less experience rate their job satisfaction as "very high," up almost 20% from just a few years earlier, and did not differ among elementary and secondary school teachers (Markow & Martin, 2005).

What exactly is it that teachers find satisfying and dissatisfying about teaching? We have already mentioned what teachers most often identify as the major satisfactions of teaching: the joy of working with children and the feeling that they are making a difference in the life of a student and in the larger society. Teachers also often talk about the sense of accomplishment they feel and the reward it brings when they watch children learn and progress (see, e.g., Brunetti, 2001; Markow & Martin, 2005). Many teachers find the autonomy they exercise in their classrooms and the control they have over their own time to be attractions. For others it is the opportunity to have a lifelong association with their subject field. And for still others the security of the position and the feeling of camaraderie and cooperation they share with their colleagues are important attractions. Teaching is one of the few professions where competition is virtually nonexistent.

1929–30	1939–40	1949–50	1959–60	1969–70	1979–80	1989–90	1999–2000	2001–02
25,678	25,434	25,112	36,087	45,550	41,651	40,543	46,851	47,672
880	912	963	1457	2286	2406	2986	3820	3989
843	875	920	1393	2195	2300	2860	3683	3829
140	195	196	404	711	782	—	—	—
703	681	724	989	1484	1518	—	—	—

ASK YOURSELF

Do I Want to Be a Teacher?

1. What reasons do you have for wanting to teach? Are they all negative (e.g., because the schools are oppressive, or because you need a job and working as a teacher is more respectable than working as a cab driver or salesperson)? What are the positive reasons for wanting to teach? Is there any pleasure to be gained from teaching? Knowledge? Power?

2. Why do you want to spend so much time with young people? Do you feel more comfortable with children? Have you spent much time with children recently, or are you mostly fantasizing about how they would behave? Are you afraid of adults? Intimidated by adult company? Fed up with the competition and coldness of business and the university?

3. What do you want from the children? Do you want them to do well on tests? Learn particular subject matter? Like each other? Like you? How much do you need to have students like you? Are you afraid to criticize them or set limits on their behavior because they might be angry with you? Do you consider yourself one of the kids? Is there any difference in your mind between your role and that of your prospective students?

4. What do you know that you can teach or share with your students?

5. With what age youngster do you feel the greatest affinity or are you most comfortable with?

6. Do you have any gender-based motives for wanting to work with young people? Do you want to enable them to become the boy or girl you could never be? For example, to free the girls of the image of prettiness and quietness and encourage them to run and fight, mess about with science, and get lost in the abstraction of math? Or to encourage boys to write poetry, play with dolls, let their fantasies come out, and not feel abnormal if they enjoy reading, acting, or listening to music?

7. What kind of young people do you want to work with?

8. What kind of school should you teach in?

9. How comfortable would you be teaching in a multiracial or multicultural setting? Do you feel capable of working with a culturally diverse student population?

Source: Kohl, 1976

Among the extrinsic factors that have been associated with teacher satisfaction and dissatisfaction are salary, level of support from parents and administrators, availability of resources, class size, degree of student misbehavior, and school safety (U.S. Department of Education, 1997; Wadsworth, 2000). And, although very few teachers are motivated by salary to enter teaching, salary can influence teachers' level of satisfaction or dissatisfaction in the position, as well as their desire to remain in or leave teaching.

Teachers are no different from other professionals in wanting to have input into the decisions that affect them and to have control over their immediate environment. Although teachers feel they are in the best position to recognize the needs of their students, they often are excluded from participation in the decision-making process regarding their students. Fortunately, an increasing number of districts nationwide are adopting site-based management (see Chapter 13), allowing teachers a greater role in the decisions that affect their professional lives.

Last, inadequate resources, the constant bane of teachers, inhibits the ability of teachers to meet the needs of individual students and prepare all students for higher levels of educational attainment or successful participation in the workforce.

Perhaps the ultimate indication of teacher job satisfaction or dissatisfaction is whether, given the opportunity to make the decision again, a person would become a teacher. When teachers are asked this very question, 60% of public school teachers said they "certainly" or "probably" would. Only 6% said that, if given the opportunity to make the decision to teach again, they "certainly would not" (U.S. Department of Education, 2004a).

Teacher Preparation

The standards and accountability movement that has driven the reform of K–12 curriculum and assessment now dominates the conversation about teacher preparation, professional development, and assessment as well as institutional and teacher certification. The standards movement in teacher education has been led by the Interstate New Teacher Assessment and Support Consortium (INTASC), a group of more than 30 states and professional associations, the National Commission on Teaching and America's Future (NCTAF), and the National Council for the Accreditation of Teacher Education (NCATE). Each of these organizations has developed standards that detail what teachers should know and be able to do. The INTASC standards for beginning teachers are presented in Table 1.3 as well as on the inside front and back covers of this text. The INTASC standards have provided the organizational framework for many teacher education programs. Standards for experienced teachers that parallel the INTASC standards have been developed by the National Board for Professional Teaching Standards (NBPTS) and have also influenced the design of teacher preparation programs. (These standards are reflected in the 10 standards presented in Table 1.3.)

There are a number of ways to become a teacher. The most common is to complete an approved 4-year baccalaureate teacher education program. At some institutions, undergraduates majoring in fields other than education are able to accumulate enough teacher education credits to qualify for certification. An extended, or 5-year preservice, teacher education program has been implemented at a number of institutions. These programs typically emphasize field experiences, and most award a master's degree upon completion.

For the increasing number of individuals who have noneducation college degrees and want to enter the profession without earning another undergraduate degree, a number of alternative routes are available ranging from enrolling in a compressed certification program to enrolling in a master's degree program leading to teacher certification. In the next section, we will review baccalaureate teacher education programs, the most common avenue into the profession, as well as the increasingly popular alternative certification program option.

Baccalaureate Teacher Education Programs

From its beginnings at the Columbian School in Concord, Vermont, (see the *Historical Note* on page 10) the formal preparation of teachers has grown to an enterprise that takes

Table 1.3 — Interstate New Teacher Assessment and Support Consortium Standards Related to Professional Expectations of Teachers

Standard 1:	The teacher understands the central concepts, tools of inquiry, and structures of the discipline(s) he or she teaches and can create learning experiences that make these aspects of subject matter meaningful for students.
Standard 2:	The teacher understands how children learn and develop and can provide learning opportunities that support their intellectual, social, and personal development.
Standard 3:	The teacher understands how students differ in their approaches to learning and creates instructional opportunities that are adapted to diverse learners.
Standard 4:	The teacher understands and uses a variety of instructional strategies to encourage students' development of critical thinking, problem solving, and performance skills.
Standard 5:	The teacher uses an understanding of individual and group motivation and behavior to create a learning environment that encourages positive social interaction, active engagement in learning, and self-motivation.
Standard 6:	The teacher uses knowledge of effective verbal, nonverbal, and media communication techniques to foster active inquiry, collaboration, and supportive interaction in the classroom.
Standard 7:	The teacher plans instruction based upon knowledge of subject matter, students, the community, and curriculum goals.
Standard 8:	The teacher understands and uses formal and informal assessment strategies to evaluate and ensure the continuous intellectual and social development of the learner.
Standard 9:	The teacher is a reflective practitioner who continually evaluates the effects of his/her choices and actions on others (students, parents, and other professionals in the learning community) and who actively seeks out opportunities to grow professionally.
Standard 10:	The teacher fosters relationships with school colleagues, parents, and agencies in the larger community to support students' learning and well-being.

The Interstate New Teacher Assessment and Support Consortium (INTASC) standards were developed by the Council of Chief State School Officers and member states. Copies may be downloaded from the Council's website at http://www.ccsso.org.

Council of Chief State School Officers. (1992). Model standards for beginning teacher licensing, assessment, and development: A resource for state dialogue. Washington, DC: Author. http://www.ccsso.org/content/pdfs/corestrd.pdf.

place in about 1,200 different departments, schools, or colleges of education in the United States. Teacher education programs usually consist of four areas: (1) general studies, (2) content studies in a major or minor, (3) professional studies, and (4) field experiences and clinical practice. The general studies or liberal arts and science portion of the program, as well as the academic major portion, are generally similar to those required of other students at the college or university. Typically students are not admitted into the teacher education program until they have completed, or substantially completed, the general studies requirement with a grade point average (GPA) of at least 2.5.

Preparation programs for elementary school teachers are somewhat different from those for secondary school teachers. In about two-thirds of the states, students completing preparation programs for secondary school teachers are required to have a major in education. In the remaining states, students may major in education or in the subject field to be taught. The number of hours in the major will usually constitute two-thirds of the hours taken in the upper division, with the other one-third in the professional education sequence.

For Your Reflection and Analysis

How did you determine your preference for elementary or secondary teaching?

To submit your response online, go to http://www. prenhall.com/webb.

CW

HISTORICAL NOTE

The Columbian School: The First Formal Teacher Training Institution

Most histories of education identify the Columbian School at Concord, Vermont, established by the Reverend Hall in 1823, as the first formal teacher training institution in the United States. Hall had gone to Concord as a supply (temporary) pastor in 1822 and in the first year observed the poor condition of the schools and came to believe that better teachers were central to any school improvement. When he accepted the pastorate in 1823 he did so with the stipulation that he be allowed to open a school to train teachers. Beginning in the unused part of a store, the school soon moved to a new brick building provided by the town.

At the Columbian School, Hall offered a review of the subjects taught in the common (elementary) school, plus advanced mathematics, chemistry, natural and moral philosophy, logic, astronomy, and the "art of teaching." In 1829 Hall published the first professional textbook on teacher education in the English language, *Lectures on Schoolkeeping*. A partial chapter outline of the book was as follows:

Chapter III.	Requisite qualifications of teachers.
Chapter IV.	Nature of the teacher's employment. Responsibility of the teacher. Importance of realizing and understanding it.
Chapter V.	Gaining the confidence of the school. Means of gaining it. The instructor should be willing to spend all his time when it can be rendered beneficial to the school.
Chapter VI.	Government of a school. Prerequisites. Manner of treating scholars. Uniformity in government. Firmness.
Chapter VII.	Government, continued. Partiality. Regard to the future as well as the present welfare of the scholars. Mode of intercourse between teacher and

	scholars, and between scholars. Punishments. Rewards.
Chapter VIII.	General management of a school. Direction of duties.
Chapter IX.	Mode of teaching. Manner of illustrating subjects. Spelling. Reading.
Chapter X.	Arithmetic. Geography. English Grammar. Writing. History.
Chapter XI.	Composition. General subjects, not particularly studies. Importance of improving opportunities when deep impressions are made on the minds of the school.
Chapter XII.	Means of exciting the attention of scholars. Such as are to be avoided. Such as are safely used.
Chapter XIII.	To female instructors.

Source: Outline from *Lectures on Schoolkeeping* by Samuel R. Hall is from Cubberly, E. P. (1934). *Readings in public education in the United States* (pp. 324–325). New York: Houghton Mifflin.

To research and explore this topic further, go to the *Historical Note* module for this chapter of the Companion Website at **http://www.prenhall.com/webb**.

Although one-fourth of the states require that students preparing to be elementary school teachers have a major in a content area, in the vast majority of states elementary education is considered the major. It is assumed that elementary education students acquire knowledge of the subject matter through the liberal arts and science requirements. Another option used by a few institutions is to require an interdisciplinary major for elementary teachers that would ground them in the core subjects they will be expected to teach (American Federation of Teachers, 2000).

The professional studies component of the teacher preparation program is that specialized body of knowledge and skills required by the profession. The typical professional studies component includes courses in the foundational studies in education (e.g., introduction to education, history, sociology, philosophy of education, educational psychology, child and adolescent development, comparative education, multicultural education) and the pedagogical studies, which concentrate on teaching and learning theory, general and specialized methods of instruction, and classroom management.

The fourth component of the teacher preparation program, clinical field experiences, includes laboratory and practicum experiences designed to provide students with the opportunity to "apply their knowledge, skills, and dispositions in a variety of settings appropriate to the content and level of their program" (NCATE, 2002, p. 27). **Clinical field experiences** are those opportunities for students to observe, assist, tutor, instruct, or conduct applied research that are provided early in the program, whereas **clinical practice** "includes student teaching and internships that provide candidates with experiences that allow for full immersion in the learning community so that candidates are able to demonstrate proficiencies in the professional roles for which they are preparing" (NCATE, 2002, p. 28).

Student teaching, or the internship, is required for certification in almost every state. The number of weeks required varies in length from 5 to 30; the typical length is 10 to 12 weeks ("Improving Teaching Quality," 2002). Typically, the student teacher is assigned to a cooperating teacher, who is selected based on a reputation as an "expert" teacher. A college or university professor is assigned to supervise the student teaching experience and makes periodic observations and visitations with the student and the cooperating teacher. During the student teaching experience, the student gradually assumes greater responsibility for instruction under the guidance of the cooperating teacher. Whereas the amount of time that the student teacher actually spends teaching may vary considerably (in part a function of the demonstrated ability of the student teacher and in part a function of the nature of the classroom), on average, student teachers will spend about 60% of their time teaching. The remaining time is spent observing, record keeping, and assisting in various classroom activities. The student teaching experience is consistently rated by practicing teachers as the most important part of their preparation program. Figure 1.1 graphically depicts the typical

Practicing teachers rate their student teaching experience as the most important part of their preparation program.

Figure 1.1 — Elementary and Secondary Education Program Requirements

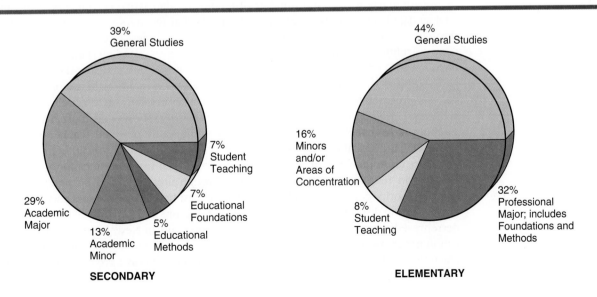

SECONDARY

- 39% General Studies
- 7% Student Teaching
- 7% Educational Foundations
- 5% Educational Methods
- 13% Academic Minor
- 29% Academic Major

ELEMENTARY

- 44% General Studies
- 16% Minors and/or Areas of Concentration
- 8% Student Teaching
- 32% Professional Major; includes Foundations and Methods

preparation programs for elementary and secondary teachers and gives the percentage of each program devoted to each area. As indicated, the general studies and student teaching requirements are approximately the same for both programs; they differ in the percentage of time spent in professional studies and in other academic studies. On average, secondary education students require 10 semester hours more to complete their program than do elementary education majors.

Alternative Teacher Preparation Programs

In response to the shortage of qualified teachers in some teaching areas, 46 states have adopted alternative teacher preparation/certification programs to certify candidates who have subject-matter competence without completion of a formal teacher preparation program. This represents a dramatic increase from 27 states in 1997 and only 8 in 1986 (Feistritzer, 2005). These programs are designed to attract to the teaching profession qualified recent college graduates or persons with at least a bachelor's degree from other professions who have been the victims of layoffs and downsizing in the private sector, or have retired from the military (e.g., Troops to Teachers) and may want to change careers. Many such programs are intended to recruit teachers for underserved rural or inner-city districts or subject areas experiencing teacher shortages.

Nationally, more than 200,000 teachers have been licensed through alternative teacher preparation programs in the last two decades, with an average of 25,000 per year in the last 5 years. Several states have been particularly aggressive in developing and utilizing alternative routes for licensing teachers: 24% of new hires in New Jersey, 24% of new hires in Texas, and 18% of new hires in California have entered the profession through alternative certification programs (Education Commission of the States, 2005).

Alternative certification programs may be offered through the local school district, a college or university, the state department of education, or a partnership of any of these. The typical alternative certification program includes (1) a rigorous selection process to ensure the selection of qualified applicants; (2) preservice training in methodology, classroom management, and human development; and (3) a structured, supervised internship that includes guidance by a mentor teacher (Duhon-Hayes, Augustus, Duhon-Sells, & Duhon-Ross, 1996). There is considerable variation among the states as to what course work is required of those seeking alternative certification, as well as how long the internship must be and how much supervision and support are given to novice teachers.

The merits of alternative certification programs are a topic of some debate and the research is mixed. For example, Linda Darling-Hammond, former director of the National Commission on Teaching and America's Future and one of the major critics of alternative certification, has reviewed a number of studies of alternative certification programs as well as data from various programs and reports that teachers who enter the profession through short-term alternative certification programs are less effective in developing student learning than are traditionally certified teachers (Darling-Hammond, Chung, & Frelow, 2002) and are less likely to remain in the profession (Darling-Hammond, 2000). Other reports show no discernible difference between traditionally prepared and alternatively prepared teachers on various measures of observable teaching behaviors, student achievement, and self-perceptions of competence. It also shows that alternatively certified teachers have a higher retention rate than traditionally certified teachers (Feistritzer, 2005). One indisputable and positive finding is that alternative certification programs tend to attract more men and minorities than do traditional teacher education programs. For example, in Texas 41% of teachers entering through alternative certification programs are from a minority population, and in California almost half of the teachers certified through university and district alternative certification programs are members of ethnic groups underrepresented in the teaching force and 29% are male. In New Jersey, alternative certification programs have been the biggest source of minority teachers: A total of 20% of the teachers certified and hired by public and nonpublic schools have been from a minority population (Feistritzer & Chester, 2001).

VIDEO INSIGHT

Teacher Shortage: Alternative Certification

This ABC News video introduces the issue of providing alternative routes to teacher certification as a strategy to meet the current and projected teacher shortage. The focus in this short video is on the benefits of attracting second-career individuals into teaching. What is left out are the concerns many educators have about many of these programs.

1. What do you see as the major concerns about trying to prepare individuals to enter the classroom in such an abbreviated time frame?
2. What are some alternative strategies that might be used to attract qualified individuals to the teaching profession?
3. Why have they not gained in popularity as has alternative certification?

CW To submit your answers online, go to the *Video Insight* module for this chapter of the Companion Website at **http://www.prenhall.com/webb**.

Minority Representation in the Teaching Force

Minority teachers are needed in the schools for a variety of reasons, perhaps the most important being their presence as role models for all students. Minority children, many of whom come from impoverished backgrounds (see Chapter 8), derive an obvious benefit from seeing minorities in professional positions. But it is also important that all children see minorities in professional roles, rather than overly represented in nonprofessional roles. Otherwise, they will be implicitly taught that majority people are more intelligent or better suited for positions of authority than minorities (Branch, 2001; Villegas & Clewell, 1998). Another negative effect of the underrepresentation of minority teachers is that there are fewer teachers who have the cultural frameworks to make instruction more culturally relevant and effective. Minority teachers often have what Miller (cited in Torres, Santos, Peck, & Cortes, 2004) terms "culture comprehensive knowledge." According to Miller, this culture comprehensive knowledge "is composed of a person's cultured and gendered understanding of their experiences and how that understanding alters their worldview.

Reflection about this knowledge in turn influences their instructional planning and decision making" (Torres et al., 2004, p. 20).

One of the major concerns of teacher preparation programs today is that fewer minority students are entering the programs. What once was one of the few professions open to minorities must now compete with all of the professions with higher salaries and status to attract capable minority students. Various studies among blacks, Hispanics, and Asian Americans have consistently cited teaching's lack of prestige and the associated low earning potential as major reasons minorities do not enter teaching. Other reasons cited, especially by Asian Americans, was fear of discrimination and fear of working outside a comfort zone defined by language and culture (Torres et al., 2004).

The decline in minority enrollment in teacher education is especially distressing

Minority enrollments in the public schools are expected to increase at a faster rate than the percentage of minority teachers.

because it has been occurring simultaneously with increasing minority enrollments in the public schools. It has been predicted that by the year 2020, 50% of the students in our nation's schools will be minorities. In fact, it is predicted that in the next decade 1 in 3 students will be a minority, whereas only 1 in 20 teachers will be minority (Stephens & Harris, 2000). The underrepresentation of minority teachers "almost guarantees that most students will end their formal public school experiences without ever having had or met a teacher of color" (Stephens & Harris, 2000, p. 5).

Strategies for Increasing Diversity.   In an attempt to address the critical shortage of minority teachers, educators and policy makers at the local, state, and national levels have initiated a number of programs aimed at eliminating obstacles to participation and recruitment. Strategies aimed at removing obstacles to participation include increasing scholarship, loan, and loan forgiveness programs; increasing support services and retention efforts; and ensuring that testing and evaluation programs minimize the influences of race and ethnicity on entry to the profession.

A number of strategies designed to increase the number of minorities in teaching go beyond traditional recruitment efforts to strategies aimed at increasing the pool of minority teacher education students. One such strategy involves identifying and encouraging interested students before their senior year in high school. This is done through Future Educator clubs, teacher cadet programs, and even magnet schools that offer a college preparatory program for students who are interested in becoming teachers (e.g., the High School for the Teaching Professions in Cincinnati and the Austin High School for the Teaching Professions in Houston). Most programs target junior high or senior high school students and are designed to engage students in learning about teaching through both classroom activities and actual teaching experiences. Such programs often provide financial aid, support services, and, in some cases, transferable credits that may be taken while in high school.

An increasingly popular recruitment strategy operated as a joint venture between a college or university and local school districts is the "grow your own" program for paraprofessionals. Under the typical program, teacher aides or other professionals continue in their regular jobs, taking courses offered with flexible scheduling arrangements after school, on the weekend, and during the summer. Some districts provide time off with pay to attend classes. Tuition is often reduced or paid for by the district. And, perhaps most important, graduates are guaranteed employment in the district upon successful completion of the program and certification.

Increasing the pool of minority teacher education students is not enough if they do not stay in the profession. Minority teachers leave the profession in alarming numbers. One reason for this is that minority teachers are more likely to be placed in the inner cities where working conditions are often the poorest and stress the highest. Among the efforts that are being implemented to increase the retention of minority teachers are the mentoring programs discussed in Chapter 2.

Teacher Certification

Successful completion of a teacher training program does not automatically qualify an individual to teach. To become qualified for teaching, administrative, and many other positions in the public schools and many private schools, individuals must acquire a valid certificate or license from the state where they wish to practice. The **certification** or licensure requirement is intended to ensure that the holder has met established state standards and is therefore qualified for employment in the area specified on the certificate. The federal No Child Left Behind Act of 2001 stipulates that by 2005–06 all newly hired teachers in schools receiving Title I funds must be certified in the level or subject to be taught and may not have any certification requirement waived on an emergency, temporary, or professional basis.

The certification process is administered by the state education agency. The certificate can be obtained in one of two ways: (1) The candidate can make application to the state agency who will make an assessment of the candidate's transcripts and experiences against state requirements, or (2) more typically, the applicant can be recommended for certification after graduation from a state-approved teacher preparation program. The certificate, when issued, may be good for life or, more commonly, must be renewed every 3 to 5 years. A certificate does not guarantee employment, it merely makes the holder eligible for employment.

Specific certification requirements vary from state to state, but they typically include a college degree (all states require a bachelor's degree as a minimum), a minimum number of credit hours in designated curricular areas (35 states specify course requirements in the field of education), recommendation of a college or employer, a student teaching experience, "good moral character," attainment of a minimum age, U.S. citizenship, the signing of a loyalty oath affirming support of the government, and the passing of a state-prescribed exam to assess pedagogical skills and subject-matter mastery. In 2005 some form of state testing for initial certification was required by 43 states.

Several states have moved to a "staged" certification system. The initial certificate, often called a probationary or provisional certificate, is issued to beginning teachers who satisfy the requirements for initial certification, and it is good for a limited number of years. The standard or "professional" certificate is issued to teachers upon successful performance on an assessment performed by a local school district team or by the state, utilizing videotaped lessons, portfolios, or classroom observations. In a three-tier system, an advanced or "master" certificate is issued to teachers based on experience and demonstrated higher levels of professional performance. One way this can be obtained in most states that have the advanced certificate is to receive certification by the NBPTS, as described later.

Assessment for Initial Certification and Licensure

Public concern about the quality of the teaching force in recent years, combined with the influence of the No Child Left Behind Act, has led to an increase in state testing of teachers. Testing for certification is seen as a necessary accountability measure to ensure that prospective teachers have met the INTASC or other standards adopted by the state and are qualified to enter the classroom. The No Child Left Behind Act requires that all newly hired teachers in schools that receive federal funds be "highly qualified." For new elementary teachers this means that they must pass a "rigorous" state test that covers the elementary curriculum and teaching skills. New middle and high school teachers must pass a "rigorous" state test in the academic subject matter they teach or complete an academic major in every subject they will teach.

The most commonly used tests for certification are the Praxis II® examinations developed by the Educational Testing Service. The first part of the Praxis II® examinations measures core content knowledge in more than 20 areas. The second part measures knowledge of teaching and learning in four areas (see Table 1.4). Some states also require prospective teachers to submit a portfolio demonstrating their teaching effectiveness that is evaluated by experienced teachers.

Emergency Certification

Forty-nine states have some provision for granting **emergency (temporary) certificates** to persons who do not meet the requirements for standard certification when districts cannot employ fully qualified teachers. Emergency certificates are issued with the presumption that the recipient teacher will obtain the credentials or will be replaced by a regularly certified teacher. In most states, before the emergency certificate is granted, the district must show that an effort has been made to hire a regularly certified teacher. Although the spread of **alternative teacher certification** programs has reduced the rate at which emergency certificates are issued, nationwide tens of thousands of individuals enter teaching each year on emergency or temporary certificates. Unfortunately, in many instances these teachers are concentrated in poor urban schools or rural areas.

Emergency certification does not require any professional education training prior to the assumption of teaching duties and often does not require the passage of a subject-matter test, although some states do require the passage of a basic skills test. Many professional educators question the ethics and safety of hiring untrained persons to teach: No other state-licensed profession issues "emergency" certificates to untrained persons.

Table 1.4 — Praxis II® Examination Principles of Learning and Teaching: Topics and Components

I. Students as Learners
   A. Student Development and the Learning Process
   B. Students as Diverse Learners
   C. Student Motivation and the Learning Environment
II. Instruction and Assessment
   A. Instructional Strategies
   B. Planning Instruction
   C. Assessment Strategies
III. Communication Techniques
   A. Basic, Effective, Verbal, and Nonverbal Communications in the Classroom
   B. Effect of Cultural and Gender Differences on Communications in the Classroom
   C. Types of Communications and Interactions that Can Stimulate Discussion in Different Ways for Particular Purposes
IV. Profession and Community
   A. The Reflective Practitioner
   B. The Larger Community

Source: Credit Line: PRAXIS materials from The Praxis Series: Test At A Glance—Principles of Learning and Teaching. Reprinted by Permission of Educational Testing Service, the copyright owner.

Disclaimer: Permission to reprint PRAXIS materials does not constitute review or endorsement by Educational Testing Service of this publication as a whole or of any other testing information it may contain.

However, despite the recognition that this practice undermines efforts to increase the professional status of teaching (Darling-Hammond, 2000), given the shortage of teachers discussed later in this chapter, it seems unlikely that the practice will be abandoned in the foreseeable future.

Recertification

Acquiring certification once does not mean that a teacher is certified for life. Teachers are required to periodically renew their certificates to ensure they are knowledgeable about new developments in their fields. In the past teachers could be recertified by earning a specified number of continuing education units (CEUs), which could be earned by taking approved college courses or by attending workshops, in-service training, or other acceptable activities. Increasingly, however, some states are taking measures to ensure that recertification requirements include more directed, research-proven career growth activities. For example, some states will not accept a master's degree for recertification unless it directly relates to the teacher's content knowledge or teaching skill (Education Commission of the States, 2005). About half the states accept NBPTS certification as the basis for granting recertification. In three states (Texas, Arkansas, and Georgia) passage of a competency test is required for recertification.

Interstate Certification

A matter of concern related to state certification for any profession is whether the certification granted by one state will be recognized by another. The increasing mobility of teachers has encouraged state certification authorities to establish **interstate reciprocity,** which allows teachers who are certified in one state to be eligible for certification in another. It is to the advantage of each state to facilitate the employment of qualified educators and to increase the availability of educational personnel, not to establish barriers to employment. To this end, 44 states and the District of Columbia have signed an Interstate Certification Contract under the auspices of the National Association of State Directors of Teacher Education and Certifications (NASDTEC) to make it possible for an individual with a certificate issued by one state to receive an equivalent certification without meeting additional course work requirements. (Iowa, Minnesota, Nebraska, New York, South Dakota, and Wisconsin are not signers.)

Regional interstate reciprocity agreements are also in place in a couple of areas. Six states in the northeast (Connecticut, Massachusetts, New Hampshire, New York, Rhode Island, and Vermont) have agreed to recognize a Northeast Regional Credential, and in the Midwest seven states (Arkansas, Iowa, Kentucky, Missouri, Nebraska, Oklahoma, and South Dakota) have formed a regional exchange agreement where each state's minimum certification standards are protected but the teacher applicant is given an initial 2-year license by the receiving state (National Center for Alternative Certification, 2005).

National Certification: The NBPTS

The professionalization of teaching, as well as the prospect for some form of national certification, has been greatly enhanced by the efforts of the NBPTS, not only to develop professional standards for teaching but also to develop certification in more than 30 fields. The certification fields are structured around student development levels and subject areas (see Table 1.5).

Teachers with 3 years of teaching experience who hold a state teaching license can start the certification process upon payment of a fee. The process involves preparing a professional portfolio containing videotapes of classroom practice, samples of student work, and a written commentary, and coming to one of the board's 400 assessment centers for a full day of written assessment exercises focused on the candidate's content knowledge. Successful candidates are deemed **board certified,** a term commonly used in other professions. Such certification is a public acknowledgment that the teacher possesses not only the requisite knowledge but also the demonstrated ability to teach in the areas or levels of certification specified. NBPTS certification is issued for a period of 10 years and may be renewed upon satisfying a renewal requirement. As discussed in Chapter 2, a major incentive for teachers to undertake this process is

> **For Your Reflection and Analysis**
>
> How likely are you to seek national board certification when you become eligible?
>
> *To submit your response online, go to http://www. prenhall.com/webb.*
>
> CW

Table 1.5 — National Board Standards and Certification by Developmental Level

Standards Subject Area	Early Childhood Through Young Adulthood: Ages 3–18+	Early Childhood: Ages 3–8	Middle Childhood: Ages 7–12	Early & Middle Childhood: Ages 3–12	Early Adolescence: Ages 11–15	Adolescence & Young Adulthood: Ages 14–18+	Early Adolescence Through Young Adulthood: Ages 11–18+
Generalist		X	X				
Art				X			X
Career and technical education							X
English as a new language				X			X
English language arts				X	X	X	
Exceptional needs	X						
Library media	X						
Mathematics					X	X	
Music				X			X
Physical education				X			X
School counseling	X						
Science					X	X	
Social studies–history					X	X	
World languages other than English	X						

Source: Reprinted with permission from the National Board for Professional Teaching Standards, (2004). Standards & National Board Certification/Standards. Retrieved November 13, 2004 from NBPTS Website: www.nbpts.org. All rights reserved.

that 35 states and hundreds of school districts offer financial incentives to teachers who receive board certification and almost all states offer licensure incentives. Since its inception in 1995, more than 40,000 teachers have received national board certification (NBPTS, 2005).

Teacher Supply and Demand

School districts nationwide are facing an unprecedented demand for teachers at all levels. The demand for teachers that began in the mid-1980s is expected to continue through the first decade of the 21st century, creating a demand for 2.2 million teachers in the next 10 years. The projected demand for additional teachers is a result of projected record increases in enrollment (see Figure 7.2 on page 178), as well as the record number of vacancies created by the retirement of an aging teacher population. More than 40% of the teaching force is 50 years of age or older and many teachers are beginning to retire: 22% of teachers expect to retire by 2010 (National Center for Education Information, 2005). The problem created by retirements is further compounded by the growing number of teachers, both new and experienced, who leave the profession each year.

The continued lowering of pupil–teacher ratios has also contributed to an increased demand for teachers. Pupil–teacher ratios in the public schools have declined from 17.4 in 1993 to 16.3 in 2003 and are projected to decline to 14.6 by the year 2014 (Hussar, 2005).

Although the demand for teachers is expected to increase, the projected supply of new teachers is not expected to be sufficient to meet the demand. The supply of newly hired teachers is a function of (1) the number of new college graduates entering teaching, (2) delayed entrants (first-year teachers who engage in other activities between graduation from college and entering teaching), (3) transfers from one state or district to another, and (4) the number of former teachers reentering teaching. In recent years, first-time teachers have come to represent a smaller percentage (30%) of newly hired public school teachers (new graduates, 18%; delayed entrants, 12%). Returning teachers make up 24% of the newly hired teachers, whereas transfers comprise about 53% of the new hires (Provasnik & Dorfman, 2005). One of the major unknowns in projecting teacher supply is what number of individuals trained as teachers will actually enter the profession. In recent years, only about 60% of newly prepared teachers actually entered teaching (Darling-Hammond, 2000). How many of these individuals, or other prepared or interested individuals, would enter teaching if salaries and working conditions were improved and the status of the profession were enhanced is an important policy issue.

The increased demand for teachers in some areas has led many school districts to extensive and intensive recruiting.

Although a shortage of teachers is expected nationwide, supply and demand will vary among states, school districts, and disciplines. In the South and West, states with growing populations will have a greater demand for teachers. States in the South such as Florida, Georgia, and the Carolinas have shortages, while states in the Midwest and Northeast, with large numbers of teacher colleges, have surpluses. Urban and rural districts in particular are expected to experience teacher shortages. Shortages continue in most areas of special education, some foreign languages, bilingual education, English as a second language, the sciences, and mathematics, while surpluses exist in kindergarten, dance, social studies, health and physical education (American Association for Employment in Education, 2005). And, as always, there is a high demand for male teachers at the elementary level.

Figure 1.2 — Average Classroom Teacher Salary, 1985–2005

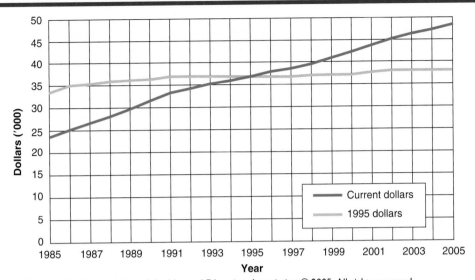

Source: Reprinted with permission of the National Education Association © 2005. All rights reserved.

Salary and Other Compensation

Historically, teachers' salaries have lagged behind those of other professionals with comparable training and responsibility, as well as those of many of the technical and semi-skilled occupations. However, with renewed public interest in the quality of education, teacher compensation has generally improved. Beginning in 1986, teacher salaries increased at a higher rate than inflation. Figure 1.2 depicts the trend in average annual salaries of elementary and secondary teachers since 1985 in 2005 dollars and 1995 dollars. Although the current dollar increases appear substantial over this 20-year period, from $23,600 in 1984-85 to $47,750 in 2004-05, in adjusted dollars salaries grew by only $2,677 (11%). And, as can be seen, during the last several years, salaries have remained almost flat or actually decreased slightly in constant dollars. This may be due to the fact that large numbers of teachers are retiring and being replaced with newer, lower paid teachers, bringing the average salary down. In 2005, salaries ranged from more than $55,000 in California, Connecticut, New Jersey, and New York to under $35,000 in South Dakota (National Education Association, 2005c). Salaries were highest in states in New England, the Midwest, and the Far West, and lowest in the Southeast and the Southwest.

The specific salary a teacher receives depends on a number of factors, including supply and demand, union activity, the prevailing wage rate in neighboring districts, and the wealth of the district as determined by the tax base. School districts with a higher assessed value of property per pupil will typically pay higher salaries than those with lesser assessed value of property per pupil. However, many poor districts, in terms of assessed valuation, have chosen to levy higher tax rates in order to pay teachers competitive salaries.

Salary Schedules[1]

More than 90% of teacher salary schedules across the nation are based on the **single salary schedule** format. The single salary schedule pays equivalent salaries for equivalent preparation and experience. The trend toward the adoption of a single salary schedule for teachers began in the first quarter of the 20th century, and before the end of the third quarter had come to dominate direct compensation. The position system it replaced based salaries on positions within the school system (elementary teacher, secondary

---

[1] Discussion of salary schedules is based on Educational Research Service. (1987). *Methods of scheduling salaries for teachers.* Arlington, VA: Author.

teacher, librarian, counselor, etc.). The single salary schedule has not always been favored by teachers' groups, but it is popular with boards of education because it is easy to understand and to administer.

There are two basic dimensions to the single salary schedule: a horizontal dimension made up of columns that correspond to levels of academic preparation (e.g., bachelor's degree, master's degree, master's degree plus 30 hours, doctorate degree), and a vertical dimension of rows of "steps" that correspond to the years of teaching experience. There is no standard number of columns or rows in a teacher's salary schedule, although there are usually more rows than columns so that the schedule tends to form a vertical matrix (see Table 1.6).

Initial Placement.   The initial vertical placement of a new teacher on a specific vertical step on a scale is determined by several factors, the most common of which is previous teaching experience. To receive credit for any previous years of teaching, usually the teacher must have taught for 75% of the school year. Most school districts place a limit on the number of years of teaching experience credited toward initial placement on the salary schedule. Factors that affect this decision are whether the experience is in or out of the district and in or out of the state.

Other factors that are considered in making the initial placement on the schedule are credit for related experience, credit for military service, and credit for other experience. Some districts recognize related experience such as public library experience for librarians or recreational experience for physical educators. Others grant full or partial credit for military service or for experience in the Peace Corps, Volunteers in Service to America (VISTA), or the National Teachers Corps.

Advancement.   Horizontal advancement across columns in a salary schedule is dependent on earned academic credit beyond the bachelor's degree. Vertical advancement from one step to the next within the scale is normally automatic after a stipulated period of time (usually 1 year), although longer periods may be required for advancement to the higher steps. Although teachers' groups have continued to advocate automatic advancement, in an increasing number of districts certain restrictions are being placed on vertical advancement. For example, advancement at specified points may be made contingent on (1) the attainment of additional units of academic credit or completion of in-service training programs or (2) satisfactory performance or merit.

To provide for teachers who have reached the maximum number of steps in a particular scale, some salary schedules also provide for supermaximum or long-term service increments beyond the highest step in the scale. Whereas in most instances the awarding of this increment is based solely on the attainment of a specific number of years' experience above the highest number recognized on the schedule, in some cases a performance or merit evaluation is required before the award is made.

Performance-based and Competency-based Pay Plans

The growing recognition of the importance of teacher quality to student performance has led to increased efforts to link teacher pay to student performance or to a demonstrated increase in professional competence. This strategy is seen as a way to both attract and retain good teachers and motivate them to greater performance.

Performance-based pay plans are of two types: those that reward the individual teacher and those that reward the performance of the school as a whole. School-based performance award programs have been instituted in a growing number of states and school districts. School-based performance reward programs provide financial rewards to individual schools that meet certain prescribed standards or outcomes in such areas as student achievement, dropout rates, graduation rates, or absenteeism. Some programs restrict the use of the funds to school improvement or other education purposes, whereas others allow funds to be used for salary bonuses. Individual performance pay plans that link teacher pay to student performance have been firmly opposed by most teacher groups and have been adopted by only a limited number of districts. The major arguments for and against individual performance-based pay are presented in the *Controversial Issue* feature presented on page 22.

For Your Reflection and Analysis

Should performance-based rewards based on student achievement go to individual teachers or to the school as a whole?
To submit your response online, go to http://www. prenhall.com/webb.

CW

Table 1.6 — Central Consolidated (NM) Certified Teacher Salary Schedule (Includes Nurse with Bachelor's in Nursing or Related Field, Librarians, and Counselors)

Salary Step	BA + 0 Hours	BA + 15 Hours	BA + 30 Hours	BA + 45/MA Hours	MA + 15 Hours	MA + 30 Hours	MA + 45 Hours Ph.D.
0	32,683	33,912	34,548	35,737	36,918	37,612	38,414
1	33,166	34,413	35,059	36,265	37,464	38,168	38,982
2	34,132	35,414	36,080	37,321	38,555	39,280	40,118
3	35,000	35,469	36,136	37,376	38,610	39,335	40,173
4	35,200	36,105	36,782	38,019	39,273	40,012	40,850
5	35,143	36,740	37,429	38,661	39,937	40,690	41,526
6	36,027	37,376	38,078	39,307	40,602	41,367	42,206
7	36,458	37,861	38,562	39,813	41,147	41,907	42,773
8	36,889	38,346	39,048	40,321	41,693	42,444	43,339
9	37,320	38,831	39,533	40,827	42,237	42,984	43,905
10	37,751	39,316	40,018	41,333	42,782	43,522	44,472
11	38,183	39,801	40,503	41,839	43,327	44,061	45,038
12	38,614	40,287	40,988	42,346	43,872	44,601	45,605
13	39,045	40,771	41,472	42,852	44,417	45,139	46,171
14	39,476	41,256	41,958	43,359	44,962	45,679	46,737
15	39,476	41,740	42,442	43,865	45,506	46,217	47,304
16	39,476	42,226	42,928	44,372	46,052	46,757	47,871
17	39,476	42,711	43,412	44,880	46,597	47,295	48,437
18	39,476	43,196	43,898	45,386	47,141	47,833	49,003
19	39,476	44,187	44,891	46,390	48,147	48,839	50,008
20	39,476	45,179	45,886	47,395	49,154	49,843	51,013
21	39,476	46,170	46,880	48,400	50,160	50,848	52,018
22	39,476	47,162	47,874	49,405	51,165	51,854	53,022
23	39,476	47,162	47,874	50,409	52,171	52,857	54,027
24	39,476	47,162	47,874	51,414	53,177	53,862	55,032
25	39,476	47,162	47,874	52,419	54,183	54,867	56,037
26	39,476	47,162	47,874	53,424	55,189	55,873	57,040
27	39,476	47,162	47,874	54,428	56,196	56,876	58,046
28	39,476	47,162	47,874	55,433	57,201	57,881	59,051
29	39,476	47,162	47,874	56,438	58,206	58,887	60,056
30	39,476	47,162	47,874	57,443	59,213	59,891	61,061
31	39,476	47,162	47,874	58,447	60,219	60,895	62,065
32	39,476	47,162	47,874	59,452	61,226	61,900	63,070
33	39,476	47,162	47,874	60,456	62,230	62,905	64,075
34	39,476	47,162	47,874	61,462	63,236	63,910	65,080
35	39,476	47,162	47,874	62,467	64,243	64,914	66,084
36	39,476	47,162	47,874	63,471	65,248	65,920	67,088
37	39,476	47,162	47,874	64,476	66,255	66,924	68,094
38	39,476	47,162	47,874	65,481	67,261	67,929	69,099
39	39,476	47,162	47,874	65,985	67,765	68,433	69,603
40	39,476	47,162	47,874	66,489	68,268	68,938	70,106
41	39,476	47,162	47,874	66,743	68,523	69,191	70,361
42	39,476	47,162	47,874	66,996	68,776	69,445	70,614

Competency-based pay, also referred to as *skills-based pay,* or *knowledge- and skills-based pay,* rewards employees with salary increases as they acquire new knowledge or skills, or as they demonstrate higher level competence at existing abilities. Although under competency-based pay salary increases are not linked to student performance, there is an expectation that more competent employees will perform at higher levels and, subsequently, so will their students. Knowledge- and skills-based pay is also seen as a way to

CONTROVERSIAL ISSUE

Individual Performance-based Pay

Several reform reports have advocated performance-based pay for teachers. Performance-based pay requires part or all of a teacher's pay to be based on student performance. However, although the public supports the practice, teachers, as a whole, do not support performance-based pay. The reasons often given in favor of or against individual performance-based pay are as follows:

Reasons For

1. Such pay would reward good teachers and provide the incentive for them to stay in education.
2. The public would be more willing to support the schools if they knew that teachers were paid according to performance.
3. Rewarding performance is consistent with the standard applied to other workers and professions.
4. Teachers would be encouraged to improve their performance and students would be the beneficiaries.

Reasons Against

1. There is little agreement about what is good teaching or how it should be evaluated.
2. Evaluation systems are often subjective and potentially inequitable.
3. Student performance is subject to too many variables beyond the control of the school.
4. The contribution of one teacher to a student's performance is difficult to determine with any accuracy—or at least with the accuracy necessary to justify differential pay.

Why do you oppose or favor performance-based pay? Are you familiar with a school system where such pay is in operation? What effect has it had on education in that system?

 To answer these questions online, go to the *Controversial Issue* module for this chapter of the Companion Website at **http://www.prenhall.com/webb**.

align the teacher reward system with the previously discussed standards for professional teaching practice developed by the NBPTS, INTASC, and others, as well as a way to promote the development of specific skills that might be valued or needed by the school district. Teacher groups have tended to support competency-based plans because, unlike individual performance-based pay plans, under competency-based plans potentially all teachers can earn salary increases. Most districts incorporate knowledge and skills into the salary structure as an "add on" to the single salary structure. For example, as previously mentioned, many school districts provide salary supplements to teachers who receive NBPTS certification.

Compensation for Supplemental Activities

In addition to a base salary, approximately one-third of the public school teaching force receives compensation during the school year for supplemental activities such as coaching, student activity sponsorship, or teaching an extra class or evening class. The amount of the supplemental pay normally depends on some consideration of the activity involved: The more student contact hours involved, students involved, and equipment and budget involved, the larger the supplement. For example, the supplement for a senior high football coach or band director may be 8% to 10% of a fixed point on the teachers' salary schedule, whereas that of the chorus director or cheerleading coach may be 4% to 5%.

Salaries for Administrative and Support Personnel

Many teachers begin their educational careers in the classroom and then move into administrative or supervisory positions or into positions such as counselor or librarian. Most of these positions are 10- to 12-month positions and command significantly higher

Table 1.7 — Deer Valley (Arizona) Unified School District 2005–2006 Professional Staff Starting Salaries

Superintendent (contract salary)	$140,835
Assistant Superintendent for:	
Educational Services	90,000
Fiscal Services	90,000
Human Resources	90,000
Director of:	
Curriculum	80,000
Public Relations	80,000
Technology and Accountability	80,000
Principals:	
K–6 Elementary School	65,000
K–8 Elementary School	66,400
Middle School	68,000
High School	73,600
Assistant Principals:	
K–6 Elementary School	57,500
K–8 Elementary School	58,400
Middle School	60,000
High School	64,000
Nurses (BA/BS)	31,000
Psychologist	45,000

salaries, even on a monthly basis, than classroom teachers (see Table 1.7). The highest paid administrator typically is the superintendent. Superintendents in small districts earn an average of $85,000 to $100,000. Superintendents in districts with over 25,000 enrollment often earn a salary of over $175,000 per year. Principals, the administrators closest to the teacher, on the average, earn 175% of the average salary of classroom teachers. However, it must be noted that most administrative and supervisory positions do require higher levels of educational preparation and experience than that required of classroom teachers.

Indirect Compensation: Employee Benefits and Services

Many teachers receive additional compensation for supplemental activities.

Indirect compensation, commonly referred to as fringe benefits, is an important part of any teacher's compensation package and costs school districts an average of 30% of wages. Certain benefits, namely, Social Security, unemployment compensation, and workers' compensation, are required by law. Other benefits, including life insurance, health and hospitalization insurance, and long-term disability insurance, are not required by law but are voluntarily provided by the school district.

A third category of benefits includes retirement and savings plans. In most states, retirement benefits are financed jointly by teacher and public contributions. In several states, in an attempt to increase compensation without increasing state aid to education,

For Your Reflection and Analysis

Do you have any interest in becoming involved in any extracurricular activities? Which ones?

To submit your response online, go to http://www. prenhall.com/webb.

CW

school districts pay the employees' share of retirement as well as the employers' share. This benefit has great appeal to employees because it has a significant impact on net income without increasing gross taxable income. Consequently, in an increasing number of school districts this provision has become a popular item for negotiation. Also becoming increasingly popular are tax-sheltered annuities, which allow employees to invest part of their salaries, before the computation of taxes, in an annuity. This allows employees to not only reduce current taxes but also supplement any state retirement plans.

One very popular category of benefits is pay for time not worked. For public school personnel this includes sick leave, personal/emergency leave, sabbatical leave, religious leave, family and bereavement leave, civic and jury duty leave, professional leave, and military leave.

Employee services enable employees to enjoy a better lifestyle or to meet certain personal obligations at a free or reduced cost. Such services include credit unions, employee assistance programs directed at improving employee mental and emotional health, wellness programs, child care, or subsidized food services.

Rating the Schools and Teaching

Each year, the public's perceptions of the schools and issues related to the schools is assessed by the Gallup Poll of the Public's Attitudes Toward the Public Schools. The poll "has become a barometer, closely watched and debated each year by educators and policymakers" (U.S. Department of Education, 1991, p. 82). The 2005 Gallup Poll results indicated that 48% of the public surveyed gave their local schools grades of A or B, the highest in the poll's 33-year history. Table 1.8 shows the ratings given to schools in the nation as a whole, to the local schools, and to the local public school attended by the respondent's oldest child. As was true in every past poll, the more that respondents know about the school, the more likely they are to give a higher rating: Respondents gave local public schools in their communities higher ratings than the schools nationally, and the schools attended by their children were likely to be rated higher than those in the entire community.

When students in a national survey were asked to rate the teaching skills of their teachers, the results showed some interesting—and sometimes disturbing—similarities and dissimilarities across racial and ethnic groups. As the data in Table 1.9 indicate, overall, students in rural areas and white students tended to rate their teachers higher than those in urban and suburban areas or black and Hispanic students. The most disturbing finding was that across all groups, less than 40% of students surveyed gave teachers a grade of A or B for their efforts to "make learning interesting for everyone," and only one-fourth gave them an above average grade for "taking an interest in students' home and personal lives" (Harris & Associates, 1996).

PROFESSIONAL REFLECTION

The great joy of teaching is seeing a student's face light up when he finally grasps a new concept. The satisfaction of teaching is when former students return and tell me that they have graduated from high school and are attending technical college or working. (I am a special education teacher so the majority of my students do not attend a 4-year college.) They are so proud of themselves and I know that in middle school, I helped give them a foundation for success.

Chandler L. Boyd
National Board Certified
Teacher, South Carolina

To analyze this reflection, go to the *Professional Reflection* module for this chapter of the Companion Website at **http://www.prenhall.com/webb.**

Table 1.8 — Ratings Given the Public Schools, 2004

Ratings	Nation's Public Schools	Local Public Schools	Public School of Oldest Child
A&B	24	48	69
A	2	12	31
B	22	36	38
C	46	29	21
D	13	9	6
Fail	4	5	4
Don't know	13	9	—

Source: Rose, L. C., & Gallup, A. M. (2005). The 37th annual Phi Delta Kappa/Gallup poll of the public's attitudes toward the public schools. *Phi Delta Kappan, 87,* 41–54. Used by permission.

Table 1.9 — Public School Students' Ratings of Teachers and Teaching Skills, by Race/Ethnicity: 1996 (in percentages)

	Total	School Location			Race/Ethnicity		
		Urban	Suburban	Rural	White	Black	Hispanic
Teacher quality							
Excellent	16	18	17	11	15	19	16
Pretty good	57	51	56	68	62	47	51
Only fair	20	23	20	16	17	25	24
Poor	5	7	5	5	5	6	5
Don't know	1	2	2	0	1	3	4
Teaching skills							
Understanding of subject	77	71	80	83	81	68	73
Helping students who are having trouble with studies	70	67	70	74	72	67	63
Treating students with respect	65	63	63	70	67	59	61
Keeping control and discipline	65	59	66	71	68	59	56
Caring about students' futures	62	60	65	62	63	62	61
Encouraging students' academic interests	58	51	64	59	61	49	47
Making learning interesting	39	41	38	38	38	42	44
Taking an interest in students' home and personal lives	27	26	25	31	26	31	28

Source: Louis Harris and Associates. (1996). *The Metropolitan Life survey of the American teacher Part II: Students voice their opinion of their education, teachers and schools.* New York: Metropolitan Life Insurance Co. Used by permission.

Summary

There are as many definitions of *teacher* as there are reasons for becoming a teacher. It is important that those considering the profession evaluate their perceptions and expectations of teaching and their motives for considering teaching as their chosen profession.

After a period of serious criticism of the teaching profession and teacher preparation, the status of the profession appears to be improving. And a greater percentage of the practicing teaching force reports being satisfied with teaching as a career. There is still a shortage of minority teachers, but more and more bright and talented individuals are entering the teaching profession, either through traditional baccalaureate programs or through the growing number of alternative certification programs.

As the current demand for teachers intensifies, various proposals for differential compensation, including performance-based pay and competency-based pay, are being adopted in an effort to attract qualified individuals to teaching. The next chapter discusses other efforts to make teaching more attractive by increasing professionalization and reviews other professional opportunities available to teachers.

Key Terms

Alternative teacher
  certification, 15
Board certified, 17
Certification, 14
Clinical field experiences, 11

Clinical practice, 11
Competency-based pay, 21
Emergency (temporary)
  certificate, 15
Employee services, 24

Indirect compensation, 23
Interstate reciprocity, 16
Performance-based pay, 20
Single salary schedule, 19

PROFESSIONAL DEVELOPMENT WORKSHOP

Prepare for the Praxis™ Examination

Tom Metcalf, a general science teacher, and Bill Rosak, a chemistry teacher, were in discussion during their prep period in the teacher's lounge at Carlton High School. Tom had just returned from Dallas where the annual professional meeting of Secondary Teachers of Science took place. The meeting is always held on the Friday following Thanksgiving. This year he was able to take his wife, Sally, and they were able to spend Thanksgiving with her parents who live in Dallas. Tom was very excited about a new curriculum series that he had learned about at the conference that provided more hands-on projects that his students could even do at home without any formal scientific equipment. Tom was also impressed by the fact that the curriculum included a number of projects that could be adapted for students with disabilities because he has been having difficulty designing lessons that are appropriate for students with learning and physical disablties in his general science class. Tom asked Bill if he would be willing to join him in requesting that the district purchase the series for use the next year.

Toward the latter part of Tom's remarks, Bill began to shake his head. "You must be crazy, Tom," he said. "There is no way I would let any kid with a physical disability come near any chemicals. Nor do I want to be responsible for some learning disabled kids hurting themselves trying to do some take-home science experiment!" Bill went on.

Not discouraged, the very next day Tom made a request to the district textbook adoption committee that this new textbook series be approved for purchase for the following year. While waiting for the committee's response, Tom seeks the advice of his assigned mentor.

1. Under what conditions can teachers be held responsible for the injury of a student? What can teachers do to reduce their liability?

2. What approaches might Tom's mentor recommend he use to accommodate various learning styles, intelligences, or exceptionalities in his general science class? Base your response on principles of varied instruction for different kinds of learners.
3. Suggest formal and informal assessments that Tom might use to allow all students to demonstrate their accomplishments on the take-home science projects.

 To submit your responses online, go to the *Prepare for the Praxis™ Examination* module for this chapter of the Companion Website at **http://www.prenhall.com/webb**.

Build Your Knowledge Base

1. What is your perception of what a teacher is and does? How is your perception reflected in your responses to the questions at the end of the opening vignette?
2. Was there any single event or experience that motivated you to choose teaching as a career?
3. What are the advantages and disadvantages of teaching as a career? Which are the most important to your decision to consider teaching as a career?
4. What strategies should be used to attract more top-quality students to teaching?
5. Should people be required to complete a teacher training program to become a teacher? Should there be any minimum requirements?
6. The public has increasingly expressed support for the competency testing of teachers. In your opinion, should prospective teachers be required to pass a competency test?
7. The public has also shown increasing support for competency-based pay for teachers. What are the pros and cons of competency-based pay? To what extent are financial incentives likely to improve job performance?

Develop Your Portfolio

The Professional Portfolio

The professional portfolio can be used as a self-evaluation strategy, as an assessment tool to evaluate candidates for teaching positions, and to document competence for licensing/certifying agencies. The National Board for Professional Teaching Standards (NBPTS) has used the portfolio as a basis for national certification of master teachers, and a number of states require teacher portfolios prior to receiving a permanent teaching certificate.

The portfolio is an organized, goal-driven collection of evidence or artifacts. The purpose of the portfolio is to demonstrate the teacher's knowledge, skills, and abilities. The audience can be either the teacher or external reviewers. The artifacts include a wide variety of materials: lesson plans, units of study, written reports, self-reflections, essays, videotapes, photographs, and other professional documents. Reflections include written thoughts about the evidence contained in the portfolio. The portfolio serves as both a record of accomplishments and a tool for evaluating professional growth over time. You should continue to revisit/revise your portfolio throughout your education and career.

Organizing Your Professional Portfolio

One of the first steps in developing a portfolio is to consider how you will organize the types of evidence or artifacts that you choose to include. The artifacts can be displayed in either print or electronic format. Most teachers include both formats in their portfolios.

Allow yourself ample time to develop and organize your professional portfolio into a series of appropriately labeled files. Organizing and setting up your portfolio filing system may be one of the more time-consuming portfolio tasks. However, once the system is in place you will not have to repeat this exercise again unless you decide to modify and improve on its filing system. First you will need to prepare a series of 10 files, each labeled with one of the 10 INTASC standards presented in Table 1.3 on page 9. As you read each chapter of the text you will be directed to develop a portfolio activity that will address one or more of the INTASC standards.

Three-ring binders, labeled file folders, or some form of electronic storage (e.g., CDs or DVDs) is typically used for organizing the materials that will comprise your portfolio. Should you plan to share your portfolio with an audience other than your immediate supervisor or state licensing agency, you will need to consider the legal issues involved with sharing such information. Release forms signed by parents/guardians are necessary if you plan to share any samples of students' work, or photographs or videotapes of students. An important rule of thumb is to make sure that you have blocked out any student's name. It is especially important to protect the identity of any student with special needs.

To view examples of portfolios that have been developed by other preservice teachers, as well as by beginning teachers and teachers who have received national board certification, visit http://www2.ncsu.edu/unity/lockers/project/portfolios/portfoliointro.html.

1. There are multiple reasons why individuals select teaching for a career. Reflect on Herbert Kohl's questions for prospective teachers presented in the *Ask Yourself* feature on page **7**. Using these reflections as a guide, write an essay about your own reasons for choosing to pursue or continue a career in teaching. Revisit Kohl's questions and your essay throughout your training and career to determine how your early ideas have shaped your thoughts or experiences. Place your essay in the portfolio folder labeled **INTASC Standard 9, Reflective Practice and Professional Growth.**

2. Because there are a number of ways to become a teacher, it is important to maintain a detailed record of your educational program, including general studies courses, content studies in a major or minor, professional studies, and field experiences such as clinical practice, internship, or student teaching. One of the most important items to include in your portfolio is a *dynamic résumé* that will continue to evolve throughout your education and career. As your education progresses, list important details or summaries of your education, experiences, and skills, and pursue letters of reference and recommendations. As an in-service teacher, continue to update all sections of your résumé file and include certifications, employment experience, and continuing education.

To complete these activities online, go to the *Develop Your Portfolio* module for this chapter of the Companion Website at **http://www.prenhall.com/webb**.

Explore Teaching and Learning: Field Experiences

1. Arrange to shadow a teacher for a day. Keep a detailed log of the activities and tasks in the teacher's day.
   a. How much time is spent in instruction?
   b. How much time is spent in interaction with individual students or small groups of students?
   c. How much time is spent in interaction with colleagues? What were the topics?
   d. How much time is spent in interaction with the principal? What were the topics?
   e. How much time is spent on administrative duties (taking attendance, lunch count, recording grades, completing reports for the principal, etc.)?
   f. How much time is spent on student discipline?

2. Arrange an interview with an experienced teacher and a beginning teacher using questions such as the following:
   a. What are some of the most satisfying aspects of teaching?
   b. What parts of your job are most frustrating?
   c. What steps can you take to improve your working conditions?
   d. *For the experienced teacher:* What have you done to help beginning teachers?
   e. *For the beginning teacher:* What did experienced teachers do to help you in your early days of teaching?

Professional Development Online

CW Visit this text's Companion Website at **http://www.prenhall.com/webb** to gain access to a variety of questions, activities, and exercises to help build your knowledge of this chapter's content. Below are just a few items available at this text's Companion Website:

- Classroom Video—To see actual classroom footage and work through activities and questions to analyze the content of the video, click on the *Classroom Video* module for this chapter.
- Teaching Tolerance—To go to this organization's website and complete activities to explore issues and topics dealing with how to teach tolerance to students, click on the *Teaching Tolerance* module for this chapter.
- Self-Test—To review terms and concepts presented in this chapter, click on the *Self-Test* module for this chapter.
- Internet Resources—To link to websites related to topics in this chapter, go to the *Internet Resources* module for this chapter.

CHAPTER 2

*A teacher who is attempting to teach without inspiring the child
to learn is hammering on a cold iron.*
—Horace Mann (1796–1859)

DEVELOPMENT OF THE PROFESSION

Mike, a new first-year middle school teacher and drama coach, has been contacted about joining the local teachers' organization and its state and national affiliates. He has also been contacted about joining the informal county drama coach's association and the state association. Mike has limited funds and does not feel that he can afford membership in all three groups. Mike is also concerned about the differ-

ence between being a "joiner" or being an active contributing member in the organization(s).

What principles and values should guide Mike's decision about membership? What are the relative benefits of joining the local teachers' organization or the organization for one's subject area or grade level? What responsibilities do you assume when you join a professional organization?

Teaching is considered by many to be "work of the most demanding sort, for teachers must make dozens of decisions daily, command a wide body of knowledge and skill, learn to react instantly, and be disposed to act wisely in difficult situations" (National Board for Professional Teaching Standards [NBPTS], 2005, p. 3). Teaching is a complex craft, calling for ongoing personal and professional reflection and commitment. This chapter focuses on teaching as a profession. The major sections of this chapter address (1) the requirements of a profession, (2) the factors working to improve the professionalization of teaching, (3) professional development for teachers, (4) evaluation of teacher performance, and (5) professional organizations for teachers. As you read and discuss this chapter and the related activities, consider the following outcome objectives and their impact on you as a potential teacher:

- Evaluate the duties of elementary and secondary school teachers in terms of the recognized criteria for a profession.
- Identify developments in the professionalization of teaching in your state.
- Develop a personal plan for professional development.
- Identify the factors that should be considered in teacher evaluations.
- Distinguish between a career ladder salary schedule for teachers and a traditional salary schedule based on education level and experience.
- Identify the programs and services provided by the major teacher organizations in your state and local school districts.
- Describe the programs and services provided by the professional organization for your teaching field.

Teaching as a Profession

Is teaching a profession? Many references are made to the profession of teaching, but the actual status of teaching as a profession continues to be a matter of discussion and debate. Few would contend that teaching has attained the status of medicine or law, but some argue that teaching as an occupation compares favorably with the ministry, accounting, engineering, and similar professions. While educators and others debate whether teaching is a profession, sociologists have developed what is known as the *professional model—* "a series of organizational and occupational characteristics associated with professions and professionals and, hence useful to distinguish professions and professionals from other kinds of work and workers" (Ingersoll, 2004, p. 103). These characteristics or requirements for a job to be considered a profession are discussed in the following sections.

Requirements of a Profession

Among the most commonly considered criteria for classifying an occupation as a **profession** are those presented in Figure 2.1. The criteria discussed in this chapter include specialized knowledge and preparation, provision of essential services to society, exercise of discretion, autonomy and freedom from direct supervision, a code of professional standards, and a professional code of ethics.

Specialized Knowledge and Preparation

Professions are sometimes referred to as "knowledge-based" occupations (Ingersoll, 2004). Teaching is clearly that. Teaching requires professionals who possess specialized knowledge acquired during a period of specialized study. While policy makers and members of the academic community do not all agree on the course of study that best produces a teacher, there is general agreement that this specialized knowledge should include:

> a broad grounding in the liberal arts and sciences; knowledge of the subjects to be taught, of the skills to be developed, and of the curricular arrangements and materials that organize and embody that content; knowledge of general and subject-specific methods for teaching and for evaluating student learning; knowledge of students and human development; skills in effectively teaching students from racially, ethnically, and socio-economically diverse backgrounds; and the skills, capacities and dispositions to employ such knowledge wisely in the interest of students. (American Federation of Teachers, 2000)

Figure 2.1 — Criteria for Classifying an Occupation as a Profession

According to the National Labor Relations Act, the occupation must:

- Be an intellectual endeavor
- Involve discretion and judgment
- Have an output that cannot be standardized
- Require advanced knowledge
- Require a prolonged period of specialized study

In addition, the American Association of Colleges of Teacher Education calls for:

- Provision of essential services to society
- Decision making in providing services
- Organization into one or more professional societies for the purpose of socialization and promotion of the profession
- Autonomy in the actual day-to-day work
- Agreed-upon performance standards
- Relative freedom from direct supervision

When and how this knowledge and skills should be acquired and developed are the subjects of some debate. Some education reform reports have advocated that professional education courses be delayed until completion of general education and academic major requirements, or even until after completion of the baccalaureate degree. Other reformers have suggested that college graduates with no professional education courses should be permitted to serve as intern teachers, but with a higher level of supervision than that traditionally provided for beginning teachers. For most teachers the route to the profession has been one of the preparation programs for elementary and secondary teachers, as described in Chapter 1. As discussed there, the content of the programs has been heavily influenced by the professional standards developed by the Interstate New Teacher Assessment and Support Consortium (INTASC), the standards for colleges of education developed by the National Council for the Accreditation of Teacher Education (NCATE), and the content of the Praxis™ tests used in most states as a requirement for teacher certification.

Provision of Essential Services to Society

Most Americans would acknowledge that teachers provide an essential service to society. The importance of education in a democratic society has always been recognized: "If a nation expects to be ignorant and free in a state of civilization, it expects what never was and never will be." This often-quoted statement by Thomas Jefferson reinforces the importance of education to the preservation of the nation. Teachers play a critical role in ensuring an educated populace.

This underlying belief about the role of the teacher was supported in a 2004–05 survey of new teachers, in which 85% believed that they could make a difference in the lives of their students (Markow & Martin, 2005). Other surveys of the attitudes of teachers with 1 and 2 years experience found that while this initial optimism had remained positive, it declined to about 70% (Markow & Martin, 2005).

For Your Reflection and Analysis

How has a teacher made a difference in your life?
To submit your response online, go to http://www. prenhall.com/webb.

CW

The Exercise of Discretion

Given the relative isolation of individual classrooms and the variety of decisions that a teacher must make during the typical school day, teachers routinely exercise discretion and judgment in providing services to their students. Teachers in schools with empowered site councils have even more workplace influence. However, teachers are not free agents. They function in an educational environment that is larger than an individual classroom, constrained by school policies and regulations, district curriculum guides, and state requirements. Such district-wide concerns as scope and sequence of instruction must be considered. The typical teacher has a group of students for 1 year, but the educational experiences in that classroom during that year provide the foundation for future learning. Thus, teachers' instructional decisions need to be in harmony with those of their peers as well as the state and the district's curriculum standards and assessment policies.

Autonomy and Freedom From Direct Supervision

Teachers have a relatively high degree of autonomy in their actual day-to-day work, and the degree of direct supervision is rather limited. Still, teachers function in the social setting of a school with other teachers, and the culture of the school requires a degree of structure and interaction among both teachers and students. In addition, parents and taxpayers have an interest in ensuring that teachers act as responsible professionals. Some degree of supervision is necessary to provide the desired assurances.

Code of Professional Standards

Many professions have adopted a code of professional standards that is monitored and enforced by its members sitting as boards or commissions (e.g., a state board of psychologist examiners). To date, the teaching profession does not police its own members through an independent body. However, teachers are policed by public agencies, typically at the state

Figure 2.2 — Code of Ethics of the Education Profession

Preamble

The educator, believing in the worth and dignity of each human being, recognizes the supreme importance of the pursuit of truth, devotion to excellence, and the nurture of democratic principles. Essential to these goals is the protection of freedom to learn and to teach and the guarantee of equal educational opportunity for all. The educator accepts the responsibility to adhere to the highest ethical standards.

The educator recognizes the magnitude of the responsibility inherent in the teaching process. The desire for the respect and confidence of one's colleagues, of students, of parents, and of the members of the community provides the incentive to attain and maintain the highest possible degree of ethical conduct. The *Code of Ethics of the Education Profession* indicates the aspiration of all educators and provides standards by which to judge conduct.

The remedies specified by the NEA and/or its affiliates for the violation of any provision of this *Code* shall be exclusive and no such provision shall be enforceable in any form other than one specifically designated by the NEA or its affiliates.

Principle I: Commitment to the Student

The educator strives to help each student realize his or her potential as a worthy and effective member of society. The educator therefore works to stimulate the spirit of inquiry, the acquisition of knowledge and understanding, and the thoughtful formulation of worthy goals.

In fulfillment of the obligation to the student, the educator–

1. Shall not unreasonably restrain the student from independent action in the pursuit of learning.

2. Shall not unreasonably deny the student access to various points of view.

3. Shall not deliberately suppress or distort subject matter relevant to the student's progress.

4. Shall make reasonable effort to protect the student from conditions harmful to learning or to health and safety.

5. Shall not intentionally expose the student to embarrassment or disparagement.

6. Shall not on the basis of race, color, creed, sex, national origin, marital status, political or religious beliefs, family, social or cultural background, or sexual orientation unfairly–

    a. Exclude any student from participation in any program

    b. Deny benefits to any student

    c. Grant any advantage to any student

7. Shall not use professional relationships with students for private advantages.

8. Shall not disclose information about students obtained in the course of professional service, unless disclosure serves a compelling purpose or is required by law.

level. Such bodies are referred to as professional practices boards or commissions. Their purpose is to take appropriate disciplinary action against teachers following a review or report of questionable professional conduct. Typically their membership includes teachers and public members.

Professional Codes of Ethics

Many professions also have **codes of ethics** that serve as standards for behavior of members of the profession. Codes of ethics do not have the status of law, but they indicate the aspirations of members of the profession and provide standards by which to judge members' conduct. In some instances, a professional organization monitors and enforces the code of ethics for its membership. In others, a public agency may assume the monitoring and enforcement role. Reporting of noncompliance can come from a variety of sources, including professional peers, clients, supervisors, and the public.

Figure 2.2 — Continued

Principle II: Commitment to the Profession
The education profession is vested by the public with a trust and responsibility requiring the highest ideals of professional service.

In the belief that the quality of the services of the education profession directly influences the nation and its citizens, the educator shall exert every effort to raise professional standards, to promote a climate that encourages the exercise of professional judgement, to achieve conditions which attract persons worthy of the trust to careers in education, and to assist in preventing the practice of the profession by unqualified persons.

In fulfillment of the obligation to the profession, the educator—

1. Shall not in an application for a professional position deliberately make a false statement or fail to disclose a material fact related to competency and qualifications.

2. Shall not misrepresent his/her professional qualifications.

3. Shall not assist any entry into the profession of a person known to be unqualified in respect to character, education, or other relevant attribute.

4. Shall not knowingly make a false statement concerning the qualifications of a candidate for a professional position.

5. Shall not assist a noneducator in the unauthorized practice of teaching.

6. Shall not disclose information about colleagues obtained in the course of professional service unless disclosure serves a compelling professional purpose or is required by law.

7. Shall not knowingly make false or malicious statements about a colleague.

8. Shall not accept any gratuity, gift, or favor that might impair or appear to influence professional decisions or actions.

Source: From National Education Association. (2002). *Code of ethics of the education profession* (pp. 1–3). Washington, DC: Author. Reprinted by permission.

The ethical considerations for teaching are different from other professions. As noted by the NBPTS (2000):

> Unique demands arise because a client's attendance is compulsory and, more importantly, because the clients are children. Thus, elementary, middle and high school teachers are obligated to meet a stringent ethical standard. Other ethical demands derive from the teacher's role as a model of an educated person. Teaching is a public activity; a teacher works daily in the gaze of his or her students, and the extended nature of their lives together in schools places special obligations on the teacher's behavior. Students learn early to draw and read lessons from their teacher's character. Teachers, consequently, must conduct themselves in a manner students might emulate. Their failure to practice what they preach does not long elude students, parents, or peers. Practicing with this additional dimension in mind calls for a special alertness to the consequences of manner and behavior. Standards for professional teaching ought, therefore, to emphasize its ethical nature. (p. 1)

The National Education Association (NEA) has adopted a code of ethics for the education profession. The NEA Code of Ethics, presented in detail in Figure 2.2, contains two sections: commitment to students and commitment to the profession. The student section notes the expectations of fair, equitable, and nondiscriminatory treatment of students. The section on commitment to the profession contains standards of personal conduct in the performance of professional duties and relationships to others.

In the past, codes of conduct for teachers were adopted by local school boards. These codes often were related to personal as well as professional conduct, regulating such things as marital status, style of clothing, and places in the community that were "off limits" to teachers. In those days, failure to abide by the requirements was used as justification for dismissal or other punitive action against teachers. The requirements of yesteryear are quite different from the current concept of codes of ethics that focus much more on professional conduct than on out-of-school behavior.

For Your Reflection and Analysis

Do you think that teachers should have a dress code if there is one for students?

To submit your response online, go to http://www.prenhall.com/webb.

The Increased Professionalization of Teaching

Great strides in the professionalization of teaching were made in the last decade of the 20th century. The factors that have contributed to the increased professionalization of teaching include these:

1. Standards for teacher education programs have been raised.
2. State licensing requirements have been increased.
3. Entry-level examinations for teachers have been mandated in most states.
4. Professional certification programs such as national board certification have been implemented.
5. Performance-based pay programs with the potential of both increasing the financial rewards of teaching and recognizing those teachers who are taking steps to increase their competencies have been implemented in some states and a growing number of school districts.
6. Teaching has come to be viewed as a career with opportunities for advancement.

Some of these were discussed in Chapter 1. Those that were not are discussed here: the widespread adoption of professional standards for teachers, the establishment of standards and certification for advanced practice, and increased opportunities for professional development and career advancement.

Development of Professional Standards

The interest in and acceptance of national standards for both student and teacher performance has been in large part an outcome of the school reform movement. The National Board for Professional Teaching Standards (NBPTS) has developed standards for experienced teachers; INTASC has developed standards for beginning teachers; NCATE has developed standards for institutions that prepare educators; states have developed teacher education program approval standards; and content standards have been developed by a variety of content specialist organizations such as the National Council of Teachers of Mathematics. The INTASC standards presented in Table 1.3 describe the "core" knowledge, dispositions, and performances all teachers are expected to possess and demonstrate. The standards have been translated into standards for a number of subject areas and still others are being developed. These standards have been adopted or adapted for teacher licensure in a number of states.

National Board Certification.   The development of standards for experienced teachers has been the work of the NBPTS. The first group of teachers received NBPTS **national board certification** in 1995. By 2004, 40,000 teachers had become board certified. National board certification is valid for 10 years; the purpose of the process is to complement, not replace, state licensing of teachers (NBPTS, 2001).

Rather than relying on a series of field experiences and satisfactory performance on a standardized test, the individualized portfolio is the centerpiece of the national certification process (NBPTS, 2002). To achieve national board certification, the teacher must have completed a minimum of 3 years of teaching, participated in a variety of personal and professional self-reflection activities, and completed performance-based assessments. The process assesses not only the teacher's knowledge, but also the demonstration of skills and professional judgment in the classroom. The focus is on what teachers should know and be able to do.

While the 40,000 board-certified teachers represent only a very small percentage of the teaching force, their numbers are growing rapidly. This can be attributed in no small part to the professional and financial rewards associated with achieving board certification. In 2005, 39 states were providing financial incentives and 49 states provided licensure incentives for teachers to secure national board certification (Skinner, 2005). State incentives vary considerably. For example, Texas gives no financial incentive, but passage of an NBPTS assessment may be used in lieu of Texas exams for persons certified outside of Texas; whereas North Carolina, the state with the highest number of board-certified teachers, pays the certification fee ($2,300 in 2005), provides 3 days of release time to allow

Figure 2.3 — Number of Board Certified Teachers in Each State, 2005

State	Number
WASHINGTON	577
OREGON	147
IDAHO	317
MONTANA	40
NORTH DAKOTA	23
MINNESOTA	255
MICHIGAN	167
VERMONT	77
MAINE	72
NEW HAMPSHIRE	NH-12
MASSACHUSETTS	MA-422
RHODE ISLAND	RI-164
CONNECTICUT	CT-107
NEW JERSEY	NJ-97
DELAWARE	DE-250
MARYLAND	MD-498
WISCONSIN	267
NEW YORK	477
SOUTH DAKOTA	31
WYOMING	53
NEBRASKA	41
IOWA	461
ILLINOIS	1239
INDIANA	121
OHIO	2376
PENNSYLVANIA	180
NEVADA	183
UTAH	77
COLORADO	203
WEST VIRGINIA	203
VIRGINIA	723
CALIFORNIA	3083
KANSAS	177
MISSOURI	248
KENTUCKY	789
NORTH CAROLINA	8280
ARIZONA	237
NEW MEXICO	145
OKLAHOMA	1084
ARKANSAS	239
TENNESSEE	127
SOUTH CAROLINA	3866
COLORADO	194
LOUISIANA	578
MISSISSIPPI	2113
ALABAMA	780
GEORGIA	1780
FLORIDA	6370
HAWAII	78
ALASKA	52
PUERTO RICO	

teachers time for portfolio and assessment center exercises, and awards a 12% increase for those who achieve national board certification. In addition to state incentives, local school districts may provide various incentives; for example, a laptop computer in Graham County, North Carolina; a $2,000 one-time bonus in Flippen School District (Arkansas); or a salary increase of $2,500 per year for the life of the certificate in the Milbank (South Dakota) School District. The total number of board-certified teachers in each state is depicted in Figure 2.3.

Although research on board-certified teachers has been limited, most studies have found positive outcomes for both teachers and for students. One study of board-certified teachers suggested that as a result of the process the teachers had developed greater professional confidence, improved their ability to analyze instruction, had a clearer focus on student outcomes, and exhibited a greater commitment to professional growth (Bohen, 2001). Another study of North Carolina's board-certified teachers found that these teachers were more likely to have higher teacher licensure test scores and more likely to be teaching in more affluent districts and in districts with higher achieving students (Goldhaber, Perry, & Anthony, 2004).

Professional Development

Beyond preservice training and mentoring of beginners, professions typically require ongoing professional development of its members. "The assumption is that achieving a

For Your Reflection and Analysis

What kind of professional development should you secure for yourself; what kind should the school district provide?

To submit your response online, go to http://www.prenhall.com/webb.

CW

professional-level mastery of complex skills and knowledge is a prolonged and continuous process and, moreover, that professionals must continually update their skills as the body of technology, skill, and knowledge advances" (Ingersoll, 2004, p. 107). The need for **professional development** of teachers has been recognized. Most experts recognize that teaching is a complex endeavor that requires continued learning about the content and process of teaching.

Recognizing the importance of professional development, both the federal government and many state governments have increased their support of professional development for teachers. In 2004–05, federal funds for staff development were available through the No Child Left Behind (NCLB) Act, and state legislatures and state departments of education were encouraging professional development in different ways. For example, in 11 states local school districts were required to set aside time for the professional development of teachers, and in 27 states state funds were being provided to support general professional development activities (Skinner, 2005).

In addition to these state activities, teachers have numerous avenues available for personal and professional development. Many choose to join the professional organization most closely related to their teaching field. This membership provides access to professional materials, but perhaps the most important benefit is the contact with other teachers, which can create a professional peer support network. Other options for professional growth include conferences, focused workshops, ongoing action research projects, and participating in school district professional development programs. Another approach to professional development is to enroll in an advanced degree program in a college or university. The challenge of this approach is to develop an individualized program and to select components that will improve the competencies needed by the individual as a teacher, and at the same time meet degree requirements.

For both the novice and master teacher, action research projects (i.e., research projects designed to answer specific school-related questions), either through graduate study, mentoring of interns, or an individual project, provide insight into the ways in which research and practice can be linked to bring about school improvement. Initial efforts can be simple with more complex projects evolving with experience and confidence. The process can be enriched by a team approach and the sharing of the results with others in formal or informal settings.

In addition to the professional development activities initiated by individual teachers, school districts are devoting increased resources to planning and conducting well-conceived relevant professional development programs for their staffs. Staff development has become increasingly important because of the expanded use of a combination of technology and the accountability, standards, and assessment movements.

The National Staff Development Council (NSDC) serves as a clearinghouse for school districts and other public and private organizations on professional development issues. The council has developed a set of content, process, and context standards to guide the professional development of teachers. The standards provide directions through which educators can acquire necessary knowledge and skills. NSDC's approach to professional development is built on the assumption that teachers must continue their pursuit of knowledge and that this can best be accomplished through learning communities in which networks of communication are initially developed in the formal professional development setting(s) but are maintained and supported long after the formal session(s). The NSDC recognizes, as do all those experienced in staff development in local, state, and

Teachers participate in professional development activities throughout their professional careers.

national educational organizations and agencies, that to be effective and produce sustainable results staff development must be results driven, standards based, and job embedded.

Mentoring Programs. In contrast to other professions in which an entry-level employee often enters as a junior member of a team consisting of persons with a range of experience, the beginning teacher typically is assigned a classroom of students in an elementary school or a series of classes in a secondary school and is expected to assume the same responsibilities as an experienced teacher. To assess beginning teachers in their transition from student to teacher, by 2005, 44 states had mandated some type of mentoring program for beginning teachers (Skinner, 2005).

The concept of **mentoring** usually involves the development of a support relationship between a beginning and an experienced teacher. An important function is to provide a colleague through which the novice teacher receives basic information about the operation of the school, as well as advice, counsel, and support that the beginner may seek when confronted with routine problems. The goal of beginning teacher mentor programs is to establish a relationship and an initial professional contact that will provide a foundation and attitude of trust through which the relationship can focus on instruction and the classroom. A recent national study of principals and new teachers found that more than 80% of new teachers were assigned a mentor during their first year of teaching, and that the assignment of a skilled, experienced teacher as a mentor was helpful to new teacher development (Markow & Martin, 2005).

Mentoring is important to the success of many beginning teachers.

The implementation of a mentoring program for new teachers should not be interpreted as suggesting that their preparation program was insufficient. Teaching is a complex process, and some aspects of teaching can be learned only through experience. Teachers are more likely to remain in the profession if they are involved in an induction program that is focused on instructional skills. Both the mentor and the novice teacher can benefit and grow from the relationship, and the professional interaction can reinforce a culture of inquiry among the professional staff of a school (Danielson, 2001).

When in a mentor relationship, rather than being in isolation, teachers are involved in helping each other, and fledgling teachers view this as a positive experience. Because of the proven success of mentoring, some states and many school districts have extended their mentoring program beyond just beginning teachers. For example, Florida not only provides a 10% salary increase to board-certified teachers, the teachers are given an additional 10% salary increase if they will spend the equivalent of 12 working days providing mentoring and related services to teachers who are not national board certified.

Self-Renewal. The routine of teaching is tempered by the excitement of new students arriving each semester or school year. However, the continuing pressures of the classroom and the possibilities of teaching the same grade level or the same subject for several decades can have a depressing effect on even the most enthusiastic person. Traditionally, **self-renewal** has been viewed as the responsibility of the individual teacher; however, experience suggests that school districts can benefit from the development of joint self-renewal or professional renewal efforts with teachers (Cain, 2001).

Local school districts use a variety of approaches to address teachers' need for renewal. Among the renewal programs available in school districts across the country are:

- Sabbaticals for advanced study
- Periodic change of school or teaching assignment
- Attendance at workshops or professional conferences
- Visitation programs.

Another option involves providing teachers with alternative assignments in curriculum or staff development programs. The purpose of such programs is to recognize outstanding teachers by providing them with a break from the classroom while continuing to engage in professionally challenging experiences of benefit to the local school district.

Teachers who have participated in formal renewal programs bring an enhanced perspective to the classroom and the school, as well as a greater sense of professionalism. Cain (2001) noted that teachers who have participated in renewal programs tended to have a stronger philosophical center; a greater sense of personal responsibility; a sense of collegiality; and a commitment to students, lifelong learning, and their school. They also seemed to have developed a strong appreciation for all aspects of life and the ability to see and appreciate people as individuals. In addition, they have enhanced their ability to communicate, developed a sense of leadership, and demonstrated the ability to separate their egos from their work.

Career Advancement

Traditional career opportunities in teaching probably were more accurately defined as career opportunities in education. Elementary and secondary school teaching was often viewed as a necessary entry-level experience before one became a school administrator or college professor. Changes in teacher salaries, teacher roles, and retirement benefits have improved the professional opportunities and rewards available to teachers and allowed them to advance in their chosen profession without abandoning the classroom.

Career Ladders.   Various states and local school districts have adopted **career ladder** programs to make teaching more attractive, increase the reward system for outstanding teachers, and promote quality control of the profession. Although each district's or state's plan is unique, there are three basic types of career ladder programs:

- *Performance-based ladders.*   As teachers demonstrate increased competence, they progress to more difficult or more complex levels of work.
- *Job-enlargement ladders.*   Teachers expand their job responsibilities to include additional activities such as curriculum development, mentoring teachers, acting as department chairs, and taking up lead teacher roles.
- *Professional development ladders.*   Advancement is based on obtaining additional knowledge and skills through professional development. Such activities might include advanced degrees, staff development activities, or pursuing national board certification.

The concept of career ladders assumes different forms such as status title, pay levels, and length of contract for teachers at different levels. A typical career ladder has four stages or levels. The first level is the beginning probationary, or *apprentice teacher.* These entry-level teachers normally are on renewable annual contracts. At the end of a 3- to 5-year apprenticeship, if the teacher were to be retained, promotion would be made to the second level, *professional teacher.*

The second-level professional teacher would receive a higher base salary with additional limited annual step increases. Depending on the details of the program, a teacher could stay at this level for a minimum of 3 years if performance is satisfactory, but could stay at this level throughout a career.

The third level, often referred to as the *senior teacher* level, would receive a higher base salary with additional annual step increases. A teacher might stay at this level for a period of 5 years and, if performance were satisfactory, could stay at this level throughout a career. The assumption in most programs is that the majority of the district's experienced teachers would be at this level. Additionally, on a case-by-case basis, senior teachers could be placed on an extended contract during the summer months to work on curricular or other projects.

Attainment of the fourth level of **master teacher** typically is more complicated and may include a formal application with a portfolio that is reviewed by school district administrators and other master teachers. The decision to seek master teacher status is voluntary. These teachers are often on a full-year contract with program development responsibilities. The first step on the pay scale of master teachers might be two times the first step on the salary schedule. This status enables the school district to keep outstanding teachers in the classroom.

New Mexico has recently adopted a three-tiered licensure system in which novice teachers *may* seek advanced licenses after 3 years of service, but *must* do so after 5 years of teaching. To remain in the system and advance to the second level, novice teachers are observed annually in the classroom and must complete professional development dossiers

For Your Reflection and Analysis

What effect might a career ladder program have on the collegial environment of the typical school?

To submit your response online, go to http://www. prenhall.com/webb.

CONTROVERSIAL ISSUE

Teacher Tenure

Teacher tenure is possibly one of the most maligned and misunderstood terms in education. Originally, tenure statutes were enacted to protect teachers from political or personal abuses and to provide for a more stable teaching force. In some instances, teaching jobs were awarded as political patronage by elected school board members, superintendents, or other public officials. A school board election could result in the wholesale dismissal of teachers and principals. As teacher organizations and school districts have entered into negotiations leading to a formal agreement, tenure has become less important because those agreements typically stipulate the conditions under which a teacher may be dismissed.

Pros—Positions in Support of Tenure Include:

1. Tenure is essential to protect the teacher from arbitrary and capricious dismissal for reasons unrelated to performance in the classroom.
2. Tenure statutes protect the rights of the individual and provide for an orderly review and due process.
3. Tenure statutes stipulate the legal procedures under which a teacher's right to employment may be reviewed and terminated.
4. Tenure statutes and regulations ensure that the teacher understands the deficiency (problem) and has an opportunity to correct the problem.
5. The security of tenure status may encourage some persons to enter teaching.

Cons—Positions in Opposition to Tenure Include:

1. Teachers in probationary status remain in the classroom and continue to teach.
2. Cumbersome and extensive dismissal procedures result in the retention and/or rotating assignments of incompetent teachers from one school to another or from teaching to some support role in the schools.
3. Tenured teachers often are not evaluated as often as probationary teachers.
4. Persons may be less interested in teaching as a career if tenure is not available.

What do you think? Should tenure be retained or repealed? Should student performance be considered in decisions about retention or dismissal of teachers? Should a person's tenure status be subject to review periodically, for example, after a 5-year cycle?

 To answer these questions online, go to the *Controversial Issue* module for this chapter of the Companion Website at **http://www.prenhall.com/webb**.

that are scored by trained reviewers. After 3 years of service at the second level, teachers with advanced licenses may, but are not required to, seek advancement to the third level. If these latter teachers choose to seek the third level, they must (1) hold a post-baccalaureate degree or national board certification, (2) have demonstrated instructional leadership competence, (3) submit a second professional dossier to the trained reviewers, and (4) provide other supportive documentation (NMSA, 2005).

   Teacher-Leaders. The components of the various school improvement models discussed in Chapter 15 project teachers into various leadership roles in school improvement efforts and call for teachers to assume a more active role in determining the direction of a school's program. Expanded roles for teachers are also consistent with the positions of the major teacher organizations. The term **teacher-leader** has become a term commonly associated with this expanded role.

   The opportunities for teachers to assume leadership roles are many and diverse; they range from the formal roles of department chair or officer in teachers' organizations to an informal role as adviser or mentor to those in formal leadership roles. Some serve as mentors, peer evaluators, and interveners who assist fellow teachers in need of support and coaching. In addition to providing leadership at the building level, some teachers work at the district or state level in curriculum development or professional development programs, policy development or revision projects, or writing grants to public or private agencies to support student or faculty growth. Because effective teacher leaders model what needs to be done in schools, these teachers have a level of enhanced credibility (Kauchak & Eggen, 2005).

Evaluating Teacher Performance

The standards-driven education reform movement has provided momentum for the development and refinement of teacher evaluation systems. Almost all states have now adopted legislation that requires the evaluation of teachers. At the same time, the focus on improving student achievement and state mandated standards-based assessment have led to the adoption of teacher evaluation systems that include student performance. In fact, as was discussed in Chapter 1, several states and a number of school districts have adopted compensation plans that directly link teacher pay to teacher as well as student performance.

The two types of teacher evaluation are *summative evaluation* and *formative evaluation.* Summative evaluation is conducted at the end of an activity or time period and is designed to assess terminal behaviors or overall performance. Summative evaluation is used to make such personnel decisions as contract renewal, the awarding of tenure, performance pay, or assignment to levels on a career ladder. Formative evaluation, unlike summative evaluation, is ongoing. It is intended to provide continuing feedback to the person being evaluated for the purpose of self-improvement or professional development. Most teacher evaluation systems are designed to provide multiple options for teachers to participate in a variety of self-growth activities based on their individual needs. Examples of these self-growth activities include peer coaching, conducting action research projects in the classroom, developing portfolios, and developing personal professional development plans (Danielson, 2001; Painter, 2001). These multiple options recognize that teachers not only have different teaching styles but also have different learning styles as well.

Observation of classroom performance by a supervisor is an important part of teacher evaluation.

Teachers are evaluated using a set of criteria developed by the state or local school district. Many states have adopted or adapted the **Praxis**™ or INTASC standards in formulating the criteria for the evaluation of beginning teachers. An example of the evaluation criteria used by the Clark County (Nevada) School District is shown in Figure 2.4.

By far the most common method used to collect data for the evaluation is the observation of teaching. The beginning teacher will normally be observed several times during the school year, usually by the principal or assistant principal. The observation is typically scheduled and may be for an entire lesson or period or shorter, more frequent observations may be conducted. Teacher self-evaluation, teacher portfolio assessment, and peer evaluation are also commonly used in combination with teacher observation.

Teachers' Organizations

Teachers often are confronted with the choice of which and how many professional organizations to join. They may affiliate with one of the national teachers' organizations and/or the state affiliate. They may also affiliate with organizations whose focus is on a particular subject or educational specialty. In some districts, there may be only one active teacher organization; in others, the new teacher may have the opportunity to choose among two or more organizations. Affiliation is often seen as an indication of the commitment to teaching as a profession and as a career.

Figure 2.4 — Example of Evaluation Criteria

9998-500008

CLARK COUNTY SCHOOL DISTRICT
LICENSED EMPLOYEE APPRAISAL REPORT

CCF-8 MS (Rev07/03)

Employee's Name: _____   School/Location: _____

Social Security No.: _____   Assignment: _____   Years in CCSD: _____   Location: _____

Observation Dates: From _____ to _____   Conference Date: _____   Page 1 of _____

Report and analysis of observations, performance, and other factors which may be pertinent to performance; probationary/postprobationary status, date of last evaluation, and directions.

LEVELS OF PERFORMANCE

Level 4	Performance exceeds standards consistently at a distinguished level.	**Level 2**	Performance approaches standards and/or does not consistently meet standards.*
Level 3	Performance consistently meets standards and may occasionally exceed standards in some areas.	**Level 1**	Performance is below standards and is not satisfactory.*

*Any area(s) marked Level 1 or 2 require documentation. Any area(s) marked Level 1, or 8 or more areas marked Level 2 results in an overall rating of "Not Satisfactory."

PROFESSIONAL DOMAINS

PLANNING AND PREPARATION	4	3	2	1
PROFESSIONAL STANDARDS				
1. Instructional planning was documented in written lesson plans and based on adopted curriculum documents and standards.				
2. Content knowledge was demonstrated in planning.				
3. Planning, reflected knowledge of student achievement, access/equity, students' interests and backgrounds, and other site-specific demographic data.				

ASSESSMENT OF STUDENT ACHIEVEMENT	4	3	2	1
PROFESSIONAL STANDARDS				
1. Student achievement, access/equity, and other site specific demographic data were analyzed.				
2. Desired results for student learning/achievement were identified, measurable, and used for instructional planning to determine and monitor student progress.				
3. Assessment regulations and guidelines were followed.				

LEARNING ENVIRONMENT	4	3	2	1
PROFESSIONAL STANDARDS				
1. An academic focus and on-task behavior were maintained.				
2. A classroom management/discipline plan was in place, communicated and maintained.				
3. Respect and courtesy were modeled by the teacher in student and parent interactions.				
4. The physical environment supported the teaching/learning process.				

INSTRUCTION	4	3	2	1
PROFESSIONAL STANDARDS				
1. The components of an effective lesson and the basic principles of learning were used when providing instruction.				
2. Varied instructional strategies, approaches, and resources, aligned with instructional objectives, engaged students in learning.				

INSTRUCTION (continued)	4	3	2	1
3. Lessons had a clearly defined structure and pacing was appropriate.				
4. Flexible instructional groupings were utilized.				
5. Accommodations and/or modifications were used in alignment with instructional objectives to meet the needs of students.				
6. Feedback to students was provided and promoted student success and achievement.				

PROFESSIONAL RESPONSIBILITIES	4	3	2	1
PROFESSIONAL STANDARDS				
1. The employee participated in the school improvement process and implemented school improvement goals.				
2. The employee addressed identified individual improvement goals/directions.				
3. The employee participated in on-going professional development to improve content knowledge and pedagogical skills.				
4. The employee participated in required job-related meetings and activities and performed assigned duties.				
5. The employee maintained student records.				
6. The employee provided communication to parents/guardians and students related to behavior and achievement.				
7. The employee worked professionally with administration, staff, parents, and community.				
8. The employee used multicultural resources, materials and activities to support multicultural literacy, awareness, and appreciation.				
9. The employee complied with all school and district policies and regulations, as well as state and federal laws applicable to teachers.				

A narrative, which includes a PERFORMANCE SUMMARY and IMPROVEMENTGOALS/DIRECTIONS, must be included on the following page.

I certify that I have supervised and evaluated the professional performance of the above named ☐ probationary   ☐ post probationary employee,

and I certify that to date this school year his/her overall performance ☐ is   ☐ is not satisfactory.

_____   _____
*Signature of Employee   Date

_____   _____
Signature of Supervising Administrator   Date

☐ A response will be made (within 30 working days).

☐ A response was submitted on _____   _____   _____
                                Date   Signature of Supervising Administrator Receiving Response   Date

*A signature on this summary does not necessarily mean the licensed employee agrees with the opinions expressed, but merely indicates the employee has read the analysis, had an opportunity for discussion with his/her immediate supervisor, and understands that he/she has the privilege of discussing it with the Human Resources Division.

031 DISTRIBUTION: Original – Licensed Personnel   1st copy -- Supervising Administrator -- Work Location File   2nd copy -- Licensed Employee

CCF-8 (Rev. 07/03 MSWord)

The challenge for new teachers is to choose carefully from among the options and make the choices that will benefit them most as they begin their teaching careers. An important consideration may be at the teacher's level of commitment to the organization and its program or the extent to which the teacher intends to become involved in the organization's activities.

National Organizations for Teachers

There are two major national organizations for teachers: the National Education Association (NEA) and the American Federation of Teachers (AFT). The NEA is the larger of the two national teachers' organizations. Formed in 1857 as a professional association, NEA members work at every level of education and are found in all types of school districts. In contrast, the AFT has fewer total members, and its activities are concentrated in the nation's urban areas. The membership of both organizations includes an increasingly diverse group of persons working in education as well as classroom teachers. Some persons hold memberships in both organizations. The NEA's membership is about 2.7 million in more than 14,000 local communities and affiliates in all states; the AFT's membership is about 1.3 million; the AFT has more than 3,000 local affiliates and 43 state affiliates. The AFT's membership also includes local, state, and federal government employees and health care professionals (NEA, 2005a; AFT, 2005b).

For almost 100 years, the NEA was the umbrella organization for college and university faculty as well as elementary and secondary education teachers and administrators. (See the Historical Note for a short history of the NEA.) Various teacher specialty and administrator organizations were under the NEA umbrella, and individuals held memberships in the specialty group and the overarching organization. Until the 1960s, leadership roles in the NEA and its state affiliates often were held by school superintendents and higher education personnel. Starting in the 1960s, elementary and secondary school classroom teachers began to assume the leadership roles. The organization's program now focuses

HISTORICAL NOTE

The Birth of Teachers' Unions

In 1857, teachers' organizations from 10 states joined to form the National Teachers Association (NTA). In 1870, the NTA merged with the American Normal School Association and the National Association of School Superintendents to form the National Education Association. Although the NEA was concerned with broad educational issues, it was initially dominated primarily by college presidents and school superintendents and had no division for classroom teachers. The organization did not concern itself with teacher welfare. Indeed, NEA leaders would not have thought that such action was professional. At this point, the NEA was in no sense a labor union.

The first teachers' labor union was the Chicago Teachers Federation (CTF), formed in 1897. In 1902,

the CTF affiliated with the Chicago Federation of Labor, an action that was condemned by the Chicago school board. The CTF eventually severed the tie when it lost a battle against the school board's arbitrary decision against union membership. Even with this setback, the CTF continued to grow. In New York City, another union, the Interborough Association of Women Teachers, claimed 12,000 members in the early 1900s and was the largest local teachers' union in the country. Unions were also formed in many other cities as teachers sought to follow the lead of the growing labor union movement and improve their working conditions through organizational representation and membership.

more on services to teachers and state and local teacher organizations. The NEA advocates
for improvement in teacher education programs, pushes for higher standards in teacher
licensure, and assumes greater control of the
professional development of teachers.

After considering a merger for several
years, in 2000, the NEA and AFT formed a
partnership under which each organization
would be free to differ and operate separately
and independently. The partnership, referred
to as the NEAFT, is governed by a joint council
that has the authority to make decisions and
to advance goals that are in conformity with
the policies and directives of each organization's governing body (NEA, 2005b).

Both the NEA and the AFT provide a variety of professional development activities
and services for their members. Publications
include national research reports, journals for

*National teachers organizations work to improve the status and working
conditions of teachers.*

members (the NEA's *Today's Education* and the AFT's *Changing Education*) and a variety of handbooks and related documents. Most of these publications are oriented toward
improving teacher performance and working conditions, or providing source information
about the status of American education. Both organizations conduct annual conferences
at the state and national levels and provide a variety of workshop training activities related
to either professional or organizational development.

The primary goals of both organizations have been to enhance the professional status
and working conditions of teachers and to create a more positive attitude toward teachers and education. As both organizations have become more involved in public policy issues and have attempted to influence state and federal legislation, they have been
subjected to criticism as being at odds with the sentiment of rank-and-file members on
school standards and accountability (King, 2004).

State Organizations for Teachers

Both the NEA and the AFT have units at the state level. The NEA has affiliates in all states
that serve as advocates for teacher tenure and certification statutes, revisions in state
school finance programs, federal aid for education, and related educational improvements.
The AFT also supports many similar activities, but the general perception has been that
the AFT's strength has been concentrated in the organizational units at the local school
district level. The AFT has affiliates in 43 states.

Local Organizations for Teachers

Local organizations provide many benefits, including the opportunity to interact with fellow professionals in both professional and social activities. Other benefits are related to
the collective representation of the teachers in discussions with the school board and
administration.

At the school district level, both the NEA and the AFT have encouraged teachers to negotiate salaries and working conditions with local school district administrators and
school boards. The AFT has been bargaining virtually since its creation; the NEA started
major professional negotiations or collective bargaining initiatives in the 1960s. During
the intervening years, in most of the states, teachers have become actively involved in formal and informal negotiations with school boards. In some states, the negotiations are voluntary; in others, school boards are required by state law to enter into a contract with the
local teachers' organizations about salaries and working conditions. The result has been
an increase in the control and input that teachers have over issues related to their salaries
and conditions of employment.

**For Your Reflection
and Analysis**

As a new teacher, what
kinds of assistance
do you expect from
the local teachers'
organization?

*To submit your response
online, go to http://www.
prenhall.com/webb.*

CW

Subject-Matter Organizations for Teachers

In addition to the general organizations for all teachers, professional organizations have been formed for each discipline. Professional development activities provided by the subject-matter organizations typically include publications, conferences, and workshops for members. These subject-matter organizations are independent of the U.S. Department of Education, state educational agencies, and local school districts. They are less prone to be politically active than the two national teacher organizations.

Some specialized organizations such as the Council for Exceptional Children (CEC) include as their members parents and interested citizens as well as professional educators. Others, such as the National Conference of Teachers of English (NCTE), the National Council of Teachers of Mathematics (NCTM), the National Council for the Social Studies (NCSS), and the National Science Teachers Association (NSTA), draw their members from teachers at all levels of education. Subject-matter organizations typically do not become involved in direct discussions with school officials about working conditions of teachers; however, they may adopt statements of principles or standards about total teaching load, textbook selection procedures, and selection and use of instructional materials. The subject-matter groups are involved in the development of the content standards for their subject areas. In this way, the specialized organizations do assume an advocacy role for changes in state or federal legislation related to their teaching area.

Examples of other organizations oriented to specific support roles in the schools include the American Library Association (ALA) and the American Association for Counseling and Development (AACD). A broader based organization is the Association for Supervision and Curriculum Development (ASCD), which includes teachers, administrators, and college professors. Specialized organizations for school district central office personnel and building principals include the American Association of School Administrators (AASA), the National Association of Secondary School Principals (NASSP), and the National Association of Elementary School Principals (NAESP). With some exceptions, these groups tend to be stronger at the state and national levels. Both the NASSP and the AASA have recently initiated assessment programs to improve the professional knowledge and skills of administrators.

PROFESSIONAL REFLECTION

Teaching is as much a profession as law or medicine. The difference is that teaching is a very public act that everyone has experienced. While we only periodically observe doctors or lawyers at work, most of us have seen teachers at work through our own education. Teachers must go through a licensing process, as do doctors, lawyers, and architects. Teachers must document their growth in expertise over time, as the profession demands one to stay current with research and best instructional practice. Most importantly, the teacher's work day or year is not defined by the direct contact hours with the consumer; while students may be at school for 6.5 hours per day, 180 days a year—teachers engage in professional duties all the time.... A teacher spends 2 hours planning for every hour she or he teaches—with most of this time occurring outside of the school day. Teachers perceive their work as extending well beyond the actual lesson, as one lesson or teaching moment may lay the groundwork for a child's future educational and life choices. A teacher introduces him- or herself to a stranger more often than not with a short, but powerful sentence following close behind: "I teach."

Laura King
National Board Certified
Teacher, Vermont

To analyze this reflection, go to the *Professional Reflection* module for this chapter of the Companion Website at **http://www.prenhall.com/webb**.

Teachers' Organizations and Public Policy Issues

The range of federal and state proposals related to accountability, standards, and assessment has placed greater pressures on the major teachers' organizations. In an effort to respond with a broader base, the AFT and NEA formed the NEAFT partnership. The NEAFT is governed by a joint council with members from both organizations. The council has the authority to make decisions and to advance goals that are in conformity with the policies and directives of each organization's governing body. This arrangement will enable the organizations to be more effective in representing their membership and presenting a united front on public policy issues on areas of agreement; however, each organization also would be free to differ and operate separately and independently. This effort at collaboration enables the two organizations to advocate, support, and coordinate mutually agreed-on national, state, regional, and local activities (NEA, 2005b).

Other professional groups such as the CEC, NSTA, and NCTM have had a continuing interest in the passage and implementation of both state and federal legislation. These groups and other educational interest groups have an interest in the effects of NCLB, state school finance proposals, and federal and state elementary and secondary education programs for students with disabilities, educationally disadvantaged students, and at-risk youth.

Summary

One outcome of the school accountability movement has been an increased expectation of teachers. Advances have also been made in procedures for evaluating teachers, and local school districts are providing increased opportunities for professional development. The effect of accountability on teacher quality and quantity is not known. Enforcement of higher standards may cause teachers to leave the profession or may attract more as the reputation of the profession is enhanced. The old view of teaching as a stepping stone to careers in administration and higher education is being replaced by the perception of teaching as a career in itself. As job rewards and leadership opportunities have increased, other changes in working conditions have made the teaching profession more attractive.

In Chapter 3, you will have the opportunity to reflect on the major philosophies and the influence of these philosophies on the current educational process and profession.

Key Terms

Career ladder, 40
Code of ethics, 34
Master teacher, 40
Mentoring, 39

National Board Certification, 36
Praxis™, 42
Profession, 32

Professional development, 38
Self-renewal, 39
Teacher-leader, 41

PROFESSIONAL DEVELOPMENT WORKSHOP

Prepare for the Praxis™ Examination

Jason Schein has been a psychology teacher at Albert Einstein High School for the past 7 years. He is an alumnus of Albert Einstein High School and also completed his student teaching at the school. Known for his unique and innovative teaching methods, Mr. Schein was recently named the Teacher of the Year by his school district. For the past 5 years he has volunteered to accept a student teacher from the local university, which has had the reputation of preparing excellent teachers.

This semester Mr. Stephen Weissman, a senior who is completing his degree in education, was assigned to do his student teaching at Albert Einstein High School under the supervision of Mr. Schein. Following 2 weeks of observation and participation in Mr. Schein's advanced placement psychology class, tomorrow Stephen is scheduled to introduce an 8-week unit on "Psychological Disorders." Last Friday Stephen met with Mr. Schein and discussed his overall unit goal as well as each of his weekly lesson plans. He assured Mr. Schein that he had incorporated the American Psychological Association's (APA's) National Standards for High School Curricula in designing the unit.

Later this afternoon, during his regularly scheduled meeting with Mr. Schein, Stephen will ask him to review the handout that he plans to distribute tomorrow. The handout briefly describes the goals for the unit and provides a brief summary of each of the following weekly lessons: Weeks 1–2: Characteristics and Origins of Abnormal Behavior; Weeks 3–4: Research Methods Used in Exploring Abnormal Behavior; Weeks 5–6: Major Categories of Abnormal Behavior; and Weeks 7–8: Impact of Mental Disorders.

Tomorrow Stephen also plans to share with the class the unit homework assignments as well as the criteria that will be used for grading. While Stephen has not yet finalized his decision about assignments, he is considering asking each student to choose a psychological disorder, identify the symptoms of the disorder as classified in the APA's *Diagnostic and Statistical Manual,* and develop an appropriate treatment plan from each of the following orientations: (1) behavioral, (2) cognitive, (3) psychoanalytic, (4) humanistic, (5) feminist, and (6) biomedical. In addition to this written assignment, Stephen is also considering using the objective and essay examination that accompanies the textbook at the end of the unit.

Mr. Schein's Observation Notes of Mr. Weissman

First Day. Stephen Weissman briefly shared information about himself and why he chose to teach the unit on "Psychological Disorders." While it was obvious that Stephen was very enthusiastic about the topic, it was also evident that several of the students in class were not paying close attention. However, when Stephen began to talk about the assignments and grading, most of the disinterested students began to pay more attention. For a moment the entire room was silent. Then, the silence changed to loud murmurs as several students voiced their opinion: "No way. This isn't college."

Stephen continued with a PowerPoint presentation on mental illness that provided an overview of the unit. The presentation lasted until the end of the class. His presentation was sensitive, humorous, and thoughtful. He included excellent visuals including graphics, cartoons, video, and photographs. Throughout the presentation Stephen incorporated segments of music that seemed to be popular with the students as evidenced by their body movements and desk tapping sounds. The presentation ended with three questions: (1) What exactly is "a psychological disorder"? (2) Who determines what is "normal" and "abnormal" behavior? and (3) How have judgments about abnormality changed throughout history? Most students were attentive to the PowerPoint presentation.

(A scheduled faculty meeting that afternoon followed by a doctor's appointment for Mr. Schein precluded a meeting at the end of Stephen's first day of teaching.)

Second Day. Stephen again used a PowerPoint presentation that lasted the entire period to present the lesson. About halfway through the presentation several students at the back of the class (James, Ashley, and Helen) began to whisper and pass notes and Robbie appeared to be falling asleep. By the end of the class, desks were being shuffled and several students were not even pretending to pay attention to Stephen's presentation.

Mr. Schein's Notes From Meeting With Stephen Weissman

I complimented Stephen on his excellent PowerPoint presentation and his command of the subject matter but noted that he should have included some opportunities for student engagement during the lesson. I also mentioned that there were numerous new concepts presented and suggested that they may need to be reinforced throughout the unit. I also told Stephen that I thought the three questions he posed to his students at the end of his PowerPoint presentation were excellent and asked him how he plans to address these basic questions in future lesson plans.

Lastly we talked about classroom management and discussed alternatives for dealing with disruptive students.

1. Recommend TWO different strategies that Stephen might use to engage his students to become active participants throughout the unit. Explain your rationale for recommending the two strategies and why you are convinced that those strategies will be effective.

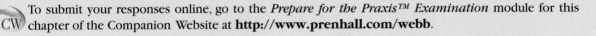

2. Describe an overall assessment plan that Stephen might use in evaluating his students' progress. Because his students are accelerated and gifted, should his criteria for grading differ from the criteria for grading used with a regular heterogeneous class? Give reasons why or why not.

3. What classroom management techniques might Mr. Schein suggest to Stephen to address disruptive behavior in the classroom?

To submit your responses online, go to the *Prepare for the Praxis™ Examination* module for this chapter of the Companion Website at **http://www.prenhall.com/webb**.

Build Your Knowledge Base

1. Which professional organization(s) do you plan to join as a new teacher, and for what reasons?
2. In what ways does teaching differ from professions such as law, medicine, and accounting?
3. To what extent will you have the knowledge and skills expected of a teacher?
4. What are the provisions for collective bargaining for teachers in your state?
5. What responsibility does the beginning teacher have for continued professional development? What are the professional development requirements for teachers in school districts with which you are familiar?
6. What steps can you take to make your teacher evaluation a positive experience that will help you improve your performance?
7. What steps are taken to monitor the extent to which teachers comply with codes of ethics in your local school districts?
8. What reasons might there be for not joining a professional organization?

Develop Your Portfolio

1. Examine Standard 9: "The teacher is a reflective practitioner who continually evaluates the effects of his/her choices and actions on others (students, parents, and other professionals in the learning community) and who actively seeks out opportunities to grow professionally." As a preservice or prospective teacher, begin recording examples of professional development activities in which you have participated during the past year. For example, you might have attended an educational lecture presented by a noted educational authority on a topic relevant to your discipline. You may choose to attend a professional organization meeting. Write a 2- to 3-page essay that includes a brief description of the activity, along with a detailed list of the concepts, ideas, or questions you considered because of the experience. How has the experience influenced your thinking? Place your essay in your portfolio under **INTASC Standard 9, Reflective Practice and Professional Growth.**

2. Odden (2000) proposed that the schools follow the example of private-sector, high-performance organizations, and incorporate into their structure incentives for teachers or schools in which student performance has improved. On the other hand, Holt (2001) has raised questions about the merits of discarding the traditional salary schedule in favor of performance pay. Prepare a brief position paper of 1 to 2 pages listing the pros and cons of both Odden's and Holt's proposals. Place your position paper in your portfolio under **INTASC Standard 9, Reflective Practice and Professional Growth.**

To complete these activities online, go to the *Develop Your Portfolio* module for this chapter of the Companion Website at **http://www.prenhall.com/webb**.

Explore Teaching and Learning: Field Experiences

1. Arrange an interview with the principal and an experienced teacher in the same school concerning the teacher evaluation process that is being used in the school. Possible questions include the following:
   a. What is the purpose of the teacher evaluation process?
   b. What role does the person being evaluated have in determining the content of the evaluation process?

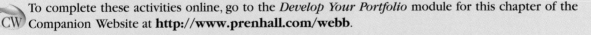

    c. What are the components of the evaluation process, that is, portfolio of classroom materials and lesson plans, pre-observation conference, observation, post-observation conference? Ask the teacher if you may examine the portfolio.

    d. To what degree are other teachers involved in the evaluation?

    e. What specific positive actions can be attributed to the evaluation process?

2. In a school near you, interview teachers and administrators to identify the dominant teachers' organization. Arrange an interview with the organization's leader(s). Develop an interview protocol of five questions. Possible questions include the following:

    a. What is your organization doing to improve working conditions for teachers?

    b. What benefits would I receive by becoming a member of your organization?

    c. What is your organization's position on the employment of teachers who do not qualify for a regular teacher's license or certificate?

    d. What is your organization's position on the courses and experience that should be required for teacher certification?

Professional Development Online

Visit this text's Companion Website at **http://www.prenhall.com/webb** to gain access to a variety of questions, activities, and exercises to help build your knowledge of this chapter's content. Below are just a few items available at this text's Companion Website:

- Classroom Video—To see actual classroom footage and work through activities and questions to analyze the content of the video, click on the *Classroom Video* module for this chapter.
- Teaching Tolerance—To go to this organization's website and complete activities to explore issues and topics dealing with how to teach tolerance to students, click on the *Teaching Tolerance* module for this chapter.
- Self-Test—To review terms and concepts presented in this chapter, click on the *Self-Test* module for this chapter.
- Internet Resources—To link to websites related to topics in this chapter, go to the *Internet Resources* module for this chapter.

PART

2

PHILOSOPHY AND ITS IMPACT ON THE SCHOOLS

CHAPTER 3

"The philosophy of the classroom is the philosophy of the government in the next generation."
—Abraham Lincoln

THE MAJOR PHILOSOPHIES

It is late Friday afternoon and classes have been dismissed at John F. Kennedy High School. A few students are left in the chemistry laboratory cleaning equipment and in the visual arts and industrial arts classrooms putting finishing touches on semester projects that are due Monday. The sound of a lonely basketball dribbling in the nearby gymnasium echoes down the corridor. The school seems rather eerie in its stark quietude—a far cry from the loud sounds and activities of an hour before.

The faculty lounge also is empty except for a group of four teachers engaged in a heated discussion. Ms. Jenkins, who has taught an introductory biology course for the past 7 years, appears agitated over the school district's new policy concerning electives. She makes a passionate argument to the rest of her colleagues at the table, alleging that it is a mistake to allow students a choice in determining their own program of study. Her major thesis is that adolescents are not capable of making such choices and that, if left to their own whims, they will opt for the easiest, least demanding courses and will avoid the mathematics, life science, and physical science courses that most colleges and universities require. Mr. Rhodes, a soft-spoken and gentle individual who has taught courses in anthropology, sociology, and psychology for the past 3 years, attempts to argue an opposing viewpoint. He directs his comments to the entire group, but his attention is focused primarily on Ms. Jenkins. His counterargument is that adolescents, and even very young children, are capable of decision making. In fact, according to Mr. Rhodes, most individuals, if left on their own, will choose what is good for them and are capable of making quality educational decisions at a very early age.

Do you agree with Ms. Jenkins or Mr. Rhodes? What additional arguments might you give to support your position?

The opposing viewpoints expressed by these teachers regarding decision making and choice are examples of basic philosophic issues. Their different points of view concerning choice reflect both their personal philosophies as well as their philosophies of education.

For many, philosophy connotes a certain type of abstract or theoretical thinking that seems far removed from the day-to-day life of the elementary or secondary classroom teacher. However, every teacher and every classroom reflects a set of assumptions about the world. Those principles or assumptions comprise one's personal philosophy as well as one's educational philosophy. In this chapter, we will outline some of the basic philosophic questions and review some of the major traditional (idealism, realism, and neo-Thomism) philosophies and contemporary (pragmatism and existentialism) philosophies. Last, we will describe the analytic approach to the study of philosophy, along with its application to educational practice.

As you study the philosophies outlined in this chapter, you may begin to question your personal philosophy. To help you better understand the philosophies and where your personal philosophy fits within that framework, consider the following objectives:

- Explain the relationship between personal philosophy and philosophy of education.
- Describe the three branches of philosophy.
- Compare the metaphysics of idealism, realism, neo-Thomism, pragmatism, and existentialism.
- Compare the epistemology of idealism, realism, neo-Thomism, pragmatism, and existentialism.
- Compare the axiology of idealism, realism, neo-Thomism, pragmatism, and existentialism.
- Identify the philosophies that take an optimistic view of human nature and those that take a pessimistic view.
- Explain philosophic analysis in education.
- Discuss your philosophy of life and how it has changed over time.

What Is Philosophy?

One formal definition of philosophy as a discipline of inquiry states that philosophy is "the rational investigation of the truths and principles of being, knowledge, or conduct" (*Random House Webster's College Dictionary,* 2001). Perhaps the most simple, yet comprehensive, definition is that philosophy is the "love of wisdom and the search for it."

The formal study of philosophy enables us as human beings to better understand who we are, why we are here, and where we are going. Whereas our personal philosophy of life enables us to recognize the meaning of our personal existence, our **philosophy of education** enables us to recognize certain educational principles that define our views about the learner, the teacher, and the school. To teach without a firm understanding of one's personal philosophy and philosophy of education would be analogous to painting a portrait without the rudimentary knowledge and skills of basic design, perspective, or human anatomy. Although you may not have thought about your personal philosophy in a formal sense, you certainly have personal beliefs that have shaped your life. After you have studied and discussed this chapter, you should be able to better articulate your personal philosophy of life.

Branches of Philosophy

Although there is much debate and little agreement about which of the schools of philosophy are most accurate, relevant, or even complete, there is general agreement concerning the basic components or branches of philosophy: metaphysics, epistemology, and axiology. These branches are concerned with the answers to the following three basic questions that are important in describing any philosophy:

• What is the nature of reality?
• What is the nature of knowledge?
• What is the nature of values?

The framework these questions provide enables us to study the major schools of philosophy from a descriptive approach. These branches and questions are discussed in the following section and summarized in Figure 3.1.

Figure 3.1 — Summary of Branches of Philosophy

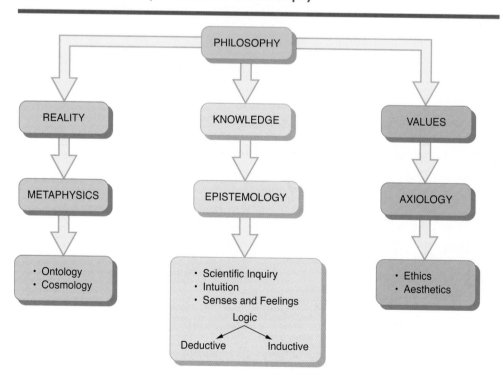

Metaphysics: What Is the Nature of Reality?

Of the three basic questions, *What is the nature of reality?* is perhaps the most difficult to answer because the elements of reality are vague, abstract, and not easily identifiable. Despite its abstraction and vagueness, most philosophers would agree that the study of the nature of reality (meaning of existence) is one of the key concepts in understanding any philosophy.

That branch of philosophy that is concerned with the nature of reality and existence is known as **metaphysics**. Metaphysics is concerned with the question of the nature of the person or the self. It addresses such questions as whether human nature is basically good, evil, spiritual, mental, or physical.

Metaphysics can be subdivided into the areas of ontology and cosmology. **Ontology** raises fundamental questions about what we mean by the nature of existence and what it means for anything "to be." **Cosmology** raises questions about the origin and organization of the universe, or cosmos.

Epistemology: What Is the Nature of Knowledge?

The branch of philosophy that is concerned with the investigation of the nature of knowledge is known as **epistemology**. To explore the nature of knowledge is to raise questions about the limits of knowledge, the sources of knowledge, the validity of knowledge, the cognitive processes, and how we know. There are several "ways of knowing," including scientific inquiry, intuition, experience, sensing, feeling, trial and error, and logic (Eisner, 1985). **Logic** is a key dimension in the traditional philosophies. Logic is primarily concerned with making inferences, reasoning, or arguing in a rational manner, and includes the subdivisions of deduction and induction. **Deductive logic** is reasoning from a general statement or principle to a specific point or example. **Inductive logic**, on the other hand, is reasoning from a specific fact or facts to a generalization. Figure 3.2 further describes these two types of logic.

For Your Reflection and Analysis

Should schools concern themselves with questions regarding the origin of the universe? Why or why not?
To submit your response online, go to http://www.prenhall.com/webb.

CW

Figure 3.2 — Types of Logic

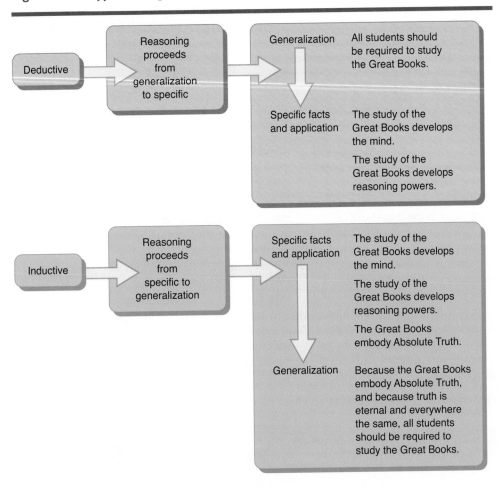

Axiology: What Is the Nature of Values?

Whereas epistemology explores the question of knowledge, **axiology**—the study of the nature of values—seeks to determine what is of value. To evaluate, to make a judgment, to value, literally means applying a set of norms or standards to human conduct or beauty. Axiology is divided into two spheres: ethics and aesthetics. **Ethics** is concerned with the study of human conduct and examines moral values—right, wrong, good, or bad. **Aesthetics** is concerned with values in beauty, nature, and the "aesthetic experience." The creative production of beauty is usually associated with music, art, literature, dance, theater, or the so-called fine arts.

One of the ongoing debates in education centers around the question of whether moral education, character education, ethics, or values education should be a responsibility of the school. The accompanying Controversial Issue feature poses arguments for and against the place of moral education, character education, ethics, or values education in the classroom; the Ask Yourself box on page 57 lists a number of questions that are asked by the three branches of philosophy. The questions provide a framework for you to examine and perhaps articulate your own philosophy of life. Your answers to these questions also reflect some of the basic assumptions you hold about the purpose of schooling, what should be taught and how, the nature of the learner, and the role of the teacher. Your

CONTROVERSIAL ISSUE

Should Moral Education, Character Education, Ethics, or Values Education Be a Responsibility of the School?

Although axiology, or the study of values, is a major component or branch of all philosophies, the question of whether moral education, character education, ethics, or values education should be taught in the school is a controversial issue today despite the fact that through most of American history the didactic teaching of moral values, including religious values, was once considered to be a basic feature of the school. The No Child Left Behind Act's support for the teaching of character education has brought the topic more squarely into public debate.

Today, some parents and educators are suggesting that ethical questions and moral dilemmas do indeed have a place in the educational enterprise. Others have expressed strong opinions against the school's role in moral or values education. The arguments, pro and con, concerning moral education, character education, ethics, or values education are as follows:

Arguments For

1. The teaching of values is not a new phenomenon and follows the earlier works of Plato, Aristotle, Dewey, and Piaget, who linked values to cognitive development, which has a place in the classroom.
2. A character education curriculum is a powerful tool for teaching basic American values.
3. The discussion of moral dilemmas integrates critical thinking and ethics, developing moral reasoning skills.
4. The school is the best place for assisting learners to understand their own attitudes, preferences, and values. The role of the school is to help students sort through value confusion so they can live by their values.
5. Students should excel in their core academic subjects. They should also excel in the basic virtues or morals.

Arguments Against

1. The teaching of values is not the purview of the school, but that of the family and church.
2. Too many teachers lecture their students about the importance of certain "appropriate" values without demonstrating those values by their own actions or behaviors.
3. No individual is "valueless," thus all teachers, by the nature of their position, have the potential of imposing their values on their students.
4. The function of the school is to educate, not proselytize or indoctrinate; therefore, moral education, character education, and values education do not belong in the classroom.

What is your view of moral education, character education, ethics, or values education?

To answer this question online, go to the *Controversial Issue* module for this chapter of the Companion Website at **http://www.prenhall.com/webb**.

ASK YOURSELF

What Is My Philosophy of Life?

Philosophic Questions	Branches of Philosophy
1. Are human beings basically good or is the essential nature of the human being evil?	What is the nature of reality? (Metaphysics—ontology)
2. What causes certain events in the universe to happen?	What is the nature of reality? (Metaphysics—cosmology)
3. What is your relationship to the universe?	What is the nature of reality? (Metaphysics—cosmology)
4. What is your relationship to a higher being (God)?	What is the nature of reality? (Metaphysics—ontology)
5. To what extent is your life basically free?	What is the nature of reality? (Metaphysics—ontology)
6. How is reality determined?	What is the nature of reality? (Metaphysics—ontology)
7. What is your basic purpose in life?	What is the nature of reality? (Metaphysics—ontology)
8. How is knowledge determined?	What is the nature of knowledge? (Epistemology)
9. What is truth?	What is the nature of knowledge? (Epistemology)
10. What are the limits of knowledge?	What is the nature of knowledge? (Epistemology)
11. What is the relationship between cognition and knowledge?	What is the nature of knowledge? (Epistemology)
12. Are there certain moral or ethical values that are universal?	What is the nature of values? (Axiology—ethics)
13. How is beauty determined?	What is the nature of values? (Axiology—aesthetics)
14. What constitutes aesthetic value?	What is the nature of values? (Axiology—aesthetics)
15. Who determines what is right, just, or good?	What is the nature of values? (Axiology—ethics)

philosophy of life and philosophy of education are interdependent and provide a basis for your view of life, as well as your view of teaching.

Traditional Philosophies and Their Educational Implications

The so-called traditional philosophies include the oldest Western philosophies of idealism, realism, and theistic realism (neo-Thomism). These philosophies all include the belief in certain preestablished metaphysical truths.

Idealism

Idealism is considered the oldest philosophy of Western culture, dating back to ancient Greece and Plato. For the idealist, the world of the mind, ideas, and reason is primary.

Metaphysics.   Idealism stresses mind over matter. For the idealist, nothing exists or is real except for an idea in the mind of the person or the mind of God, the Universal Mind. The universe can be explained as a creative and spiritual reality. One of the basic tenets of idealism is that mind is prior; that when we seek what is ultimate in the world, if we push back behind the veil of immediate sense experience, we will find that what is ultimate in the universe is of the nature of mind or spirit, just as it is mind that is ultimate in the world of personal experience (Wingo, 1974).

If the mind is prior, in the sense that it is ultimate, then material things either do not exist (i.e., are not real), or if they do exist, their existence depends in some fashion on the mind. For example, an idealist would contend that there is no such thing as a chair, there is only the idea of a chair.

The idealist's concept of reality considers the self as one in mind, soul, and spirit. Such a nature is capable of emulating the Absolute or Supreme Mind.

Epistemology.   Because idealism accepts a primarily mental explanation for its metaphysics or reality, it is not surprising that idealists also accept the premise that all knowledge includes a mental grasp of ideas and concepts. And, because the mind is the primary reality, it is important to master the science of logic because logic provides the framework for unifying our thoughts. Although traditional idealists consider reason, logic, or revelation to be the primary ways of "knowing," modern idealists also accept intuition as a way of knowing.

Some idealists believe that the search for truth, rather than truth itself, is the ultimate challenge. But they also believe that most of us resort to the lowest level (mere opinions about truth) and never reach "Ultimate Truth." Nonetheless, although we may never grasp Ultimate Truth, we do have the potential to aspire to wisdom, to improve the quality of our ideas, and to move closer to Ultimate Truth.

Axiology.   For the idealists, values are rooted in existence and are part of reality. Order is also an important element of reality, and is considered a basic principle of values. Moreover, idealists believe that values can be classified and ordered into a hierarchy or classification system.

Idealists believe that human behavior is intentional and not merely the response to external stimuli. Rather, within the human self is an inherent urge for self-realization that provides the basic motivation for behavior. Because behavior is intentional, we cannot escape the need to value (or devalue) the things and events that we experience (Wingo, 1974).

Idealists contend that values are absolute; that there are universal standards of moral behavior that have been applied throughout history and that apply equally to all people everywhere. "What is true, and beautiful does not depend on where you live or when you live. Goodness, truth, and beauty are found in the nature of the universe" (Gutek, 2004, p. 39). Figure 3.3 provides an overview of idealism and its educational implications.

For Your Reflection and Analysis

If you were an idealist, what eternal ideas would you recommend be taught in the schools? *To submit your response online, go to http://www. prenhall.com/webb.*

CW

Figure 3.3 — Idealism at a Glance

The Nature of Reality (Metaphysics)	The Nature of Knowledge (Epistemology)	The Nature of Values (Axiology)	The Nature of the Learner	Purpose of Schooling	Curriculum and Instruction
The mind and eternal ideas that represent perfect order	A rational, orderly body of truth	Absolute, eternal, and universal; a reflection of the ideal—God	A mind, soul, and spirit capable of emulating the Absolute Mind	Education should stress eternal ideas of the past and promote spiritual and intellectual development	The liberal arts and Great Books taught by lecture, discussion, and Socratic dialogue

Leading Proponents.   The Greek philosopher Plato (427–347 B.C.), a disciple of Socrates, is considered the father of idealism. Plato believed that individuals should be attentive to the search for truth, which is perfect and eternal and cannot be found in matter because it is uncertain and subject to change. In his famous "Allegory of the Cave," found in *The Republic* (1958/360 B.C.), Plato inferred that each of us lives in a cave of shadows, doubts, and distortions about reality. However, through education and enlightenment, the real world of pure ideas can be substituted for those distorted shadows and doubts.

Judaism and Christianity were both influenced by the philosophy of idealism. Judeo-Christian teaching suggests that ultimate reality could be found in God through the soul. Augustine (354–430), a prominent theologian of the fourth and fifth centuries, applied a number of Plato's assumptions to Christian thought, providing the rationale for the religious idealism that influenced Western thought for centuries (Ozmon & Craver, 2003).

Idealist thought influenced the writings of a number of major philosophers, including René Descartes, Immanuel Kant, and Georg Wilhelm Friedrich Hegel. The French philosopher Descartes (1596–1650), in his famous dictum *"Cogito, ergo sum"* (I think, therefore I am), declared that as humans we may doubt everything but we cannot doubt our own existence. Descartes not only accepted the place of the finite mind and ideas as advanced by Plato, but determined that all ideas, save one, depend on other ideas. The only idea that does not depend on any idea other than itself is the idea of a Perfect Being or God. The process used by Descartes, later known as the *Cartesian method*, involved the derivation of axioms on which theories could be based by the purposeful and progressive elimination of all interpretations of experience except those that are absolutely certain. This method came to influence a number of fields of inquiry, including the sciences (Ozmon & Craver, 2003).

Immanuel Kant (1724–1804), also incorporated the major tenets of idealism into his thinking. Kant believed there were certain universal moral laws known as **categorical imperatives** that guide our actions or behaviors. One of Kant's categorical imperatives was "treat each person as an end and never as a mere means." This moral maxim became one of the primary principles in moral training or character development in education (Ozmon & Craver, 2003).

The German philosopher Hegel (1770–1831) approached reality as a "contest of opposites" such as life and death, love and hate, individual and society. According to Hegel, each idea (thesis) had its own opposite (antithesis). The confrontation between the thesis (e.g., man is an end in himself) and its antithesis (e.g., man cannot be merely an end to himself—he must also live for others) produces a resolution or synthesis (e.g., man fulfills his true end by serving others). This synthesis becomes a new thesis, which when crossed with a new antithesis, forms a new synthesis, and so on (Morris & Pai, 1976).

For Your Reflection and Analysis

Can you think of examples of categorical imperatives that might be espoused by idealists, and that would be relevant to education today?

To submit your response online, go to http://www. prenhall.com/webb.

CW

Although we may never grasp Ultimate Truth, we have the potential to aspire to wisdom.

HISTORICAL NOTE

Plato's Academy

Contrary to the popular use of the word or the depiction in Raphael's fresco *The School of Athens,* shown at the beginning of Chapter 5, Plato's academy was not a formal institution of learning. Rather, the academy (*akademeia*) was the name of a beautiful public park named after the hero Akademos and located about a mile from the center of Athens. The area had been planted with olive trees, adorned with statues and temples, and was the site of various festivals and athletic contests.

About 387 B.C. Plato began writing and meeting his followers there. Eventually they took over the site and established a school for the study of philosophy and mathematics. Plato taught there for the next 40 years. Students came from all over Greece to study with Plato but he accepted only those "intoxicated to learn what was in their souls" (Planeaux, 1999, p. 2). Aristotle came to study at the *akademeia* and stayed 20 years. Once at the *akademeia,* a student listened as Plato walked about the gardens reading from his *Dialogues* (philosophical discussions or debates) and lecturing, "and they all enjoyed moderate but pleasant banquets.... The meals were conducted according to an elaborate set of rules, but Platon (sic) did not hold these feasts simply to celebrate to dawn. He held his banquets so "that he [and his companions] might manifestly honor the gods and enjoy each other's company and chiefly to refresh themselves with learned discussion" (Planeaux, 1999, p. 2).

When Plato died in 427 B.C. he was buried on the grounds of the *akademeia.* Headed by a series of individuals elected for life, the *akademeia* continued unto Roman times.

To research and explore this topic further, go to the *Historical Note* module for this chapter of the Companion Website at **http://www.prenhall.com/webb.**

Realism

Realism, like idealism, is one of the oldest philosophies of Western culture, dating back to ancient Greece and the time of Aristotle. Classical or Aristotelian realism is the antithesis of idealism. For the realist, the universe exists whether or not the human mind perceives it. Matter is primary and is considered an independent reality. The world of things is superior to the world of ideas.

Metaphysics. Realism stresses the world of nature or physical things and our experiences and perceptions of those things. For the realist, reality is composed of both matter (body) and form (mind). Matter can only be shaped or organized into being through the mind. Moreover, the interaction of matter and form is governed not by God but by scientific, natural laws. Unlike the idealists, who believe reality is in the mind and internal, realists believe reality is external and can be verified.

Epistemology. The major ways of knowing for realists are perception, rational thinking, and sensing. **Sense realism** is a school of realism that asserts that knowledge comes through the senses, which gather data and transmit them to the mind to be sorted, classified, and categorized. From these data we make generalizations. Some realists, such as Aristotle, believed that perception (knowledge through the senses) was not sufficient to understand reality. Aristotle argued that the use of deductive logic is more effective than perception in understanding the physical world. The process of deduction entails the establishment of a first or major premise, followed by a second or minor premise, and the drawing of a conclusion (*syllogism*) from them. For other realists, knowledge is established by the **scientific method**, which includes the systematic reporting and analysis of what is observed and the testing of hypotheses formulated from the observations.

Axiology. Realists believe that values are derived from nature. Natural law and moral law are the major determinants of what is good; that which is good is dependent on leading a virtuous life, one in keeping with these natural or moral laws.

Although realism does not adhere to any hard and fast set of rules, realists believe that deviating from moral truth will cause injury both to persons and to society. To protect the common good, certain codes of conduct or social laws have been written and must be followed (Power, 1982).

For Your Reflection and Analysis

Consider yourself a realist. To what extent might you use the scientific method as a basis of inquiry in a beginning music class? In a class of preschoolers?
To submit your response online, go to http://www.prenhall.com/webb.

Figure 3.4 — Realism at a Glance

The Nature of Reality (Metaphysics)	The Nature of Knowledge (Epistemology)	The Nature of Values (Axiology)	The Nature of the Learner	Purpose of Schooling	Curriculum and Instruction
Physical things or nature and our experience or perception of those things	The discovery of logical, orderly truth of the external world via sensing and the scientific method	Natural law or moral law governing what is good	An orderly, sensing, and rational being capable of understanding the world of things	Develop reason, teach natural law, and help students master the principles of scientific inquiry	Liberal arts and sciences taught through lecture, discussion, and scientific method

For the realist, aesthetics is the reflection of nature. What is valued is that which reflects the orderliness and rationality of nature. Figure 3.4 provides an overview of realism and its educational implications.

Leading Proponents.   Aristotle (384–322 B.C.), a pupil of Plato, is considered the father of realism. Aristotle disagreed with Plato's premise that only ideas are real. For Aristotle, reality, knowledge, and value exist independent of the mind and their existence is not predicated by our ideas. Aristotle believed that knowledge can be acquired through the senses and that to obtain knowledge one had to first understand the physical world (Dunn, 2005).

Two other advocates of realism were Francis Bacon (1561–1626) and John Locke (1632–1704). Bacon, a philosopher and a politician, advanced a rigorous form of inductive reasoning that included empirical observation, analysis of observed data, inference leading to hypotheses, and verification of hypotheses through observation and experimentation (Dunn, 2005). Following a similar path, Locke's advocacy of realism stemmed from his study of human knowledge. One of Locke's major theories was the concept of the *tabula*

Today's students follow the precepts of Aristotle by formulating, testing, and discovering knowledge through the scientific method.

rasa, which proposed that there are no such things as innate ideas. When we enter the world, our mind is like a blank sheet of paper, a *tabula rasa.* Knowledge is acquired not by the mind, but by the use of our five senses and reflection (Ozmon & Craver, 2003).

Other major philosophers who contributed to realism were the Czech educator and theologian John (Jan) Amos Comenius (1592–1670), and Jean-Jacques Rousseau (1712–1778), the French philosopher known for his political and educational theories (both discussed in Chapter 6). Another realist and follower of Rousseau was Johann Heinrich Pestalozzi (1746–1827), the Swiss educator known for his child-centered philosophy discussed in Chapter 6. Pestalozzi along with Rousseau had a profound influence on the progressive educators of the early 20th century.

Neo-Thomism

The third of the traditional philosophies is **neo-Thomism**. Neo-Thomism, or its antecedent, Thomism, dates to the time of Thomas Aquinas (1225–1274). Neo-Thomism, also referred to as theistic realism, incorporates both theism (belief in God) and realism (belief in objective reality guided by rational law) (Gutek, 2004). For the neo-Thomist, God exists and can be known through faith and reason.

Metaphysics.   Neo-Thomists believe that God gives meaning and purpose to the universe. God is the Pure Being that represents the coming together of essence and existence. Things exist independently of ideas. However, both physical objects and human beings, including minds and ideas, are created by God. Thus, although both physical objects and God are real, God is preeminent. Neo-Thomists conceive of the essential nature of human beings as rational beings possessing souls, modeled after God, the Perfect Being.

Epistemology.   Although some philosophers believe that one can come to know God only through faith or intuition, neo-Thomists believe that it is through both our faith and our capacity to reason that we come to know God. They also believe there is a hierarchy of knowing. At the lowest level is scientific or synthetic knowing. At the second level there is analytic or intuitive knowing. At the highest level there is mystical or revelatory knowing (Morris & Pai, 1976). Thomas Aquinas clarified that truth or knowledge could not deviate from, or be inconsistent with, revelation (Jacobsen, 2003).

Axiology.   For the neo-Thomist, ethically speaking, goodness follows reason. That is, values are unchanging moral laws established by God that can be discerned by reason. As a corollary, ignorance is the source of evil. If people do not know what is right, they cannot be expected to do what is right. If, on the other hand, people do know what is right, they can be held morally responsible for what they do. In terms of aesthetics, the reason, or intellect, is also the perceiver of beauty: That which is valued as beautiful is also found pleasing to the intellect (Morris & Pai, 1976). Figure 3.5 provides an overview of neo-Thomism and and its educational implications.

Figure 3.5 — Neo-Thomism at a Glance

The Nature of Reality (Metaphysics)	The Nature of Knowledge (Epistemology)	The Nature of Values (Axiology)	The Nature of the Learner	Purpose of Schooling	Curriculum and Instruction
Physical objects and human beings, including our minds and ideas, are a creation of God	Faith and reason enable us to know God	Goodness follows reason. Beauty follows knowledge. Ignorance is the source of evil	A rational being with a soul modeled after God, perfection	Cultivate the intellect and develop spirituality through a relationship with God	Basic skills, liberal arts, and theology taught through drill and practice, demonstration, and recitation

Leading Proponents. Thomas Aquinas, the 13th-century theologian from which neo-Thomism takes its name, is credited with interfacing the secular ideas of Aristotle and the Christian teachings of Augustine. Aquinas, like Aristotle, viewed reality via reason and sensation. Aquinas believed God created matter out of nothing and gave meaning and purpose to the universe. In his most noted work, *Summa Theologica,* he used the rational approach suggested by Aristotle to answer various questions regarding existence and Christianity. Aquinas found no conflict between finding truth via faith and reason and finding truth via rational observation and study. Many of the supporting arguments of Christian beliefs rely on Aquinas' works, and Roman Catholicism considers Thomism its leading philosophy (Ozmon & Craver, 2003).

Contemporary Philosophies and Their Educational Implications

The modern or contemporary philosophies have their beginnings in the early 20th century and include pragmatism, existentialism, and analytic philosophy. These philosophies share the belief that there are no preestablished truths. At best there is a relative truth.

Pragmatism

Pragmatism, also known as **experimentalism,** focuses on experience or the things that work. Primarily viewed as a philosophy of the 20th century developed by Americans such as John Dewey (see Chapter 7), pragmatism has its roots in European and ancient Greek tradition.

Metaphysics. Unlike the traditional philosophers, who view reality as a given, pragmatists regard reality as an event, a process, a verb (Morris & Pai, 1976). As such, it is subject to constant change and lacks absolutes. Meaning is derived from experience, which is simply an interaction with one's environment (Garrison, 1994).

Epistemology. According to pragmatism's theory of knowledge, truth is not absolute but is determined by function or consequences. In fact, pragmatists shun the use of the word *truth* and at best speak of a "tentative truth" that will serve the purpose until experience evolves a new truth. Knowledge is arrived at by scientific inquiry, testing, questioning, and retesting—and is never conclusive.

For Your Reflection and Analysis

Have you ever attended or known anyone who attended parochial school? How did that experience compare with attendance at a public institution? *To submit your response online, go to http://www. prenhall.com/webb.*

CW

The teaching of Dewey is evident in classrooms where children actively participate in projects and social activities.

For Your Reflection and Analysis

An 80-year-old woman who is dying of cancer has requested assistance from her son, husband, physician, and the Hemlock Society to aid her in the design of her own suicide. How might a pragmatist deal with this ethical dilemma?
To submit your response online, go to http://www. prenhall.com/webb.

CW

Axiology.   Whereas traditional philosophers concentrate on metaphysics and episte-mology, pragmatists focus primarily on axiology or values. As with truths, values to the pragmatist are only tentative. They are constructed from experience and are subject to testing, questioning, and retesting. For the pragmatist, whatever works, or leads to desir-able consequences, is ethically or morally good. The focus on consequences is not to im-ply that the pragmatist is concerned only with what works for the self. In fact, the pragmatist is concerned with social consequences. "What works" is what works for the larger community. For Dewey, democracy was the key component of pragmatism. He was convinced that democracy could not exist without community. Democracy is more than government; it includes a free community capable of influencing the political, social, and economic institutions that affect its citizenry (Brosio, 2000).

Regarding aesthetic values, for pragmatists what is beautiful is not determined by some objective ideal but by what we experience when we see, feel, and touch. Accordingly, art is a creative expression and shared experience between the artist and the public. Figure 3.6 presents an overview of pragmatism and its educational implications.

Leading Proponents.   In the 19th century, the two individuals who had the greatest impact on pragmatist philosophy were Auguste Comte (1798–1857) and Charles Darwin (1809–1882). Comte influenced pragmatism by suggesting that science could solve social problems. For pragmatists, problem solving is a key ingredient in scientific inquiry. Darwin's theory of natural selection implied that reality was open ended, not fixed, and subject to change. Pragmatists applied Darwin's ideas to education, which they inferred was also open ended and subject to biological and social development (Ozmon & Craver, 2003).

Pragmatism is primarily associated with the Americans Charles Sanders Peirce (1839–1914), William James (1842–1910), and John Dewey (1859–1952). Peirce, a mathematician and logician, believed that true knowledge depends on verification of ideas through experience. Ideas are merely hypotheses until tested by experience. Peirce regarded learning, believing, and knowing as intimate parts of doing and feeling and lamented that educators often ignored this important relationship (Garrison & Neiman, 2003).

William James, a psychologist and philosopher, incorporated his view of pragmatism in both psychology and philosophy. James emphasized the centrality of experience. Ac-cording to James, there are no absolutes, no universals, only an ever-changing universe. He suggested that experience should take precedence over abstractions and universals be-cause experience is open ended, pluralistic, and in process (Ozmon & Craver, 2003).

James's contemporary, John Dewey, had the greatest influence on American pragma-tism. As discussed in more detail in Chapter 4, for Dewey (1916), experience, thought, and consequence were interrelated:

Figure 3.6 — Pragmatism at a Glance

The Nature of Reality (Metaphysics)	The Nature of Knowledge (Epistemology)	The Nature of Values (Axiology)	The Nature of the Learner	Purpose of Schooling	Curriculum and Instruction
Experience and interaction with environment	Tentative truth determined by the scientific method or function	Ethical conduct and moral codes are determined by what works; aesthetics are determined by experimental consequences	An evolving and active being capable of interacting with the environment	Education should stress function or experience; model a democratic society	An integrated curriculum taught through problem solving, group projects, and discussion

[Thought] is the discernment of the relation between what we try to do and what happens in consequence. No experience having a meaning is possible without some element of thought.... We simply do something, and when it fails, we do something else, and keep on trying until we hit upon something which works, and then we adopt that method as a rule of thumb measure in subsequent procedures. (pp. 169–170)

Existentialism

Existentialism appeared as a revolt against the mathematical, scientific, and objective philosophies that preceded it. Existentialism voices disfavor with any effort directed toward social control or subjugation. Existentialism focuses on personal and subjective existence. For the existentialist, the world of existence, choice, and responsibility is primary.

Metaphysics. Unlike the realists and neo-Thomists, who believe that essence precedes existence, the existentialist believes that existence precedes essence. For the existentialist there is neither meaning nor purpose to the physical universe. We are born into the universe by chance. Moreover, according to existentialism, because there is no world order or natural scheme of things into which we are born, we owe nothing to nature but our existence (Kneller, 1971). Since we live in a world without purpose, we must create our own meaning (Gutek, 1988).

In addition to existence, the concept of choice is central to the metaphysics of existentialism. To decide who and what we are is to decide what reality is. Is it God? Reason? Nature? Science? By our choices we determine reality. According to existentialists, we cannot escape from the responsibility to choose, including the choice of how we view our past.

Epistemology. Similar to their position concerning reality, existentialists believe that the way we come to know truth is by choice. The individual self must ultimately decide what is true and how we know. Whether we choose logic, intuition, the scientific method, or revelation is irrelevant; what matters is that we must eventually choose. The freedom to choose carries with it a tremendous burden of responsibility that we cannot escape. Because there are no absolutes, no authorities, and no single or correct way to the truth, the only authority is the authority of the self.

The search for meaning, purpose in life, and individual existence continues to challenge contemporary youth as it challenged Kierkegaard in the nineteenth century.

Axiology. For the existentialist, choice is imperative, not only for determining reality and knowledge but also for determining value. Every act and every word is a choice and hence an act of value creation. And here is the dilemma, say the existentialists: Because there are no norms, standards, or assurances that we have chosen correctly or rightly, choice is at times frustrating and exasperating. It is often much easier to be able to look to a standard or benchmark to determine what is right, just, or of value than to take responsibility for the choices we have made. Yet, the existentialists suggest, this is a very small price we pay for our free will. Figure 3.7 presents an overview of existentialism and its educational implications.

Leading Proponents. The leading proponent, indeed the "father of existentialism," was the Danish philosopher-theologian Soren Kierkegaard (1813–1855). Kierkegaard renounced scientific objectivity for subjectivity and personal choice. He believed in the reality of God and was concerned with individual existence.

Another expositor of existentialism was Martin Buber (1878–1965), a Jewish philosopher-theologian. He incorporated the principle described as an "I-Thou" relationship whereby each individual recognizes the other's personal meaning and reality. Buber suggested that both the divine and human are related, and that through personal relationships with others, one can enhance one's spiritual life and relationship with God (Ozmon & Craver 2003).

Also contributing to existential thought were Edmund Husserl (1859–1938) and Martin Heidegger (1889–1976). Husserl focused his attention on philosophy as an empirical study of meaning through what he termed "intuitive conscious experience." According to Husserl, to get to this level of consciousness, one must strip away the assumptions and presuppositions of the culture and get back to the immediate original consciousness. He referred to this method as **phenomenology**. Heidegger expanded and revised phenomenology to create another philosophical method known as **hermeneutics**, or the interpretation of lived experience (Ozmon & Craver, 2003). Phenomenology had a major influence on the critical theory and postmodern movements that followed.

Undoubtedly, the most widely known existentialist was Jean-Paul Sartre (1905–1980). Sartre claimed that free choice implies total responsibility for one's own existence. There are no antecedent principles or purposes that shape our destiny. Responsibility for our existence extends to situations of the gravest consequence, including the choice to commit suicide. Sartre's major philosophic work, *Being and Nothingness* (1956), is considered one of the major philosophic treatises of the 20th century. According to Sartre, because there is no God to give existence meaning, humanity exists without any meaning until we construct our own.

Existentialism had a major impact on educators such as John Holt (1981), Charles Silberman (1970), and Jonathan Kozol (1972, 1991), who were supporters of the open schools, free schools, and alternative schools that flourished during the mid-1960s. One of the most well-known educational existentialists was A. S. Neill (1883–1973), who founded

Figure 3.7 — Existentialism at a Glance

The Nature of Reality (Metaphysics)	The Nature of Knowledge (Epistemology)	The Nature of Values (Axiology)	The Nature of the Learner	Purpose of Schooling	Curriculum and Instruction
Existence precedes essence; the individual determines personal reality by choice	The individual is responsible for personal knowledge	Values consist of personal choices	A free individual capable of authentic and responsible choices	Education should stress individual responsibility and choice	Humanities, values education taught through self-discovery, decision making, and the Socratic method

Summerhill School outside London shortly after World War I. Summerhill offered an educational experience built on the principle of learning by discovery in an atmosphere of unrestricted freedom (Neill, 1960).

One of the current spokespersons for the existential philosophy of education is Nel Noddings. Noddings (1992) offered an existential educational model that stresses the *challenge to care:*

> As human beings, we care what happens to us. We wonder whether there is a life after death, whether there is a deity who cares about us, whether we are loved by those we love, whether we belong anywhere; we wonder what we will become, who we are, how much control we have over our own fate. For adolescents these are among the most pressing questions: Who am I? Who will love me? How do others see me? Yet schools spend more time on the quadratic formula than on any of these existential questions. (p. 20)

Analytic Philosophy

As we study the major philosophies and their corollary educational theories, it becomes evident that these descriptive schools of thought, or "isms" as they are often called, are very broad in their aims, are quite eclectic, and at times appear lacking in clarity. Critics of the descriptive approach to philosophy point out that the philosophies of idealism, realism, neo-Thomism, and the like have major limitations in that they try to prescribe certain things and make normative judgments. Moreover, they render educational statements that are jargon ridden and unverifiable. For these reasons, a number of philosophers began to move away from traditional thinking about philosophy and theory as disciplines and focused their attention on analytic philosophy or clarification of the language, concepts, and methods that philosophers use (Ozmon & Craver, 2003; Partelli, 1987). The resulting so-called analytic movement was less concerned with the underlying assumptions about reality, truth, and values addressed by descriptive philosophy than with the clarification, definition, and meaning of language. That is, analytic philosophers are not interested in which values are true, which behaviors are good, or which art is most beautiful. They are only concerned with questions such as "Can these values or behaviors be tested empirically and do the terms used have clear meaning to the reader?"

Analysis in philosophy began in the post–World War I era when a group of European natural scientists and social scientists formed what became known as the Vienna Circle. These scholars were particularly concerned about the alienation between philosophy and science that existed at that time. One of the major outcomes of the work of the Vienna Circle was the clarification of the joint roles of both science and philosophy. For example, it was determined that if the testing of hypotheses through experimentation and observation were to be the purview or charge of science, then the proper role of philosophy should be the analysis of the logical syntax of scientific language (Magee, 1971).

The concept of **logical positivism**, or **logical empiricism**, grew out of the thinking of the Vienna Circle. Logical positivism suggests that the language of science consists of two types of expressions: logical and empirical. Eventually, the concept of logical positivism became associated with the *principle of verification,* which asserts that no proposition should be accepted as meaningful unless it can be verified on formal grounds, logical or empirical (Magee, 1971).

PROFESSIONAL REFLECTION

My personal values include respect, honesty, responsibility, best effort, logical thinking, organizational skills, positive thinking, and the importance of being a positive role model. As a teacher I am constantly aware of the fact that "what I do speaks louder than what I say," therefore I attempt to be a positive role model showing students how all these values are exemplified in daily life. On the students' part, I expect and accept nothing less than organized work that reflects their best logical thinking. Students are encouraged to request assistance in an affirmative manner by stating "Will you help me please?" My personal values are an innate part of what influences not only my teaching, but also, who I am.

Mary L. Keizer
National Board Certified Teacher
Nevada

To analyze this reflection, go to the *Professional Reflection* module for this chapter of the Companion Website at **http://www.prenhall. com/webb.**

One of the most important logical positivists was Ludwig Wittgenstein (1889–1951). Wittgenstein (1953) argued that the role of the sciences should be to discover true propositions and facts, whereas the role of philosophy should be to resolve confusion and clarify ideas. The assumptions that were made by the logical positivists became so rigid and restrictive that their popularity began to wane. Today, very few individuals identify themselves as logical positivists.

By the 1950s, logical positivism shifted to linguistic analysis, or the analytic philosophy movement. **Analytic philosophy** assumes that language statements have immediate meaning because of their inner logic, or that they have the possibility of being made meaningful by being stated in empirical terms that can be verified and tested. According to analytic philosophers, if language has no method of verification, it has no meaning. Many of the words or statements we use are emotional or subjective and have meaning specific to the person who used them (Gutek, 2004). For example, the terms *adaptation, inclusion, adjustment, professionalism, reform, growth,* and *tolerance* imply multiple meanings and would be defined in different ways by different disciplines. Similarly, in philosophy, statements such as "Existence precedes essence" or "Self-actualization is the highest goal for mankind" are not verifiable and hence have limited meaning.

An early spokesperson for the analytic philosophy movement was Israel Scheffler (b. 1923). In his first major work, *The Language of Education* (1960), Scheffler focused attention on how **philosophic analysis** can help teachers formulate their beliefs, arguments, and assumptions about topics that are particularly important to the teaching and learning process. Scheffler and other analytic philosophers concerned with education believed that each prospective teacher should learn the art or science of philosophic analysis. One of the first steps in learning this process is to raise questions about the assumptions we make, the values we hold, the theories we propose, the procedures we use, and the methods we trust. According to Soltis (1978):

> The analytic temperament and techniques should prove very useful to all practicing educators in getting them to think through with care and precision just what it is they are buying from theorists, and more importantly, just what it is they're after and how best it might be achieved. (p. 88)

Since the 1970s analytic philosophy has focused its attention on political philosophy, ethics, and philosophy of the human sciences. The impetus for this shift was to better understand the connections between concepts and ethical values. An example of some of the analytic work that has focused on complex ethical and political problems is an examination of "Who should have the right to determine the form and content of children's education? Should it be the state? Parents?" (White & White, 2001).

For Your Reflection and Analysis

Do you consider yourself to have an analytic temperament? Explain.

To submit your response online, go to http://www.prenhall.com/webb.

CW

Summary

The study of philosophy enables us to better understand our philosophy of life. One of the most effective methods of developing a philosophy of life is to respond to three basic questions: What is the nature of reality? What is the nature of knowledge? What is the nature of values? These three questions and their accompanying responses comprise the branches of philosophy.

The philosophies of idealism, realism, and neo-Thomism are considered the classical or traditional philosophies, whereas pragmatism and existentialism represent the contemporary or modern philosophies. The traditional philosophies are more concerned with the past, truths, and absolutes, whereas the contemporary philosophies are more concerned with the present or future and do not subscribe to the idea of "absolute truths."

Although the study of descriptive philosophy provides a mechanism for translating basic philosophic tenets into educational practice, it is quite restrictive. Most philosophies are too broad in scope and lack precise meaning and clarity. Today, many philosophers and educators believe that a more effective way to study philosophy is by philosophic analysis, which is concerned with clarifying the language we use to describe our educational concepts and assumptions.

In the next chapter, we will examine how these basic philosophic views have led to a number of theories of education. We will also explore the impact of these theories on educational programs and practices.

Key Terms

Aesthetics, 56
Analytic philosophy, 68
Axiology, 56
Categorical imperatives, 59
Cosmology, 55
Deductive logic, 55
Epistemology, 55
Ethics, 56
Existentialism, 65

Hermeneutics, 66
Idealism, 58
Inductive logic, 55
Logic, 55
Logical positivism (logical
  empiricism), 67
Metaphysics, 55
Neo-Thomism (theistic
  realism), 62

Ontology, 55
Phenomenology, 66
Philosophic analysis, 68
Philosophy of education, 54
Pragmatism
  (experimentalism), 63
Realism, 60
Scientific method, 60
Sense realism, 60

PROFESSIONAL DEVELOPMENT WORKSHOP

Prepare for the Praxis™ Examination

It was a typical Monday morning in late April. The 7:00 A.M. morning traffic had already slowed down to a "snail's pace." The driver, Jose Santora, had been teaching American history at the same junior high school since he graduated from college 6 years earlier. For the past 3 years he had carpooled with three other teachers from the same school: Bruce Parlius, who taught social studies; Shana Cohen, a science teacher; and Cal Crane, an English teacher.

On this particular morning, while en route to school, Shana seemed very quiet and withdrawn. Cal asked Shana if there was something wrong. He had noticed she was not her usual animated self. At first there was a long silence and she hesitated before answering. Finally, she answered by relaying the following incident. Over the weekend she had been shopping at her local supermarket near the school when she ran into her principal, Phil Aronsky. Phil told her that late Friday afternoon he received a telephone call from the mother of one of her students. Phil explained that the mother was quite upset after learning from her son that Shana had spent the entire class period talking about the importance of evidence-based research in the sciences, especially medicine. Phil told Shana that the mother was irate because her son had come away from her class feeling that any alternative to science, relative to health and well-being, was not acceptable.

Jose was the first to speak. As he spoke, his words were carefully directed at Shana. "You know, I have been teaching history for the past six years. The first day of every class I always tell my students that there is no 'single' nor 'right' interpretation of history. Each historian interprets the events from his or her own reality or experience. One of my goals is to teach tolerance and acceptance of different viewpoints. This lesson stretches beyond history. It impacts life in general."

Cal immediately interrupted Jose and said, "I never told you guys about the incident that happened to me two years ago. Shortly after I introduced a new unit on American literature, one of my seventh-grade students told his parents that I was a 'racist.' The student came to this conclusion based on my assigned reading of *The Adventures of Huckleberry Finn* by Mark Twain, which he inferred had deprecated his values, his family values, and the values of our country. I was called in by our former principal to explain my decision making relative to the assigned reading. What happened was that I had to meet with the parents of the seventh grader and explain why I felt it important for the students to read Twain's work.

Shana, who had been very quiet and attentive to her colleagues' comments said, "This whole experience has really soured me about teaching. I decided to become a teacher when I was in first grade. I loved school, I loved my teachers. And, I love teaching now. I was motivated to help others grow to love learning like I did. After this experience, I am beginning to have some doubts about my professional goals. If I have to justify every professional decision I make regarding the curriculum and what I choose to teach, then it is not worth it! I'd rather pursue some other profession and not have to put up with having to explain myself every time I make a professional decision.

Bruce had been listening quietly to all the comments and finally spoke. He was sitting in the backseat next to Shana. He put his arm around her shoulder and said, "Shana, I have not had the experiences that you, Jose, and Cal have had relative to the issue of professionalism and the right to choose the curriculum and assignments. So, on that level, I really cannot make any comment. But, I can tell you this. What is going on here is a difference in philosophy. It doesn't really have anything to do with professionalism. What is going on here is a variety of views about how we come to know what is 'right' and what is 'good,' for us and our students. In short, there is no 'right' answer because we are all right in making the choices we make even though those choices may contradict your choice or my choice. What is most important is that we are able to articulate to the student, parent, administration, and the public why we believe it is important that we teach what we teach. The bottom line is that we must be able to have a strong rationale for the decisions we make knowing that oftentimes our decisions may be in direct conflict with another person's values or decisions. Shana, when you go into that meeting this afternoon and face both Phil and the mother of your student, you need to relax and just be your usual calm and articulate self. Tell the parent that you respect her values and her desire for the best education for her son. But, also communicate that as a teacher your role is to prepare her son to be able to tolerate and accept different viewpoints based on different philosophies even though those differences may contradict theirs. If we as teachers can get that lesson across, then we will have made one of the most important contributions to teaching and learning."

1. Which philosophies do you think are exemplified by Shana's classroom presentation on the importance of evidence-based research in science? Least exemplified? Give reasons why.
2. Do you agree or disagree with Bruce's conclusion that what is really at stake here is a difference in philosophies? Which philosophy would you attribute to Shana? To Jose? To Cal? To Bruce?
3. What advice would you give Shana in preparation for her meeting with her principal and the mother of her student?
4. How has your philosophy of life influenced your priorities and values?

To submit your responses online, go to the *Prepare for the Praxis™ Examination* module for this chapter of the Companion Website at **http://www.prenhall.com/webb**.

Build Your Knowledge Base

1. Consider the vignette at the beginning of this chapter. Which philosophy would you ascribe to Ms. Jenkins? To Mr. Rhodes? Explain.
2. Which of the philosophies discussed in this chapter is most like your own? In what ways? Which is the most unlike your own? In what ways?
3. List all the ways of knowing. Does what is to be known (i.e., the subject matter) dictate the approach to knowing? Explain.
4. Construct an argument using deductive logic (deductive reasoning) to explain the following statement: "Teaching does not imply education and education does not imply learning."
5. The metaphor "learning is essentially growing" depicts which philosophy? Name three other metaphors that depict three other major philosophies.
6. Give examples of words or phrases in your discipline that could be considered jargon or have subjective multiple meanings.

Develop Your Portfolio

1. As a professional educator, one of the most important questions that you will be asked throughout your career is "What is your philosophy of education?" To help you begin to think about your philosophy of education, it is important to first consider some of the basic underlying philosophical questions about life such as those included in the Ask Yourself feature "What Is My Philosophy of Life?" on page 57. Prepare a two- to three-page reflection paper titled "My Philosophy of Life." In your paper respond to the following questions: (a) Are human beings basically good or evil? (b) How is knowledge determined? (c) Are there certain moral or ethical values that are universal? Place the reflection paper in your portfolio under **INTASC Standard 1, Knowledge of Subject.**

2. Group Activity: Divide into groups of five. Each member of the group will research and prepare a response to the question "What kinds of educational activities best help students develop their thinking and reasoning skills?" from the point of view of one of the following philosophers: Plato, Aristotle, Thomas Aquinas, John Dewey, and Soren Kierkegaard. As a group discuss the various points of view. Record the discussion on audio or videotape. Following the discussion, each participant should prepare a reflection paper that summarizes the dialogue and includes his or her reactions and thoughts to the original question. Include which position or school of thought you tend to agree with the most, which you agree with the least, and what experiences or feelings influenced your position. Title your paper "Philosophy of Education" and place it in your portfolio under **INTASC Standard 1, Knowledge of Subject.**

CW To complete these activities online, go to the *Develop Your Portfolio* module for this chapter of the Companion Website at **http://www.prenhall.com/webb.**

Explore Teaching and Learning: Field Experiences

1. Contact the principal of a nearby school and request a copy of the school's written mission, goals, and curriculum. See if you can identify the primary philosophic principles that undergird the school's approach to teaching and learning.
2. Interview three teachers at different grade levels on the topic of values education. Ask the following questions: What values guide you in your daily relationship with students? In your teaching, how do you model the values that you expect of your students? What values do you want students to practice in the classroom, on the playground, or in school activities?

Professional Development Online

CW Visit this text's Companion Website at **http://www.prenhall.com/webb** to gain access to a variety of questions, activities, and exercises to help build your knowledge of this chapter's content. Below are just a few items available at this text's Companion Website:

- Classroom Video—To see actual classroom footage and work through activities and questions to analyze the content of the video, click on the *Classroom Video* module for this chapter.
- Teaching Tolerance—To go to this organization's website and complete activities to explore issues and topics dealing with how to teach tolerance to students, click on the *Teaching Tolerance* module for this chapter.
- Self Test—To review terms and concepts presented in this chapter, click on the *Self-Test* module for this chapter.
- Internet Resources—To link to websites related to topics in this chapter, go to the *Internet Resources* module for this chapter.

CHAPTER 4

The roots of education are bitter, but the fruit is sweet.
—Aristotle, 4th century B.C.

THE IMPACT OF EDUCATIONAL THEORIES ON EDUCATIONAL PRACTICE

During a typical micro-teaching session in a methods class, six prospective teachers had just finished presenting a 20-minute lesson in their subject field using the instructional technique of their choice. What was surprising to the instructor was that no two students had used the same technique.

Jim, a physical education major, had chosen demonstration as the major technique for his 20-minute session on chipping in golf. Beth, an art major, had used the group project as the technique for her lesson on basic design, and Sam, a history major, had used lecture as the principal instructional technique to teach about the Spanish-American War. During the class critique, all three students expressed how well prepared they felt they had been and how appropriate each of their instructional techniques had proven to

be. The class concurred with their self-assessments. Then, in a surprise move, Beth turned to Sam and added, "You know, even though I felt that your lesson on the Spanish-American War was excellent and your mini-lecture held my attention, I would not feel comfortable giving a lecture to an art class."

"What do you mean?" asked Sam, rather flabbergasted at her comment.

"Just what I said, Sam," Beth replied. "Maybe it's the subject matter of art or maybe it's just me. It just doesn't fit with basic design!"

Do you agree with Beth? What is the relationship between the preferred method or instructional technique used by teachers and their philosophy of education?

Like Beth, many students enrolled in preprofessional teacher education programs do not recognize the relationship between the study of philosophy and educational practice. One explanation for this is that much of the subject matter of teacher education is taught in a fragmented fashion, with little or no connection to theory and practice. As a result, the student or novice teacher is unable to discern how educational concepts such as the purpose of schooling, nature of the learner, curriculum, instructional methods, classroom management, assessment, and the role of the teacher are associated with both educational philosophy and one's philosophy of life. For, as Hogan and Smith (2003) point out, "no teacher, beginner or experienced, is wholly innocent of theory, of having an underlying philosophy" (p. 177).

In this chapter, you will be introduced to several major educational theories or *applied philosophies* and their impact on educational practice. Based on these theories and their application to practice, you will be encouraged to formulate your own philosophy of education. Information regarding the impact of the major educational theories on the purpose of schooling, nature of the learner, curriculum, instructional methods, classroom management, assessment, and the role of the teacher will be presented.

To help you study these important concepts, consider the following outcome objectives:

- Define an educational theory and explain its relationship to philosophy as a discipline.
- Identify the various underlying protests that led to the establishment of the theories of perennialism, progressivism, behaviorism, essentialism, social reconstructionism, and postmodernism.
- Compare the purpose of schooling from a perennialist, progressivist, behaviorist, essentialist, social reconstructionist, and a postmodernist perspective.

- Describe the nature of the learner from a perennialist, progressivist, behaviorist, essentialist, social reconstructionist, and a postmodernist perspective.
- Compare the curricula of perennialism, progressivism, behaviorism, essentialism, social reconstructionism, and postmodernism.
- Compare the instructional methods that characterize perennialism, progressivism, behaviorism, essentialism, social reconstructionism, and postmodernism.
- Compare the preferred classroom management methods of perennialism, progressivism, behaviorism, essentialism, social reconstructionism, and postmodernism.
- Compare the assessment strategies of perennialism, progressivism, behaviorism, essentialism, social reconstructionism, and postmodernism.
- Describe the role of the teacher from a perennialist, progressivist, behaviorist, essentialist, social reconstructionist, and a postmodernist perspective.
- Formulate your educational theory (philosophy of education).

Having examined the assumptions that underlie the major philosophies, it is now appropriate to examine how these basic assumptions translate to educational theories and practice. The major traditional and contemporary philosophies that were discussed in Chapter 3 each have a corollary educational theory. It is the combination of philosophy and theory that will enable you to frame your own philosophy of education.

Theories of Education

The term *theory* can be defined in two ways. First, a theory is a hypothesis or set of hypotheses that has been verified by observation or experiment. Second, a theory is a general synonym for systematic thinking or a set of coherent thoughts. Thus, a **theory of education** is a composite of systematic thinking or generalizations about schooling (Kneller, 1971). A well-thought-out theory of education is important, for it helps to explain our orientation to teaching and allows us to defend our position with respect to how learning takes place. In short, a theory of education enables teachers to explain what they are doing, and why. It provides academic accountability. As you become acquainted with each of the theories of education, you may conclude that most teachers incorporate several theories in their practice.

The major theories of education examined in this chapter are perennialism, progressivism, behaviorism, essentialism, social reconstructionism, and postmodernism. Each theory was developed as a protest against the prevailing social and educational climate of the time. For example, perennialism came about as a protest against secularization and the excessive focus on science and technology, at the expense of reason, that dominated society and its educational institutions at the time.

As you review each educational theory, keep in mind the similarities and differences among the theories and the reason or rationale behind the protest that led to its development.

Perennialism

Eternal or perennial truths, permanence, order, certainty, rationality, and logic constitute the ideal for **perennialism.** The philosophies of idealism, realism, and neo-Thomism are embedded in the perennialist theory of education. The educational focus of perennialism is on the need to return to the past, namely, to universal truths and such absolutes as reason and faith. The views of Plato, Aristotle, and Thomas Aquinas are reflected in this educational theory. (The *Historical Note* gives a brief look at Aquinas's life.) Although perennialism has been historically associated with the teachings of neo-Thomism, it has also received widespread support from lay educators.

Purpose of Schooling

Perennialists consider the purpose of schooling to be to teach the eternal truths, cultivate the rational intellect, and develop the spiritual nature of the individual. For the ecclesias-

HISTORICAL NOTE

St. Thomas Aquinas

St. Thomas Aquinas was born of a noble family in Roccasecca, Italy, in 1224. From 1239 to 1244 he attended the University of Naples, where he came in contact with the Dominican order. Against the violent opposition of his parents, Aquinas became a Dominican friar in 1244. During the years 1245 to 1252, he studied philosophy and theology under the tutelage of the German theologian St. Albertus Magnus. From 1252 to 1259 and again from 1269 to 1272 he taught at the University of Paris, where he was known as "The Angelic Doctor." Between 1259 and 1269 he taught at the Papal Curia in Italy. Aquinas's two most influential works were the *Summa Contra Gentiles,* which expressed the doctrine of scholasticism, or Christian philosophy, and his most important work, *Summa Theologica.* In the latter work, Aquinas attempted to explain the truth of Christian theology and advanced the proposition that conflict need not exist between reason and faith.

Aquinas believed that the government had a moral responsibility to assist the individual to lead a virtuous life. He further postulated that governments must not violate human rights, including the right to life, education, religion, and reproduction. Laws passed by human beings must be in concert with divine laws.

Aquinas died in 1274. In 1323, Pope John XXII canonized him and since then his philosophy has become the official doctrine of the Roman Catholic Church. In 1567, Pope St. Pius V proclaimed him a Doctor of the Church. He has also been proclaimed the patron saint of all Catholic schools, colleges, and universities.

CW To research and explore this topic further, go to the *Historical Note* module for this chapter of the Companion Website at **http://www.prenhall.com/webb.**

tical perennialists, the highest goal of education is union with God. They also believe that education is preparation for life and that—although formal education may end—learning is a lifelong process.

Nature of the Learner

Perennialists believe that all students are rational beings who exemplify value and worth. Ecclesiastical perennialists also believe that students have been endowed with both an intellect and a soul.

Curriculum

For the ecclesiastical perennialist, Christian doctrine is an important aspect of the curriculum. The holy scriptures, the catechism, and the teaching of Christian dogma play a significant role. Wherever possible, theistic works would take precedence over purely secular works (Morris & Pai, 1976). The cultivation of the intellect while stressing faith and reason through a relationship with God best describes the curriculum of the ecclesiastical perennialist.

Both ecclesiastical and lay (secular) perennialists emphasize a strong liberal arts curriculum that includes such cognitive subjects as philosophy; mathematics (especially algebra and geometry); history; geography; political science; sociology; theology, languages, and literature (in particular the **Great Books**); physical and life sciences; and the fine arts and humanities. Mastery of these subjects is considered necessary for the training of the intellect. In addition, perennialists contend that character training and moral development have an appropriate place in the design of the curriculum.

More contemporary perennialists such as Mortimer Adler (1902–2001) have placed less emphasis on subject matter. Rather, they view the curriculum as the context for developing intellectual skills, including reading, writing, speaking, listening, observing, computing, measuring, and estimating. These perennialists maintain that education involves confronting the problems and questions that have challenged people over the centuries.

For Your Reflection and Analysis

If you were a perennialist, what 10 books would you choose as the Great Books? At what grade level(s) should they be introduced to students?

To submit your response online, go to http://www. prenhall.com/webb.

CW

Instructional Methods

Adler (1984) suggested three specific methods of instruction: (1) didactic instruction, (2) coaching, and (3) the Socratic method described in Chapter 5. Each method is carefully chosen to develop the student's intellect.

Prior to studying the great works of literature, philosophy, history, mathematics, and science, students would be taught methods of critical thinking and questioning strategies to prepare them to engage in "dialogue" with the classical writers. For the ecclesiastical perennialists, any type of teaching method that brings the learner into direct contact with the Supreme Being would be encouraged.

Classroom Management

Perennialists are concerned with training not only the intellect, but also the will. They believe that the teacher has the obligation to discipline the student in order to train the will. They would consider the most appropriate classroom environment for training the will to be one that reinforces time on task, precision, and order. In addition to orderliness and structure, for the ecclesiastical perennialist the learning environment would also reflect an appreciation for prayer and contemplation.

Assessment

The objective examination would be the favored evaluation tool of the perennialist teacher. Because the study of the classical tradition of the Great Books promotes an exchange of ideas and insights, the essay examination would also be utilized.

The Perennialist Teacher

Perennialists view the teacher who is well educated in the liberal arts to be the authority figure and the instrument that provides for the dissemination of truth. And if the teacher is the disseminator, then the student is the receptacle for learning. The metaphor "director of mental calisthenics" has been used to describe the perennialist teacher (Morris & Pai, 1976).

Another metaphor that describes the perennialist teacher is the "intellectual coach" who can engage students in the Socratic dialogue. The perennialist teacher must be a model of intellectual and rational powers. He or she must be capable of logical analysis, be comfortable with the scientific method, be well versed in the classics, possess a good memory, and be capable of the highest forms of mental reasoning.

Leading Educational Proponents

Jacques Maritain (1882–1973), a French Catholic philosopher who served as ambassador to the Holy See, was perhaps the best spokesperson for the ecclesiastic perennialist position. According to Maritain (1941), intelligence alone is not sufficient to fully comprehend the universe. One's relationship to a Spiritual Being is necessary to understand the cosmos or universe. Robert M. Hutchins (1899–1977), former chancellor of the University of Chicago, was a noted spokesperson for the lay perennialist perspective. Both Maritain (1943) and Hutchins (1936) argued that the ideal education is one that is designed to develop the mind, and this can be best done by a curriculum that concentrates on the Great Books of Western civilization.

As discussed in Chapter 7, the 1980s saw a resurgence of perennialism. In his *Paideia Proposal: An Educational Manifesto* (1982), Mortimer Adler advocated a curriculum that would be appropriate for all students. Adler, like Hutchins, opposed differential curricula (e.g., vocational, technical, academic) and contended that all students in a democratic society should have access to the same high-quality education that includes language, literature, mathematics, natural sciences, fine arts, history, geography, and social studies. Also like Hutchins, Adler favored the Great Books tradition and maintained that by studying the great works of the past, one can learn enduring lessons about life.

Allan Bloom, another prominent perennialist of the 1980s, was concerned with what he perceived as the intellectual crisis of liberal education, particularly in the university. In

Both Robert Hutchins (left) and Mortimer Adler (right) advocated the Great Books and the enduring lessons of the past.

his book *The Closing of the American Mind* (1987), Bloom refers to "cultural illiteracy" as the crisis of our civilization. Like Hutchins and Adler, Bloom advocates teaching and learning about the Great Books, because they provide knowledge and information that have lasting significance.

Today the perennialist curriculum can be found in low-income multicultural public schools as well as elite academies. The curriculum of St. John's College at Annapolis, Maryland, and Santa Fe, New Mexico, which emphasizes the importance of studying the Great Books of the Western tradition, is an excellent example of the perennialist curriculum. Figure 4.1 presents an overview of perennialism.

For Your Reflection and Analysis

As a response to Allan Bloom's perceived "crisis in our civilization," what suggestion would you make for revamping the general studies curriculum at the university level?
To submit your response online, go to http://www. prenhall.com/webb.

CW

Progressivism

Progressivism focuses on real-world problem-solving activities in a democratic and co-operative learning environment. This view of education is grounded in the scientific method of inductive reasoning. As an educational theory, it encourages the learner to seek out those processes that work and to do those things that best achieve desirable ends. Progressivism came about as a protest against the emphasis on universal truth and the past at the expense of experience and social relevance. The philosophy of pragmatism is embedded in the progressivist theory of education.

Purpose of Schooling

Progressivists believe that the school should model life, particularly a democratic society. Dewey envisioned such a democratic community to be pluralistic in nature and include moral, economic, educational, and political goals. To prepare students to best operate in this democracy and in the larger democratic society, the school should encourage cooperation, not competition, and develop problem-solving and decision-making skills.

Nature of the Learner

Progressivism embraces the notion that the child is an experiencing organism who is capable of "learning by doing." Progressivists perceive students to be evolving and active

Figure 4.1 — Perennialism at a Glance

Purpose of Schooling	Nature of Learner	Curriculum	Instructional Methods	Classroom Management	Assessment	The Perennialist Teacher	Leading Proponents
Teach eternal truth Cultivate intellect Develop spiritual nature Prepare for life	Rational being with soul Exemplify value and worth	Christian doctrine Liberal arts Philosophy Mathematics History Geography Political science Sociology Theology Foreign language Science Fine arts and humanities Great Books Character training Moral development	Didactic instruction Coaching Socratic method Critical thinking Questioning strategies Discussion Lecture	Training the will Time on task Precision Order Structure Regularity Prayer Contemplation	Objective exam Essay exam	Educated in liberal arts Authority figure Disseminator of "truth" "Director of mental calisthenics" "Intellectual coach" Rational Logical Well versed in classics Scholar	Jacques Maritain Robert Hutchins Mortimer Adler Allan Bloom

beings capable of interacting with their environment, setting objectives for their own learning, and working together to solve common problems. They are also capable of establishing rules for governing their classrooms, and testing and evaluating ideas for the improvement of learning (Noddings, 1995).

Curriculum

The progressivist curriculum can best be described as experience centered, relevant, and reflective. Such a curriculum would not consist of a given set of predetermined facts or truths to be mastered, but rather a series of experiences to be gained. For Dewey (1963) "anything, which can be called a study, whether arithmetic, history, geography, or one of the natural sciences, must be derived from materials which at the onset fall within the scope of ordinary life-experiences" (p. 73). However, while he maintained that experience was the basis of education, Dewey (1938) cautioned that not all experiences are equal:

> The belief that all genuine education comes about through experience does not mean that all experiences are genuinely or equally educative. Experience and education cannot be directly equated to each other. For some experiences are mis-educative. Any experience is mis-education that has the effect of arresting or distorting the growth of further experience. (p. 25)

The curriculum of progressivism would integrate several subjects but would not reflect universal truths, a particular body of knowledge, or a set of prescribed core courses. Rather, it would be responsive to the interests, needs, and experiences of the individual, which would vary according to the situation. Lerner (1962) described such a curriculum as child centered, peer centered, growth centered, action centered, process and change centered, and equality centered. It is also community centered. It would feature an **open classroom** environment in which students would spend considerable time in direct contact with the community or cultural surroundings beyond the confines of the classroom or school. Students would experience the arts by frequenting museums and theaters. They would experience social studies by interacting with individuals from diverse social groups and social conditions. They would experience science by exploring their immediate physical world. All students would be involved in a "social" mode of learning (Westheimer & Kahne, 1993).

The progressivist is not interested in the study of the past but is governed by the present. Unlike the perennialist or the essentialist who advocate the importance of the cultural and historic roots of the past, the progressivist advocates that which is meaningful and relevant to the student today.

Instructional Methods

For the progressivist, because there is no rigid subject-matter content and no absolute standard for what constitutes knowledge, the most appropriate instructional methods include group work and the project method. The experience-centered, problem-solving curriculum lends itself to cooperative group activities whereby students can learn to work together on units or projects that have relevance to their own lives. Katz and Chard (2000) recommend that as early as the first grade, project work can complement systematic instruction. The instructional strategy that would be used with the project method is the scientific method. However, unlike the perennialist or the essentialist who views the scientific method as a means of verifying truth, the progressivist views scientific investigation as a means of verifying experience.

Because the progressivist curriculum is an emerging rather than static curriculum, any teaching method that fosters individual and group initiative, spontaneity of expression, and creative new ideas would be used. Classroom activities in critical thinking, problem solving, decision making, and cooperative learning are examples of some of the methods that would be incorporated in the curriculum. For the progressivist, "teaching is . . . exploratory rather than explanatory" (Bayles, 1966, p. 94).

Classroom Management

Progressivism views learning as educating "the whole child," including the physical, emotional, and social aspects of the individual. As a result of this holistic view of education, the environment is considered fundamental to the child's nature. The type of classroom management that would appeal to a progressivist would be an environment that stimulates or invites participation, involvement, and the democratic process. The atmosphere of the classroom would be active, experience directed, and self-directed (Dewey, 1956).

The progressivist teacher would foster a classroom environment that practices democracy and emphasizes citizenship. Students and parents would be encouraged to form their own councils and organizations within the school to address educational issues and to advance social change. Teachers would advocate parental involvement, site-based management, and democratic decision making with regard to the administration of the school.

Assessment

Because progressivism supports the group process, cooperative learning, and democratic participation, its approach to evaluation differs from the more traditional approaches. For example, the progressivist would engage in formative evaluation, which is process oriented and concerned with ongoing feedback about the activity under way, rather than the measurement of outcomes. Monitoring what the students are doing, appraising what skills they still need to develop, and resolving unexpected problems as they occur would be typical examples of the type of evaluation used by the progressivist.

The Progressivist Teacher

The metaphor of the "teacher as facilitator" or "director of learning" might best describe the progressivist teacher. Such a teacher is not considered to be the authority on, or disseminator of, knowledge or truth, like the perennialist or essentialist teacher. Rather, the teacher serves more as a guide who facilitates learning by assisting students to sample direct experience. Although the teacher is always interested in the individual development of each student, the role of the progressivist teacher is focused beyond the individual. Progressivism by its very nature is socially oriented; thus, the teacher would be

For Your Reflection and Analysis

What type of process-oriented evaluation would you be most comfortable using in your teaching?
To submit your response online, go to http://www.prenhall.com/webb.

CW

a collaborative partner in making group decisions, keeping in mind their ultimate consequences for the students. The teacher's role is to help the students to acquire the values of the democratic system.

Leading Educational Proponents

As discussed in Chapter 7, while progressivism traces its roots to Pestalozzi and Rousseau, the term *progressive education* is associated with a movement that gained momentum in the first decades of the 20th century at a time when many liberal thinkers alleged that American schools were failing to prepare all students to be effective participants in the social, economic, and political life of a democratic society. As discussed in that chapter, Francis W. Parker (1837–1902), superintendent of schools in Quincy, Massachusetts, and later head of the Cook County Normal School in Chicago, is considered the father of progressive education. However, as is also discussed, John Dewey (1859–1952), perhaps more than any other American educator, is credited with having advanced progressivism. Dewey's approach to progressivism differed from earlier progressive educators in that, rather than emphasizing the individual learner, Dewey emphasized the importance of the teacher–student interaction and the social function of the school as a model of democracy. Dewey's work at the laboratory school at the University of Chicago as well as his position at Teachers College, Columbia University, provided the clinical testing ground for his educational theory for almost a half a century.

Ella Flagg Young (1845–1917), a colleague of Dewey's at the University of Chicago and superintendent of the Chicago Public Schools, also served as an important spokesperson for progressivism by emphasizing the central role of experimentation and democracy in the classroom and the school. William H. Kilpatrick (1871–1965) further advanced progressive education by introducing the experience-centered curriculum, including the project method.

Progressivism fell into disfavor in the years following World War II, but as Ravitch (2000) has noted, it has never disappeared. Vestiges of progressivism could be found in **nongraded schools,** alternative schools, the whole-child movement, and **humanistic education.** In the last decades of the 20th century, progressive education was given

A century apart, both Ella Flagg Young and Theodore Sizer advance the principles of progressive education.

Figure 4.2 — Progressivism at a Glance

Purpose of Schooling	Nature of Learner	Curriculum	Instructional Methods	Classroom Management	Assessment	The Progressivist Teacher	Leading Proponents
Model a democratic and pluralistic society Encourage cooperation Develop problem-solving and decision-making skills Educate physical, emotional, and social needs	Experiencing organism Capable of learning by doing Evolving and active being Capable of interacting with environment Capable of setting objectives for learning Capable of cooperative problem solving Capable of establishing classroom rules Capable of testing and evaluating ideas	Experience centered Relevant Reflective Integrated Problem solving Responsive to student's interests and needs Child centered Growth centered Action centered Process centered Equality centered Community centered	Group activities Project method Critical thinking Problem solving Decision making Cooperative learning	Democratic and participatory Self-directed	Formative evaluation Ongoing feedback Monitoring student progress Appraising skills	Teacher as facilitator Director of learning Guide Collaborative partner	Francis W. Parker John Dewey Ella Flagg Young William H. Kilpatrick

renewed attention. The most visible examples can be found in Theodore Sizer's Coalition of Essential Schools. Coalition schools promote:

- Personalized instruction to address individual needs and interests;
- Small schools and classrooms where teachers and students know each other well and work in an atmosphere of trust and high expectations;
- Multiple assessments based on performance of authentic tasks;
- Democratic and equitable school policies and practice; and
- Close partnerships with the school community. (Coalition of Essential Schools, 2005, p. 1)

As these goals demonstrate, 50 years after his death, John Dewey is still very much alive in American schools.

Figure 4.2 presents an overview of progressivism.

Behaviorism

Behaviorism is an educational or learning theory that is predicated on the belief that human behavior can be explained in terms of responses to external stimuli. The basic principle of behaviorism is that education can best be achieved by modifying or changing student behaviors in a socially acceptable manner through the arrangement of the conditions for learning. For the behaviorist, the predictability and control of human behavior are paramount concepts. The control is obtained not by manipulating the individual but by manipulating the environment.

The basic principles or philosophical foundations of behaviorism are as follows:

1. Most behaviors are learned.
2. Most behaviors are stimulus specific.
3. Most behaviors can be taught, changed, or modified.
4. Behavior change goals should be specific and clearly defined.
5. Behavior change programs should be individualized.
6. Behavior change programs should focus on the here and now.
7. Behavior change programs should focus on the child's environment. (Zirpoli, 2005, p. 13)

There are two major types of behaviorism: (1) **classical conditioning** or stimulus substitution behaviorism, and (2) **operant conditioning,** or response reinforcement behaviorism. Classical conditioning, based on the work of the Russian physiologist Ivan Pavlov (1849–1936) and the American experimental psychologist John B. Watson (1878–1958), demonstrates that a natural stimulus that produces a certain type of response can be replaced by a conditioned stimulus. For example, Pavlov found that in laboratory experiments involving dogs, a natural stimulus such as food will produce a natural response such as salivation. However, when Pavlov paired the natural stimulus (food) with a conditioned stimulus (bell), he found that eventually the conditioned stimulus (bell) produced a conditioned response (salivation). Watson eventually used Pavlov's classical conditioning model to explain all human learning.

The operant conditioning model can best be described by the work of psychologists E. L. Thorndike (1874–1949) and B. F. Skinner (1904–1990). Both Thorndike and Skinner suggested that any response to any stimulus can be conditioned by immediate reinforcement or reward. Skinner later determined that an action or response does not have to be rewarded each time it occurs. In fact, Skinner found that random reward, or intermittent reinforcement, was a more effective method for learning than continuous reward. Skinner concluded that behavior could be shaped by the appropriate use of rewards.

As a theory of education, behaviorism came into being as a protest against the importance placed on mental processes that could not be observed (e.g., thinking, motivation). Today, behaviorism continues to be a viable theory not only in the classroom but in clinical settings as well. For example, cognitive-behavioral therapy has emerged as an effective therapeutic intervention in the field of psychology for identifying and modifying faulty thinking, attitudes, and problem behaviors.

B. F. Skinner advocated reinforcement as a method of shaping behavior.

Purpose of Schooling

Behaviorists' view of the purpose of schooling is to increase appropriate behaviors, decrease inappropriate behaviors, and teach new behaviors by incorporating a variety of behavioral techniques (Zirpoli, 2005). The school sets the stage for modifying and reinforcing behaviors.

Nature of the Learner

Behaviorists believe that "most behaviors are learned, are stimulus-specific, and can be taught and modified. They also believe that students have the capacity and disposition to change" (Zirpoli, 2005, p. 34).

Curriculum

Unlike the curricula of perennialism, which prescribes a particular subject matter, or essentialism, which emphasizes a core of fundamental knowledge, the behaviorist curriculum is not interested in content per se, but is interested in environmental variables such as teaching materials, instructional methods, and teacher-classroom behaviors, because they directly influence the learner's behavior (Wittrock, 1987). The behaviorist curriculum includes cognitive problem-solving activities whereby students learn about their belief systems, recognize their power to influence their environment, and employ critical thinking skills.

Instructional Methods

Behaviorist theory is primarily concerned with the process of providing contingencies of reinforcement as the basis for any instructional strategy or method. According to the behaviorists, if there are appropriate opportunities for the learner to respond, and appropriate reinforcers that are readily available, then learning will occur. Behaviorists employ a variety of instructional methods to promote generalization and maintenance of learned behaviors. Computer-assisted instruction, or any type of interactive method that provides immediate feedback and reinforcement, would be favored by behaviorists. Other instructional methods employed by behaviorists include strategies such as problem solving, anger control, self-instruction, and self-reinforcement training. These strategies have been effectively used to modify both cognition and behavior (Zirpoli, 2005).

Classroom Management

For the behaviorist, classroom management is an integral part of the process of learning. Emmer (1987) described two general principles that guide the behaviorist teacher in classroom management:

1. Identify expected student behavior. This implies that teachers must have a clear idea of which behaviors are appropriate and which are not appropriate in advance of instruction.
2. Translate expectations into procedures and routines. Part of the process of translating expectations into procedures is to formulate some general rules governing conduct. (pp. 438–439)

Other components of good management include careful monitoring or observation of classroom events; prompt and appropriate handling of inappropriate behavior; using reward systems, penalties, and other consequences; establishing accountability for completion of assignments; and maintaining lesson or activity flow (Emmer, 1987). Behaviorism is widely used in special education and mainstream classroom environments.

Assessment

Measurement and evaluation are central to the behaviorist teacher. Specified **behavioral objectives** (e.g., the behaviors or knowledge that students are expected to demonstrate or learn) serve not only as guides to learning for the student but as standards for evaluating the teaching–learning process. For the behaviorist teacher, only those aspects of behavior that are observable, and preferably measurable, are of interest to the teacher. Advocates of behavioral objectives claim that if teachers know exactly what they want students to learn and how they want them to learn, then the use of behavioral objectives can be an efficient method for gauging how much learning has occurred. Measurement and evaluation also provide a method for obtaining accountability from teachers because they are pivotal to the learning process. Two other types of evaluation commonly used by behaviorist teachers are performance contracting and teaching students to record their own progress.

The Behaviorist Teacher

Because education as behavioral engineering entails a variety of technical and observational skills, the behaviorist teacher must be skilled in a variety of these techniques. Moreover, because behavioral engineering depends on psychological principles, the teacher must be knowledgeable about psychology, in particular educational psychology that emphasizes learning. Because behaviorism focuses on empirical verification, the teacher must also be well versed in the scientific method.

For Your Reflection and Analysis

What types of problem-solving activities would you use to help students learn about their belief systems?

To submit your response online, go to http://www.prenhall.com/webb.

CW

The behaviorist teacher is very concerned about the consequences of classroom behavior. Therefore, the teacher must be able to recognize which reinforcers are most appropriate. In addition, the behaviorist teacher must be skilled in using a variety of schedules of reinforcement that are effective and efficient in shaping and maintaining desired responses.

To establish the behaviors that will be most beneficial to the learner, behaviorist teachers are most concerned with the student achieving specific objectives or competencies. For this reason the teacher must be capable of planning and using behavioral objectives, designing and using various types of instruction, reinforcement strategies, and intervention strategies. Two of the most appropriate metaphors for describing the behaviorist teacher are "the controller of behavior" and "the arranger of contingencies."

Leading Educational Proponents

As previously noted, classical conditioning had its beginnings with Pavlov and Watson, both of whom maintained that classical conditioning was the key mechanism underlying all human learning. Also as previously discussed, the behaviorists Thorndike and Skinner are known for the concept of operant conditioning, which suggests that reinforcement of responses (operant behavior) underlies all types of learning. Another noted behaviorist, psychologist David Premack, determined that organisms often freely choose to engage in certain behaviors rather than other behaviors. Consequently, providing access to the preferred activities can serve as reinforcement for not engaging in nonpreferred activities. To apply the **Premack principle** in the classroom, the teacher first must observe and carefully record the behavior that students more often freely choose to perform as well as the relative frequency of competing behaviors (Bates, 1987). Figure 4.3 provides an overview of behaviorism.

Figure 4.3 — Behaviorism at a Glance

Purpose of Schooling	Nature of Learner	Curriculum	Instructional Methods	Classroom Management	Assessment	The Behaviorist Teacher	Leading Proponents
Increase or reinforce appropriate behavior Modify or change inappropriate behavior Increase or reinforce new behavior	Capable of and disposed to modifying or changing behavior Capable of learning new behavior	Individualized Cognitive problem solving	Classical conditioning Operant conditioning Computer-assisted instruction Problem solving self-instruction Self-reinforcement training	Identifying expected behavior Translating expectations into procedures Formulating rules of conduct Monitoring Observing Responding promptly to inappropriate behavior Using rewards Using penalties Establishing accountability	Behavioral objectives Performance contracting Student self-evaluation	Skilled in variety of technical and observational skills Trained in educational psychology Skilled in scientific method Plans and uses behavioral objectives Designs and uses various types of instruction, schedules of reinforcement, and intervention strategies	Ivan Pavlov John W. Watson E. L. Thorndike B. F. Skinner David Premack

Essentialism

As described in Chapter 7, **essentialism** began in the 1930s as a protest against the perceived decline of intellectual rigor and moral standards in the schools. Essentialists then and now often base their criticisms of American education on comparisons with other countries such as Japan and Germany. They have argued that the curriculum in American schools was watered down and full of frills, and that in an attempt to provide equality, educational standards had been lowered and the more able students were badly served. Moreover, they contended that the schools had not only lost sight of their major purpose, to train the intellect, but they were failing in their responsibility to transmit the culture and traditions that are the basis of the American tradition (Wingo, 1974). The philosophies of idealism and realism are embedded in the essentialist theory of education.

For Your Reflection and Analysis

What subjects might be considered a "frill" by an essentialist?
To submit your response online, go to http://www. prenhall.com/webb.

CW

Purpose of Schooling

For the essentialist the primary purposes of schooling are to train the intellect and teach students the culture and traditions of the past. It should also provide students with the knowledge and skills necessary to successfully participate in a democratic and technological society.

Nature of the Learner

Essentialists believe that students have the capacity to become culturally literate and to develop disciplined minds. To do so, rigorous academic and moral training are required to overcome their natural tendencies.

Curriculum

The essentialist philosophy supports the belief that there is a critical core or body of knowledge that all students should possess. The curriculum of the essentialist school would provide instruction in these "essentials," which would include those "skills and subjects that have contributed to human survival, productivity, and civility" (Gutek, 2004, p. 281). At the primary level this would include reading, writing, and mathematics. At the upper elementary grades, history, geography, natural science, and foreign languages would be added. At the secondary level, the curriculum would place a major emphasis on a common core that includes 4 years of English, 3 years of mathematics, 3 years of science, 3 years of social studies, and a half year of computer science. For the college-bound student, foreign languages would be required. Overall, essentialists maintain that the educational program should not permit any "frivolous subjects," but rather should adhere to sound academic standards and return to the "basics."

Like the perennialists, who advocate intellectual discipline as well as moral discipline, the essentialists also maintain that moral development and character training deserve an important place in the curriculum. William Bennett (1993), former U.S. secretary of education, strongly endorsed essentialism because it advocates moral literacy. Bennett proposed the use of stories, poems, essays, and other works to help children achieve moral literacy and learn to possess the traits of character that society most admires.

Instructional Methods

The methods of instruction to support such a curriculum include the more traditional instructional strategies such as lecture, recitation, discussion, and the Socratic dialogue. Written and oral communication also occupy prominent places in the instructional milieu of the essentialist school. Like perennialists, essentialists view books as an appropriate medium for instruction. Essentialists have also found various educational technologies supportive of their educational theory.

In general, essentialists prefer instructional materials that are paced and sequenced in such a way that students know what they are expected to master. Detailed syllabi, lesson plans, learning by objectives, competency-based instruction, and computer-assisted instruction are other examples of teaching strategies that would be acceptable to the modern-day essentialist.

Classroom Management

For the essentialist, students attend school to learn how to participate in society, not to manage the course of their own instruction. They prepare for life by being exposed to fundamental knowledge and values, as well as by exercising discipline. Thus, the essentialist teacher would take great pains in designing and controlling a classroom environment that creates an aura of certainty, an emphasis on regularity and uniformity, and a reverence for what is morally right. The essentialist classroom would emphasize discipline and character training with clear expectations for behavior and respect for others.

Assessment

Of all the theories of education, essentialism is perhaps most comfortable with assessment, evaluation, and testing. In fact, the entire essentialist curriculum reflects the influence of the testing movement. The increased use of IQ tests, standardized achievement tests, diagnostic tests, and performance-based competency tests, as well as the current "high-stakes testing" mandated by the No Child Left Behind Act (2001), are all examples of the influence of the testing and measurement movements supported by essentialists. Competency, accountability, mastery learning, and performance-based instruction have gained increasing acceptance by many educators as a result of essentialists' influence on educational practice.

The Essentialist Teacher

The essentialist teacher, like the perennialist teacher, is an educator who has faith in the accumulated wisdom of the past. Rather than having majored in educational pedagogy, the essentialist teacher would probably have majored in a subject-matter discipline in the liberal arts, sciences, or the humanities. The essentialist educator is viewed as either a link to the so-called "literary intellectual inheritance" (idealism) or a "demonstrator of the world model" (realism). An essentialist teacher would be well versed in the liberal arts and sciences, a respected member of the intellectual community, technically skilled in all forms of communication, and equipped with superior pedagogical skills to ensure competent instruction. One of the most important roles of the teacher is to set the character of the environment in which learning takes place (Butler, 1966).

Leading Educational Proponents

Essentialism's greatest popularity emerged in the twentieth century. As noted in Chapter 7, in the 1930s and 1940s William C. Bagley and Arthur E. Bestor led the essentialist criticism of the progressivism of Dewey and his followers. They formed the Essentialist Committee for the Advancement of American Education. In the 1950s, Admiral Hyman G. Rickover (1900–1986) became the spokesperson for the essentialists. According to Rickover (1963), the quality of American education declined considerably as a result of "watered-down" courses and "fads and frills." He called for a return to the basics, with particular emphasis on mathematics and science.

A major revival of essentialism occurred with the **back-to-basics movement,** which gained support in the 1970s and was echoed in the education reform reports of the 1980s. *A Nation at Risk* (National Commission on Excellence in Education, 1983), the premier example of these reports, recommended a core of "new basics": English, mathematics, science, social studies, and computer sciences, and for the college-bound student, a foreign language.

One of the individuals most identified with the contemporary essentialist movement is E. D. Hirsch, Jr. Hirsch's 1987 best-selling *Cultural Literacy: What Every American Needs to Know* became a manifesto for the back-to-basics movement. In *Cultural Literacy*

Two prominent 20ᵗʰ-century spokespersons for Essentialism include Admiral Hyman Rickover and Diane Ravitch.

Hirsch identified 5,000 names, dates, facts, and concepts from the fields of art, religion, science, and culture that he maintained an individual must know to be considered educated. **Cultural literacy,** he claimed, had become the "common currency for social and economic exchange in our democracy" and is therefore "the only available ticket to citizenship" and "the only sure avenue of opportunity for disadvantaged children" (p. xiii). *Cultural Literacy* was such a success in the popular press that Hirsch followed it with a dictionary of cultural literacy and books about what children should know at various grade levels. Hirsch also developed a Core Knowledge curriculum, which offered the same academic credit to students in more than 1,000 Core Knowledge schools nationwide.

In a similar vein was Diane Ravitch and Chester Finn's *What Do Our 17 Year Olds Know?* (1987). After analyzing the results of the history and literature sections of the National Assessment of Educational Progress (NAEP), Ravitch and Finn concluded that the students had failed in both subjects. They then advanced the essentialist position that there is a body of knowledge that is so important it should be possessed by all Americans.

Another very visible essentialist is William Bennett, secretary of education during much of Ronald Reagan's second term. From his position Bennett designed the curriculum for the model essentialist high school, *James Madison High School* (1987), and the model elementary school, *James Madison Elementary School* (1988). According to Bennett's design, all students except those in vocational programs would have the same curriculum of high academic standards.

The success of the essentialist position is evidenced by the steps taken in a number of states to mandate curricula, strengthen graduation requirements, and increase student assessment. Essentialism is the dominant philosophy in our schools today. Figure 4.4 presents an overview of essentialism.

Social Reconstructionism

Throughout history there have been individuals who have aspired to improve, change, or reform society, including its educational institutions. Social reconstructionists differ

Figure 4.4 — Essentialism at a Glance

Purpose of Schooling	Nature of Learner	Curriculum	Instructional Methods	Classroom Management	Assessment	The Essentialist Teacher	Leading Proponents
Train intellect Teach past culture and tradition Teach knowledge and skills	Capable of becoming culturally literate Capable of a disciplined mind	Critical body of knowledge Reading Writing Mathematics Upper elementary History Geography Natural science Foreign language Secondary common core English Mathematics Science Social studies Computer science Foreign language Back to basics Moral development Character training	Lecture Recitation Discussion Socratic dialogue Written communication Oral communication Books Computer-assisted instruction Paced and sequenced materials Detailed syllabi Lesson plans Learning by objectives Competency-based instruction	Discipline Clear behavior expectations Respect for others	IQ tests Standarized achievement tests Performance-based tests Competency-based tests "High-stakes tests" Mastery learning	Well versed in liberal arts, sciences, or humanities Intellectual Skilled communicator Superior pedagogical skills	William C. Bagley Arthur E. Bestor Hyman G. Rickover E. D. Hirsch, Jr. William J. Bennett Chester Finn Diane Ravitch

from these revolutionaries in that they believe not only that society is in need of change or reconstruction, but that education must take the lead in the reconstruction of society. **Social reconstructionism** began in the 1930s with a group of progressive educators known as the "Frontier Thinkers." These educational reformers looked to the schools for leadership in creating a "new" and "more equitable" society than that which led up to the Depression. They advocated changes beyond what Dewey envisioned in his theory of progressivism; his emphasis was on the democratic social experience, theirs was on social reform. Social reconstructionism can be traced to the philosophies of both pragmatism and existentialism.

Purpose of Schooling

Social reconstructionists consider the purpose of schooling to be to critically examine all cultural and educational institutions and recommend change and reform as needed. In addition, the school's purpose is to teach students and the public not to settle for "what is," but rather to dream about "what might be." Most important, the purpose of schooling is to prepare students to become change agents.

Nature of the Learner

Social reconstructionists believe that students are the critical element in bringing about social change. They contend that students are capable of initiating and adapting to change especially if they are influenced by appropriate adult role models.

Curriculum

Because the majority of social reconstructionists believe in the importance of democracy
and the proposition that the school is the
fundamental institution in modern society,
the curriculum of the social reconstructionist
school would reflect democratic ideals. It
would also emphasize **critical theory** and
the development of **critical literacy** or critical thinking skills. The curriculum would provide an opportunity for students to gain
firsthand experiences in studying real social
issues and community problems. Such a curriculum denounces any form of the politics of
exclusion. Instead, it challenges all unequal
power relationships and focuses on power as
applied to class, gender, sexuality, race, and nationalism (Blake & Masschalein, 2003). Rather
than concentrate on separate subjects, stu-

Social reconstructionists aspire to improve, change, and reform society.

dents would consider societal problems such as the place of biomedical ethics in improving the quality of life, the need to conserve our natural resources, and the issues of foreign
policy and nationalism. In addition to the formal or official curriculum, attention would be
given to the "hidden curriculum" (see discussion in Chapter 14), which "represents the
knowledge, claims and values of the dominant group or class that controls the schools"
(Gutek, 2004, p. 319).

Instructional Methods

The instructional methods of the social reconstructionist would include problem solving
and critical thinking. The focus would be on activities outside the school such as tutoring
younger students, public cleanup projects, or promoting consumer legislation. Activities
such as these contextualize skills learned at school in a way that helps students appreciate
their usefulness (Kincheloe, Slattery, & Steinberg, 2000). Instead of merely reading and
studying about the problems of society, students would spend time in the community becoming acquainted with and immersed in society's problems and their possible solutions.
They would analyze, research, and link the underlying issues to institutions and structures
in the community and larger society. Finally, they would take some action or responsibility
in planning for change.

Classroom Management

The classroom environment of the social reconstructionist would be a climate of inquiry
in which teachers and students question the assumptions of the status quo and examine
societal issues and future trends. The social reconstructionist would strive to organize the
classroom in a classless, nonsexist, and nonracist manner. There would be less emphasis
on management and control, and more focus on community building (Kincheloe et al.,
2000). An atmosphere that promotes analysis, criticism, and action research would best describe this type of classroom environment. Conflict resolution and differences in world
views would be encouraged and reinforced.

Assessment

The type of assessment that would be favored in a social reconstructionist school would
be **authentic assessment,** including formative evaluation, and would include a cooperative effort between student and teacher, student and student, teacher and administrator or
supervisor, and community and teacher. Information would be shared regularly during periodic formal and informal conferences, and the student or teacher being evaluated would
be an active participant in the process. Such an assessment requires participants to have

the ability and willingness to think in critical terms and to expose underlying assumptions and practices. Social reconstructionists oppose standardized testing of both students and teachers and use it only if mandated by local, state, or federal authorities.

The Social Reconstructionist Teacher

The metaphors "shaper of a new society," "transformational leader," and "change agent" aptly describe the social reconstructionist teacher. According to George S. Counts (1933), a leading figure in social reconstructionism in the 1930s, teachers "cannot evade the responsibility of participating actively in the task of reconstituting the democratic tradition and of thus working positively toward a new society" (p. 19).

For Your Reflection and Analysis

How comfortable are you with ambiguity? Constant change? *To submit your response online, go to http://www. prenhall.com/webb.*

CW

Social reconstructionist teachers must also be willing to engage in ongoing renewal of their personal and professional lives. They must be willing to critique and evaluate the conditions under which they work and extend their educative role outside the domains of the classroom and school. They must have a high tolerance for ambiguity, be comfortable with constant change, and be willing to reflect on their own thinking and the cultural and psychosocial forces that have shaped it. As an educational reformer, such a teacher detests the status quo and views the school as a particular culture in evolution. Moreover, he or she views the larger society as an experiment that will always be unfinished and in flux. The social reconstructionist teacher must be willing to engage in and form alliances with community groups, neighborhood organizations, social movements, and parents to critique and question the practice of school democracy and school policy.

Leading Educational Proponents

Modern social reconstructionism had its beginnings in Marxist philosophy. According to Karl Marx (1818–1883), capitalism and its emphasis on competition and the control of property in the hands of a few led to an alienated workforce who found little meaning or purpose in their work. Marx's later writings recommended a total social revolution against the ruling class by the working class. Two decades later, following the onslaught of the Great Depression, the American social reconstructionists, George S. Counts, Theodore Brameld (1904–1987), and Harold Rugg, called on the schools to take the lead in planning for the reconstruction of society and building a more ideal and more equitable social order. Counts, in his famous 1932 speech before the Progressive Education Association titled "Dare the Schools Build a New Social Order," called on the schools to focus less on the child and more on the social issues of the time, to "face squarely and courageously every social issue, come to grips with life in all its stark reality . . . develop a realistic and comprehensive theory of welfare, fashion a compelling and challenging vision of human destiny" (p. 7).

Two more contemporary spokespersons for the social reconstructionist theory of education were Ivan Illich (b. 1926) and Paulo Freire (1921–1997). Illich (1974), in his *Deschooling Society,* maintained that because schools have corrupted society, one can create a better society only by abolishing schools altogether and finding new approaches to education. Illich called for a total political and educational revolution. Freire, who was born, educated, and taught in Latin America, proposed that education be drawn from the everyday life experiences of the learners. From his students, the illiterate and oppressed peasants of Brazil and Chile, Freire drew his theory of *liberation pedagogy* and reconstructionism (Gutek, 2004). In his *Pedagogy of the Oppressed* (1973), Freire maintained that students should not be manipulated or controlled but should be involved in their own learning. According to Freire, by exchanging and examining their experiences with peers and mentors, students who are socially, economically, and politically disadvantaged can plan, initiate, and take action for their own lives.

Although few current educators would consider themselves to be social reconstructionists, many have beliefs and practices that are consistent with the principles of social reconstructionism. In addition, many principles of social reconstructionism are reflected in the critical theory and postmodern movements discussed next.

Figure 4.5 presents an overview of social reconstructionism.

Figure 4.5 — Social Reconstructionism at a Glance

Purpose of Schooling	Nature of Learner	Curriculum	Instructional Methods	Classroom Management	Assessment	The Social Reconstructionist Teacher	Leading Proponents
Examine cultural and educational institutions Recommend change and reform Prepare change agents	Capable of initiating change Capable of adapting to change	Democratic ideals Critical literacy Critical thinking Political/social awareness Community problems Hidden curriculum	Problem solving Critical thinking Community projects Becoming immersed in social problems Analyzing and researching problems Planning for change	Establishing a climate of inquiry Questioning the status quo Community building Conflict resolution Encouraging criticism and differences	Authentic assessment Formative evaluation Ongoing feedback Periodic formal and informal conferences	Shaper of a new society Transformational leader Change agent Tolerance for ambiguity Comfortable with change Educational reformer Engaged in community alliances	Karl Marx George S. Counts Theodore Brameld Harold Rugg Paulo Freire Ivan Illich

Postmodernism

Postmodernism, also called *postmodern constructivism,* has been defined as a contemporary philosophy, ideology, movement, and process. It represents a combination of the philosophies of pragmatism, existentialism, social reconstructionism, and critical pedagogy, which incorporates the technique of *critical theory.* As previously mentioned, critical theory is a process of analyzing and critiquing political, economic, social, and educational institutions. Critical theorists make assumptions and generalizations about the political nature of those institutions. They raise such questions as these: Who controls the school? Who chooses the curriculum? Who hires the teachers? Who chooses the textbooks? Who writes the textbooks? In short, who has the power? From their analyses, they uncover examples of disequity between the dominant culture (male, white, middle class) and disenfranchised, disadvantaged, or marginal groups (e.g., women, racial and ethnic minorities, homosexuals, immigrants, the aged, the poor).

Postmodernists believe that there are no eternal universal truths and values. They suggest that reality is subjective; it is not found in our ancient past, but in the eye of the beholder.

Postmodernists believe that individuals construct their own meaning from personal experience and that history is itself a construction (Newman, 1998). This theme is prevalent throughout the writing of postmodernists such as Jacques Derrida (1976), Jean-Francois Lyotard (1985), and Richard Rorty (1998).

Postmodernists also question "scientific realism" by refuting epistemological claims that science (in particular, the scientific method) is objective and unbiased. They claim that objective observation is not possible because the observer affects what is observed. Postmodernists suggest that the way we arrive at knowledge is not by science alone but by examining "the human past and present to see how claims of truth have originated, been constructed and expressed, and have had social, political and educational consequences" (Gutek, 2004, p. 130). They question the dominance of objectivity, universal explanations, truth, and rationality (Kincheloe et al., 2000). In their place they substitute critical inquiry and political awareness (Henderson, 2001); diversity, inclusion, and multiplicity (McLaren & Torres, 1998); and the limitations of language or the meaning of words (Biesta, 2001).

Purpose of Schooling

Postmodernists perceive the purpose of schooling to be to prepare students for critical citizenship and critical inquiry. To accomplish these tasks, the school must prepare

For Your Reflection and Analysis

Give examples of other "myths" that are perpetuated by the schools and by other institutions.

To submit your response online, go to http://www. prenhall.com/webb.

CW

students to recognize that schools, like other social institutions, are not value free. They have perpetuated certain myths and have reinforced a social order that is patriarchal, Eurocentric, and biased by social class and the "free market ideology" of capitalism. The school also has a responsibility to make students aware that certain groups in society have been excluded, marginalized, and exploited.

Nature of the Learner

Postmodernists believe that students have the right to voice and question the purpose of the major institutions in society including the school. Moreover, they believe students have the capacity to understand that humans are responsible for the phenomena of wars, poverty, violence, corruption, and social, political, economic, and ecological injustices (Martusewicz, 2001).

Curriculum

Postmodernists believe that historically the curriculum has not been unbiased. It has functioned to name and honor particular histories and experiences and has done so in such a way as to marginalize or silence the experiences of subordinate groups (Aronowitz & Giroux, 1991). In the postmodernist curriculum, any form of the politics of exclusion, including elevating Eurocentrism as a model for cultural literacy, would be unacceptable. Rather, curriculum topics such as "suffering and social justice" would be emphasized. The main focus of the curriculum would be one of cultural politics that would challenge all unequal power relationships (class, gender, sexuality, race, ethnicity, and nationalism). Its purpose would be to teach *literacy,* not *cultural literacy* but *critical literacy* (McLaren, 2003), which would empower all students.

Postmodernists encourage reading a wide variety of materials. For example, postmodernists might suggest the reading of the Great Books. However, they would not use the Great Books as a model for truth as do the perennialists, but as a model for questioning, critiquing, and analyzing what constitutes truth and who has the power to decide.

Instructional Methods

Postmodernists incorporate the learning theory of **constructivism,** whereby students construct their own knowledge and meaning via hands-on, problem-solving activities. Constructivism has its roots in the philosophy of pragmatism (Dewey) and the cognitive developmental theories of Jerome Bruner (1966) and Jean Piaget (1950).

Postmodernists would also include any method that would help the student recognize and understand the notion of **hegemony,** where the dominant culture is able to exercise domination over subordinate classes or groups with the partial consent of the subordinate group (Wink, 2005). It would encourage students to not only question, critique, and examine the culture and its institutions, but to also recognize and pay particular attention to the contradictions and variable meanings of the language we use in our discourse and text (Derrida, 1976).

An analysis and exploration of the students' own autobiographical histories, languages, and cultures would be highlighted. The **hidden curriculum,** or "unexpressed perpetuation of the dominant western culture through institutional processes," would also be examined (Wink, 2005, p.46). Lastly, the use of *text,* or "any set of symbolic objects through which we attempt to communicate something and through which we create meaning (classrooms, film, books, clothing)" would be incorporated (Martusewicz, 2001, p.11).

Classroom Management

The postmodernist classroom environment would be nonthreatening, supportive, and open to discussions of many controversial subjects and topics, where students are expected to value and treat each other with dignity and respect. Students are encouraged to reflect on their experiences and share their personal stories and narratives. Questioning and critiquing are not interpreted as negative actions or behaviors. Rather, they are perceived as positive actions toward bringing about change. The learning environment would stimulate group problem solving, collaboration, and experimental group activities. At the same time it would encourage self-discipline and reinforce individual choice and responsibility.

Assessment

Postmodernists would be most comfortable using various forms of authentic assessment to evaluate their students' ability to apply knowledge and skills in solving real-life problems. Some of the forms of authentic assessment that might be incorporated would be journals, personal narratives, independent and group portfolios that include photographs, videos, audiotapes, and art projects, as well as traditional writing samples. Students would also be encouraged to evaluate their own progress to determine how well they have grasped the important aspects of the learning activities (McNergney & McNergney, 2004). They would also be invited to evaluate the teacher.

Michael Apple is one of the leading critical theorists.

The Postmodernist Teacher

The terms "scholar-practitioner leader" (Horn, 2004), "critical thinker," and "change agent," are metaphors that describe the postmodernist teacher. The postmodernist teacher's role is to practice and model the "doing of critical theory." These teachers practice and model questioning, critiquing, and analyzing. At the same time, they recognize the power and influence they have over their students, their peers, parents, and the larger community. As professionals, they constantly check how they are communicating to determine whether they are alienating or offending others, while always respecting the rights of all individuals to take issue and disagree.

Leading Educational Proponents

Critical theory was first associated with the Frankfurt School of philosophy and social theory, which began in the 1920s, flourished in the 1930s in Germany, the 1940s in the United States, and continued throughout the 1950s and 1960s (Kincheloe, 2004). The Frankfurt School included the melding of philosophy and psychoanalysis. Some of the leading proponents included Karl Marx, Theodor Adorno, Max Horkheimer, Herbert Marcuse, Jurgen Habermas, and Eric Fromm.

The contemporary philosophy of postmodernism is one of the most influential philosophies in education today. Leading proponents include Michael Apple, Jacques Derrida, Michel Foucault, Henry A. Giroux, Jean-Francois Lyotard, and Richard Rorty. Figure 4.6 presents an overview of postmodernism.

Identifying Your Philosophy of Education

Educational philosophies and educational theories do not remain static, but constantly change depending on the social, economic, and political climate at the time. Upon visiting any school, it quickly becomes evident that a variety of philosophies and theories of education can coexist in the same school, or even in the same classroom. Few teachers operate from a single philosophical or theoretical perspective. Most educators are eclectic and sample a variety of ideas, propositions, principles, or axioms that represent a smorgasbord of views.

Figure 4.6 — Postmodernism at a Glance

Purpose of Schooling	Nature of Learner	Curriculum	Instructional Methods	Classroom Management	Assessment	The Postmodernist Teacher	Leading Proponents
Critically examine all institutions in society Develop critical literacy Question "scientific realism" Question objectivity truth & rationality	Capable of becoming aware of the disequity in society Capable of understanding social, economic, political, & ecological injustices	Cultural politics that challenge all unequal power relationships Hidden curriculum	Constructivism Critique & examine autobiographical histories, languages, & cultures Examine hegemony & hidden curriculum	Non-threatening Supportive Open Self-discipline Individual choice Responsibility	Authentic assessment Journals Narratives Portfolios Writing Samples Student self-evaluation Teacher-evaluation	Scholar-practitioner leader Critical thinker Change agent Doing critical theory Sensitive to and aware of their influence on students Respect right of students to disagree	Jacques Derrida Jean-Francois Lyotard Richard Rorty Michael Apple Michel Foucault Henry A. Giroux

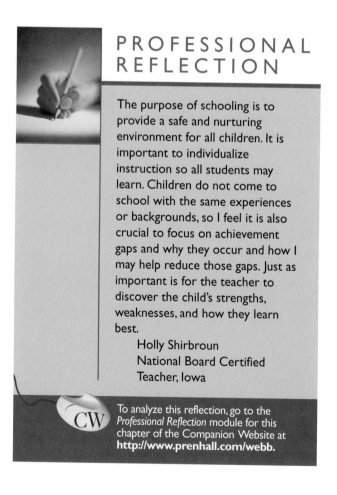

PROFESSIONAL REFLECTION

The purpose of schooling is to provide a safe and nurturing environment for all children. It is important to individualize instruction so all students may learn. Children do not come to school with the same experiences or backgrounds, so I feel it is also crucial to focus on achievement gaps and why they occur and how I may help reduce those gaps. Just as important is for the teacher to discover the child's strengths, weaknesses, and how they learn best.

Holly Shirbroun
National Board Certified Teacher, Iowa

CW To analyze this reflection, go to the *Professional Reflection* module for this chapter of the Companion Website at **http://www.prenhall.com/webb.**

Identifying and developing your philosophy of education may appear to be a formidable task. However, it is one of the most important tasks that you will probably be asked to perform as a prospective teacher. It is not uncommon to be asked to articulate your philosophy of education on job applications or in job interviews. School districts may require that you express your philosophical ideas and compare them to the philosophy or mission of the school district.

In Chapter 3 you were asked to respond to a series of questions that reflected your personal philosophy of life. You were also advised that the answers to those questions represented some of the assumptions you hold about teaching and learning. The time has come to combine philosophy, theory, and practice in constructing your philosophy of education. Your responses to the basic theoretical questions in the *Ask Yourself* feature reflect your philosophy of education. As you ask yourself these questions, recall the importance of clarity and meaning in the language you choose. Your ideas about education may change before you enter the teaching profession, and may change one or more times during the course of your career. Nevertheless, it is vitally important that you begin to conceptualize those ideas at this stage of your professional development.

ASK YOURSELF

What Is My Philosophy of Education?

To assess your preference for an educational philosophy, answer the following questions:

1. Are students intrinsically motivated to learn?

2. Should education be the same for everyone?

3. Are there certain universal truths that should be taught?

4. What determines morality?

5. What is the ideal curriculum?

6. What is the purpose of schooling?

7. If you were to choose one method or instructional strategy, what would it be?

8. What type of classroom environment is most conducive to learning?

9. How do you know when your students have learned?

10. What is the most important role of the teacher?

11. What is the role of the student?

12. How should prospective teachers be prepared?

Summary

There are six major theories of education: perennialism, progressivism, behaviorism, essentialism, social reconstructionism, and postmodernism. Educational theories influence educational practice by their impact on curriculum, instructional methods, classroom management, assessment, and the role of the teacher. Each theory developed from a particular philosophy or philosophies. Most theories were formulated as a protest against the prevailing social and cultural forces at the time. The educational theories of perennialism and essentialism have much in common in that they underscore the importance of a liberal education and the wisdom of the past. Behaviorism differs from the other educational theories in that its proponents believe all behaviors are both objective and observable.

Progressivism, social reconstructionism, and postmodernism share a common theme in that each of them is more concerned with the study of the present and future than the past. Unlike the perennialist and essentialist, who emphasize the important cultural and historic roots of the past, the progressivist, social reconstructionist, and postmodernist stress that which is meaningful and relevant to the student today.

In the next chapter, you will explore the historical origins of Western education. You will also examine the beginnings of American education as it evolved in the 13 original colonies.

Key Terms

Authentic assessment, 89
Back-to-basics movement, 86
Behavioral objectives, 83
Behaviorism, 81
Classical conditioning, 82
Constructivism, 92
Critical literacy, 89
Critical theory, 89

Cultural literacy, 87
Essentialism, 85
Great Books, 75
Hegemony, 92
Hidden curriculum, 92
Humanistic education, 80
Nongraded schools, 80
Open classroom, 78

Operant conditioning, 82
Perennialism, 74
Postmodernism, 91
Premack principle, 84
Progressivism, 77
Social reconstructionism, 88
Theory of education, 74

PROFESSIONAL DEVELOPMENT WORKSHOP

Prepare for the Praxis™ Examination

The Copper Creek School District is an urban district that in the past two decades has been transformed from a manufacturing-based to a technology-based economy. During the end of the 2004–05 school year, the Educare Traditional K–5 Magnet School became a reality. The impetus for the school came from several members of the business community who were concerned about what they considered a lack of rigor in the schools and the fact that many graduates of the Copper Creek schools came to them unable to read, spell, or compute at a level that was demanded of them in their daily assignments.

Three focus groups and two public open hearings had been held, and numerous editorials for and against the establishment of the magnet school were printed in the local *Copper Creek Examiner.* The unexpected surprise was that some of the most vocal critics of the schools were alumni of the Copper Creek schools.

Within 6 months after the first focus group meeting, the Copper Creek school board passed a resolution to establish Educare Traditional K–5 Magnet School. There was immediate agreement on the underlying philosophy of the school. True to its name, it would be a school that would embrace the classical tradition with an emphasis on the basic core subjects. Special features of Educare would include teacher-directed instruction in self-contained classrooms, regular homework assignments, teaching and modeling of study skills, weekly progress reports, and active participation of parents.

Several of the faculty who were selected to staff the new Educare Traditional School were appointed to the curriculum committee. Representatives of the business community and parents were also asked to serve on the committee. The task of the curriculum committee is to design a model traditional curriculum with particular attention given to the basic core subjects.

1. Which basic core subjects should the curriculum committee propose that would be in keeping with the philosophy of the new school? Give a rationale or justification for your choices.
2.   a. Which educational theory or theories should guide their decision making and recommendations?
     b. Which underlying philosophies are aligned with the educational theory or theories selected?
3. Describe two approaches the school district might use to improve its communication with parents and the community and to encourage their support for the new magnet school. Base your answer on some principles of communication.

To submit your responses online, go to the *Prepare for the Praxis™ Examination* module for this chapter of the Companion Website at **http://www.prenhall.com/webb**.

Build Your Knowledge Base

1. Reflect on the vignette at the beginning of this chapter. Which theory of education would you ascribe to Jim? To Beth? To Sam? Explain.
2. Describe the relationship between philosophy of life, educational theory, and philosophy of education.
3. Which of the theories of education presented in this chapter is most similar to your theory of education? In what ways is it different?
4. B. F. Skinner and other advocates of operant conditioning have been criticized for their emphasis on control. Are freedom and control incompatible concepts in the classroom? Explain.
5. As a social reconstructionist, list five major changes that you would propose for education and schooling in the 21st century. Should teachers and students be involved in promoting these changes? Why or why not?

6. Choose a leading educational proponent of essentialism and, using that individual's theory, construct a letter to the editor of a newspaper suggesting how the current training of teachers should be reformed.

Develop Your Portfolio

1. Examine INTASC Standard 4: "The teacher understands and uses a variety of instructional strategies to encourage students' development of critical thinking, problem solving, and performance skills." Review each of the educational theories discussed in this chapter (perennialism to postmodernism) and reflect on which educational theorist(s) provide(s) the most effective instructional strategies (instructional methods) to encourage students to develop critical thinking skills. Prepare a reflection paper that both describes the critical thinking skills you believe are most important in your discipline or subject area and the instructional strategies (instructional methods) you might use to help your students develop their critical thinking skills. Place the reflection paper in your portfolio under **INTASC Standard 4, Instructional Strategies.**

2. Review the basic questions in the *Ask Yourself* feature on page 95. In preparation for constructing your philosophy of education, reflect on the question, "Are students intrinsically motivated to learn?" Prepare a reflection paper that summarizes your response to this question. Place the reflection paper in your portfolio under **INTASC Standard 2, Student Learning and Development.**

To complete these activities online, go to the *Develop Your Portfolio* module for this chapter of the Companion Website at **http://www.prenhall.com/webb.**

Explore Teaching and Learning: Field Experiences

1. Visit a classroom, observe a lesson, review the teacher's lesson plan, and see if you can determine which of the six educational philosophies discussed in this chapter was used in the development of the lesson.

2. Review each of the major educational philosophies discussed in this chapter. Then interview the chair of the teacher education department or the associate dean for teacher education at your college or university to determine which, if any, of these educational philosophies is reflected in the teacher education program at your institution.

Professional Development Online

Visit this text's Companion Website at **http://www.prenhall.com/webb** to gain access to a variety of questions, activities, and exercises to help build your knowledge of this chapter's content. Below are just a few items available at this text's Companion Website:

- Classroom Video—To see actual classroom footage and work through activities and questions to analyze the content of the video, click on the *Classroom Video* module for this chapter.
- Teaching Tolerance—To go to this organization's website and complete activities to explore issues and topics dealing with how to teach tolerance to students, click on the *Teaching Tolerance* module for this chapter.
- Self-Test—To review terms and concepts presented in this chapter, click on the *Self-Test* module for this chapter.
- Internet Resources—To link to websites related to topics in this chapter, go to the *Internet Resources* module for this chapter.

CHAPTER 5

Only the educated are free.
—Epictetus, Roman slave and Stoic philosopher, *The Discourses* (101 A.D.)

AMERICAN EDUCATION: EUROPEAN HERITAGE AND COLONIAL EXPERIENCE

In his tenth Annual Report, the great American educator Horace Mann said, "I believe in the existence of a great, immutable principle of natural law . . . which proves the absolute right of every human being that comes into the world to an education; and which, of course, proves the correlative duty of every government to see that the means of that education are provided for all."

The U.S. Supreme Court, in Brown v. Board of Education of Topeka (1954), stated:

Today education is perhaps the most important function of state and local governments. Compulsory school attendance laws and the great expenditures for education both demonstrate our recognition of the importance of educa-

tion to our democratic society. It is required in the performance of our most basic public responsibilities, even service in the armed forces. It is the very foundation of good citizenship. . . . Such an opportunity [of an education], where the state has undertaken to provide it, is a right which must be made available to all on equal terms.

However, because the Constitution makes no mention of education, the question of whether it should be considered one of the implicitly guaranteed fundamental rights has been the subject of continued debate.

In your opinion, is the right to an education one of those inalienable rights that should be guaranteed by the government? Why? What are the implications of your decision?

When the courts consider cases that involve interpretation of the Constitution or specific laws, they often review historical records and consider the context of the time to try to determine the intent of the lawmakers. Similarly, studying the history of education helps educators to understand the development of educational thought and practice and to evaluate present educational institutions, theories, and practices in the light of past successes and failures. To help you develop insights into the European and colonial background of American education presented in this chapter, keep the following learning objectives in mind:

■ Contrast Spartan and Athenian education.
■ Compare the educational philosophies of Socrates, Plato, and Aristotle.
■ Explain the contribution of Quintilian to the development of European educational thought and practice.
■ Describe the influence of Arab scholars on Western education.
■ Discuss the impact of the Reformation on the provision of education.
■ Identify the contributions of Bacon, Comenius, Locke, Rousseau, Pestalozzi, Herbart, and Froebel to current educational practice.
■ Describe the curriculum in colonial elementary and secondary schools and the forces that shaped it.
■ Compare education in the New England, Middle Atlantic, and Southern colonies.

European Background of American Education
Education in Ancient Societies

The oldest known schools were those of Sumer, an area located between the Tigris and Euphrates rivers in Mesopotamia. These schools date from the third millennium B.C. Most of these schools were connected with a temple and taught writing and some calculations. The Sumerian language was not alphabetic, but consisted of 600 or more characters. Writing was done on clay tablets called cuneiform tablets, so a school was called the Tablet House or *edubba*.

Temple schools were also operated in ancient Egypt and were attended almost exclusively by the children of the upper class. Their purpose was to prepare the educated bureaucracy needed to administer the vast Egyptian empire and to further the technologies needed to build the architectural monuments for which Egypt is so well known. The curriculum of the Egyptian school at the lower level emphasized writing, music, religion, astronomy, and mathematics. After 6 to 10 years, a limited number of students went on to advanced studies in religion, medicine, and architecture. Students were taught using an elaborate system of pictographic script known as *hieroglyphics*. Lower level students used clay tablets, whereas students at the upper level used papyrus, a form of paper made from reeds that was invented by the Egyptians.

Although the Sumarians and Egyptians did operate schools, the Greeks are considered the first real educators in the Western world, "for they were the first western peoples to think seriously and profoundly about educating the young, the first to ask what education is, what it is for, and how children and men should be educated" (Castle, 1967, p. 11). However, although the Greeks were interested in education, they were not all in agreement as to what form it should take. For example, the content and approach to education in the two principal Greek city-states, Sparta and Athens, were quite different.

Education in Greece. Sparta was predominantly a military state, and education reflected Spartan life. The maintenance of military strength was the most important goal of the government. The welfare of the individual came second to the welfare of the state, life was regimented by the state, and severe limits were placed on individual freedoms. Creative or strictly intellectual pursuits were discouraged. The aim of the educational system, which began at age 7 for boys, was to inculcate patriotism and the ideal of the sacrifice of the individual to the state, as well as to develop and train physically fit and courageous warriors.

Whereas Sparta was renowned for its military preeminence, Athens was a democracy that held the individual in the highest regard. There was no compulsory education in Athens, except for 2 years beginning at age 18 when military training was required of all men. Athenian schools were private and restricted to those who could afford the fees.

Education in Athens prior to 479 B.C. (the defeat of Sparta), referred to as "the old education," consisted of sending boys ages 7 to 14 to several schools: the *didascaleum* or music school; the home or building of the *grammatistes* for the study of reading, writing, and arithmetic; and the *palestra* for physical education. Formal education stopped after age 14, although some youth continued their education at the gymnasia, where they received more demanding physical training, somewhat military in nature. From ages 18 to 20, a program involving military, public, and religious service was required of all young men; on completion of this service, full citizenship was granted. The aim of educating men in the Athenian state was to prepare a cultivated, well-mannered, physically fit, and agile individual ready for participation in Athenian citizenship.

The traditional view of the education of girls in Athens, as in Sparta, is that they received instruction only in the home. Yet archaeological evidence suggests otherwise. Various pottery and statues depict girls going to school, as well as reading, writing, and engaging in sports. However, it is uncertain how widespread these practices were (Beck, 1964).

The "new Greek education" (after 479 B.C.) continued in much the same vein as the "old" education at the elementary level. At the secondary level, however, a new element was introduced—the Sophists, traveling teachers who charged admission to their popular lectures. In the absence of a legal profession, some Sophists developed the practice of *logography,* the writing of speeches that their clients could deliver in courts of law. Sets

For Your Reflection and Analysis

What aspects of the educational systems of Sparta and Athens do you find appropriate for today's students? *To submit your response online, go to http://www.prenhall.com/webb.*

CW

of speeches and handbooks on rhetoric were sold. Schools of rhetoric grew in size and number.

Socrates (470–399 B.C.).   In contrast to the Sophists, Socrates did not commercialize his teaching and accepted no fees. He also disagreed with the use of knowledge merely to achieve success or gain power, but believed that knowledge was ethically and morally important to all men. According to Socrates, knowledge was a virtue that was both eternal and universal.

Socrates believed that the purpose of education was not to perfect the art of rhetoric but to develop in the individual his inherent knowledge and to perfect the ability to reason. Socrates believed that education and society were inextricably related: Society was only as good as its schools. If education was successful in producing good citizens, then society would be strong and good.

Socratic Method.   Socrates employed a dialectical teaching method that has come to be known as the **Socratic method** and is similar to the inquiry method practiced today. Using this method, Socrates would first demolish false or shaky opinions or assumptions held by the student while disclaiming any knowledge himself. Then, through a questioning process based on the student's experiences and analyzing the consequences of responses, he led the student to a better understanding of the problem. Finally, he brought the student to a discovery of general ideas or concepts that could be applied to new problems.

> "What is courage?" he would casually ask a soldier.
> "Courage is holding your ground when things get rough."
> "But supposing strategy required that you give way?"
> "Well, in that case you wouldn't hold—that would be silly."
> "Then you agree that courage is neither holding or giving way."
> "I guess so. I don't know."
> "Well, I don't know either. Maybe it might be just using your head. What do you say to that?"
> "Yes—that's it; using your head, that's what it is."
> "Then shall we say, at least tentatively, that courage is presence of mind—sound judgment in time of stress?"
> "Yes." (Meyer, 1972, p. 26)

Plato.   Socrates' most famous pupil was Plato. Plato founded the academy described in Chapter 3. Fees were not charged, but donations were accepted. As a teacher, Plato practiced a variety of methods. Sometimes he employed the Socratic method. At other times he assigned individual exercises and problems. Sometimes he lectured, although according to Meyer (1972), he was too technical and lecturing was not his best performance. Plato's theory of education is most clearly put forward in *The Republic* (1958) and the *Laws*.

In *The Republic* Plato begins by accepting Socrates' premise that "knowledge is virtue." He then expounds on the nature of knowledge and lays out the framework for both a political and social system, including an educational system. Plato believed that the state should operate the educational system. The aim of the school was to discover and develop the abilities of the individual, to aid the individual in discovering the knowledge of truth that is within each of us, and to prepare the individual for his or her role in society. The curriculum was to include reading, especially the classics, writing, mathematics, and logic. Plato also emphasized the physical aspects of education. However, games and sports, as well as music, were important not for the purpose of entertainment but to improve the soul and achieve moral excellence.

Although Plato advocated universal education, he presumed that few possessed the capacity to reach its final stages. Those who passed the successive selection tests and reached the highest levels of wisdom and devotion to the state were to rule the state— the philosopher was to be king (Good & Teller, 1969). Thus, education is the means by which one arrives at the ultimate good. In the process, it promotes the happiness and fulfillment of the individual (because the individual is sorted into the social office to which he or she is most fitted), as well as the good of the state. Plato's belief in leadership by the

---

For Your Reflection and Analysis

Can you recall an example from your own educational experience of the application of the Socratic method?

To submit your response online, go to http://www. prenhall.com/webb.

CW

Aristotle studied with Plato for a number of years at Plato's Academy in Athens.

most intelligent has since been espoused by countless others including some of the founders of our nation. His belief in unchanging ideas and absolute truths has earned him the title of "the Father of Idealism."

Aristotle. Aristotle was Plato's most famous student. For 20 years he studied and taught at the Academy. However, as the picture at the beginning of this chapter aptly reminds us, and as discussed in Chapter 3, Plato and Aristotle differed in some important respects. In the picture Plato is shown pointing heavenward as Aristotle points earthward. And that, metaphorically, was the main difference between them: Plato was the idealist, the lover of the metaphysical, whereas Aristotle was a realist, the more scientific of the two (Winn & Jacks, 1967).

It is probably fair to say that Aristotle has had more of an impact on education than either Socrates or Plato, perhaps because he gave the most systematic attention to it. Aristotle is credited with the introduction of the scientific method of inquiry. He systematically classified all branches of existing knowledge and was the first to teach logic as a formal discipline. He believed that reality was to be found in an objective order.

Like Plato, Aristotle believed in the importance of education to the functioning of society and that education should be provided by the state; unlike Plato, he did not believe in educating girls. The aim of education, he felt, is the achievement of the highest possible happiness of the individual by the development of the intellect through the cultivating of habits and the specific use of inductive and deductive reasoning (Bowen, 1972). An additional aim is to produce the good person and good citizen.

Last, Aristotle believed that there was a common "core" of knowledge that was basic to education, which included reading, writing, music, and physical education. This belief in a core of knowledge has prevailed through the centuries and is the basis for the core course requirements in American schools and colleges today.

Education in Rome. The Roman conquest of Greece in the second century B.C. brought thousands of Greek slaves to Rome and exposed Romans to Greece and its culture. The educational theories of the Greeks had a great impact on the Romans, and by the end of the first century these theories dominated Roman education. The formal Roman school system that evolved (and that influenced education throughout Europe for centuries) was composed of the elementary school, known as the *ludus,* and the secondary school or **grammar school.** At the ludus children ages 7 to 12 years were taught reading, writing, and accounting. Girls could attend the ludus, but usually that was as far as their education extended. Grammar schools were attended by upper class boys ages 12 to 16 years who learned grammar (either Greek or Latin) and literature. From ages 16 to 20, boys attended the school of rhetoric, where they were instructed in grammar, rhetoric, dialectic, music, arithmetic, geometry, and astronomy. Universities were founded during the early years of the Roman Empire. Philosophy, law, mathematics, medicine, architecture, and rhetoric were the principal subjects taught.

Quintilian (35–95 A.D.). The most noteworthy Roman educator was Quintilian, tutor to the emperor's grandsons. His influence on Roman schooling has had a subsequent impact on education through the centuries. Quintilian was so respected that he was made a senator and was the first known state-supported teacher (Wilkins, 1914). His *Institutio Oratoria (Education of the Orator)* is considered to be "the most thorough, systematic and scientific treatment of education to be found in classical literature, whether Greek or Roman" (Monroe, 1939, p. 450).

Quintilian believed education should be concerned with a person's whole intellectual and moral nature, and should have as its goal the production of the effective moral man in practical life (Monroe, 1939). Accordingly, in addition to instruction in grammar and rhetoric, Quintilian recommended a broad literary education that included music, astronomy, geometry, and philosophy. Such an education was to take place in the schools, preferably the public schools, not at home with private tutors as had been the earlier practice in Rome. Public (i.e., group) education, he maintained, provided the opportunity for emulation, friendships, and learning from the successes and failures of others. Progressive for his time, Quintilian disapproved of corporal punishment:

> first because it is a disgrace . . . and in reality . . . an affront; secondly, because if a boy's disposition be so abject as not to be amended by reproof, he will be hardened . . . (by) stripes. Besides, after you have coerced a boy with stripes, how will you treat him when he becomes a young man, to whom such terror cannot be held out? (Monroe, 1939, pp. 466–467)

The *Ask Yourself* feature below will help you examine your position on corporal punishment in today's schools.

In many other respects Quintilian's views seem remarkably modern. Recognizing that "study depends on the good will of the student, a quality that cannot be secured by compulsion," Quintilian supported holidays because "relaxation brings greater energy to study, and also games because it is the nature of young things to play" (Castle, 1967, p. 138). He believed in the importance of early training to child development. Of the proper methods of early instruction Quintilian said: "Let his instruction be an amusement to him; let him be questioned and praised; and let him never feel pleased that he does not know a thing . . . let his powers be called forth by rewards such as that age prizes" (cited in Monroe, 1939, p. 455). He also maintained that children should not be introduced to specific subject matter until they are mature enough to master it. Last, Quintilian emphasized the importance of recognizing individual differences when prescribing the curriculum. He charged the teacher to "ascertain first of all, when a boy is entrusted to him, his ability and disposition . . . when a tutor has observed these indications, let him consider how the mind of his pupil is to be managed" (cited in Monroe, 1939, p. 465).

The Roman system of education eventually spread throughout Western Europe. The schools of medieval Europe retained the standard curriculum of the Roman schools: grammar, rhetoric, logic, mathematics, geometry, music, and astronomy. Figure 5.1 provides an overview of education in Sparta, Athens, and Rome.

> **For Your Reflection and Analysis**
>
> Should Quintilian's works be required reading for teacher education students today? Why or why not?
>
> *To submit your response online, go to http://www. prenhall.com/webb.*
>
> CW

ASK YOURSELF

Does Corporal Punishment Have a Place in the Schools?

Quintilian vehemently opposed corporal punishment. The U.S. Supreme Court has said that corporal punishment does not violate the Constitution. Still, a number of states have abolished corporal punishment in the schools. In others, the decision to administer corporal punishment and the procedure to be followed in its administration have been delegated to local school districts. What is your position on corporal punishment? Ask yourself the following questions:

1. Does corporal punishment serve as a deterrent to undesirable behavior?

2. If it is practiced, for what infractions should it be reserved?

3. Who should administer it?

4. Should a teacher or administrator who administers excessive corporal punishment be held liable to prosecution under child abuse statutes?

5. Would you administer corporal punishment if required by the district? (If, for example, district policy stated that after three unexcused tardies to any one class, the student is to be given three swats by the teacher of the class.)

6. If struck by a student, how would you respond?

Figure 5.1 — Education in Ancient Societies

EDUCATION IN SPARTA

- Goal of education: to promote patriotism and train warriors
- Welfare of individual is secondary to the welfare of the state
- Curriculum emphasized exercise and games, military training, dance, and music

CONTRIBUTION TO WESTERN EDUCATION

- Recognition of importance of physical and moral training

EDUCATION IN ATHENS

- Goal of education: to prepare the well-rounded individual for participation in citizenship
- Emphasis on the development of reason
- Curriculum: reading, writing, mathematics, logic, physical education, music, and drama
- Schools: *didascaleum* (music school); *grammatistes* (reading, writing, and arithmetic)

- Concept of liberal education
- The Socratic method as a teaching method
- Importance of reason/the scientific method

EDUCATION IN ROME

- Goal of education: to develop the intellectual and moral citizen
- Emphasis on education for citizenship
- Curriculum: reading, writing, arithmetic, grammar, literature, music, rhetoric, astronomy, geometry, and philosophy
- Schools: *ludus* (elementary); grammar school (secondary); schools of rhetoric (from ages 16–20); universities

- Roman curriculum and organization adopted throughout Europe
- Recognition of individual differences
- Recognition of importance of play and relaxation

The philosophy of Thomas Aquinas provided the foundation for Roman Catholic education. Source: Dagli Orti/Picture Desk, Inc./Kobal Collection

Education in the Middle Ages

The period between the end of the Roman Empire (476 A.D.) and the 14th century is known as the Middle Ages. The Germanic tribes that conquered the Romans appropriated not only their land but much of their culture and their Catholic religion. The Roman Catholic Church became the dominant force in society and in education. By the end of the 6th century, public education had all but disappeared, and what remained took place under the auspices of the church. At the secondary level, monastic schools, originally established to train the clergy, educated boys in the established disciplines of the Roman schools. Theology was studied by those preparing for the priesthood. One important function of the monastic schools was preserving and copying manuscripts. Had it not been for the monastic schools, many of the ancient manuscripts that survive today would have been lost.

Thomas Aquinas.   The most important scholar and philosopher of the Middle Ages was the Dominican monk St. Thomas Aquinas. As discussed in Chapter 3, his philosophy, called scholasticism or neo-Thomism, is the foundation of Roman Catholic education. Aquinas was able to reconcile religion with the rationalism of Aristotle. He believed that human beings possess both a spiritual nature (the soul) and a physical nature (the body). He also maintained that man is a rational being and that through the deductive process of rational analysis man can arrive at truth. When reason fails, man must rely on faith. Thus, reason supports what man knows by faith: Reason and faith are complementary sources of truth. In accordance with this philosophy, the schools were to teach both the principles of the faith and rational philosophy. The curriculum was to contain both theology and the liberal arts.

The Medieval Universities.   During the later Middle Ages, as the Crusades opened Europe to other parts of the world and as many of the Greek masterpieces that had disappeared from Europe but had been preserved by Arab scholars were rediscovered, an intellectual revival occurred that manifested itself not only in scholasticism but in the establishment of several of the world's great universities. The University of Salerno, established in 1050 A.D., specialized in medicine; the University of Bologna (1113 A.D.) in law; the University of Paris (1160 A.D.) in theology; and Oxford University (1349 A.D.) in liberal arts and theology. By the end of the Middle Ages, some 80 universities were in existence (Meyer, 1972). Some, such as the University of Paris, grew out of a cathedral school, in this case Notre Dame. Others evolved from associations called *universitas,* which were chartered corporations of teachers and students, organized for their protection against interference from secular or religious authorities.

Initially, most universities did not have buildings of their own but occupied rented space. The curriculum at the undergraduate level followed the seven liberal arts. Classes started soon after sunrise. The mode of instruction was lecture in Latin, with the teacher usually reading from a text he had written. Student guilds or unions, commonplace at the time, ventured to tell the professors how fast to speak. At Bologna the students wanted to get full value for their fees and required the professors to speak very fast. By contrast, the Parisian students insisted on a leisurely pace, and when the authorities ordered some acceleration, the students not only "howled and clamored" but threatened to go on strike (Meyer, 1972). More exciting than the lectures were the disputations at which students presented and debated opposing intellectual positions. The disputations also served to prepare students for the much dreaded day when they would defend their theses. The *Historical Note* on page 108 provides a brief glimpse of the life of the university student in medieval times. Note the differences and similarities with present-day student life.

Of all the institutions that have survived from medieval times to the present, with the exception of the Catholic Church, the university bears the closest resemblance to its ancient ancestors. As it was then, it is still an organization of students and professors dedicated to the pursuit of knowledge. It still grants the medieval degrees: the bachelor's, the master's, and the doctor's. In most universities students are still required to study a given curriculum, and if they seek the doctorate, they are required to write a thesis or dissertation and to defend it publicly. The gowns worn at academic ceremonies today are patterned after those worn by our medieval ancestors. Deans, rectors, and chancellors still exist, although their duties have changed (Meyer, 1972).

Influence of Arab Scholars.   Although it is true that "without the Arabs much of the Greek philosophical tradition would have been lost to the world" (Ulich, 1971, p. 193), their contribution to Western education goes beyond that. Motivated in part by a desire to spread their Islamic faith, Arab scholars carried both their religious and their intellectual ideas and scientific advancements throughout northern Africa, as far east as India, and as far west as Spain. Libraries were established in all of their principal towns (the library of one Arab ruler was so large that the catalog alone was said to fill 40 volumes), and to each mosque was attached a public school (Draper, 1970). The scholars in these schools as well as the Arab universities produced copious dictionaries, lexicons, pharmacopoeias, and encyclopedias, as well as all forms of literature and treatises on topics ranging from algebra (an Arab word) and astronomy to commerce and agronomy (Draper, 1970).

The Arab contribution to the advancement of medicine and medical education is particularly noteworthy. Not only did the Arabs establish hospitals throughout their far-flung empire, but also, as early as the beginning of the 10th century, Arab physicians were required to pass an examination and possess a license (Totah, 1926). The most famous and influential Arab philosopher-scientist of the late 10th and early 11th centuries, Avicenna (Ibn Sina) (980–1037), wrote more than 100 treaties on Aristotelian philosophy and medicine. Of his two most famous works, *Encyclopedia Britannica* declares the *Kitab ash-Shita,* which covers logic, metaphysics, and the natural sciences, to be the "largest work of its kind ever written by one man," and *The Canon of Medicine* to be "the most famous single book in the history of medicine both East and West" ("Avicenna," 1997, p. 740). The

For Your Reflection and Analysis

If the student guild or union were in effect today, what changes might it recommend for undergraduate education?

To submit your response online, go to http://www. prenhall.com/webb.

CW

HISTORICAL NOTE

Life of the Medieval University Student

Although academic life was rigorous, students had many privileges. They were exempt from military service and from paying taxes. A student who shaved his head and assumed a few other burdens became one of the clerical class and was allowed some of the benefits associated with it. For example, if he broke what would be considered civil law, he was tried under church law, not civil law. However, in keeping with his clerical status the student was required to be celibate. If he did stray, he could continue with his studies, but lost his privileges and could receive no degree.

Medieval students were not without vices. Taverns often surrounded the universities and at the taverns were women and gambling. More seriously, students at Oxford were said to roam the streets at night, assaulting all who passed. In Rome the students went from tavern to tavern committing assault and robbery. At Leipzig they were fined for throwing stones at professors, and at Paris they were excommunicated for shooting dice on the altars of Notre Dame.

Although these acts were the exception rather than the rule, such actions, as well as the attitude of the students, who held townspeople in low regard, were sufficient to lead to open hostilities between "town" and "gown." Some separation still exists between town and gown in many university communities today, perhaps a legacy from our medieval ancestors.

Source: Based on accounts in Meyer, A. E. (1972). *An educational history of the Western world.* New York: McGraw-Hill.

 To research and explore this topic further, go to the *Historical Note* module for this chapter of the Companion Website at **http://www.prenhall.com/webb.**

latter "served as the guide for medical education throughout Europe and was still in use as late as 1650" (Totah, 1926, p. 7).

Numerous other advances in mathematics and science made by Arab scholars were adopted by Western educators and European culture. One of the most enduring examples is the adoption of the Arabic numbering system to replace the cumbersome Roman numbering system, which used Latin letters. Last, it should be noted that the institutions of higher education established by the Arabs throughout Spain, in Egypt, and in the Middle East provided the model for those that were established in Europe during the Middle Ages (Ulich, 1971).

Education During the Renaissance

The Renaissance, which began in the 14th century and reached its high point in the 16th century, was so called because it represented a renaissance or rebirth of interest in the cultures of ancient Greece and Rome. It was a period of great change: the decline of the feudal system; the rise of nation-states and nationalism; the growth of cities; a revival of commerce; the introduction of gunpowder, new forms of art, literature, and architecture; and the exploration of new worlds. The dominant philosophy of the Renaissance was **humanism.** Humanism viewed human nature as its subject. It stressed the dignity of the individual, free will, and the value of the human spirit and all nature. Rejecting scholasticism and the model of the scholar-cleric as the educated man, the humanists considered the educated man to be the secular man of learning described in the classics. They also looked to the classics, primarily the works of Quintilian, for commentary on education. Quintilian's *Institutio Oratoria (Institutes of Oratory)* had been found and brought to Italy by Byzantine scholars when Constantinople (Istanbul) fell to the Muslims in 1453.

The foremost humanist of the Renaissance and the one with the greatest impact on educational thought was Desiderius Erasmus (1466–1536) of the Netherlands. Erasmus studied at the University of Paris and Oxford University and was a professor at Cambridge in

England. Like other humanists, Erasmus believed in the importance of teaching Latin and Greek. His *Colloquies* used dialogues to not only teach Latin style but to instruct in religion and morals, and were among the most important textbooks of his time. The use of text to teach both language and Christian doctrine and morals provided a model for the *New England Primer,* which was to become the most important textbook in colonial America.

In the *Education of Young Children,* Erasmus argued for early childhood education. In *Upon the Method of Right Instruction,* he proposed the systematic training of teachers who he believed must be both broadly educated and experts in their subjects, of gentle disposition, and have unimpeachable morals. His views on pedagogy are found in his treatise *Of the First Liberal Education of Children,* in which he asserted that the needs and interests of the student take precedence in the selection of materials and methods, not those of the church or the medieval guilds. In this treaty he, as had Quintilian 15 centuries earlier, deplored the use of corporal punishment and promoted the value of play and games.

Erasmus's philosophy expresses a belief in the potential of the individual to improve himself (Erasmus does not address the education of females), as well as the importance of education to the development of the intellect and morality. In his emphasis on individuality and inherent human rights, Erasmus was ahead of his time and pointed the way to the Enlightenment that was to follow.

The first products of the Renaissance in education can be seen in the famous Italian court schools connected to the courts of reigning families, perhaps the best known being the ones operated by Vittorino da Feltre at Mantua from 1423 to 1446 and by Guarino da Verona at Ferrara from 1429 to 1459. Like many modern preparatory boarding schools, they housed boys age 8 or 10 to age 20. They emphasized what Woodward (1906) called the "doctrine of courtesy"—the manners, grace, and dignity of the antique culture. At the court schools a humanist curriculum was taught that included the so-called **seven liberal arts** (grammar, logic, rhetoric, arithmetic, geometry, astronomy, and music), as well as reading, writing, and speaking in Latin, study of the Greek classics, and, for the first time, the study of history. Following the teachings of Quintilian, games and play were also emphasized, individual differences were recognized, and punishment was discouraged. The goal was to produce well-rounded, liberally educated courtiers—the ideal personality of the Renaissance—for positions as statesmen, diplomats, or scholars.

The classical humanist curriculum, if not the humanist student-centeredness, is reflected in the Latin grammar school, the dominant form of secondary education in colonial New England. Moreover, the humanist belief that the human condition could be improved by education is reflected in the educational writings of many of the Founding Fathers. And, although the Protestant reformers discussed later in this chapter are generally not considered humanists, they also shared the humanist belief in the importance of education, the importance and responsibility of the individual in determining his destiny, and the role of the school in teaching moral principles.

Education During the Reformation

That period of history known as the Reformation formally began in 1517 when an Augustinian monk and professor of religion named Martin Luther nailed his *Ninety-five Theses* questioning the authority (and abuses)of the Roman Catholic Church to the door of the court church in Wittenburg, Germany. In the years that followed, a religious revolution swept the European continent, resulting in a century of war and the reformation of the Roman Catholic Church. Those who protested the authority of the Church came to be known as Protestants. The invention of the printing press enabled their doctrine and the Bible translated in the vernacular to be spread rapidly. Where the Renaissance produced educational thought and practice that presaged secondary education in America, the Reformation did the same for elementary education.

Martin Luther (1483–1546). One of the major practices rejected by Martin Luther and other leaders of the Reformation was that the Scriptures were read almost exclusively by the

For Your Reflection and Analysis

Which, if any, of the seven liberal arts should be required subjects today? Why?

To submit your response online, go to http://www. prenhall.com/webb.

CW

For Your Reflection and Analysis

Speculate on the impact of the invention of the printing press on education.

To submit your response online, go to http://www. prenhall.com/webb.

CW

The nailing of Luther's theses on the door of the church at Wittenburg marked the beginning of the Reformation.

priests and interpreted to the people by them because most of the people were illiterate. Luther not only objected to the power and authority this provided the church, but he believed that every individual was responsible for his or her salvation, a salvation that came through faith, not works, and that could best be obtained by prayer and reading and studying the Scriptures. To do this, however, it was necessary that every child be provided a free and compulsory elementary education. Luther believed that education should be supported by the state, and that the state should have the authority and responsibility to control the curriculum, the textbooks, and the instruction. In his 1524 *Letters to the Mayors and Aldermen of All Cities of Germany in Behalf of Christian Schools,* Luther stressed the spiritual, economic, and political benefits of education. The curriculum he recommended was to include classical languages, grammar, mathematics, science, history, physical education, music, and didactics (moral instruction). Theology was also to be taught and the study of Protestant doctrines accomplished through the catechism (a question-and-answer drill).

Although formal schooling was important to the establishment of a "priesthood of believers," Luther thought it should occupy only part of the day. At least 1 or 2 hours a day should be spent at home in vocational training, preparing for an occupation through an apprenticeship. Secondary schools, designed primarily as preparatory schools for the clergy, taught Hebrew as well as the classical languages, rhetoric, dialectic, history, mathematics, science, music, and gymnastics. A university education, whose purpose was seen as providing training for higher service in the government or the Church, was available only to those young men who demonstrated exceptional intellectual abilities.

John Calvin (1509–1564).   One of the major theologians of the Protestant Reformation, and perhaps the one most important to American history, was John Calvin. Raised as a French Catholic, Calvin, like Luther, came to reject the authority of the Catholic Church and accepted the doctrine of salvation by faith through prayer and the study of the Scriptures. Calvin's views on education were very similar to those of Luther. He too stressed the necessity of a universal, compulsory, state-supported education that would not only enable all individuals to read the Bible themselves and thereby attain salvation, but would profit the state through the contributions of an orderly and productive citizenry. The school was also seen as a place for religious indoctrination through catechistic instruction. Calvin also supported a two-track educational system consisting of common schools for the masses and secondary schools teaching the classical, humanist curriculum for the preparation of the leaders of church and state.

Calvin's influence was widespread, both in the Europe of his day and later in the colonies of the New World. His advocacy of a universal primary education provided by the vernacular schools described later was adopted by Protestant theologians and educators throughout Europe and was brought to the New World by the Puritans (English Calvinists who sought to purify or reform the Church of England) who settled in New England, as well as members of the Dutch Reformed Church who settled in New York, and Presbyterian Scotch Calvinists who settled in the Middle and Southern colonies. The efforts of each of these groups reflect the Calvinist emphasis on the importance of education to the religious, social, and economic welfare of the individual and the state. The legal mandates adopted by Calvinist communities in Europe (e.g., holding parents responsible for the education of their children) became the models for similar laws in the New England colonies. And, the Calvinist proposal for state-supported education had great appeal to the growing middle classes in Europe and the American colonies.

Vernacular Schools.   The initial product of the belief that it was necessary for each person to be able to read the Scriptures was the establishment of **vernacular schools**— primary or elementary schools that offered instruction in the mother tongue or "vernacular." Instruction in the native tongue also reflected and served to reinforce the spirit of nationalism that had begun to emerge during the Renaissance. The vernacular schools provided a basic curriculum of reading, writing, mathematics, and religion.

Vernacular schools were established throughout Germany by Philip Melanchthon and Johann Bugenhagen following Luther's teachings. Elementary schools that followed the teachings of Calvin also began to appear in other Protestant strongholds, especially those in the Netherlands, Scotland, and Switzerland. And, it was the vernacular school that served as the model for the elementary schools that were established in colonial America.

Later European Educational Thought

The Reformation opened the door not only to the questioning of superstition and religious dogma, but also to investigation of the laws of nature. The Reformation gave way to the Age of Enlightenment or Reason, so called because of the great reliance placed on reason and scientific inquiry. Philosophers and scholars believed that observation and scientific inquiry were the avenues to the discovery of the "natural laws" that dictated the orderly operation of the universe.

Francis Bacon.   The English philosopher Francis Bacon (mentioned in Chapter 3) was central to this movement. He was also important to education because of the emphasis he placed on scientific inquiry, rather than on accepting previously derived hypotheses. He emphasized the need for education to develop what today is termed *critical thinking skills.* The Utopia described in Bacon's *The New Atlantis* envisioned a research university not inconsistent with modern ideas.

Jan Amos Comenius (1592–1670).   Bacon had a major influence on Jan Amos Comenius, a Moravian bishop. Like Bacon he was a proponent of what is termed **sense realism,** which is the belief that learning must come via the senses through observational experience. Accordingly, education must allow children to observe for themselves and experience by doing. The notion of sensory learning was later expanded by Locke, Rousseau, and Pestalozzi.

Comenius also shared Bacon's belief in the scientific method and in an ordered universe that could be discovered through reason and experience. Comenius attempted to identify the developmental stages of children and is said to be the first educator to propose a theory of child growth and development. He proposed a set of teaching methods that incorporated both the deductive method and whatever instructional method was most appropriate for the specific developmental stage of the child.

Comenius proposed that teaching be straightforward and simple and proceed from concrete examples to abstract ideas, that it deal with things before symbols, and that it have practical application. He affirmed Quintilian's beliefs with regard to individual differences, motivation, and corporal punishment. Finally, he believed in a general learning, *paideia*, which should be possessed by all educated persons.

Comenius was perhaps the first educator to propose universal public education. He had a profound effect on Western education through his influence on the thinking of such educational leaders as Johann Pestalozzi, Horace Mann, John Dewey, and Mortimer Adler (1984) who dedicated his *The Paideia Program: An Educational Syllabus* to Comenius.

John Locke.   Although the English philosopher John Locke is best known for his political theories, which served as the basis for the American and French constitutions, he also had a profound influence on education. As discussed in Chapter 3, Locke taught the **tabula rasa** concept of the human mind, which says that we come into the world with our minds a blank slate. We then learn through sensation. Locke recommended a curriculum that included, beyond the "three Rs," history, geography,

For Your Reflection and Analysis

What are the disadvantages of teaching in the vernacular?
To submit your response online, go to http://www. prenhall.com/webb.

CW

ethics, philosophy, science, and conversational foreign languages, especially French. Mathematics was also emphasized, not to make the scholar a mathematician but to make him a reasonable man.

The curriculum Locke recommended anticipated that of the academy described in the next section. And, as is evidenced in the writings of the Founding Fathers on which he had such an influence, Locke believed the goal of education was to create the moral, practical individual who could participate effectively in the governing process.

Locke's political philosophy, in keeping with his respect for the lessons of science, proposed that there were inherent laws of nature and that associated with these natural laws man had certain natural rights. These natural rights came from God or nature, not from rulers or governments. Among these rights, according to Locke, were those espoused in the Declaration of Independence: life, liberty, and the pursuit of happiness.

Jean-Jacques Rousseau (1712–1778).   A century later, another philosopher who is best remembered for his political theories, but who also had a profound effect on educational theory, Jean-Jacques Rousseau, continued to advance the natural law argument. Rousseau is associated with an educational movement called **naturalism.** Its emphasis on freedom and the individual has had a significant influence on educational theory and practice. Rousseau's book *Social Contract* had a major influence on the thinking of those involved in both the French and American revolutions.

Rousseau expounded a theory and philosophy of education that influenced many educators, including John Dewey and other progressive educators. Rousseau has also been called the "father of modern child psychology" (Mayer, 1973). Like Comenius, Rousseau believed in stages of children's growth and development and in the educational necessity of adapting instruction to the various stages. His major thoughts on education are contained in his novel *Emile,* which puts forth the ideal education for a youth named Emile. The education of Emile was to be child centered, concerned with developing his natural abilities. He was to learn by his senses through direct experience and was not to be punished. Emile's education was to progress as he was ready and as his interests motivated him and is to be concerned with his physical growth and health. Finally, Emile is to be taught a trade in order to prepare him for an occupation in life.

Johann Pestalozzi (1746–1827).   Johann Heinrich Pestalozzi, a Swiss educator, put Rousseau's ideas into practice. Pestalozzi has had a profound impact on education throughout much of the Western world. The Prussian government sent teachers to be instructed by him, and educators came from all over the world, including the United States, to observe and study his methods. Horace Mann and Henry Barnard came under his influence. Edward A. Sheldon, superintendent of schools in Oswego, New York, established a teacher training school at Oswego in 1861 that followed Pestalozzi's methods.

Pestalozzi's philosophy of education incorporated the child-centered, sensory experience principles of Rousseau. Like Rousseau, he believed in the natural goodness of human nature and the corrupting influence of society. He also supported Rousseau's idea of individual differences and "readiness" to learn. His belief in the development of the total child to the child's maximum potential was given its greatest recognition during the second half of the 20th century in the movement for the education of disadvantaged students.

Perhaps more than Rousseau, Pestalozzi recognized the importance of human emotions in the learning process. It was important, he believed, that the child be given feelings of self-respect and emotional security. It also was important that the teacher treat students with love. In fact, it can be said that the ideal of love governs Pestalozzi's educational philosophy. Pestalozzi was especially fond of poor children and recognized the need to provide them with a school environment that addressed their physical and emotional needs.

Like Comenius, Pestalozzi believed that instruction must begin with the concrete and proceed to the abstract. Materials should be presented slowly, in developmental order from simple to complex, from known to unknown. The **object lesson** centers on concrete materials within the child's experience, involves discussion and oral presentation, and replaces rote learning (Gillett, 1966).

Johann Herbart (1776–1841).   One of the Prussian educators who studied under Pestalozzi was Johann Friedrich Herbart. Herbart believed that the aim of education should be the development of moral character. His pedagogical theory included three key concepts: interest, apperception, and correlation. Instruction can be successful only if it arouses interest. Interests are derived from both nature and society; thus, the curriculum should include both the natural and social sciences. All new material presented to the child is interpreted in terms of past experiences by the process of apperception. Additionally, ideas are reinforced and organized in the mind by the process of correlation (Gillett, 1966).

Herbart maintained that any suitable material could be learned if presented systematically. The five steps in the Herbartian methodology are as follows:

1. *Preparation*—preparing the student to receive the new material by arousing interest or recalling past material or experiences;
2. *Presentation*—presenting the new material;
3. *Association*—helping students see the relationship between old and new ideas;
4. *Generalization*—formulating general ideas or principles; and
5. *Application*—applying the ideas or principles to new situations.

Herbart's ideas had a significant influence on American education. Before the end of the century, teachers across the country were organizing lessons around the five steps in the Herbartian methodology. Although the Herbartian movement was short lived, the Herbartian ideas and pedagogy had a profound influence on teaching methods and the curriculum, particularly at the elementary level, long after the movement itself faded (Kliebard, 1995). As late as the 1950s the Herbartian steps could be found in teacher education tests (Connell, 1980). But, perhaps most important, 200 years later his theories of learning have been incorporated into constructivism and validated by what emerging brain research has revealed about how we learn (see discussion in Chapter 14).

Friedrich Froebel (1782–1852).   Friedrich Froebel was the third member of what Gillett (1966) called the 19th century's "famous pedagogical triumvirate" that broke with subject-centered instruction and created a new concern for the child. Froebel is known for the establishment of the first kindergarten (1837) and for providing the theoretical basis for early childhood education. Although Froebel accepted many of Pestalozzi's ideas associated with child centeredness, Froebel was more concerned with activity than Pestalozzi, but less concerned with observation. According to Froebel, the primary aim of the school should be self-development through self-expression, which would take place through games, singing, or any number of creative and spontaneous activities that were to be part of an **activity curriculum.** Froebel was also concerned with the development of creativity in children. He viewed the classroom as a miniature society in which children learned social cooperation.

Froebel developed highly stylized educational materials that were mass produced and used throughout the world. They were designed to aid self-expression and bring out the "divine effluence" (the fundamental unity of all nature with God) within each child. Materials referred to as *gifts* and *occupations* were used. The gifts were objects that did not change their form (e.g., wooden spheres, cubes), symbols of the fundamentals of nature. The occupations were materials used in creative construction or design whose shape changed in use (e.g., clay, paper). Used together they were said to ensure the progressive self-development of the child.

One of Froebel's pupils, Margaretha Schurz, opened the first kindergarten in the United States in Watertown, Wisconsin. John Dewey adopted many of Froebel's principles and used them in his famous laboratory school at the University of Chicago. Today, the kindergarten is recognized for its importance in the educational process and as a socializing force. It is the cornerstone of the American educational system.

Table 5.1 gives an overview of the educational theorists we have discussed and their influence on Western education.

For Your Reflection and Analysis

Recall your own experience in the primary grades. To what extent was your education similar to Froebel's activity curriculum?

To submit your response online, go to http://www. prenhall.com/webb.

CW

Table 5.1 — Western European Educational Thought (1200–1850)

Theorist	Educational Theories	Influence on Western Education
Aquinas (1225–1274)	Human beings possess both a spiritual and a physical nature. Man is a rational being. Faith and reason are complementary sources of truth.	Provided basis for Roman Catholic education.
Erasmus (1466–1536)	The liberally educated man is one educated in the seven liberal arts, steeped in the classics and in rhetoric. Systematic training of teachers is needed. Follower of Quintilian.	Advanced the need for the systematic training of teachers and a humanistic pedagogy. Promoted the importance of politeness in education.
Luther (1483–1546)	Education is necessary for religious instruction, the preparation of religious leaders, and the economic well-being of the state. Education should include vocational training.	Provided support for concept of free and compulsory elementary education. Promoted concept of universal literacy.
Calvin (1509–1564)	Education serves both the religious and political establishment: elementary schools for the masses where they could learn to read the Bible and thereby attain salvation; secondary schools to prepare the leaders of church and state.	Concept of two-track system and emphasis on literacy influenced education in New England and ultimately the entire nation.
Bacon (1561–1626)	Education should advance scientific inquiry. Understanding of an ordered universe comes through reason.	Provided major rationale for the development of critical thinking skills. Proposed the concept of a research university.
Comenius (1592–1670)	Learning must come through the senses. Education must allow the child to reason by doing. There is a general body of knowledge (*paideia*) that should be possessed by all.	Provided theory of child growth and development. Concept of *paideia* profoundly influenced numerous Western educational leaders.
Locke (1632–1704)	Children enter the world with the mind like a blank slate (*tabula rasa*). The goal of education is to promote the development of reason and morality.	Provided support for the concept of the reasonable man and the ability and necessity for the reasonable man to participate in the governing process.

Education in the "New" Old World Before Jamestown

The English, the predominant settlers of the American colonies, had the greatest influence on the educational system that emerged in the colonies, but the French and Spanish also played a role. The French empire in the New World spread from Canada to Louisiana. French priests, particularly the Jesuits, followed explorers and fur traders into the wilderness to convert and educate the Native Americans. The Catholic influence on education, which can still be seen today in cities as far apart as Quebec and New Orleans, can be traced to the Jesuits, a teaching order that had been influential in establishing a number of secondary schools and universities in Europe, and to orders of teaching sisters.

The Spanish empire in the New World was no less vast, encompassing at various times the entire Southwest, Florida, and California. Spanish Catholic priests, especially the Franciscans, followed the explorers and established a vast network of missions throughout the Southwest where they sought to convert and educate the Native Americans. On the heels of the priests came Spanish settlers migrating north from Mexico. By 1800 almost 25,000 Spanish-speaking people were living in the Southwest. What little formal education most children of these settlers received took place at one of the missions established by the priests. These missions also often taught Native Americans not only the Spanish language but also agricultural and vocational skills. Children of more affluent settlers were schooled at home by tutors or were sent to schools in Mexico or Spain.

Theorist	Educational Theories	Influence on Western Education
Rousseau (1712–1778)	Major proponent of naturalism, which emphasized individual freedom. The child is inherently good. Children's growth and development goes through stages, which necessitates adaptation of instruction. Education should be concerned with the development of the child's natural abilities.	Naturalism provided the basis for modern educational theory and practice. Father of modern child pyschology.
Pestalozzi (1746–1827)	Education should be child-centered and based on sensory experience. The individual differences of each child must be considered in assessing readiness to learn. Children should be educated to reach their maximum potential. Ideal of love emphasized the importance of emotion in the learning process. Instruction should begin with the concrete and proceed to the abstract.	Concept of maximum development of each child provided support for education of the disadvantaged. Pestalozzian methods were exported throughout Europe and to the United States. One of the earliest theories of instruction formally taught to teachers.
Herbart (1776–1841)	The aim of education should be the development of moral character. Any material can be learned if presented systematically: preparation, presentation, association, generalization, and application. Instruction must arouse interest to be successful. Education is a science.	Elevated the study of educational psychology. Demonstrated the significance of methodology in instruction. Advanced the concept that education is a science and can be studied scientifically.
Froebel (1782–1852)	The aim of education should be to ensure self-development through self-expression. Self-expression takes place through an activity curriculum. The school should promote creativity and bring out "divine effluence" within each child.	Established first kindergarten. Provided theoretical basis for early childhood education.

Pictograph on Arizona canyon wall shows Spanish soldiers and priest exploring the Southwest.

Figure 5.2 — Native American Culture Groups

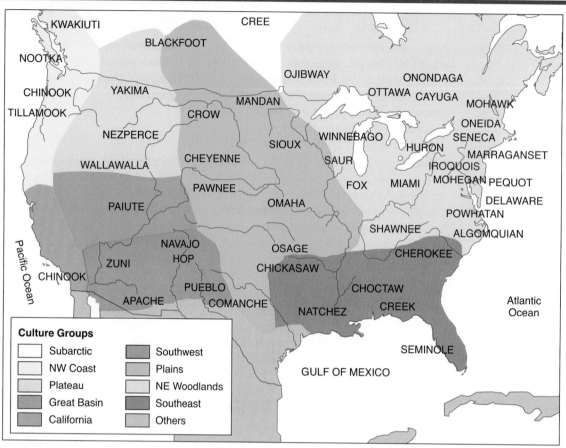

Source: Stefoff, R. (2001). *The colonies.* Tarrytown, NY: Benchmark Press, p. 21. Copyright © Marshall Cavendish Corporation. Reprinted from *The Colonies* with permission of Marshall Cavendish Benchmark.

Native American Education

When the Spanish, French, and later English came to what was to be called the "New World," the land already had as many as 11 million inhabitants representing 300 different tribes and 200 different languages (see Figure 5.2). The education of these millions of native peoples did not originate with the mission schools. In fact, prior to the arrival of Europeans in the New World, each native group had a comprehensive formal and informal system for educating and training their children and youth in what Tuscarura has described as the "three basic courses" of native education: (1) economic or survival skills, (2) knowledge of cultural heritage, and (3) spiritual awareness (Szasz, 1999). However, the free and spontaneous nature of Native American education, which relied on oral tradition, not the written word, was very different from the more formalized approach of the Europeans. As a result, the European colonists perceived it as unreliable and as a lesser form of education than the traditional school model they employed (Hale, 2002).

Education in Colonial America

The first English settlement in North America was at Jamestown (Virginia) in 1607. In 1620, the Pilgrims, a group of Separatist Puritans (Protestants who wanted not only to purify but to separate from the Church of England), settled at Plymouth (Massachusetts). Ten years later a group of nonseparatist Puritans founded the Massachusetts Bay Colony. This colony became a focal point of migration, and other New England colonies (Rhode Island, New Haven [Connecticut], New Hampshire, Maine) developed from this base (Cohen, 1974). Many of the colonists who came to the New World were filled with a sense of religious commitment, largely Protestant, which shaped their views on life and education. However, the settlers in other regions did not all share their economic and political traditions, religion, society, or education. These variations are explored in the following sections.

Education in the New England Colonies

According to Cubberley (1934), the Puritans who settled New England "contributed most that was of value for our future educational development" (p. 14). The New England colonists, who were generally well educated themselves, sustained a vigorous emphasis on education even in the hostile new environment. In fact, by 1700 the New England colonies could boast of literary rates that were often superior to those in England (Cohen, 1974).

Initially, the Puritans attempted to follow English practice regarding the establishment and support of schools by relying on private benefactors and limiting the role of the state. However, the general absence of wealthy Puritan migrants soon led to the abandonment of this practice and, because of fears that parents were neglecting the education of their children, to a more direct role for the state (Cohen, 1974).

First Education Laws.   The Massachusetts Law of 1642 ordered the selectmen of each town to ascertain whether parents and masters (of apprentices) were, in fact, providing for the education of their children. The selectmen were also to determine what the child was being taught. The child of any parent or master failing to meet his obligation could be apprenticed to a new master who would be required to fulfill the law. Although the law neither specified schools nor required attendance, it is said to have established the principle of compulsory education. Five years later, the Education Law of 1647 ordered every township of 50 households to provide a teacher to teach reading and writing, and all townships of 100 or more households to establish a grammar school. Although there was no uniform compliance or administration of these laws, they show how important education was to the Puritans and demonstrate their belief in the necessity of a literate citizenry for the functioning of political society. The laws also served as models for other colonies and are considered the first education laws in America.

Religious Influence.   In New England, as in the other colonies, the institutions of secular government, including education, were closely aligned with the dominant religious group. The Puritans brought with them many of the educational views of the Reformation, namely, that education was necessary for religious instruction and salvation as well as for economic self-reliance and the exercise of citizenship by an educated laity. As the Massachusetts Law of 1642 explained, there was a need to ensure the ability of children "to read and understand the principles of religion and the capital laws of this country." This purpose is also evidenced by the first words of the Massachusetts Education Law of 1647, also called the "old Deluder Satan Law": "It being one chief project of that old deluder, Satan, to keep men from knowledge of the Scriptures." The founding of Harvard College in 1636 was also based on religious motives: to ensure that there would be an educated ministry for the colony. The colonists were fearful that there would be no replacements for the ministers who first came with them, and they dreaded "to leave an illiterate Ministry to the churches, when our present Ministers should lie in the Dust" (Cubberley, 1934, p. 13).

Elementary Schooling.   The New England colonists not only shared Calvin's view of the aim of education but they also adopted the two-track system advocated by Calvin and other scholars of the Reformation. Town schools and dame schools were established to educate the children of the common folk in elementary reading, writing, and mathematics. The **dame schools** were held in the kitchen or living room of a neighborhood woman, often a widow, usually a person with minimal education herself, who received a modest fee for her efforts. Girls were allowed to attend the dame schools, and some did attend the town schools, but most received only a minimal education. In Puritan New England the view was that a little reading, spelling, and needlework was all the education that was needed or appropriate for females. Girls needed to be able to read so that they could study the Bible, but writing, arithmetic, grammar, and geography were considered unnecessary.

For Your Reflection and Analysis

Give examples of existing education laws or policies that are directed at maintaining or strengthening the social order. How effective are they?
To submit your response online, go to http://www. prenhall.com/webb.

CW

For Your Reflection and Analysis

How do the basic purposes of education in Colonial America compare with those of today?
To submit your response online, go to http://www. prenhall.com/webb.

CW

The dame school provided the only education many colonial children received.

So-called writing or reading schools were concerned with the teaching of these disciplines and operated on a fee basis. **Charity** or **pauper schools** were operated by various denominations or wealthy benefactors for the children of the poor who could not afford to attend other schools.

Education was also made available as a result of the apprenticeship system whereby a child was apprenticed to a master to learn a trade. In addition, the master was required by the terms of the indenture to ensure that the apprentice received a basic education. For some children this was the avenue by which they learned what little reading and writing they knew.

Instruction in the schools was primarily religious and authoritarian. Students learned their basic lessons from the **hornbook,** so called because the material was written on a sheet of parchment, placed on a wooden board, and covered with a thin sheath of cow's horn for protection. The board was shaped like a paddle and had a handle with a hole in it so it could be strung around the child's neck.

The New England Primer. The *New England Primer* was used with slightly older children. The primer is an excellent example of the interrelationship between education and religion. Although different editions of the primer varied somewhat in the 150 years of its publication, which began in 1690, it usually featured an alphabet and spelling guide, followed by one of the things that made the primer famous—24 little pictures with alphabetical rhymes as illustrated in Figure 5.3.

The primer also included the Lord's Prayer, the Apostles' Creed, the Ten Commandments, a listing of the books of the Bible, and a list of numbers from 1 to 100, using both Arabic and Roman numerals. Another prominent feature of the primer was a poem, the exhortation of John Rogers to his children, from John Foxe's *Book of Martyrs,* with a picture of the martyr burning at the stake as his wife and children look on. The primer ended with a shortened version of the Puritan catechism (Ford, 1962).

Secondary Grammar Schools. Secondary grammar schools existed for the further education of the male children of the well-to-do. They also served as preparatory schools for the university where the leaders of the church and political affairs were to be trained and which required proficiency in Latin and Greek for admission. The Boston Latin School, established in 1635, became the model for similar schools throughout New England.

Education at the grammar school was quite different from that at the dame or town school. The emphasis was on Latin, with some Greek and occasionally Hebrew. Other disciplines included those necessary for the education of the Renaissance concept of the educated man. The course of study in the grammar school was fairly intensive and lasted for 6 to 7 years, although students "tended to withdraw and return, depending on familial need and circumstances; and since school was conducted on a year-round basis and instruction organized around particular texts, it was fairly simple for a student to resume study after a period of absence" (Cremin, 1970, p. 186).

University Education. Education in the university in the early colonial period was also based on the classically oriented curriculum of English universities. As Cohen (1974) described it:

> The undergraduate courses revolved around the traditional Trivium and Quadrivium but without musical studies, the Three Philosophies (Metaphysics, Ethics, Natural Science), and Greek, Hebrew, and a chronological study of ancient history. As in English universities logic and rhetoric were the basic subjects in the curriculum. . . . Compositions, orations, and disputations were given the same careful scrutiny as at English universities. (p. 66)

Figure 5.3 — An Alphabet Including Both Religious and Secular Jingles

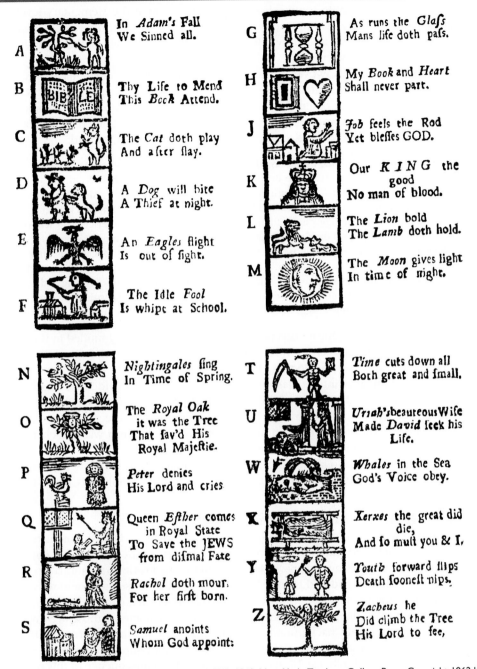

A   In *Adam's* Fall
We Sinned all.

B   Thy Life to Mend
This *Book* Attend.

C   The *Cat* doth play
And after flay.

D   A *Dog* will bite
A Thief at night.

E   An *Eagles* flight
Is out of fight.

F   The Idle *Fool*
Is whipt at School.

G   As runs the *Glafs*
Mans life doth pafs.

H   My *Book* and *Heart*
Shall never part.

J   *Job* feels the Rod
Yet blefses GOD.

K   Our *KING* the good
No man of blood.

L   The *Lion* bold
The *Lamb* doth hold.

M   The *Moon* gives light
In time of night.

N   *Nightingales* fing
In Time of Spring.

O   The *Royal Oak*
it was the Tree
That fav'd His
Royal Majeftie.

P   *Peter* denies
His Lord and cries

Q   Queen *Efther* comes
in Royal State
To Save the JEWS
from difmal Fate

R   *Rachel* doth mour.
For her firft born.

S   *Samuel* anoints
Whom God appoint:

T   *Time* cuts down all
Both great and fmall.

U   *Uriah's* beauteous Wife
Made *David* feek his
Life.

W   *Whales* in the Sea
God's Voice obey.

X   *Xerxes* the great did
die,
And fo muft you & I,

Y   *Youth* forward flips
Death fooneft nips.

Z   *Zacheus* he
Did climb the Tree
His Lord to fee,

Source: From *The New England Primer* by P. L. Ford (Ed.), 1962, New York: Teachers College Press. Copyright 1962 by Teachers College Press. Reprinted by permission.

Education in New England During the Later Colonial Period.

Social and Economic Changes.   The Age of the Enlightenment or Age of Reason that swept the Western world in the 17th century had found its way to the shores of the American colonies by the 18th century. As in Europe, it brought greater concern for independent rationality, a repudiation of supernatural explanations of phenomena, and a greater questioning of traditional dogma. At the same time that the Enlightenment was sweeping the colonies, the population of the colonies increased rapidly and their economy outgrew their localized base of farming and fishing. Trade and commerce increased and a new mercantile gentry emerged (Cohen, 1974). The mercantile activities of the new middle class called for a freer environment and increased religious toleration.

Birth of the Academy.   It was inevitable that the educational system would change to meet the needs of the intellectual, economic, and social order. The writing and dame schools began to give way to town schools. The curriculum at the elementary level, although still dominated by reading and writing, now placed greater importance on arithmetic. Greater concern was also shown for practical and vocational training at both the elementary and secondary levels.

Many grammar schools, however, refused to change their classical curricula. As a result, numerous academies and private venture schools sprang up in the larger towns, teaching subjects useful in trade and commerce. If the prestigious Boston Latin School would not teach mathematics, others would. Advertisements for these schools filled the newspapers of the time. One such 1723 advertisement appearing in New York City read:

> There is a school in New York, in the Broad Street, near the Exchange, where Mr. John Walton, late of Yale College, Teacheth Reading, Writing, Arethmatick, whole Numbers and Fractions, Vulgar and Decimal, The Mariners Art, Plain and Mercators Way; Also Geometry, Surveying, the Latin Tongue, the Greek and Hebrew Grammers, Ethicks, Rhetorick, Logick, Natural Philosophy and Metaphysicks, all or any of them for a Reasonable Price. The School from the first of October till the first of March will be tended in the Evening. If any Gentlemen in the Country are disposed to send their Sons to the said School, if they apply themselves to the Master he will immediately procure suitable Entertainment for them, very Cheap. Also if any Young Gentlemen of the City will please to come in the Evening and make some Tryal of the Liberal Arts, they may have the opportunity of Learning the same things which are commonly Taught in Colledges. (Seybolt, cited in Rippa, 1997, pp. 61–62)

Growth of Colleges.   During this period, several colleges were founded in the New England colonies: Collegiate School, now Yale University, in 1701; the College of Rhode Island, now Brown University, in 1764; and Dartmouth College in 1769. The colleges of this era also reflected the growing secularism of the society. This was evidenced in a broadened curriculum. In 1722 Harvard established its first professorship in secular subjects: mathematics and natural philosophy. By 1760 the scientific subjects accounted for 20% of the student's time. Another manifestation of the growing secularism was the change in graduates' careers. Theology remained the most popular career, but an increasing number of graduates were turning to law, medicine, trade, or commerce as the New England colleges became centers of independence, stimulation, and social usefulness (Cohen, 1974).

Education in the Mid-Atlantic Colonies

Whereas the New England colonies had been settled primarily by English colonists who shared the same language, traditions, and religion, the settlers of the mid-Atlantic colonies (New York, New Jersey, Pennsylvania, Delaware) came from a variety of national and religious backgrounds. Most had fled Europe because of religious persecution and were generally more distrusting of secular authority than the New England colonists. Thus, whereas the schools in the mid-Atlantic colonies were as religious in character as those in New England, their diverse religious backgrounds made it impossible for the government in any colony to agree on the establishment of any one system of state-supported schools. Thus, it fell to each denomination to establish its own schools. The consequence of this pattern was the absence of any basis for the establishment of a system of public schools or for state support or regulation of the schools. As a result, many young people, especially those in rural areas, had no access to education beyond what might be provided in the home.

New York.   The colony of New Netherlands was established in 1621 by the Dutch. Initially, New Netherlands was similar to the New England colonies. Schools were supported by the Dutch West India Company and were operated by the Dutch Reformed Church. After the colony was seized by the British and became the royal colony of New York (1674), state responsibility and support were withdrawn and, except for a few towns that maintained their own schools, formal schooling became a private concern. Education at the elementary level was by private tutors for the upper class, private venture schools for the middle class, and denominational schools for the lower class.

Most notable of the denominational schools were those operated by a missionary society of the Church of England, the Society for the Propagation of the Gospel in Foreign

For Your Reflection and Analysis

Which would you prefer to attend: the Boston Latin School or Mr. Walton's school? Why?

To submit your response online, go to http://www. prenhall.com/webb.

CW

Parts (SPG). The apprenticeship system also was very strong in New York and provided the means by which some children gained an education. However, because few towns established their own schools and the provision of education was principally left to the will or ability of parents to send their children to private or denominational schools, illiteracy rates were high (Cohen, 1974).

Education at the secondary level was even more exclusively private or parochial. The private venture secondary schools were few in number and questionable in quality.

Higher education was absent for any but the few who could afford to leave the colony. It was not until 1754 that the first institution of higher education, Kings College, now Columbia University, opened in the colony.

New Jersey.   New Jersey was originally part of New York. As in New York, education in New Jersey was primarily private and denominational. The religious diversification was great and each of the sects—Dutch Reformed, Puritan, Quaker, German Lutheran, Baptist, Scotch-Irish Presbyterian—established its own schools. The SPG also operated schools for the poor. A few towns, mainly those in the eastern region settled by the Puritans, established town schools. Secondary education was limited. Because of the primarily rural, agrarian economy, the private venture secondary schools found in the other mid-Atlantic colonies were lacking. However, the proximity to New York and Philadelphia did provide access to their secondary institutions for those who could afford it (Cohen, 1974).

It is in the realm of higher education that the colony of New Jersey most distinguished itself. Prior to the Revolution more colleges were founded there than in any other colony: the College of New Jersey, now Princeton University (1746), and Queens College, now Rutgers University (1766).

Pennsylvania.   The Pennsylvania colony was founded in 1681 by a Quaker, William Penn. The Quakers, or Society of Friends, were very tolerant of other religions; consequently, a number of different religious groups or sects settled in Pennsylvania. William Penn advocated free public education, and the Pennsylvania Assembly enacted a law in 1683 providing that all children be instructed in reading and writing and be taught "some useful trade or skill." Yet the colony did not develop a system of free public education, primarily because of the great diversity among the settlers. A few community-supported schools were established, but as in the other mid-Atlantic colonies, formal education was primarily a private or denominational affair.

However, the major difference between Pennsylvania and the other mid-Atlantic colonies was that the various denominations did, in fact, establish a fairly widespread system of schools in Pennsylvania. The SPG founded a number of charity schools, including a school for black children in Philadelphia. The Moravians also established a number of elementary schools, including the first nursery school in the colonies, a boarding school for girls, and were active in efforts to Christianize and educate the Native Americans. They devised a script for several Native American languages and translated the Bible and other religious materials into these languages. In their pedagogical practices they were influenced by the educational philosophy of Comenius, who was a Moravian bishop.

The Quakers were the most significant denomination in terms of educational endeavors. Their belief that all people were created equal under God led not only to the education of both sexes and to the free admission of the poor, but also to the education of blacks and Native Americans. A school for black children was established in Philadelphia as early as 1700. Because the Quakers do not have a ministry, they were not as interested in the establishment of secondary schools leading to that vocation. In their secondary schools they emphasized practical knowledge rather than the classical curriculum studied at most secondary schools at that time.

Schools were also established at the secondary level by other denominations. A number of private secondary schools were opened during the later colonial period, many offering such practical subjects as navigation, gauging, accounting, geometry, trigonometry, surveying, French, and Spanish. Among them was Benjamin Franklin's Philadelphia Academy, opened in 1751.

Benjamin Franklin (1706–1790).   Franklin was strongly influenced by the writings of John Locke and was a proponent of practical education to prepare the skilled craftsmen, businessmen, and farmers needed by the colonies. In his 1747 *Proposals Relating to* *the Education of Youth in Pennsylvania,* he outlined the plan for a school in which English, rather than Latin, was to be the medium of instruction. This break with tradition was important, for in effect it proposed that vernacular English could be the language of the educated person. Franklin also proposed that students be taught "those Things that are likely to be most useful and most ornamental. Regard being had to the several Professions which they are intended" (Gillett, 1969, p. 138).

From this statement of principle, Franklin went on to detail what should be the specific subject matter of the academy:

> All should be taught "to write a fair hand" and "something of drawing"; arithmetic, accounts, geometry, and astronomy; English grammar out of Tillotson, Addison, Pope, Sidney, Trenchard, and Gordon; the writing of essays and letters; rhetoric, history, geography, and ethics; natural history and gardening; and the history of commerce and principles of mechanics. Instruction should include visits to neighboring farms, opportunities for natural observations, experiments with scientific apparatus, and physical exercise. And the whole should be suffused with a quest for benignity of mind, which Franklin saw as the foundation of good breeding and a spirit of service, which he regarded as "the great aim and end of all learning." (Cremin, 1970, p. 376)

As time passed, Franklin's academy gave less emphasis to the practical studies and came to more closely resemble the Latin grammar school. Before he died Franklin declared the academy a failure as measured against his initial intent (Cremin, 1970).

Franklin was also instrumental in the founding in 1753 of the College of Philadelphia, now the University of Pennsylvania. Unlike its sister institutions, the College of Philadelphia was nonsectarian in origin (although it later came under Anglican control). The curriculum of the college was perhaps more progressive than those at other institutions. Students were allowed a voice in the election of courses, and the curriculum emphasized not only the classics but also mathematics, philosophy, and the natural and social sciences. A medical school was established in connection with the college.

Delaware.   Delaware, founded in 1638 as a Swedish colony, New Sweden, fell under Dutch control in 1655, then under the rule of the English with their conquest of New Netherlands. Education in Delaware was greatly influenced by Pennsylvania. Pennsylvania's general abandonment of the responsibility for the provision of education to private or denominational groups after 1683 was followed in Delaware. Although a number of elementary schools were established in the colony, the level of literacy remained low. During the colonial period, formal secondary education was available on a very limited basis and no institution of higher education was established in Delaware (Cohen, 1974).

Education in the Southern Colonies

Influence of Social and Economic Systems.   The Southern colonies (Maryland, Virginia, the Carolinas, and Georgia) differed significantly from the New England and Mid-Atlantic colonies. The Southern colonies were royal colonies administered by governors who were directly accountable to the king. Unlike the New England Puritans, who sought to reform the Church of England, the colonists in the Southern colonies accepted the Church of England as the established church. (The exception was Maryland, which was founded by Lord Baltimore as a refuge for English Catholics.) And, the Church of England asserted that it was the responsibility of parents to educate their children, not the government. Consequently, local governments were not required to establish or support schools. Whereas religious dissatisfaction was the principal motivation for the settling of New England, the reasons for settlement of the Southern colonies were primarily economic.

Rather than small farms and commerce, the economy of the Southern colonies was based on the plantation and slave system. The plantation system created distinct classes dominated by the aristocratic plantation owners. The relatively small population of the Southern colonies was widely dispersed. This factor limited the growth of any public or universal system of education.

Elementary and Secondary Education.   As a result of the social and economic structure of the Southern colonies, educational opportunities were largely determined by social class. The children of the plantation owners and the wealthy commercial classes in the Tidewater cities received their education from private tutors or at private Latin grammar schools before being sent to a university. In the early colonial period, it was common for the children of the plantation aristocracy to be sent to England to receive their secondary or, more often, their university education. However, as the number of colonial colleges grew in the later colonial period, this practice declined.

For the majority in the less affluent classes, the only education available was at the elementary level, informally through the apprenticeship system, or formally at endowed (free) schools, charity schools, denominational schools, or private venture schools. Virginia was the most active of the Southern colonies in attempting to ensure the education of apprenticed children, especially orphaned children. Often this education took place in so-called "workhouse schools."

The endowed or free schools were few in number and actually were not free except to a small number of poor boys. The charity schools were primarily those operated by the SPG. The influence of the SPG in the Southern colonies was significant and represented "the nearest approach to a public school organization found in the South before the Revolution" (Cohen, 1974, p. 129). Schools operated by other denominations were also established in the Southern colonies. In some rural areas where other schooling was not available, several small planters or farmers might build a schoolhouse on an abandoned tobacco field. These "old field schools" generally charged a fee and offered only the most basic education.

At the secondary level, except for the private venture schools and a few public grammar schools in the larger towns or cities, few schools existed. And even the number of private venture schools was limited. As a result of the public neglect of education, overall the educational level of the Southern colonies was below that of most of the Northern colonies, especially those in New England.

Higher Education: The College of William and Mary. The only institution of higher education established in the South prior to the Revolutionary War was the College of William and Mary, established in 1693 to train ministers for the Church of England and bring Christianity to Native Americans. Like Harvard, the only older institution of higher education in the colonies, it also originally offered the traditional curriculum. However, by the first quarter of the 18th century it began to broaden its curriculum. It was the first college to offer an elective system and, perhaps foreshadowing Virginian supremacy in the public affairs of the country, William and Mary emphasized law and politics earlier than any other college in the country.

Figure 5.4 presents an overview of education in colonial America.

PROFESSIONAL REFLECTION

I find that, as a history teacher, it is easy to slip into a routine where one is simply shoveling content at the students to make sure that it is covered, but this accomplishes little since the students retain very little and do not come away either more skilled or considerably more knowledgeable. (Jay Leno points this out on a regular basis.) The learner by nature is curious, and we quash that curiosity when we throw unrelated facts at students or simply use the textbook explanation, which is often dry and devoid of controversial but interesting details. Engaging students in activities that immerse them in the history they are about to study piques their curiosity (such as what it was like to be a spy during World War II or a radio announcer during the 1920s or an imperialist around the turn of the century). When this is then coupled with a presentation of the content that focuses on cause and effect—satisfying the curiosity of the student about why things happened and how they are related to the way the world is today, giving them a satisfying big picture—they are hooked. (How many adults who almost slept through their history classes are hooked on the History Channel because they are still curious?) The final element is where, through an assignment such as an essay or a National History Day Project, students essentially become historians themselves for a time by delving into history's puzzle pieces (primary sources) and drawing a picture that makes sense using their logical and analytical thinking skills in constructing a thesis essay, documentary, exhibit, etc.

Scott L. Johnson
National Board Certified Teacher, Iowa

To analyze this reflection, go to the *Professional Reflection* module for this chapter of the Companion Website at **http://www.prenhall.com/webb.**

Figure 5.4 — Education in Colonial America

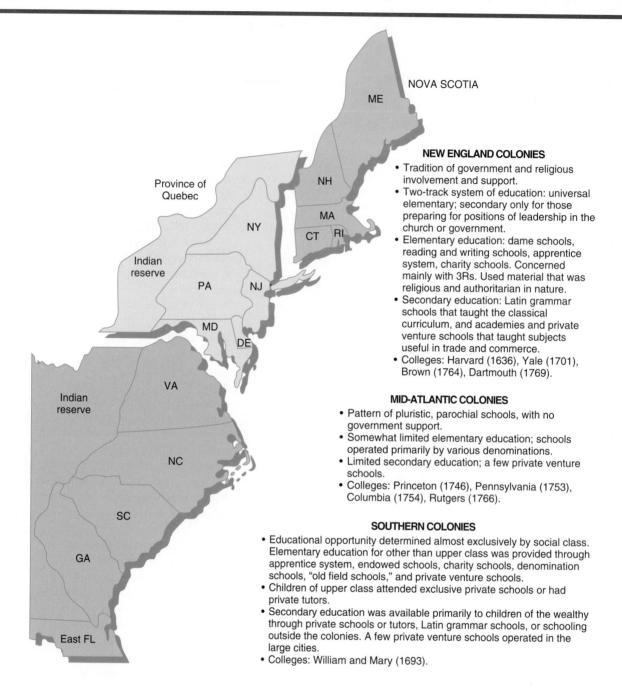

NOVA SCOTIA

ME

Province of Quebec

Indian reserve

NH

MA

NY

CT   RI

PA   NJ

MD

DE

VA

Indian reserve

NC

SC

GA

East FL

NEW ENGLAND COLONIES

- Tradition of government and religious involvement and support.
- Two-track system of education: universal elementary; secondary only for those preparing for positions of leadership in the church or government.
- Elementary education: dame schools, reading and writing schools, apprentice system, charity schools. Concerned mainly with 3Rs. Used material that was religious and authoritarian in nature.
- Secondary education: Latin grammar schools that taught the classical curriculum, and academies and private venture schools that taught subjects useful in trade and commerce.
- Colleges: Harvard (1636), Yale (1701), Brown (1764), Dartmouth (1769).

MID-ATLANTIC COLONIES

- Pattern of pluristic, parochial schools, with no government support.
- Somewhat limited elementary education; schools operated primarily by various denominations.
- Limited secondary education; a few private venture schools.
- Colleges: Princeton (1746), Pennsylvania (1753), Columbia (1754), Rutgers (1766).

SOUTHERN COLONIES

- Educational opportunity determined almost exclusively by social class. Elementary education for other than upper class was provided through apprentice system, endowed schools, charity schools, denomination schools, "old field schools," and private venture schools.
- Children of upper class attended exclusive private schools or had private tutors.
- Secondary education was available primarily to children of the wealthy through private schools or tutors, Latin grammar schools, or schooling outside the colonies. A few private venture schools operated in the large cities.
- Colleges: William and Mary (1693).

Summary

The schools of the United States can trace their ancestry to those of ancient Greece and Rome. Educational idealism is based on the philosophy of Plato. The scientific method popularized in the 20th century is rooted in the philosophy of realism espoused by Aristotle. And a number of the more progressive educational positions of this century were advanced by the Roman educator Quintilian: opposition to corporal punishment, advancement of the concept of readiness learning, and support for the recognition of individual differences in learners. The concept of universal public education that we enjoy today was a product of the Reformation. It was brought to New England by the Puritans, who held the view that education was necessary for religious instruction and salvation as well as for good citizenship. However, the earliest American educational systems were not free, were limited at the secondary levels and, in ways that would be prohibited today, were dominated by the religious establishment. In the next chapter we will continue to trace the evolution of the American educational system from the Revolution to the 20th century.

Key Terms

Activity curriculum, 113
Charity (pauper) school, 118
Dame schools, 117
Grammar school, 104
Hornbook, 118

Humanism, 108
Naturalism, 112
Object lesson, 112
Paideia, 111
Sense realism, 111

Seven liberal arts, 109
Socratic method, 103
Tabula rasa, 111
Vernacular schools, 111

PROFESSIONAL DEVELOPMENT WORKSHOP

Prepare for the Praxis™ Examination

Mr. George Theosolis is a fifth-grade teacher at the Eleanor Roosevelt Elementary School where he has been teaching for the past decade. Although George enjoys being in a self-contained classroom and teaching a variety of subjects, his real love is history. Because of George's commitment and creativity, numerous students throughout the school have been actively engaged in several major history projects including the construction of a huge diorama to be unveiled in late May that will showcase America's colonial history.

During the past decade, George has developed a reputation for being the in-house historian. His finest moments have occurred when he dresses up as one of history's most noteworthy figures. He has gone so far as having studied the speech and idiosyncratic mannerisms of many American spokespersons, including several American presidents. Today, George Theosolis is Ben Franklin and in a few minutes is scheduled to enter his fifth-grade class dressed as Franklin to introduce a new unit entitled *America's Break with Tradition.* George is not sure how much his students already know about Franklin, and his objective is for his students to become acquainted with Franklin's multiple, important contributions to America's past, present, and future.

Besides his love of history, George Theosolis has become the school's guru on *constructivist* teaching. Last summer he took a professional development class at the university entitled "Jean Piaget: Constructivism & Creativity." Since that experience, George has been convinced that Piaget's theories about learning styles are key to motivating children to learn. According to Piaget, students are not passive bystanders in relationship to their environment, nor to their educational experiences. Rather, when they become involved in their education by either relating to it or experiencing it, they gain personal meaning.

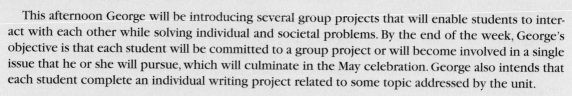

This afternoon George will be introducing several group projects that will enable students to interact with each other while solving individual and societal problems. By the end of the week, George's objective is that each student will be committed to a group project or will become involved in a single issue that he or she will pursue, which will culminate in the May celebration. George also intends that each student complete an individual writing project related to some topic addressed by the unit.

1. Give examples of various writing projects that George Theosolis might assign his fifth-grade students. Describe the benefits of those assignments and the criteria he would use for grading the writing projects.
2. What form of preassessment should George use to determine what students know about Benjamin Franklin before beginning the unit? Defend your choice.
3. What are the essential elements of constructivist teaching? Which of these have been incorporated into George Theosolis's instruction?

To submit your responses online, go to the *Prepare for the Praxis™ Examination* module for this chapter of the Companion Website at **http://www.prenhall.com/webb**.

Build Your Knowledge Base

1. How would Aristotle and Plato answer the question posed at the beginning of this chapter: Should the right to an education be guaranteed by the government?
2. What impact did the Reformation have on the education of common people?
3. What ideas of Pestalozzi and Froebel are in practice in the schools of your community?
4. Describe the status of higher education in colonial America.
5. Contrast education in the New England, mid-Atlantic, and Southern colonies. Do any legacies of these differences remain today?
6. What was the contribution of the apprenticeship system to education in the colonies?

Develop Your Portfolio

1. Rousseau believed in stages of children's growth and development, and in the educational necessity of adapting instruction to the various stages. Review INTASC Standard 2: "The teacher understands how children learn and develop and can provide learning opportunities that support their intellectual, social, and personal development." Faced with the reality that, in any given class, you will probably be faced with students who are at various stages of growth and development, prepare an artifact that demonstrates how you will be sensitive to adapting your instruction to your students' needs. Place your artifact in your portfolio under **INTASC Standard 2, Student Learning and Development.**
2. Johann Friedrich Herbart, who studied under Pestalozzi, believed that the aim of education should be the development of moral character. Review the Controversial Issues feature in Chapter 3, page 56, "Should Moral Education, Character Education, Ethics, or Values Education Be a Responsibility of the School?" Reflect on the pros and cons of this issue and develop a position paper that summarizes your views on this subject. Place your paper in your portfolio under **INTASC Standard 1, Knowledge of Subject.**

To complete these activities online, go to the *Develop Your Portfolio* module for this chapter of the Companion Website at **http://www.prenhall.com/webb**.

Explore Teaching and Learning: Field Experiences

1. Check out a book on the history of education in the colonial period, explore Internet resources, and prepare a 3- to 5-page summary of the history of the American kindergarten movement. How does today's program compare with the program in which you were a student? What are the differences and similarities?
2. Using public library materials, newspaper reports, interviews with local citizens, and governmental records, summarize the evolution of public and private precollegiate and collegiate education in your community. What factors influenced decisions about the location and mission of educational institutions in your region?

Professional Development Online

Visit this text's Companion Website at **http://www.prenhall.com/webb** to gain access to a variety of questions, activities, and exercises to help build your knowledge of this chapter's content. Below are just a few items available at this text's Companion Website:

- Classroom Video—To see actual classroom footage and work through activities and questions to analyze the content of the video, click on the *Classroom Video* module for this chapter.
- Teaching Tolerance—To go to this organization's website and complete activities to explore issues and topics dealing with how to teach tolerance to students, click on the *Teaching Tolerance* module for this chapter.
- Self-Test—To review terms and concepts presented in this chapter, click on the *Self-Test* module for this chapter.
- Internet Resources—To link to web sites related to topics in this chapter, go to the *Internet Resources* module for this chapter of the Companion Website.

CHAPTER 6

Those who cannot remember the past are condemned to repeat it.
—Santayana

AMERICAN EDUCATION: FROM REVOLUTION TO THE TWENTIETH CENTURY

The Boston Examiner   Thursday, July 13, 1867

"New U.S. Commissioner of Education Deplores Training of Teachers"

In an address last evening to the National Education Association meeting in New York, Mr. Henry Barnard, the newly appointed United States Commissioner of Education, commented on the inadequate training possessed by the vast majority of teachers who teach our young. According to Commissioner Barnard: "Too many of those we have entrusted to guide and guard our nation's youth have little knowledge beyond that which they are attempting to impart. Indeed, we might well

question whether their knowledge is superior to that of many of their fellow tradesmen. Not only is the depth and breadth of their knowledge of the curriculum matter a subject of concern, but where knowledge is possessed, there exists most often an absence of any training in pedagogy." The commissioner went on to say that "teachers will not be elevated to that place in society and receive that compensation they so richly deserve until they are required to undertake a special course of study and training to qualify them for their office."

Do these comments sound familiar? Which of the concerns expressed by Barnard remain concerns today? Which are no longer concerns?

At the time Henry Barnard made these remarks the nation was less than 100 years old but had already more than tripled in size and increased tenfold in population. Before the century was over, the population would double again. The educational system grew with the nation, sometimes responding to, sometimes leading, social and economic changes.

As you study the history of American education from the birth of the nation to the beginning of the 20th century, think about the following objectives:

- Describe the impact of Thomas Jefferson and Noah Webster on American education in the early 19th century.
- Identify the contributions that monitorial schools, Sunday schools, infant schools, and free school societies made to the expansion of educational opportunities in the early national period.
- Compare the curriculum and purposes of the academy with those of the grammar school and the high school.
- Discuss the development of common schools in the United States and the roles that Horace Mann, Henry Barnard, Emma Willard, and Catherine Beecher played in that development.
- Outline the development of secondary education in the United States.
- Discuss the factors leading to the growth of higher education in 19th-century America.
- Compare the educational opportunities provided to Native Americans, Hispanic Americans, and black Americans in the 19th century.
- Trace the development of teacher education in the United States.

Education in the Early National Period

On July 4, 1776, the 13 colonies declared their independence from England. Education was one of the casualties of the war that followed. Illiteracy increased as rural schools closed their doors, and even the larger town Latin grammar schools were impacted. Almost all schools suffered from a shortage of funds and teachers (Pulliam & Van Patten, 2003). Institutions of higher education lost professors and students to fight on both sides of the conflict. Many schools were taken over by the war effort, others became casualties of the war.

After the Revolutionary War the leaders of the new nation set about the business of devising a government that would encompass the ideas for which they had fought. The first attempt at self-governance under the Articles of Confederation provided little authority to the central government and established no executive or judicial branches. When this government proved inadequate, delegates from each state met in the summer of 1787 and drafted the Constitution, which after ratification in 1789 launched the new republic. Perhaps because of the former colonists' suspicion of a strong central government, or perhaps because of the association of education with theology, neither the Articles of Confederation nor the Constitution mentioned education.

Northwest Land Ordinances

Despite the fact that neither the Articles of Confederation nor the U.S. Constitution mentioned education, there can be no doubt that the nation's founders recognized the importance of education to a country in which the quality of representation depended on its citizens' ability to make informed choices at the ballot box. To ensure that the settlers in the Northwest Territory did not neglect education, Congress passed perhaps the most important piece of legislation under the Articles of Confederation, the Land Ordinance of 1785. This ordinance prescribed the terms of admitting new states into the union from the Northwest Territory, and required that the 16th section of land in each township in the Territory be set aside for the support of education. The land could be sold or leased, but the proceeds were to go to fund education. The 16th section, which was the section closest to the geographical center of the township (see Figure 6.1), was a strategic choice for the possible location of a school. Two years later, Article Three of the Northwest Ordinance, which incorporated the Northwest Territory, proclaimed: "Religion, morality, and knowledge being necessary to good government and the happiness of mankind, schools and the means of education shall be forever encouraged."

Nationalism and Education

The spirit of nationalism that dominated the new republic shaped the views of the Founding Fathers regarding what type of education was needed for the new nation. Whereas the primary purpose of colonial education had been sectarian, emphasis was now placed on citizenship and the nation-state. Education was seen as the best way to both prepare citizens to participate in a republican form of government and maintain order.

The Founding Fathers were aware that changing their form of government was only the beginning of the revolution. As Benjamin Rush, a proponent of universal education, remarked: "We have changed our form of government, but it remains to effect a revolution of our principles, opinions, and manners, so as to accommodate them to the forms of government we have adopted" (Cremin, 1982, p. 1). Rush and his compatriots worked untiringly at devising endless versions of political and educational arrangements.

Although they differed on many details, there were at least four beliefs common to their discussions: (1) that the laws of education must be relative to the form of government, hence a republic needs an educational system that motivates citizens to choose public over private interest; (2) that what was needed was a truly American education purged of all vestiges of older, monarchical forms and dedicated to the creation of a cohesive and independent citizenry; (3) that education should be genuinely practical, aimed at the improvement of the human condition, with the new sciences at its heart; and (4) that American education should be exemplary and a means through which America could teach the world the glories of liberty and learning (Cremin, 1982).

Figure 6.1 — Northwest Territory and Township. The 16th Section of Each Township in the Northwest Territory was Set Aside for the Support of Education.

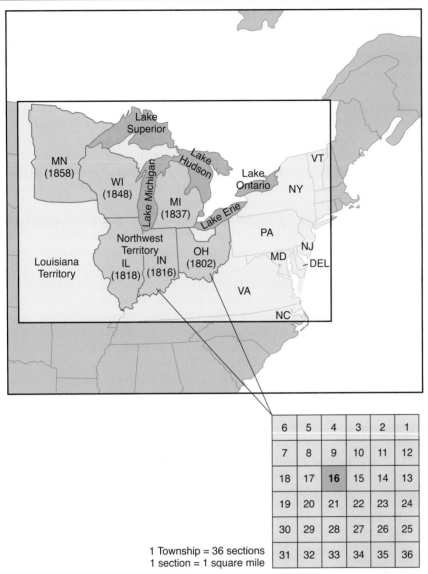

1 Township = 36 sections
1 section = 1 square mile

Source: Webb, L. Dean, History of American Education, The: A Great American Experiment, 1st, © 2005. Electronically reproduced by permission of Pearson Education, Inc. Upper Saddle River, New Jersey.

Thomas Jefferson. Although many of the Founding Fathers expressed their views on the importance of education, perhaps none is so well known for his educational views as Thomas Jefferson (1743–1826). Jefferson, who was strongly influenced by the philosophy of Locke, believed that government must be by the consent of the governed and that men were entitled to certain rights that could not be abridged by the government. Jefferson was one of the chief proponents of the addition of a Bill of Rights to the Constitution. As Rippa (1997) noted, "Few statesmen in American history have so vigorously strived for an ideal (liberty); perhaps none has so consistently viewed education as the indispensable cornerstone of freedom" (p. 55).

Plan for a State Education System. Jefferson's *Bill for the More General Diffusion of Knowledge,* introduced in the Virginia legislature in 1779, provided for the establishment of a system of public schools that would provide the masses with the basic education necessary to ensure good government, public safety, and happiness. Under the bill each county would be subdivided into parts called *hundreds;* each hundred was to provide an elementary school, supported by taxes. Attendance would be free for all white children, male and female, for 3 years. The curriculum would be reading, writing, arithmetic, and history. The bill also proposed that the state be divided into 20 districts with a public boarding grammar school built in each district. Those attending would be not only those boys whose families could afford the tuition, but the brightest of the poorer students from the elementary schools whose tuition would be paid by the state. The curriculum of the grammar school was to include Latin, Greek, geography, English, grammar, and higher mathematics. Finally, on completion of grammar school, 10 of the scholarship students would receive 3 years' study at the College of William and Mary at state expense. The remaining scholarship students, according to Jefferson, would most likely become masters in the grammar schools.

Although this plan, viewed in today's light, appears strikingly elitist, in Jefferson's day it was considered excessively liberal and philanthropic. In fact, it was defeated by the Virginia legislature, no doubt in large part because of the unwillingness of the wealthy to pay for the education of the poor. Nonetheless, the plan is considered important because it removed the stigma of pauperism from elementary schooling (Rippa, 1997) and proposed a system of universal, free, public education—if only for 3 years.

Founding the University of Virginia. Jefferson's interest in education also extended to establishing the University of Virginia. After leaving the presidency in 1809, he devoted much of his energies to that effort. Sometimes called "Mr. Jefferson's University," no college or university ever bore so completely the mark of one person. He created the project in every detail: He designed the buildings and landscape (even bought the bricks and picked out the trees to be used as lumber), chose the library books, designed the curriculum, and selected the students and faculty. The university opened in 1825, a year before Jefferson's death on July 4, 1826, exactly 50 years after the adoption of the immortal document he wrote—the Declaration of Independence (Rippa, 1997).

Benjamin Rush. Benjamin Rush (1745–1813), a medical doctor and professor, was a graduate of both the University of Edinburgh (Scotland) and Princeton. At the outbreak of the Revolutionary War he was a professor at the College of Philadelphia. Rush was deeply interested in education as well as a broad range of social issues: He was strongly opposed to the death sentence and encouraged penal reform and the establishment of institutions for the mentally ill. Together with Benjamin Franklin, he organized the first abolition society in Philadelphia, the Society for the Relief of Free Negroes Unlawfully Held in Bondage.

Rush wanted to establish a system of schools in Pennsylvania and eventually the entire nation that would provide public support for a system of free schools. According to the plan he laid out in *A Plan for the Establishment of Public Schools and the Diffusion of Knowledge in Pennsylvania,* a plan similar to Jefferson's plan for Virginia, Rush proposed that in every town of 100 or more families a free school be established where children would be taught to read and write English and German as well as arithmetic. An academy was to be established in each county "for the purpose of instructing youth in the learned languages (Latin and Greek), and thereby preparing them to enter college." The higher education provisions of the plan included four colleges where males would be instructed in mathematics and the "higher branches of science" as well as one university located in the state capital where "law, physic, divinity, the law of nature and nations economy, etc. be taught . . . by public lectures in the winter season, after the manner of the European universities." Rush's educational plan was intended to tie together the whole educational system: The university would supply the masters for the academies and free schools, while the free schools, in turn, would supply the students for the academies.

For Your Reflection and Analysis

How different are the wealthy of today from the wealthy of Jefferson's time in terms of their willingness to pay additional taxes to support the public schools?

To submit your response online, go to http://www. prenhall.com/webb.

CW

The Founding Fathers recognized the importance of education to the preservation of the new republic.

Rush was an advocate of the education of women and founded one of the first female academies in the United States, the Young Ladies Academy of Philadelphia. However, he was not an egalitarian. To a large extent, Rush's support of women's education was based on his view of their particular duties in a republic. In his *Thoughts Upon Female Education* (1787) Rush espouses the idea of "republican motherhood," the idea that a woman's primary duty was to bring up her sons to be virtuous citizens and that to do this they must themselves be educated.

Rush was also an advocate for the education of blacks. Rush saw the education of blacks to be a moral and economic imperative: "let the young negroes be educated in the principles of virtues and religion . . . let them be taught to read and write—and afterward instructed in some business whereby they may be able to maintain themselves" (Binderman, 1976, p. 21).

Noah Webster.   It was a teacher, Noah Webster (1758–1843), who had the greatest influence on education in the new republic. Whereas the nation's founders had sought political independence from England, Webster sought cultural independence. Webster believed that the primary purpose of education should be the inculcation of patriotism, and that what was needed was a truly American education rid of European influence (Madsen, 1974). These goals could best be accomplished, he believed, by creating a distinctive national language and curriculum. To this end, Webster prepared a number of spelling, grammar, and reading books to replace the English texts then in use; an American version of the Bible; and what became the world-famous *American Dictionary of the English Language.*

Of his textbooks, the most important was the *Elementary Spelling Book,* published in 1783, often referred to as the "blue-back speller" because of the color of the binding. By 1875, 75 million copies of the speller had been sold (Spring, 2005), many of which were used again and again. The book included both a federal catechism with political and patriotic content, and a moral catechism whose content was related to respect for honest work and property rights, the value of money, the virtues of industry and thrift, the danger of drink, and contentment with one's economic status (Rippa, 1997; Spring, 2005). According to the noted historian Henry S. Commager, "No other secular book had ever spread so wide, penetrated so deep, lasted so long" (cited in Rippa, 1997, p. 60).

Webster supported the concept of free schools in which all American children could learn the necessary patriotic and moral precepts. As a member of the Massachusetts legislature, he worked for the establishment of a state system of education and is credited by some as initiating the common school movement, which culminated in Horace Mann's work in the 1830s (Spring, 2005). He also supported the education of women, because they would be the mothers of future citizens and the teachers of youth. However, he envisioned a rather limited and "female" education for them and counseled parents against sending their daughters to "demoralizing" boarding schools. A staunch patriot whose proposals sometimes bordered on the fanatic (e.g., the proposal that the first word a child learned should be "Washington"), Webster has been called the "Schoolmaster of the Republic."

Educational Innovations

Although Webster and others promoted the establishment of a uniquely American education, some of the major innovations in American education in the first quarter of the 19th century were of European origin. Among these were the monitorial school, the Sunday school, and the infant school. The period also witnessed the efforts of the free school societies and, more important, the rise of the academies. Each of these made a contribution, but the primary pattern of schooling that developed in the first half of the 19th century emerged from the common school movement, which is discussed in the next section. However, a review of these alternatives illustrates how the country, in the absence of established state systems, was searching for a suitable educational pattern for the new and developing nation (Gutek, 1991).

Monitorial Schools.   **Monitorial schools** originated in England and were brought to America by a Quaker named Joseph Lancaster. In the Lancasterian monitorial system,

For Your Reflection and Analysis

What textbook or book from your elementary or secondary education had the greatest influence on you? Why?
To submit your response online, go to http://www.prenhall.com/webb.

CW

one paid teacher instructed hundreds of pupils through the use of student teachers or monitors who were chosen for their academic abilities. Monitorial education was concerned with teaching only the basics of reading, writing, and arithmetic. The first monitorial school in the United States was opened in New York City in 1806, and the system spread rapidly throughout the states. One such school in Pennsylvania was designed to accommodate 450 students:

> The teacher sits at the head of the room on a raised platform. Beneath and in front of the teacher are three rows of monitors' desks placed directly in front of the pupils' desks. The pupils' desks are divided into three sections . . . and each section is in line with one of the rows of monitors' desks . . . a group of pupils would march to the front of the room and stand around the monitors' desks, where they would receive instruction from the monitors. When they finished, they would march to the rear part of their particular section and recite or receive further instruction from another monitor. While this group was marching to the rear, another group would be marching up to the front to take their places around the monitors. When finished, the pupils would march to the rear, and the group in the rear would move forward to the second part of their section to receive instruction from yet another monitor. Because each of the three sections had a group in front, one in the rear, and one in the middle working on different things, a total of nine different recitations could be carried on at one time. (Spring, 2005, p. 59)

The monitorial system was attractive not only because it provided an inexpensive system for educating poor children, but because submission to the system was supposed to instill the virtues of orderliness, obedience, and industriousness. As already noted, the system gained wide appeal. However, in time the system declined. It appeared to be suited only for large cities with large numbers of students rather than small towns and rural areas. It was also criticized because it afforded only the most basic education. However, instead of being an educational dead end, as depicted by many educational historians, Lancasterian monitorialism may have been the model for the factory-like urban schools that emerged in the United States in the late 19th century (Gutek, 1991).

Free School Societies: Charity Schools. The Lancasterian system was considered ideal for the schools operated by the various free school societies. These societies operated charity schools for the children of the poor in urban areas. In some instances, as in New York City, they received public support. Overall they were not a major factor in the history of education; nonetheless, for a period they did provide the only education some children received. For example, by 1820 the Free School Society of New York City (renamed the Public School Society in 1826 and placed under the city department of education in 1853) was teaching more than 2,000 children (Cremin, 1982).

Sunday Schools. Another educational plan introduced to America was the **Sunday school,** begun by Robert Raikes in 1780 in England. The first Sunday school in America opened in 1786 in Virginia. Its purpose was to offer the rudiments of reading and writing to children who worked during the week, primarily in the factories of the larger cities, and to provide them with an alternative to roaming the streets on Sunday. Although the Bible was commonly its textbook, originally the Sunday school was not seen as an adjunct of the church and was not intended to promote conversion. By 1830, however, the initial practical purpose had been superseded by religious interests and these schools had become primarily religious institutions operated by Sunday school societies with an evangelical mission. They grew in number, reaching out to the frontier and becoming available to children from homes of all sorts. In new communities they often paved the way for the common school (Cremin, 1982).

Infant Schools. The **infant school** was originated in England by Robert Owen, who also established one of the first infant schools in the United States at his would-be Utopia, a collective at New Harmony, Indiana. Established primarily in the eastern cities, these schools were taught by women and were designed for children ages 4 to 7 who, because they would go to work in a factory at a very early age, probably would not receive any other schooling. The primary schools designed along this model did not survive long. However, in a few cities the primary schools had been designed as preparatory to entry into the elementary school and often became part of the town school system.

For Your Reflection and Analysis

What virtues do the schools attempt to instill today?

To submit your response online, go to http://www.prenhall.com/webb.

In the 1850s, the followers of Froebel revived the idea behind this form of infant school in the form of the kindergarten.

The Growth of the Academy

More significant in foreshadowing the coming changes in patterns of formal schooling was the growth of the academy. Although the current concept of academy evokes the image of an exclusive private institution with a college-preparatory curriculum, or perhaps military training, in the late 18th and 19th centuries the term was more broadly applied. As we have seen, Franklin's academy and similar institutions were interested in providing an alternative to the traditional curriculum of the Latin grammar schools by providing a "practical" education.

The variations among academies were great. Some were indeed prestigious and exclusive, whereas others were nothing more than log cabins. Stimulated by the founding of the United States Military Academy at West Point in 1802 and the Naval Academy at Annapolis in 1848, many academies were established as military schools. Admission to some was open to all comers, whereas others catered to special clients. Some were boarding schools, some were day schools. Some were teacher owned, others were organized by groups of parents or individuals, and yet others by denominations or various societies. In several states public support was given to the academies.

The curriculum of the academy usually depended, at least in part, on the students who were enrolled, but most offered an education beyond the three Rs. In the larger academies, Latin and Greek were offered along with English grammar, geography, arithmetic, and other studies deemed "practical" or in demand. By the end of the early national period, some of the larger academies were also offering courses designed to provide preparation for teaching in the common schools (Cremin, 1982; Madsen, 1974).

Academies for Women.   A number of the academies were established for women and are important for the role they played in providing females the opportunity for an education beyond the elementary school. Some of these academies bore the name *seminaries* and were important in the training of female teachers, teaching being about the only profession open to women at the time. In 1821 the Troy Female Seminary in New York was opened by Emma Willard, a lifelong activist for women's rights. Opposed to the finishing school curriculum of the female boarding schools, Willard proposed a curriculum that was "solid and useful."

Mount Holyoke Female Seminary in Massachusetts, founded in 1837 by Mary Lyon, provided a demanding curriculum that included philosophy, mathematics, and science. To be admitted to Mount Holyoke, as at many of the leading seminaries, students had to demonstrate mastery of not only the basics, but also Latin. Mount Holyoke, like Troy, was oriented to the training of teachers. Its success is indicated by the fact that more than 70% of the alumnae from the first 40 years taught at one time.

Catherine Beecher, the sister of Harriet Beecher Stowe, founded both the Hartford (Connecticut) Female Seminary (1828) and the Western Institute for Women (1832) in Cincinnati, and was instrumental in the founding of female seminaries in Iowa, Illinois, and Wisconsin.

Following the path forged by the female seminaries in New England, seminaries sprang up in other regions of the country, being especially popular in the South. By the mid-19th century there were more than 6,000 academies in the United States enrolling 263,000 students. The academy is considered by most educational historians as the forerunner of the American high school. Its broad range of curricular offerings responded to the demands of the growing middle class and demonstrated that there was an important place in the educational system for a secondary educational institution for non-college-bound as well as college-bound youth. The broadened curriculum, combined with the more liberal entrance requirements, allowed the entrance of people of various religious and social backgrounds and were major steps in the democratization of American secondary education (Rippa, 1997). Figure 6.2 gives an overview of the 19th-century educational institutions discussed in this chapter.

> **For Your Reflection and Analysis**
>
> Do you support publicly funded single-sex schools? Why or why not?
> *To submit your response online, go to http://www.prenhall.com/webb.*
>
> CW

Figure 6.2 — Nineteenth-Century Educational Innovations and Their 20th-Century Descendants

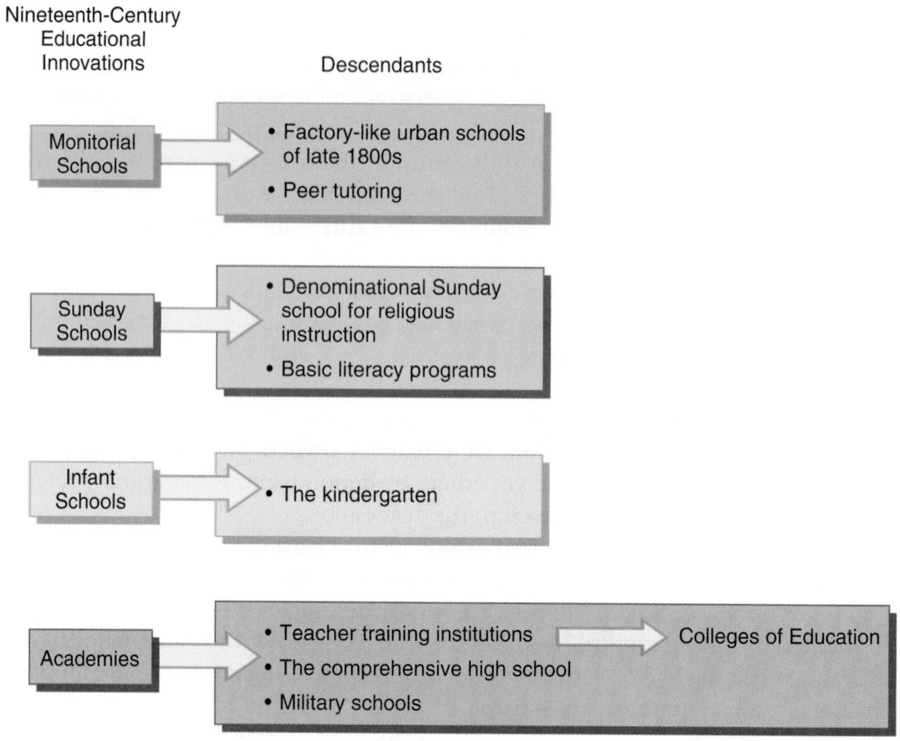

Nineteenth-Century
Educational
Innovations

Descendants

Monitorial Schools → • Factory-like urban schools of late 1800s
• Peer tutoring

Sunday Schools → • Denominational Sunday school for religious instruction
• Basic literacy programs

Infant Schools → • The kindergarten

Academies → • Teacher training institutions → Colleges of Education
• The comprehensive high school
• Military schools

The Common School Movement

The period from 1830 to 1865 has been designated the age of the **common school** movement in American educational history. During this period, the American educational system as we know it today began to take form. Instead of sporadic state legislation and abdication of responsibility, state systems of education were established. State control as well as direct taxation for the support of the common schools—publicly supported schools attended in common by all children—became accepted practices. The common school movement was the product of a variety of economic, social, and political factors.

Moving Forces

Changing Demographics: A Larger and More Urban Population. Between 1830 and 1860, 1,234,566 square miles of territory were added to the United States. During the same period, the population exploded from 13 million to 32 million (see Table 6.1). Of this growth, 4 million came from immigration. Not only was there an increase in immigration, but the national origins of the immigrants were different. Before this era the majority of immigrants had come from Northern Europe and shared much of the same cultural and religious backgrounds as the inhabitants of their new homeland. Beginning in the 1830s and 1840s larger numbers came from Ireland, Germany, and Southern Europe and were often Roman Catholic and often spoke a language other than English. Most settled in the larger cities of the Northeast and Midwest, providing the much needed labor for the growing industrial complex, but at the same time contributing to the problems facing growing urban areas.

At the same time the United States was growing rapidly in size, it was becoming increasingly urban. Not only did the new immigrants tend to settle in the cities, but more and more people moved from the farm to the city. Improved methods of agriculture made farming less labor intensive at the same time that employment opportunities were created by the growing number of factories. In 1820 there were only 12 cities in the then 23 states

Table 6.1 — Area and Population of the United States, 1790–1890

Year	Land Area (square miles)	Population
1790	864,746	3,929,214
1800	864,746	5,308,483
1810	1,681,824	7,239,881
1820	1,749,462	9,638,453
1830	1,749,462	12,865,020
1840	1,749,462	17,069,453
1850	2,940,042	23,191,876
1860	2,969,640	31,443,321
1870	2,969,640	39,818,449
1880	2,969,640	50,155,783
1890	2,969,640	62,947,714

Source: U.S. Bureau of the Census. (1975). *Historical statistics of the United States, colonial times to 1970* (p. 8). Washington, DC: U.S. Government Printing Office.

with a population of over 10,000; by 1860 the number had increased to 101 and 8 had a population of over 100,000 (Binder, 1974).

The growth in the cities was a result of the growth in industrialization. For example, in 1807 only 15 cotton mills were in operation in the United States; by 1831 there were 801 mills employing 70,000 workers (Rippa, 1997). These changing economic and social patterns gave rise to an increasing urban population, which included concentrations of children who needed schooling, a more industrialized economy that required a trained workforce, and in certain areas a Roman Catholic population that challenged Protestant domination.

Demands of the Working Class. In this context the common schools were seen by the working class, who could not afford to educate their children at private expense, as avenues for upward social and economic mobility. Critical of pauper or charity schools, the newly emerging workingmen's organizations were open in their support of tax-supported common schools. The common schools were seen as providing the education necessary for protection against the tyranny of the upper class and for equal participation in a democracy. The leaders of business and industry also supported common schools. They saw them as a means of ensuring a supply of literate and trained workers.

Social Control. The dominant English-speaking, upper-class Protestants saw a different merit in the common schools. This group viewed the common schools as agencies of social control over the lower socioeconomic classes. According to Gutek (1991), social control in this context meant

imposing by institutionalized education the language, beliefs, and values of the dominant group on outsiders, especially on the non-English speaking immigrants. Common schools were expected to create such conformity in American life by imposing the language and ideological outlook of the dominant group. For example, by using English as the medium of instruction, the common schools were expected to create an English-speaking citizenry; by cultivating a general value orientation based on Protestant Christianity, the schools were expected to create a general American ethic. (pp. 87–88)

Most social groups also saw the common schools as a means of controlling crime and social unrest. Knowledge was seen as "the great remedy for intemperance: for in proportion as we elevate men in the scale of existence . . . so do we reclaim them from all temptation of degrading vice and ruinous crimes" (Binder, 1974, p. 32).

The Frontier Movement. Interest in the establishment of common schools was not limited to the industrialized regions of the East. As the frontier moved ever westward, the one-room schoolhouse, often the only public building in a community, became the symbol of civilization and the center of efforts to keep literacy, citizenship, and civilization alive in the wilderness (Gutek, 1991).

The spirit of the frontier movement itself also contributed to the common school movement. The frontier movement was fueled by individuals who placed more value on the worth of the individual than on his or her social class. The frontier was also a place where a practical education was more important than the ability to read or write Latin. In effect, the philosophy of the common school was consistent with and supportive of the values of the frontier.

Extended Suffrage.   On the political front, the age of the common school coincided with the age of the common man. In the early years of the republic, the right to vote in many states was limited to those who owned property. Gradually this began to change and many states, especially those on the frontier, extended suffrage to all white males. The result of the extension of suffrage was not only increases in the number of common men holding public office, but increases in the pressure for direct taxation to support common schools.

Education Journals and Organizations.   Two of the most important mechanisms for spreading the ideology of the common school were educational periodicals and educational organizations. Between 1825 and 1850 more than 60 educational journals came into existence (Spring, 2005). Among the most important were the *Massachusetts Common School Journal* and the prestigious *American Journal of Education.* Although many of these journals did not survive, collectively they served both to popularize education and to keep teachers informed of educational innovations and ideas from home and abroad.

Of the educational organizations, the most noteworthy were the American Institute of Instruction, the Western Literary Institute and College of Professional Teachers, and, on a more national scale, the American Lyceum. The latter was founded in 1826 by a Connecticut farmer, Josiah Holbrook, as an organization devoted to advancing the education of children and adults. By 1839 there were 4,000 to 5,000 local **lyceums** in the United States actively presenting programs, demonstrations, mutual instruction, and informative lectures by notable speakers. Many of these speakers, Horace Mann among them, were in favor of school reforms and in support of the common school. Cremin (1982) credits educational organizations with spearheading the common school movement, "articulating its ideals, publicizing its goals, and instructing one another in its political techniques; indeed, in the absence of a national ministry of education, it was their articulating, publicizing, and mutual instruction in politics that accounted for the spread of public education across the country" (p. 176).

Protestant Religious Accommodation.   Religious intolerance had been part of American life since the earliest colonial days. Roger Williams and Anne Hutchinson, the founders of Rhode Island, were banished from the Massachusetts Bay Colony because of their disagreement with Puritan practices. Historically, public support for the schools had been rejected if the result would be support being given to another's religion. Common school reformers addressed the problem by proposing that the schools practice nondenominational Protestantism. Thus, as will be discussed later in this chapter, although Catholicism would be excluded, the schools would not be Protestant nonsectarian. They would promote republican virtues and Christian morality, but free of the doctrine and without the interpretation of any particular Protestant denomination (Kaestle, 1983). Although this accommodation was criticized in those parts of the country where sectarian bias was strong, support for the common schools could not have been obtained without it.

Leading Proponents of the Common School

Horace Mann.   If any one person were to be given the title "Father of American Education," that person would be Horace Mann (1796–1859). Elected to the Massachusetts legislature in 1827, Mann, a brilliant orator, soon became the spokesperson for the common school movement. He led a campaign to organize the schools in Massachusetts into a state system and to establish a state board of education.

Upon the creation of the state board of education in 1837, Mann gave up his political career and a chance at the governorship to become the board's first secretary and the chief state school officer. He served in this position for 12 years and used it as a platform for proclaiming the ideology of the common school movement, as well as other educational ideals. In addition to his numerous lectures, editorships, and other writings, each year Mann wrote a report to the legislature reciting current educational practice and conditions and making recommendations for improvement. These reports were distributed in other states and abroad, and were significant in influencing educational legislation and practice throughout the country.

In his own state, Mann campaigned vigorously to increase public support for education and public awareness of the problems facing education in the form of dilapidated, unsanitary facilities and substandard materials, as well as the shortcomings of the local school committees. Mann was also critical of the status of the teaching profession and the training of teachers. As a result of his efforts, state appropriations to education were doubled, 50 new secondary schools were built, textbooks and equipment were improved, and teachers' salaries in Massachusetts were raised more than 50%. Mann also fought for the professional training of teachers and established three **normal schools** (teacher training institutions), the first such schools in America. The first of these normal schools was established in 1839 at Lexington, Massachusetts.

In his Tenth Annual Report (1846), Mann asserted that education was the right of every child and that it was the state's responsibility to ensure that every child was provided an education. Although Mann himself did not promote compulsory attendance but rather regular attendance, this report was instrumental in the adoption by the Massachusetts legislature of the nation's first compulsory attendance law in 1852.

Like several prominent educators of his time, Mann had visited the Prussian schools and observed the Pestalozzian methods. His Seventh Report (1843) gave a positive account of his observations. He was particularly impressed with the love and rapport shared by the teachers and students involved in these schools. He also shared Pestalozzi's and Catherine Beecher's belief that women were better teachers than men for the common schools.

Mann's view of the role of the common school in promoting social harmony and ensuring the republic would be guided by an intelligent, moral citizenry was not original or unique. However, at a time when the common school movement was spreading across the nation, when it came to defining its basic principles and articles of faith, he was unquestionably its chief spokesperson (Binder, 1974).

Henry Barnard.   Another major leader of the common school movement was Henry Barnard (1811–1900). Like Mann, he served in the state legislature (for Connecticut), worked to establish a state board of education, and then became the board's first secretary (1838–1842). He then served in a similar capacity in Rhode Island (1845–1849) and later became the first U.S. commissioner of education.

Much of Barnard's influence on educational theory and practice came through his numerous lectures and writings and, more important, through his editorship of the *American Journal of Education.* Barnard is also credited with initiating the teachers' institute movement discussed later in this chapter. Barnard's greatest successes lay in his democratic philosophy ("schools good enough for the best and cheap enough for the poorest") and as a disseminator of information about better schools. He is sometimes called the "Father of American School Administration" (Pulliam & Van Patten, 2003).

Catherine Beecher.   Catherine Beecher (1800–1878), the founder of the Hartford Female Seminary and the Western Institute for Women, was a strong supporter of the common

For Your Reflection and Analysis

Who in contemporary America could be considered a champion of education? Name some of that person's activities.

To submit your response online, go to http://www.prenhall.com/webb.

CW

District schools enrolled male and female children of all ages.

school and saw her task as focusing attention on the need for a corps of female teachers to staff the common schools. She set forth a plan for a nationwide system of teacher training seminaries. Although the plan was not adopted, her efforts on behalf of the common school were a force in its acceptance, and her work on behalf of women pointed to a new American consensus concerning female roles (Cremin, 1982).

Growth of State and Local Support and Supervision

Increased State Support.   The idea of having universal common schools was one thing, but paying for them through direct taxation of the general public was another. Until the 1820s or 1830s, the only really free education was that provided by the charity schools, or in certain other schools if the parents were willing to declare themselves paupers. Often local or county taxes levied on specific activities, for example, liquor licenses or marriage fees, provided partial support for the schools, but the remainder of the expenses were charged to the parents in the form of a **rate bill.** The rate bill was, in effect, a tuition fee based on the number of children in the family attending school. Even though the fee might be small, poor parents often could not afford it, so their children either did not attend school or took turns attending.

One of the major goals of the common school movement was to secure greater state support for the common schools. Beginning in the first quarter of the 19th century, several states began to provide aid for public schools. Funds came from the permanent school fund (derived largely from the sale of public lands), direct taxation, or appropriations from the general fund. Conditions were usually placed on the receipt of funds; for example, that local support must equal or exceed state support, or that the schools must be kept open a minimum length of time.

By 1865 systems of common schools had been established throughout the northern, midwestern, and western states, and more than 50% of the nation's children were enrolled in public schools. The lowest enrollments were in the South, where the common school movement had made little progress. As enrollments grew, the pressure to make these schools completely tax supported increased. In 1827 Massachusetts became the first state to abolish the rate bill. Pennsylvania's Free School Act of 1834 was a model for eliminating the pauper school concept. Other states soon followed these examples and by constitutional or legislative enactment adopted the concept of public support for public schools open to all children. But it was not until 1871 that the last state (New Jersey) abolished the rate bill, making the schools truly free.

Creation of State Boards and State Superintendents of Education.   As is usually the case, increased support is accompanied by increased efforts to control. The effort to establish some control or supervision was marked by the creation of an office of state superintendent, or commissioner of education, and a state board of education. In 1812 New York became the first state to appoint a state superintendent, Gideon Hawley. His tenure in office was filled with such controversy that in 1821 he was removed from office and the position was abolished and not re-created until 1854. Nonetheless, by the outbreak of the Civil War, 28 of the 34 states had established state boards of education and chief state school officers. By and large, these officers and boards were vested with more supervisory power than real control. Initially their major responsibilities involved the distribution of the permanent school funds and the organization of a state system of common schools.

Creation of Local School Districts and Superintendents.   The creation of a state system of common schools paralleled the establishment of school districts and the establishment of local and county superintendents. The New England states instituted the district system in the early years of the 19th century and it spread westward during the next three decades. Initially the districts were administered by a school committee, then by the district or county superintendent, whose primary duty was to supervise instruction. The development of the position of county superintendent of schools helped bring about some degree of standardization and uniformity in areas that had numerous small, rural school districts (Gutek, 1991).

The evolution of the office of city school superintendent quickly followed that of the district and county office. The first city superintendent was appointed in Buffalo in 1837, and was soon followed in Louisville, St. Louis, Providence, Springfield, Cleveland, Rochester, and New Orleans. The early superintendents functioned mostly as assistants or representatives of the school board. Most boards continued to operate as both an executive and legislative body. Many school board members were businessmen and were reluctant to delegate any of their executive functions to the superintendent. They considered themselves more competent to conduct the financial affairs of the district than the superintendent (American Association of School Administrators, 1952). It was not until the second half of the 19th century that superintendent and school board relationships began to change and the superintendent began to assume the powers and duties associated with a chief executive officer.

Organization and Curriculum

The common schools varied in terms of size, organization, and curriculum, depending on their location. In rural areas the one- or two-room school was dominant; progress was not marked by movement from one grade to another but by completing one text and beginning another. In larger cities and towns, grading had been introduced. On the frontier the curriculum was often limited to the three Rs; in larger cities it tended to be more broad. In the second quarter of the 19th century, a greater variety of textbooks appeared for use in the common schools. For example, the extremely popular *McGuffey Readers* continued to teach "the lessons of morality and patriotism, but the stern, direct preachments of earlier schoolbooks were replaced or supplemented by stories and essays designed to appeal to youthful interest" (Cremin, 1982, p. 96). Rote learning, drill, and practice did not disappear from the classroom, but a more Pestalozzian approach that placed value on the sensitivities and individuality of the child was making some inroads.

> **For Your Reflection and Analysis**
>
> What would be the advantages and disadvantages of attending a one- or two-room rural school over a large, urban school?
>
> *To submit your response online, go to http://www. prenhall.com/webb.*
>
> CW

Secondary School Movement

Public **secondary schools** offering education beyond the elementary school did not become a firmly established part of the American educational scene until the last quarter of the 19th century. However, the beginnings of the movement occurred well before the Civil War. Perhaps not unexpectedly, the lead was taken by those states that had been first to establish systems of common schools. Boston inaugurated the high school movement in 1821 with the opening of the English Classical School, renamed the Boston English High School in 1824. The school was open to boys only and was intended to be an alternative to the Latin grammar school and to provide a "practical education." Such an education, as we have seen, could otherwise be obtained only at a private academy.

The success of the English High School for boys led education reformers to push for a high school for girls. The school opened in 1828 and, although very successful—in fact, because it was so successful—was closed after only 3 years. The girls who enrolled in the school tended to stay, and being "neither trade- nor profession-minded, and unlike the boys, rarely obtained employment or other opportunities before they graduated from school. Thus, . . . was but a waste of taxpayers' money" (Herbst, 1996, p. 44). (See the Controversial Issue feature on page 142 for the arguments for and against single-sex schools and classes.)

In 1831, the first American **comprehensive** (and coeducational) **high school,** offering both English and classical courses of study, was opened in Lowell, Massachusetts. In 1838 Philadelphia opened a coeducational high school with three tracks: a 4-year classical curriculum, a 4-year modern language curriculum, and a 2-year English curriculum.

Slow Beginnings

In the years before the Civil War, the high school movement expanded slowly. By 1860 there were only 300 high schools in the nation compared with more than 6,000 academies; of the former, more than 100 were located in Massachusetts, the only state to require communities of 50 families or more to provide secondary-level education.

The initial slow growth of the high school movement can be partially explained by the fact that, unlike the common school, the high school was not being overwhelmingly

CONTROVERSIAL ISSUE

Single-Sex Schools and Classes

While Title IX has helped correct some of the blatant discrimination and disequity that has existed in educational institutions, its efforts to bring about gender equity have not been totally successful. The proposal for single-sex schools has been suggested as a possible remedy to ensure that both males and females obtain equal educational opportunities. The reasons stated by opponents on each side include the following:

Pro

1. Girls who attended private, single-sex schools have higher levels of academic achievement in reading, mathematics, and science compared to those who attended coeducational private or public schools.
2. Girls in single-sex schools are more likely to explore nontraditional subjects such as computer science, advanced physics, and advanced mathematics. They are also inclined to participate on athletic teams and play in a variety of sports.
3. Boys in single-sex schools are more likely to study subjects such as English, foreign languages, art, music, and drama.
4. Both boys and girls tend to have a more positive attitude toward learning when they attend single-sex schools.
5. In their respective single-sex schools, girls are more confident, and boys display fewer discipline problems. Single-sex schools have great potential for high-risk students from low-income and underprivileged backgrounds (Riordan, 1990).

Con

1. Single-sex schools fail to prepare the student for "real-life" experiences where males and females are in direct competition with one another for grades, honors, and admission to competitive and prestigious academic programs and institutions.
2. Allowing single-sex institutions runs the risk of dismantling the public school system and replacing it with the private school model.
3. Currently the majority of single-sex schools are private, which may make them more vulnerable to a return to the past where sexual stereotypes and traditional gender roles prevailed.
4. There is no need for a single-sex school since the federal government has published new guidelines that support single-sex classes under certain conditions.
5. Educational gender inequity continues to exist in spite of the numerous educational, social, and legal efforts that have been initiated to bring about needed change. There is no guarantee that establishing a single-sex school will resolve or eliminate the multiple inequities that exist relative to gender and schooling.

Have you ever attended a single-sex class or school or known someone who has? If so, how effective was the experience for you or for them? What is your position on single-sex schools?

 To answer these questions online, go to the *Controversial Issue* module for this chapter of the Companion Website at **http://www.prenhall.com/webb.**

demanded by the masses. It appeared to be more a reformer's response to urbanization and industrialization. Middle- or upper-class reformers, adopting the philosophy and rhetoric of the common school advocates, viewed their efforts as democratizing secondary education, providing a means of maintaining social values, and promoting economic progress. Prior to the Civil War, most high schools were located in urban areas where there were a sufficient number of students and tax support to support them.

The Movement Grows as Industry and the Economy Grow

In the years after the Civil War, however, a number of factors came together to create a greater demand for secondary education. These factors were similar to those that fueled the common school movement: population growth due in large part to increased immigration and a rapid growth in industry and technological change, which intensified the demand for skilled workers. At the same time, a high school education was increasingly seen as necessary to the full realization of one's social and economic goals. This was as true for artisans and small entrepreneurs in the cities and for businessmen and professionals in rural communities (Herbst, 1996). Last, economic growth created a larger tax base that could be used to support an expanded educational system.

The convergence of these factors created a demand for secondary education that brought a dramatic increase in the number of public high schools; from about 500 in 1870 to 6,000 in 1900. During the 1880s the number of high schools increased tenfold and surpassed the number of academies (see Figure 6.3). By the end of the century, free public high schools had pushed out the majority of fee-paying academies. Although still only a small percentage of the eligible population attended high school, in 1900 more than half a million students were enrolled and 62,000 graduated.

Figure 6.3 — The Development of Secondary Schools in the United States, 1630–1930

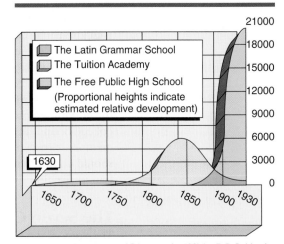

Source: From *The History of Education* (p. 699) by E. P. Cubberly, 1948. Cambridge, MA: Riverside Press. Copyright Riverside Press. Reprinted by permission.

Tax Support, Compulsory Attendance, and the Decline of Illiteracy

The public secondary school movement was given further impetus by the decision of the Michigan Supreme Court in the famous *Kalamazoo* case (1874). By its ruling that the legislature could tax for the support of both elementary and secondary schools, the court provided the precedent for public support of secondary education. And, in the decade between school years 1879–80 and 1889–90, total expenditures for the public schools increased 81%, from $78 million to $141 million (U.S. Department of Education, 2004a). By the end of the century, the publicly supported high school had replaced the academy in most communities and had become an established part of the common school system in every state.

The *Kalamazoo* decision having quashed the argument that public funds could not be used for secondary education, compulsory attendance laws soon followed. The passage of child labor laws was also instrumental in driving the adoption of compulsory attendance laws. By 1918, all states had enacted laws requiring full-time attendance until the child reached a certain age or completed a certain grade. By 1900 children attended school an average of 99 days per year, twice as many as they had a century earlier (U.S. Department of Education, 2004a).

One result of this increase in school attendance was a decline in the illiteracy rate from 20% of all persons over 10 years of age in 1870 to 7.7% in 1910 (Graham, 1974). However, illiteracy rates varied by segment of the population. As a result of the pre–Civil War prohibition on teaching blacks in most southern states and inadequate education after the war, blacks had the highest illiteracy rate: 30.4% in 1910. The illiteracy rate was also high among the older population, which had not been the beneficiary of universal, compulsory education. Whites who were the children of a foreign-born parent had the lowest illiteracy rate, 1.1%. Literacy rates also varied by region. The South, which not only had the highest population of blacks but also had been the slowest in developing systems of common schools, had the highest illiteracy rate (Graham, 1974).

The Committee of Ten

As previously noted, in its origins the high school had been viewed as a provider of a more practical education. The need to assimilate the children of the new immigrants, and the more technical demands of industry, placed additional pressures on the schools to include a curriculum that could be immediately useful and that included vocational training

(Graham, 1974). However, some educators did not share this esteem for the "practical curriculum." In 1892, in an effort to standardize the curriculum, the National Education Association established the Committee of Ten. The committee was chaired by Charles Eliot, the president of Harvard University, and was largely composed of representatives of higher education. The committee recommended an early introduction to the basic subjects and uniform subject matter and instruction for both college-bound and terminal students, with few electives. In addition, although four curricula were recommended (classical, Latin-scientific, modern language, and English), the entire curriculum was dominated by college-preparatory courses. Using the psychology of mental discipline as a theoretical rationale, the committee claimed that the recommended subjects would be used profitably by both college-bound and terminal students because they trained the powers of observation, memory, expression, and reasoning (Gutek, 1991). Vocational training, they believed, should come after high school. The committee also recommended that each course meet four or five times weekly for 1 year, for which the student would receive a **Carnegie unit.**

The Seven Cardinal Principles of Secondary Education

For Your Reflection and Analysis

Of the seven cardinal principles, which ones have the most relevance today?
To submit your response online, go to http://www.prenhall.com/webb.

CW

The view of the Committee of Ten was immediately challenged by many educators, and within 25 years there was little support for its position. In 1918 the National Education Association appointed another committee, the Commission on the Reorganization of Secondary Education (CRSE), to review the curriculum and organization of secondary education in light of the many changes that had swept American society. Unlike the Committee of Ten, which was made up almost exclusively of university representatives, the majority of the members on the CRSE represented elementary and secondary schools. The commission issued its seven *Cardinal Principles of Secondary Education,* which identified what should be the objectives of the high school curriculum: (1) health, (2) command of fundamental academic skills, (3) worthy home membership, (4) vocational preparation, (5) citizenship, (6) worthwhile use of leisure time, and (7) ethical character. Compared with the recommendations of the Committee of Ten, only one of these seven principles, command of fundamental processes, was concerned with college preparation; and unlike the Committee of Ten report, which focused on goals outside the curriculum, the curriculum was seen as the instrument through which students would achieve the goals.

The cardinal principles received wide agreement and represented significant revision of the curriculum philosophy of the high school. After a decade of debate over whether secondary education in the United States should follow the European model of dual systems (academic and vocational/industrial) or a unitary, "democratic" system, the *Cardinal Principles* provided the blueprint for the American comprehensive high school and its distinguishing feature—academic and vocational studies under the same roof (Wraga, 2000).

By the mid-1920s four basic patterns of curricular organization were in evidence in the comprehensive high school: (1) the college preparatory program, which included courses in English language and literature, foreign languages, mathematics, the natural and physical sciences, and history and social sciences; (2) the commercial or business program, which offered courses in bookkeeping, shorthand, and typing; (3) the industrial, vocational, home economics, and agricultural programs; and (4) a modified academic program for students who planned to terminate their formal education on high school completion. The typical high school program was 4 years and was attended by students ages 14 to 18. Exceptions were the 6-year combined junior-senior high schools (Gutek, 1991).

The Junior High School

The 2-year and 3-year **junior high schools** that began to appear in some urban districts, offering grades 6 and 7 or grades 6 through 8, were an outgrowth of the Committee of Ten's recommendation that academic work begin earlier and that elementary schooling be reduced from 8 to 6 years. Their growth was also encouraged by the work of G. Stanley Hall, who wrote the first book on adolescent development and emphasized the developmental differences between childhood and preadolescence that would justify a reorganization of the 8–4 system (8 years of elementary school and 4 years of high school). The concept appealed to a group of reformers who were concerned about attrition and preparing students for the world of work. They felt the junior high school would prevent dropping out and would provide students the opportunity to explore their vocational interests or even receive vocational training before high school.

The first junior high school was established in Columbus, Ohio, and another followed the next year in Berkeley, California. Other cities followed suit, but it was not until after World War II and a rapid growth in enrollments and new school construction that school reorganization driven by overcrowding and space availability brought an end to the dominance of the 8–4 pattern and cemented this rung of the U.S. educational system ladder.

Developments in Higher Education

As discussed in the preceding chapter, nine colleges were founded during the colonial period. In the period following the Revolutionary War, the same nationalistic, democratic spirit that gave rise to the common school also produced an increase in public institutions of higher education. The increase was also spurred by people moving westward who wanted colleges close at hand as well as some denominations choosing to establish their own colleges rather than have their members educated at colleges operated by other denominations. Thus, of the colleges founded before 1860, fewer than 10% were state institutions.

By and large, the colleges were very small. For example, it was not until after the Civil War that Harvard had a graduating class of 100. During the late colonial and early national periods, the curriculum of the colleges became more "liberal," but it retained its heavy classical overlay and its emphasis on religion.

The first state institutions of higher education were established in the South: the University of Georgia in 1785, the University of North Carolina in 1789, the University of Tennessee in 1794, and the University of South Carolina in 1801. In the second quarter of the 19th century, the same nationalistic, democratic spirit that gave rise to the common school also produced an increase in public institutions of higher education. These appeared primarily in the Midwest: Indiana University in 1820, the University of Michigan in 1837, and the University of Wisconsin in 1848.

In both public and private institutions, lecture and recitation remained the most common modes of instruction, and discipline remained strict. Also, although the curriculum of public institutions gave more emphasis to the sciences and modern languages than the curriculum in the denominational institutions, over growing objection, the classical curriculum remained dominant in both public and private institutions of higher education in the early national period. The classical curriculum was supported by the *Yale Report* of 1828, a report by Yale scholars which argued that the classical curriculum helped develop mental discipline and proper character and provided the best preparation for professional study.

The Dartmouth College Case

In 1816 the New Hampshire legislature, dominated by the liberal Jeffersonian Republicans and concerned by what appeared to be the antiliberal sentiments of the board of trustees, enacted legislation to convert Dartmouth College from a private to a state institution. In the *Dartmouth College* case (1819), the U.S. Supreme Court upheld the original contract from the king of England that had given private status to the college. The case was important not only in affirming the constitutional principle that the state could not impair contracts, but to provide a strong foundation for the system of private colleges secure from government control that we have today.

The Morrill Acts and the Establishment of Land-Grant Institutions

By the mid-19th century, there was growing recognition among farmers and laborers of the importance of an education to improving their social and economic status. Because these groups found the majority of existing colleges unresponsive and irrelevant to their needs, they urged the establishment of a new institution, the industrial college. In

For Your Reflection and Analysis

Did you attend a junior high school? If so, what educational experiences do you recall that reinforce the positive value of the junior high school over other organizational plans? *To submit your response online, go to http://www. prenhall.com/webb.*

CW

response, the first Morrill Act was passed by Congress and signed by President Lincoln in 1862. The act granted 30,000 acres of land to each state for each senator and representative it had in Congress based on the 1860 census. The act specified that the income from the land was to be used to support at least one college that would "teach such branches of learning as are related to agriculture and mechanical arts, . . . in order to promote the liberal and practical education of the industrial classes in the several pursuits and professions of life."

A Second Morrill Act of 1890 provided for direct annual grants of $15,000 (increasing annually to $25,000) to each state for the support of land-grant colleges. The bill also provided that no grant would be given to any state that denied admission to its land-grant colleges because of race without providing "separate but equal" institutions.

As a result of the Morrill Acts, 65 new land-grant colleges were established. Among the first of the new institutions of higher education were the universities of Maine (1865), Illinois and West Virginia (1867), California (1868), Purdue and Nebraska (1869), Ohio State (1870), and Arkansas and Texas A&M (1871). Seventeen states, mostly in the South, also established separate land-grant colleges for blacks under the provisions of the Second Morrill Act. Together, the Morrill Acts provided the incentive for both a shift to a new type of curriculum and for greatly expanded state systems of higher education.

Higher Education for Women

Significant developments were also being made in the higher education of women during this period. As discussed earlier, a number of women's seminaries or colleges had been opened prior to the Civil War. A few coeducational colleges also existed before the Civil War (e.g., Oberlin, 1833; Antioch, 1853; and the State University of Iowa, 1858). However, only 3,000 women in the entire nation were attending colleges or universities that offered A.B. degrees (Newcomer, 1959). It was not until the Civil War that women's higher education really began to flourish. Several women's colleges (e.g., Vassar, 1861; Wellesley, 1875; Smith, 1875; Radcliffe, 1879; and Bryn Mawr, 1880) were established that offered pro-

After the Civil War, women increasingly sought higher education.

grams comparable to those found in the colleges for men. In addition, perhaps in part because of the impact of the Civil War casualties on enrollments and finances, an increasing number of formerly all-male institutions began admitting women, albeit selectively. By 1880 almost one-half of the colleges and universities admitted women (Pulliam & Van Patten, 2003). However, although a wide curriculum was open to women, severe restrictions were placed on their access to facilities, libraries, and lectures. In the end, teaching remained the most accessible and socially acceptable career option for women.

The Emergence of the Modern University

Some historians have called the period between the end of the Civil War and the beginning of the 20th century the "Age of the University." During this period more than 200 new colleges were established in the United States. Not only did the number of institutions of higher education grow, so did their role. Many of the new institutions, as well as many of the older institutions, bore the name *university*. In contrast to the small, single-purpose, largely undergraduate colleges, the emerging universities were large and multi-purpose with graduate departments and they emphasized research, influenced by the German universities where many of their faculty had studied. By the end of the 19th century, the American university had come to look much as we know it today, with an undergraduate college of liberal arts and sciences, a graduate college, and various professional colleges.

Founding of Junior Colleges

The initiative for the establishment of **junior colleges** came in the late 19th century from a number of university presidents. Some viewed the first 2 years of higher education as more appropriate to secondary education. They wanted to free their faculty from what they considered secondary education responsibilities so that they could devote themselves more to research and graduate education. Others, such as President William Rainey Harper who had put a 2–2 plan (2 years under class, 2 years upper class) in place at the University of Chicago, felt the arrangement would meet the needs of those who could not afford to attend 4 years, as well as those who were not interested in research or were not academically qualified for it.

In 1901 the first free-standing public junior college was established, the Joliet (Illinois) Junior College. Although initially established to offer courses that would transfer to 4-year institutions, it soon began to offer terminal and vocational programs as well (Gutek, 1991). In 1907 California passed a law permitting school boards to offer high school graduates courses similar to those required during the first 2 years of college (Rippa, 1997). By the early 1920s, the concept of the junior college was well established. During the late 1920s, encouraged by the Smith-Hughes Act, which provided federal aid to vocational education, junior colleges developed more extensive vocational and technical education programs. In subsequent decades they not only expanded rapidly, but as their goal was expanded to include serving the broad-based needs of the community, they became transformed into today's community colleges (Gutek, 1991).

> ### For Your Reflection and Analysis
>
> Did you attend a community or junior college? Would you support the movement toward having all lower division education take place at these institutions?
>
> *To submit your response online, go to http://www. prenhall.com/webb.*
>
> CW

Education of Minorities

The progress of education in the United States has not been uniform across all regions, socioeconomic classes, or races. To many, the schoolhouse door was closed and the promise of equal educational opportunity an unrealized dream. Native Americans, Hispanic Americans, Asian Americans, and black Americans in particular have had to struggle to realize the promise of an equal education.

Education of Native Americans

The formal education of Native Americans was initiated by missionaries who equated education with Christianity and the virtues of civilized life. The Society for the Propagation of the Gospel and the Moravians were among the more active of the missionary groups.

Just as education for the white colonists was primarily for the purpose of training for the ministry, so too was it hoped that education would equip Native Americans to become missionaries to their people. However, the efforts of missionary or philanthropic groups were limited, and the town and grammar schools enrolled few Native Americans. Efforts to provide any higher education were even more limited. In 1653 a college was founded at Harvard to instruct Native American students in the same classical education received by whites. Dartmouth College was originally established for the education of Native Americans, but was soon dominated by the children of the white colonists.

The initial response of Native Americans to the formal, traditional education offered by the colonists was distrust and rejection. Benjamin Franklin quoted one Native-American leader as saying:

> Several of our young people were formerly brought up at the colleges of the Northern Provinces; they were instructed in all your Sciences; but, when they came back to us, they were bad Runners, ignorant of every means of living in the Woods, unable to bear either Cold or Hunger, knew neither how to build a Cabin, take a Deer, or kill an Enemy, spoke our Language imperfectly, were therefore neither fit for Hunters, Warriors, nor Counsellors; they were totally good for nothing. (cited in Kidwell & Swift, 1976, p. 335)

Treaties and Mission Schools.   During the first century of the new republic, much of the education of the Native Americans came about as a result of federal legislation or negotiated treaties. According to the terms of the treaties, 389 of which were signed with various tribes between 1778 and 1871, in return for relinquishing their land, Native Americans were given money payments, guarantees of the integrity of the land they retained, and promises of educational services (Kidwell & Swift, 1976). The predominant means by which the federal government met its obligation to provide educational services was through support of mission schools operated on the reservations by religious groups. The objective of the education was to assimilate Native Americans into American society. Most of the schools followed a program of studies known as the 50/50 curriculum: Half of the time was spent in the traditional common school academic subjects, as well as the religion of the sponsoring denomination, and the other half of the time in vocational and agricultural training for boys and domestic arts for girls. Native language and culture were excluded from the curriculum (Hale, 2002).

The mission school experience was not a positive one for most Indians or for the missionaries. The missionaries failed to recognize that Indians were intensely religious and were invested in preserving their religion and culture at all cost (DeJong, 1993). The federal government provided a little money but no standards. The net result of 100 years of effort and hundreds of thousands of dollars was "a small number of poorly attended mission schools, a suspicious and disillusioned Indian population, and a few hundred alumni who for the most part were considered outcasts by whites and Indians alike" (DeJong, 1993, p. 59). In 1917 this arrangement, which in effect constituted government support of sectarian education, ended (Butts, 1978).

Boarding Schools.   After the Civil War the **assimilation** approach became popular. As discussed in Chapter 8, this approach advocated the immersion of Native Americans into the predominant white culture and was established on the belief that the most lasting and efficient way to advance this assimilation was to remove Native American children from their tribal setting and subject them, in a strict disciplinary setting, to an infusion of American values, language, and customs.

The first major boarding school was established in 1879 at Carlisle, Pennsylvania, by General Richard Pratt. At the boarding school students were given new names and forbidden to speak in their native tongue. Vocational and industrial training were emphasized at this and other off-reservation boarding schools. By the turn of the century, 25 off-reservation boarding schools had been established (Szasz, 1977). However, they were subject to much criticism. The physical and living conditions were often inadequate and the discipline strict and harsh. Disease and death were common. The dropout rate was high. Students often returned to the reservation rather than enter white society, and upon return to the reservation they found that they were unable to apply the training they had received or that it was irrelevant.

Class at Carlisle Indian boarding school, circa 1900.

Reservation Day Schools and Public Schools.   In the last quarter of the 19th century, in part as a response to the criticisms of the boarding schools, government schooling expanded rapidly in the form of Bureau of Indian Affairs (BIA)-operated day schools on the reservation. The reservation day schools offered several advantages over the off-reservation boarding school; not only were they less expensive, they were more acceptable to parents. Consequently, day schools increased in number after the turn of the 20th century.

Although Native Americans in the eastern United States who were not under the jurisdiction of the federal government had already been attending off-reservation public schools, a newer phenomenon was the public school located on the reservation. These schools initially had been built to accommodate the white people who rented land on the reservation. The on-reservation public schools tended to encourage not only assimilation but learning. As one Indian agent wrote, "Indian children progress much faster when thrown in contact with white children than they do when they are all kept together with whites excluded" (Szasz, 1977, p. 11).

The Meriam Report.   In 1924 Congress granted U.S. citizenship to all Native Americans. At the same time, the appalling living conditions and reprehensible treatment of Native Americans were brought to public view by a number of reformers determined to improve their plight. In response the BIA commissioned the Brookings Institution to conduct an independent study of Native American life in the United States. The Meriam Report, issued in 1928, documented the intolerable conditions of Native American life and noted that much of their poverty was caused by their loss of land. It also criticized the BIA educational program, exposing the inadequate industrial training, overcrowded dormitories, inadequate diet, and physical punishment in the boarding schools. The report discouraged the practice of boarding schools and encouraged the construction of day schools that could also serve as community centers. It accused the reservation system of creating isolation and concluded that the best way to improve the living standards of Native Americans was to educate them so they could be assimilated into white society (Kidwell & Swift, 1976).

The Meriam Report marked the beginning of a change in BIA policy. After 1928, BIA appropriations for education increased dramatically, efforts were made to deal with conditions in government schools, and curriculum reform was initiated. Soon a major share of

For Your Reflection and Analysis

How successful have been efforts to assimilate Native Americans into mainstream society?
To submit your response online, go to http://www.prenhall.com/webb.

CW

the BIA's budget was allocated to education, with the goal of assimilating Native Americans into mainstream society.

Education of Hispanic Americans

The story of the involvement of the United States in the education of Hispanics is largely to be told in relation to the Spanish-speaking peoples of the southwestern United States and begins with the acquisition of this territory from Mexico in 1848 at the end of the Mexican-American War. For the Mexicans who chose to remain in the territory after the U.S. takeover, or for those who fled across the border in the years that followed, life became marked by discrimination, prejudice, and segregation. The education provided Hispanic students, like that provided Native American students, was designed to promote, if not force, assimilation and deculturalization. Instruction in the segregated schools was in English and the use of Spanish was forbidden, even on the playground.

During the Depression years, many rural Mexican Americans moved to the cities, bringing their problems to a wider consciousness. Often they settled in poverty-ridden barrios. Until right after World War II the segregation of Hispanics was permitted in California and other states. Then, in 1944 Gonzalo Mendez moved his family to a farm he was to run for its Japanese owners who were in an interment camp. When the Westminster school district refused to enroll his children, he joined other parents in suing Westminster and three other school districts. In 1946 the U.S. district court rejected the school district argument that the segregation was not based on race but the need to provide special instruction to Hispanic children (a defense that had been successfully used by the Del Rio School District in Texas in 1930). In fact, the court said, the only special instruction these students needed was to learn English and this was actually impeded when they are segregated (*Mendez v. Westminster School District*, 1947). Accordingly, the court determined that segregation was illegal because it had no basis in state law or educational need. Although some, including the NAACP and its attorney, Thurgood Marshall, who had filed an *amicus curiae* brief in the case, were disappointed that the court did not overturn "separate but equal," the decision did have a broad impact. Encouraged by the decision, the segregation of Mexican Americans was challenged in the courts in other states and within 2 years *de jure* **segregation** had been overturned in Texas and Arizona. However, despite these and other court victories, the desegregation of Hispanic children was far from being achieved and equality of opportunity still an unrealized dream.

Education of Asian Americans

Asian immigration to the United States in any significant numbers did not occur until the mid-1850s when Chinese workers were recruited as cheap labor to work in the mines and railroads of the West. Throughout the 19th century and well into the 20th century, Asian Americans experienced much of the discrimination in the schools and the larger society as did other minorities. For example, from 1871 to 1885, by their deliberate exclusion from the state school law, Chinese children were excluded from the public schools in California. When the decision of the state supreme court in *Tape v. Hurley* (1885) forced a change in the law, most school boards responded by providing segregated, so-called Oriental schools. Typically, these facilities were inferior to the facilities attended by white students. Sometimes Asian Americans were allowed to attend white schools but were segregated in different rooms or on a different floor. In the classroom the special language needs of students were largely ignored as school systems attempted to force mastery of the English language and were reluctant to employ Asian American teachers or staff. The result was that many Asian American children experienced serious difficulties (Weinberg, 1997).

Following World War I the rigid policy of segregation began to break down as parents became more persistent and Chinese students were regularly admitted to public high schools. However, elementary schools remained highly segregated, in large part because of housing patterns and attendance zones. Even in the years after World War II when many middle-class Chinese moved out of segregated neighborhoods and into integrated neighborhoods, schools in the many ethnic neighborhoods (Chinatowns) remained basically segregated. Instruction in these schools was typically in English only, leading to the *Lau* case discussed in Chapter 7.

Education of Black Americans

Although blacks came to America before the Puritans—20 arrived at the Jamestown colony in 1619, not as slaves but as indentured servants—their educational history was anything but similar. The vast majority of blacks living in the United States during the first 300 years of its history lived in the South and, until after the Civil War, as slaves. On the eve of the Civil War, there were about 4 million black slaves and 500,000 free blacks out of a total U.S. population of 31 million.

Education of Slaves and Free Blacks Prior to the Civil War.   For the vast majority of slaves, education was virtually nonexistent. A few slave owners educated their slaves, and missionary or philanthropic groups such as the SPG provided limited and sporadic schooling. However, by the third decade of the 19th century, the rise of militant abolitionism and the fear of slave revolts if the slaves "got too high an opinion of themselves" had led to the enactment of the so-called Black Codes which, among other things, prohibited the education of slaves.

The education of free blacks was also was very limited. In the decades preceding the Civil War, as common school systems were developed in the North, blacks more often than not found themselves in segregated schools. An important legal support for this segregation (and also the legal basis for segregation for the remainder of the century) was provided by the Massachusetts Supreme Court decision in *Roberts v. City of Boston* (1850), which said that separate-but-equal schools did not violate the rights of black children.

Despite the difficulties, some free blacks did obtain an education. In some communities the children of freed slaves attended public schools or the private schools established by various religious, philanthropic, or abolitionist societies. The outbreak of the Civil War in 1861 found about 4,000 blacks in schools in the slave states and 23,000 in the free states (West, 1972). A few blacks even obtained a higher education. A small number went abroad to England or Scotland, a few attended the limited number of American colleges that admitted blacks (notably Oberlin in Ohio and Berea in Kentucky), and others attended one of the three black colleges established before 1860: Cheyney State College (1839) and Lincoln University (1854) in Pennsylvania and Wilberforce University (1856) in Ohio.

Many of the free blacks who gained a higher education prior to 1860 did so under the auspices of the American Colonization Society, which was established in 1817 to send free blacks to the colony of Liberia in Africa, founded by the society in 1822. The education of the free blacks was undertaken to provide the doctors, lawyers, teachers, clergy, and civil servants needed by the colony. Although not all those educated by the society went to the colony, or if they went did not remain, enough did so as to provide the colony and the Republic of Liberia, established in 1847, with its leadership elite (Pifer, 1973).

Education During Reconstruction.   During the post–Civil War period known as Reconstruction (1865–1877) hundreds of teachers supported by various northern churches, missionary societies, and charitable **educational foundations** moved to the South to educate newly liberated blacks. The first of these educational foundations, established in 1867, was the Peabody Fund for the Advancement of Negro Education in the South. It later merged with the Slater Fund to support industrial education and teacher preparation. Among the others, the largest was the General Education Board set up by John D. Rockefeller in 1902 (Pifer, 1973; West, 1972).

Another major force affecting the education of blacks in the South during Reconstruction was the Freedmen's Bureau. The bureau was responsible for the establishment of some 3,000 schools, and by 1869 some 114,000 students were in attendance at these schools. (The Historical Note on page 152 gives an account of one teacher in a freedmen's school.) These schools followed the New England common school model in terms of their curriculum (reading, writing, grammar, geography, arithmetic, and music) and moral outlook (the importance of certain values and the responsibility of citizenship), but added a new dimension—industrial training. In the view of northern educators, industrial training would prepare blacks for the occupations they were considered most suited to perform in the South (Gutek, 1991).

For Your Reflection and Analysis

Why was assimilation a goal of Native American education but not of African American education?
To submit your response online, go to http://www.prenhall.com/webb.

CW

HISTORICAL NOTE

Zeal for Learning Among Freedmen, 1868

Dear Brethren and Sisters;

Since I last wrote I have commenced my school and have now been teaching just four weeks. Everything was finally arranged so that on Monday Nov. 30th I opened school with twenty-five scholars. Since then the number has been steadily increasing and now it numbers forty-two with a prospect of large additions after their great holiday Christmas week is past.

From all the accounts of Freedmen's schools which I had heard and read previous to coming here I expected to find them anxious to learn but after all, I confess I was unprepared for the amount of zeal manifested by most of them for an education. I can say as one did of old, "The half had not been told me." I am surprised each day by some new proof of their anxiety to learn. Nearly all ages, colors, conditions and capacities are represented in my school. Ages ranging from five to sixty-five; Colors from jet-black with tight curling hair to pale brunette with waving brown hair.

Some, a few of them could read quite readily in a second reader and many more knew the alphabet and were trying patiently to spell out short easy words, while by far the greater number could not distinguish a letter. I have had as many as nineteen in my alphabet class at one time but it is now reduced to four.

One old woman over sixty, after spending three weeks on the alphabet and finally conquering it, said she wanted to learn to spell Jesus first before spelling easy words for said she, "Pears like I can learn the rest easier if I get that blessed name learned first." So now she looks through the Bible for that name and has learned to distinguish it at sight from other words. The older members of the school are as quiet and orderly as I could desire but the children are not so very different from other children. They love mischief and play and the prevailing vice among them is deceit. But education has all the charm of novelty to them and they learn with astonishing rapidity. They come to school as well provided with books as children usually do.

Your Sister in Christ,
Pamelia A. Hand

Source: The Black American and Education (pp. 73–74) by Earle H. West. Copyright © 1972 by Merrill Publishing Company. Reprinted by permission.

To research and explore this topic further, go to the *Historical Note* module for this chapter of the Companion Website at **http://www.prenhall.com/webb.**

The Higher Education Debate: Booker T. Washington and W. E. B. DuBois. One of the first and most important institutions of higher education for blacks in the immediate post–Civil War period was the Hampton Normal and Agricultural Institute, founded in 1868 by General Samuel Chapman Armstrong, a representative of the Freedmen's Bureau. The Hampton Institute was founded for the education of blacks, but beginning in 1878 also admitted Native Americans. Industrial education was the basic mission of the Hampton Institute. Booker T. Washington (1856–1915) was one of the hundreds of young blacks who flocked to the few normal schools or colleges that admitted blacks. At Hampton, Washington developed the educational ideas that led to his establishment of the Tuskegee Institute in 1881. Washington emphasized the dignity of labor and, rather than an academic education, advocated a practical education that would provide blacks the marketable skills that would allow them to be self-sufficient.

Others, such as W. E. B. DuBois (1868–1963), the first black to earn a Ph.D. from Harvard, disagreed with Washington and what they considered a position of accommodation or compromise. They argued that such a position was wrong and that it undermined the achievement of civil and political equality for blacks to be given only one educational direction (industrial) and whites several. DuBois encouraged political activism and in 1909 joined a multiracial group of social activists in founding the National Association for the Advancement of Colored People.

Whether Washington's accommodation approach to civil rights or DuBois' militant approach hindered the movement, or whether any other approach would have made any dif-

For Your Reflection and Analysis

Do you consider Booker T. Washington a realist or an accommodationist? Explain.

To submit your response online, go to http://www.prenhall.com/webb.

ference, is open to conjecture. What is known is that by the time Washington began his work at Tuskegee, Reconstruction had not only begun to decline, but a backlash against blacks had begun. The education he advanced was perhaps the only one that would have been permitted and supported in the openly racist political and social climate that pervaded the South at the end of the 19th century.

Washington's efforts were successful: Ten years after its founding, Tuskegee had a faculty of 88 and a student body of 1,200, making it one of the largest institutions of higher education in the South. It is also significant to note that Tuskegee and, even more so, the Hampton Institute were important as centers for the training of black teachers. The traditional attention given to Tuskegee and Hampton as agricultural and industrial schools has obscured the fact they were founded and

Booker T. Washington and students at the Tuskegee Institute.

maintained primarily to train black teachers for the South. Indeed, between 1872 and 1890, 604 of Hampton's 723 graduates became teachers (Anderson, 1978). Many of these and Tuskegee's alumni were instrumental in not only establishing and teaching in the public schools, but in establishing normal schools in rural areas throughout the South.

In addition to Hampton and Tuskegee, several other distinguished black colleges and universities were established in the immediate post–Civil War years. These include Atlanta University, founded in 1865 by the American Baptist Mission Society; Howard University, chartered in 1868 by the Congregationalists; Fisk University, established in 1866 by the American Missionary Association; and Mehary Medical College, originally Walton College, founded in 1865 by the Methodist Episcopal Church. Somewhat later, as a result of the Second Morrill Act of 1890, black land-grant colleges were established in each of the southern and border states—17 in all (Pifer, 1973).

Segregated Public Schools.   Yet another factor changing the face of education in the South during the Reconstruction period was legislation leading to the establishment of tax-supported public or common school systems. Many freedmen recently elected to state legislatures were a force in this movement. Many of these black legislators as well as some white legislators advocated integration in the newly established schools. In fact, many of the state statutes or constitutional provisions established the schools without making reference to either integration or segregation. However, none of the southern states actually instituted an integrated system, and the segregation that began as custom became law in all the southern states. Yet the efforts of the various groups and agencies did result in a dramatic reversal of the educational status of black Americans from a literacy rate estimated at 5% or 10% at the outbreak of the Civil War to one of 70% by 1910.

From the end of Reconstruction through the turn of the century, a system of racial segregation was established in the South that remained in effect until the desegregation movement of the 1950s and 1960s. The practice of segregation was sanctioned by the 1896 U.S. Supreme Court decision in *Plessy v. Ferguson,* which said that separate railroad cars did not violate the Constitution. But the "separate but equal" doctrine, while always producing separate, rarely produced equal. Nonetheless, after the 1870s the federal government effectively withdrew from the promotion of the civil and educational rights of blacks.

During this same period, ever-increasing numbers of white children from immigrant and lower socioeconomic families were entering the enlarged public school system; between 1880 and 1895 white enrollment in the public schools increased 106% compared to 59% for black enrollment (Fraizer, cited in Hare & Swift, 1976). The "rise of the poor whites" placed increased financial demands on public revenues and often resulted in funds being diverted from black schools to improve other schools (Gutek, 1991). To this was added the disenfranchisement of blacks by many southern states and the delegation of authority to local school boards to divide state education funds as they saw fit. From the court approval of segregation, the loss of political power, and the decreased financial support emerged the "separate but inferior" system that dominated so much of the South until well after the mid-20th century.

Teacher Education

The formal training of teachers in the United States did not begin until the 19th century. In colonial America, teachers at the elementary level were often young men who taught for only a short time before studying for the ministry or law. Given the strong relationship between church and education, more often than not they were chosen more for their religious orthodoxy than their educational qualifications. In fact, they were often viewed as assistant pastors and in addition to their teaching they were expected to perform various duties related to the functioning of the church. In many small communities, the minister himself was the schoolmaster.

Unfortunately, too often the "career teachers" were individuals who had been unsuccessful at other occupations or those whose personal character and civil conduct left something to be desired. It was also not uncommon in colonial America to find teachers who were indentured servants—persons who had sold their services for a period of years in exchange for passage to the New World. Perhaps the closest thing to any teacher preparation was that received by those individuals who entered teaching after serving as apprentices to schoolmasters. In fact, some historians refer to the apprenticeship training received by Quaker teachers as the first teacher education in America (Pulliam & Van Patten, 2003).

A distinction was made between teachers at the elementary level and those at the secondary level, not in the teacher training they received but in the higher status the secondary teachers held in society and the higher education they possessed. Teachers in the Latin grammar schools and academies typically were graduates of secondary schools and, not uncommonly, had received some college education, whereas those at the elementary level very often had little more than an elementary education themselves.

As noted in Chapter 1, most histories of education consider the Columbian School at Concord, Vermont, to be the first formal teacher training institution. However, a good argument can be made that the first such institution was actually the previously mentioned Troy Female Seminary opened by Emma Willard in 1821 (Spring, 2005). Willard established the seminary to train female teachers in both the subject areas and pedagogy. She also wrote a textbook on pedagogy, as did Catherine Beecher, the head of Mount Holyoke. Each graduate of the Troy Female Seminary received a signed certificate confirming her qualifications to teach. Long before the first state-supported normal schools in Massachusetts were opened by Horace Mann, the Troy Seminary had prepared 200 teachers for the common schools (Rippa, 1997). In fact, this and other academies were responsible not only for expanding educational opportunities for women but for preparing a large number of individuals for the teaching profession, and thus were strongly supported by Horace Mann.

Establishment of Normal Schools

The greatest force, however, in increasing the professional training of teachers was the establishment of normal schools. As we have seen, Horace Mann, Henry Barnard, Catherine Beecher, and others who worked for the establishment of common school systems recognized that the success of such systems was dependent on the preparation of a sufficient quantity of adequately trained teachers. This, in turn, demanded the establishment of institutions for the specific training of teachers, that is, normal schools. These educational leaders also believed that the teaching force for the common schools should be female, not only because women supposedly made better teachers at the elementary level but because they were less expensive to hire. The fact that at least the latter was true is shown in Table 6.2, which compares the salaries of men and women teachers from 1841 to 1864, as well as the salaries of teachers in rural areas with those in cities.

Table 6.2 — Average Weekly Salaries of Teachers, 1841–1864

Year	Rural		City	
	Men	Women	Men	Women
1841	$4.15	$2.51	$11.93	$4.44
1845	3.87	2.48	12.21	4.09
1850	4.25	2.89	13.37	4.71
1855	5.77	3.65	16.80	5.79
1860	6.28	4.12	18.56	6.99
1864	7.86	4.92	20.78	7.67

Source: From *The American School, 1642–1985: Varieties of Historical Interpretation of the Foundations and Development of American Education* by Joel Spring. Copyright © 1986 by Longman Publishing Group. Reprinted with permission of McGraw-Hill, Inc.

The growing enrollments in the common schools also created a growing demand for teachers. The response in one state after another was the establishment of normal schools. The New York State Normal School at Albany, the next established (1844) after those in Massachusetts, was headed by David P. Page. His book, *Theory and Practice of Teaching or the Motives and Methods of Good School Keeping,* published in 1847, became the standard text in teacher education. In addition to state-supported schools, to meet the ever-increasing demand for teachers in urban areas, a number of larger cities operated normal schools. These normal schools typically had higher entrance requirements than the state or private schools (generally the completion of 2 or 3 years of high school) and also provided the opportunity for much more observation and practice experience. In most instances they were authorized to issue teaching certificates (Augus & Mirel, 2000). By 1865 more than 50 normal schools were in operation and by 1900 a reported 350 normal schools were operating in 45 states.

Admission to most normal schools required only an elementary education and was free to residents of the state. The course of study lasted 1 or 2 years and included a review of material to be taught in the elementary school, instruction in methods of teaching, "mental philosophy" (i.e., educational psychology), and classroom management. Overriding the curriculum was a concern for the development of moral character. A prominent feature of the normal school was the model school, the forerunner of the laboratory school, where students could practice teaching.

Teacher Institutes

Despite the spread of normal schools, as late as 1900 only a bare majority of teachers had attended normal schools. Before this time, the most important institution in the training of teachers was the **teacher institute.** A common practice of school districts was to hire individuals with no formal training, with the condition that their continued employment depended on attendance at a teacher institute. The typical institute met once or twice a year and lasted from several days to 4 weeks, usually in the summer months. In less populous areas the institutes were often conducted by the county superintendent of schools. Some were offered in connection with institutions of higher education. The primary purpose of many institutes was to provide a brief course in the theory and practice of teaching, with great emphasis placed on elevating the moral character of the teacher (Spring, 2005). At some institutes, teachers were inspired by noted educators, instructed in new techniques, and informed of the most modern material (Binder, 1974).

Normal School Curriculum and Standards Strengthened

Toward the end of the 19th century, the character of the normal school began to change. The growing population had not only created an increased demand for elementary or common school teachers, but the secondary school movement created a concomitant demand for secondary school teachers. To meet this demand, normal schools began to broaden

For Your Reflection and Analysis

Are you attending or have you attended an institution that began as a normal school? What influence has this history had on the institutional climate?

To submit your response online, go to http://www.prenhall.com/webb.

CW

PROFESSIONAL REFLECTION

Education is an ever evolving pursuit. In the quote at the beginning of the chapter, Santayana is discussing the impact of things that have been on things that are yet to come. In education, many theories are presented and tested, but an educator must remember the successes and failures to be effective. Remembering the techniques that helped a child to learn and those that never worked are what ultimately create effective instruction. As new brain studies develop and new insights into learning are gained, it is still important to remember the successes achieved *without* the new knowledge. If we do not remember the components of Maslow's hierarchy of needs or Piaget and Dr. Maria Montessori's insights, we are destined to teach rote facts and routines without the capability of critical and divergent thinking developing. If we forget the foundations of education that were constructed by former educators, famous and not, then we are creating a society that cannot educate itself beyond what we teach them. We are creating a society with no inventors or musicians or artists or scientists.

If you think of the teachers who most inspired you to think and grow and learn and strive for more than you thought you could be, you will realize that being an expert in the curriculum or master of the current "buzz" in the field of education was not what made them so inspiring. It was knowing where to meet the needs of their students and believing that they could achieve. Now remember the teacher whose class you could not wait to leave or even dreaded attending and think of the things that made that teacher so different from the one you remember with fondness and respect. If you do not remember which teacher you want to be, you will become the one you do not want to be. Your history impacts a child's tomorrow.

Sandra L. Bixby
National Board Certified Teacher,
Maryland

To analyze this reflection, go to the *Professional Reflection* module for this chapter of the Companion Website at **http://www.prenhall.com/webb.**

their curriculum to include the training of secondary school teachers. At the same time, they began to require high school completion for admission. The passage of teacher certification statutes that specified the amount and type of training required of teachers contributed to the expansion of the normal school program from 2 to 3 years, and eventually, during the 1920s, to 4 years. By this time normal schools were beginning to call themselves state teachers' colleges. In time, with the broadening of the curriculum to embrace many of the liberal arts, the "teacher" designation was dropped and most became simply "state colleges." Some of these former normal schools have become the largest and most respected universities in the United States.

Universities Enter Teacher Training

During the late 19th century, the universities became increasingly involved in teacher education. Teacher training at the college or university level had been offered at a limited number of institutions as early as the 1830s, but it was not until toward the end of the 19th century that universities entered the field of teacher preparation to any measurable extent. Their involvement stemmed in part from the increased demand for secondary school teachers. The universities had always been institutions for the education of those who taught in the grammar schools, academies, and high schools. However, they prepared these students not as teachers per se, but as individuals who had advanced knowledge of certain subject matter. The increased demand for secondary school teachers, the late entrance of the normal schools into the training of secondary school teachers, and the growing recognition that the professionalization of teaching demanded study of its theory and practice led to the increased involvement of universities in teacher education. The University of Iowa established the first chair of education in 1873; other midwestern universities followed, and in 1892 the New York College for the Training of Teachers (Teachers College) became a part of Columbia University. After the turn of the century, teacher training departments became commonplace in most universities.

Summary

The Founding Fathers recognized the importance of education to the development of the new nation. As the nation marched through the 19th century and became an industrial giant, the demand for skilled workers and the demand of the working class, who saw education as a path to success, combined to expand the offering of publicly supported education through the secondary school. The growth of higher education can also be attributed to these forces. Indeed, today it is the recognition of education's importance to our national prominence and its vital role in assuring our continued economic prosperity that has served as the motivation for much of the current activity to reform our nation's schools.

Unfortunately, although the educational opportunities afforded much of the population were greatly expanded in the 19th century, the history of the education of minorities was basically one of neglect and segregation. It would not be until the third quarter of the 20th century that any marked progress would be made in improving the education of Native Americans, Asian Americans, Hispanic Americans, and Black Americans. In the next chapter, many of these efforts will be detailed, as well as those designed to improve the professional training of teachers.

Key Terms

Assimilation, 148

Carnegie unit, 144

Common school, 136

Comprehensive high
  school, 141

De jure segregation, 150

Educational foundations, 151

Infant school, 134

Junior college, 147

Junior high school, 144

Lyceum, 138

Monitorial schools, 133

Normal school, 139

Rate bill, 140

Secondary school, 141

Sunday school, 134

Teacher institute, 155

PROFESSIONAL DEVELOPMENT WORKSHOP

Prepare for the Praxis™ Examination

Terry Wosinski, a second-year social studies teacher at Daniel Webster Junior High School, has become increasingly concerned about the conduct of one student in his third period history class who is having a negative effect on the entire class. Terry is worried that he is on the verge of either "losing his cool" or losing control of the class. At issue is the inappropriate and aggressive behavior of a large 13-year-old boy named Forrest. Forrest consistently gets out of his seat and on his way to pick up a dropped pen, sharpen a pencil, or put something in the trash will poke someone on the arm, thump them on the head, or in some other way make physical contact—not enough to really harm, but enough to disrupt and annoy. When he is seated he talks to or at students around him. Forrest rarely completes an assignment, but when he does his work, it is well above average.

Terry has tried to get to know Forrest better to see if there is anything happening outside the school that would be contributing to his behavior, but Forrest has been reluctant to share anything about his home or family situation. Terry repeatedly and sternly tells Forrest to stay in his seat and to not do whatever inappropriate thing he is doing. He has also made Forrest stay after school for detention on numerous occasions but after a day or two at best Forrest resumes his misbehaviors. Terry is reluctant to go to Neil Jones, the assistant principal, for advice or intervention because he does not want to be seen as not being able to manage his class.

1. Describe behavioral theories of classroom management that might be used to manage Forrest's behavior.

2. Explain the importance of clear expectations and consistency in administering consequences to classroom management.
3. Give examples of several desist behaviors that Terry might use to deal with Forrest's physical and verbal misbehaviors.

To submit your responses online, go to the *Prepare for the Praxis™ Examination* module for this chapter of the Companion Website at **http://www.prenhall.com/webb**.

Build Your Knowledge Base

1. In what ways do Henry Barnard's concerns in the opening of the chapter echo the concerns regarding teacher education expressed in the media today?
2. In what ways were Thomas Jefferson's plans for an educational system elitist? Egalitarian?
3. What was the significance of each of the following to expanding educational opportunities in the United States?
   a. Monitorial schools
   b. Sunday schools
   c. Infant schools
   d. Free school societies
4. Describe the contributions of Horace Mann and Henry Barnard to the common school movement.
5. What influence did Prussian educators have on American education in the early 19th century?
6. Describe the impact of the Second Morrill Act on the provision of education for minorities in the United States.
7. What impact has the historical neglect of the education of minorities had on their education and on the educational system today?
8. What was the contribution of Emma Willard to women's education? To teacher education?
9. Compare the role of the university with that of the normal school in the education of teachers.

Develop Your Portfolio

1. We gain much insight about contemporary education through our reading of the history of education. Read an article from the professional education literature for the period from 1850 to 1890, and an article on the same or a similar topic in a recent journal (2000 or later). Prepare an artifact that compares and contrasts the educational concepts, methodologies, and general ideas presented in both journals. Place your artifact in your portfolio under **INTASC Standard 1, Knowledge of Subject.**
2. In 1918 the National Education Association appointed a Commission on the Reorganization of Secondary Education. The commission issued seven cardinal principles of secondary education which identified what should be the objectives of high school curriculum: (1) health, (2) command of fundamental academic skills, (3) worthy home membership, (4) vocational preparation, (5) citizenship, (6) worthwhile use of leisure time, and (7) ethical character. Reexamine the educational theory of social reconstructionism, particularly the contributions of critical theory as presented in Chapter 4. Prepare a table that lists each cardinal principle in the left column and summarizes how a critical theorist might react to it in the right column. Place your artifact in your portfolio under **INTASC Standard 4, Instructional Strategies.**

To complete these activities online, go to the *Develop Your Portfolio* module for this chapter of the Companion Website at **http://www.prenhall.com/webb**.

Explore Teaching and Learning: Field Experiences

1. Arrange interviews with key local citizens and review historical information so that you can write a 3- to 5-page history of the organization and development of the school district from which you graduated, a local district, or one in which you might teach.
2. Identify two to three colleges and universities in your community. Contact the institutions for information, and trace their development from their original sponsor, mission, and source of funds to their current status. Indicate the kinds of changes that have taken place.

Professional Development Online

Visit this text's Companion Website at **http://www.prenhall.com/webb** to gain access to a variety of questions, activities, and exercises to help build your knowledge of this chapter's content. Below are just a few items on this text's Companion Website:

- Classroom Video—To see actual classroom footage and work through activities and questions to analyze the content of the video, click on the *Classroom Video* module for this chapter.
- Teaching Tolerance—To go to this organization's website and complete activities to explore issues and topics dealing with how to teach tolerance to students, click on the *Teaching Tolerance* module for this chapter.
- Self-Test—To review terms and concepts presented in this chapter, click on the *Self-Test* module for this chapter.
- Internet Resources—To link to websites related to topics in this chapter, go to the *Internet Resources* module for this chapter.

Human history becomes more and more a race between education and catastrophe.
—H. G. Wells. *The Outline of History* (1920)

MODERN AMERICAN EDUCATION: FROM THE PROGRESSIVE MOVEMENT TO THE PRESENT

In the 1930s, faculty and students at Oglethorpe University created a "time room" where artifacts from the history of civilization were preserved in their original form, on film and paper. Film footage was also included that presented a verbal and visual condensed version of significant events in the history of the world up to that time.

Suppose you and your classmates were requested to create a time room on the history of American education. What artifacts would you include in your room? If you made a video chronicle of education, what would it include?

As you may have discovered in answering the preceding questions, capturing the most noteworthy happenings from a period of time, whether in a capsule, a room, or a chapter, is a challenge. The challenge becomes greater the more rapidly changing the times and the more diverse the areas to be included.

In this chapter, discussion of the history of American education begun in Chapters 5 and 6 is brought to the present. Although from a historical perspective this period encompasses a relatively short amount of time, it has witnessed the most rapid expansion of education in our nation's history and some of the most marked changes. So much has taken place that this text cannot focus in detail on every contributing personality or intervening variable. Consider the following objectives as you study this chapter:

- Identify the major economic, political, and social forces affecting education in the 20th century.
- Describe the progressive education movement in the United States.
- Compare the impact of the Great Depression, World War II, and the Cold War on education.
- Evaluate the progress of the Civil Rights movement and the War on Poverty.
- Outline the developments in education during the 1970s, 1980s, and 1990s.
- Trace the fluctuation of federal support for education in the 20th century.
- Describe the major provisions of the No Child Left Behind Act and their impact on the schools.

The Twentieth Century Unfolds
The People and the Nation Grow

The 20th century brought marked changes in American social, economic, political, and educational life. Population growth continued at a staggering rate: from 50 million in 1880, to 76 million in 1900, to 106 million in 1920. Although birthrates declined, improvements in medicine and sanitation led to lower infant mortality and a lower overall death rate. As in the last decades of the previous century, a significant portion of the population growth was the result of immigration. In the first two decades of the 20th century, the average number of immigrants arriving in this country doubled from the previous two decades, from an average of 450,000 immigrants per year to an average of almost 900,000 per year. Continuing with the trend that had begun in the last century, the majority of these "new" immigrants were from southern and eastern Europe—Italy, Poland, Russia, Austria-Hungary—and were primarily Catholic or Jewish. Concerns that the new immigrants were of an undesirable "racial stock" and tended to be illiterate, criminal, and "ill-fitted to the demands of a Teutonic civilization" led to demands in the popular media that immigration be restricted (Ravitch, 2000, p. 65).

At the same time that the population was experiencing rapid growth, it was becoming increasingly urban. According to the 1920 census, for the first time in our nation's history, the number of those living in towns of 2,500 or more (54.2 million) exceeded those living in rural areas (51.6 million). Much of the growth of the cities came from the new immigrants. The immigrants tended to congregate in crowded segregated neighborhoods in tenement houses. Living conditions in the slums and tenements in many of the major American cities equaled or exceeded the squalor, poverty, and unsanitary conditions of the European slums the immigrants had left behind.

America experienced growth not only at home but also on the international scene. In the last years of the 19th century and the beginning of the 20th century, the United States acquired Guam, the Philippines, Puerto Rico, Hawaii, the Virgin Islands, and the Panama Canal Zone. The nation also engaged in a war with Spain; landed troops in Mexico, Nicaragua, and Haiti; helped put down a revolt in China; and in 1917 entered the fight to "make the world safe for democracy."

Economic Growth

The economic growth of the United States during this period was even more profound than the population growth. Whereas the population increased less than fourfold in the post–Civil War to pre–World War I period, production increased tenfold (Gray & Peterson, 1974). This was a period of rapid growth for the railroads and other transportation and communication industries. The expansion of the railroads brought an end to the frontier and linked all parts of the nation, as did an ever-expanding network of telephone lines. At the same time, the trans-Atlantic cable and transworld shipping linked America with other nations. The expansion in the transportation industry opened up new markets for the growing agricultural and manufacturing industries. By 1920 the United States had become the largest manufacturing nation in the world.

Paradoxically, this period of stellar economic growth is also regarded as a dark chapter in American history because of the abuses in industry (Gray & Peterson, 1974). The business leaders who helped bring about the growth and contributed to the abuses have been referred to as "robber barons," and the business and political corruption of the era touched every aspect of American life. The plight of workers (including children) in factories, the unsafe and unsanitary working conditions, the horrors of industrial accidents, and descriptions of life in the poverty-ridden slums filled the tabloids and stirred political and social reforms.

Politics and Reform

Antitrust legislation was enacted in an attempt to control monopolies and their unfair business practices. The progressive movement that emerged at the turn of the century was responsible for a flood of labor legislation addressed at regulating the labor of women

For Your Reflection and Analysis

What are some of today's most pressing problems facing "new immigrants" to the United States?

To submit your response online, go to http://www.prenhall.com/webb.

CW

and children, wages and hours, and health and safety conditions. Workers also sought to improve their plight through labor unions. Increased union activity met with harsh resistance and persecution; violence and loss of life were not uncommon. Yet by 1920 one-fifth of all nonagricultural workers in the nation were organized, a considerable achievement in light of employer hostility (Kirkland, 1969).

In the political arena, the progressive movement gained momentum in the years after 1900. Decrying the excesses of big business, the progressives challenged the cherished ideal of limited government and urged the government to protect consumers against unfair monopolistic practices, workers (particularly women and children) against exploitation, and the less fortunate against any form of social injustice. Reform became the "order of the day" on the local, state, and national levels as progressives sought to wrest control of government from the business community and use it to bring about social change.

Changes in Education

Significant changes in the educational arena accompanied those in the social, economic, and political arenas. The urbanization of the population and the popularity of the automobile made possible the building of larger schools and contributed to the consolidation of rural school districts. The number of school districts in the United States gradually decreased from more than 130,000 at the turn of the 20th century to approximately 15,500 in 2000. State control of education increased in a number of areas: certification of teachers, requirements for teacher education programs, curricular requirements for the schools, standards for school facilities, and provisions for financial support.

At the same time, the size of the school population increased more rapidly than the overall population. In the three decades between 1890 and 1920 the school-age population increased 49% and school enrollments 70%. A significant portion of the increase in school enrollment, especially in the larger cities, came from the new immigrants or the children of new immigrants.

The growth in the student population was accompanied by an 80% growth in the number of teachers and other nonsupervisory personnel. During the same period, the average length of the school term increased by 27 days. More teachers and longer terms translated into significant increases in expenditures (see Table 7.1).

Progressivism in Education

The Beginnings of Progressive Education

The progressive reform movement, which had such a widespread impact on political, social, and economic life, also found expression in education. In the pre–World War I period, paralleling the call of the social and political reformers, education reformers called for curricular and administrative reforms. They also called for making the schools, particularly those in the cities, more sanitary, more open to air and sunlight, and more conducive to creative activity. They asked for lowered pupil–teacher ratios and added the provision of basic health care and food services to the responsibilities of the school. Progressivism also sought to improve the operational efficiency of school districts and rid them of political corruption.

Pedagogical progressivism traces its intellectual roots to Rousseau and its beginnings in America to Francis W. Parker (1837–1902), superintendent of schools in Quincy, Massachusetts, and later head of the Cook County Normal School in Chicago. Parker studied in Europe and became familiar with the work of Pestalozzi and Froebel. He shared their belief that learning should emanate from the interests and needs of the child and that the most appropriate curriculum was an activity-based one that encouraged children to express themselves freely and creatively.

The practice school of the Cook County Normal School was organized as a model democratic community. Art was an integral part of the curriculum, as were nature studies, field trips, and social activities. Rather than deal with multiple, discrete subject matter, the curriculum attempted to integrate subjects in a way that made it more meaningful to the learner. In all things Parker's aim was to make the child the center of the educational process.

For Your Reflection and Analysis

For a number of years the average length of the school term has been 180 days. Do you support efforts to extend the school year? Why or why not?

To submit your response online, go to http://www. prenhall.com/webb.

CW

Table 7.1 — Historical Summary of U.S. Public Elementary and Secondary School Statistics, 1870–1930 (all dollars unadjusted)

	1870	1880	1890	1900	1910	1920	1930
Enrollments							
Total school age (5–17 yrs.) population (thous.)	12,055	15,066	18,543	21,573	24,009	27,556	31,417
Total enrollment in elementary and secondary schools (thous.)	6,872	9,867	12,723	15,503	17,814	21,578	25,678
Percent of population aged 5–17 enrolled in public schools	57.0	65.5	68.6	71.9	74.2	78.3	81.7
(in private schools)	(NA)	(NA)	(9.5)	(6.4)	(5.2)	(4.9)	(7.8)
Attendance							
Average daily attendance (thous.)	4,077	6,144	8,154	10,633	12,827	16,150	21,265
Average length of school terms (in days)	132.2	130.3	134.7	144.3	157.5	161.9	172.7
Average number of days attended per pupil enrolled	78.4	81.1	86.3	99.0	113.0	121.2	143.0
Instructional staff							
Total classroom teachers/ nonsupervisory staff (thous.)	201	287	364	423	523	657	843
Men	78	123	126	127	110	93	140
Women	123	164	238	296	413	565	703
Average annual salary of instructional staff	$189	$195	$252	$325	$485	$871	$1,420
Finance							
Total revenue receipts (thous.)	(NA)	(NA)	$143,195	$219,766	$433,064	$970,120	$2,088,557
Percent of revenue receipts from:							
Federal government	(NA)	(NA)	(NA)	(NA)	(NA)	.3	.4
State government			18.2	17.3	15.0	16.5	16.9
Local government			67.8	67.7	72.1	83.5	82.7
Total expenditures per pupil in ADA	$16	$13	$17	$20	$33	$64	$108

Source: U.S. Department of Education, National Center for Education Statistics. (2005). *Digest of Education Statistics 2004* (Table 36). Washington, DC: U.S. Government Printing Office.

John Dewey

Among the parents of children at Parker's school in Chicago was John Dewey, professor of philosophy and pedagogy at the University of Chicago. Dewey was impressed with the philosophy and methods of the school and in 1896 established his own laboratory school at the University of Chicago. Through his many writings and articulation of his philosophy, Dewey provided the intellectual foundation for progressive education. In fact, Dewey was said to be "the real spokesman for intellectual America in the Progressive Era" (Bonner, 1963, p. 44).

Dewey's progressivist educational theories are discussed in Chapter 4. He rejected the old, rigid, **subject-centered curriculum** in favor of the **child-centered curriculum** in which learning came through experience, not rote memorization. The problem-solving method was the preferred approach, and motivation was at the center of the learning process. The goal of education was to promote individual growth and to prepare the child for full participation in a democratic society.

Dewey maintained that the child should be viewed as a total organism and that education is most effective when it considers not only the intellectual but also the social, emotional, and physical needs of the child. He thought that education was a lifelong process and that the school should be an integral part of community life, a concept that gave support to the development of the community school. Dewey wrote some 500 articles and 40 books. His influence was felt not only in philosophy and education, but also in law, political theory, and social reform. He left an imprint on American education that was unparalleled in the 20th century. His classic *Democracy and Education* (1916) provided perhaps the strongest statement of his educational theories and provided the rationale for a generation of educators who were part of what was to be known as the progressive education movement.

Ella Flagg Young

Ella Flagg Young, who is featured in the Historical Note on this page, was an important figure in the progressive education movement, both in her own right and through her influence on Dewey. Dewey acknowledged that he was constantly getting ideas from Young: "More times than I could say I didn't see the meaning or force of some favorite conception of my own until Mrs. Young had given it back to me . . . it was from her that I learned that freedom and respect for freedom mean regard for the inquiring and reflective processes of individuals" (McManis, 1916, p. 121). Like Dewey, Young proposed that teaching methods give fullest expression to the individual interests of the child, that education recognize the total experiences the child brings to the school, and that the "curriculum must provide the child with experience that builds on his or her natural interests and tendencies" (Webb & McCarthy, 1998, p. 231).

From her positions as principal of the Chicago Normal School, superintendent of Chicago schools, and president of the National Education Association, as well as through

For Your Reflection and Analysis

To what extent did your elementary school experience reflect the progressive child-centered philosophy?
To submit your response online, go to http://www.prenhall.com/webb.

CW

HISTORICAL NOTE

Ella Flagg Young, Pioneer School Administrator

Ella Flagg Young served as a teacher, principal, and area superintendent of schools before receiving her doctorate from the University of Chicago. From 1899 to 1904, she was a professor of pedagogy at the University of Chicago and a colleague of John Dewey, with whom she collaborated on several published works. She also served as supervisor of instruction at Dewey's laboratory school at the university. Dewey regarded Young as the "wisest person on school matters" with whom he had ever come in contact.

In 1905, Young became principal of the Chicago Normal School, and from 1907 to 1915 served as the superintendent of schools for Chicago, the first woman to head a large city school system. In 1910, she was elected president of the National Education Association, the first woman to hold this office.

Throughout her career, Young sought to improve the training and condition of teachers. She espoused

democratic administration and organized teachers' councils to provide teachers with a greater voice in decision making. She worked for higher teachers' salaries and once resigned as a superintendent because of the board of education's policies regarding teachers' organizations and salaries. At the outbreak of World War I, she became chairman of the Women's Liberty Loan Committee and, although over 70 years old, traveled throughout the country on its behalf. While on one trip, she became ill and died on October 18, 1918.

Young's capable administration of both the National Education Association and Chicago's schools was a victory for all women educators. She inspired many women to seek positions of leadership and led many men (and women) to reconsider the capabilities of women as administrators.

To research and explore this topic further, go to the *Historical Note* module for this chapter of the Companion Website at **http://www.prenhall.com/webb.**

her numerous presentations and publications, Young was able to play a visible and important role in education in the years leading up to World War I. She strove to bring greater democracy to education by providing teachers with a greater voice and by encouraging the extension of the principles of democracy to the classroom.

Progressive Education Association

The formation of the Progressive Education Association (PEA) in 1919 gave progressivism a vigorous organizational voice (Cremin, 1962). The association adopted seven guiding principles: (1) the child's freedom to develop naturally, (2) interest provides the motivation for all work, (3) the teacher as guide in the learning process, (4) the scientific study of pupil development, (5) greater attention to everything that affects the child's physical development, (6) cooperation between the school and home in meeting the natural interests and activities of the child, and (7) the progressive school should be a leader in educational movements (*Progressive Education*, 1924, pp. 1–2).

For Your Reflection and Analysis

What activity in your educational experience was the best example of creative self-expression? Was it intended as such by the teacher, or did it take place by accident? *To submit your response online, go to http://www.prenhall.com/webb.*

CW

The PEA published the journal *Progressive Education* from 1924 to 1955. In its early years, *Progressive Education* devoted considerable space to the concept of "creative self-expression." According to Harold Rugg, professor at Teachers College, Columbia University, and a leading spokesperson for the PEA, creative self-expression was the essence of the progressive education movement (Cremin, 1962).

Another well-known spokesperson for progressive education, William H. Kilpatrick, was also on the faculty at Teachers College. Kilpatrick translated Dewey's philosophy into a practical methodology, the **project method.** The project method was an attempt to make education as "lifelike" as possible. At the heart of the educative process was to be "wholehearted purposeful activity," activity consistent with the child's own goals. Kilpatrick shared Dewey's belief in the importance of problem solving, but went beyond Dewey in his child-centered emphasis and in his rejection of any organized subject matter (Cremin, 1962).

During the 1930s (1932–1940), the PEA conducted a study of almost 3,000 students from progressive and nonprogressive high schools regarding the schools' effectiveness in preparing graduates for college. The results of the study, *The Eight Year Study,* showed that students from progressive high schools not only achieved higher than students from traditional high schools but also were better adjusted socially.

Influence of the Progressive Movement on Higher Education

The influence of the progressive education movement was also felt in higher education. The great model of progressive higher education was the University of Wisconsin. The Wisconsin model was based on the idea that "the obligation of the university was to undertake leadership in the application of science to the improvement of the life of the citizenry in every domain" (Cremin, 1988, p. 246). This was accomplished through faculty research and service, the training of experts, and extended education.

College and university enrollments rose steadily during the pre–World War I years and then surged after the war, partly as a result of those who had come to higher education as part of the Student's Army Training Corps and then stayed after the war ended. Enrollments rose from almost 600,000 in 1919–20 to 1.1 million in 1929–30.

Most of these students were seeking a professional or technical education, primarily in education, business, and engineering, and enrolled not in the universities but in the growing number of junior colleges and the teacher education institutions. The number of junior colleges increased from 52 in 1920, to 277 in 1930, to 456 in 1940 (U.S. Bureau of the Census, 1975); the number of colleges for teachers grew from 45 in 1920 to four times that number by 1940 (Pulliam & Van Patten, 2003). The normal schools across the country were as typical of the progressive service orientation in higher education as the state universities: "they presumed to prepare scientifically trained experts; they extended their learning to all comers; and they prided themselves on their sensitivity to popular need" (Cremin, 1988, p. 248).

The Child Study Movement

During the first two decades of the 20th century, as the progressive movement was gaining momentum, two related movements were taking place that would have far-reaching consequences: the child study and measurement movements. The child study movement began with the pioneering work of G. Stanley Hall. Hall established a center for applied psychology at Johns Hopkins University in 1884, the year Dewey graduated from the same institution. Later, as president of Clark University, he brought together the first group of scholars interested in the scientific study of the child through the observation of children at various stages of development.

Hall and his colleagues recognized that emotional growth and personality development were just as important as cognitive development in understanding the child. They saw the child as an evolving organism and believed that once educators understood how the child developed, they would be better able to foster that development (Perkinson, 1977). These early efforts were important in laying the foundation for educational psychology and developmental psychology and for the recognition and inclusion of this discipline in teacher education. Child study, the stage theory of learning propounded by theorists such as Jean Piaget, the specialties of child, adolescent and developmental psychology, and the study of exceptional children can all trace their beginnings to Hall.

The Measurement Movement

Another cornerstone of educational psychology was laid by Lewis M. Terman, Edward L. Thorndike, and other psychologists involved in the development of the measurement movement. Although intelligence and aptitude tests had been in use for some time, the real breakthrough came when the French psychologists Alfred Binet and Theodore Simon developed an instrument based on an intelligence scale that allowed comparison of individual intelligence to a norm. Of the many adaptations of the Binet-Simon scale the most important for education was the so-called Stanford revision by Lewis Terman of Stanford University. It was also Terman who developed the **intelligence quotient (IQ),** a number indicating the level of an individual's mental development. Meanwhile, Thorndike and his students at Columbia developed scales for measuring achievement in arithmetic, spelling, reading, language, and other areas (Cremin, 1962).

World War I was a major factor in the growth of the measurement movement. The military needed a massive mobilization of manpower. It also needed a way to determine which men were suited for service and for what type of service. Out of this need, a number of group intelligence tests were developed and ultimately were administered to hundreds of thousands of recruits. One unexpected result of this massive testing was the discovery of a large number of young men with educational (as well as physical) deficiencies: approximately one-quarter of all recruits were judged illiterate. Deficiencies were particularly high among rural youth.

Within a decade of the end of the war, the measurement movement had become a permanent part of American education. According to Heffernan (1968), the "apparent objectivity of the test results had a fascination for school administrators and teachers. Certainty seemed somehow to attach to these mathematically expressed comparisons of pupil achievement" (p. 229). Throughout the country students were classified, assigned, and compared on the basis of tests results.

The testing of World War I recruits was a major step in the development of intelligence tests.

Often the tests were wisely used to diagnose learning difficulties and assess individual differences. Unfortunately, they were also used to make comparisons without consideration of differences in school populations, to make judgments about the quality of teaching, and, most distressing, to make subjective judgments about students' potential (Heffernan, 1968). Regrettably, these misuses of tests continue today.

Education During the Great Depression

The crash of the stock market in October 1929 ushered in the greatest depression our nation has ever experienced. The period was marked by the failure of banks and businesses, the closing of factories, mass unemployment, bread lines, soup kitchens, and tent cities. Unemployment was particularly high among minorities and young people. As many as 6 million young people were out of school and unemployed in 1933 to 1935. Many had no occupational training or experience. In a labor market overrun with experienced workers, they had few opportunities for employment (National Policies Commission, 1941).

For Your Reflection and Analysis

What were probably the greatest challenges faced by teachers during the Great Depression?

To submit your response online, go to http://www. prenhall.com/webb.

CW

The Great Depression also had a serious impact on the operation of schools. In many states, especially in the hard-pressed South and Southwest, schools were closed or the school year shortened. By the first quarter of 1934 an estimated 20,000 schools nationwide, including 85% of the public schools in Alabama, had closed, affecting more than 1 million pupils. Ten states were estimated to have schools with school terms of less than 3 months and 22 with terms of less than 6 months (National Education Association [NEA], 1933). As the Depression deepened, students were increasingly asked to bring their own supplies or, in extreme cases, to pay tuition. In school districts throughout America, the local school boards were unable to pay their teachers and issued them promissory notes agreeing to pay them when revenues were collected. And in almost every school district the number of teachers was reduced, class size increased, and the number of courses in the high school curriculum cut (Gutek, 1991).

Until the Great Depression, the relationship of the federal government to education was clear: Education was viewed as a function of the states and local school districts. These entities were responsible for operating educational programs. Beginning in 1933, with the creation of the Civilian Conservation Corps (CCC) and later the National Youth Administration (NYA), this established relationship changed markedly. The CCC and the NYA were two of the federal emergency agencies created under President Franklin D. Roosevelt's New Deal to provide "work relief" for the unemployed. The CCC provided temporary work for more than 2 million people 18 to 25 years of age on various conservation projects. The NYA administered two programs: (1) a work relief and employment program for needy, out-of-school youth ages 16 to 25 and (2) a program that provided part-time employment to needy high school and college students to help them continue their education. At its peak in 1939–40, approximately 750,000 students in 1,750 colleges and 28,000 secondary schools participated in NYA programs.

When it became clear to officials of both the CCC and the NYA that many participants lacked not only vocational skills but basic skills in reading, writing, and arithmetic, they moved to meet these needs by means of educational activities operated and controlled by the agencies themselves. Although both of these measures were terminated as the war economy stimulated employment, the fact that the federal government actually operated and controlled educational activities that could have been offered by state or local educational systems marked a departure from the past that was of concern to many educators, including the NEA (National Policies Commission, 1941).

Other New Deal programs provided relief to the financially depressed schools. The Public Works Administration (PWA) provided assistance for the building of numerous public buildings, including almost 13,000 schools. The Works Projects Administration (WPA, originally the Works Progress Administration) provided employment for 100,000 teachers in adult education, art education, and the 1,500 WPA-operated preschools. The WPA adult education program served as many as 4 million adults primarily in their own communities. Perhaps its most important program was the adult literacy program. Between 1933 and 1938, 1.5 millions adults were taught to read, about one-third of them black. In addition, under a program that became the forerunner of the National School Lunch Program, the Department of Agriculture distributed surplus foods to the schools.

Indian New Deal.   Several New Deal measures were directed at improving the plight of Native Americans and became known as the Indian New Deal. The Indian New Deal was an attempt to remedy the conditions described by the Meriam Report (see Chapter 6). Among the actions taken was the cessation of the sale of allotted Indian land, the organization of tribal councils as legal bodies, the investment of the Bureau of Indian Affairs (BIA) with the right to contract with states for educational services, and the ending of the boarding school system (although because of distance constraints, several off-reservation boarding schools still exist). The Johnson-O'Malley Act of 1934 provided supplemental funds to public schools to provide for the special costs associated with transportation, school lunches, or activities such as graduation (Kidwell & Swift, 1976).

Native American education was also the beneficiary of other programs of Roosevelt's New Deal—WPA, PWA, and CCC—because they provided job training, income, and improvements on the reservations, including construction of schools and roads and conservation of land, water, and timber. The total result of the New Deal was "the most dynamic program of Indian education in the history of the Indian Service" with a "curriculum more suited to the needs of the child; . . . community day schools and a decreased emphasis on boarding schools; and a better qualified faculty and staff" (Szasz, 1977, p. 48).

George S. Counts and Social Reconstructionism

The experience of the Depression had a significant impact on many progressive educators who came to believe that the schools had a responsibility to redress social injustices. At the 1932 convention of the PEA, in an address entitled "Dare Progressive Education Be Progressive?" George S. Counts challenged the child-centered doctrine and urged educators to focus less on the child and more on society, to "face squarely and courageously every social issue, come to grips with life in all its stark reality . . . develop a realistic and comprehensive theory of welfare, fashion a compelling and challenging vision of human destiny" (Perkinson, 1977, p. 205). In effect, Counts asked the schools to take the lead in planning for an intelligent reconstruction of society. Although the social reconstructionism movement never gained much of a foothold in American education, it served to associate progressive education in the minds of many people with "an economic radicalism that smacked of socialism and communism" and ultimately contributed to its growing unpopularity in the postwar years (Spring, 1976, p. 8).

Counts was joined in his deep concern about the socioeconomic conditions in America and his belief that educators should do something to address these conditions by liberal progressive educators such as William H. Kilpatrick and Harold Rugg. In 1935, these individuals joined with other social reformers to form the John Dewey Society for the Study of Education and Culture, and began publishing a journal, *The Social Frontier,* which became the focus of educational extremism during the 1930s. The position of Counts and his contemporaries was sharply criticized by many conservative progressives and was responsible for a deepening schism within the PEA.

William C. Bagley and the Essentialists

Although progressive education and innovations such as the community school and the project method were popular, protests against the child-centered ideal and its lack of emphasis on fundamentals gained momentum under another professor of education at Teachers College, William Bagley, and other educators associated with the educational theory of **essentialism** discussed in Chapter 4. Like Arthur Bestor in the 1950s and the reform reports in the 1980s, Bagley looked at American education and judged it weak, lacking in rigor, full of "frills," and inadequate in preparing youth for productive participation in society. The essentialists were also critical of the social reconstructionists and argued that instead of attempting to reconstruct society, educators would serve society better by preparing citizens who possessed the knowledge of the fundamental skills and subjects that provide a basis for understanding, and for the collective thought and judgment essential to the operation of our democratic institutions (Bagley, 1938).

For Your Reflection and Analysis

Would Bagley be supportive of the seven cardinal principles of education? Why or why not?
To submit your response online, go to http://www. prenhall.com/webb.

CW

The Influence of the Second World War

As the war with Nazi Germany spread in Europe, and American factories were increasingly called on to supply the Allied war effort, the American economy began to recover from the Depression. Once this country entered the war, every institution, including the schools, was dominated by the war effort (see Figure 7.1). According to a statement made by the NEA shortly after the Japanese attack on Pearl Harbor,

> When the schools closed on Friday, December 5, they had many purposes, and they followed many roads to achieve those purposes. When the schools opened on Monday, December 8, they had but one dominant purpose—complete, intelligent, and enthusiastic cooperation in the war effort. (Education Policies Commission, 1942, p. 3)

Impact on Schools.   The war had a heavy impact on the schools. Not only did large numbers of teachers leave the classroom for the battlefield, but enrollment also dropped significantly as youth chose not to return to school or to go to work. By the end of the war more than one-third of the teachers employed in 1940–1941 had left teaching (Kandel, 1948). High school enrollments declined from 6.7 million in 1941 to 5.5 million in 1944 (Knight, 1952). In addition, financial support, which was already low because of the Depression, was further reduced as funds were diverted from education to the war effort. Some assistance was provided by the Lanham Act of 1941 to school districts overburdened by an influx of children from families employed in defense industries or on military bases. The so-called impact aid continues today under the provisions of Public Laws 815 and 874.

Colleges and universities were also affected by the war. Enrollments declined sharply; the enrollment of civilian students was cut almost in half between 1940 and 1944. There was also a severe reduction in instructional staff and revenues. Institutional income in 1944 and 1945 was 67% of what it had been in 1940 (Knight, 1952). Income would have been reduced even more dramatically had it not been for the specialized training and large research projects commissioned by the federal government. These vast research enterprises transformed many universities into what Clark Kerr (1963) has termed "federal grant universities."

Colleges and universities also played a vital role in preparing men for military service, for war industries, and for essential civilian activities. By the end of 1943, 380,000 men were involved in specialized training in 489 colleges and universities, many as part of the Army Specialized Training Program or the Navy College Training Program (Knight, 1952).

For Your Reflection and Analysis

Which of the educational institutions (elementary–secondary or higher education) felt the most negative impact of World War II? Explain.
To submit your response online, go to http://www. prenhall.com/webb.

CW

For Your Reflection and Analysis

What is your position in the debate about the appropriateness of ROTC on college and university campuses?
To submit your response online, go to http://www. prenhall.com/webb.

CW

Figure 7.1 — A War Policy for American Schools, A Statement of the Educational Policies Commission of the National Education Association

The responsibilities of organized education for the successful outcome of the war involve at least the following activities:

- Training workers for war industries and services.
- Producing goods and services needed for the war.
- Conserving materials by prudent consumption and salvage.
- Helping to raise funds to finance the war.
- Increasing effective manpower by correcting educational deficiencies.
- Promoting health and physical efficiency.
- Protecting school children and property against attack.
- Protecting the ideals of democracy against war hazards.
- Teaching the issues, aims, and progress of war and the peace.
- Sustaining the morale of children and adults.
- Maintaining intelligent loyalty to American democracy.

Source: Educational Policies Commission. (1942). *A war policy for American schools.* Washington, DC: National Education Association. Reprinted by permission.

The Postwar Years

Toward the end of the war, in an effort to assist veterans whose schooling had been interrupted by military service, the Servicemen's Readjustment Act of 1944 was passed. The G.I. Bill of Rights, as it became known, provided benefits to 7.8 million veterans of World War II to help them further their education. The benefits were subsequently extended to veterans of the Korean, "Cold," and Vietnam wars; eventually almost 15 million veterans were involved. The G.I. Bill also initiated a great postwar popularization of higher education. More men and women representing a greater age range and varied social, economic, cultural, and racial groups attended colleges and universities than ever before (Cremin, 1988) (see Table 7.2).

While returning servicemen filled college and university classrooms, within a decade the postwar "baby boom" hit the public schools. Between 1946 and 1956, kindergarten and elementary school enrollments increased 37%, from 17.7 million to 24.3 million.

The Critics and the Decline of Progressive Education

One of the foremost critics of progressive education in the postwar years was Arthur Bestor. In his most famous critical study, *Educational Wastelands,* Bestor deplored the anti-intellectual quality of American schools, which he argued had been caused by progressive education. Bestor advocated a rigorous curriculum of well-defined subject-matter disciplines and the development of the intellect as the primary goal of education. Bestor later became one of the founders of the Council on Basic Education, an organization dedicated to the promotion of a basic academic curriculum. Two other leading critics of the contemporary educational scene were Robert Hutchins and Admiral Hyman Rickover, the father of the atomic submarine. Both Hutchins and Rickover advocated a return to a the classical liberal arts curriculum. Rickover also favored the multitrack, ability grouping of most European schools to the American comprehensive high school and focused his attention on the academically talented, who he believed were central to maintaining America's competitive edge with the Soviets.

Progressive education was also hurt by its identification with an educational program known as **life adjustment education.** Focusing on the youth who do not attend college, life adjustment education stressed functional objectives, such as vocation and health, and rejected traditional academic studies. Critics of progressive education found in life adjustment education a perfect target: "it continued an abundance of slogans, jargon, and various anti-intellectualism; it carried the utilitarianism and group conformism of latter-day progressivism to its ultimate trivialization" (Ravitch, 1983, p. 70).

However, in the end it was not its critics that killed progressive education. It died because it was no longer relevant to the time. The great debate about American education

Table 7.2 — Degree-Granting Institutions of Higher Education, Faculty, and Enrollments, 1919–20 to 2001–02

Year	Total Institutions	Total Faculty	Total Enrollment
1919–20	1,041	48,615	597,880
1929–30	1,409	82,386	1,110,737
1939–40	1,708	146,929	1,494,203
1949–50	1,851	245,722	2,659,021
1959–60	2,008	380,554	3,639,847
1969–70	2,525	450,000	8,004,660
1979–80	3,152	675,000	11,569,899
1989–90	3,535	824,220	13,538,560
1999–2000	4,084	1,027,830	14,791,224
2001–02	4,197	1,113,183	15,927,087

Source: U.S. Department of Education, National Center for Education Statistics. (2004). *Digest of Education Statistics 2003* (Table 17B) Washington, DC: U.S. Government Printing Office.

continued until 1957 when the Soviet Union launched *Sputnik,* the first space satellite. Then, in a nation suddenly concerned with intelligence and the need for increased science and mathematics skills, progressive education seemed out of step. By the time it disappeared in the mid-1950s, progressive education had strayed far from the "humane, pragmatic, open-minded" approach proposed by Dewey (Ravitch, 1983).

The Montessori Movement

Concerns about academic standards also contributed to a revival of an approach to early childhood education developed by the Italian physician and educator, Maria Montessori. Although Montessori's approach had been introduced in this country before World War I, it was not until the 1950s that a second and more widespread interest led to the establishment of hundreds of Montessori schools. Its resurgence in the 1950s was fueled in part by parents searching for more academically oriented early childhood programs than those found in most public schools. Its movement gained further attention in the 1960s as many Head Start programs adopted the Montessori approach (Gutek, 2001).

Although they were different in many ways, Montessori shared with Froebel a belief that "children possessed an interior spiritual force that stimulated their self-activity" (Gutek, 2001, p. 334). In keeping with this belief, the Montessori method emphasizes sensory training and the use of didactic materials, learning episodes, and physical exercises in a structured environment. Interest and motivation are at the heart of the method. Materials are intended to arouse the student's interest, and interest provides the motivation for learning. Instruction is highly individualized and is designed to develop self-discipline and self-confidence. The role of the Montessori teacher is to be aware of the child's readiness to learn, to make sure the child has the materials to learn, and to guide the child through experiences.

From *Sputnik* to the New Federalism

Few times in history has a single event had such an impact on education as the launching of *Sputnik* in October 1957. The event seemed to confirm the growing fear that the United States was losing the Cold War technological and military races with the Soviet Union because of a shortage of trained teachers, engineers, and students.

Curriculum Reforms

Reacting to public pressure, in 1958 the federal government passed the National Defense Education Act (NDEA). By directing significant federal funding to specific curricular areas, particularly mathematics, science, and modern foreign languages, the federal government for the first time attempted to influence the curriculum in general elementary and secondary education. The NDEA sponsored the efforts of academic specialists to revise the curriculum according to the latest theories and methods. Soon the "new math," "new chemistry," "new grammar," and other "new" revisions were being developed and introduced in the schools. Summer institutes were held to train teachers in the use of the new materials and methods. The NDEA also provided funding for science, mathematics, and foreign language laboratories; media and other instructional material; and improvement of guidance, counseling, and testing programs, especially those efforts directed at identification and encouragement of more capable students. Student loans and graduate fellowships were also funded under the NDEA.

The curriculum reforms initiated by the NDEA of 1958 and an expanded version of that act in 1964 were further stimulated by James Conant's widely publicized study of secondary education, *The American High School Today* (1959), which recommended increased rigor and an academic core of English, mathematics, science, and the social sciences. Underlying these curricular reforms was the learning theory of Jerome Bruner, which stressed the teaching of the structure of the disciplines (i.e., the major concepts and methods of inquiry of the discipline) and the stage concept of child development formulated by Jean Piaget (1970). According to Bruner (1966), some form of the structure of a discipline could be taught to students at each stage of their cognitive development. These theories provided the rationale for the **spiral curriculum** sequencing pattern, whereby subject matter is presented over a number of grades with increasing complexity and abstraction. His theories of the way children construct knowledge provided the theoretical framework for the constructivist theory discussed in Chapter 4.

The NDEA set the stage for the federal government's increased involvement in education. In the decade that followed, the federal government waged another war in which it became, for perhaps the first time in our nation's history, a major force in the educational arena. This war was the War on Poverty.

Education and the War on Poverty

In the early 1960s, large numbers of Americans became aware that at least one-quarter of the population had been bypassed by the postwar prosperity and lived in dire poverty. The results were rising crime rates, a decline in qualified manpower for military service, and a number of other social and economic problems. Books, reports, and high-impact media coverage such as Edward R. Murrow's documentary on migrant farm workers, "Harvest of Shame," brought a flood of interest in the elimination of poverty. As a result, the Democratic administrations of John F. Kennedy in 1963 and Lyndon B. Johnson in 1964 declared a War on Poverty. In an effort to win this "war," federal legislation was passed to subsidize low-income housing, improve health care, expand welfare services, provide job retraining, undertake regional planning in depressed areas such as Appalachia, and improve inner-city schools (Church & Sedlak, 1976).

Education was viewed as a major factor in the elimination of poverty. Poor children as well as those of certain minority groups, it was noted, consistently failed to achieve. In the optimistic view of many politicians, social scientists, and educators, the "cultural deprivation" (i.e., lack of middle-class attitudes and incomes) of the poor was attributable to a lack of education, and if the poor were provided the skills and education for employment, they could achieve middle-class economic and social status and break the "cycle of poverty" (Zigler & Valentine, 1979).

Federal Education Legislation. On the education front, the War on Poverty was waged by a number of initiatives. The Vocational Education Act of 1963 more than quadrupled federal funds for vocational education. The purpose of the act was to enhance occupational training opportunities for persons of all ages by providing financial assistance to vocational and technical programs in high schools and nonbaccalaureate postsecondary institutions. The Manpower Development and Training Act, enacted the same year, was directed at providing retraining for unemployed adults.

The Economic Opportunity Act (EOA) of 1964 established the Job Corps to train youth between 16 and 21 years of age in basic literacy skills and for employment, and also established a type of domestic Peace Corps, Volunteers in Service to America (VISTA). Perhaps the most popular and controversial component of the EOA was Project Head Start, a program aimed at disadvantaged children 3 to 5 years of age who would not normally attend preschool or kindergarten. President Johnson predicted that Head Start would "strike at the basic cause of poverty" by addressing it at its beginnings—the disadvantaged preschool child. As the name suggests, the intent of the program was to give disadvantaged children a head start in the educational race so that once in school they might be on equal terms with children from nondisadvantaged homes. Although the Head Start Program has perhaps not lived up to all of President Johnson's expectations, it has proved to be the most successful of the compensatory education programs.

The centerpiece of the education legislation enacted as part of the War on Poverty was the Elementary and Secondary Education Act of 1965 (ESEA). The most far-reaching piece of

Presidents Kennedy and Johnson declared a war on poverty, using education as a major weapon in the fight.

federal education legislation to date, the ESEA provided more than $1 billion in federal funds to education. The ESEA included five major sections or titles. The largest, receiving about 80% of the funds, was Title I, which provided assistance to local school districts for the education of children from low-income families. The compensatory education programs funded through Title I were intended to maintain the educational progress begun in Head Start. Other sections of the ESEA provided funds for library resources, textbooks, and instructional materials; supplemental education centers; educational research and training; and strengthening state departments of education. The act was expanded in 1966 and 1967 to include programs for Native American children, children of migrant workers, students with disabilities (Title VI), and children with limited English-speaking ability (Title VII).

In the same year that the ESEA was enacted, Congress passed the Higher Education Act, which provided direct assistance to institutes of higher education for facility construction and library and instructional improvement, as well as loans and scholarships to students. The year 1965 also saw the establishment of the National Foundation of the Arts and the Humanities to promote and encourage production, dissemination, and scholarship in the arts and humanities.

Between 1963 and 1969, Congress passed more than two dozen major pieces of legislation affecting education. These laws dramatically increased federal involvement in education and provided vast sums of money for elementary and secondary schools, vocational schools, colleges, and universities. In 1963–64, federal funds for elementary and secondary schools totaled almost $900 million. By 1968–69 this amount had skyrocketed to $3 billion, and the federal government's share of the financing of education had risen from 4.4% to 8.8%. Perhaps equally as important as the increased funding was the shift in emphasis from identification of gifted students, which had marked the 1950s, to a concern for disadvantaged students.

The Civil Rights Movement

The Brown Decision.   Not only were the schools given a major role in the War on Poverty but they also became a stage for much of the drama of the Civil Rights movement. In the landmark *Brown v. Board of Education of Topeka* (1954) decision, the U.S. Supreme Court ruled that segregated educational facilities have no place in public education and generate a feeling of inferiority that affects the child's motivation to learn. However, instead of being the climax of the struggle for racial equality in education, *Brown* marked the beginning of the Civil Rights revolution. Although the Civil Rights movement began with blacks, perhaps because the basic vision of what was wrong was most visible in the history of blacks in America, the general principles of the movement were later applied to advancing the rights of women, racial and ethnic groups, the aged, and the disabled (Sowell, 1984).

The *Brown* decision met with massive nationwide resistance in the form of legal maneuvers and violence, resulting in countless confrontations between federal authorities who sought to enforce the law and local police or citizens who sought to obstruct it. The most dramatic physical confrontation in the struggle to integrate the public schools took place in Little Rock, Arkansas, when President Eisenhower sent federal troops to ensure that, over the objections of the governor, Orval Faubus, nine black students were safely enrolled in Central High School. A more violent confrontation involving the integration of higher education resulted in the loss of two lives when federal marshals were required to enroll James Meredith at the University of Mississippi, again over the objections of the state's governor, Ross Barnett.

In the early years of school desegregation, attention was focused on the *de jure* segregated districts in the southern states.

One of the most dramatic moments in school desegregation was the integration of Little Rock Central High School.

Initially, districts attempted to accomplish desegregation by adopting freedom of choice plans. In most instances, these plans had little impact on the level of segregation, and a decade after *Brown,* little progress toward integration had been made.

At the same time that school desegregation was making limited progress, the Civil Rights movement was gaining momentum on other fronts. Freedom rides, sit-ins, boycotts, and other forms of nonviolent protest appealed to the national conscience and focused national attention on a movement that would not be denied. President John F. Kennedy pressed for the passage of a federal civil rights statute that would end segregation in public facilities, attack discrimination in employment, and require nondiscriminatory practices in programs and institutions receiving federal funds. Five days after President Kennedy was assassinated, his successor, Lyndon B. Johnson, appeared before Congress and sought its passage, declaring it the most fitting honor of his memory. The Civil Rights Act of 1964, when passed, became one of the most significant pieces of social legislation in the United States in the 20th century (Spring, 1976).

The Civil Rights Act and Desegregation.   The Civil Rights Act of 1964 further involved the federal government in the activities of the schools. Title VI of the act prohibits discrimination against students on the basis of race, color, or national origin in all institutions receiving federal funds. Title VII forbids discrimination in employment based on race, religion, national origin, or sex. The act authorized the withholding of federal funds from any institution or agency violating the law. It also authorized the U.S. attorney general to take legal action to achieve school desegregation and provided federal financial assistance to school districts attempting to desegregate.

The passage of the Civil Rights Act of 1964 and the education acts of 1965 combined with the growing intolerance of the Supreme Court to the resistance to the *Brown* decision led to the creation of a "carrot-and-stick" mechanism that dramatically increased the pace of school desegregation. The carrot was the increased federal expenditures for education, which increased from $2.0 billion in 1965–66, to $4.9 billion in 1970, to $4.4 billion in 1974. The Civil Rights Act of 1964 and a series of Supreme Court decisions between 1968 and 1972 that favored more aggressive measures to integrate in the South (e.g., *Swann v. Charlotte-Mecklenburg Board of Education* [1971], which allowed forced busing) and attacked **de facto segregation** in the North were the stick. The Supreme Court ruled that *de facto* segregation created by local zoning ordinances, housing restrictions, attendance zones, *gerrymandering,* or other deliberate official actions designed to segregate African Americans were just as illegal as *de jure* segregation (*Keys v. School District No. 1 of Denver, Colorado,* 1973).

VIDEO INSIGHT

The Reunion

This ABC News video examines the lasting effects of school integration that began during the 1960s Civil Rights struggle. *The Reunion* celebrates the reuniting of classmates who participated in a controversial social experiment on school integration that took place in one of America's wealthiest suburbs, Shaker Heights, Ohio. Each of the former students had the opportunity to live and attend school in a racially mixed community starting from kindergarten through high school.

1. How comfortable would you have been had you been asked to participate in a similar experiment on school integration?
2. What factors contributed to the success of this experiment?
3. What were the most enduring effect(s) of the experiment on the lives of the participants?

CW   To submit your answers online, go to the *Video Insight* module for this chapter of the Companion Website at **http://www.prenhall.com/webb.**

Further Advances in Civil Rights in Education.   The Civil Rights Movement in education also made advances in several other areas. Previously, instruction in most schools was given only in English. In the 1960s, however, attention was turned to the growing Hispanic population of the large cities and in the Southwest. In 1968 the Bilingual Education Act was passed, giving federal funds to school districts to provide bilingual education to low-income students with limited English proficiency. Additional support for bilingual education was provided by the U.S. Supreme Court ruling in *Lau v. Nichols* (1974), which said that schools must provide special language programs for non-English-speaking children. In response, Congress passed the Bilingual Education Act of 1974, which provided for bilingual education for all children with limited English ability, as a means of promoting their participation in the regular classroom as soon as possible.

While litigation and legislation were expanding the educational opportunities afforded black and language-minority students, Native Americans were attempting to gain greater control and assume greater responsibility for the education of their youth as well as to restore native language and culture to the curriculum. Self-determination came closer to reality with the passage of the Indian Education Act of 1972, which established the Office of Indian Education, and the Indian Self-Determination and Educational Assistance Act of 1975, which expanded the rights of Native Americans with regard to the education of their youth, and sought to ensure increased educational opportunity for those youth.

On other fronts, Title IX of the 1972 Education Amendments, which prohibited sexual discrimination against employees and students in educational programs receiving federal funds, was a major victory in the extension of the Civil Rights movement to women. Another victory in the movement to extend civil rights to women came in the same session of Congress when Title VII of the Civil Rights Act of 1964, which prohibited discrimination in employment, was extended to cover academic institutions. With the legal support of Title IX and Title VII, women brought political pressure on local school districts and colleges and universities in an attempt to end sex discrimination in admissions, access to courses, extracurricular activities, instructional materials, counseling and counseling materials, employment, and policies and regulations governing the treatment of students and employees.

In 1975, the landmark Education for All Handicapped Children Act (EHA) established the right of all children with disabilities to a free and appropriate education. The EHA, often referred to as the Bill of Rights for Handicapped Children, served not only to guarantee the educational rights of children with disabilities, but to define and expand the rights of all children. Each of these topics is covered in greater detail in later chapters.

Social Unrest.   The late 1960s and early 1970s also saw a series of urban riots and the sometimes passive, sometimes violent student rights and anti–Vietnam War movements. College campuses were the scenes of sit-ins, marches, and even the bombing and burning of campus buildings. Both student rights and antiwar movements tended to have a negative impact on the Civil Rights movement through a subliminal process of guilt by association. Many members of academia as well as the larger society became disenchanted with the Civil Rights movement, "not because they disagreed with or were unsympathetic to its legitimate claim, but because the Student Rights movement, which they strongly opposed, got its impetus, simulation, and example from the Civil Rights Movement" (Tollett, 1983, p. 57). A campaign against demonstrations and riots and for the restoration of law and order helped put Richard Nixon in the White House in 1969 and reelect him in 1972.

During the 1980s the Civil Rights movement was slowed considerably by the actions of both the courts and the Reagan administration. The budget of the Office of Civil Rights was cut, investigations were "cursory," and enforcement and compliance were loosened. The Department of Justice not only seemed uninterested in enforcing civil rights plans, it attempted to block efforts to broaden the scope of civil rights and to strengthen affirmative action and opposed even the continuation of existing desegregation plans. Magnet schools, which attempted to attract white students to predominantly minority schools, were one of the favored strategies of the Reagan administration in out-of-court settlements of desegregation cases.

For Your Reflection and Analysis

In what ways have males benefited from the extension of civil rights to females?
To submit your response online, go to http://www.prenhall.com/webb.

CW

The 1970s: Retreat and Retrenchment

During the Nixon administration (1969–1974), support for many of the initiatives begun during the Kennedy and Johnson administrations was reduced. The Nixon administration represented a conservative reaction to student demonstrations and the demands of the Civil Rights movement. "The conservative reaction included a retreat from the programs of the War on Poverty . . . a renewed emphasis on the power of the educational expert, the spread of the concept of accountability in education, increased emphasis on testing, and the use of behavioral psychology in the classroom" (Spring, 2005, p. 449). On the other hand, the 1970s witnessed increased attention to the needs of people with disabilities. The Vocational Rehabilitation Act of 1973 sought to increase the physical access of persons with disabilities to educational institutions, vocational training, and employment. During the Ford administration (1974–1977), the Education for All Handicapped Children Act of 1975 (now the Individuals with Disabilities Education Act), which is discussed in Chapter 9, was enacted.

The Carter administration (1977–1981) was unable to secure the passage of any major education legislation, but was able to oversee an increase in the federal education budget, from 8.8% of the total elementary and secondary revenues in 1977 to 9.8% in 1980 (see Table 7.3). And, under Carter's administration a Department of Education was established.

Table 7.3 — Public Elementary and Secondary School Revenues, by Source, 1940–2005 (in thousands of dollars)

School Year Ending	Federal Amount	Federal Percent of Total	State Amount	State Percent of Total	Local Amount	Local Percent of Total	Total
1940	39,810	1.8	684,354	30.3	1,536,363	68.0	2,260,527
1950	155,848	2.9	2,165,689	39.8	3,115,507	57.3	5,437,044
1960	651,639	4.4	5,768,047	39.1	8,326,932	56.5	14,746,618
1962	760,975	4.3	6,789,190	38.7	9,977,542	56.9	17,527,707
1964	896,956	4.4	8,078,014	39.3	11,569,213	56.3	20,544,182
1966	1,996,954	7.9	9,920,219	39.1	13,439,886	53.0	25,356,858
1968	2,806,469	8.8	12,275,536	38.5	16,821,063	52.7	31,903,064
1970	3,219,557	8.0	16,062.776	39.9	20,984,589	52.1	40,266,923
1972	4,467,969	8.9	19,133,256	38.3	26,402,420	52.8	50,003,645
1974	4,930,351	8.5	24,113,409	41.4	29,187,132	50.1	58,230,892
1976	6,318,345	8.9	31,776,101	44.6	33,111,627	48.5	71,206,073
1978	7,694,194	9.4	35,013,266	43.0	38,735,700	47.6	81,443,160
1980	9,503,537	9.8	45,348,814	46.8	42,028,813	43.4	96,881,165
1982	8,186,466	7.4	52,436,435	49.7	49,568,346	45.0	110,191,257
1984	8,567,547	6.8	60,232,981	47.8	57,245,892	45.4	126,055,419
1986	9,975,622	6.7	73,619,575	49.4	65,532,582	43.9	149,127,779
1988	10,716,687	6.3	84,004,415	49.5	74,840,873	44.1	169,561,974
1990	12,700,784	6.1	98,238,633	47.1	97,608,157	46.8	208,547,573
1992	15,493,330	6.6	108,783,449	46.4	110,304,605	47.0	234,581,384
1994	18,341,483	7.1	117,474,209	45.2	124,343,776	47.8	260,159,468
1996	19,104,019	6.6	136,670,754	47.5	131,928,071	45.9	287,702,844
1998	22,201,965	6.8	157,645,372	48.4	146,128,674	44.8	325,976,011
2000	24,304,600	6.9	188,360,448	50.9	155,994,731	42.1	368,659,779
2002	32,100,922	7.7	206,138,670	49.5	178,514,436	42.8	516,753,028
2004	38,856,224	8.6	217,139,989	48.0	196,798,990	43.5	552,794,703
2005	41,415,719	8.8	229,227,924	48.6	201,371,862	42.7	412,015,505

Source: U.S. Department of Education, National Center for Education Statistics. (2004). *Digest of Education Statistics, 2003* (Table 157). Washington, DC: U.S. Government Printing Office; National Education Association. (2005). *Rankings & Estimates.* Washington, DC: Author.

Figure 7.2 — Actual and Projected Enrollment in Elementary and Secondary Schools (by grade level: fall 1965 to fall 2014)

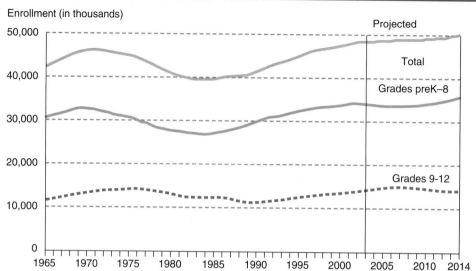

Source: U.S. Department of Education, National Center for Education Statistics. (2005) *Projections of education statistics to 2014* (Figure 2). Washington, DC: U.S. Department of Education.

Carter kept his campaign promise to the NEA and overcame congressional opposition, and in 1979 the Office of Education was elevated to department status, making its secretary a member of the president's cabinet. Carter appointed Shirley Hufstadler, a federal appeals court judge, as the first secretary of education.

The decade of the 1970s was a time of financial uncertainty for the schools. Not only were schools faced with spiraling operating costs but teachers hurt by inflation were becoming more strident in their salary demands. At the same time, revenues for the schools were actually declining. The decline in revenues was a result of two forces: (1) the "revolt" of taxpayers against rising taxes, especially property taxes, which are the major source of tax revenues for the schools; and (2) a decline in enrollments, which brought with it a reduction in state revenues, because most states, to a large extent, base their aid to local school districts on enrollment. In 1971, for the first time since World War II, the total number of elementary and secondary students enrolled in the public schools declined (see Figure 7.2).

Revenues and enrollments were not the only things in education declining during the 1970s; test scores and public confidence in the schools were also declining. The decline in Scholastic Aptitude Test (SAT) scores witnessed in the 1960s continued into the 1970s: SAT scores fell almost 60 points from 1970 to 1980. Concern about the lower academic achievement of students led many parents and politicians to call for a "back-to-basics" curriculum and to seek greater accountability from the schools. Parents in poor schools began to look to the courts to remedy the inequalities that were reflected in inferior schools and reduced educational opportunity. In 1973 the California Supreme Court handed down a decision in *Serrano v. Priest* that has since been followed by the courts in almost two dozen states. In *Serrano,* the court held that the quality of a child's education could not depend on the wealth of the district. The concern for student achievement, the push for a back-to-basics curriculum, and the demand for greater accountability that began in the 1970s have continued unabated to the present.

The 1980s: Renewed Conservatism and Reform

The election of Ronald Reagan to the presidency in 1980 brought a resurgence of conservatism in both politics and education. Reagan's New Federalism called for reduced taxes and reduced federal spending for social programs, including education, and encouraged a greater role for state and local governments, as well as a greater involvement of the business community in supporting schools and setting goals and standards. The National Education Consolidation and Improvement Act of 1981 sought to consolidate the massive array of federal aid programs into several large block programs. However, Reagan's proposal for the entire block was less than what formerly had been spent for the ESEA alone. In fact, in every budget request made while he was in office, President Reagan proposed reductions in federal spending for education, and from fiscal years 1980 to 1989, federal funds for elementary and secondary education declined by 17%, and for higher education by 27% (U.S. Department of Education, 1989). Reagan's conservative education agenda included not only a reduced federal role but also the elimination of the Department of Education, high standards, greater accountability, increased parental support, a return to the basics, and a return of prayer to the classroom.

Much of the conservative agenda regarding federal aid to education stemmed from the fact that many conservatives blamed the schools for the social unrest of the 1960s and early 1970s and for many of the social problems that were seen as undermining the very moral fabric of the country. The conservative response to the presumed educational excesses of the 1960s and 1970s led to a continuation of the public debate about the condition of education. Whereas *Sputnik* and technological competition with the Russians had focused attention on the educational system in the 1950s, it was economic competition with the Japanese that brought the educational system into the forefront of public debate in the 1980s. In response to the growing belief that the decline in the quality of the educational system was a major factor in the nation's declining economic and intellectual competitiveness, President Reagan appointed a National Commission on Excellence in Education. Its report, *A Nation at Risk: The Imperative for Educational Reform* (1983), in strong and stirring language described a "rising tide of mediocrity" and declared that it would have been seen as "an act of war" if any unfriendly power had imposed our educational system on us.

A Nation at Risk has been described by some as a "bombshell" on the American educational scene, by others a "call to action," and by still others as a "conservative call to arms" (Horn, 2002). However it is described, there is no question that *A Nation at Risk* was a landmark report in the history of educational reform in the United States. *A Nation at Risk* and the series of reports that followed collectively are responsible for what has been referred to as the "Educational Reform Movement of the 1980s." This reform movement has been characterized as having two waves. The first wave responded to the recommendations of *A Nation at Risk* and similar reports and acted on the assumption that what was wrong with schools could be fixed by top-down state actions directed at improving achievement and accountability. States enacted higher graduation requirements, standardized curriculum mandates, increased the testing of both teachers and students, and raised certification requirements for teachers. School districts throughout the nation increased their emphasis on computer literacy, homework, and basic skills; established minimum standards for participation in athletics; and lengthened the school day and the school year.

The second wave of reform, beginning in 1986, focused not on the state level, on state mandates and centralization of authority, but on the local level and on the structure and processes of the schools themselves. A major theme of the second wave was the redistribution of power among the critical stakeholders of the schools. The belief was that the most effective reforms were those that emanated from those closest to the students, namely, educators and parents. The recommendations from the second wave of reform, coming from such noted educators as John Goodlad, Theodore Sizer, and Ernest Boyer, called for change from the bottom up, not from the top down, and dealt with such issues as decentralization, site-based management, teacher empowerment, parental involvement, and school choice. The second wave of reform was associated with a number of prescriptions: year-round schools, longer school days and school years, recast modes of governance, alternative funding patterns, all-out commitments to technology, and various combinations of these and other proposals (Kaplan, 1990). This wave of reform also sought to balance the concern over the impact of education on the economy and the push for excellence of the first wave with a concern for equity and the disadvantaged students who might become further disadvantaged by the "new standards of excellence." Other

For Your Reflection and Analysis

Which of the initiatives from the first wave of reform are still emphasized today? *To submit your response online, go to http://www.prenhall.com/webb.*

CW

state and local responses to the second wave of reform continued into the 1990s and are discussed in the chapters that follow.

The 1990s: National Goals, National Standards, and Choice

By the end of the 1980s the adoption of the myriad of reform initiatives had not produced any significant change in educational outputs. As a result, the quality of education and the perceived need to "fix it" remained major topics of public debate. Responding to the on-going criticism of both education and his administration's failure to offer any remedies, in the fall of 1989 President Bush co-convened, with the National Governors Association, an "education summit" at Charlottesville, Virginia, chaired by Arkansas Governor Bill Clinton. As an outcome of the meeting, in early 1990 the National Governors Association and the Bush administration approved six national education goals to be accomplished by the year 2000. However, President Bush was unable to gain congressional support for his plan for implementing the goals, largely because of the controversy surrounding a key feature of the plan: vouchers to promote school choice.

The 1992 election saw education assume a place of prominence on the political agenda not previously held. As observed by Terrel H. Bell (1993), secretary of education under President Reagan:

> George Bush proclaimed himself to be the "Education President" during his successful 1988 campaign. President Bill Clinton brought the less-than-spectacular Bush record in education to the attention of the voters during the campaign of 1992 and promised to be a more effective "Education President." This has never happened in the nation's history. Education is now a major, high priority national concern, as well as a state and local responsibility. (p. 595)

The Clinton administration's plan to implement the national goals was called the Goals 2000: Educate America Act. Goals 2000 adopted the six goals articulated by the National Governors Association and added two new goals related to parent participation and teacher education and professional development (see Figure 7.3). The act not only for-

The 1990 Education Summit led to the establishment of the first national education goals.

Figure 7.3 — The National Education Goals

1. *School Readiness.* By the year 2000, all children in America will start school ready to learn.

2. *High School Completion.* By the year 2000, the high school graduation rate will increase to at least 90 percent.

3. *Student Achievement and Citizenship.* By the year 2000, all students will leave grades 4, 8, and 12 having demonstrated competency over challenging subject matter including English, mathematics, science, foreign languages, civics and government, economics, arts, history, and geography, and every school in the United States will ensure that all students learn to use their minds well, so they may be prepared for responsible citizenship, future learning, and productive employment in our Nation's modern economy.

4. *Teacher Education and Professional Development.* By the year 2000, the Nation's teaching force will have access to programs for the continued improvement of their professional skills and the opportunity to acquire the knowledge and skills needed to instruct and prepare all American students for the next century.

5. *Mathematics and Science.* By the year 2000, United States students will be first in the world in mathematics and science achievement.

6. *Adult Literacy and Lifelong Learning.* By the year 2000, every adult American will be literate and will possess the knowledge and skills necessary to compete in a global economy and exercise the rights and responsibilities of citizenship.

7. *Safe, Disciplined, and Alcohol- and Drug-Free Schools.* By the year 2000, every school in the United States will be free of drugs, violence, and the unauthorized presence of firearms and alcohol, and will offer a disciplined environment conducive to learning.

8. *Parental Participation.* By the year 2000, every school will promote partnerships that will increase parental involvement and participation in promoting the social, emotional, and academic growth in children.

Source: H. R. 1804 Goals 2000 Educate America Act, Sec. 101. (1994).

malized the national education goals but also formalized the development of national standards and new assessment systems and established a "new federal partnership to reform the nation's educational system" (U.S. Department of Education, 1994).

The adoption of Goals 2000 also marked a turning point in the aim of state and federal education policy: "Emphasis shifted from educational inputs to educational outcomes and from procedural accountability to educational accountability. Equity was reconceptualized as ensuring all students access to high-quality educational programs rather than providing supplemental and often compensatory services" (Goertz, 2001, p. 62). The reauthorization of the ESEA, included under the Goals 2000 umbrella as the Improving America's Schools Act, encouraged comprehensive reform at the state and local levels to meet the national goals. A major provision of the act required states (with the input of local school districts) to develop school improvement plans that establish challenging content and performance standards, implement assessments to measure student progress in meeting these standards, and adopt measures to hold schools accountable for the achievement of the standards. Unlike previous federal programs that bypassed state education policies, these initiatives were designed to be integrated with state and local reform initiatives (Goertz, 2001).

Throughout the remainder of the 1990s, the calls for school reform continued and standards and accountability became the key words in promoting school reform. However, states and local school districts faced a number of challenges in their efforts to establish challenging academic standards and accompanying assessment systems. In state after state, standards became the battleground for ongoing "curriculum wars" as educators and policy makers faced off over such issues as whole language versus phonics or whose history to teach (Campbell, 2000). However, despite the challenges, and in no small part due to the work of the various curriculum organizations in establishing content standards in each of the major academic disciplines (see Chapter 14), by 2000 academic standards were in place in 48 states and schools were expected to align their curriculum with these standards.

The push for standards was accompanied by the enactment in almost every state of so-called **"high-stakes testing"** that would determine who would be promoted and who would graduate from high school. However, as the testing was initiated, several states experienced serious problems associated with test construction and, more important, with the high numbers of students who were being failed by the tests. In most states the students who performed the poorest on the exams were low-income and minority students, especially those with limited English speaking ability and children from low-income, mostly urban districts—the victims described in Kozol's *Savage Inequalities* (1991). Lost in the focus on standards and improving performance was the question of whether the standards movement would lead to school improvement for many marginalized students (Campbell, 2000).

The fall of 1996 saw not only the reelection of President Bill Clinton but also record enrollments in the public schools. The impact of the "baby boom echo"—the children of the 76 million baby boomers born between the end of World War II and 1964—was strengthened by continued immigration, pushing school enrollments beyond the record 1971 baby boom enrollments of 51.3 million. Enrollments in the fall of 1996 reached 51.7 million, grew to 53.2 million by the turn of the century, and were projected to decrease to 50 million by the year 2014 (see Figure 7.2) with the greatest increases occurring in the South and West. The growing enrollments combined with growing teacher retirements to worsen the teacher shortages already impacting many districts.

School Choice

The Republican takeover of the U.S. Congress and many state legislatures in the 1994 elections put Goals 2000 in conflict with a renewed conservative agenda, "Contract with America," which had as a key feature support for choice and privatization in education. And, although some indicators, such as SAT scores, improved throughout the 1980s and 1990s in the wake of the reform movements, large numbers of parents continued to be dissatisfied with school systems that valued diversity over diction and affirmative action over arithmetic and were demanding the right to send their children to the school of their choice funded at public expense. Support for school choice came from parents across the socioeconomic and ideological spectrum. Low-income and minority parents saw choice as a way to extend educational opportunities to students who historically had not had the resources to choose between public and private schools, or even among public schools. (The *Controversial Issue* feature on p. 183 discusses the pros and cons of school choice.) Other parents saw choice as providing the opportunity to protect their children from the violence in the schools or to provide them with a more academically challenging or enriched experience. Religious conservatives saw choice as a way to support schools that promoted a particular religious ideology. However, while almost all parents and politicians supported the concept that parents should be given greater choice in the school their child attended, how this was to be achieved was very much in debate. The most often seriously considered approaches were school vouchers, charter schools, and privatization. Each of these is discussed next and in more detail in Chapter 13.

The use of vouchers, including their use at private schools, was upheld by the U.S. Supreme Court in 2002 (*Zelman v. Simmons-Harris,* 2002). Following the *Zelman* decision, voucher supporters anticipated their widespread adoption elsewhere. However, this has not occurred. A major reason seems to be that the growing array of alternative school choice options (see Figure 7.4), in particular charter schools, contributed to a decreased interest in pursuing the contentious voucher alternative (Metcalf & Legan, 2002).

A less controversial proposal for increasing parental choice, one that gained increased favor in the 1990s was **charter schools.** As discussed in Chapter 13, charter schools are publicly supported schools established upon the issuance of a charter from the state, local school board, or other designated entity. In 1997 President Clinton lent support to the movement by pledging $100 million to help create 3,000 more charter schools by the year

For Your Reflection and Analysis

What would influence your decision to work in a charter school if you were asked to do so?

To submit your response online, go to http://www. prenhall.com/webb.

CONTROVERSIAL ISSUE

Parental Public School Choice

One of the most popular proposals of the **restructuring** movement is the proposal to let parents choose the public school their children will attend. According to a Gallup Poll, 60% of Americans favor public school choice. However, a number of educational groups, as well as many in the lay public, oppose choice plans. The reasons stated by proponents of each side include the following:

Arguments For

1. Breaks the monopoly of the public schools and makes them more responsible to the forces of the marketplace.
2. Competition will promote efficiency and excellence in operation.
3. Encourages diversity in programs.
4. Students achieve better in schools they have chosen to attend.
5. Parents are more satisfied with and committed to the schools when they have a choice.
6. Teacher satisfaction and morale is higher in schools of choice.

Arguments Against

1. Will lead to ethnic, racial, and socioeconomic segregation.
2. Conditions will worsen in poorest districts as students leave and take their per-pupil state aid with them.
3. Transportation costs will be dramatically increased.
4. Potential for fluctuations in enrollments make planning for staffing and budgeting difficult.
5. Most parents would not be able to make an informed choice among the alternative schools.

What, if any, support for parental choice is there in your state? How has it been evidenced? What is your position on parental public school choice?

 To answer these questions online, go to the *Controversial Issue* module for this chapter of the Companion Website at **http://www.prenhall.com/webb**.

2000. In fact, by 2003 approximately 2,500 charter schools were in operation in 37 states and the District of Columbia (U.S. Department of Education, 2004a).

Although not expanding the choice option of attending a different school, another favorite among choice advocates was to allow private contractors to bid to provide various services to the schools. The practice of contracting for services with private companies or individuals outside the school systems for services has been around since

Figure 7.4 — The Choice Continuum

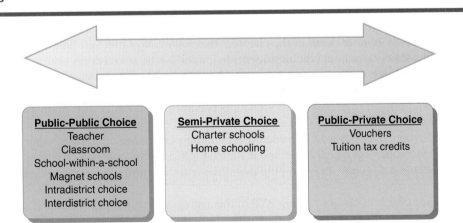

Public-Public Choice
Teacher
Classroom
School-within-a-school
Magnet schools
Intradistrict choice
Interdistrict choice

Semi-Private Choice
Charter schools
Home schooling

Public-Private Choice
Vouchers
Tuition tax credits

Source: Metcalf, Kim K., Muller, Patricia A., Legan, Natalie A. (2001). *School choice in America: The great debate.* Bloomington, IN: Phi Delta Kappa International, 2001, p. 4. Reprinted by permission of Phi Delta Kappa International.

the New England schools but has typically not been for the delivery of instructional or administrative services. However, in the 1990s a number of school districts experimented with more expanded forms of privatization, often over the objections of teacher groups. Some districts contracted with for-profit firms to operate one or more schools on a for-profit basis. Other districts contracted with various providers for leadership or instructional services.

The End of a Presidency, the End of a Century

During President Clinton's second term, debate at the federal level continued over whether there should be a federal Department of Education, voluntary national testing, and private school choice. Faced with a larger Republican majority in Congress, and weakened by personal scandals and threats of impeachment, Clinton was able to hold off any significant reductions in federal spending for education, but was unable to advance any of his major education proposals.

The final year of the 20th century brought a tragedy that captured the nation's attention like no other event on school grounds since the days of forced integration. That event was the massacre at Columbine High School that resulted in the deaths of 14 students and one teacher. This event came to symbolize what was increasingly being acknowledged as a crisis in education: violence in the schools (see Chapter 10). Fighting in the schools was matched by fighting in the courts, in legislatures, and in school board meetings as the battles over the curriculum, the role of religion in the schools, standards and testing, and the provision of choice continued into the new century.

A New Century Begins

The new century began where the last one left off—with the public as well as the educational establishment divided over the issues of state and national standards, accountability, school choice, and the place of religion in the schools. Despite the fact that the 1990s had witnessed rising test scores and unparalleled economic prosperity that had been said to be at risk as a result of the quality of the schools, the cries for educational reform continued.

No Child Left Behind

The reform offered by the first president of the new century, George W. Bush, was embodied in his education plan, the No Child Left Behind (NCLB) Act. No Child Left Behind, the most sweeping education reform legislation since the ESEA of 1965, did what a Democratic administration could never have done: create "a much larger federal presence in educational policy and funding and set the foundation for a national testing system" (Lewis, 2002, p. 423). Although some of the major provisions of NCLB applied only to schools receiving Title I funds, because states and school districts could not practically require things of one school or group of teachers and students it did not require of all its schools, the impact of the provisions of NCLB were universal.

As discussed in more detail in the chapters that follow, No Child Left Behind required that by the 2005–06 school year all students in grades 3–8 be tested every year in reading and math and one more time in grades 10–12 (additional tests have since been added), that the tests be aligned with state content and academic achievement standards, and that the school population as a whole as well as its subgroups make adequate yearly progress (AYP) toward meeting established achievement goals. If even one of the subgroups fails to make AYP the entire school is considered to be underperforming. NCLB also requires that 95% of each subgroup take the test, and if, for example, a school only had 10 Native American students and 1 were absent on the day of the test the entire school would be labeled underperforming.

Sanctions for schools not making AYP in the aggregate or for any of the major student subgroups range from notifying parents that the school had failed to make AYP and offering them the option of transferring their children to another school and the provision of supplemental services to students from low-income families, to replacing staff, state takeover, conversion to a charter school, or hiring a private contractor to manage the school. The act also requires that all students reach a state-established "proficient" level on the state assessments by 2014.

States faced a number of challenges in meeting the mandates of NCLB. First and foremost was the 20% to 30% increase in the state education budget that was necessary to meet the requirements and the goals. Federal funding is expected to provide less than half of these increased costs. In state departments of education and local school districts that are already facing budget shortfalls, "unfunded mandates" became perhaps the most common objection to NCLB. Some states have requested waivers or greater flexibility in meeting goals. The National Conference of State Legislatures (NCSL) has pushed the federal government to recognize that the "one-size-fits all" method to judge school effectiveness is impractical (NCSL, 2005). In April 2005 the NEA joined school districts in Michigan, Texas, and Vermont in suing the U.S. Department of Education by challenging the enforcement of the mandates based on a provision of the law that said states were excused if not fully funded by the federal government. As of this writing, this issue had not been resolved.

One of the major factors driving up the cost of meeting NCLB mandates was the fact that many states did not have in place a system for testing at every grade level for grades 3–8 and these tests had to be developed or adapted. And, of course, the tests had to be administered and scored. The test requirements produced many challenges in addition to the funding issue. Numerous states encountered problems with the development or scoring of tests. For example, questions of accuracy and scoring led Georgia to cancel the statewide exam for fifth-graders 3 years in a row because of test accuracy (Henriques, 2003). In Connecticut, the private firm scoring the tests made so many errors the state had to suspend publication of school ratings (Tucker & Toch, 2004). More serious consequences befell students in Minnesota where scoring errors by NCS resulted in 8,000 students being inaccurately failed, including 525 seniors who were denied diplomas.

An accompanying issue has been defining what is to be considered "proficient on the state assessment." Because of the variation in the rigor of state tests, as well as in the setting of state proficiency levels, states differed dramatically in the way they viewed school performance and in the percentage of students categorized as proficient. Because of these variations, the number of schools identified as in need of improvement varied significantly from state to state. Michigan identified more than 1,500 schools and California more than 1,000, whereas Wyoming and Arkansas identified no schools. In Florida, 87% of the schools, including 22% of the "A" schools, failed to make AYP under NCLB guidelines. Urban districts serving high proportions of minority and poor students, as well as rural districts, reported the highest percentage of schools in need of improvement.

One of the most contentious provisions of NCLB is its requirement that all public schools have "highly qualified" teachers in place by 2005–06. As noted in Chapter 1, new elementary teachers were required to pass "rigorous" state tests in the core elementary subjects and teaching skills. New middle and high school teachers had to pass either a "rigorous" state test in the academic subject matter, or have an academic major, graduate degree, or advance certification in the subject(s) they plan to teach. Veteran teachers may demonstrate content knowledge by any of these means or by meeting the requirements of a "high, objective, uniform state standard of evaluation" (HOUSSE).

The regulations implementing NCLB did not specify what constitutes "rigorous testing" or HOUSSE but left this up to the states. Given this leeway, what has emerged is the perpetuation of a system of widely differing requirements and practices. Some states have said that having a state license is all that is necessary to be considered highly qualified, whereas others have established elaborate evaluation systems. At the beginning of the 2005–2006 school year, most states reported that more than 90% of their teachers were highly qualified (Feller, 2005). Many districts, especially poor districts, have had problems complying with the NCLB mandate. For these districts having any teacher in the classroom was a challenge; having a "highly qualified" teacher in every classroom seemed impossible, especially given the estimated 20% to 50% additional cost associated with attracting these teachers (Olson, 2003).

For Your Reflection and Analysis

How realistic is the goal of having all students achieving at grade-level proficiency by 2014?
To submit your response online, go to http://www.prenhall.com/webb.

CW

For Your Reflection and Analysis

What can a district with limited resources do to attract high-quality teachers?
To submit your response online, go to http://www.prenhall.com/webb.

CW

As the states have attempted to meet the requirements of NCLB, they have done so against the backdrop of major changes in the demographics of the student population, the resegregation of schools, and the never-ending challenge of funding the schools equitably and adequately. The school population (ages 5 to 17) has become increasingly minority, a trend that is projected to continue, from approximately 22% in 2005 to 28% in 2020 (U.S. Department of Education, 2005c).

At the same time that the minority population is growing, the progress in closing the achievement gap between whites and minorities seems to have not only stalled, but, as discussed in Chapter 8, in some instances it has grown. What also has not improved, and what may be a contributing factor to the achievement gap, is the resegregation of the public schools. In fact, the resegregation has not only resulted in the loss of the gains in integration of African Americans that were made in the 1960s and 1970s, but Hispanics have become even more segregated, not only by race, but by language. In 2000, more than 75% of Hispanics and 70% of blacks attended predominantly minority schools, and 37% of each attended schools that are 90% to 100% minority, an increase for Hispanics from the pre-busing level of 1968 (23%) (Orfield, 2001). In effect, while the overall school enrollment has become increasingly diverse, the nation's schools are becoming increasingly segregated.

Changing Roles

As discussed in more detail in Chapter 13, No Child Left Behind marked a major expansion and change in the direction of federal involvement in education. It also created a vastly expanded regulatory role for state and local school districts. In the past federal programs had been directed at specific populations (e.g., students with disabilities, migrant children), but NCLB was directed at all children. Moreover, for the first time in history, the federal government became involved in determining the qualifications of instructional personnel.

At the state level, the states have continued to become more and more involved in issues that have traditionally been the responsibility of local school boards. School finance reform has resulted in the state assuming greater financial responsibility. The school reform movement and the standards, testing, and accountability measures that accompanied the 1994 ESEA expanded the state role, and NCLB gave the state an even larger role. Not only did the state have the responsibility for testing, sanctions, and ensuring teacher quality, more importantly, since it is the state that has the legal responsibility to provide for education, it is ultimately the state's responsibility to ensure that all children in the state reach the proficient level by 2014.

PROFESSIONAL REFLECTION

I feel *Brown v. Board of Education* had the greatest influence on American education in the 20th century. The case initiated educational and social reform throughout the United States and was instrumental in launching the Civil Rights movement. Those who fought for the desire to see equity and freedom for African Americans in our country led the way for all other cultures and races to have access to public education. We have all, regardless of race or religion, reaped the benefits of this case through the thinkers and inventors who bloomed in an integrated educational system, and we are a better nation for recognizing the value in diversity. I know the value of this case personally because without integration I would not have been in my fifth-grade teacher's class. Georgia Meadows was an African American teacher who, in 1970, had broken the color barrier and was teaching in a predominantly white, rural school. Mrs. Meadows loved us all equally and saw each of us, regardless of color, as individuals. It is because of Mrs. Meadows, a black teacher who took an interest in a white student, me, that I am a teacher today.

Sara Zeek
National Board Certified
Teacher, Virginia

To analyze this reflection, go to the *Professional Reflection* module for this chapter of the Companion Website at **http://www.prenhall.com/webb.**

Some historians have interpreted the events of the last decade as a sign of the end of the common school (Spring, 2005). Others take a less pessimistic view, but, like the authors of this text, share a concern over what appears to be the continued criticism of the public schools as they face the daunting task of educating an increasingly multicultural and multiracial/multiethnic society, meeting the needs of at-risk students, implementing the most effective curriculum designs and instructional strategies, and responding to a myriad of other challenges. Many of these issues and challenges are discussed in the chapters that follow.

Summary

Much of the history of education in this century can be seen in terms of a swing from one view of education to another. The progressive education movement, which began at the turn of the century and continued to gain popularity through the 1930s, gave way in the post–World War II years to a more conservative view of the purpose of education, which was a response to a perceived decline in the nation's technological supremacy. In the 1960s, the tide turned again in favor of a more liberal and child-centered approach and schools became a vital weapon in the War on Poverty. The schools were also placed center stage in the Civil Rights struggles of the 1960s and 1970s.

The late 1970s and 1980s once again saw renewed interest in the basics and a national cry for reform of the entire educational system. At the beginning of the 1990s, education assumed an unprecedented place on the political agenda and played a major role in the election of Bill Clinton, "Education President," in 1992. Education remained on the political agenda but took a different direction with the Republican takeover of Congress in the mid-1990s, which led to renewed efforts at the federal and state levels to advance a conservative education agenda that included support for increased choice, vouchers, privatization, and school prayer. These efforts continued throughout the 1990s and into the new century. The standards and accountability movements that began in the 1990s gained momentum in the new century with the passage of the No Child Left Behind Act. NCLB created new and expanded roles for the state and federal governments as well as challenges and opportunities for school districts. Some predictions of what lies ahead for education in the United States are discussed in Chapter 16.

Key Terms

Charter schools, 182
Child-centered curriculum, 164
De facto segregation, 175
Essentialism, 169

High-stakes testing, 182
Intelligence quotient (IQ), 167
Life adjustment education, 171
Project method, 166

Restructuring, 183
Spiral curriculum, 173
Subject-centered
  curriculum, 164

PROFESSIONAL DEVELOPMENT WORKSHOP

Prepare for the Praxis™ Examination

Ms. Knight is a third-year science teacher at John Dewey High School. Her class contains students at all ability levels as well as three limited English language learners. Ms. Knight is attempting to design science projects that are based on student interests and that build on experiences and materials common to the daily lives of the students. She believes this would be consistent with the constructivist perspective she has been taught at State College. As her first major student assignment, she has asked students to collect a minimum of six different materials and design a project using these materials, to make

a class presentation of the project, and to submit a written paper describing the project and the science supporting it. Ms. Knight reserved the computer lab for two classes to give students the opportunity to do research on the Internet.

On the scheduled day student presentations varied considerably, with some students making PowerPoint presentations, others poster displays, and still others reading a short and poorly written paper. Several students had nothing ready to present or a paper to turn in. Three students said they forgot it was due that day; three others said they did not understand the assignment. As each student made their presentation Ms. Knight tried to make some positive and encouraging comments. Her efforts were undermined by Jeff Smith and Larry Hughes, two of the students who did not have a presentation ready. They made jokes and comments throughout the presentations and laughed at students when they misspoke or when their demonstrations did not go as planned.

Ms. Knight is discouraged with the results of this first assignment. She wonders if instead of trying to be creative she should have just prepared a lecture or PowerPoint presentation.

1. What accommodation should Ms. Knight have made for the varying ability levels of the students?
2. What criteria should Ms. Knight use to assess the class presentations? The writing projects? Justify your choices.
3. a. What strategies can Ms. Knight use to try to ensure that students understand and complete assignments?
   b. How should Ms. Knight deal with the disruptive behavior of Jeff and Larry?

To submit your responses online, go to the *Prepare for the Praxis™ Examination* module for this chapter of the Companion Website at **http://www.prenhall.com/webb.**

Build Your Knowledge Base

1. What criteria did you use in deciding what artifacts to include in your "time room" or video on the history of education?
2. Compare the high school curricula of 1930, 1960, 1990, and 2006.
3. Describe the impact of the two world wars on American higher education.
4. To what extent did the schools either change society or adapt to changes in society in the 20th century?
5. Trace the changing involvement of the federal government in education in the 20th century. What has been the impact of declining federal financial support?
6. What is your response to Joel Spring's (2005) assertion that the end of the common school is at hand?
7. What have been the most significant positive and negative changes in education during your lifetime? What changes/reforms do you think need to be made?

Develop Your Portfolio

1. Review INTASC Standard 8: "The teacher understands and uses formal and informal assessment strategies to evaluate and ensure the continuous intellectual and social development of the learner." Gather information on the current use of academic content standards in your discipline or subject field. If you are not familiar with the content standards in your subject area, contact your state department of education or specialized organizations such as the Council for Exceptional Children, the National Conference of Teachers of English, or the National Council for Teachers of Mathematics. Next, interview a teacher in your discipline regarding his or her views on the use of academic standards. How successful has this teacher been in aligning the curriculum with the standards? What steps has he or she taken to address the problem of those students who have performed the poorest on the high-stakes testing? Summarize the teacher's responses and incorporate your views regarding standards, testing, and accountability. Place your reflection paper in your portfolio under **INTASC Standard 8, Assessment.**
2. Using photos, illustrations, news clippings, or other materials, create an artifact that displays what you perceive to be the most important noteworthy happening that took place during the

period of modern American education from the progressive movement to the present. Describe the event and how the noteworthy happening has impacted education today. Place your artifact in your portfolio under **INTASC Standard 1, Knowledge of Subject.**

CW To complete these activities online, go to the *Develop Your Portfolio* module for this chapter of the Companion Website at **http://www.prenhall.com/webb.**

Explore Teaching and Learning: Field Experiences

1. Using the following online source (**http://www.unlv.edu/projects/ohpsp/index.html**), compare and contrast the recorded views of principals across three decades: the 1970s, the 1980s, and the 1990s. For guidance, you might focus on questions such as the following:
   a. What were the primary issues or concerns expressed by the principals? Did the concerns differ? How were they similar?
   b. Across the three decades, were there differences in the ways that principals discussed issues related to student learning?
2. Divide the 20th century into five periods (1900–1919, 1920–1939, 1940–1959, 1960–1979, and 1980–1999). Identify and trace shifts/changes in the dominant economic, social, political, and educational issues through these five periods of history.

Professional Development Online

CW Visit this text's Companion Website at **http://www.prenhall.com/webb** to gain access to a variety of questions, activities, and exercises to help build your knowledge of this chapter's content. Below are just a few items on this text's Companion Website:

- Classroom Video—To see actual classroom footage and work through activities and questions to analyze the content of the video, click on the *Classroom Video* module for this chapter.
- Teaching Tolerance—To go to this organization's website and complete activities to explore issues and topics dealing with how to teach tolerance to students, click on the *Teaching Tolerance* module for this chapter.
- Self-Test—To review terms and concepts presented in this chapter, click on the *Self-Test* module for this chapter.
- Internet Resources—To link to web sites related to topics in this chapter, go to the *Internet Resources* module for this chapter of the Companion Website.

In teaching there should be no class distinctions.
—Confucius (551–478 B.C.)

THE SOCIAL AND CULTURAL CONTEXTS OF SCHOOLING: THEIR INFLUENCE AND CONSEQUENCE

It was almost midnight and Ms. Cohen had one more term paper to read before retiring. It was an exhausting time before finals. Each semester she vowed that she would not assign a 20-page term paper to her senior social studies honors class. But each semester she made the same assignment—and each semester she was glad that she did.

This semester she seemed to have an exceptionally gifted class. Of her 25 honors students, at least 75% had received admission and scholarships to more than one college or university. She glanced at her grade book and noticed some of the titles of the students' term papers. They read like a list of college theses, she thought, as she picked up the last term paper. It was David Marshall's paper and she smiled as she read his title: "Equal Educational Opportunity and the American Dream: You've Got to Be Kidding!"

As she turned to his introduction, Ms. Cohen was struck by the thoughtful perceptions and insights of this 17-year-old. His introduction read as follows:

To assume that the school as an institution can rectify the problems and concerns of the poor is either naive or sheer ignorance. The truth of the matter is that schools not only reflect the classes within the society, but they do everything they can to reinforce those divisions. Until we recognize that the basic concept of society must be reconceptualized and that social classes must be eliminated, the goal of equal educational opportunity will continue to be, at best, a fantasy or myth.

If David Marshall had written such an introduction to a term paper for your class, how might you respond? To what extent do you agree or disagree with David's assumptions about equal educational opportunity? About social class? Why or why not?

The issues that David Marshall has raised are central to any discussion of the relationship between the school and society. In this chapter, various dimensions of the relationship between the school and society are explored. First, the various aspects of socialization—the school, the family, the peer group, religion, and the mass media—are examined. Then, the purposes and expectations of schooling from different perspectives are compared. Last, the diversity of the student population in terms of social class, ethnicity, race, gender, exceptionality, and language proficiency is described. Comparisons of the educational achievement and attainment of these major population subgroups are presented. After you study this material you should be able to do the following:

- Explain the relationship between the school and the society it serves.
- Explain how the school, the family, peer group, religion, and the mass media socialize children and youth.
- Compare the functionalist, conflict, and interactionist perspectives on the purposes and expectations of education.
- Describe the social class system in the United States.
- Compare the educational achievement and attainment of social class groups, ethnic and racial groups, and males and females.
- Discuss the factors contributing to the gaps in the achievement and attainment of social class groups, ethnic and racial groups, and between males and females.
- Describe the demographic profile of students with exceptionalities.
- Explain the educational challenges faced by language-minority students.

The Relationship Between School and Society

The term **society** refers to a group of persons who share a common culture, government, institutions, land, or a set of social relationships. A person may be a member of several societies at the same time: a religious society, a professional society, and a social society. Each of these societies has its own culture or subculture. **Socialization** is the process by which persons are conditioned to the customs or norms of a particular culture. The schools most often reflect the society they serve. In democratic societies schools are locally governed by democratically elected boards and are concerned with promoting and protecting individual rights and freedoms. In totalitarian societies governance is imposed from above and individual creativity and freedom take a back seat to the perceived needs of the state.

As discussed later in this chapter, schools play a major role in the socialization of the young. In fulfilling its socialization role, the school is constantly challenged to assume a major role in either (1) inculcating or reinforcing the past or present values of the social order, or (2) encouraging the adoption of new and emerging values for the culture. Often, the school is called on to reinforce and transmit the common values of the past and, at the same time, to implement social change.

Agents of Socialization

The concept of education is very similar to the concept of socialization, because both aim to preserve and transmit the intellectual, moral, and aesthetic values of the society. In addition, both socialization and education take place not only in school but also through a variety of other institutions outside the school (see Figure 8.1). Of these, the family, the peer group, the church/religion, and the mass media seem to be particularly important and are examined in the sections that follow.

The School

The school plays a major role in socializing the young in the norms and values of society. The school trains children for responsible citizenship and socializes them for their future adult roles. In short, the school prepares the individual for life. Through curricula, classroom rules, and interactions with teachers and other adults, children learn the symbols and rituals of patriotism and the values of our democratic society. They also learn the behaviors that are supported and valued by the system.

Within the culture of the school, teachers exercise significant control over how the culture is transmitted to the young. It is the teacher who ultimately determines what subject matter will be taught and the manner in which the subject matter will be conveyed. As a result of this control, teachers are one of the central figures in the socialization process. The teacher is the symbol of authority to the child. Within the social system and reward structure created by teachers in their classrooms, children learn the beliefs, values, and expectations of the larger society. As Goodlad (2004) observed, while teachers "are not democracy's anointed stewards . . . (they do) have potentially powerful roles to play in ensuring that our public educational institutions provide the apprenticeship that responsible citizenship requires" (p. 2)

The Family

Although the organization of the family varies from culture to culture and from one period of history to the next, there are certain basic functions that all families serve. One of

Figure 8.1 — Socializing Agents That Transmit Culture

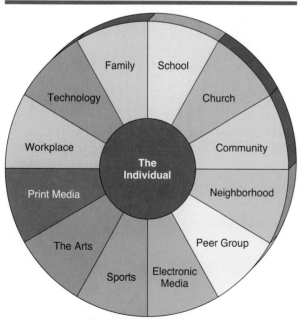

Source: *Human Diversity in Education: An Integrative Approach* (p. 66) by K. Cushner, A. McClelland, & P. Safford, 1996. New York: McGraw-Hill. Copyright 1996 by McGraw-Hill. Reprinted by permission.

those is the socialization function. Children are born into families and, for a significant period in their life, in particular their early years, the family is the only world that the children know. Thus, the family is the major socializing agent for the young. It is the family that first introduces the child to the world at large, and it is the family that transmits a particular culture's values to the young. Parents pass on their perceptions, values, beliefs, attitudes, experiences, and understandings to their children. These primary impressions are long lasting and very difficult to modify or change. They also have significant impact on children's later educational development and success in school. Parent–child interactions, the use of language in the home, child-rearing practices, and how gender roles are perceived in the home are a few of the many influences that are associated with a child's later educational achievement or attainment (Webb & Sherman, 1989).

Although the family has traditionally been the major instrument of socialization for the young, in the last quarter century increasing responsibility for socialization has been transferred to the school or other institutions. The major reason schools and other institutions have taken on a greater role as socializing agents is the changing structure of the family.

The Changing Family.   When we refer to "the American family," we are referring to a wide range of possible familial structures. During the past three decades, the family configuration has changed dramatically. Demographic, economic, and cultural changes have altered the very definition of "family" as we currently perceive it. The "plurality of family forms" is evident in the following configurations: *nuclear family* with husband, wife, and their children; dual-career family; single-parent family; gay and lesbian family; *blended* or *reconstituted family,* in which spouses from former marriages live together as a single nuclear family; *bi-nuclear family,* in which each divorced parent establishes a separate household and their children spend time at both households; and *extended family* where two or more generations of kin function as an independent social and economic unit (Curry, Jiobu, & Schwirian, 2005). While there has been historical evidence of a variety of these family structures, social recognition and support for some of these structures continue to be challenged (Elliott & Umberson, 2004).

Today's families spend less time together than they did in the past. In many families both parents work outside the home, often in more than one job. When they do spend time together, it is often spent watching television. Little family interaction occurs and less time is given to teaching children acceptable values and behaviors. As a result, the school has

For Your Reflection and Analysis

What were the child-rearing practices in your home during your formative years? How were gender roles perceived?
To submit your response online, go to http://www.prenhall.com/webb.

For Your Reflection and Analysis

Has your family configuration changed during the past two decades?
To submit your response online, go to http://www.prenhall.com/webb.

 VIDEO INSIGHT

Family Lost, Family Found: Children Raised by Their Grandparents

This ABC News video segment explores the lives of children from four families whose parents abandoned them due to drug abuse, incarceration, mental illness, or other social problems. Besides having all been deserted by their parents, the children have one other experience in common. They are all being raised by their grandparents or great-grandparents. Several are raising as many as five grandchildren. Plagued with insurmountable challenges, these children survive. The video depicts the true meaning of love, compassion, and devotion on the part of the grandparents and great-grandparents, one of whom is 82 years of age.

1. How do you account for the resiliency of the children who have been abandoned by their parents?
2. Why did the grandparents choose to raise the grandchildren rather than let them be placed in foster homes where they would have been eligible for more adequate financial assistance from the government?

 To submit your answers online, go to the *Video Insight* module for this chapter of the Companion Website at **http://www.prenhall.com/webb.**

Extended families play a major role in the socialization of children in many cultures.

taken on the function of teaching certain subjects that were once considered the purview of the family. For example, sex education and values education, domains that were traditionally considered the responsibility of the family and church, have been transferred to the school.

The Peer Group

The peer group, which consists of friends who are approximately the same age and social status, is one of the most important institutions for shaping the child's values and behaviors (Pugh & Hart, 1999). Each peer group has its own set of rules and regulations, its own social organization, its own customs, and, in some cases, its own rituals and language. Children develop friendship patterns at a very early age. By the age of 11, these friendship groups are fairly well established. Although the peer group relationship may be transitory in nature, its influence can be profound. Unlike the family influence, which tends to lessen with time, the peer group becomes more influential with the advancing age of the child or adolescent (Levine & Levine, 1996).

By adolescence, many youth begin to question their family values and attitudes and become more influenced by the values and attitudes of their peers. The peer group often influences the teen's decision making regarding drug and alcohol use, sexual activity, gangs, and participation in violence toward others (Henniger, 2004). The peer group also reflects and reinforces what constitutes appropriate gender roles and social behavior in the culture (Curry et al., 2005).

Religion

From its very beginning as a nation, religion has been a major force in American society. Religion influenced Roger Williams and Ann Hutchinson to leave the Massachusetts Colony and found the colony of Rhode Island and the followers of Joseph Smith to cross the unsettled West to establish a settlement near a great salt lake in what was to become Utah. More currently, 74% of American adults have indicated that religion is an important part of their daily lives (Carroll, 2004), as did 60% of high school seniors (Wallace, Forman, Caldwell, & Willis, 2003). Religious institutions serve as primary agents for the transmission of values and function as agents of social control by reward and punishment (Gollnick & Chinn, 2006).

Religion, with its accompanying beliefs and values, serves as an important socializing agent. Religion provides a moral code or plan for living; provides social and emotional support when needed; and chronicles and ritualizes such important events as birth, marriage, and death. And, to many, it provides answers regarding the meaning of life, existence, and the afterlife (Curry et al., 2005). Religion influences our attitudes regarding the role of the family, sex roles, discipline, child rearing, and our political identities.

The Mass Media

Mass media refers to television and videos, electronic media (video and computer games), popular music, movies, music videos, radio, newspaper, and magazine industries. The socialization effects of both television and the electronic media stand out since they have become almost as strong as those of the home, school, and neighborhood in their influence on children's development and behavior.

The relationship between exposure to media violence and violent behavior has been researched for several decades. Although a direct cause-and-effect relationship has not

For Your Reflection and Analysis

Describe the peer groups in your early life that served as an agent of socialization for you.

To submit your response online, go to http://www.prenhall.com/webb.

CW

been established, there is compelling evidence that exposure to televised acts of aggression can have a negative influence on very young children. The major pediatric, psychiatric, and medical associations cited more than 1,000 studies in the past 30 years that suggest children can become sensitized to media violence, tend to copy and model what they view, and their values may be influenced by it (Sappenfield, 2002).

One such study, a 17-year research study of television viewing and aggressive behavior, found a significant association between the amount of time spent watching television during adolescence and early adulthood and the likelihood of subsequent aggression toward others. Adolescents who viewed television for 1 hour per day were four times more likely to later commit aggressive acts compared to those who viewed television for less than 1 hour per day. For those who viewed television for more than 3 hours per day, 28% were later found to be involved in a variety of aggressive behaviors (assaults, robberies, and fights). The association was significant after controlling for previous aggressive behavior, child neglect, low family income, neighborhood violence, parental education, and psychiatric disorder (Johnson, Cohen, Smailes, Kasen, & Brook, 2002). Yet another study found a strong relationship between viewing television at an early age and subsequent bullying (Zimmerman, Gleu, Christakis, & Katon, 2005).

Other research has confirmed that being exposed to video games and computer games with violent themes and content may also desensitize both children and youth to violent feelings and aggressive behaviors (Anderson, 2004). Among elementary and middle school students, boys play video games an average of 13 hours per week compared to girls who play an average of 5.5 hours per week. Young children, age 7, play an average of 43 minutes per day (Gentile & Walsh, 2002). Research has also shown that the more children play violent games, the more likely they are to have a hostile personality and to be physically aggressive (Gentile & Gentile, 2005).

Television and School Achievement.   The relationship between television viewing and school achievement is also a matter of concern. Except for limited evidence that television viewing may increase vocabulary, most studies that have examined the relationship between television viewing and school achievement have found a negative correlation between the amount of viewing and the level of achievement, especially at the higher levels of viewing. For example, data from the National Assessment of Educational Progress show that among 8th graders, those who watch 2 or fewer hours of television per day had an average reading score of 288, whereas those who watch 6 hours or more had an average score of 264; at the 12th-grade level, the comparable scores were 313 and 286 (U.S. Department of Education, 2005b). In addition, many teachers also complain that increased television viewing interferes with homework and creates in children an expectation that they must be entertained.

Of equal concern with test scores is the effect of television viewing on attention. A 2004 study led by Christakis found that for each hour a child between 1 and 3 years of age watches television, the risk the child will have attention problems is increased by 10% (Barton, 2004).

The Purposes and Expectations of Schooling

Just as there are a variety of theories of education that influence how we view the teaching and learning process, there are also a variety of theories or perspectives on the primary purposes and expectations of schooling. Sociologists and others commonly refer to three distinct perspectives on the purposes and expectations of schooling: the *functionalist perspective,* the *conflict theory perspective,* and the *interactionist perspective.* The functionalist perspective emphasizes the benefits of education to the social and economic order. The conflict perspective emphasizes the role of education in the perpetuation of social inequality. The interactionist perspective looks at the interactions in the schools to understand their effect on school processes and students.

Functionalist Perspective

Functionalists believe the role of the school is to preserve a common set of values that foster social unity and maintain social order. According to the functionalist perspective, the purpose of the school is to teach the economic, political, and cultural practices and norms of the dominant society (Feinberg & Soltis, 2004). These lessons are not limited to the formal curriculum, but include the hidden curriculum as discussed in Chapter 14.

The functionalists see the school as the institution where students can best acquire the necessary knowledge and skills to become responsible and productive citizens and to compete in the global economy. (The importance placed on education in terms of our nation's global standing is attested to by the attention given to, and the debate over, the achievement of American students compared with that of students in other countries.) Although there is disagreement as to what body of knowledge and which skills are the most important for students to master, philosophers, educational theorists, teachers, parents, and individuals across the economic, social, and political spectrum have underscored this purpose of schooling.

According to functionalists, education contributes to economic growth and development primarily through its effect on productivity by upgrading the skills of the labor force. They point to the research that has shown that more educated workers (1) are less likely to lose time because of unemployment and illness; (2) are more likely to innovate and be aware of, and receptive to, new ideas and knowledge; (3) produce better goods and render services with greater skill; and (4) produce more goods and services in a given period of time because of their skill, dexterity, and knowledge (Webb, McCarthy, & Thomas, 1988). Schools also prepare children to support the economic system by enhancing the development of personal attributes compatible with the industrial workplace. This purpose of schooling, aimed at training students as future workers, emphasizing the need for planning, punctuality, time on-task, cooperation, independence, and following the rules, has also been referred to as its *social efficiency* goal (Labaree, 2000),

Functionalists point out that it is not just the larger society or the employer that enjoys the benefits of schooling, but that education pays off handsomely for the individual. For example, the average annual earnings of workers ages 18 and older with a degree beyond the bachelor's level is $74,602 compared to $51,206 for those with a bachelor's degree, $27,915 for those with a high school diploma, and $18,734 for those with less than a high school diploma (U.S. Census Bureau, 2005a).

The functionalists also believe that schools play an important role in developing moral character. This was an explicit expectation of the schools throughout much of America's history. The textbooks and curriculum of the school were directed toward the development of character and moral behavior. Teachers were expected not only to exhibit high ethical and moral principles but also to teach those principles to their students. Although the continued push for separation of church and state has greatly eliminated the religious involvement that was once the significant vehicle for much of this training, the emphasis on moral development continues to be one of the important expectations of schooling. And, as the family has relinquished more and more of its role in transmitting moral responsibility, the school has, in part, assumed this function.

Conflict Theory Perspective

Those who espouse the conflict theory perspective believe that schools cannot agree on a common set of values and are influenced by which groups have the most power and who benefits most from the system. Conflict theorists are concerned with the conflict between social classes, the workers and the "capitalists," the powerless and the powerful (Feinberg & Soltis, 2004).

Conflict theorists, similar to the Marxists, neo-Marxists, and critical theorists, believe that the schools essentially serve the wealthy and powerful at the expense of the disadvantaged. They contend that the schools serve the upper socioeconomic classes by socializing the working and lower classes to conform to the values and beliefs that are necessary to maintain the existing social order. Critical theorists argue that the classroom, with its extrinsic reward system and hierarchical relationship between teacher and student, is like a miniature factory system. Through the hidden curriculum, students are taught the goals and ideology of the capitalist system. According to conflict theorists, the hidden curriculum works against working class students because it instructs them not to

Table 8.1 — Comparison of the Three Theoretical Perspectives on Education

Perspective	View of Education	Key Concepts and Processes
Functionalist	Sees education as essential for an orderly and efficient society	Socialization and other functions Official and hidden curriculum
Conflict Theory	Sees educational system as perpetuating social inequality	Prestige hierarchy of schools Cultural capital
Interactionist	Sees education as interaction in the social setting of the school	Labeling Self-fulfilling prophecy

Source: Adapted from: T. Curry, R. Jiobu & K. Schwirian, © 2005, *Sociology for the Twenty-First Century*, 4th., Upper Saddle River, NJ: Pearson Prentice Hall, p. 364.

challenge authority" (Curry et al., 2005, p. 362). Critical theorists further contend that the real purpose of schooling, which they contend is controlled by the elite, is to train the workers needed for business and industry, not to promote the movement of disadvantaged youth into the upper classes (Spring, 2004).

Interactionist Perspective

The interactionist perspective is both a critique and an extension of both the functionalist and the conflict perspectives. Interactionists criticize functionalists and conflict theorists for being too abstract in their depictions of what schools offer students and what teachers offer schools and for failing to address what goes on in the schools on a day-to-day basis. They miss the interactional aspects of school life, what takes place between students and students and between students and teachers. "For example, the processes by which students are labeled 'gifted' or 'learning disabled' are, from an interactionist point of view, important to analyze because such processes carry with them the many implicit assumptions about learning and children" (Ballentine & Spade, 2004, p. 13).

Interactionist perspective is often combined with functionalist or conflict perspectives to provide a more complete picture of society and its institutions, including the schools. Applied by the discipline of educational sociology, interaction theory has contributed to our understanding of the effect that teacher expectations and assumptions about students based on race, ethnicity, class, and gender have on student's self-concept and achievement, as well as on the school processes and interactions that are important to decisions related to ability grouping and tracking. Combining the findings of conflict theory with the interactionist perspective, sociologists have been able to demonstrate how school processes at the organizational level actually result in inequality and social stratifications at the classroom level. In effect, "the system of public education in reality perpetuates what it is ideologically committed to eradicating—class barriers which result in inequality in the social and economic life of citizenry" (Risk, cited in Sadovnik, 2004, p. 14).

A comparison of the three theories of the purposes of education from a sociological perspective is presented in Table 8.1.

The Diverse Student Population

The schools reflect the society they serve. The student population is made up of children from all of the social classes, religions, races, ethnicities, languages, and exceptionalities found in the larger society. The conditions of each of these groups are reflected both in the diverse student groups and in their impact on educational achievement and attainment. Although there is practically no limit to the number of diverse groups found in the student population of our nation's schools, the most common groupings are those defined by social classes, ethnicity, race, language, exceptionality, and gender.

Social Class

Sociologists maintain that a number of social classes exist within most societies, distinguishable by great differences in wealth, prestige, and power. The **social class** system in the United States has traditionally been represented by a hierarchy of five classes or groups: upper class, upper middle class, lower middle class, upper working class, and lower working class. (See the Historical Note below for a review of the concept of social class.) One's social class, or **socioeconomic status** (SES), is determined by a number of variables, including wealth and income, education, occupation, power, and prestige. When asked to which social class they belong, the majority of Americans identify themselves as being middle class. Over the years, differences between certain classes have disappeared. For example, blue-collar workers of the working class have enjoyed greater gains in income than lower middle class White-collar workers, thereby eliminating some of the earlier distinctions between the two groups. At the same time, in recent years both the high income and high status upper class and the low income low status lower class have grown, creating an ever widening gulf between the very rich and the very poor.

Although changes are occurring among the different classes, the five-class structure still remains a viable and convenient method of differentiating one group from another. The *upper class,* which comprises only 3% of American society, includes those individuals who control great wealth, power, and influence. Members of the *upper middle class,*

HISTORICAL NOTE

The Concept of Social Class

The concept of social class and social stratification can be found as early as the time of Plato and Aristotle. Although Plato and Aristotle did not attempt to advance any particular theory to explain the causes and consequences of such stratification, they did recognize the different classes that existed in their social structures. Both Plato and Aristotle discussed social class distinctions in the ideal society. Plato envisioned a utopian society that was divided into three social classes: guardians, auxiliaries, and workers. According to Plato, the guardians would be a disinterested ruling elite. Aristotle acknowledged three social classes including the very wealthy, the very poor, and the middle class. According to Aristotle, in the ideal political system, the middle class would be the dominant or ruling class.

By the 17th and 18th centuries, the concept of social class was an important subject for discussion. During this period, John Locke developed a theory of social class that identified two separate classes: property owners and laborers. In 1755, the French philosopher Jean-Jacques Rousseau recognized the existence of social

classes by describing what he referred to as natural inequalities and those inequities that resulted from the social order.

Perhaps more than any other political philosopher, Karl Marx was able to demonstrate the relationship between social class and the political economy. For Marx, what distinguishes one type of society from another is the mode of production (i.e., technology and the division of labor). Marx hypothesized that each mode of production creates a particular class system whereby one class controls the process of production and the other class or classes become the producers or service providers for the dominant/ruling class. Marx was primarily concerned with modern capitalist society. He envisioned a successful working class revolution and the birth of a new classless society.

Identify your social class and indicate what impact your socioeconomic status has had on your educational achievement and attainment.

To research and explore this topic further, go to the *Historical Note* module for this chapter of the Companion Website at **http://www.prenhall.com/webb.**

which includes 22% of society, do not have the family background of the upper class. They are generally leading professionals, high-level managers, or corporate executives who are well educated and financially well off. The *lower middle class,* accounting for 34% of the population, consists of middle income businesspeople; white-collar clerical workers and salespersons; skilled workers such as factory foremen; farm owners; and some building, electrical, and plumbing contractors. The *upper working class* is largely made up of blue-collar workers in skilled and semiskilled jobs and represents 28% of the population. The *lower working class* consists of that 13% of society who are often referred to as the *underclass* and is composed of individuals with incomes at or below the poverty level who are usually poorly educated and often unemployed. The underclass includes the 2% hard-core unemployed who have lived in poverty for a lengthy period of time, such as 8 out of the last 10 years, and excludes those individuals who are temporarily poor due to loss of a job or other unfortunate circumstances (Rose, 2000).

The socioeconomic distinctions among the social classes, specifically the existence of poverty, affect not only lifestyles, patterns of association, and friendships but patterns of school achievement and attainment. In 2003 nearly 13 million children in the United States were living in poverty. Of these, nearly 4 million lived in low-income households where neither parent had been employed during the past year (Annie E. Casey Foundation, 2005).

The effects of poverty are seen early in the child's development and academic career. Children in poverty have lower birth weight, which is associated with delayed motor and social development (Barton, 2004). They also tend to have poor vision, poor oral hygiene, more lead poisoning, more asthma, poor nutrition, less adequate pediatric care, and more exposure to secondhand smoke—all of which are likely to have a significant impact on cognitive functioning and academic achievement (Rothstein, 2004). Poverty's adverse effects on achievement are visible as early as the first grade, and the differences appear to increase as the child progresses through school. Low-income children are 1.4 times as likely as their higher income peers to have a learning disability, 1.3 times more likely to be at risk for parent-reported emotional and behavioral problems, 3.1 times more likely to experience teen pregnancy, 6.8 times more likely to be victims of child abuse and neglect, and 2.2 times more likely to become a victim of violent crime (Duncan & Brooks-Gunn, 2001).

Millions of families of all races and cultures live in poverty.

Parental income is also highly correlated with school readiness. Kindergartners from low-income homes typically start school at least one full year behind others in reading and have a vocabulary of only 5,000 words compared to 20,000 words for their middle class peers (Evans, 2005). A number of factors are thought to be related to this lack of readiness, including the fact that these children are not as likely to attend preschool and that low-income parents, on the average, read less to their children and speak less to them (e.g., 600 words per hour for low-income parents compared to 2,100 words per hour for parents who are professionals) (Evans, 2005).

The Social Class Achievement and Attainment Gaps.   Notwithstanding the popular rhetoric that schools advance economic growth, economic productivity, and **social mobility,** the goal of equal educational opportunity for all has never been fully achieved in the United States. While the attention given to the achievement disparities between students in the public schools has focused on the achievement gaps between white and Asian American students and black and Hispanic students, the achievement and attainment gaps between rich and poor students and upper and lower class students are equally persistent and challenging.

A number of indicators of school success, including the sometimes controversial standardized tests (see *Controversial Issue* on page 202), have been linked to various indicators of socioeconomic status. For example, the **National Assessment of Educational Progress (NAEP)** annually tests a national representative sample of students in public

For Your Reflection and Analysis

Identify your social class and indicate what impact your socioeconomic status has had on your educational achievement and attainment.
To submit your response online, go to http://www. prenhall.com/webb.

CW

CONTROVERSIAL ISSUE

Standardized Testing

The use of standardized tests—always a controversial issue—has been even more broadly debated as a number of states and school districts have adopted so-called "high-stakes tests" and as the testing requirements of the No Child Left Behind Act have been enforced. Some of the most commonly given arguments for and against standardized tests follow.

Pros

1. They improve the accountability of students, teachers, and schools.
2. Student weaknesses can be identified and addressed early.
3. Schools can identify their weaknesses and focus improvement efforts on the areas of greatest need.
4. Allows for the necessary comparisons across schools, districts, and over time that are needed for public policy purposes.
5. Helps parents know how well their children are learning.
6. Leads to improvement in teaching and student achievement.

Cons

1. Tests are inherently biased against certain learning styles and work to the disadvantage of poor and minority students.
2. Test results are misleading: Tests do not have the reliability or validity to accurately measure the proficiency of students across the ability, racial, ethnic, and socioeconomic spectrums.
3. Teachers spend too much time "teaching to the test" at the expense of other material or teaching for understanding.
4. Tests are expensive to develop and administer and take money needed for other educational programs.
5. Test results are used to make decisions that cannot be adequately informed by one measure.
6. Students and schools in poor districts, which are subject to numerous conditions beyond their control, are unfairly stigmatized and sanctioned.

What is your position? Will high-stakes testing improve education or harm it? Which students are hurt the most by such tests?

 To answer these questions online, go to the *Controversial Issue* module for this chapter of the Companion Website at **http://www.prenhall.com/webb**.

and private schools in certain subject and skill areas. The NAEP reports, referred to as the "Nation's Report Card," have consistently shown that, in general, achievement is related to parental education and student eligibility for free and reduced lunch, two indicators of socioeconomic status. According to the findings, the NAEP proficiency scores of free and reduced lunch–eligible students were consistently lower than those of noneligible students, and proficiency scores at each age level also consistently increased as level of parental education increased. For example, in 2004 the average NAEP mathematics score for the eighth-grade children of high school dropouts was 262, compared with 271 for the eighth-grade children of high school graduates, and 292 for the eighth-grade children of college graduates (U.S. Department of Education, 2005b).

As shown in Figure 8.2, on another indicator, the Scholastic Assessment Test (SAT), the test most frequently taken by college-bound seniors, the relationship between parental education and SAT scores is also evident: The lower the parental educational level, the lower the SAT scores.

Social class as measured by the educational and occupational levels of parents has also been found to be the most significant predictor of educational attainment. Regardless of race or ethnicity, students from low-income or underclass families were more likely to repeat a grade and to drop out of school than those from middle or upper class families. In 2001, young people from families in the lowest 20% of family income were six times more

Figure 8.2 — 2005 Mean SAT Scores Vary with Parental Education

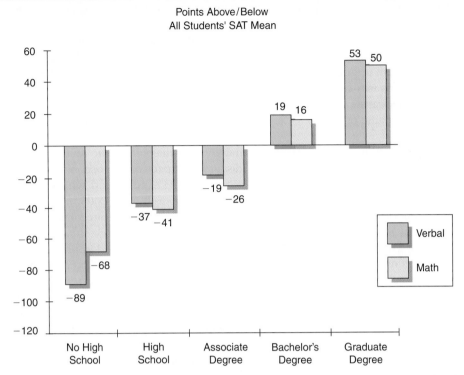

Points Above/Below
All Students' SAT Mean

Source: 2005 Mean SAT Scores Vary with Parental Education. Copyright © 2005, CollegeBoard.com. Reproduced with permission. All rights reserved. www.collegeboard.com.

likely to drop out of school than those from the highest 20% of income (U.S. Department of Education, 2005d). Students whose parents completed a bachelor's degree or higher were more than twice as likely to enroll in college immediately after high school graduation than students whose parents had less than a high school diploma (U.S. Department of Education, 2005d).

Hispanic Americans

Ethnic groups are subgroups of the population that are distinguished by having a common cultural heritage (e.g., language, customs, history). The 41 million Hispanics in the United States, who make up 14% of the population, comprise the largest ethnic group in the country and the second largest and fastest growing minority group. One of every two people added to the nation's population is Hispanic (U.S. Census Bureau, 2005c). Since 2000 the Hispanic population has expanded three times faster than the population as a whole. Immigration and a high birthrate are responsible for the rapid growth in the Hispanic population.

Hispanic Americans are a diverse group made up of Mexican Americans (65% of Hispanics), Puerto Ricans (9%), Cubans (3%), and "Other," which includes persons from Spain, Central and South America, the Caribbean, and those who identify themselves as Latino, Hispano, Spanish American, and so on. The median age of the U.S. Hispanic population, 27 years, is 13 years younger than that of the non-Hispanic, white population (Kamman, 2005). Thirty-four percent of the Hispanic population is under the age of 18. Hispanics have the highest concentration of preschoolers of any racial or ethnic group. By

Hispanics are the fastest growing minority in the United States.

2050, the number of Hispanic Americans is projected to grow to 98 million and represent 24% of the U.S. population (U.S. Census Bureau, 2005c).

Hispanic Americans are geographically concentrated in three separate regions: the West, the South, and the Northeast. Hispanic Americans of Mexican origin are more likely to live in the West (57%) and South (33%). Puerto Ricans are most likely to reside in the Northeast (64%). Cubans tend to be concentrated in the South (80%), whereas people of Central American origin are found in all of these three regions of the United States. Hispanic Americans may be of any race. About 14% of whites, 3% of African Americans, 2% of Asians Americans and Pacific Islanders, and 11% of Native Americans and Alaska Natives are of Hispanic origin (U.S. Census Bureau, 2005c; World Book Special Census Edition, 2002).

The low educational achievement and attainment of many Hispanic American youth is no doubt associated with the previously discussed impact of socioeconomic status. In 2003, the poverty rate for Hispanic Americans was 23%, compared with 8% for non-Hispanic whites and 12% for Asian Americans (U.S. Census Bureau, 2005c). Also, whereas Hispanic American children represent 16% of the children in the United States, they constitute 29% of all children living in poverty (U.S. Census Bureau, 2005c).

Nationally, Hispanic American children are also underrepresented in preprimary education programs, such as Head Start, which may explain their lack of readiness to participate in elementary school. They are also underrepresented in gifted and college preparation courses and overrepresented in remedial and vocational tracks (Walker, 2004).

A significant explanation for the poorer academic performance of some Hispanic American children may also be their limited English-speaking ability. Other factors that may contribute to the low achievement and low attainment of these students include the following:

- High mobility (Between the first and third grades, 25% of Hispanic students change schools three or more times compared to 13% of whites [Evans, 2005].);
- Understaffed, poorly equipped, and poorly funded schools, often segregated and staffed by mostly non-Hispanic teachers;
- The limited education of parents, which makes it difficult for them to effectively participate in their children's education;
- A lack of family support in terms of monitoring homework and other school-related activities (Schmid, 2001);
- Higher level of television viewing (Twenty percent of Hispanic students watch 6 or more hours of TV per day compared to 13% of white students [U.S. Department of Education, 2005b].);
- High incidence of single-parent families; and
- Recent immigration.

African Americans

The 39 million African Americans in the United States make up 13.3% of the total population (U.S. Census Bureau, 2005b). The African American population is expected to reach 61.4 million, or 15% of the U.S. population, by 2050 (U.S. Census Bureau, 2005b). Many African Americans are immigrants from Africa, Central or South America, and the Caribbean. Thirty-two percent of the black population is under the age of 18, making it the second youngest racial or ethnic group (U.S. Census Bureau, 2005b); see Figure 8.3.

As in the case of Hispanic Americans, explanations for the lower levels of academic achievement and attainment of African Americans (relative to whites and Asian Americans) are linked to the lower socioeconomic status and the social milieu of African American families. For example, in 2003, the poverty rate for African Americans, 24%, was about the same as that of Hispanic Americans (U.S. Census Bureau, 2005b). Lower average levels of parental education and lower levels of parental availability are also contributory factors. Only 38% of black students compared to 75% of white students live with two parents. Many live in a single-mother household below the poverty level, "a consideration that puts children from any ethnic group at risk for, among other problems, poor attendance and achievement and behavior problems" (Evans, 2005, p. 586).

African American children, like Hispanic children, disproportionately reside in tax-poor, high-poverty districts and are thus disadvantaged relative to resources available to their schools. They are also less likely to be enrolled in preprimary education, have higher placement in remedial and vocational classes, are less likely to be enrolled in gifted and college preparatory classes, change schools more often, and experience higher school expulsion rates (Borja, 2001; Walker, 2004).

Asian Americans and Pacific Islanders

Asian Americans are defined as those Americans whose ancestry can be traced to such Asian countries as Cambodia, China, India, Japan, Korea, Laos, Malaysia, Pakistan, the Philippine Islands, Thailand, and Vietnam. The U.S. Census Bureau combines Asian Americans with Pacific Islanders for reporting purposes. Pacific Islanders include Polynesians, Micronesians, or Melanesians, Samoans, Guamanians, Native Hawaiians, Tahitians, Northern Mariana Islanders, Palauans, and Fijians. Chinese Americans (21%), Filipino Americans (21%), and Japanese Americans (19%) comprise the largest ethnic groups of Asian Americans (Zirpoli & Melloy, 2001). Approximately 53% of the total Asian American population lives in the western part of the United States; 96% live in metropolitan areas. In 2002, approximately 24% of Asian Americans were under age 18, the same as non-Hispanic whites (UCLA Asian American Studies Center, 2005).

Although their percentage of the U.S. population is relatively small (5%), the 13.5 million Asian Americans are one of the fastest growing racial groups in the United States. It is anticipated that by the year 2050, the Asian American population will more than double, to 36 million, and will represent 9% of the U.S. population (U.S. Census Bureau, 2005e).

Much of the research that has been done on Asian American students' achievement and attainment has concentrated on the factors contributing to their success. Cultural factors have been found to be among the most important variables. Among the cultural variables noted are high expectations of parents and teachers, a supportive home learning environment that reinforces academic success, a high level of parental supervision, and a high value placed on self-control and education for self-improvement and family honor (Chiang, 2000; Weinberg, 1997). Southeast Asian children are taught from an early age to develop a sense of moral obligation and loyalty to the family that demands unquestioning loyalty and obedience not only to parents but also to all authority figures, including teachers and other school personnel (Morrow, 1991).

Asian American students are often stereotyped as "the model student" or the "whiz kid." This stereotype can sometimes work to their disadvantage. That is, when Asian American students do have educational problems, their problems often go unnoticed (Chiang, 2000).

Native Americans (American Indians and Alaska Natives)

Native Americans are a diverse population composed of American Indians and Alaska Natives (Eskimos and Aleuts). They include more than 554 different tribes, each with its own culture, and 250 surviving languages. Nearly one-half of the nation's American Indians and Alaska Natives reside in the Western states. The states with the largest percentages are Alaska (19%), New Mexico (11%), Oklahoma (11%), South Carolina (9%), and Montana (7%) (U.S. Department of Education, 2005f).

The Native American population, which currently makes up almost 1.5% of the total population, has been growing at a faster rate than the overall population. Since 1990 the Native American population has increased 14% compared to an 8% increase in the U.S. population as a whole and is expected to reach 3.2 million by 2050 (U.S. Department of Education, 2005f). During the next two decades, the Native American population is

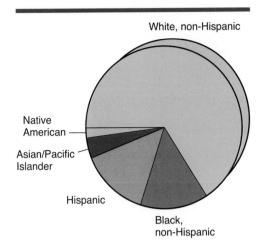

Figure 8.3 — Racial/Ethnic Composition of U.S. Population, 2004

White, non-Hispanic

Native American

Asian/Pacific Islander

Hispanic

Black, non-Hispanic

projected to increase at a faster rate than either the white or African American populations, but at a slower rate than the Asian American population. The Native American population is also younger than the overall population: Approximately one-third of the Native American population is under 18 years of age, with a median age of 29 years, 7 years younger than the median age for the total population (U. S. Department of Education, 2005f).

The majority of Native American children and youth (approximately 90%) attend public schools. The remainder attend one of 171 Bureau of Indian Affairs (BIA)–operated schools in Arizona, New Mexico, North Dakota, and South Dakota. A study of student achievement at BIA schools indicated that students attending BIA schools scored considerably lower on standard tests than Native American students who attended public schools (Zehr, 2001).

There are a number of explanations for the lower levels of educational achievement and attainment of Native Americans. For one thing, Native American children have the highest rate of absenteeism of any racial or ethnic group. They also have the second highest rate of suspensions or expulsions, placing them at higher risk for dropping out (U.S. Department of Education, 2005f). In addition, many Native American children come from homes of lower socioeconomic status: About 24% of the American Indian and Alaska Native population is classified as living in poverty (U.S. Department of Education, 2005f). The limited English proficiency of many Native American parents, coupled with the English-only instruction in many schools, may also exacerbate the problems of Native American students and prevent their parents from becoming involved in their children's educational experience. In addition, the curriculum in many schools, which is primarily Euro-American in focus, is often perceived by Native American students and their families not only as irrelevant and insensitive to their needs, but actually detrimental to their own culture, language, and identity (Chavers, 2000; National Education Association, 2001a; St. Charles & Costantino, 2000).

One explanation for the relatively low academic achievement and attainment of Native American students that has gained wide acceptance among educational researchers and theorists is the *cultural difference theory.* According to this theory, the relatively low academic achievement and attainment of Native American students results from discontinuities between the culture and language of their homes and communities and those of the mainstream society and the schools. In effect, many Native American students come from backgrounds that equip them with linguistic, interactional, and learning styles that are not typically supported or rewarded by the traditional American school. Many Native American students also face a discontinuity between the varieties of English they speak, so-called "Indian English," and that spoken by their non-Indian peers and teachers. The result of all these discontinuities is a systematic and chronic miscommunication in the classroom, as well as a failure to recognize and build on the knowledge and skills that the Native American students bring with them to school (St. Charles & Costantino, 2000).

Several additional factors identified in the literature that help explain the underachievement and lower attainment of Native American students include these:

- The lack of well-trained teachers and administrators;
- Low student and/or parent motivation;
- Inadequate funding of the schools attended by Native Americans, many of which are small, rural schools or schools on reservations;
- Test bias, inadequate preparation for testing, and test anxiety;
- High student and staff mobility in their schools; and
- Higher rates of school violence and substance abuse (Beaulieu, 2000; Gilbert, 2000).

It is important to note that not only are there differences between Native American students and students of the dominant culture, but there are significant differences among Native American students from different tribal groups. These differences (for example, the family's attitudes toward traditionalism, whether the student is from a multitribal home, the degree of monolingualism or bilingualism in the family, and the parents' educational background) may all impact educational outcomes as much as any of the factors previously mentioned (Callahan & McIntire, 1994).

The Racial and Ethnic Achievement Gap

Student differences and differences in the quality of their educational experiences have combined to produce what has become perhaps the most persistent and difficult issue in education in the United States—the achievement gap. "Closing the gap is widely seen as important not just for our educational system but ultimately for our economy, our social stability, and our moral health as a nation" (Evans, 2005, p. 582).

Although in the half century since *Brown* the attainment and achievement of minorities have improved significantly, a large achievement gap between Asian Americans and other minorities and between Whites and Hispanics and Blacks has remained. The evidence supporting the achievement gap is typically the results of standardized tests, specifically tests such as the NAEP, the SAT, or the ACT. When scores on these tests over time are examined, the indication is that after improving for a number of years the gap between some subgroups is increasing. For example, as seen in Figure 8.4, the average gap in the reading and math scores of 17-year-old white and black students reached a record low in 1988 before beginning to increase, and the gaps are currently 29 and 28 points, respectively. One positive observation is that, although the NAEP scores of black students lag behind those of their white peers, their scores have increased at a faster rate than those of white students. The achievement gap between white and Hispanic students, as evidenced by NAEP scores, shows a similar trend (see Figure 8.5). That is, the gap in scores between Hispanic and white students declined steadily into the 1980s before beginning to increase in the 1990s. However, unlike the black–white achievement gap, the gap in Hispanic–white scores has shown signs of a continued decline. For example, the gap between both the reading and math scores of 17-year-old Hispanic and whites has actually increased since 1999, as has the gap in the reading scores of 13-year-olds. Still, as was true for blacks, while the gap remains, overall the NAEP scores of Hispanics have increased at a faster rate than those of whites.

Not shown on these graphs are the NAEP scores of Asian Americans and Native Americans, which for many years were not separately reported. In recent years, including 2005, the reported data have shown that Asian American students had the highest NAEP mathematics scores at each grade level reported (4th grade = 246, 8th grade = 291). And, Asian Americans were second only to whites in NAEP performance in reading.

Native American children and youth typically have lower achievement scores than white or Asian American students in reading and mathematics but higher scores than those of Hispanic American or African American students. For example, the 2003 NAEP reading scores for Native American fourth graders was 202, compared to 229 for whites, 200 for Hispanics, and 198 for blacks (U.S. Department of Education, 2005f).

Table 8.2 provides trend data for another common measure of academic achievement, the SAT. The 2005 SAT scores were the highest ever, and taken by a record 148 million high school seniors. During the 10 year period from 1995 to 2005, math and verbal scores increased for almost all racial and ethnic groups. However, Mexican Americans and "Other Hispanics" showed smaller gains than all other racial or ethnic groups. In fact, Mexican Americans showed no gain in the SAT verbal between 1995 and 2005. The largest 10-year verbal score gains were for Asian Americans, whose scores rose 19 points, and Puerto Ricans, with a gain of 12 points. Asian Americans also had the largest gain in math scores (25 points), followed by American Indians/Alaska Natives (up 17 points), whites (15 points), and Puerto Ricans (13 points).

Despite the record scores in 2005 and the 10-year gains, significant gaps remain: The 10 year composite score increase of black students was still 12 points below that of whites. In addition, a gap of 152 points existed between the 2005 composite SAT scores of Mexican American seniors and white seniors.

For Your Reflection and Analysis

Did you take the SAT or ACT? To what extent do you feel that your scores were affected by your race, ethnicity, gender, or social class?

To submit your response online, go to http://www. prenhall.com/webb.

CW

Figure 8.4 — Black–White Achievement Gap

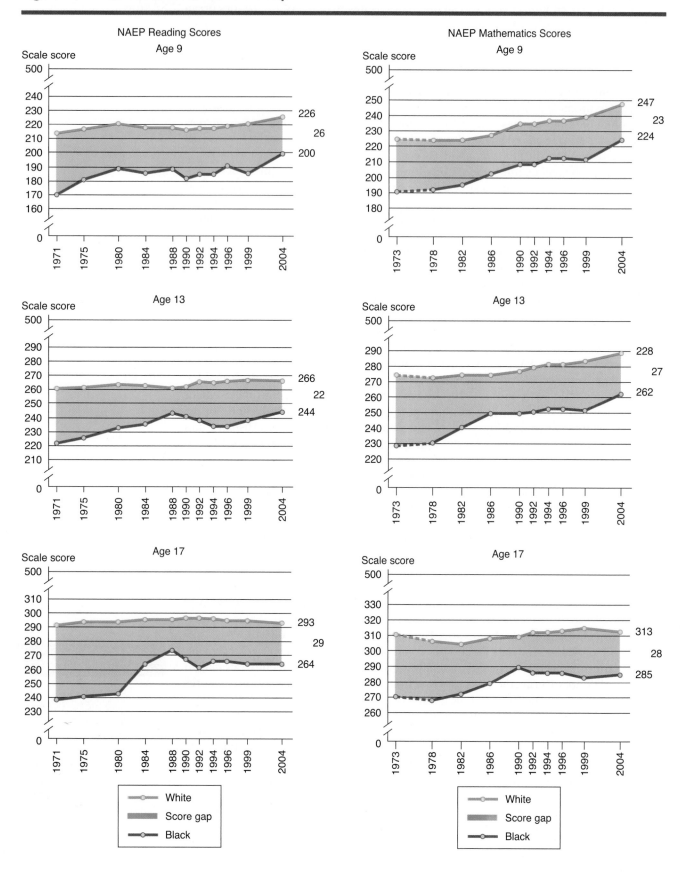

Figure 8.6 — Percentage of 16- to 24-Year-Olds Who Were High School Dropouts, by Race/Ethnicity: Selected Years, 1990 to 2003

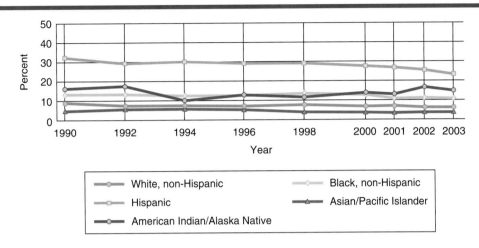

Figure 8.7 — Percentage Distribution of Adults Ages 25 and Over, by Highest Level of Education and Race/Ethnicity: 2003

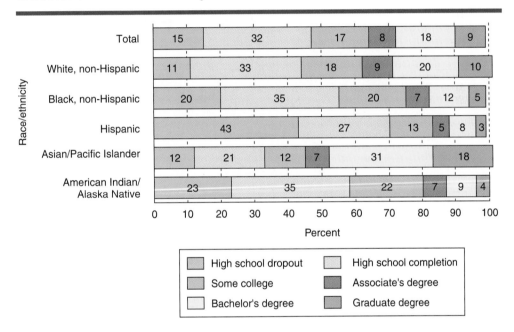

Asian Americans have the highest percentage of postsecondary education completion of any racial or ethnic group—and they are completing their schooling at an ever-increasing rate. As shown in Figure 8.7, in 2003, approximately 49% of Asian Americans age 25 years and older had completed a bachelor's degree or higher, and 18% had completed an advanced degree, almost twice the percentage of whites and almost four times the percentage of all other racial or ethnic groups.

The Declining Gender Gap

Since the passage of Title IX in 1972, the large gaps that existed between males and females in educational achievement and attainment have seen a significant decline, and in some cases have been eliminated. In fact, on the NAEP assessment of reading proficiency (see Figure 8.8), females outscored males in each age as they have since the test began. The opposite occurred in mathematics proficiency where a small but consistent gap in math scores between male and female students persists (see Figure 8.8). In science, the

Figure 8.8 — Gender Achievement Gap

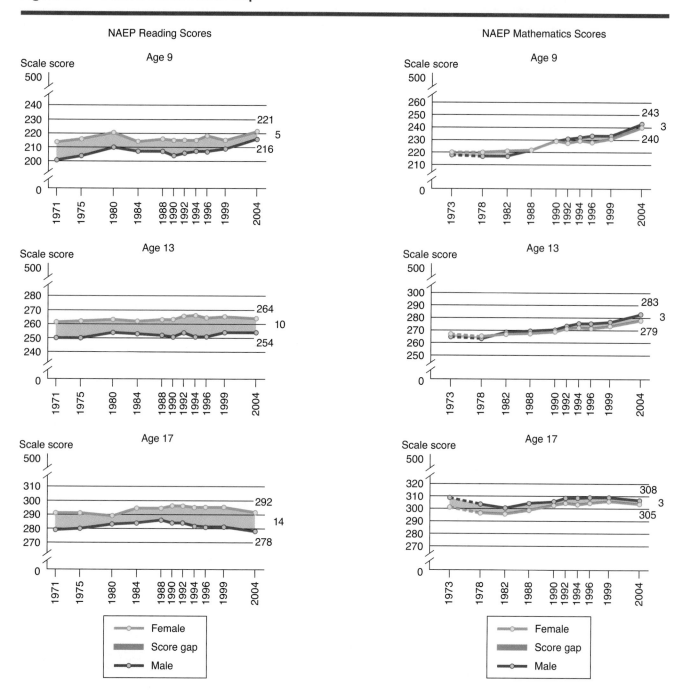

achievement gap between the NAEP scores of males and females was more pronounced. Male students outperformed females in each age group (9-, 13-, and 17-year-olds) on the most recent NAEP assessment (U.S. Department of Education, 2005b).

The comparative achievement of males and females on the SAT also demonstrates a clear pattern of gender difference (see Figure 8.9). Moreover, not only have males consistently outscored females on both the verbal and mathematics sections of the SAT, the gap scores in both areas have increased in the last decade.

During the past three decades, females have made significant gains in both secondary and postsecondary attainment. In 2003, for the second year in a row, females 25 years old and older had a higher high school completion rate (85%) than males (84%).

At the postsecondary level, educational attainment also increased for both males and females. For example, the postsecondary attainment for the population 25 years old and

Figure 8.9 — Average SAT Verbal Scores and Math Scores of College-Bound Seniors By Gender, 1975–2005

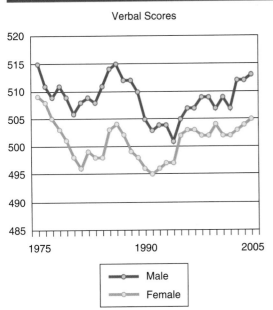

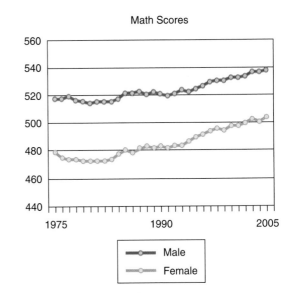

older has increased from approximately 5% in 1950 to 53% in 2003. However, female attainment has increased at a faster pace than male attainment, and by 1985 females were essentially equal to males in the percentage of bachelor's and master's degrees awarded. By 2005 the percentage favored women, with women projected to earn 54% of the bachelor's degrees and 58% of the master's degrees and approaching near parity in the percentage of doctoral degrees awarded (U.S. Census Bureau, 2005d). The success of women in postsecondary education is noteworthy in that they represent 60% or more of students with characteristics that place them at a disadvantage for completion: low income, older, married with children, or single parent (Peter & Hern, 2005). In effect, the attainment gap between males and females, or at least one that favored males, had disappeared.

Although female participation in higher education has increased, females are still underrepresented in majors such as computer and information sciences, engineering, mathematics, and the physical sciences and overrepresented in the somewhat lower paying fields like education.

A number of theories have been suggested as to why males and females achieve differently. The most common explanations are that the differences can be largely attributed to the gender-role socialization that children receive from parents and the gender-role stereotyping and sexism they experience in school and in society. Parents are the first to teach gender

Females now receive the majority of postsecondary degrees.

roles beginning with their simple choice of clothing or dress, the child's living space, their toys, and so forth. Parents also interact with males and females differently. For example, research suggests that preschool girls are read to more than boys, which may contribute to later higher reading achievement for females. As children grow older, their peer groups and the media influence and reinforce certain gender roles (Curry et al., 2005).

The school experience also contributes to gender socialization, but impacts differently on the achievement of males and female students. For example, boys are more likely than girls to experience serious behavioral problems at school and engage in risky behaviors such as drug use. They are also more apt to be diagnosed with a learning disability or emotional disturbance and to be bullied, be in a physical fight, be victimized, or carry a weapon (U.S. Department of Education, 2005g). Other factors that have been identified in the research as contributing to the differential achievement and attainment of male and female students include the following:

1. Modes of classroom interaction: Boys are called on and interact more with teachers, and "the power of the teacher's time and attention means that boys reap the benefits of a more intense educational climate" (Sadker, 2001, p. 82).
2. The sexual abuse and sexual harassment of females in schools: As noted in Chapter 12, 80% of females experience some form of sexual harassment at school and 20% report being physically and sexually abused—all of which can have an impact on the student's academic performance and even desire to remain in school.
3. Females are less likely to repeat a grade or drop out of school. However, girls who do repeat a grade are more likely to drop out of school than boys, and girls who drop out (often due to pregnancy) are less likely to return than boys.
4. Boys are more likely to be enrolled in gifted math and science programs, whereas girls are more often enrolled in gifted programs that focus on language arts (Sadker, 2001).
5. Boys are more likely than girls to be enrolled in higher level high school mathematics courses (i.e., calculus) or related courses such as physics.

Students With Exceptionalities

Students with exceptionalities include both gifted and talented students and students with mental and physical disabilities. Gifted and talented students are estimated to make up 6.3% of the student population (U.S. Department of Education, 2005c). Students with mental and physical disabilities who are enrolled in federally supported programs comprise 13.8% of the student population of the public schools in the United States (U.S. Department of Education, 2005c).

Education for students with disabilities has grown steadily since the 1970s when two historic cases (*Pennsylvania Association of Retarded Citizens v. Commonwealth of Pennsylvania,* 1972, and *Mills v. Board of Education of the District of Columbia,* 1972) mandated services for special education students. In addition, two major federal laws, Section 504 of the Rehabilitation Act of 1973 and the Education for All Handicapped Children Act (EHA) of 1975, provided federal support for a wide range of programs and services for students with disabilities.

Since the passage of the EHA, renamed the Individuals with Disabilities Education Act (IDEA), the number of children served by federally supported programs has tripled. The IDEA recognizes the 13 categories of disabilities listed in Table 8.3. The growth in the number of students served under the IDEA is due not only to an increase in the total student population, but in large part to the growth in the number of students classified as having a learning disability. A child is considered to have a learning disability if he or she has a disorder or delayed development in one or more of the processes of thinking, speaking, reading, writing, listening, or performing arithmetic operations. As shown in Table 8.3, the number of students with disabilities classified as learning disabled tripled and their percentage in the disabled student population rose from 22% in 1977 to 43% in 2004. The second largest category or enrollment for students with disabilities was speech or language impairment, followed by mental retardation.

American Indians/Alaska Natives and blacks are more likely than any other racial or ethnic group to receive services under the IDEA. About 12% of American Indian/Alaska Native children and 11% of black children received services in 2003, compared to 8% of white and Hispanic children and 4% of Asian/Pacific Islander children (U.S. Department of Education, 2005f).

Table 8.3 — Children 3 to 21 Years Old Served in Federally Supported Programs for the Disabled, by Type of Disability: Selected Years, 1976–77 to 2001–02 (numbers in thousands)

Type of Disability	1976–77	1980–81	1990–91	1995–96	1997–98	1999–2000	2001–02	2003–04
All disabilities	3,694	4,144	4,710	5,573	5,903	6,190	6,407	6,633
Specific learning disabilities	796	1,462	2,129	2,579	2,725	2,830	2,846	2,831
Speech or language impairments	1,302	1,168	985	1,022	1,056	1,078	1,084	1,441
Mental retardation	961	830	535	570	589	600	592	593
Emotional disturbance	283	347	390	438	453	468	476	489
Hearing impairments	88	79	58	67	69	70	70	79
Orthopedic impairments	87	58	49	63	67	71	73	77
Other health impairments	141	98	55	133	190	254	337	464
Visual impairments	38	31	23	25	25	26	25	28
Multiple disabilities	—	68	96	93	106	111	127	140
Deaf-blindness	—	3	1	1	1	2	2	2
Autism and traumatic brain injury	—	—	—	39	54	80	118	186
Developmental delay	—	—	—	—	4	19	45	305
Preschool disabled	—	—	390	544	564	582	612	—

Source: U.S. Department of Education, National Center for Education Statistics. (2005). *Digest of Education Statistics, 2004.* Washington, DC: U.S. Government Printing Office.

One group of students that is *not* included under the IDEA but is present in almost every classroom are students with attention deficit–hyperactivity disorder (ADHD). ADHD is the most commonly diagnosed childhood psychiatric disorder, affecting 3% to 7% of the population. ADHD is a condition characterized by symptoms of inattention or hyperactivity-impulsivity "for at least 6 months and to a degree that is maladaptive and inconsistent with developmental level" (American Psychiatric Association, 2000, p. 80). Some students with ADHD may also have a learning or emotional disability and be receiving support under the IDEA or Section 504, but ADHD itself is not recognized as a disability under the IDEA. Boys are more likely to be diagnosed with ADHD than girls, but recent research indicates that the incidence of ADHD in girls may be higher than previously thought, but with subtly different symptoms (Friend, 2005).

Another group of exceptional students not included under the IDEA are students who are gifted and talented. The U.S. Department of Education (1993) defines gifted and talented students as:

> children and youth with outstanding talent to perform or show the potential for performing at remarkably high levels of accomplishment when compared with others of their age, experience, or environment. These children and youth exhibit high performance capability in intellectual, creative, and/or artistic areas, possess an unusual leadership capacity, or excel in specific academic fields. They require services or activities not ordinarily provided by the schools. (pp. 20–21)

There is no federal legislation requiring states to provide services to gifted and talented students and, unfortunately, most states (29) and school districts do not offer any funding for gifted education, making the number of gifted and talented students in the United States difficult to estimate. However, the Council of State Directors of Programs for the Gifted (2000) has estimated that on the average 12% of the student population could be classified as gifted or talented, whether or not they have been identified or are being served. As previously stated, blacks and Hispanics are underrepresented in programs for the gifted and talented, as are females.

Language Diversity

For many students in the public schools, English is not their native language. Many of these **language-minority** students are immigrants and face the double challenge of attempting

PROFESSIONAL REFLECTION

I think one of the largest factors contributing to the issue of the achievement gap is that teachers fail to recognize the cultural aspects that are at play in the classroom, especially in cases where middle class teachers are responsible for children of poverty.

Megan Fuller
National Board Certified
Teacher, Virginia

CW To analyze this reflection, go to the *Professional Reflection* module for this chapter of the Companion Website at **http://www.prenhall.com/webb.**

to adapt to a different culture and learn a new language. In 2003 almost 10 million school-age students, 19% of the children 5–17 years of age, spoke a language other than English at home, up 5 points from a decade earlier. Spanish is the native language of 77% of these students. Many of these children have not mastered English and are referred to the schools as being limited English proficient (LEP). In 2003–04 there were an estimated 5.1 million LEP students in grades K–12, representing approximately 9.6% of the total K–12 population (U.S. Department of Education, 2005c).

In addition to the challenges associated with having limited English proficiency, LEP students often are characterized by a number of the previously discussed factors found to be associated with underachievement and underattainment. For example, LEP children often have not attended preschool and begin school less ready to learn than their non-LEP peers, they have been read to less by their parents, and they are more likely to live in households in poverty with the associated health risks.

As described in the next chapter, 80% of LEP students, approximately 4 million students, are enrolled in language instruction education programs designed to ensure that they attain English proficiency and meet the same standards for academic achievement expected of all students.

Summary

In this chapter, the schools, the family, the peer group, religion, and the mass media were examined as agents of socialization. Of these institutions, the family has undergone the most significant changes since World War II. As a result of those changes, many of the earlier functions of the family have now been transferred to the school. At the same time, as children spend more time viewing television, its influence on their behavior and school achievement has increased.

There are a number of perspectives on the primary purposes and expectations of schooling; the functionalist prespective, the conflict theory perspective, and the interactionist perspective. Among these, the issue of whether the schools promote social selection or social mobility remains the most controversial.

Many people would agree that there are numerous opportunities for education, but most believe that equal educational opportunity is more a myth than a fact in the American educational system. The myth of equal educational opportunity is particularly evident when one examines differences in the educational achievement and attainment of socioeconomic groups, ethnic groups, racial groups, and males and females and the challenges faced by students with disabilities and language-minority students. In the next chapter, we will look at some of the strategies that have been employed to increase equality of educational opportunity and ameliorate against the effects of economic and cultural discrimination.

Key Terms

Ethnic group, 203
Language minority, 215
Mass media, 196
National Assessment of
  Educational Progress
  (NAEP), 201

Social class, 200
Social mobility, 201
Socialization, 194

Society, 194
Socioeconomic status, 200

PROFESSIONAL DEVELOPMENT WORKSHOP

Prepare for the Praxis™ Examination

Kelly Fuller is a second-year, fourth-grade teacher at Martin Luther King Middle School (MLKMS), an inner-city school. MLKMS has a student body that is 15% Hispanic, many of whom are recent immigrants and non-English speakers, and 4% African Americans whose families have lived in the neighborhood for decades and whose parents also probably attended MLKMS.

Kelly Fuller had just received the results of the state standardized test for her students in reading and mathematics. She was alone when she turned to the large sealed manila envelope that held the test results. Her students were still at the library working on their a book report assignment so she had time to carefully review the scores of each student.

Mrs. Fuller was disappointed to see that the majority of her students had made only a slight gain in reading and no gain in mathematics: Reading scores had increased from the 48th percentile to the 49th percentile while their mathematics scores remained at the 43rd percentile. Kelly had worked hard all year on improving student math skills and had really expected to see an improvement in students' math scores. She is concerned about how her students, their parents, and school and district administrators will receive the test results.

As she continued to stare at the test results, Kelly's memory flashed back to 2 years ago and her interview with Joe Edwards, the principal. Joe had said, "Kelly, I want you to know that one of the most difficult parts of your job here at Martin Luther King Middle School will be to not get discouraged and disappointed. In their few short years on this earth, the kids that you will be teaching have known disappointment far beyond what you and I can even imagine. Our job is to build them up and instill in them a purpose for trying, no matter what the outcome. Students are more than just test scores to us."

Moments later, her students filed back into the class, still energized and excited about their book reports. Tommy Sanchez and Billy Middleton could hardly contain their excitement when asking Mrs. Fuller if they could do a combined book report on *The Latest Discovery of Extinct Reptiles in the Sonoran Desert.* Responding, she puts aside her thoughts and disappointment regarding the state test results, and refocused her attention on the 26 nine-year-olds who were getting settled back in their seats.

1. Differentiate between the two major types of standardized tests. Discuss the advantages and disadvantages of each approach.
2. How can Kelly best communicate the results of the state tests to students and parents to ensure that they understand the limits of the tests?
3. Statewide testing programs generally serve different purposes than teachers' classroom assessments. Explain the major purposes of a teacher's classroom assessment program.

To submit your responses online, go to the *Prepare for the Praxis™ Examination* module for this chapter of the Companion Website at **http://www.prenhall.com/webb**.

Build Your Knowledge Base

1. In response to the opening vignette that describes David Marshall's paper, what are some of the possible ways he might reconceptualize the basic concept of society?
2. Describe some of the ways in which the structure of your family has changed over time. To what extent have those changes been positive? To what extent have they been negative?
3. How could you, as a teacher, attempt to mitigate against the negative influence of television on children's aggressive behavior? What suggestions would you make to parents?
4. Reflect on the high school from which you graduated. To what extent did it promote upward social mobility? In what ways did it resemble a miniature factory system?
5. Discuss what is meant by the cycle of poverty. What can the schools do to break this cycle?

6. Discuss the impact of differing cultural values on school achievement and attainment. Give specific examples.
7. Discuss the common factors contributing to the underachievement of Hispanic Americans, African Americans, and Native Americans and Alaska Natives.
8. What are the levels of educational attainment of the females in your family? The males? What factors account for any differences that may exist between the two groups? To what extent are the factors evident today?

Develop Your Portfolio

1. Review the purposes and expectations of schooling. To what extent do you tend to agree or disagree with the purposes and expectations described? Imagine that you have been asked to write an editorial for the local newspaper regarding what you believe are the purposes and expectations of schooling. Prepare your editorial from the perspective of a critical theorist. Place your editorial in your portfolio under **INTASC Standard 4, Instructional Strategies.**
2. After examining INTASC Standard 3, review the various ethnic and racial differences in school achievement that are discussed in this chapter. Begin to collect artifacts (instructional materials) that have been adapted to diverse learners, including those learners who represent a variety of ethnic, racial, and social class differences. Place your artifacts in your portfolio under **INTASC Standard 3, Adapting Instruction for Diverse Learners.**

To complete these activities online, go to the *Develop Your Portfolio* module for this chapter of the Companion Website at **http://www.prenhall.com/webb.**

Explore Teaching and Learning: Field Experiences

1. Identify three schools with different student body characteristics in a nearby district. Compare and review the most recent school report cards or accountability reports for each. How do the schools differ in student performance, socioeconomic characteristics, and other data as reflected in the report cards? What generalizations are suggested by the data?
2. Identify a middle school in a low personal income area and a middle school in a high personal income area. Visit the schools to determine if there is an observable difference in the access that students have to computers, laboratories, scientific equipment, and instructional materials.

Professional Development Online

Visit this text's Companion Website at **http://www.prenhall.com/webb** to gain access to a variety of questions, activities, and exercises to help build your knowledge of this chapter's content. Below are just a few items available at this text's Companion Website:

- Classroom Video—To see actual classroom footage and work through activities and questions to analyze the content of the video, click on the *Classroom Video* module for this chapter.
- Teaching Tolerance—To go to this organization's website and complete activities to explore issues and topics dealing with how to teach tolerance to students, click on the *Teaching Tolerance* module for this chapter.
- Self-Test—To review terms and concepts presented in this chapter, click on the *Self-Test* module for this chapter.
- Internet Resources—To link to websites related to topics in this chapter, go to the *Internet Resources* module for this chapter.

CHAPTER 9

As a son of a tenant farmer, I know that education is the only valid passport from poverty. As a former teacher—and I hope a future one—I have great expectations of what this law will mean for all of our young people . . . I believe deeply no law I have signed or will ever sign means more to the future of America.

—President Lyndon Johnson, upon signing the Elementary and Secondary Education Act, April 1, 1965

RESPONDING TO DIVERSITY

At the end of the second week of school, a student, Linda Wilson, comes to the counseling office with a problem. She complains that she has been the subject of harassment by the teacher and students in the auto mechanics class. According to Linda, the boys refuse to work with her on small group projects, ignore her when she talks to them, and on various occasions have hidden her tools or put grease in her book. One day when she went to her car, she found all the air let out of her tires with a note on the windshield saying, "Do it yourself if you're such a red-hot mechanic!" She says she knows Mr. Thompson, the teacher, is aware of the students' behavior but just ignores it. According to Linda, Mr. Thompson acts as if she's stupid when she asks a question, always refers to the class as "You men," and when discussing employment opportunities makes it clear that auto mechanics is for men only. Linda says she's really interested in auto mechanics, but under the circumstances wants to drop the course.

Do you agree with Linda that she should drop the course? Why or why not? What other options would you suggest to Linda? What evidence is there of sexism, sex-role stereotyping, or sex discrimination?

As we have seen in previous chapters of this text, a variety of circumstances have combined in society and the schools to restrict the educational opportunities of many students, including students such as Linda Wilson. This chapter presents an overview of a number of programs and strategies for responding to a diverse and multicultural society while combating inequity and inequality in education. As you review these strategies, consider the following learning objectives:

- Differentiate the concepts of multiculturalism, assimilation, cultural pluralism, and multicultural education.
- Discuss the various types of bilingual education and the controversy surrounding the education of linguistic minority children.
- Describe the major compensatory education programs and their current status.
- Outline the principles inherent in the Individuals With Disabilities Education Act and their impact on American education.
- Discuss the progress of gender equity in education and the process for its attainment.

Diversity and Culture

Multiculturalism is simply a demographic fact. Teaching only those students who share a teacher's or a community's background is neither desirable or likely to happen. And teaching diverse groups of students only from a teacher's or community's perspective (as if all shared the same past) is unacceptable. For American teachers, *multicultural* cannot be just a lesson, a curriculum, a teaching style, or a philosophy. In the 21st century, nonwhite and immigrant voices and languages will be heard or ignored, honored or derided, but they will not be silenced or assimilated out of existence. (Oakes & Lipton, 2004, p. vii)

The diversity of the U.S. population in terms of race, ethnicity, socioeconomic status, gender, and exceptionalities was discussed in the preceding chapter. There are, of course, many other ways in which the population differs, including age, religion, sexual orientation, and geography. One very important difference in the population is their cultural identity. **Culture** is defined as the behavioral patterns, ideas, values, attitudes, norms, religions and moral beliefs, customs, laws, language, institutions, art, artifacts, and symbols characteristic of a given people at a given period of time.

The concept of culture can be used in a macro and micro sense. All members of a society share, to some extent, some broad ideals that define them a as member of a specific *macroculture.* For example, if introduced to someone in another country you would probably identify yourself as "American" before you would identify your religion or political affiliation. In complex societies such as the United States, individuals will also be members of various subgroups, or *microcultures,* that are distinguished by their ethnic, racial, religious, geographic, social, economic, or lifestyle traits. Most people are members of a variety of microcultures. For example, you might be a visually impaired, Asian American male from an upper middle class background who is Catholic and lives in the South. The interaction of the macroculture and various microcultures can be conceived as depicted in Figure 9.1.

Culture is made up of different elements or layers that together make up a complex system of language, symbols, customs, values and beliefs. Teachers need to understand these elements and how they influence student learning. These elements are:

Figure 9.1 — Macroculture and Microcultures

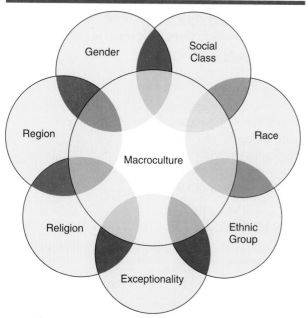

Source: Adapted from Banks, J. A. (2006). Cultural diversity and education: Foundations, curriculum, and teaching (5th ed.). Boston: Allyn & Bacon, page 77. Reprinted with permission of James A. Banks.

- *Language, Symbols, and Artifacts* (means of communication)—language, dialects preferred, proverbs, signs, sayings, jokes, stories, myths, analogies, folklore, art forms, heros, dances, rituals, children's games, currency, holidays, history (family, national, and global).
- *Customs, Practices and Interactional Patterns* (means of interaction)—verbal (tone of voice, phrases used) and nonverbal (eye contact, proximity of stance, gestures) communication patterns, family behaviors, governmental and social institutions, conversational styles (formal-business, casual, ritualized), friendship patterns, community roles, and gender roles.
- *Shared Values, Beliefs, Norms, and Expectations* (values driving people, groups)—attitudes, cultural values, religious and spiritual beliefs, fears, laws, standards, norms, levels of political participation, and expectations. (Pang, 2005, pp. 39–40)

Children learn the language, customs, beliefs, norms, and expectations of their culture by the process of **enculturation.** They are taught to them formally and informally by their parents and other adults. Children or adults who are outside the dominant culture, or are new to the dominant culture because of their minority or immigrant status, learn the dominant culture by a process of assimilation. Throughout much of the history of the United States, the schools attempted to force the assimilation of minorities and immigrants by encouraging English-only classrooms, the Anglicization of names, and the prohibition of the native language, even outside the school environment. Many school districts attempted to replace parental and community values with the values of the Anglo middle class (Stein, 1986).

Cultural Influences on Teaching, Learning, and Behavior

Culture influences almost every aspect of the teaching and learning process. Cultural views on gender roles have been a major factor in the dominance of males in administrative positions in schools systems as well as their underrepresentation in elementary classrooms. Culture also influences the selection of curriculum materials, what and who they portray, and how they portray the content. Culture influences the way teachers teach, how they attempt to motivate, and the very assumptions they have about students. Culture also influences how those outside the school view the teaching profession, the appropriate role of government in the educational process, and more fundamentally, the purpose of schooling.

Culture also has a major influence on how students think, process information, and learn—in effect, their **cognitive styles.** Differences in cognitive styles may be found between those who are characterized as field-independent analytic thinkers and those who are characterized as field-dependent descriptive thinkers. Field-independent students prefer to work on independent projects, like competition, and approach tasks on a step-by-step sequence. In contrast, students with a field-dependent style will be more likely to attend to global or holistic aspects of the curriculum and prefer group as well as multiple or cooperative activities (Cushner, McClelland, & Safford, 2000; Salend, 2005).

Research has shown that differences in learning and cognitive styles may be related to cultural factors. For example, there is some evidence that members of the dominant cultural group in the United States tend to be more field independent, whereas many members of the oppressed groups tend to be more field dependent. Research has also shown that children from cultures where children are subject to more control and pressure to conform are more field dependent. If teachers are aware of their students' preferred learning styles and sensitive to the importance of cultural factors on learning, they will be able to design learning activities that accommodate those differences in learning styles (e.g., group versus individual learning, concrete versus abstract presentations). If teachers are unaware of or misunderstand their students' cultural learning styles, they may underestimate the students' cognitive abilities and unknowingly misplace or mistreat them (Bennett, 2002). At the same time, teachers should avoid stereotyping students and remember that within-group differences can be just as different as between-group differences. Table 9.1 provides an overview of some aspects of the preferred learning styles of African American, Hispanic, and Native American students.

Where there are significant differences between the culture of the student and the culture of the school, a *cultural dissonance* may occur. For example, many lessons that focus on skill development are presented in isolation and rely heavily on step-by-step analytical thinking. However, students with field-sensitive (i.e., field-dependent) cognitive styles may not perform well, "not necessarily because of lack of ability but rather because the instructional approach did not relate well with their strengths. If such lessons are the rule rather than the exception, over time the academic performance of the field-sensitive learner may be artificially depressed" (Friend, 2005, p. 90).

Many aspects of a student's behavior and a teacher's response to it may also be influenced by culture. For example, in some cultures it would be acceptable for students to be very animated and socially engaged when working on a group project. However, many teachers would find this behavior unacceptable and would ask the group to "tone it down" or "work quietly." Some other cultural considerations related to student behavior are briefly described in Figure 9.2.

For Your Reflection and Analysis

Did you or any of your ancestors come to the United States as immigrants? What was your assimilation experience like?
To submit your response online, go to http://www. prenhall.com/webb.

CW

For Your Reflection and Analysis

Identify your cognitive style and how it has influenced your learning.
To submit your response online, go to http://www. prenhall.com/webb.

CW

Table 9.1 — Learning Styles of African American, Hispanic, and Native American Learners

African American Learners Tend To	Hispanic Learners Tend To	Native American Learners Tend To
Respond to things in terms of the whole instead of isolated parts Prefer inferential reasoning as opposed to deductive or inductive Approximate space and numbers rather than adhere to exactness or accuracy Focus on people rather than things Be more proficient in nonverbal than verbal communication	Prefer group learning situations Be sensitive to the opinions of others Be extrinsically motivated Prefer concrete representations to abstract ones	Prefer visual, spatial, and perceptual information rather than verbal Learn privately rather than in public Use mental images to remember and understand words and concepts rather than word associations Watch and then do rather than employ trial and error Value conciseness of speech, slightly varied intonations, and limited vocal range

Source: Irvine and York (1995) as cited in Dilworth, M. E., & Brown, C. E. (2001). Consider the difference: Teaching and learning in culturally rich schools. In V. Richardson (Ed.), *Handbook of research on teaching* (4th ed.). Washington, DC: American Educational Research Association, p. 656.

Culturally Relevant Teaching

In most classrooms today the teacher will encounter students from various microcultures, be they racial, ethnic, religious, or socioeconomic, bringing with them the cultural influences just discussed. Understanding and responding to the cultural context of these students is one of the most difficult challenges many teachers face. However, while it is not possible to create an environment that is culturally congruent for all students all the time, it is possible to create an affirming environment that values and respects the culture of the student and that integrates information about various cultures into the curriculum (Pang, 2005). Research has shown that perhaps the best way this can be accomplished is through culturally responsive and relevant teaching. The term **culturally relevant teaching** has been defined as:

an approach to instruction that responds to the sociocultural context and seeks to integrate the cultural content of the learner in shaping an effective learning environment. Cultural content includes aspects such as experiences, knowledge, events, values, role models, perspectives, and issues that arise from the community. Cultural context refers to the behaviors, interactional patterns, historical experiences, and underlying expectations and values of students. Culturally literate teachers develop an insider perspective of a cultural community. They understand that cultural elements operate simultaneously and respond in congruence with their students. Culturally knowledgeable teachers are keen

Schools are becoming increasingly multicultural.

Figure 9.2 — Cultural Influences on Behavior

Interactional Styles

- **Degree of directness.** In some cultures, it is preferable to "get right to the point" or "say what you have to say" in the most unequivocable manner possible—without sharing information that is not central to the point and without considering how the listener might feel about what you have to say. In other cultures, such an interactional style may be considered rude, and preference is given to less direct communication styles that include more elaborate introductory or intervening discourse and greater deference to how the message is received by the listener.

- **Level of emotionality.** Some cultural variation exists in the extent to which outward signs of emotion are displayed in interactions with others. For example, in some cultures there may be a dramatic display of emotions through voice volume, voice tone, gestures, and facial expressions. Consequently, cross-cultural interpretations of the intensity of emotion felt can become difficult.

- **Degree of movement and vocalizations.** In some cultures, it is not uncommon or viewed as disrespectful for more than one person to speak at a time. In other cultures, this practice is seen as rude. Likewise, in some cultures, a higher level of physical activity and verbal exchange may be a natural accompaniment to cognitive activity. In other cultures, there may be a greater compartmentalization of these activities (i.e., doing only one thing at a time).

- **How consideration of others is shown.** In some cultures, consideration of others is shown by refraining from behaviors that may offend the sensibilities of others. In other cultures, consideration is more often shown by being tolerant of the behaviors of others that you might personally find unpleasant or offensive. For example, in some cultures one may show consideration of others by not playing music loudly (because others may be disturbed by it). In other cultures, there may be more of a tendency to show consideration by learning to tolerate loud music if someone else is enjoying it.

- **Attitudes toward personal space.** The level of tolerance for others entering the space immediately around the body varies across cultures. In some cultures, it is customary for speakers to remain at least two feet apart when speaking to one another. Failure to recognize this is often interpreted as a desire to seek intimacy or as a prelude to aggression. In other cultures, closer interactions are common and physically distancing oneself may be interpreted as aloofness.

- **Attitudes toward sharing.** Ideas about personal ownership vary by culture and consequently influence attitudes and values related to sharing. Some cultures may emphasize communal property rights and reinforce the notion that "What's mine is yours and what's yours is mine." Other cultures may be less inclined to embrace this philosophy. Conflicts can occur when there is not a shared understanding on this issue.

Response to Authority Figures

- **Perceptions of authority figures.** Perceptions regarding what constitutes an authority figure are culturally influenced. In some cultures status may be a determining factor. For example, students may view all adults as authority figures by virtue of their status as adults. In other cultures, position may be a primary determiner. For example, students may view teachers or police officers as authority figures by virtue of their positions rather than their status as adults. In still other cultures, designation as an authority figure must be earned by behavior and is not accorded based solely on status or position.

- **Manner in which respect is shown to authority figures.** Deference to authority figures also is culturally influenced. For example, in some cultures students show respect for authority figures by not making eye contact; in other cultures, the opposite is true. Likewise, in some cultures questioning authority figures would be considered disrespectful; in other cultures this practice may be valued as an indicator of critical thinking.

- **Response to varying management styles.** In some cultures, permissive management styles are viewed as a way to encourage the child's individuality and self-expression. In other cultures, such a management style would indicate weakness or lack of concern.

In considering these cultural influences on behavior, what examples can you think of that illustrate how they may be displayed in classroom behaviors? What are the implications for educators?

Source: From Marilyn Friend. *Special Education: Contemporary Perspectives for School Professionals.* Published by Allyn and Bacon, Boston, MA. Copyright © 2005 by Pearson Education. Reprinted by permission of the publisher.

observers, understand the importance of context and can read nonverbal communication cues such as facial expressions or the hand gestures of students. (Pang, 2005, p. 337)

As this description implies, culturally relevant teachers must be observant and alert to the classroom behaviors and communications, verbal and nonverbal, of students. There is no "one-size-fits-all" approach to culturally relevant teaching. Every student must be studied individually and stereotypes about a particular group discarded: Black students from rural Mississippi are as different from black students in Watts as second-generation Cuban Americans are from new Mexican American immigrants. Nor will a piecemeal sprinkling of colorful aspects of a culture create culturally relevant teaching. Culturally relevant teaching only occurs when teachers are sensitive to cultural differences and when culture is naturally integrated into the curriculum, into instructional and assessment practices, and into classroom management.

For Your Reflection and Analysis

Can you think of a teacher who could be described as a culturally relevant teacher? Defend your choice.
To submit your response online, go to http://www.prenhall.com/webb.

CW

Strategies for Teaching Culturally Diverse Students

A variety of strategies are available for teaching culturally diverse students. Among those the research has identified as being most effective are the following:

Emphasizing verbal interactions. Use activities that encourage students to respond verbally to the material in creative ways such as group discussions, role plays, storytelling, group recitations, choral, and responsive reading, and rap.

Teaching students to use self talk. Encourage and teach students to learn new material by verbalizing it to themselves.

Facilitating divergent thinking. Encourage students to explore and devise unique solutions to issues and problems through activities such as brainstorming group discussions, debates, and responding to open-ended questions.

Using small-group instruction and cooperative learning. Allow students to work in small groups, and use cooperative learning arrangements including peer tutoring and cross-age tutoring.

Employing verve in the classroom. Introduce *verve,* a high level of energy, exuberance, and action, into the classroom by displaying enthusiasm for teaching and learning, using choral responding, moving around the classroom, varying your voice quality, snapping your fingers, using facial expressions, and encouraging students to use their bodies to act out and demonstrate content.

Focusing on real-world tasks. Introduce content, language, and learning by relating them to students' home, school, and community life, and to their cultures and experiences.

Promoting teacher–student interactions. Use teaching methods based on exchanges between students and teachers. Ask frequent questions, affirm students' responses, give feedback, offer demonstrations and explanations, and rephrase, review, and summarize material. (Salend, 2005, pp. 359–360)

Creating culturally relevant teaching and effective classrooms is a process that involves virtually every aspect of educational practice. And, while the processes are challenging and sometimes frustrating, they are vital to the fullest development of all children of every microculture.

Multicultural Education

Multicultural education represents a broader response to diversity than culturally relevant teaching. Multicultural education is an approach to teaching and learning that is based on recognizing, accepting, and affirming a broad view of human differences and similarities. The two primary goals of multicultural education are (1) to promote educational equality for all students, male and female, minority or majority, abled or disabled, and (2) to enable all students to learn and develop the knowledge, skills, and attitudes needed to successfully participate in and contribute to an increasingly diverse society (Banks, 2002).

James Banks (2002), a leading expert on multicultural education, describes multicultural education as having five dimensions:

1. The *content integration dimension,* which deals with the extent to which teachers use examples, data, and other information from a variety of cultures and groups to illustrate the key concepts, principles, generalizations, and theories in the subject or discipline.
2. The *knowledge construction process dimension,* which relates to the way teachers help students to understand, investigate, and determine the implicit cultural assumptions, frames of reference, perspectives, and biases within a discipline that influence the construction of knowledge.
3. The *prejudice reduction dimension,* which focuses on the characteristics of children's racial attitudes and on strategies that can be used to help students develop more positive racial and ethnic attitudes.
4. The *equity pedagogy dimension,* which exists when teachers use techniques and teaching methods that facilitate the academic achievement of students from diverse racial and ethnic groups and from all social classes.

5. The *empowering school culture and social structure dimension,* which would require the restructuring of the culture and organization of the school so that students from diverse racial, ethnic, and social-class groups will experience equality and a sense of empowerment. (pp. 25, 27)

Approaches to Multicultural Education

To accomplish the goals inherent in these dimensions, multicultural education employs a variety of curricular, instructional, and other educational practices. Sleeter and Grant (2002) have developed a typology of the five most commonly used approaches to multicultural education. Some approaches emphasize making the curriculum more inclusive, others on improving intergroup relations. The five approaches are discussed next and illustrated in Figure 9.3.

Teaching the Exceptional and Culturally Different Approach. The goal of the *teaching the exceptional and culturally different approach* to multicultural education is to assimilate or mainstream students of all races, classes, abilities, language dominance, and sexual orientation into the same classroom. Sleeter and Grant (2002) criticize this approach because of its identification of students as being "at risk" or with "special needs," because these terms endorse teacher expectations of academic deficits or behavioral problems.

Human Relations Approach. The *human relations approach* to multicultural education is the approach Sleeter and Grant (2002) say is the most popular among white elementary teachers. The human relations approach attempts to help students understand the commonalities among all people and to accept their differences. Its goal is social cohesion (harmony) and tolerance. Unfortunately, this approach can often be simply a "tourist curriculum" teaching primarily the food, clothing, and folk stories of other cultures.

Single Group Studies Approach. Using the curriculum model developed in higher education in the 1980s and 1990s, the goal of the *single group studies approach* to multicultural education is for students to learn and appreciate the histories and contemporary issues facing certain oppressed groups (e.g., minorities, women, immigrants, the poor, gays, and lesbians). The approach endorses the teaching of women's studies, African American studies, Chicano studies, Asian studies and Native American studies separate from Anglo studies and in so doing, according to Grant and Sleeter (2002), run the risk of celebrating diversity over unity.

Inclusive Multicultural Education Approach. The goal of the *inclusive multicultural education approach* to multicultural education is to reflect cultural pluralism in a democracy. The inclusive multicultural education approach to multicultural education involves not just the curriculum but the entire educational institution. The faculty mirrors the diversity of the larger population, tracking and labeling of students are eliminated, multicultural materials and curricula are integrated, and differential learning styles accommodated.

Educational Multiculturalism and Social Reconstructionism Approach. The *educational multiculturalism and social reconstructionism approach* to multicultural education is the model that Sleeter and Grant (2002) advocate. The goal of this approach,

Figure 9.3 — Five Approaches to Multicultural Education

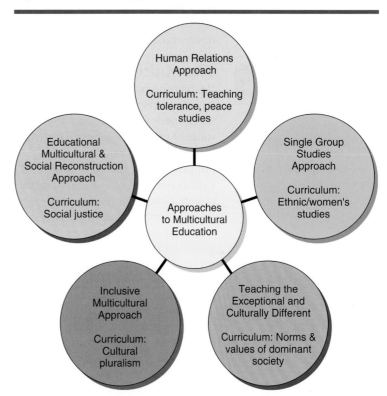

Source: Based on Sleeter, C. E., & Grant, C. A. (2002). *Making choices for multicultural education: Five approaches to race, class, and gender* (4th ed.). New York: John Wiley & Sons.

similar to that of the social reconstructionists of the 1930s, is to restructure schools in ways that will promote social justice. At the core of this model is the use of critical theory whereby students are taught to critically question classism, sexism, racism, Eurocentrism, and other social inequities.

The Multicultural Education Debate

Despite the progress being made in integrating the principles of multicultural education into the curriculum, multicultural education continues to be attacked by critics who view it as a costly and unnecessary entitlement program for minorities. Glazer (1997) highlights some of the critics' other major fears: "An emphasis on multiculturalism will teach our children untruths; it will threaten national unity; it will undermine civic harmony; it will do nothing to raise the achievement of the groups expected to benefit from it" (p. 34). Individuals such as Diane Ravitch, Arthur Schlesinger, Jr., William Bennett, and E. D. Hirsch argue that although the teaching of other cultures may be valuable, educators should not lose sight of our European tradition, which has served as the centerpiece for our government and its institutions (Howe, 1997; Spring, 2004).

Supporting English Language Learners

As noted in Chapter 8, there are an estimated 5.1 million limited English proficient (LEP) students enrolled in U.S. schools. About 80% of these students receive language instruction from programs supported, in part, from Title III of the No Child Left Behind (NCLB) Act of 2001. Perhaps no other federal grant program was as fundamentally changed by the NCLB act as was what was previously Title VII of the Elementary and Secondary Education Act (ESEA), the Bilingual Education Act. Since its inception in 1968, Title VII provided grants to schools and school districts on the basis of a competitive grant program. Not all school districts received funding. This changed with NCLB. Funds are no longer distributed on a competitive basis but on a formula that considers the number of LEP students in the state (80%) and the number of immigrant students enrolled in the state (20%). The change means that many more districts are receiving federal funds.

Title III of the NCLB act also brought a very significant change in the program focus, a change that many educators believe to be more important than the change in funding. The change in the title of the legislation, from the Bilingual Education Act to the English Language Acquisition Act, tells the story. The focus has moved from **bilingual education,** where the student is taught the content in their native language while learning English, to a focus on English acquisition and achievement (in English) on state academic standards. Bilingual education aims at developing literacy in two languages and includes several different program options, including those detailed in Figure 9.4. All bilingual education programs employ **English as a second language (ESL)** as an instructional methodology to help students acquire English. ESL is also used to teach English when there are not enough speakers of one language to make the provision of bilingual education feasible.

Bilingual education came under increasing attack in the 1990s. Concerns were voiced by a significant number of individuals, including immigrant parents. Their concerns focused on the fact that children routinely remained segregated in bilingual programs for 3 years or more, and in some cases more than 6 years. Nowhere had the opposition been more

For Your Reflection and Analysis

What arguments would you add to the multicultural education debate?

To submit your response online, go to http://www.prenhall.com/webb.

CW

Bilingual education incorporates instruction in two languages.

Figure 9.4 — Bilingual Education Programs

Programs that focus on developing literacy in two languages include
- **Two-way immersion or two-way bilingual**
  - The goal is to develop strong skills and proficiency in both LI (home language) and L2 (English)
  - Includes students with an English background and students from one other language background
  - Instruction is in both languages, typically starting with smaller proportions of instruction in English, and gradually moving to half in each language
  - Students typically stay in the program throughout elementary school
- **Dual language**
  - When called "dual language immersion," usually the same as two-way immersion or two-way bilingual
  - When called "dual language," may refer to students from one language group developing full literacy skills in two languages—LI and English
- **Late exit transitional, developmental bilingual,** or **maintenance education**
  - The goal is to develop some skills and proficiency in LI and strong skills and proficiency in L2
  - Instruction at lower grades is in LI, gradually transitioning to English; students typically transition into mainstream classrooms with their English-speaking peers
  - Differences among the 3 programs focus on the degree of literacy students develop in the home language
- **Early exit transitional**
  - The goal is to develop English skills as quickly as possible, without delaying learning of academic core content
  - Instruction begins in LI, but rapidly moves to English; students typically are transitioned into mainstream classrooms with their English-speaking peers as soon as possible
- **Heritage language** or **Indigenous language program**
  - The goal is literacy in two languages
  - Content taught in both languages, with teachers fluent in both languages
  - Differences between the two programs: heritage language programs typically target students who are non-English speakers or who have weak literacy skills in LI; indigenous language programs support endangered minority language in which students may have weak receptive and no productive skills; both programs often serve American Indian students

Programs that focus on developing literacy in only English include:
- **Sheltered English, Specially Designed Academic Instruction in English (SDAIE),** or **Content-based English as a Second Language (ESL)**
  - The goal is proficiency in English while learning content in an all-English setting
  - Students from various linguistic and cultural backgrounds can be in the same class
  - Instruction is adapted to students' proficiency level and supplemented by gestures, visual aids
  - May be used with other methods, e.g., early exit may use LI for some classes and SDAIE for others
- **Structured English Immersion (SEI)**
  - The goal is fluency in English, with only LEP students in the class
  - All instruction is in English, adjusted to the proficiency level of students so subject matter is comprehensible
  - Teachers need receptive skill in students' LI and sheltered instructional techniques
- **English language development (ELD)** or **ESL Pull-out**
  - The goal is fluency in English
  - Students leave their mainstream classroom to spend part of the day receiving ESL instruction, often focused on grammar, vocabulary, and communication skills, not academic content
  - There is typically no support for students' home languages

Source: Modified from work by R. Linquanti (1999), *Fostering academic success for English language learners: What do we know?* San Francisco: WestEd. Retrieved January 29, 2005, from http://www.wested.org/policy/pubs/fostering/models.htm and N. Zelasko and B. Antunez (2000), *If your child learns in two languages: A parent's guide for improving educational opportunities for children acquiring English as a second language.* Washington, DC: National Clearinghouse for English Language Acquisition, The George Washington University.

heated than in California, where in 1998 voters approved Proposition 227, which mandated that LEP students be taught in a special English immersion program for no more than 1 year before being mainstreamed into the regular English classrooms. Similar initiatives followed in other states and were also approved by the voters. By 2001, George W. Bush and the Republican Congress, who not only believed that schools should teach English without any attempt to preserve the native language but that bilingual education had actually retarded English language acquisition, were successful in including the English

VIDEO INSIGHT

Controversy Over Bilingual Education

In this ABC News video segment, you are introduced to an experiment in education that has produced its own deep, persistent controversy, namely, bilingual education.

1. In the video, English-only instruction is portrayed as being superior to bilingual education based on recent student achievement test scores. How might you explain the rapid success of English-only instruction compared to bilingual instruction? What factors other than instruction might have contributed to the improved test scores of a million California children who were taught by English-only instruction?
2. Bilingual education includes several program options involving two languages of instruction. Review the program options in Figure 9.4 and state the strengths and weaknesses of each of the options.

To submit your answers online, go to the *Video Insight* module for this chapter of the Companion Website at **http://www.prenhall.com/webb.**

Language Acquisition Act in NCLB and by so doing, some feel, gave support to the anti-bilingual education agenda (Spring, 2004).

The stated goal of the English Language Acquisition Act is to "help ensure that children who are limited English proficient, including immigrant children and youth, attain English proficiency, develop high levels of academic attainment in English, and meet the same challenging State academic content and student academic achievement standards as all children are expected to meet." In addition, consistent with other major NCLB programs that include provisions to ensure states comply with the intent of the act, Title III of the NCLB states that state and local education agencies and schools will be held accountable for attaining achievement benchmarks.

All programs supported by Title III have the same overall goals, for LEP students: (1) to attain English proficiency so that they can achieve in the core academic content areas and (2) to meet the academic achievement targets set by each state. Among the program options supported by Title III and listed in Figure 9.4, the most commonly used programs (used by at least 30 states) were sheltered English instruction, pull-out ESL, content-based ESL, structured English immersion, dual language, and transitional bilingual education. Less frequently used were two-way immersion, heritage language, and developmental bilingual education.

Services to Immigrant Children and Youth

As previously noted, 20% of Title III funds are to be spent on services to immigrant children and youth. During the 1990s, more immigrants arrived in the United States than at any other time in the nation's history (see Figure 9.5). The growth has been fueled by the increases in legal admission ceilings, the acceptance of political refugees, and the large-scale undocumented immigration that began in the 1970s and has continued to grow.

Immigrant children, the majority of whom are English language learners, face a number of obstacles and barriers, not the least of which are the anxiety of learning a new language, adjusting to a new culture, and understanding the Eurocentric curriculum and unique pedagogy used in the schools (Miller & Endo, 2004). Other problems noted by Salend (2005) include the following:

> In school, they often encounter racial tension and rejection from peers that takes the form of physical attacks (fights, robberies, and so on), mimicking, and verbal harassment. Immigrant youth also may fear authority figures such as the principal because the child or a family member has an undocumented status. As a result, these youth may be reluctant to make

Figure 9.5 — Immigrants Admitted, Fiscal Years 1900–2003

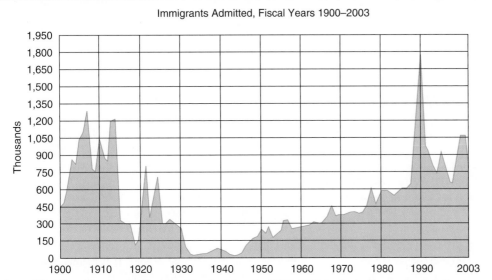

Immigrants Admitted, Fiscal Years 1900–2003

Source: U.S. Office of Immigration Statistics, Homeland Security. (2004). *2003 Yearbook of Immigration Statistics,* Washington, DC: Author, p. 5.

friends with others, to seek help from and interactions with professionals, to attempt to gain recognition or excel in programs, or to draw attention to themselves. (p. 118)

According to Frieman (2001), one of the major challenges faced by immigrant children is "keeping a healthy ethnic identity while developing an American identity" (p. 182).

Undocumented immigrant students have the same right as U.S. citizens to attend public schools and cannot be treated differently based on their immigration status; see discussion of the U.S. Supreme Court decision in *Plyler v. Doe* (1982) in Chapter 11. In fact, school personnel are prohibited from inquiring about the immigration status of students or their families or asking students to provide Social Security numbers, which could identify their status.

Although many immigrant children quickly become acclimated to American schooling and achieve at levels equal to or greater than that of American students, many others need assistance to succeed. Title III provides this assistance through a variety of programs that provide enhanced instructional opportunities for immigrant students. Among the programs are the following:

Meeting the special needs of migrant children is a challenge faced by a growing number of districts.

- Family literacy, parent outreach, and training programs;
- Tutorials, mentoring, and academic career counseling;
- Identification and acquisition of curricular materials, software, and technologies;
- Support for personnel, including teacher aides, to provide services for immigrant children and youth; and/or
- Basic instructional services for immigrant children and youth. (U.S. Department of Education, 2005a)

HISTORICAL NOTE

Tape v. Hurley: The Chinese Struggle for Education

Except for a brief period (1859–1871) when a segregated school for Chinese children was in operation, the only education most Chinese children received in the United States in the late 1800s was by private tutors or Bible classes with the Protestant missions in Chinatown. Neither of these provisions satisfied Chinese parents. Countless letters and petitions in support of public education for Chinese children were directed to the school board and county board of supervisors, but were ignored or denied.

In 1878, seven years after the closing of the Chinese public school, more than 1,300 merchants in San Francisco, Sacramento, and other California Chinatowns petitioned the state to provide a school—even a segregated one—for Chinese students. They noted that although they paid taxes, 3,000 Chinese were being denied an education. Their petition was denied.

In 1884, after a federal district court ruled that immigration officials could not deny reentry to a natural-born citizen of the United States who was Chinese, the Chinese community turned to citizenship status as the key to pressing for the provision of education. The week after the decision, Joseph and Mary Tape attempted to enroll their 8-year-old daughter Mamie, a natural-born citizen of the United States, at the Spring Valley School in San Francisco near their residence. The principal, Jennie Hurley, refused admission and the Tape family filed suit. The state superintendent of public instruction supported the board's decision, noting that the California constitution declared Chinese to be

"dangerous to the well-being of the state." On January 9, 1885, the trial court supported Mamie's request and ruled that to deny American children born in the United States the right to attend public school would be a violation of the Fourteenth Amendment. On March 3, 1885, the California Supreme Court upheld the decision.

On April 7, 1885, in a scene foretelling the desegregation of schools in the 1950s, Mamie, accompanied by her parents and attorneys and with the Supreme Court decision in hand, again attempted to enroll at the Spring Valley School. Once again Principal Hurley denied admission, arguing that Mamie needed a health certificate before she could be admitted. When threatened with legal action she then said the classes were already overcrowded, in violation of district policy, and that Mamie would be placed on a waiting list. In the meantime, responding to the court's decision, the San Francisco School Board persuaded the legislature to pass a bill allowing districts to establish segregated schools for "Mongolians," and on April 13, 1885, the Chinese Primary School was opened at Jackson and Powell Streets. In the end the Tapes had won the battle, but lost the war.

Sources: Fung, F. A. (2004, May). Lessons from the past: *Tape v. Hurley. CHSA Bulletin,* pp. 3–4; and Webb, L. D. (2006). *The history of American education: A great American experiment.* Upper Saddle River, NJ: Merrill/Prentice Hall.

 To research and explore this topic further, go to the *Historical Note* module for this chapter of the Companion Website at **http://www.prenhall.com/webb.**

Compensatory Education for Disadvantaged Students

Compensatory education programs designed to overcome the deficiencies associated with educational and socioeconomic disadvantages have been an important part of federal educational policy and funding since the passage of the Elementary and Secondary Education Act in 1965. Title I of that act was the centerpiece of President Johnson's Great Society education program and was viewed as an important weapon in the War on Poverty. And, it is Title I of the 2001 reauthorization of the ESEA, the No Child Left Behind Act, that has provided the most far-reaching provisions related to standards, student testing, and highly qualified teachers.

Title I, Part A, provides assistance to enable children in low-socioeconomic-level schools to meet state academic content and performance standards. This assistance reaches approximately 12.5 million students in both public and private schools. Still, Title I serves only about half the students who are eligible to receive services. Services are especially limited at the secondary level. Title I funds may be used for children from pre-school through high school. A total of 65% of the students served are in grades 1 through 6 and 12% are in preschool and kindergarten programs. This is the largest elementary and secondary education program with a fiscal year 2005 budget of $13.3 billion.

Types of Programs

Compensatory education programs encompass a variety of educational services delivered primarily in program-eligible schools during school hours. These are the most common programs:

1. Programs under Early Head Start, which provide infant education and family support services.
2. Early childhood readiness programs such as Head Start, which prepare children between the ages of 3 and 5 for school. Head Start is a comprehensive program that combines educational programs, medical and nutritional benefits, parent involvement, and social services.
3. Programs for primary students such as Transition Head Start, which continue Head Start services into the second grade.
4. Programs for secondary education students such as Upward Bound, which are directed at dropout prevention and at increasing the preparation and participation of disadvantaged youth for postsecondary education through tutoring, instruction in basic skills, and counseling services.
5. Enrichment programs in subject areas. Almost all Title I districts offer programs in reading (e.g., Reading First). Most also offer programs in mathematics, and a lesser percentage offer programs in language arts.
6. Programs for students with disabilities. Almost three-fourths of the Title I districts provide services to students with disabilities. In most districts, these students must be eligible for Title I to receive services.
7. Bilingual education and ESL. Both options of instruction are offered to LEP students. Again, normally the students must be eligible for Title I to receive services.
8. Programs for migrant students. Most such programs are found in larger school districts.
9. Psychological and social services for disadvantaged students.
10. Education for Homeless Children and Youth program. The purpose of this program is to ensure that all children and youth who experience homelessness have equal access to the same free, appropriate education, including public preschool education, that is provided to other children and youth.

Most Title I instruction is provided through the "pullout" method, in which eligible students are removed from the regular classroom to receive additional instruction, usually in reading, mathematics, and language arts. Instruction lasts about 30 minutes and is delivered in smaller classes by separately hired "Title I teachers," often with the assistance of aides and with more equipment and materials than are available in the regular classroom. Even though there is some criticism of pullout models, they are popular with school districts because they are the safest way of meeting the requirement that Title I funds be spent only on eligible students. However, in the last decade changes in Title I regulations have made it easier for a growing number of districts to replace pullout programs with co-ordinated programs that allow in-class assistance.

> **For Your Reflection and Analysis**
>
> What are the advantages and disadvantages of pulling students out of the regular class to receive compensatory instruction?
> *To submit your response online, go to http://www.prenhall.com/webb.*
>
> CW

Creating Equal Educational Opportunities for Students With Disabilities

Students with mental and physical disabilities who are receiving services in federally supported programs comprise approximately 14% of the students in public schools (U.S. Department of Education, 2005c). As noted in Chapter 8, in 1975 Congress passed the Education for All Handicapped Children Act (EHA) (PL 94-142). The EHA, often referred to as the Bill of Rights for Handicapped Children, and its successors have served not only to guarantee the rights of children with disabilities but also to expand the rights of all children. In 1990 the EHA was reauthorized and renamed the Individuals With Disabilities Education Act (IDEA).

The Individuals with Disabilities Education Act

The IDEA applies to all children with disabilities between the ages of 3 and 21 and includes preschool, elementary school, secondary school, and vocational education. The statute defines "disabled children" as those with mental retardation, hearing impairments, speech or language impairments, visual impairments, emotional disturbance, orthopedic impairments, autism, traumatic brain injury, multiple disabilities, or specific learning disabilities.

To receive services under the IDEA, a student must not only have a disability, but the condition must have an impact on the student's education to an extent that requires the delivery of special education programs and related services (i.e., services necessary for the student to benefit from the special education). The major principles that are included in the IDEA are (1) the right to a free and appropriate education, (2) identification and nondiscriminatory evaluation, (3) an individualized education program, (4) least restrictive environment, and (5) procedural due process.

Free and Appropriate Education.   Perhaps the most fundamental and important principle of the IDEA is that all children ages 3 to 21 years with disabilities, regardless of the nature or severity of their disabilities, must have available to them a free and appropriate education and related services designed to meet their unique needs. The IDEA does not say what programs or services must be provided to satisfy the guarantee of an appropriate education. Rather, this must be decided on a case-by-case basis through the decision-making process required for developing the student's individualized education program (IEP). The question of what should be included in the IEP has been the subject of considerable litigation. Some guidance was provided by the U.S. Supreme Court in *Board of Education v. Rowley* (1982), in which the Court stated that a free and appropriate public education did not mean "an opportunity to achieve full potential commensurate with the opportunity provided to other children," but rather "access to specialized instruction and related services which are designed to provide educational benefit to the handicapped child." Since *Rowley,* the courts have continued to support parents in their attempts to expand services to their children with disabilities, but they do tend to accept the most reasonable program rather than require the best possible program.

Identification and Nondiscriminatory Evaluation.   The first obligation imposed on the schools by the IDEA is to take affirmative steps to identify children with disabilities who may be entitled to special education. A teacher or other educator who has reason to believe a student has a disability and is in need of special education services may refer the student for a comprehensive evaluation to describe the child's functioning and determine whether the child has a disability. The evaluation, which assesses all areas related to the suspected disability, is to be carried out by a multidisciplinary team. Placement in any special education program cannot be made on the basis of a single test, but on multiple measures and procedures. Additionally, whatever evaluation mechanisms are used must be nondiscriminatory in terms of culture, race, and language, and must be designed for assessment with specific handicaps (e.g., tests for non-English speakers or tests for students with visual impairments).

If the evaluation determines that the student is not eligible for services under the IDEA, he or she may still be eligible for special education services under Section 504. On the other hand, if as a result of evaluation the team decides that the student requires special education services, an individualized education program must be prepared.

Individualized Education Program.   The IDEA requires that an **individualized education program (IEP)** be prepared for each child who is to receive special education services. The IEP is designed to meet the unique needs of the child for whom it is developed and is prepared at a meeting that, under the requirements of the IDEA, must include the student's parents, teachers (special education and regular education), special education specialists or others who may contribute to the individually tailored learning plan, and, if appropriate, the student. The IEP includes a description of present performance; a statement of annual goals, including short-term objectives; a statement of special education and related services (e.g., transportation, physical therapy) to be provided and their duration; evaluation criteria and procedures to determine if the objectives are being achieved; and a statement of any testing accommodations that the student will need to participate in state or district-wide assessments. IEPs are reviewed annually and provide the means for ensuring parent involvement in the educational decisions affecting their children, the means for accountability, the delivery of services, and a record of progress.

Least Restrictive Environment. The IDEA requires that the student receive the special education services in the **least restrictive environment (LRE).** The least restrictive environment principle does not require all children with disabilities to be *mainstreamed* in the regular classroom. However, the language of the IDEA establishes a clear preference for educating children with disabilities, to the maximum extent possible, in the regular classroom where they have contact with children without disabilities. "To the maximum extent appropriate, children with disabilities . . . are educated with children who are nondisabled." The courts have interpreted this provision to mean that children with disabilities should not be removed from the regular educational setting unless the nature or severity of the disability is such that education in the regular classroom, even with the use of supplemental aides and services, cannot be satisfactorily achieved. In every case, a child with a disability cannot be moved from the regular classroom without a due process hearing, and schools have been required to provide supplemental services in the regular classroom before moving the child to a more restrictive environment.

The LRE principle does not require mainstreaming; in fact, the IDEA does not mention mainstreaming. What the principle does call for is the careful consideration of all possible placement alternatives for each child with a disability before a final placement is made. In the end, it may be necessary to place the child in a segregated setting in order to provide the

The inclusion of children with disabilities is a fundamental principle of the IDEA.

most appropriate education, or in order to prevent the disruption of the educational process for other students. Students may also be placed in private schools at public expense if the district is not able to provide an appropriate placement. Schools must ensure a continuum of alternative placements such as that shown in Figure 9.6.

Procedural Due Process. The extensive procedural requirements of the IDEA are designed to ensure children with disabilities a free and appropriate education and to protect them from improper evaluation, classification, and placement. Parents have the right to obtain an individual evaluation of their child in addition to that conducted by the school district and to be involved in every stage of the evaluation, placement, and educational process. Parents must be informed of the IEP conference and encouraged to attend. In addition, the school district must inform parents in writing, or in a format understandable by them, before it initiates, changes, or refuses to initiate or change the identification, evaluation, or educational placement of the child.

When the parents and school disagree on a decision, each has the right to request a due process hearing. The request can be filed at almost any point in the process. A due process hearing is conducted by an impartial hearing officer determined in accordance with each individual state's statutory procedures for implementing the IDEA. If disagreement continues after the due process hearing, appeal may be made to the courts. While any proceedings are occurring, the child must "stay put." In other words, the child remains in the current—or last agreed-on placement—pending the outcome of the proceedings.

For Your Reflection and Analysis

The IEP concept has been very successful in working with students with disabilities. How might it be used with other students?

To submit your response online, go to http://www. prenhall.com/webb.

CW

Figure 9.6 — Continuum of Educational Placements for Students with Disabilities

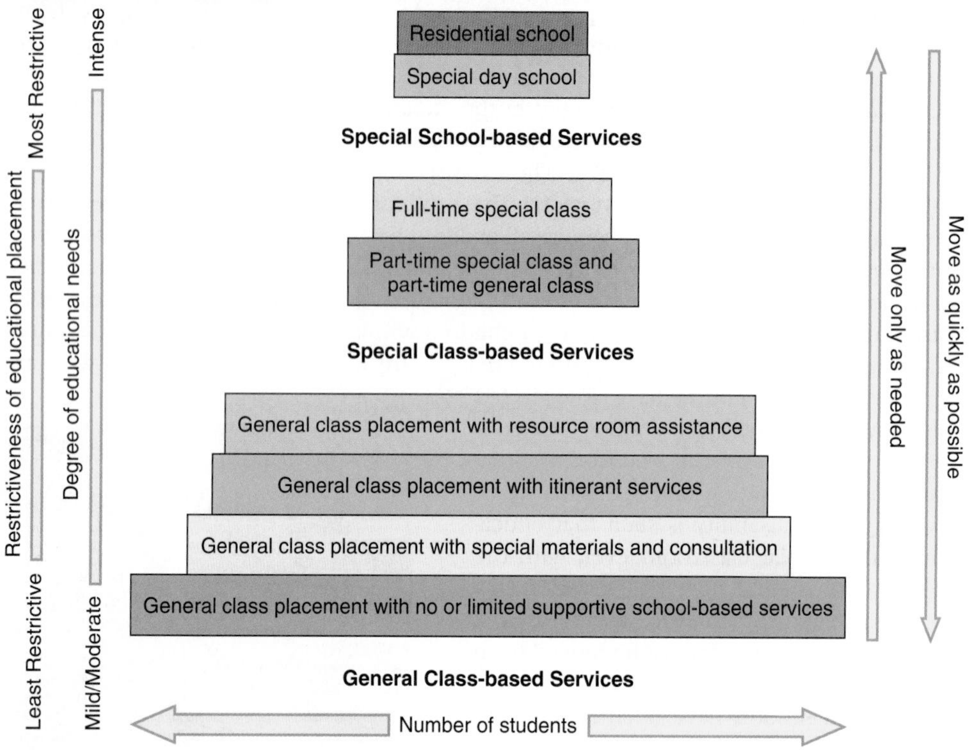

Source: Mercer, C.D., and Pullen, P.C. (2005). *Students with learning disabilities* (6th ed), p. 213. Upper Saddle River, NJ: Merrill/Prentice Hall. Copyright 2005 by Pearson Education. Reprinted by permission.

Section 504 of the Rehabilitation Act

Section 504 of the Rehabilitation Act is a civil rights law that prohibits educational institutions that receive federal financial assistance from discriminating in the delivery of programs and activities, employment, and access to facilities. Section 504 is broader than the IDEA and is intended to prevent discrimination against, rather than just provide services to, students with disabilities. Section 504 seeks to remove physical and programmatic barriers to participation in schools. Under Section 504 schools must make reasonable accommodations for students with disabilities.

Section 504 is applicable to any student with a physical or mental impairment that substantially limits any major life activity, or who is regarded as having, or has a history of, such impairment. Included could be students with communicable diseases, attention deficit–hyperactivity disorder (if the student is not in need of special education and related services under IDEA), or students with lifelong health conditions such as epilepsy, diabetes, asthma, arthritis, or allergies.

Students who qualify for services under IDEA are also afforded the protections under Section 504. In addition, some children who do not qualify for special education under IDEA because they are over 21 (Section 504 covers the entire life span) or do not have a condition serious enough to qualify for IDEA services may be protected by Section 504.

Although Section 504 does not require the development of an IEP, it does require the development of a Section 504 accommodation plan. Many districts follow many of the procedures in developing the accommodation plan as they do in developing the IEP; that is, it is prepared by a team that is familiar with the student, the assessment data, and with the placement and accommodations options. In addition, parents have a right to participate in any identification and placement decisions as well as to a hearing by an impartial party if they disagree with the identification, education, or placement of their child.

The Inclusion Debate

Just as the IDEA does not define what is meant by an appropriate education but leaves the issue to be decided on a case-by-case basis, it also does not define what is meant by the "least restrictive environment" but leaves this to be decided on an individual basis. The least restrictive environment issue has been central to expanded efforts to increase the number of students with disabilities who are included in regular classroom settings.

The broader concept of **inclusion** has replaced the concept of **mainstreaming.** Inclusion consists of serving students with a variety of abilities and disabilities in the regular classroom along with the appropriate support services. It is considered to be a full-time placement. Those who support inclusion argue that not only does it contribute to the academic and social progress of children with disabilities, but it also creates greater tolerance on the part of students without disabilities and better prepares them to live in an integrated society. As a result of the inclusion movement, more and more students are spending more of their time in a regular classroom than in any other school setting. The NCLB act supports inclusion and makes it clear that *all* students are general education students. Federal special education policy aims at closing the achievement gap between special education students and their peers.

The inclusion movement has generated some debate over the extent to which students are being integrated without the support necessary to make the transition successful. Many educators and parents are also concerned that inclusion is being used to save money at the expense of providing needed services to students with disabilities, and that it may have a detrimental effect on the learning of students without disabilities. Others are concerned that inclusion has resulted in accommodation to the extent that students are not being challenged to achieve more independence (Kauffman, McGee, & Brigham, 2004).

To assess your support for the concept of inclusion, complete the checklist in the "Ask Yourself" below.

For Your Reflection and Analysis

How prepared are you to have a student with a severe disability included in your class?

To submit your response online, go to http://www. prenhall.com/webb.

CW

ASK YOURSELF

Inclusion Checklist

The following checklist for practicing (or prospective) teachers reflects an inclusion philosophy. The more "yes" answers, the more positive toward responsible inclusion is the respondent.

1. Are you (would you be) willing to have age-appropriate students with disabilities in your class?

2. Do (would) you modify your curriculum, instructional methods, and materials to meet the diverse needs of students in your class?

3. Are you (would you be) open to suggestions and modifications in your teaching and classroom management?

4. Are you (would you be) willing to share your teaching responsibilities with other professionals?

5. Do you expect students with disabilities to be as successful in meeting their own goals as students without disabilities are in meeting theirs?

6. Do (would) you call on students with disabilities as much as you (would) call on other students in your class?

7. Do (would) you use heterogeneous grouping?

8. Do (would) you use peer tutoring?

9. Do (would) you use adaptive technology and customized software?

10. Have you attended training sessions about responsible inclusion?

Source: Lombardi, T. P. (1994). *Responsible inclusion of students with disabilities.* Bloomington, IN: Phi Delta Kappa Educational Foundation.

For Your Reflection and Analysis

Give personal examples of differential treatment that you have experienced in elementary school, secondary school, or college.

To submit your response online, go to http://www.prenhall.com/webb.

CW

Promoting Gender Equity

Despite the gains that have been made in gender achievement and attainment noted in Chapter 8, differences in the educational experiences of boys and girls remain very much a reality and impact on them in ways that affect them in every aspect of their school experience.

Throughout the 1990s much of the research on gender differences in the schools focused on gender bias against girls. However, by the turn of the century researchers were increasingly acknowledging that both girls and boys are victims of gender bias in the schools. In fact, some studies suggested that boys experience the most gender bias and neglect in the schools (see, e.g., Sommers [2000], *The War Against Boys*). The emerging field of brain research has also helped us to understand that there are both functional and structural differences between the brains of boys and girls that have a profound effect on learning (Gurian & Stevens, 2004). For example, one explanation given by Gurian and Henley (2001) for why males tend to do better on the SAT is that:

> The male brain is better at storing single-sentence information (even trivia) than in the female. On game shows like "Who Wants to Be a Millionaire?" men outperform women in

Table 9.2 — How Boys and Girls Are Better Off at School

How Boys Are Better Off:

Boys outperform girls in science and mathematics.

Boys are represented in higher numbers in mathematics and science gifted programs.

Boys are more represented in computer science and engineering "high-income" careers.

Boys are overrepresented in National Merit Scholars.

Boys often avoid some of the inner struggles that can lead to depression and eating disorders in adolescent girls.

Teenage boys who become parents are more likely to remain and complete high school than teenage girls who become parents.

Boys are twice as likely than girls to participate in team sports.

Boys are less likely than girls to be the victims of sexual harassment and abuse.

Boys get more teacher attention of the kind that is likely to foster student achievement.

How Girls Are Better Off:

Girls are less likely than boys to drop out of school.

Girls are less likely than boys to be diagnosed with attention deficit–hyperactivity disorder (ADHD).

Girls receive higher grades than boys.

Girls are less likely than boys to be diagnosed as having a learning disability.

Girls outperform boys in reading and writing.

Girls are more focused on education as a goal and are more likely to pursue college degrees.

Girls are less likely than boys to repeat a grade.

Girls are less likely than boys to have their parents contacted by the school about an academic or behavioral problem.

Girls are less likely to be the victims of violence in the school.

Girls have a lower rate of suicide.

Girls are more likely to participate in community service activities.

Source: Suggested by, among others, "Trends in Educational Equity of Girls and Women" by Y. Bae, S. Choy, C. Geddes, J. Sable, & T. Snyder, Summer 2000, *Educational Statistics Quarterly*, pp. 1–9; *Boys and Girls Learn Differently: A Guide for Teachers and Parents* by M. Gurian & P. Henley, 2001, San Francisco: Jossey-Bass; *American Education* (11th ed.), by J. Spring, 2004, New York: McGraw-Hill; and "The Chilly Climate: Subtle Ways in Which Women Are Often Treated Differently at Work and in Classrooms," by B. R. Sandler, 2004, in J. Z. Spade and C. G. Vallentine (Eds.), *The Kaleidoscope of Gender: Prism, Patterns, and Possibilities* (pp. 187–191), Belmont, CA: Wadsworth/Thomson Learning.

large part because of the brain advantage. The male brain holds a visual advantage in working with lists (as in multiple choice), and in making quick deductive decisions in lists. The female brain thinks more inductively (less like a deductive reasoner) and thus often needs substantial information to make a decision. This puts the female at a disadvantage in testing that requires very quick decision making in a short time. (pp. 59–60)

The American Association of University Women (AAUW) in its publication *Beyond the Gender Wars* (2001) acknowledged that "both boys and girls as groups are simultaneously thriving in some areas of school life and struggling in others" (p. 21). Table 9.2 provides a partial list of some of the ways in which boys seem to be better off or advantaged in school and some of the ways in which girls seem to be better off in school.

Strategies for Achieving Gender Equity

While the socialization that takes place outside the school to a large extent shapes interactions in the school, teachers need to be aware of and understand the ways in which they and the culture of the school can reinforce gender inequities. "Increased awareness of the often unconscious interpersonal dynamics by which we 'do gender' is particularly important if teachers wish to create gender-neutral classrooms" (Spade, 2004, p. 293). Numerous strategies have been proposed to achieve gender-neutral classroom and **gender equity** in the schools. These include, but are not limited to, the following:

- Eliminate inequitable practices (e.g., encourage girls to take advanced science and mathematics courses to correct limited access in the past).
- Resist gender-role stereotyping (e.g., invite males and females in nontraditional roles as guest speakers; encourage girls to pursue careers in science, math, and computing and boys to pursue careers in elementary teaching).
- Ensure that curriculum materials are free of gender bias and represent males and females of all races and in all walks of life.

PROFESSIONAL REFLECTION

Today's teachers face multiple challenges, including a large English language learner (ELL) population, with not one or two language groups, but sometimes many language groups in the same classroom. I had 5 Russian or Ukrainian students, one from Vietnam, one from Samoa, one from India, and one who was born in the United States, but whose language at home was Spanish. Yes, they had some similarities in learning needs: building vocabulary, reading comprehension, writing development. Some of my "regular" kids had the same issues, but for different reasons, so I learned to not group ELL students with other struggling learners because their concerns were based on language acquisition, while the others' learning issues were from other causes . . . .

Another large challenge area is the ever-growing group of students who need learning support due to learning delays, learning disabilities, or other reasons beyond their control. In my classroom, which also included a Highly Capable group, the reading levels included readers at the low end of the second-grade reading level and several students who read at an upper high school level, with comprehension at a commensurate level. This presents enormous challenges when trying to instruct each student at his or her appropriate learning level.

Other than in the classroom, the challenges come in the form of a more diverse group of parents, many of whom didn't have a positive school experience or had a very different kind of experience, as with the parents of students from the former Soviet Union. Other parents find it next to impossible to make time for homework, or aren't sure how best to help their students. . . . The diverse population of today demands accomplished teaching for all of the reasons above. It takes energy, will, time for professional development, and enough caring to keep on trying new ways to reach and teach our kids ever more effectively.

Janet M. Dondelinger
National Board Certified Teacher,
Washington

To analyze this reflection, go to the *Professional Reflection* module for this chapter of the Companion Website at **http://www.prenhall.com/webb.**

- Be sensitive to gender issues (e.g., provide for the discussion of sexism, gender stratification, and the feminization of poverty).
- Provide gender-neutral affirmation of skills and abilities (e.g., praise a female student for her good problem-solving ability and reinforce a male student for his sensitivity to others).
- Utilize positive instructional strategies (e.g., make a concerted effort to reinforce gender equity in the classroom and playground).
- Use a variety of instructional strategies that recognize the diverse and multiple learning styles of boys and girls.
- Ensure that testing accurately assesses the abilities of both boys and girls.
- Provide training to all instructional and support personnel in recognizing and preventing sexual harassment and in dealing with gender issues in all areas of education. (AAUW, 1998, 2001; Gurian & Stevens, 2004; Spade, 2004)

Another somewhat controversial strategy that has been suggested to remedy the problem of sexism is single-sex education. (See the Controversial Issue feature on page 142 for some of the pros and cons of single-sex classes and schools.) As described in Chapters 5 and 6, single-sex instruction was the norm for much of the first 200 years of our nation's history. The U.S. Department of Education is working on issuing guidelines for the operation of single-sex classes and schools.

The attainment of gender equity should be one of the primary goals of all educational institutions. As Americans attempt to remain competitive in the 21st century's world markets, Plato's words of 2,500 years ago seem remarkably relevant: "Nothing can be more absurd than the practice . . . of men and women not following the same pursuits with all of their strength and with one mind, for thus the state . . . is reduced to a half" (Laws, VII, p. 805).

Summary

Educating children with disabilities and language minority students and ensuring gender equity are strategies for achieving equality of educational opportunity. The presence of each of these strategies in the American educational system has served to expand the educational opportunities not only for the targeted populations but for all students. It is largely through the efforts of those asserting their rights under the constitutionally based programs that the rights of all students have been expanded. The success of our educational system and, indeed, our economic and social structure depends on the full participation of all children. This chapter focused attention on strategies for increasing the equality of educational opportunity. The next chapter turns to strategies directed at specific populations of "at-risk" youth.

Key Terms

Bilingual education, 228
Cognitive styles, 223
Compensatory education, 232
Culturally relevant
    teaching, 224
Culture, 222
Enculturation, 222

English as a second language
    (ESL), 228
Gender equity, 239
Inclusion, 237
Individualized education
    program (IEP), 234

Least restrictive environment
    (LRE), 235
Mainstreaming, 237
Multicultural education, 226

PROFESSIONAL DEVELOPMENT WORKSHOP

Prepare for the Praxis™ Examination

Kevin Lewis is a third-grade teacher at Kennedy Elementary School. Kennedy is a school of 820 students in an urban school district with a predominantly minority population. Kennedy has an English language learner (ELL) population of 260 students. Spanish (68%), Vietnamese (11%), and Chinese (10%) are the most common languages spoken in the homes of the ELL students. Kevin has six ELL students in his third-grade class.

Angela Ong has been diagnosed as both LD and LEP. The statement on Angela's Level of Education Performance on her IEP developed at the beginning of the year states:

> According to the SELP test, Angela's oral proficiency level is at an emergent level, meaning Angela's speech contained numerous errors in grammar, syntax, and vocabulary. Angela has been observed speaking English with her classmates but tends to avoid initiating conversation in the classroom. Angela's writing and reading skills were assessed at a preproduction level in both English and Chinese. The learning of English for Angela will be slow and should not be expected to be at the same rate for similar LEP students given Angela's identified learning disability. Angela would benefit from ELL strategies integrated into her special education instruction.

The IEP recommendation is being followed and Angela is showing improved language acquisition. However, Angela's parents are concerned that Angela is not getting as much attention in the classroom as the Spanish speakers. They have requested a reassessment of Angela's acquisition and placement. They feel that Angela would benefit more from sheltered English instruction.

The IEP team, which includes Mr. Lewis, has met but feels that no change in the IEP is warranted. The Ongs are not satisfied and continue to insist that sheltered English would be better for Angela.

1. Is the regular classroom the best placement for Angela? Justify your response.
2. What process is required under the IDEA to resolve disagreements between the school and parents over what special education programs and services should be provided?
3. What are the advantages and disadvantages of ESL and sheltered English as instructional strategies in helping English language learners meet English proficiency standards?

To submit your responses online, go to the *Prepare for the Praxis™ Examination* module for this chapter of the Companion Website at **http://www.prenhall.com/webb**.

Build Your Knowledge Base

1. How has your cultural background influenced your learning and school experience?
2. Describe the multicultural education program in a school district with which you are familiar. What evidence exists that it has improved the academic performance of its participants? Is it viewed as helping or hindering progress toward racial or ethnic integration?
3. Currently, many youth feel alienated from the school and find little identification and meaning in the educational process. As a teacher, what can you do to reach these students?
4. Discuss ways in which the Individuals with Disabilities Education Act has benefited *all* children.
5. Compare the treatment of boys and girls in the schools with their treatment in other institutions.
6. How do the missions of multicultural education, special education, and gender equity in education complement each other?

Develop Your Portfolio

1. Review the cultural influences on behavior described in Figure 9.2 on page 225. Write a personal reflection paper that describes the interactional styles that were practiced or reinforced in your family when you were a young child as well as the expected responses to authority that were practiced in your family when you were an adolescent. Place the reflection paper in your portfolio under **INTASC Standard 3, Adapting Instruction for Diverse Learners.**

2. Research has demonstrated that differences in learning and cognitive styles may be related to cultural factors as well as socioeconomic factors. Prepare a reflection paper that describes your preferred learning and cognitive style. When did you first discover your preferred learning style? How has your learning style changed over time? What cultural or socioeconomic factors might have influenced your predisposition to a particular learning style? Place your reflection paper in your portfolio under **INTASC Standard 3, Adapting Instruction for Diverse Learners.**

To complete these activities online, go to the *Develop Your Portfolio* module for this chapter of the Companion Website at **http://www.prenhall.com/webb.**

Explore Teaching and Learning: Field Experiences

1. Identify two schools with an ethnically diverse student body. Interview the principal and two experienced teachers about the challenges of working in a school with a diverse population. Inquire about the activities/programs that a school can provide so that diversity can be viewed as an asset through which students can become more understanding of the cultural differences in the school community, the student body, and the world at large. In what ways are your observations from the field experiences consistent or inconsistent with the content of the chapter?

2. Locate two schools that practice inclusion of students with disabilities in the regular classroom. Interview teachers and administrators in the school to determine the merits of assigning students with disabilities to a regular classroom. Consider the impact on the workload of the teacher, experiences of the student(s) with disabilities, and experiences of the other students.

Professional Development Online

Visit this text's Companion Website at **http://www.prenhall.com/webb** to gain access to a variety of questions, activities, and exercises to help build your knowledge of this chapter's content. Below are just a few items available at this text's Companion Website:

*   Classroom Video—To see actual classroom footage and work through activities and questions to analyze the content of the video, click on the *Classroom Video* module for this chapter.
*   Teaching Tolerance—To go to this organization's website and complete activities to explore issues and topics dealing with how to teach tolerance to students, click on the *Teaching Tolerance* module for this chapter.
*   Self-Test—To review terms and concepts presented in this chapter, click on the *Self-Test* module for this chapter.
*   Internet Resources—To link to websites related to topics in this chapter, go to the *Internet Resources* module for this chapter.

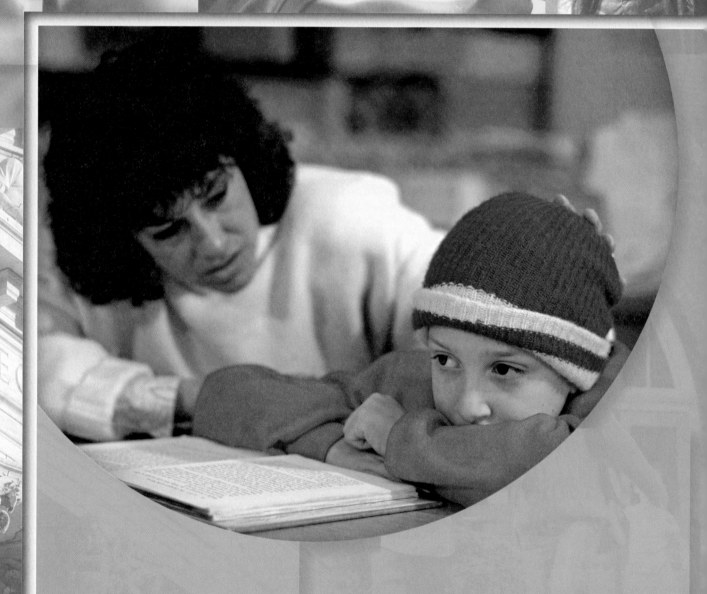

CHAPTER 10

Child abuse casts a shadow the length of a lifetime.
—Herbert Ward, 1985

STUDENTS AT RISK

It was twilight when Tom Wright finished packing the last box in his apartment. The movers had already taken the furniture. All that remained were a few boxes. As Tom lifted one of the boxes, an old photograph fell to the floor. He picked it up and smiled as he recognized his eighth-grade graduating class.

Twelve years had passed since that photo was taken. It seemed more like an eternity. He studied the photo for a long time. He immediately identified one of his best boyhood friends. Whatever happened to Jake Nash? He and Jake began kindergarten together and were like brothers for the entire 8 years of elementary school. The last time he saw Jake was the summer after the photo was taken. Tom went on to Springview High School, but Jake moved away. It was

so sudden, Tom remembered. He and Jake had planned for high school together. But that summer Jake's life was turned upside down. Jake's mother and father divorced and shortly afterward his younger sister, Karen, attempted suicide. In August Jake, his mother, and his sister moved to Michigan to be near his grandparents. He and Tom promised that they would see each other often. But that never happened. They exchanged a few letters and phone calls for a year or so, then grew apart. Tom was horrified and shocked when he later learned from Jake's former neighbor that Jake had dropped out of high school in his senior year and had been indicted on drug trafficking charges on his 21st birthday.

What, if any, clues indicated that Jake was at risk for dropping out of school? For substance abuse?

Jake is typical of millions of youth in and out of America's schools whose life experiences and situations place them at risk for educational, emotional, and physical problems. In this chapter, at-risk children and youth are described. In addition, the methods of identifying a number of at-risk conditions and behaviors are suggested. The following objectives should guide you in your study of at-risk populations:

- Identify the predictors of being an at-risk student.
- Discuss the relationship between risk, resiliency, and protective factors.
- Identify the key elements for establishing a trusting relationship with at-risk students.
- Describe the conditions or behaviors associated with substance abuse.
- Identify the suicidal child or adolescent.
- Explain the incidence and consequence of dropping out of school.
- Suggest reasons why certain adolescents are at high risk for pregnancy, HIV/AIDS, or sexually transmitted infections (STIs).
- Name the common signs or indicators of child abuse or neglect.
- Describe the extent of the problem of violence in the schools.
- Explain why gay, lesbian, bisexual, transgender, or questioning youth are at risk for a variety of self-destructive behaviors.

At-Risk Children and Youth

A variety of terms are used to describe children and adolescents who are in need of special treatment or special services. Often, they are referred to as being **at risk.** The main characteristic of this group of youngsters is that they are already achieving below grade level or are likely to experience educational problems in the future. The term *at risk* is also used to describe children and youth who are already experiencing or are likely to experience physical and mental health problems.

Identifying At-Risk Students

Early identification is the key to developing and implementing effective educational programs for at-risk students. Among the most prominent behaviors or factors that identify those children and adolescents who might become at risk for a variety of self-destructive behaviors are underachievement; retention in grade; social maladjustment; discipline problems; dropping out of school; low parental support; physical problems; using and abusing drugs or alcohol; engaging in premature, unprotected sexual activity; being a victim or perpetrator of violence; and contemplating or attempting suicide. Additional risk factors include being born to, or raised by, a mentally ill parent; suffering from the loss of a significant other; having experienced prenatal trauma or poor health status at birth; experiencing chronic poverty; living in an abject environment, such as being homeless; participating in public assistance programs; and having a parent in prison (Biglan, Brennan, Foster, & Holder, 2004; DeAngelis, 2000; LeCapitaine, 2000).

The research also indicates that a disproportionate number of ethnic/minority children, in particular black, Hispanic, and Native American children; non-English-speaking children; children of single-parent families; and gay, lesbian, bisexual, and transgender (GLBT) youth are represented among the at-risk population. Certain individuals in these groups have a high incidence of at-risk behavior, including low achievement, dropping out of school, teen pregnancy, suicide, and being a victim of violence.

Risk, Resiliency, and Protective Factors

Despite their overwhelming hardships, obstacles, and negative life events, many at-risk children and youth have been able to cope with adversity and succeed. These youngsters are resilient and have developed the necessary coping mechanisms and characteristics for success. Research on these children and youth suggests that when certain *protective factors* are present, they develop **resiliency.** According to Benard (1997), resilient children and youth share at least four common attributes:

- Social competence,
- Problem-solving skills,
- Autonomy, and
- Sense of purpose and future.

The key protective factors associated with resiliency include:

- *Supportive relationships,* particularly encouragement from school personnel and other adults;
- *Student characteristics,* such as self-esteem, motivation, problem-solving skills, conflict resolution skills, and the acceptance of responsibility;
- *Family factors,* such as parental support/concern and school involvement;
- *Community factors,* such as community youth programs (i.e., sports, clubs, hobbies);
- *School factors,* such as academic success and pro-social skills (Chavkin & Gonzalez, 2000); and
- *Cultural and religious factors* that support self-preservation instincts and a purpose of life.

As suggested by the model in Figure 10.1, those adults with whom the student has significant relationships can help students develop resiliency by providing encouragement, a

Figure 10.1 — Conceptual Model of Factors Influencing Resilient At-Risk Students

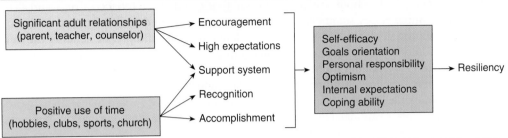

Source: "At-Risk Students and Resiliency: Factors Contributing to Academic Success" by J. H. McMillan & D. F. Reed. 1994. *Clearing House, 67,* 140. Reprinted with permission of the Helen Dwight Reid Educational Foundation. Published by Heldref Publications, 1319 Eighteenth St., N.W., Washington, DC 20036-1802. Copyright 1994.

support system, and recognition, as well as by holding high expectations for student performance. They can also help by identifying achievement reference points, aiding students in establishing long-range goals, and continually relating success to effort and ability. Students gain resiliency in classroom environments that stress high achievement while building self-esteem. Such an environment should emphasize time on task, student interaction and success, and positive reinforcement for desired classroom behaviors. Additionally, in today's climate, one of the most important ways schools can help develop resiliency is by providing a positive and safe learning environment (Christle, Jolivette, & Nelson, 2000; Waxman, Padron, & Gray, 2004).

Research suggests that the key to working with at-risk children or adolescents is to establish a trusting relationship. Figure 10.2 presents some of the keys to establishing a trusting relationship with at-risk students. The remainder of this chapter describes a number of at-risk conditions or behaviors and discusses how they might be identified. In addition, for each at-risk condition or behavior, prevention and intervention strategies are explored. The conditions or behaviors to be discussed include drug and alcohol abuse; suicide; dropping out of school; teenage pregnancy; AIDS and other STIs; child abuse and neglect; and violence. The conditions that place GLBT youth at risk for a variety of self-destructive behaviors are also discussed.

Figure 10.2 — Keys to Working with At-Risk Children and Adolescents

1. **Establish a Meaningful Connection.** Before any at-risk child or adolescent can trust or confide in a teacher, counselor, or other adult, he or she must experience a safe and meaningful connection with that adult.

2. **Be Honest and Direct.** Be honest in sharing your care, concern. However, if a child or adolescent is engaging in risky behavior, don't be afraid to challenge him or her.

3. **Seek Opportunities to Empower the Child or Adolescent.** Many children or adolescents who are at risk have internalized feelings of being "less than" and "unworthy." Compliment at-risk youngsters for the courage to talk with an adult about their problems and to seek help.

4. **Don't Be Afraid to Discuss Decision Making Relative to Sensitive Areas.** Once at-risk students have confided in you, don't be afraid to discuss their decision making relative to sensitive areas such as drug or alcohol abuse or sexual behavior.

5. **Know Your Limits.** Refer to other professionals (i.e., counselor, school psychologist, school nurse, or social worker) for their guidance and input. When you suspect a child or adolescent is at risk for self-destructive behavior such as suicide, immediately contact your school administration and the child or adolescent's parents or guardian. Follow the recommended protocol/guidelines of your school relative to appropriate intervention.

Tobacco, Drug, and Alcohol Use and Abuse

Although many high school students continue to use and abuse tobacco, drugs, and alcohol in the United States, significant decreases have been seen during the past decade. For example, among 9th- through 12th-grade students in public and private schools, the percentage of students who reported current cigarette smoking decreased from 36% in 1997 to 22% in 2003 (U.S. Department of Health and Human Services [USDHHS], 2004a). White students were significantly more likely than black and Hispanic students to report current cigarette smoking. The average smoker begins to smoke at age 13, and in less than 2 years is smoking daily (National Education Association [NEA] Health Information Network, 2001b). Perhaps not unexpectedly, cigarette smoking is highest among older youth, with 26% of 12th graders having smoked cigarettes during the 30 days preceding the latest annual Centers for Disease Control and Prevention (CDC) survey (USDHHS, 2004a).

In addition to smoking cigarettes, an estimated 7% of all high school students and 4% of middle school students currently use smokeless tobacco (chewing tobacco, which comes in the form of loose leaf, plug, or twist) and snuff (finely ground tobacco in sachets) that can be sniffed or inhaled (USDHHS, 2004b).

Alcohol use among youth and adolescents continues to be a major problem facing the schools and society. The average youth tends to take his or her first drink between the ages of 12 and 13 (NEA Health Information Network, 2001b). Forty-five percent of all high school students reported having one or more drinks during the 30 days preceding the 2004 CDC survey. Use among males and females was almost equal: 44% and 46%, respectively. Use among white and Hispanic students was also almost equal (47% and 46%, respectively) compared to 37% for black students. Perhaps more disturbing, nationwide 28% of students reported episodic heavy drinking, consuming five or more drinks in a row during the 30 days preceding the survey. Especially disturbing is that 30% of the students reported that they had ridden in a car or other vehicle with a driver who had been drinking. In addition, 12% of the students had driven a car or other vehicle while under the influence of alcohol. Despite these disturbing statistics, alcohol consumption of high school students declined from 82% in 1991 to 75% in 2003 (USDHHS, 2004d).

The use of marijuana also showed a decrease among the youth surveyed. Nationwide, 22% of students used marijuana one or more times during the 30 days preceding the CDC survey. Overall, marijuana use was higher among males (25%) than females (19%). Cocaine use was twice as high among Hispanic students (8%) as white students (4%) and four times that of black students (2%) (USDHHS, 2004d).

While there has been a steady decline in the overall use and abuse of drugs among American teenagers (600,000 fewer teens used drugs in 2004 than in 2001), the use of certain drugs has been increasing. Among these are inhalants, Ecstasy, anabolic-androgenic steroids, and painkillers. The use of inhalants (glue, shoe polish, gasoline, spray paint, nail polish remover, hair spray, and cleaning fluids) poses a particular problem since they are readily accessible, legal, and inexpensive. Inhalant use reaches its peak during the 7th through 9th grades (National Institute on Drug Abuse [NIDA], 2005c).

There has also been an increase in the use of Ecstasy and anabolic steroids. Approximately 5% of 12th graders, 3% of 10th graders, and 2% of 8th graders had used Ecstasy in 2003. Ecstasy, a synthetic psychoactive drug with both stimulant and hallucinogenic properties, is a neurotoxin and has the potential to cause injury to the brain, including memory loss (NIDA, 2005b).

Anabolic steroids are a synthetic version of the primary sex hormone, testosterone. They can be injected, taken orally, or used transdermally. When used inappropriately, they have the

Early prevention efforts are a key to combating the serious problem of drug abuse that affects adolescents of all cultures and socioeconomic classes.

Table 10.1 — Percentage of High School Students Who Use Cigarettes, Alcohol, Marijuana, and Cocaine by Sex, Race/Ethnicity, and Gender—United States, 2003

Category	Cigarette Use			Alcohol Use			Marijuana Use			Cocaine Use		
	Female	Male	Total	Female	Male	Total	Female	Male	Total	Female	Male	Total
Race/Ethnicity												
White	26.6	23.3	24.9	48.4	45.9	47.1	19.9	23.3	21.7	3.7	3.9	3.8
Black	10.8	19.3	15.1	37.0	37.5	37.4	18.1	29.8	23.9	0.9	3.3	2.2
Hispanic	17.7	19.1	18.4	48.4	42.7	45.6	20.4	27.1	23.8	5.8	5.5	5.7
Grade												
9	18.9	16.0	17.4	38.5	33.9	36.2	17.2	19.6	18.5	4.2	3.1	3.6
10	21.9	21.7	21.3	44.9	42.2	43.5	18.2	25.7	22.0	2.9	4.4	3.7
11	24.0	23.2	23.6	46.8	47.3	47.0	20.9	27.3	24.1	3.3	4.9	4.1
12	23.3	29.0	26.2	56.5	56.0	55.9	21.3	30.0	25.8	3.5	5.8	4.7
Total	21.9	21.8	21.9	45.8	43.8	44.9	19.3	25.1	22.4	3.5	4.6	4.1

Source: U.S. Department of Health and Human Services, Centers for Disease Control and Prevention. (2004). Youth risk behavior surveillance—United States, *MMWR, 53.*

potential to cause serious negative health consequences (stunted height, cardiovascular disease, liver and kidney disease, and psychiatric problems). Also, because steroids are often injected, users are at risk for contracting or transmitting HIV or hepatitis (NIDA, 2005a).

Last, the use and abuse of painkillers by teenagers is also on the increase. In 2004, Vicoden was used by 9% of 12th graders, 5% of 10th graders, and 3% of 8th graders. During the same year, OxyContin was used by 5% of 12th graders, 4% of 10th graders, and 2% of 8th graders (NIDA, 2005d). Current patterns of drug use among American high school students are presented in Table 10.1.

The Effects of Drug and Alcohol Abuse

Drug and alcohol abuse are related to a variety of at-risk behaviors, including unintentional injury (automobile accidents), school failure, unintended pregnancy, AIDS and other STIs, violent and abusive behavior, and other psychological and social problems. On an individual level, drug and alcohol abuse interfere with cognitive development and academic achievement. On a societal level, neighborhoods near schools often become the target of drug dealers, many of whom are students themselves. Additionally, crimes of violence often are associated with substance abuse, particularly among teenage gang members. Research also suggests that teenage drug abuse is a contributing factor to personal, social, and occupational maladjustment in later young adulthood. The prevention of drug use and abuse is not only a moral imperative but it also represents a cost savings to society. For example, it has been suggested that for every dollar spent on drug use prevention, communities can save four to five dollars in costs for drug abuse treatment and counseling (NIDA, 1997). The research also suggests that youth who do not use illicit drugs, alcohol, and tobacco prior to the age of 18 are likely to avoid chemical-dependency problems over their lifetime (National Clearinghouse for Alcohol and Drug Information, 1998).

Identifying Alcohol and Drug Use

Parents and school personnel are better prepared to provide early intervention when they recognize the difference between normal childhood and adolescent behavior and behavior that may indicate substance use or abuse. Among the psychological and interpersonal factors that place certain children and adolescents at risk for alcohol and drug use include low self-esteem, antisocial and aggressive behavior, lack of engagement with the school, and poor school achievement. Family factors such as substance abuse by parents or siblings, coupled with environmental factors such as poverty and violence, also make certain youngsters more vulnerable than others. However, the strongest risk predictors are attitudes toward drug use and association with peers.

The differences between so-called normal behavior and behavior that reflects substance use or abuse often are a matter of degree. For example, it is normal for a child or adolescent to spend time alone. However, it is usually not normal to exhibit sudden, almost complete withdrawal from family or peers. Overall, the best predictor of possible substance abuse is a pattern of changes, not any single behavioral change.

Prevention and Intervention Strategies

Chemical dependency has serious implications for the schools. Practically every teacher from middle school on will be confronted by students who are engaging in regular use of drugs and/or alcohol. Beginning teachers need to become familiar with the educational prevention programs offered by their district and their school (e.g., peer counseling and school-based individual and group counseling). They also need to become acquainted with the treatment programs available in the community for children, adolescents, and their families. The school counselor, social worker, school psychologist, or school nurse will be an invaluable resource to the beginning teacher who may feel unprepared to deal with this particular type of at-risk behavior.

There are literally hundreds of programs, activities, and services at the national, state, and local levels that are designed to reduce the occurrence of substance use and abuse in children and adolescents. One of the major programs at the national level is the Safe and Drug Free Schools and Communities (SDFSC) Act. The purpose of this act is to support programs that prevent violence in and around schools; that prevent the illegal use of alcohol, tobacco, and drugs; and that are coordinated with related federal, state, school and community efforts and resources aimed at providing a safe and drug-free learning environment conducive to setting high academic standards for all students. The SDFSC act supports school-based programs that promote a sense of individual responsibility and that teach the consequences of the illegal use of drugs; that most people do not illegally use drugs; how to recognize social and peer pressure to use drugs illegally, the skills for resisting illegal drug use; and the dangers of emerging drugs. Research has demonstrated that successful substance abuse prevention programs teach resistance skills while correcting erroneous perceptions about the prevalence and acceptability of drug use among peers (NIDA, 2005e).

A number of prevention initiatives have been directed at reducing risk factors associated with drug use and strengthening protective factors. The most successful of these programs attempt to address multiple risk factors. Research suggests that prevention efforts that target only one risk factor may be less effective because there are many youth who engage in multiple problem behaviors including antisocial behavior, cigarette smoking, binge drinking, marijuana use, hard drug use, and risky sexual behavior (Biglan et al., 2004). Regardless of the thrust of the prevention program, it is important that parental involvement be a component of the substance abuse prevention curriculum.

Suicide

Suicide is the third leading cause of death among youth 15 to 24 years of age; only accidents and homicides rank higher (Hoyert, Kung, & Smith, 2005). Suicide ranks as the second leading cause of death for 15- to 19-year-olds. More adolescents and young adults die from suicide than from cancer, heart disease, AIDS, birth defects, pneumonia and influenza, and chronic lung disease combined (Hoyert et al., 2005). The most recent CDC survey reported that 17% of high school students had seriously considered suicide and had even made a suicide plan. Overall, females were significantly more likely than males (19% and 14%, respectively) to have made a suicide plan (USDHHS, 2004d). Female students were also more apt to attempt suicide than male students (11% and 6%, respectively), while male students are four times more likely to complete or commit suicide. The use of firearms accounts for 54% of youth suicides (Anderson & Smith, 2003).

The rate of suicide and **suicide attempts** varies among racial and ethnic groups. For example, among female students, attempted suicide rates varied from 15% for Hispanic students to 10% for white students and 9% for black students. Of the various racial and ethnic categories, American Indian and Alaskan Natives have the highest rate of suicide in the 15- to 24-year-old age group (USDHHS, 2004d). Gay, lesbian, bisexual, and transgender youth of both sexes and all racial and ethnic groups are at increased risk for suicidal behavior.

Overall, in 2003, 3% of all students in our nation's schools actually made a suicide attempt that resulted in an injury, poisoning, or overdose that necessitated being treated by a physician or nurse during the past year. Thus, within a typical high school classroom, it is probable that three students (one boy and two girls) have attempted suicide during the past year (USDHHS, 2004d). However, because many suicide attempts go undetected or unreported, these data probably do not reflect the true magnitude of the problem.

Identifying the Suicidal Child or Adolescent

Most children and youth who are suicidal will exhibit a number of verbal and nonverbal warning signs and clues. It behooves every parent and educator to be sensitive to any one of the signs or clues, because it may be the youngster's last desperate plea for understanding or help. If one or more of these signs is observed, the parents and/or educator should talk to the child about his or her concerns and seek professional help if those concerns or problems persist. Table 10.2 presents some of the major indicators of childhood or adolescent suicidal behavior.

Table 10.2 — Indicators of Childhood or Adolescent Suicide

Psychosocial	Familial	Psychiatric	Situational
1. Poor self-esteem and feelings of inadequacy 2. Hypersensitivity and suggestibility 3. Perfectionism 4. Sudden change in social behavior 5. Academic deterioration 6. Underachievement and learning disabilities	1. Disintegrating family relationships 2. Economic difficulties and family stresses 3. Child and adolescent abuse 4. Ambivalence concerning dependence versus independence 5. Running away 6. Family history of suicide	1. Prior suicide attempt 2. Verbalization of suicide or talk of self-harm 3. Preoccupation with death 4. Repeated suicide ideation 5. Daredevil or self-abusive behavior 6. Mental illness such as delusions or hallucinations in schizophrenia 7. Overwhelming sense of guilt 8. Obsessional self-doubt 9. Phobic anxiety 10. Clinical depression 11. Substance abuse	1. Stressful life events 2. Firearms in the home 3. Exposure to suicide

Source: Adapted from © 1998. *Preventing Adolescent Suicide* by Capuzzi, D., & Golden, L. Reproduced by permission of Routledge/Taylor & Francis Group, LLC.

Recognizing and responding to depression is key to suicide prevention.

One of the most important risk factors for suicide is substance abuse. Research suggests that the use of drugs or alcohol may temper the fear of death (Wu Hoven, Liu, Cohen, Fuller, & Shaffer, 2004). A strong relationship has also been found between **major depression** and suicide. The clinically depressed child or youth is likely to exhibit signs of hopelessness, a change in eating and sleeping habits, withdrawal from family and friends, substance abuse, persistent boredom, loss of interest in pleasurable activities, neglect of personal appearance, and frequent complaints about physical symptoms. In early adolescence, depression is often masked by acting out or delinquent behavior. Older adolescents are more apt to resort to violence, drug or alcohol use, and sexual activity rather than face their emotional pain.

Students who have made a previous suicide attempt are at high risk for suicide. The child or adolescent who experiences a significant number of stressful life events (e.g., death of a parent, separation or divorce of parents, family turmoil or conflict, lack of family support, school failure, sexual or physical assault), issues of sexual identity, or interpersonal conflict with a boyfriend or girlfriend, may also be at risk. Children who tend to be preoccupied with death, know a teenager who has attempted or completed suicide, or have a family history of suicide are also at risk. This is especially true if those stressors occur in combination with alcohol and drug use and the availability of firearms.

Prevention and Intervention Strategies

All school personnel should be trained in identifying suicidal youth, but students themselves also need training. The majority of suicide prevention programs for students emphasize a curriculum of decision making, problem solving, and general life-skills training. Many of these prevention programs also include information about how students can recognize the signs and symptoms of depression and suicidal behavior among their friends and how to access help from the school and community (Children's Safety Network, 2000). Such programs are often incorporated into the health curriculum.

Some educators and parents have concerns that exposure to such programs may have a negative effect on students who are already at risk for suicide, in particular students who may have made an earlier suicide attempt. While there is no research evidence that exposure to such a curriculum has caused a suicide or suicide attempt, the research has recommended that for students who are already at risk for suicide, a prevention curriculum is not appropriate. Instead, such students need to be identified and immediately referred for treatment intervention and follow-up. The Controversial Issue on the next page lists arguments for and against the schools taking an active role in suicide prevention.

The most common suicide intervention program is the **crisis intervention team** approach. The crisis intervention team is composed of teachers, counselors, administrators, social workers, school nurses, and school psychologists who are trained to respond to a variety of crisis situations, including suicide. Their task is to work with each other to identify youngsters who appear to be depressed, overwhelmed by stress, or who display a **suicide gesture** or suicide threat. Problems are often solved at the team level; however, the crisis team may refer a student to a community mental health agency or hospital for emergency care. Other school-based intervention strategies include individual and group counseling, peer counseling, and referral to a suicide hotline for students who are in crisis when school is not in session. School personnel should not attempt to handle the suicidal student alone; they should notify parents if they suspect that a child or an adolescent is suicidal and hold the student in protective custody until the parents arrive.

CONTROVERSIAL ISSUE

The School's Role in Suicide Prevention

The extent to which the schools should assume a role in suicide prevention is debated by educators, school boards, and parents. The reasons often given in favor of or against suicide prevention in the school are as follows:

Arguments For

1. Suicide prevention programs can help students cope with stresses in their school and personal lives.
2. Suicide prevention programs usually teach coping, problem solving, and survival skills that are valuable life skills for all students.
3. Programs help teachers and students recognize warning signs of the suicidal child or adolescent, enabling them to make a timely referral if necessary.
4. Suicide prevention programs offer training in peer counseling, which has been an invaluable strategy for identifying the suicidal child or adolescent.
5. The alarming statistics concerning suicide among children and adolescents require that schools take a proactive step in addressing the problem.

Arguments Against

1. School counselors, teachers, and other professional staff do not have the time or training to deal effectively with the suicidal youngster.
2. There is little research evidence that confirms that suicide prevention programs lessen suicidal behavior.
3. The liability of the school is unclear concerning suicide prevention programming.
4. Recent research on imitative and modeling behavior raises serious questions about offering suicide prevention programs in the schools, i.e., teaching about suicide will trigger a suicide, because children and youth are so suggestible.

What is your view of suicide prevention in the school? What types of program(s) exist in a school with which you are familiar?

 To answer these questions online, go to the *Controversial Issue* module for this chapter of the Companion Website at **http://www.prenhall.com/webb.**

The crisis intervention team also plays an important role in helping the school return to normal in the aftermath of a suicide. Grief counseling, support groups, implementation of guidelines for interacting with the media, and follow-up care are examples of strategies facilitated by the crisis intervention team.

Parents and teachers are often the last to recognize that the child or adolescent is at risk for suicide. The child's peer group will probably be the first to know that the child is in need of immediate help. Teachers need to be able to establish a trusting relationship with students so that they will come forward to seek the help they need to respond to a suicidal friend. Many beginning teachers feel very inadequate and fearful of handling a suicidal student for fear that their actions may precipitate an actual suicide or suicide attempt. The truth is that talking about suicidal tendencies will not exacerbate a suicide or suicide attempt. Most youngsters at risk for suicide are relieved to be able to articulate their fears and concerns to an adult who will listen. The worst response is no response.

Dropping Out of School

The majority of states and school districts define a **dropout** as a student who leaves school for any reason before graduation or completion of a program of study without transferring to another school or institution. Although there has been a decrease in the dropout rate in the 5-year period from 1998 to 2003 (from 12% to 10%), dropping out of school remains a serious issue because of its grave consequences for the individual and society. It is estimated that during their lifetime, dropouts will earn $370,000 less than high school graduates and approximately $1.5 million less than college graduates. More

For Your Reflection and Analysis

Why might dropping out of school have a more deleterious effect on females than males?
To submit your response online, go to http://www. prenhall.com/webb.

CW

seriously, the poverty rate for dropouts (17%) is more than twice that of those with a high school diploma (7%), and they are more likely to be incarcerated and be in poor health (Wiles, 2005).

In 2003, 11% of males and 8% of females 16 through 24 years of age had dropped out of school. As discussed in Chapter 8, there are significant differences in dropout rates among racial/ethnic groups, with the dropout rate for Hispanics being more than twice that of blacks and four times that of whites. In addition to racial and ethnic differences in dropout rates, there are also significant differences in dropout rates among students from different income groups. For example, youth from families in the lowest 20% of all family incomes were six times as likely to drop out of school as those in the topmost 20% of family incomes (U.S. Department of Education, 2005d).

Identifying the Potential Dropout

Research has identified a number of factors that are associated with dropping out of school. One of the major factors is dis-identification with the school. Other commonly mentioned factors include poor academic performance; having been retained in at least one grade; lack of basic skills, particularly, reading; problems at home; a history of school transfers and family moves; having a parent or older sibling who is a dropout; dislike for school; low socioeconomic status; lack of parental involvement in the school; limited English proficiency; low self-esteem; institutional racism in the classroom; poor peer relationships; and conflict between home and school culture. In addition, dropouts are often individuals who have undiagnosed learning disabilities or emotional problems and who abuse drugs or alcohol. For adolescent girls, pregnancy is the principal reason for dropping out of school (Sutton, 2003).

Prevention and Intervention Strategies

As with other at-risk behaviors, early identification of the potential dropout is critical. The earlier the identification, the more likely dropout prevention efforts will be successful. Regrettably, some school practices, such as suspension, serve to push students out of school (Grier, 2000). Unfortunately, the current high-stakes testing movement has placed additional pressure on underachieving students to consider dropping out of school.

Fortunately, a number of strategies have been found to be effective in preventing students from dropping out. They include compensatory education programs that assist children from low-income families to qualify for alternative educational opportunities beyond the traditional high school setting. Examples include establishing a school-within-a-school or initiating career academies; placing more emphasis on vocational education by offering job skills training and practical work experience; being more attentive to the student's learning style; providing English as a second language (ESL) instruction; and making available prenatal/pregnancy counseling and child care (Lunenburg, 2000; Sutton, 2003).

Other prevention strategies include the implementation of state punitive or disincentive policies. The most controversial of these are the "No pass, no drive laws," which are intended to keep teens in school by revoking their driver's licenses if they drop out of school, are truant, or are not progressing toward graduation. Several states have passed legislation that links driving privileges to school attendance (National Commission on the States, 2005). Another negative sanction policy reduces state benefits to families on welfare if their child fails to attend school regularly. This sanction is designed to place the responsibility on parents for their children's school attendance (Lunenburg, 2000). Another proposed policy, while not punitive, would raise the compulsory attendance age to 18.

Teenage Pregnancy

The birthrate for teenagers 15 to 17 years old declined substantially from a high of 39 per 1,000 in 1991 to 22 per 1,000 (a 42% decline) in 2003 (Ventura, Abma, Mosher, & Henshaw, 2005). A similar significant decline was seen in abortion rates. The induced abortion rate high of 31 per 1,000 in 1983 decreased by more than one-half to 15 per 1,000 by 2000 (Hamilton, Martin, & Sutton 2005).

For Your Reflection and Analysis

Do you support the "dropouts don't drive law" as an intervention strategy? Why or why not?

To submit your response online, go to http://www.prenhall.com/webb.

CW

Figure 10.3 — Birth Rates By Race/Ethnicity, 15- to 17-Year-Olds, 1980–2003

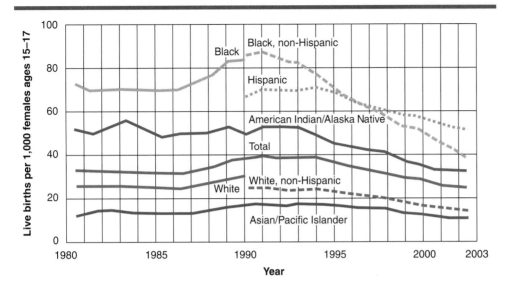

Significant racial and ethnic differences in birthrates are seen among adolescents ages 15 to 17. In 2003, the highest birthrate per 1,000 for this age group was 50 for Hispanics; 39 for black, non-Hispanics; 30 for American Indians/Alaska Natives; 12 for white, non-Hispanics; and 9 for Asians/Pacific Islanders. The birthrate for black, non-Hispanic females ages 15 to 17 dropped by more than half between 1991 and 2003 (Hamilton et al., 2005). Figure 10.3 shows the decline in birthrates for females ages 15 to 17 by race and ethnicity from 1980 to 2003.

Delayed sexual intercourse with improved contraceptive practice may account for these declines (Santelli et al., 2004). Despite these declines, the United States continues to have one of the highest teen birthrates in the Western industrialized world. The U.S. adolescent pregnancy rate is nearly twice that of Canada and Great Britain, and approximately four times that of France and Sweden (Darroch, Frost, & Singh, 2001).

Several myths surround teenage pregnancy. One myth is that teen pregnancy is an adolescent problem. In reality, a slight majority (51%) of the fathers of children born to females under age 18 were in their twenties. The second myth is that American adolescents who have had sexual intercourse have done so voluntarily. In fact, although the research data tend to be scattered and preliminary, there is growing evidence that many young women become pregnant as a result of nonvoluntary sexual intercourse (Annie E. Casey Foundation, 2001).

Pregnant teens are at increased risk for dropping out of school.

Consequences of Adolescent Pregnancy

Adolescent parenthood has profound implications for health care and social services, for poverty and crime, for family relationships, and for the institution of the school. Because so many teenage parents often lack sufficient health care insurance and the necessary funds for the delivery, they must resort to outside subsidies to meet their financial commitments. In addition, they often lack proper prenatal care, one of the major prerequisites for a healthy delivery and low infant mortality. This, coupled with inadequate nutrition, has resulted in a significant number of premature deliveries with accompanying low birth weight. These premature infants often are at risk for a host of subsequent serious health problems. The mortality rate for teenage mothers also is higher than for any age group. Because teen mothers experience so many health problems before and after the birth, they place heavy demands on the accompanying social service agencies, exacerbating the costs to the teen, her family, and society. Many of the children of teen mothers become at risk for educational and psychological problems and often are overrepresented in classes for students with learning disabilities and emotional disturbances (Bonjean & Rittenmeyer, 1987). These "children of children" often become adolescent parents themselves, repeating the cycle and worsening the problem.

The issue of teenage pregnancy has several major economic consequences. Many pregnant adolescents fail to complete the eighth grade or do not graduate from high school. And, as previously noted, dropouts have a reduced earning potential and are more likely to be on welfare and out of the labor force. Moreover, there is strong evidence that the transfer of poverty from the mother to her children perpetuates a cycle of poverty for future generations.

Prevention and Intervention Strategies

The obvious primary aim of pregnancy prevention programs is to keep teens from conceiving. Typical school-based prevention strategies include an abstinence-only health curriculum that focuses on how to resist peer pressure and abstain from sexual activity. Others provide basic information about health and human sexuality, contraception, communication, decision making, and family planning. A few school-based health clinics provide contraceptive counseling and related health services to adolescents in addition to providing counseling, physical examinations, immunization, and referrals to other community agencies. Currently, pregnancy prevention programs that target the needs of Hispanic adolescent girls, in particular Mexican-American females, are especially needed as is the need to find effective strategies to involve young men in the pregnancy prevention efforts. Despite the strong objections of some parents, a recent survey reported that, overall, parents and other adults overwhelmingly support making sexuality education part of the junior high and senior high school curriculum (Henry J. Kaiser Family Foundation, National Public Radio, & Kennedy School of Government, 2004).

The primary goals of most intervention strategies are to provide prenatal care, parenting skills, and vocational and personal counseling to adolescent mothers in an effort to reduce the cycle of repeated pregnancies and welfare dependency. Parent resource centers, which are usually coordinated with school health clinics, have proven to be a promising intervention strategy. Such parent resource centers provide pregnant and parenting students with a wide range of health, educational, and social services, including child care. The students who are referred to such resource centers typically work with a case management team that includes a social worker, teacher, and public health nurse. This team interacts with the students' parents and closely monitors the academic progress, attendance, and health of each girl and her baby.

HIV/AIDS and Other Sexually Transmitted Infections

Acquired immunodeficiency syndrome (AIDS) is a serious disease caused by the **human immunodeficiency virus (HIV),** which destroys the body's immunological system and leaves the body susceptible to infection. Two potentially fatal diseases identified in AIDS patients are *Pneumocystis carinii* pneumonia, an infection of the lungs, and *Kaposi's sarcoma,* a rare form of cancer.

Between 1985 and 2003, approximately 5,208 cases of AIDS were reported for U.S. teens 13 to 19 years of age. In 2003 alone, a total of 472 adolescents were diagnosed with AIDS. Of these, 256 (54%) were male compared to 216 (46%) female (USDHHS, 2005b). An additional 2,520 adolescents are known to be living with HIV.

Black and Hispanic adolescents are disproportionately affected by AIDS/HIV. Fifteen percent of adolescents 13 to 19 years of age are black, yet 66% of reported AIDS cases in this age group were black. Similarly, Hispanics 15 to 19 years of age represent 16% of that age group but 21% of the reported AIDS cases in 2003. Asian/Pacific Islander and Ameri-

For Your Reflection and Analysis

To what extent should the school bear the costs and responsibility for providing a pregnancy prevention and intervention program?

To submit your response online, go to http://www. prenhall.com/webb.

CW

can Indian/Alaska Native youth account for only about 1% of the reported AIDS cases (USDHHS, 2005b). The group with the highest risk for AIDS/HIV infection was young men who have sex with men, especially those of minority races and ethnicities.

The prevalence of **sexually transmitted infections (STIs)** also continues to be a major health threat in the United States, particularly among youth. It is estimated that 19 million STIs occur each year, half of them targeting youth 15 to 24 years old (Weinstock, Berman, & Cates, 2004). **Chlamydia infection,** a bacterial infection, is the most commonly reported infectious disease in the United States and can be cured with antibiotics. However, if not treated, it can cause severe health consequences for women. Similar to other STIs, chlamydia can also facilitate the transmission of HIV infection.

Youth are particularly vulnerable for AIDS and other STIs because of their at-risk sexual behavior. The CDC's Youth Risk Behavior Survey of high school students reported that in 2003, nationwide, 47% of the students reported having had sexual intercourse, with 14% having had four or more sex partners. Of the 34% currently sexually active youth, 63% reported that either they or their partner used a condom during their last intercourse and 17% reported that either they or their partner used birth control to prevent pregnancy. Not surprisingly, research has shown that teens who engage in sex after using drugs or drinking alcohol are less apt to use condoms for protection (USDHHS, 2004c).

Prevention and Intervention Strategies

Because AIDS and other STIs have far-reaching implications for our society, the schools have an obligation to offer prevention or educational strategies that address this problem. However, there is considerable controversy among school officials, health educators, governmental officials, and parents regarding the most effective approach to HIV/AIDS and STI education. Although a number of vocal community and religious groups have argued that sexual abstinence should be the only prevention method emphasized, a number of school and health officials concerned about the spread of HIV/AIDS and STIs among youth have suggested that the educational curriculum should also include information on such topics as condom use and restricting sexual activity to monogamous relationships.

A survey of successful school-based programs to reduce risky sexual behaviors concluded that the following strategies should be included:

- Targeting a specific risk behavior (e.g., unprotected sexual intercourse);
- Using social learning theory;
- Personalizing risk information, thereby making students feel more vulnerable;
- Addressing social and media influences that pressure teens into having sexual intercourse;
- Reinforcing norms against unprotected sex; and
- Providing practice in communication skills to help with refusal and negotiation (NEA Health Information Network, 2001b, p. 1).

Most communities do support AIDS and STI education in the schools. However, a number of communities have requested that parental consent be obtained before any student participates in such an educational program.

Students with HIV/AIDS cannot be excluded from school attendance unless under rare circumstances they have been found to be a risk of transmitting the disease (See Historical Note on page 258). Children (and teachers) with HIV/AIDS are protected by Section 504 of the Rehabilitation Act of 1973, which prohibits discrimination against persons with handicaps in federally assisted programs such as elementary and secondary schools (see discussion in Chapter 12). Nonjudgmental counseling for students with HIV/AIDS or STIs is one of the most important intervention strategies. In addition, schools must recognize the importance of confidentiality in working with adolescents with HIV/AIDS and other STIs.

Teachers cannot ignore the reality of HIV/AIDS or other STIs among student populations. With the increasing number of very young sexually active adolescents (7% had sexual intercourse the first time before age 13), it is very possible, whether they know it or not, that teachers will encounter a student with a STI at some time in their career and many may encounter a student with HIV/AIDS.

For Your Reflection and Analysis

Should the schools be responsible for dispensing condoms to prevent AIDS and STIs?

To submit your response online, go to http//www. prenhall.com/webb.

CW

HISTORICAL NOTE

Outcasts: Three HIV-Positive Brothers Barred From School

In 1986, in Arcadia, a small town in west central Florida, three brothers, Ricky (age 9), Robert (age 8), and Randy (age 7), Ray were diagnosed with HIV, the virus that causes AIDS. They were among the thousands of hemophiliacs who contracted the virus through tainted blood. During this time, fear, misunderstanding, and ignorance regarding HIV/AIDS prevailed. Little was known about the transfer of HIV and the residents of Arcadia had their own theories: medical conspiracies, mosquitoes, and using the same toilet.

When Clifford and Louise Ray learned of their sons' diagnosis, they notified the school district and attempted to enroll their sons in regular classes. The school board barred their admission. The boys were tutored at home at district expense. The Rays sued the school board. The next year the federal court in Tampa ruled that the Ray children could not be excluded from regular classes and ordered the De Soto County Schools to admit the three boys in the fall. In response, a group calling themselves Citizens Against AIDS in Schools encouraged parents to keep their children at home. The organization drew hundreds of local residents to a series of rallies where they demanded that the children be quarantined. The first day of school hundreds of parents, including the

mayor, kept their children out of school. Ugly protests were followed by death threats. Finally, someone set fire to the Ray home. Quiet Ricky blamed himself for the fire, and Randy, the youngest, was desolate over the loss of his stuffed monkey during the fire. The little restuffed monkey without a tail had been with him through all of his hospital stays.

After the fire the Rays moved to Sarasota where the Ray boys enrolled with little protest. Ricky died in 1992 at age 15. In 1998 the federal government passed the Ricky Ray Relief Fund Act, which acknowledged the government's lax screening of the blood supply and provided compensation for hemophiliacs (many of whom were children) who had contracted AIDS between 1982 and 1987. Robert died in 2000 at age 22 before his scheduled marriage. As of this writing, Randy Ray has full-blown AIDS but maintains an active life.

Sources: Buckley, S. (2001, September 2). Slow change of heart. *St. Petersburg Times.* Retrieved September 7, 2005, from http://www.sptimes.com/News/090201/news_pf/State/slow_chang_of_heart.shtml; and Voboril, M. (October, 1987). The castaways: Fears about AIDS drive three boys from home. Retrieved September 7, 2005, from http://www.maryellenmark.com/text/magazines/life/905W-000-030.html

CW To research and explore this topic further, go to the *Historical Note* module for this chapter of the Companion Website at **http://www.prenhall.com/webb.**

Child Abuse and Neglect

Child abuse and neglect are defined in both federal and state legislation. The Child Abuse Prevention and Treatment Act (CAPTA, 42 U.S.C. 5106g) defines **child abuse** and **child neglect** as:

> At a minimum, any recent act or failure to act on the part of a parent or caretaker which results in death, serious physical or emotional harm, or sexual abuse or exploitation. It includes an act or failure to act which presents an imminent risk of serious harm.

Based on the CAPTA guidelines, each state has developed its own definitions of child abuse and neglect, which are included in state civil or criminal statutes.

The major types of child abuse include neglect, and physical, sexual, and emotional abuse, all of which can occur separately or in combination. Emotional abuse is almost always present with other forms of maltreatment. As shown in Table 10.3, approximately 900,000 children in the United States, or 12 children in every 1,000, were victims of child abuse or neglect in 2003. Girls were more often victims than boys, and Pacific Islander or Alaskan Native children and African American children had higher rates of victimization than other population subgroups.

Child fatalities constitute the most drastic form of child abuse and neglect. In 2003, approximately 1,500 children died due to child abuse or neglect. White children accounted

Table 10.3 — Rates of Child Abuse and Neglect Victimization (victims per 1,000) by Maltreatment Type, Gender, Race, and Ethnicity, 2003

	Number of Victims	Victimization Rate
Maltreatment Type		
Physical abuse	148,877	2.3
Neglect	479,567	7.5
Medical neglect	17,945	0.3
Sexual abuse	78,188	1.2
Psychological maltreatment	38,603	0.6
Other abuse	132,993	3.7
Unknown	1,792	0.3
Gender		
Male	378,374	11.6
Female	405,505	13.1
Race/Ethnicity*		
American Indian/Alaskan Native	13,350	21.3
African American	199,723	20.4
Asian	4,652	2.7
White	419,378	11.0
Multiple Race	11,507	12.8
Hispanic	90,177	9.9

*Not all states reporting

Source: From *Child Maltreatment 2003,* by U.S. Department of Health and Human Services, Administration on Children, Youth and Families, 2005, Washington, DC: U.S. Government Printing Office.

for 43% of all child fatalities, black children accounted for 31%, and Hispanic children 15%. More than one-third of child fatalities were attributed to neglect. Physical abuse was also a major contributor to child fatalities. Seventy-eight percent of the fatalities were caused by one or more parents (USDHHS, 2005a).

Physical Abuse

It is estimated that 19% of all victims of child abuse suffered from *physical abuse.* Examples of physical abuse include punching, beating, kicking, biting, burning, shaking, throwing, stabbing, choking, hitting, and/or otherwise harming a child. The injury is considered abuse whether intentional or not (USDHHS, 2005a).

Child Neglect

Failure to provide for a child's basic physical, educational, or emotional needs is considered to be a form of child neglect. Abandonment, expulsion from home, refusal to allow a runaway to return home, inadequate supervision, and the refusal to provide health care in a timely manner are all forms of *physical neglect.* Failure to attend to a child's special educational needs, failure to enroll a child in school, and the tolerance of chronic truancy all constitute a form of *educational neglect. Emotional neglect* includes the failure to provide for the psychological well-being of the child, being inattentive to a child's needs for affection, and parental permission to use and abuse drugs or alcohol. *Neglect* accounts for 61% of the cases of child maltreatment. Female parents tend to be the major perpetrators of child neglect (USDHHS, 2005a).

Sexual Abuse

During 2003, approximately 10% of children were victims of *sexual abuse* (USDHHS, 2005a). Sexual abuse includes fondling a child's genitals, intercourse, incest, rape, sodomy, exhibitionism, and commercial exploitation through prostitution or the production of pornographic materials. Sexual abuse is considered to be the most underreported form of child maltreatment due to the "conspiracy of silence" that is often associated with such cases. Male parents are primarily identified as the perpetrators of sexual abuse for the highest number of victims (USDHHS, 2005a).

Emotional Abuse

Emotional abuse (psychological/verbal abuse/mental injury) almost always occurs with the other forms of child maltreatment already mentioned. It includes acts or omissions by the parents or caregivers that might or could cause serious behavioral, cognitive, emotional, or mental disorders. Specific examples of emotional abuse include such nonphysical abusive behaviors as blaming, disparaging, or rejecting the child; habitual scapegoating, belittling, and intimidating; treating siblings unequally; deliberately enforcing isolation such as confinement to a dark closet; and continually withholding security and affection. In 2003, 5% of victims were emotionally or psychologically maltreated (USDHHS, 2005a).

Identifying Child Abuse and Neglect

Some of the common signs or indicators of child physical abuse include unexplained injuries, fractures, bruises, bite marks, and welts. A pattern of accidents may also be an indicator. Children who have been subject to any form of abuse often exhibit a variety of behavior changes, including aggressive or withdrawn behavior, neglected appearance, attention-seeking behavior, anxiety, or fear. They may engage in self-destructive behaviors and exhibit low self-esteem, depression, and severe emotional problems. They may be socially isolated, have poor relationships with parents, repeatedly run away, and have a history of frequent tardiness or absence from school. The presence of one of these signs does not prove a child is being abused, but when they occur repeatedly or in combination, as they often will if the child is being abused, they warrant closer examination and possible reporting. Some of the physical and behavioral indicators of possible neglect and abuse that teachers should be aware of are listed in Table 10.4.

Parents or caregivers also exhibit behaviors that may be indicators of child abuse or neglect. For example, they may show little concern for the child, provide minimal supervision, see the child as burdensome, or rarely look at or touch the child. They may deny the existence of, or blame the child for, problems the child is having at home or at school. They may see the child as bad or worthless and ask teachers or administrators to use harsh physical discipline if the child misbehaves. There is increasing awareness that abuse of drugs or alcohol by parents and other caretakers may be related to abuse and neglect. Many states have responded by expanding the definition of child abuse or neglect to include exposing children to illegal drugs in the home environment.

As discussed in Chapter 12, state child abuse statutes require that child abuse be reported by school counselors, school psychologists, social workers, teachers, nurses, or administrators to the local child protective agency, department of welfare, or law enforcement agency. Teachers and counselors must report suspected abuse or neglect even though to do so would violate a confidence; they cannot claim privileged communication as a defense for failure to report.

Most state reporting statutes detail the procedures that are to be followed in making the report. In all jurisdictions the initial report may be made orally to either a law enforcement agency, child protective services, or other designated agency. It is important that teachers be familiar with the applicable state statutes and the local school district's policies on reporting child abuse and neglect. State statutes that require teachers to report suspected child abuse do not demand that reporters be certain that the child has been abused, only that there be "reasonable cause to believe" that the child is subject to abuse or neglect. Under all state statutes, school employees who report suspected child abuse or neglect are provided immunity from civil and criminal liability if the report was made in good faith.

Table 10.4 — Signs of Child Abuse and Neglect

Signs of Physical Abuse

Consider the possibility of physical abuse when the child

- has unexplained burns, bites, bruises, broken bones, or black eyes;
- has fading bruises or other marks noticeable after an absence from school;
- seems frightened of the parents and protests or cries when it is time to go home;
- shrinks at the approach of adults;
- reports injury by a parent or another adult caregiver.

Signs of Neglect

Consider the possibility of neglect when the child

- is frequently absent from school;
- begs or steals food or money;
- lacks needed medical or dental care, immunizations, or glasses;
- is consistently dirty and has severe body odor;
- lacks sufficient clothing for the weather;
- abuses alcohol or other drugs;
- states that there is no one at home to provide care.

Signs of Sexual Abuse

Consider the possibility of sexual abuse when the child

- has difficulty walking or sitting;
- suddenly refuses to change for gym or to participate in physical activities;
- reports nightmares or bedwetting;
- experiences a sudden change in appetite;
- demonstrates bizarre, sophisticated, or unusual sexual knowledge or behavior;
- becomes pregnant or contracts a venereal disease, particularly if under age 14;
- runs away;
- reports sexual abuse by a parent or another adult caregiver.

Signs of Emotional Maltreatment

Consider the possibility of emotional maltreatment when the child

- shows extremes in behavior, such as overly compliant or demanding behavior, extreme passivity, or aggression;
- is either inappropriately adult (parenting other children, for example) or inappropriately infantile (frequently rocking or head banging, for example);
- is delayed in physical or emotional development;
- has attempted suicide;
- reports a lack of attachment to the parent.

Source: From *Recognizing Child Abuse and Neglect: Signs and Symptoms,* by National Clearinghouse on Child and Neglect Information, 2004, Washington, DC: U.S. Government Printing Office. http://www.nccanch.acf.hhs.gov

Prevention and Intervention Strategies

A number of school-based prevention programs have been introduced to address child abuse, in particular, sexual abuse. The major objectives of these programs are to increase the child's and adolescent's awareness of the risk of sexual abuse or exploitation, and to identify youngsters who are in abusive situations. The key elements of such prevention programs typically include (1) an awareness of body parts and how to distinguish between "good touch," "bad touch," and "confusing touch"; (2) the development of assertiveness or refusal skills; and (3) a discussion of how and where to obtain help (Minard, 1993). Many school districts have incorporated the prevention program content into the health education curriculum in order to keep it outside the controversial sex education domain. Curriculum units on life skills, such as assertiveness training, coping with stress, decision making, problem solving, and locating community resources, are also helpful in providing youngsters with the necessary tools to address sexual abuse.

The use of humor and entertainment have also been used with all grade levels to transmit information about sexual abuse through theater performances, art, role playing, play therapy, puppets, coloring books, bibliotherapy, and so forth. **Bibliotherapy** includes the use of selected reading materials as a therapeutic prevention technique. Obtaining parental permission to participate in such a program is recommended.

Because child abuse occurs across all socioeconomic classes and ethnic/racial groups, it is likely that most teachers will be confronted with this problem at some point during their teaching career. In fact, 16% of all reports of abuse or neglect in 2003 were made by teachers. When abuse or neglect occurs, it is important to remember not only one's legal and professional obligation to report the abuse but one's obligation to the student. Although these are normally delicate and emotionally charged situations, avoidance is not the appropriate response. It is always better to err on the side of the child's welfare.

For the child or adolescent victim of abuse, the attitude of the school personnel is critical. It is important that school personnel understand and believe that the child is not to blame and communicate this to the child. The teacher, in particular, is in a unique position to create a classroom environment that is safe, nurturing, and responsive to the needs of the vulnerable youngster. The teacher can help the abused child set healthy boundaries and know that those boundaries will be respected. Teachers need to set reasonable goals, but they also need to provide the support necessary for youngsters to feel confident and successful. Because abused children often feel powerless to control their environment, the teacher's role is to help them become more resilient and regain a personal sense of control. The first step in a child's regaining control is by having basic needs met within a safe and nurturing school environment. Because abused children tend to have low self-esteem, a caring and sensitive teacher can help them learn that they have many strengths and that they are valued and accepted members of society. To facilitate a sense of belonging, teachers should make a conscious effort to include these children in a variety of classroom activities (Gullatt & Stockton, 2000).

School Violence

When we hear the term "school violence" we are immediately reminded of the 1999 Columbine High School tragedy in Littleton, Colorado, in which 12 students and a teacher were killed; the 2005 incident at Red Lake, Minnesota, that resulted in the death of 6 students, a teacher, and a security guard; or the dozen or more other widely publicized school shootings that have occurred during the last decade. However, while these events make the headlines, every day thousands of school children across the country are the victims of school violence, including serious crimes such as murder, rape, robbery, and aggravated assault. School violence may also include physical attack or fighting without a weapon, theft/larceny, and vandalism. Peer sexual harassment based on gender, sexual orientation, and disability are further examples of school violence. And, in recent years bullying has become one of the most serious problems facing the schools, a problem that touches schools in all geographic and demographic profiles.

Data on the magnitude of school violence show that in 2002 students between 12 and 18 years of age were victims of approximately 1.8 million nonfatal crimes at school. Of these, 88,100 were victims of serious crimes including rape, sexual assault, robbery, and aggravated assault. Males were twice as likely as females to be victims of serious violent crimes, and the violent crime victimization rate was highest for blacks. In addition there were 14 homicides at school. While these figures are sobering, in fact, the percentage of students who reported being victims of crime at school decreased dramatically between 1995 to 2003, from 95% to 51% (Devoe et al., 2004).

Bullying

Another form of victimization that takes place in and out of school is *bullying*. Bullying is a form of aggressive antisocial behavior that involves one or more individuals who harass another individual verbally, physically, socially, and/or psychologically repeatedly over a period of time. Bullying differs from other aggressive behavior (e.g., jostling or rough play) that is a normal part of childhood in that the latter is benign, not malicious or intended to harm or dominate the peer (Doll, Song & Siemers, 2004). As Figure 10.4 illustrates, when

Figure 10.4 — Bullying: A Continuum of Aggressive Interactions

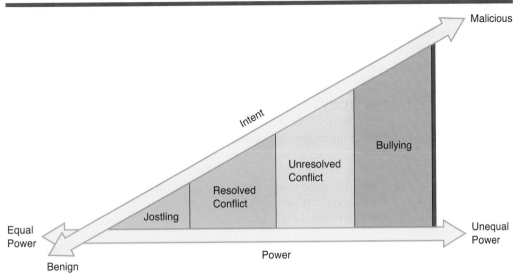

Source: Doll, B., Song, S., & Siemers, E. (2004). Classroom ecologies that support or discourage bullying. In D. L. Espelage & S. M. Swearer (Eds.), *Bullying in American Schools: A Social-ecological perspective on prevention and intervention* (pp. 161–183). Mahwah, NJ: Lawrence Erlbaum Associates.

aggressive peer interactions occur between children they will typically work to resolve the conflict, especially if it involves a friend. However, if the conflict is left unresolved, or if the opportunity presents itself in an unequal power relationship, children may resort to physical or verbal aggression or social ostracism in order to prevail over or dominate classmates (Doll et al., 2004).

Males are more likely to commit physical bullying, while females are more likely to engage in social bullying (e.g., exclusion, manipulation of friendship) (Salend, 2005). The targets/victims of bullying tend to be those who are most vulnerable because of age, gender, physical weakness, timidity, insecurity, poor self-esteem, mental capacity, or lack of protection from peers or teachers. Bullying often begins at the elementary level, peaks at middle school, and lessens at high school. Much bullying occurs when students are going to and from school, especially on the school bus. It also occurs during the school day in the hallways, bathrooms, and on the playground. It is most likely to occur when there is a lack of adult supervision and structured environment (Horn, Opinas, Newman-Carlson, & Bartolomucci, 2004). In 2003, 7% of students ages 12 to 18 reported they had been bullied at school (Devoe et al., 2004). Approximately 15% of students bully others and about half of bullies come from abusive homes (Galezewski, 2005).

A recent phenomenon of bullying has been the emergence of *cyberbullying*, which has transferred the dynamics of schoolyard bullying to the Internet. According to WireSafety.org, 50% of children reported that they or someone they knew had been victims of or were guilty of cyberbullying. Cyberbullies, mostly ages 9 to 14, use the anonymity of the Web to send belittling messages, nasty rumors, and humiliating photos via e-mail and *blogs*. The problem is aggravated by the widespread use of wireless devices such as cell phones and *BlackBerrys* which are most prevalent in upper class suburbs, where high-speed Internet use is greatest and youngsters are technically savvy. Many victims

Every day thousands of school children are victims of bullying or other forms of violence.

For Your Reflection and Analysis

Have you ever been bullied? Witnessed bullying? How did you respond? What could the school have done to prevent the incident?

To submit your response online, go to http://www. prenhall.com/webb.

CW

refrain from reporting the cyberbullying for fear that they will be barred from Internet use (Swartz, 2005).

No one explanation accounts for the rise in violence. Several factors have contributed to violent behavior such as peer pressure, need for attention or respect, feelings of low self-worth, early childhood abuse or neglect, witnessing violence at home, in the community, or media, and easy access to weapons (American Psychological Association, 2005).

Prevention and Intervention Strategies

The majority of public schools have initiated some type of formal school violence prevention and/or violence reduction program. Most of these programs attempt to reach students through a variety of in- and out-of-school activities. The most common violence prevention strategies involve the enactment and enforcement of expanded and clearly articulated discipline codes, life skills training, the establishment of peer mediation, conflict resolution, law-related education programs, and the institution of increased security measures, including security personnel and equipment on campus. Still others have adopted school uniforms.

While these strategies can be effective in reducing the frequency and intensity of school violence, the most important action schools can take to prevent violence is to recognize the early warning signs of a potentially violent youth and to get help for that troubled youth. These "early warning signs" are presented in Table 10.5. It is important to note that these warning signs should be viewed as potential indicators, not as predictors of violence. It would be inappropriate "and potentially harmful to use the early warning signs as a checklist against which to match individual children. Rather, the early warning signs are offered only as an aid in identifying and referring children who may need help" (Dwyer, Osher, & Warger, 1998, p. 8).

The Columbine tragedy and other tragedies taught educators several important lessons. Perhaps one of the most important is that "the best metal detector is the student." Students are usually the first to learn that a peer is in trouble and may be at risk for violent behavior. They may also be the first to know that a troubled peer has made a threat of violence. It is estimated that in more than 75% of school violence incidents, the attacker has told someone before acting. For this reason, schools need to emphasize to students that warning an adult or school official about the proposed violent act could save lives (Cloud, 2001). In an effort to encourage students to warn authority figures and make warning more comfortable, some schools have installed phone lines for anonymous tips. Youngsters also need to know that if they report a potential violent act, their name will be kept confidential and will not be traced.

Table 10.5 — Early Warning Signs of Potentially Violent Youth

- Social withdrawal
- Excessive feelings of isolation and being alone
- Excessive feelings of rejection
- Being a victim of violence
- Feelings of being picked on and persecuted
- Low school interest and poor academic performance
- Expression of violence in writings and drawings
- Uncontrolled anger
- Patterns of impulsive and chronic hitting, intimidating, and bullying behaviors
- History of discipline problems
- Past history of violent and aggressive behavior
- Intolerance for differences and prejudicial attitudes
- Drug and alcohol use
- Affiliation with gangs
- Inappropriate access to, possession of, and use of firearms
- Serious threats of violence

Source: Early Warning, Timely Response: A Guide to Safe Schools by K. Dwyer, D. Osher, & C. Warger, 1998, Washington, DC: U.S. Department of Education.

VIDEO INSIGHT

Action, Reaction, and Zero Tolerance: How Far Is Too Far?

In this ABC News video, you are asked a variety of questions about the effect of zero tolerance in schools. You are also asked to consider zero tolerance for anything that might be construed as a threat of violence.

1. In the video segment, you are confronted with three possible choices relative to the students playing "cowboys and indians." Should the officer have (1) just walked on by and ignored the situation? (2) intervened and counseled the students? or (3) considered the situation as a criminal matter? Give the pros and cons for each choice. What other possible choice(s) might you have recommended to the officer?

2. Consider the zero tolerance policies for various offenses other than firearms (alcohol, drugs, harassment, etc.). What are the most effective ways of ensuring that those policies are both understood and accepted by the students and their parents or guardians?

To submit your answers online, go to the *Video Insight* module for this chapter of the Companion Website at **http://www.prenhall.com/webb.**

Because most schools will experience some episode of violence, the violence prevention program should be linked to a crisis response plan. Such a plan will typically call for the establishment of a crisis response team and describe what to do both when a crisis occurs and in its aftermath. For example, members of a crisis team might be responsible for evacuating students to a safe area in the case of a violent act on campus, a bomb threat, or a natural disaster such as an earthquake; debriefing and leading a discussion or support group following the death or loss of one of the members of the school; and monitoring and supporting friends of a suicide or homicide victim (Poland & McCormick, 1999).

At the national level, in response to the rising tide of school violence in the 1990s, Congress passed the Gun Free Schools Act (1994), which requires states, as a condition of receiving federal funding for elementary and secondary education, to put in place laws whereby students who bring guns to school are expelled for at least 1 year. All states are currently in compliance with the Gun Free Schools Act. As a result, in 2002 approximately 2,554 students were expelled for bringing firearms to school (U.S. Department of Education, 2004b).

Gay, Lesbian, Bisexual, Transgender and Questioning Youth

Sexual orientation is an enduring emotional, romantic, sexual, or affectional attraction toward another human being. Because sexual orientation develops across the life span, individuals may realize at various periods in their lives that they are heterosexual, gay, lesbian, or bisexual. An individual may identify himself or herself as homosexual or bisexual without having had any sexual experience. Others, in particular adolescents, may have had sexual experiences with someone of the same gender, but not consider themselves to be gay, lesbian, or bisexual (American Psychological Association, 2005).

An estimated 5% to 6% of the student population, or as many as 2 million school-age youth, may be gay, lesbian, or bisexual (Human Rights Watch, 2005). Gay, lesbian, bisexual, and **transgender** adolescents are at risk for a variety of serious problems that have been discussed in this chapter: rejection from family and peer group, violent victimization, sexual abuse, school failure, HIV/AIDS, substance use and abuse, missing school, depression, and attempted or completed suicide. The *2003 National School Climate Survey* reported that middle and high school gay, lesbian, bisexual, and transgender youth experienced harassment at unacceptable levels and often the harassment is ignored. Eighty-four percent of the students experienced verbal harassment and more than one-third (39%) were physically harassed. More disturbing, 83% reported that faculty or staff never intervened or intervened only some of the time when they were present and homophobic remarks were made (Kosciw, 2004). Another comprehensive study of harassment based on actual or perceived sexual orientation and gender nonconformity in California schools found:

- An estimated 200,000 California students (8% of the total) in middle school and high school were harassed on the basis of actual or perceived sexual orientation.
- Of these, 32% had been harassed more than four times in the past 12 months.
- Students harassed based on actual or perceived sexual orientation were more than three times as likely than students who were not harassed to carry a weapon to school and to miss school because they felt unsafe; more than twice as likely to report depression and to seriously consider suicide; and more likely to make low grades, smoke cigarettes, drink alcohol, use other illicit drugs, or be victims of violence.
- Students harassed on the basis of actual or perceived sexual orientation also reported weaker connections to school and community and weaker support from teachers and other adults. In fact, one very disappointing finding was that 46% of the harassed students reported hearing teachers or staff make negative comments based on sexual orientation (California Safe Schools Coalition and the 4-H Center for Youth Development, University of California, Davis, 2004).

Many schools have published antiharassment policies to protect students, yet these policies are not always enforced. For example, in *Nabozny v. Podlesny* (1996), a gay male student had been subjected to years of taunts and threats at school that ultimately ended in violence. He was spat upon, urinated upon, subjected to a mock rape in a class of 20 students, and beaten and kicked resulting in internal injuries. School administrators had repeatedly failed to act to stop the harassment, telling the student that he should expect such treatment if he was going to be gay and that "boys will be boys." The court found that the district had a responsibility to protect the student and had failed to do so. The district was required to pay almost $1 million in damages.

In its *Guide to Sexual Harassment* (discussed in Chapter 12), the Office of Civil Rights provided examples of anti-gay harassment that are prohibited by Title IX. These guidelines have significant implications for all schools because schools that fail to follow the guidelines in responding to this and other forms of sexual harassment risk losing federal funding.

Improving the School Climate

Gay, lesbian, bisexual, and transgender students respond to the fear, rejection, guilt, and alienation they feel by withdrawing from friends and family, abstaining or withdrawing from school, failing to concentrate, developing low self-esteem, and, in the most serious cases, developing a major depression or attempting suicide. Teachers and parents need to be alert to these signs and symptoms and take positive steps to ensure that all students feel safe and supported in school and are able to learn.

Strategies that have been recommended to improve the school climate for GLBT students include the following:

- Staff development for school personnel should be provided, which includes a review of psychological and social research on same-sex sexual orientation, encourages an examination of beliefs and attitudes toward such orientation, and teaches staff how to help students who approach them with issues of sexual identity.
- Nondiscrimination policies that protect GLBT employees and students from harassment, violence, and discrimination should be developed by the school district and should be included in student and employee handbooks; all other policies that

For Your Reflection and Analysis

What strategies have been used in your school or school district to improve the school climate for GLBT youth?

To submit your response online, go to http://www. prenhall.com/webb.

deal with the health and welfare of students should be communicated to all those who are in contact with the students. Because a policy that is not enforced is worthless, the policy must be enforced. When violations occur, teachers, counselors, and administrators should challenge anti-gay epithets and should speak out against any form of harassment (Anderson, 1997).

- Issues of sexuality and sexual identity should be addressed in the health curriculum. In addition, the curriculum of all subjects should be an inclusive experience for all students. For example, gender equity could be discussed in a unit on civil rights in a social studies class, and gay and lesbian writers could be highlighted in an English class (Anderson, 1997).

In addition to improving the school climate, counselors, teachers, and administrators should be aware of the resources in the community that can be helpful to these youth. Among the resources that can be helpful include telephone hotlines and such organizations as Parents and Friends of Lesbians and Gays (P-FLAG), the Sex Information and Education Council of the United States (SIECUS), and Gay, Lesbian and Straight Education Network. To address the issues of gay students "is not about condoning homosexuality. It is about providing a secure environment for all students" (Frankfurt, 1999).

PROFESSIONAL REFLECTION

We must recognize that school is not a priority for students who are at risk for various reasons. It is more important for them to survive the day/week/month than it is to do their schoolwork. Our ability to change their lives outside of school is limited. However, we can control the time that they spend with us. Therefore, we must make our classroom a safe haven that is both exciting and challenging. It is our responsibility to ensure that the time students spend with us is a time without fear. Once we have established this atmosphere, the opportunities are endless.

Mary Palma
National Board Certified
Teacher, West Virginia

To analyze this reflection, go to the *Professional Reflection* module for this chapter of the Companion Website at **http://www.prenhall.com/webb.**

Summary

At-risk children and youth are a particular challenge for school personnel and mental health professionals. Because of their association with students, teachers and counselors play a vital role in identifying at-risk students. Prevention and intervention programs for a variety of at-risk behaviors have become the combined responsibility of schools, social service agencies, churches, faith communities, parent groups, and law enforcement agencies. Although for each at-risk behavior a number of prevention and intervention strategies have been devised, growing evidence supports the primacy of early identification and treatment. Creating classrooms and school environments that foster resilience and strengthen protective factors is also most important. Chapter 12 will expand the discussion of the responsibilities of teachers. We will also consider their legal rights, as well as those of their students. But first we will explore the legal basis for public education and the legal issues surrounding the church–state relationship in education in Chapter 11.

Key Terms

Acquired immunodeficiency
   syndrome (AIDS), 256
At risk, 246
Bibliotherapy, 262
Child abuse, 258
Child neglect, 258
Chlamydia infection, 257

Crisis intervention team, 252
Dropout, 253
Emotional abuse, 260
Human immunodeficiency
   virus (HIV), 256
Major depression, 252

Resiliency, 246
Sexually transmitted infections
   (STIs), 257
Suicide attempt, 251
Suicide gesture, 252
Transgender, 265

PROFESSIONAL DEVELOPMENT WORKSHOP

Prepare for the Praxis™ Examination

Mrs. Chavez, a tenth-grade math teacher at Temple High School, glanced at the clock on the wall and noted it was already 3:15 P.M. It was Friday afternoon. Just minutes before, all of her students had hurriedly left her classroom bound for the parking lot or waiting buses. As Mrs. Chavez began to organize her desk for Monday morning class, she became startled as she glanced up and saw Lucia Alvarez standing in front of her. Lucia was one of her best students and had been absent for several days and Mrs. Chavez was pleased to see her in school. However, it was clear that Lucia had been crying. Mrs. Chavez motioned to Lucia to sit in the empty chair beside her desk. Lucia slowly sat down and immediately began to weep uncontrollably. In a quiet and compassionate voice, Mrs. Chavez said, "Lucia, what's wrong? Tell me and let me try to help." After a few moments, Lucia gained her composure and told Mrs. Chavez that she was 4 months pregnant. She began to weep again. In a barely audible voice she said, "I can't tell my parents. My father is very strict. He'll kill me! Maybe I should just save him the trouble and do it myself. I really wanted to be the first in my family to graduate high school and go to college and now I'll have to drop out."

Mrs. Chavez held Lucia's hand and quietly said, "Lucia, the first thing you must do is *not* focus on handling this situation alone. Since you are fifteen years old and a minor you must tell your parents and let them help you through this. If you would like, either I, or Mrs. Radcliff, the school counselor, will be willing to be with you when you talk to your parents."

Lucia stopped crying and seemed more in control. Mrs. Chavez asked her if the father of the baby was aware of the pregnancy. Lucia said she had not told him. Mrs. Chavez asked the age of the father. Lucia said he just celebrated his 17th birthday. Mrs. Chavez asked Lucia if she knew about the pregnancy support group that Temple High had initiated during the spring semester. Lucia said she had heard about it during the summer from one of her friends, but since it did not seem relevant for her at the time, she did not think much about it except that it sounded like a good idea. Mrs. Chavez suggested Lucia talk with either Mrs. Radcliff or Ms. Hernandez, the school nurse, about the support group because both of those individuals cosponsored the group, which meets weekly after school.

Lucia got up to leave and Mrs. Chavez also got up from her chair and hugged Lucia. Mrs. Chavez's parting words were, "Lucia, let me know how either I or anyone at the school can help you." Lucia wiped away her tears and said, "Thank you. I will." After Lucia closed the door and left, Mrs. Chavez thought to herself, "Another prom baby!"

1. How should Mrs. Chavez respond to Lucia's comment about her father or her own suicide? What responsibility do teachers have to report threats of violence to self or others?
2. What family and community considerations might influence a student's decision to remain in or drop out of school?

3. If the father of the baby were 21 years of age or older, what additional responsibility would Mrs. Chavez have had relative to reporting the information?

To submit your responses online, go to the *Prepare for the Praxis™ Examination* module for this chapter of the Companion Website at **http://www.prenhall.com/webb.**

Build Your Knowledge Base

1. If you were confronted with a suicidal child in your classroom, what steps might you take to ensure that child's safety? What type of information and experiences do prospective teachers need to better prepare them to work effectively with children who are at risk for suicidal behavior?
2. What role do schools play in promoting educational resilience? What specific resilience-promoting strategies might you use in your classroom?
3. How can the school help in combating teen pregnancy? AIDS? STIs? How comfortable would you be in discussing "safe sex" with your students?
4. How does peer pressure contribute to adolescent substance abuse and youth violence? How can teachers use the power of peer influence to combat these problems?
5. How can the school and society more effectively address the problem of violence in the schools? Because the majority of youth deaths result from homicide or suicide by gunshot wounds, what can and should be done to restrict the use of firearms by minors?

Develop Your Portfolio

1. Examine INTASC Standard 10: "The teacher fosters relationships with school colleagues, parents, and agencies in the larger community to support students' learning and well-being." Interview a school counselor, social worker, school psychologist, school nurse, or special education teacher regarding their experiences in working with at-risk children and youth. Prepare a reflection paper that describes your reaction to their experiences. Include a statement regarding what steps you will take to become more knowledgeable and effective in working with at-risk students. Place your reflection paper in your portfolio under **INTASC Standard 10, School and Community Relations.**
2. Select one particular at-risk behavior (underachievement, retention in grade, discipline problems, dropping out of school, physical problems, using and abusing drugs or alcohol, engaging in premature, unprotected sexual activity, teen pregnancy, being a victim or perpetrator of violence, and contemplating or attempting suicide). Examine information and referral resources in your community that are designed to address that particular at-risk behavior. Interview a representative of one of the community agencies that provide services for that particular at-risk behavior, and inquire about the extent to which that agency interfaces and works directly with the schools. Prepare a file on "Information and Referral Resources for At-Risk Students." Include a summary of your interview in the file. Place your file in your portfolio under **INTASC Standard 10, School and Community Relations.**

To complete these activities online, go to the *Develop Your Portfolio* module for this chapter of the Companion Website at **http://www.prenhall.com/webb.**

Explore Teaching and Learning: Field Experiences

1. Arrange an interview with a social worker to identify the ways in which schools work with other child welfare agencies. What is the source of funds for these activities? What role does the school district have in coordinating the activities?
2. Building on the previous field experience, arrange an interview with a middle school or high school counselor to secure information about programs that have been started to address the special needs of students who are at risk of dropping out of school. How many staff members have been involved and what is the source of funds? Summarize the findings of your efforts for the class.

Professional Development Online

Visit this text's Companion Website at **http://www.prenhall.com/webb** to gain access to a variety of questions, activities, and exercises to help build your knowledge of this chapter's content. Below are just a few items available at this text's Companion Website:

- Classroom Video—To see actual classroom footage and work through activities and questions to analyze the content of the video, click on the *Classroom Video* module for this chapter.
- Teaching Tolerance—To go to this organization's website and complete activities to explore issues and topics dealing with how to teach tolerance to students, click on the *Teaching Tolerance* module for this chapter.
- Self-Test—To review terms and concepts presented in this chapter, click on the *Self-Test* module for this chapter.
- Internet Resources—To link to websites related to topics in this chapter, go to the *Internet Resources* module for this chapter.

PART

5

LEGAL AND POLITICAL CONTROL AND FINANCIAL SUPPORT

Chapter 11
Legal Framework for the Public Schools

Chapter 12
Teachers, Students, and the Law

Chapter 13
Governance and Financing of Elementary and Secondary Schools

The law is the true embodiment of everything that is excellent.
—W. S. Gilbert (1836–1911)

LEGAL FRAMEWORK FOR THE PUBLIC SCHOOLS

Like many schools, Oceanview High School has found it difficult to find qualified teachers to fill vacancies left by "baby boomer" retirees. In particular, Oceanview has had difficulty finding teachers for its advanced placement science courses. For this reason, Mr. Kindrick, principal of Oceanview, was particularly pleased when Jean Collins applied for an open science position. Mrs. Collins had recently moved to Oceanview with her family when her husband's company transferred him there. She had previously taught science at a private denomination high school.

After an interview and following the district's hiring process, Mrs. Collins began teaching at Oceanview. Toward the middle of the fall semester, Mr. Kindrick visited Mrs. Collins's class to conduct a scheduled performance evaluation. He found her to be an exceptionally gifted teacher who clearly cared about her students. On that occasion he did notice that Mrs. Collins was wearing a very large cross, approximately 5 to 6 inches long. A few days later he saw her at a faculty meeting and she was wearing the same cross. Within 2 weeks he received a call from Larry Kruz, the father of one of Mrs. Collins's students, complaining about the fact that, according to the student, Mrs. Collins wore the cross every day and that it was a distraction and seemed to get in the way as she wrote on the board and leaned over students' desks, exacerbated by the fact that she seemed to always be handling it. According to the father, he and the student, who were not Christians, were offended by Mrs. Collins's oversized cross and by what they considered her attempt to bring attention to it. They asked that Mr. Kindrick direct Mrs. Collins to stop wearing the cross.

What action should Mr. Kindrick take? What additional information might be important to his decision? What constitutional issues are involved? What, if any, action should Mr. Kindrick have taken prior to Mr. Kruz's complaint?

The U.S. Constitution protects Mrs. Collins's right to freedom of religious expression as well as students' rights not to be subjected to state actions that further the establishment of religion. It is within the rules of action or conduct provided by federal and state constitutional provisions, federal and state statutory law, regulations and decisions of administrative agencies, and court decisions that the framework is established for the operation of the public schools. Before going into the specifics of the law as they affect teachers' and students' rights, this chapter provides a brief overview of the major sources of school law, the federal and state court systems, and their interrelationship in forming the legal basis for public education. The second half of the chapter addresses one of the most controversial issues in education today—the appropriate relationship between religion and the schools. After reading this chapter you should be able to:

- Identify federal constitutional provisions affecting education.
- Discuss the importance of state constitutional provisions affecting education.
- Compare statutory law, case (or common) law, and administrative law.
- Describe the levels of the federal court system and those of a typical state court system.
- Explain how challenges under the establishment clause are evaluated.
- Give the current posture of the courts with regard to prayer and Bible reading, student devotional activities, compulsory attendance, and private and homeschooling.
- Distinguish between permissible and impermissible state aid to nonpublic education.

Federal Constitutional Provisions Affecting Education

Written contracts for the establishment of governments, known as **constitutions,** are uniquely American (Collins, 1969). Constitutions are the highest level of law. They are the fundamental laws of the people of a state or nation, establishing the very character and concept of their government, its organization and officers, its sovereign powers, and the limitations of its power. Constitutions are written broadly so as to endure changing times and circumstances. Although constitutions can be changed by amendment, the process is normally difficult and is seldom utilized. The Constitution of the United States, written more than 200 years ago, has served the needs of a fledgling nation and a world power, with only 26 amendments.

Education, though, is not mentioned in the U.S. Constitution. It is therefore considered to be one of the powers reserved to the states by the Tenth Amendment, which states, "The powers not delegated to the United States by the Constitution, nor prohibited by it to the States, are reserved to the States respectively, or to the people." Although the provision of education is considered one of the powers of the states, the supremacy clause of the Constitution (Article VI, Section 2) declares that the Constitution and the laws enacted by the U.S. Congress are the supreme law of the land. Thus, the states, in exercising their authority, may not enact any laws that violate any provisions of the federal Constitution.

Several important sections of the federal Constitution have an impact on the schools (see Figure 11.1). Among these are Article I, Section 8; Article I, Section 10; and the First, Fourth, Fifth, Eighth, and Fourteenth Amendments. These constitutional provisions serve as the basis for education-related cases being brought to federal courts.

Figure 11.1 — Laws Affecting the Schools

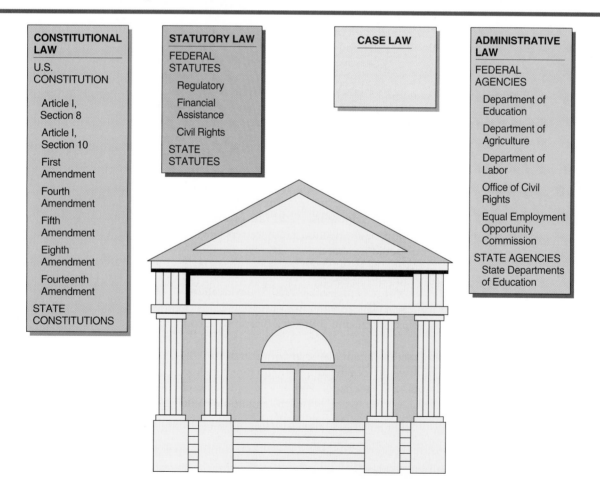

General Welfare Clause

Article I, Section 8, known as the general welfare clause, gives Congress the power to tax and to "provide for the common defense and general welfare of the United States." Over the years, the U.S. Supreme Court has interpreted the general welfare clause as authorizing Congress to tax and spend money for a variety of activities, including education, that were construed as being in the general welfare. However, the general welfare clause does not give Congress the authority to do anything it pleases to provide for the general welfare, only to tax for that purpose. In regard to education, this means that although Congress may levy taxes to provide support for education, it may not legislate control of education. However, in recent years the Supreme Court has ruled that the federal government can attach conditions to the use of federal funds that, if not complied with, may result in the denial or withdrawal of the funds.

Exercising its authority under the general welfare clause, Congress has enacted a massive body of legislation that has provided direct federal support for a variety of instructional programs, as well as providing services and programs for identified special needs students and financial assistance to prospective teachers. Article I, Section 8, has also served as the authority for the federal government to establish the U.S. military academies; operate overseas schools for dependents of military and civilian personnel; and establish schools on Indian reservations, in the U.S. territories, and in the District of Columbia. In addition, Congress may operate libraries, such as the Library of Congress, and conduct a variety of other activities and operations deemed educational in nature.

For Your Reflection and Analysis

In what way does federal support of education contribute to the "common defense" of the United States?

To submit your response online, go to http://www.prenhall.com/webb.

CW

Obligation of Contracts Clause

Article I, Section 10, the obligation of contracts clause, declares "No state shall . . . pass any Bill of Attainder, **ex post facto law,** or law impairing the obligation of Contracts." This provision of the Constitution prohibits a state legislature from passing a law relative to teacher tenure or retirement that would be to the detriment of teachers who had acquired a contractive status under existing statutes. The obligation of contracts clause also protects school personnel who have contracts from arbitrary dismissals; that is, a teacher who has a contract cannot be dismissed during the term of that contract without a showing of cause and without due process (see discussion in Chapter 12). The obligation of contracts clause also protects both the school board and those businesses and individuals with whom it does business from nonperformance relative to the terms of the contract.

First Amendment

The First Amendment addresses several basic personal freedoms. It provides that

> Congress shall make no law respecting an establishment of religion, or prohibiting the free exercise thereof; or abridging the freedom of speech or of the press; or of the right of the people peaceably to assemble, and to petition the Government for a redress of grievances.

Increasingly, the first clause of the First Amendment, the establishment and free exercise of religion clause, has become the focus of litigation in education. The schools have become a battleground for some of the most volatile disputes over the appropriate governmental relationship vis-à-vis religion (Cambron-McCabe, McCarthy, & Thomas, 2004). As discussed later in this chapter, these cases have dealt with numerous issues surrounding (1) school practices objected to on the basis of promoting or inhibiting religion (e.g., released time, prayer, Bible reading), (2) curriculum content, and (3) public funds used to provide support to nonpublic schools or to students or parents of students attending nonpublic schools.

The second clause of the First Amendment, that dealing with the freedom of speech and press, has also been the subject of a growing number of education cases in recent years. Both teachers and students have increasingly protested abridgments of their rights to express themselves in a variety of ways. Teachers have also become more concerned with what they consider attempts to infringe on their academic freedom to select textbooks and other teaching materials and to practice certain teaching methodologies.

Students and their lockers are subject to search.

The third clause of the First Amendment, which deals with the rights of citizens to assemble, has also been called into question in a number of education cases concerning the freedom of association. Both students and teachers have become more assertive of their rights to belong to various organizations, including those that may have goals contrary to that of the school system. The question of freedom of association has also been at issue in a number of cases dealing with teachers' associations or unions. Questions of non-school-sponsored student assemblies are not usually addressed under this clause but under the freedom of religion (if that is their purpose) or freedom of expression clauses.

Fourth Amendment

The Fourth Amendment provides that the right of the people to be "secure in their persons, houses, papers, and effects, against unreasonable searches and seizures, shall not be violated and no warrants shall issue, but upon probable cause." The growing problem of student possession of drugs and other contraband has led to an increasing number of student searches. As we will see in the next chapter, the Fourth Amendment has served as the basis for a number of employee and student challenges to warrantless searches of their automobiles, desks, lockers, or persons by school officials and others.

Fifth Amendment

According to the provisions of the Fifth Amendment, no person shall be "compelled in any criminal case to be a witness against himself, nor be deprived of life, liberty, or property, without due process of law; nor shall private property be taken for public use, without just compensation." The first clause of the Fifth Amendment, the self-incrimination clause, has been invoked by teachers in refusing to answer questions about their affiliations and activities outside the school. However, the courts have ruled that teachers may not use the Fifth Amendment to avoid answering questions about their activities outside the classroom that relate to their qualifications or fitness to teach (*Beilan v. Board of Public Education,* 1958).

The second clause, the due process clause, is not usually involved in education cases. Rather, the due process clause of the Fourteenth Amendment is used because it relates directly to the states.

The last clause of the Fifth Amendment is relevant in those few cases where the state or school system is seeking to obtain private property for school purposes in the exercise of the government's right of **eminent domain,** the right to take private property for public use. Thus, a school district attempting to gain property to enlarge a school may find it necessary to exercise its power of eminent domain (if such power has been given it by the state) if it has not been able to negotiate a voluntary purchase of the needed property. Whenever the power of eminent domain is exercised, just compensation must be given to the owners of the property that is taken.

Eighth Amendment

The Eighth Amendment, in part, provides protection against "cruel and unusual punishments." This amendment on occasion has been involved in challenging the practice or use of corporal punishment in schools. The Supreme Court has held, however, that disciplinary corporal punishment per se is not cruel and unusual punishment as anticipated by the Eighth Amendment (*Ingraham v. Wright,* 1977). This does not mean, however, that corporal punishment may not be prohibited by state or school district regulations or that punishment can be excessive. In fact, if the punishment causes physical harm, it may be grounds for a civil action for assault and battery.

Fourteenth Amendment

The Fourteenth Amendment is the federal constitutional provision most often involved in education-related cases because it pertains specifically to state actions and, as previously stated, education is a state function. The Fourteenth Amendment states:

> No State shall make or enforce any law which shall abridge the privileges or immunities of citizens of the United States; nor shall any State deprive any person of life, liberty, or property, without due process of law; nor deny to any person within its jurisdiction the equal protection of the laws.

As discussed in Chapter 12, the due process clause of the Fourteenth Amendment has been important to students in disciplinary actions and to teachers in negative personnel actions, and has been invoked in a wide array of issues involving student and teacher rights.

State Constitutional Provisions Affecting Education

Like the federal Constitution, state constitutions have provided the foundation for the enactment of subsequent innumerable statutes that govern the activities of the state and its citizens. However, unlike the federal Constitution, which contains no reference to education, every state constitution includes a provision for education, and all but one expressly provides for the establishment of a system of public schools. These provisions range from very general to very specific, but their overall intent is to ensure that schools and education be encouraged and that a uniform system of schools be established. For example, Article X, Section 3 (as amended, April 1972), of the Wisconsin constitution states:

> The Legislature shall provide by law for the establishment of district schools, which shall be as nearly uniform as practical; and such schools shall be free and without charge for tuition to all children between the ages of 4 and 20 years.

The constitutions of 45 states provide for the establishment of "common schools" and 35 states establish specific methods for financial support (Collins, 1969). The constitutions of 30 states expressly prohibit the use of public funds for the support of religious schools, and the constitutions of every state except Maine and North Carolina contain a provision prohibiting religious instruction in the public schools.

The wording of the state constitutional provision for education has proved to be very important to the courts in determining whether particular legislative enactments were constitutionally permissible or required. For example, an Arizona Court of Appeals ruled that the constitutional requirements that the state legislature provide for a system of "free common schools" did not require that free textbooks be provided to high school students (*Carpio v. Tucson High School District No. 1 of Pima County,* 1974). The basis for the court's decision was its interpretation that at the time the constitution was adopted the common schools consisted only of grades one through eight.

Regardless of the particular provisions related to education contained in a state's constitution, the constitution does not grant unlimited power to the state legislature in providing for the public schools. Rather, it establishes the boundaries within which the legislature may operate. The legislature may not then enact legislation exceeding these parameters or violate any provisions of the federal Constitution, which is the supreme law of the land.

Statutory Law

Statutory law is that body of law consisting of the written enactments of a legislative body. These written enactments, called statutes, constitute the second highest level of law, following constitutions. Where constitutions provide broad statements of policy, statutes establish the specifics of operation. Both the U.S. Congress and state legislatures have enacted innumerable statutes affecting the provision of education. These statutes are continually reviewed and often revised or supplemented by successive legislatures. They are also subject to review by the courts to determine their intent and whether they are in violation of the federal Constitution.

Federal Statutes

Despite the federal constitutional silence on education, during each session the U.S. Congress enacts or renews numerous statutes that affect the public schools. Some of these, such as the Occupational Safety and Health Act (OSHA), which requires employers to furnish a safe working environment, although not directed specifically at school districts, do affect their operation. Many of the statutes enacted by Congress are related to the provision of financial assistance to the schools for a variety of special instructional programs, research, or programs for disadvantaged children. Still other federal statutes, federal civil rights statutes, also have had a considerable impact on educational programs and personnel. An overview of the major civil rights statutes affecting schools is provided in Table 11.1. They are discussed in more detail in relevant sections of this text.

State Statutes

Most of the statutory laws affecting the public schools are enacted by state legislatures. The power of the state legislature is **plenary,** or absolute; it may enact any legislation that is not contrary to federal and state constitutions. Although the principle is challenged every year by local school districts, the courts have clearly established that education is a function of the state, not an inherent function of the local school district, and that the local district has only those powers delegated to it by the state legislature. The courts have also affirmed the authority of the state to regulate such matters as certification, powers of school boards, accreditation, curriculum, the school calendar, graduation requirements, facilities construction and operation, and the raising and spending of monies. In fact, the courts have made it clear that school districts have no inherent right to exist; they exist only at the will of the legislature and can be created, reorganized, or abolished at the will of the legislature.

Although the state legislature has delegated the administration of the state education system to an administrative agency, such as the state department of education, and the actual operation of the majority of the schools to the local school districts, the legislature still must pass legislation to administer the system as a whole and to provide for its financing and operation. Consequently, numerous education statutes exist in every state, and in every legislative session new statutes will be enacted that affect education.

Case Law

Case law, also referred to as **common law,** is that body of law originating with historical usages and customs, including court decisions. Case law is based on the doctrine of *stare decisis,* which means "let the decision stand." The doctrine requires that once a court has laid down a principle of law as applicable to a certain set of facts, it will apply it to all future cases where the facts are substantially the same, and other courts of equal or lesser rank will similarly apply the principle (Black, 1990). However, adherence to the doctrine of *stare decisis* does not mean that all previous decisions may never be challenged or overturned. On numerous occasions a higher or subsequent court has rejected the reasoning of a lower or earlier court. On other occasions constitutional or statutory changes have, in effect, overturned the previous decision.

Administrative Law

Administrative law consists of the formal regulations and decisions of those state or federal agencies that are authorized by law to regulate public functions. Courts grant a good deal of direction to the administrative agencies charged with implementing and monitoring state and federal statutes. The regulations issued by these agencies carry the force of law, are subject to judicial review, and will stand as law unless found to be in conflict with federal or state constitutional provisions, statutes, or court decisions.

Table 11.1 — Summary of Major Civil Rights Statutes Affecting Education

Statute	Major Provision
Civil Rights Act of 1866, 1870 42 U.S.C. §1981	Provides all citizens equal rights under the law regardless of race
Civil Rights Act of 1871 42 U.S.C. §1983	Any person who deprives another of his/her rights may be held liable to the injured party
Civil Rights Act of 1871 42 U.S.C. §1985 and 1986	Persons conspiring to deprive another of his/her rights, or any person having knowledge of any such conspiracy, are subject to any action to recover damages
Civil Rights Act of 1866, 1870 (as amended) 42 U.S.C. §1988	Courts may award reasonable attorney fees to the prevailing party in any action arising out of the above acts and Title VI of the Civil Rights Act of 1964
Civil Rights Act of 1964, Title VI 42 U.S.C. §2000(d)	Prohibits discrimination on the basis of race, color, or national origin
Equal Pay Act of 1963 29 U.S.C. §206(D)	Prohibits sex discrimination in pay
Civil Rights Act of 1964, Title VII 42 U.S.C. §2000(e)	Prohibits discrimination in employment on the basis of race, color, religion, gender, or national origin
Age Discrimination in Employment Act of 1967 29 U.S.C. §621	Prohibits discrimination against any individual with respect to employment unless age is a bona fide occupational qualification
Education Amendments of 1972, Title IX 20 U.S.C. §1681	Prohibits sex discrimination in any education program or activity receiving federal financial assistance
Rehabilitation Act of 1973 (as amended) 29 U.S.C. §791	Prohibits discrimination against any "otherwise qualified handicapped individual"
Equal Educational Opportunities Act of 1974 20 U.S.C. §1703	Prohibits any state from denying equal educational opportunities to any individual based on his/her race, color, gender, or national origin
Americans With Disabilities Act of 1990 42 U.S.C. §12112	Prohibits discrimination against persons with disabilities
Individuals With Disabilities Education Act of 1990 20 U.S.C. §1400–1485	Individuals with disabilities must be guaranteed a free appropriate education by programs receiving federal financial assistance
Civil Rights Restoration Act of 1991 42 U.S.C. §1981 et seq.	Amends the Civil Rights Act of 1964, the Age Discrimination in Employment Act of 1967, and the Americans With Disabilities Act of 1990 with regard to employment discrimination

The U.S. Department of Education is the federal agency most directly concerned with education. The regulations issued by the Office of Civil Rights of the Department of Education in regard to the implementation of Title IX are a prime example of the profound impact that administrative law can have on the operations of the schools.

Among the other federal agencies that have significant interaction with schools are the Department of Agriculture, which administers the National School Lunch Act; the Department of Health and Human Services, which administers Head Start; and the Department of Labor, which administers the Occupational Safety and Health Act. In addition, both the Office of Civil Rights of the Department of Education and another agency, the Equal Employment Opportunity Commission, are charged with enforcement of civil rights and nondiscrimination legislation.

The state agency that has the most direct control over and responsibility for education is the state department of education. A large body of administrative law is generated by this agency as a result of the promulgation of numerous rules and regulations relating to such areas as certification of teachers, accreditation of schools, adoption of textbooks, courses of study, minimum standards for specified areas, and distribution of state funds.

Powers and Organization of the Courts

The courts have three basic functions: (1) settle disputes between parties, (2) interpret laws and policies, and (3) determine the constitutionality of governmental actions. In school-related matters, the courts have generally taken the position that they will not intervene in a dispute unless all internal appeals have been exhausted. For example, where school board policy provides teachers with the right of direct appeal to the board, this avenue of appeal must be exhausted before the courts will hear the appeal. The exceptions to this provision are cases involving an alleged violation of a constitutionally protected right.

The courts cannot become involved in education cases of their own initiative. A case must be brought to the court for resolution. The most common type of school case brought to the court is one that requires the court to interpret laws within its jurisdiction. Another common type of school case requires the court to determine the constitutionality of legislative or administrative enactments.

The Federal Court System

Most education cases that come to federal courts involve alleged violations of constitutionally protected rights or interpretations of federal statutes. Sometimes a case will involve questions of both federal and state law. When this occurs, the federal court can decide on the state issue, but it must do so according to the rules governing the courts of that state.

The federal court system consists of three levels of courts of general jurisdiction: a supreme court, district courts, and courts of appeals. In addition, the federal court system includes courts of special jurisdiction, such as the Customs Court or the Tax Court. These courts normally would not be involved in education cases (see Figure 11.2).

The lowest level federal courts are district courts. There are about 100 district courts: at least one in each state, and as many as four in the more heavily populated states, such as California, New York, and Texas. Federal district courts are given names reflective of the geographic area they serve; for example, "S. D. Ohio" indicates the Southern District of Ohio. District courts are the courts of initiation or original jurisdiction for most cases filed in the federal court system, including most education cases. They are trial courts, meaning that a jury hears the case. The decisions of federal district courts have an automatic right of appeal to the next level of federal courts, U.S. Circuit Courts of Appeals.

There are 13 circuit courts of appeals in the federal system. Twelve of the circuit courts have jurisdiction over a specific geographic area (see Figure 11.3). A 13th, the Federal Circuit, has jurisdiction to hear appeals in specific areas of federal law (e.g., customs, copyright, international trade). A circuit court hears appeals from the decisions of district courts and certain federal administrative agencies. It hears arguments from attorneys, but

Figure 11.2 — Federal Court System

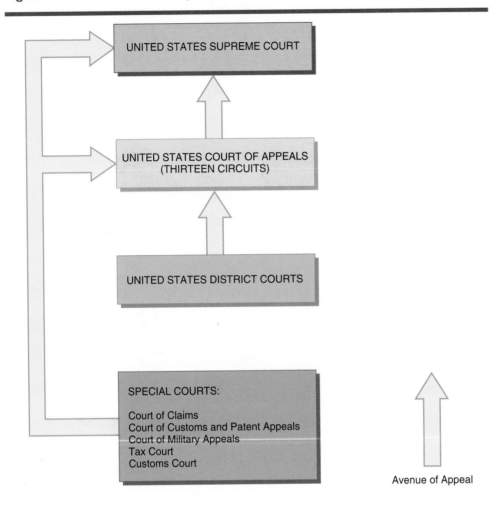

UNITED STATES SUPREME COURT

UNITED STATES COURT OF APPEALS
(THIRTEEN CIRCUITS)

UNITED STATES DISTRICT COURTS

SPECIAL COURTS:

Court of Claims
Court of Customs and Patent Appeals
Court of Military Appeals
Tax Court
Customs Court

Avenue of Appeal

it does not retry the case; there is no jury. A panel of judges, usually three, hears the case and can affirm, reverse, or modify the decision of the lower court, or remand the case back to the lower court for modifications or retrial.

The decision of a federal circuit court is binding only on federal district courts within its geographic jurisdiction. Circuit courts have no power over state courts and do not hear appeals from them, nor does the decision of one circuit court bind other circuit courts or the district courts in other circuits. Thus, it is possible, and indeed it happens quite often, that one circuit court will rule one way, whereas another circuit court will rule in the reverse.

The highest federal appeals court, indeed the highest court in the land, is the U.S. Supreme Court. Decisions of the Supreme Court are absolute: There is no appeal. If Congress or citizens do not agree with a decision of the Supreme Court, the only ways they can mediate against the effect of the decision are to pass a law or to get the Court to reconsider the issue in a later case. A notable example with regard to education of the Supreme Court reversing itself on reconsideration concerned racial segregation: In *Plessey v. Ferguson* (1896), the Court had said "separate but equal" public facilities for blacks and whites were constitutionally permitted, but in 1954 in *Brown v. Board of Education of Topeka,* the Court reversed this position and ruled that separate educational facilities for blacks and whites were inherently unequal.

The Supreme Court hears cases on appeal from lower federal courts or from state supreme courts if the state case involves questions of federal law. Although thousands of cases are appealed to the Supreme Court each year, only a small number are heard. However, in recent years the number of education cases being heard by the Supreme Court has increased.

Figure 11.3 — The Thirteen Federal Judicial Circuits

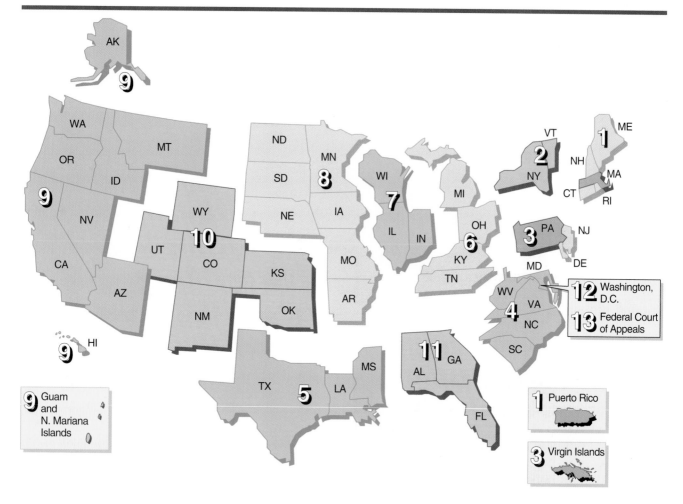

The State Court Systems

Because most education cases do not involve the federal Constitution or federal statutes, they are handled by state courts rather than federal courts. Like the federal court system, the state court system is created by the state constitution and subsequent legislative enactments. Although the specific structure of the court system and the names given to courts vary from state to state, in most respects state court systems resemble the federal court system in terms of having courts of limited and special jurisdiction and courts of appeal.

Most states have courts that are designated as courts of limited or special jurisdiction. The limitation may be related to the types of cases they may handle (e.g., probate courts, juvenile courts) or the amount in controversy (e.g., small claims courts, traffic courts). Generally, state court systems do not permit appeal of the decisions of courts of limited jurisdiction.

All states have courts of general jurisdiction. These courts are generally trial courts and as such hear witnesses, admit evidence, and, when appropriate, conduct jury trials. Depending on the state, courts of general jurisdiction may be referred to as district courts, county courts, circuit courts, superior courts, or supreme courts (in New York). Appeals from the decisions of courts of general jurisdiction are made to state appellate courts, often referred to as courts of appeals. Like the federal appellate courts, state appellate courts do not retry cases but sit as a panel of judges to review the record of the trial court and hear attorneys' arguments.

The final appeal in state court systems is to the state supreme court, the final authority on questions related to the state constitution, state law, or school district policies. If the case involves federal issues, however, appeal may be taken from the state supreme court to the U.S. Supreme Court.

HISTORICAL NOTE

Thurgood Marshall: Breaking the Color Barrier on the U.S. Supreme Court

Thurgood Marshall was born July 2, 1908, in Baltimore. He graduated from Lincoln University in Pennsylvania (1930) and was first in his class from Howard University Law School. After graduation he entered private practice while volunteering his services to the National Association for the Advancement of Colored People (NAACP). In 1936 he went to work for the NAACP and in 1940 became the chief of the organization's Legal Defense and Education Fund.

Marshall played a major role in the NAACP's efforts to end racial segregation. He won 29 of the 32 cases he argued before the Supreme Court, including the historic *Brown v. Board of Education* (1954), which opened the door for the integration of the nation's public schools, and *Sweatt v. Painter* (1950), which declared unconstitutional "separate but equal" facilities in higher education.

Marshall's reputation as the architect of the Civil Rights movement legal strategy led President John F. Kennedy to nominate him to the U.S. Court of Appeals for the Second Circuit in 1961. Opposition by Southern senators delayed his confirmation for several months. In 1965, President Lyndon B. Johnson appointed Marshall U.S. solicitor general, and 2 years later nominated him to the U.S. Supreme Court. Marshall became the first black member of the Supreme Court. He was a steadfast liberal throughout his tenure on the court and "was the principal architect of a flexible definition of equality that gave black Americans the full rights of citizenship"

Thurgood Marshall argued the historic Brown v. Board of Education *before the U.S. Supreme Court and later became a member of that court.*

(Holland, 1995, p. 367). By the time he retired in 1991, he had become part of the minority dissenting from a conservative majority. He died January 24, 1993, at the age of 84 in Bethesda, Maryland.

To research and explore this topic further, go to the *Historical Note* module for this chapter of the Companion Website at **http://www.prenhall.com/webb.**

Religion and Education

The issue of the appropriate relationship between religion and the state has been one of the most controversial in American legal history. The experience of the nation's founders with both attempts to interfere with the free exercise of religion and with state control of education prompted a desire to erect what President Thomas Jefferson called "a wall of separation between Church and State" through the very first amendment to the Constitution, which states "Congress shall make no law respecting an establishment of religion or prohibiting the free exercise thereof." Although the establishment and free exercise of the First Amendment make reference only to actions of the federal government (Congress), they are made applicable to the states by the Fourteenth Amendment, which prohibits state actions that violate the constitutional rights of citizens.

Maintaining the wall of separation without being "hostile to religion" has been the challenge faced by policy makers at every level of government, as well as by public school teachers and administrators. Often they find their actions challenged in the courts, and a number of cases have reached the U.S. Supreme Court (see Table 11.2). For more than a

Table 11.2 — Overview of Selected U.S. Supreme Court Cases Affecting Church–School Relations

Case	Decision
Cochran v. Louisiana State Board of Education (1930)	States may provide secular textbooks to children attending sectarian schools.
West Virginia State Board of Education v. Barnette (1943)	Public schools may not require the pledge of allegiance to the flag.
Everson v. Board of Education (1947)	States may use public funds to provide for transportation of children to and from private, sectarian schools where state constitution permits it.
Illinois ex rel. McCollum v. Board of Education (1948)	Released time program whereby religious instruction is provided during school hours on school grounds is unconstitutional.
Zorach v. Clauson (1952)	Released time program whereby students are released to go off campus to receive religious instruction and where no state support is provided is constitutional.
Engel v. Vitale (1962)	Public schools may not require the recitation of prayers.
School District of Abington Township v. Schempp (1963)	State may not promote Bible readings and prayers, even when participation is not compulsory.
Epperson v. Arkansas (1968)	State law forbidding the teaching of evolution is unconstitutional.
Lemon v. Kurtzman (1971)	State support to nonpublic schools, their personnel, and their students is unconstitutional if it (1) has a primarily religious purpose, (2) either advances or inhibits religion, or (3) creates an excessive entanglement between church and state.
Mueller v. Allen (1983)	State may provide income tax deduction for educational expenses of nonpublic school parents if also available to public school parents.
Wallace v. Jaffree (1985)	State laws authorizing classroom periods of silent meditation or prayer are unconstitutional.
Edwards v. Aguillard (1987)	Public schools may not be required to teach creationism.
Board of Education of Westside Community Schools v. Mergens (1990)	Schools must provide access to student-sponsored religious groups if access is provided to other student groups not directly related to the school's curriculum.
Lee v. Weisman (1992)	School-sponsored prayers at graduation exercises are unconstitutional.
Zobrest v. Catalina Foothills School District (1993)	School district provision of the services of a sign language interpreter to a student attending a sectarian school is constitutional.
Agostini v. Felton (1997)	State aid allocated to nonpublic schools on the basis of neutral, nonsectarian criteria is not unconstitutional.
Mitchell v. Helms (2000)	Federal Chapter 2 funds allocated to non-public schools for the acquisition and use of instructional materials is constitutional.
Santa Fe Independent School District v. Doe (2000)	School-sponsored, student-led, student-initiated prayer at football game is unconstitutional.
Zelman v. Simmons-Harris (2002)	Publicly financed tuition vouchers may be used at religious schools.

For Your Reflection and Analysis

Do you recall being involved in any religious activities in a public school situation? Would it pass the *Lemon* test? *To submit your response online, go to http://www.prenhall.com/webb.*

CW

quarter century, the courts used a tripartite test to evaluate claims under the establishment clause. The test, often called the **Lemon** test (from the case in which it was developed, *Lemon v. Kurtzman,* 1971), asked three questions, all of which must be answered in the negative if the policy or action is to be judged constitutional: (1) Does the policy or action have a primarily religious purpose? (2) Does the policy or action have the primary effect of advancing or inhibiting religion? (3) Does the policy or action foster an excessive entanglement between the state and religion? As will be discussed in later sections, later Supreme Courts, although not directly overturning *Lemon,* have reinterpreted it in such a way as to significantly affect its application.

The church–state issues most often contested in education can be categorized into three broad areas: religious activities, curriculum content, and public support for private schools. Other areas of importance, if not as litigious, involve released time for religious instruction and private and homeschooling. Each of these is discussed in the sections that follow.

Religious Activities in the Public Schools

Prayer and Bible Reading.   The issue of school prayer has been one of ongoing—and heated—dispute. In *Engel v. Vitale* (1962), parents challenged the use of a prayer composed by the New York Board of Regents as part of morning exercises. The denominationally neutral prayer read "Almighty God, we acknowledge our dependence upon thee, and we beg thy blessings upon us, our parents, our teachers, and our country." The Supreme Court held that "it is no part of the business of government to impose official prayers for any group of American people" and to do so constituted a violation of the establishment clause.

The following year, the Supreme Court rendered another significant decision affecting both school prayer and Bible reading. In *School District of Abington Township v. Schempp* (1963), the Court declared unconstitutional Pennsylvania and Maryland statutes that required daily Bible reading and, in Maryland, recitation of the Lord's Prayer. Although children could be exempted from participation in the Maryland case upon request by their parents, the Court held that such activities, held in public school buildings under the supervision of public school personnel, served to advance religion in violation of the establishment clause of the First Amendment. Although prohibiting Bible reading as a religious exercise, the Court in *Schempp* specifically noted that its opinion did not prevent studying the Bible as literature and studying about religion (e.g., the history of religion or comparative religion).

Not only are state-imposed prayers and Bible reading in the classroom constitutionally impermissible, so too are voluntary prayers and Bible reading, whether given by teachers or students, or even if requested by students. The courts have found little to distinguish these from state-imposed prayers in that both are sanctioned by the school.

Although state-sponsored prayer in the classroom has been disallowed, this does not mean that students cannot engage in individual prayer, as long as it is nondisruptive and does not give the appearance of school endorsement. Such has been the case in several instances where states or districts have enacted "moments of silence." For example, in a 1985 case, *Wallace v. Jaffree*, the U.S. Supreme Court concluded—in fact, the state conceded—that the intent of the Alabama statute that provided for a period of silent meditation or prayer had no secular purpose but was clearly to encourage and/or accommodate prayer, and thus violated the establishment clause. However, the Court did indicate that statutes providing for periods of silence that did not demonstrate legislative intent to encourage prayers and that demonstrated a secular purpose would probably be upheld. Accordingly, in 2001 the Supreme Court declined to review and overturn an appeal from the Fourth Circuit challenging a Virginia statute that required a daily moment of silence for students to "meditate, pray, or engage in any other silent activity" (*Brown v. Gilmore*, 2001). In refusing to block enforcement of the law, Chief Justice Rehnquist noted not only the absence of legislative intent to establish religion but its stated secular concern about violence in the schools. Before the terrorist attacks of September 11, 2001, "moment of silence" laws were in effect in about half the states. Since that time, several states and numerous school districts have moved to impose mandatory moments of silence. Although many people see these efforts as attempts to bring back government-led prayer, the legality of each is subject to determination on a state-by-state basis.

Prayer at School-Sponsored Events.   While it is clear that the school or teachers may not orchestrate prayer at the beginning of the day, in class, or within the curriculum, school districts continue to wrestle with the issue of if, and under what circumstances, prayers may be delivered at school-sponsored activities. One of the most frequently litigated areas relative to prayers has been prayers at graduation ceremonies. In the years following *Engel* and *Schempp*, some courts ruled against such practices, whereas others found no establishment clause violation, judging them to be more ceremonial in nature with no intent to indoctrinate. The issue was at last addressed by the U.S. Supreme Court in 1992 in *Lee v. Weisman*. The case involved the practice of the

For Your Reflection and Analysis

Are you in favor of a constitutional amendment to authorize prayers and Bible reading in the schools?

To submit your response online, go to http://www. prenhall.com/webb.

CW

Providence, Rhode Island school system of allowing principals to select clergy to deliver prayers at graduation ceremonies. Although the clergy were instructed that the prayers were to be nonsectarian and were given a copy of "Guidelines for Civic Occasions" prepared by the National Conference of Christians and Jews, the Supreme Court, in a five-to-four decision, ruled that the school's policy violated the establishment clause. The Court focused on the fact that the school supervised or controlled the activity by selecting the clergy to deliver the prayers and giving directions to them. The Court did not apply the *Lemon* test, but employed what has since been referred to as the *coercion test.* In the opinion of the Court, the "psychological coercion" placed on student dissenters to attend graduation ceremonies had the effect of government coercion of students to attend religious exercises. In the words of the Court:

> high school graduation is one of life's most significant occasions . . . a student is not free to absent herself from the graduation exercise in any real sense of the term, "voluntary," for absence would require forfeiture of those intangible benefits which have motivated the student through youth and all her high school years. . . . [t]he Constitution forbids the State to exact religious conformity from a student as the price of attending her own high school graduation. (pp. 2659–2660)

Lee v. Weisman left unanswered the question of the constitutionality of graduation prayers that are delivered by students. However, soon after *Lee,* the Fifth Circuit addressed this question in *Jones v. Clear Creek Independent School District* (1992). Here the court applied the *Lee* coercion test for the first time in review of a school district policy that allowed prayers offered by student volunteers selected by the graduating seniors. The court ruled that the practice was not an unconstitutional endorsement of religion because it was the decision of the seniors, not school officials, whether or not to have the prayer. It also found that the practice did not coerce participation by objectors. According to the court, because the graduating class selected the presenter, students knew that the prayers "represent the will of their peers who are less able to coerce participation than an authority figure from the state or clergy" (p. 971). The Supreme Court's refusal to review both the decision in *Jones* and the decision of the Eleventh Circuit in *Adler v. Duval County School Board* (2001), which upheld a school's policy of letting a senior class choose a classmate to deliver a graduation message (the messages need not be religious, but the vast majority were), has been interpreted as giving a green light to other school districts to initiate "voluntary, neutral" policies ("Court won't stop graduation prayers," 2001).

In the years since *Lee,* the lower courts have applied the *Lee* coercion rationale in reviewing prayer at other school-sponsored activities. In *Santa Fe Independent School District v. Doe* (2000), the U.S. Supreme Court applied the control–coercion rationale to find the delivery of a prayer over the public address system at a football game by an elected student council chaplain under the supervision of school faculty to be a violation of the establishment clause. Although noting that attendance at a football game is voluntary, the court reasoned that the social pressure or personal desire to attend does not dramatically differ from that of commencement exercises, and those in attendance may not be coerced into participating in an act of religious worship. The court also noted that the very election process itself ensured that minority view candidates would never prevail and that their views would be effectively silenced.

The issue of prayer in the public schools continues to be the subject of legal and political debate.

Although the decision in *Sante Fe* may have struck down student-led prayer at football games, it will not end the debate over student-led prayer at extracurricular activities. According to legal experts, "We can expect more cases involving student-initiated and student-led prayer at school events as advocates of such prayers attempt to craft conditions that will pass constitutional muster" (Haynes, 2001, p. 17).

Pledge of Allegiance. Two of the most controversial rulings ever made by the U.S. Supreme Court involved compulsory flag salute. In *West Virginia State Board of Education v. Barnette* (1943), the Court ruled that the compulsory flag salute violated the religious freedom of Jehovah's Witnesses. Following *Barnette,* the position of the courts has been that schools may lead the pledge of allegiance so long as student participation is voluntary. For example, in *Sherman v. Consolidated School District 21 of Wheeling Township* (1992), the Seventh Circuit Court of Appeals upheld an Illinois statute that provided for a voluntary pledge of allegiance. The court ruled that the statute did not violate the free exercise clause of the First Amendment because participation was voluntary and did not violate the establishment clause because the pledge, despite the phrase "under God," is not a religious exercise. In the wake of the terrorist attacks on September 11, 2001, a number of states and school districts have moved to enact statutes or policies that would force teachers to set aside time each day for the recitation of the pledge of allegiance. To the extent such policies included "opt-out" provisions they have not been seen to be in conflict with *Barnette*.

Religious Displays and Observances. Every year courts around the country are faced with deciding whether specific actions of school districts, teachers, or students constitute either an unconstitutional advancement or prohibition of religion. The application of the *Lemon* test led the Supreme Court to overturn a Kentucky statute that required the posting of the Ten Commandments (purchased at private expense) in every classroom in the state (*Stone v. Graham,* 1980). A similar ruling by a Michigan court found that a picture of Jesus Christ prominently displayed outside the principal's office violated the First Amendment's establishment clause (*Washegesic v. Bloomington Public Schools,* 1994). On the other hand, the Supreme Court declined to review an Eighth Circuit decision upholding a school board policy that allowed the use of religious symbols if used temporarily in an unobjectionable manner and as an example of the cultural and religious heritage of the particular holiday (*Florey v. Sioux Falls School District 49-5,* 1980).

The *Lemon* test has also been applied to challenges of religious observances in the public schools with the same general result: Public schools may not sponsor religious practices. In practice, this means that there can be recognition of a holiday, and the teacher can teach about the holiday, but any religious program must serve an educational rather than a religious purpose and cannot make any child feel excluded because of his or her religion. This does not mean that any display, program, or song that has some religious element but whose primary purpose is secular would violate the First Amendment. In fact, in *Doe v. Duncanville Independent School District* (1995), the Fifth Circuit Court stated that to prohibit the singing of certain songs that might be religious in origin, but were sung because of their recognized musical value, would be showing hostility to religion.

Those students or parents who object to classroom discussions or programs or activities on religious grounds may ask to be excused. Such requests are routinely granted and are provided for in school district policy.

Students as well as teachers may also request to be absent from school for religious reasons. In deciding whether teachers and students can be absent from school for religious holidays, although the courts have generally recognized the right of school districts to place limits on the number of such absences, they have also required that reasonable accommodation be made for the exercise of staff and student religious beliefs. For example, although the courts have held that it is within the discretion of school districts to limit the number of paid leaves that are provided employees for religious leave, they have also held that to allow employees to take unpaid leave is a reasonable accommodation for the employee's religious beliefs. Also, whereas scheduling public school holidays for periods that coincide with certain Christian religious holidays does not violate the establishment clause (*Koenick v. Felton,* 1999), designating Good Friday as a state-mandated school holidays does (*Metzl v. Leininger,* 1995). Last, schools are not obliged to schedule athletic events or other student activities such as graduation so as not to conflict with religious holidays.

For Your Reflection and Analysis

Have you participated in a program at school which had religious content? How did you respond?

To submit your response online, go to http://www. prenhall.com/webb.

CW

Wearing of Religious Attire.   Since colonial times school officials have sought to regulate both student and teacher dress. Also, as discussed in the next chapter, the courts have given schools considerable discretion in adopting student dress codes as long as they do not burden students' First Amendment rights without adequate justification. For example, in *Cheema v. Thompson* (1995), a district refused to allow three young Khalsa Sikh children to wear ceremonial knives called "kirpans" to school. The kirpans are one of the five symbols of the Khalsa Sikh that are to be worn at all times (the others were a comb, a steel bracelet, long hair, and sacred underwear). The case was settled when the parties agreed that the knives could be worn if the blade was dulled, did not exceed two and a half inches in length, and was sewn securely into a sheath and secured in a cloth pouch.

The wearing of religious garb by teachers presents a different set of issues for school officials. To deny a teacher from wearing religious garb could be construed as violating the teacher's free exercise of religion but, at the same time, to allow it could be construed as placing the school's stamp of imprimatur on that particular religion. While acknowledging the delicate balance that must be maintained between the rights of the teacher and the interest of the school, the courts have been almost unanimous in supporting school district prohibitions regarding the wearing of religious garb (see, e.g., *United States v. Board of Education for the School District of Philadelphia* [1990] where the third circuit ruled a district's compelling interest in maintaining religious neutrality was sufficient to prohibit a Muslim teacher from wearing her traditional Muslim dress). The courts have also tended to support school districts in restricting teacher dress that is intended to carry a specific religious message. For example, in *Downing v. West Haven Board of Education* (2001), the court found no violation of the teacher's rights when she was required to change clothes or cover a t-shirt with the slogan "Jesus 2000" on it. However, while disallowing religious dress, the courts have generally permitted teachers to wear *incidental* pieces of religious garb or religious symbols (e.g., a cross, crucifix, or Star of David).

Distribution of Religious Literature.   An issue of growing contention is the school's obligation to distribute or refrain from distributing religious materials to children. Absent any Supreme Court guidance as was provided for access, the majority of courts have applied the same equal access rationale and ruled that when school officials allow distribution of nonreligious literature, the same rules must be applied to the distribution of religious literature. A number of distribution cases have involved efforts by a Christian evangelical group, the Good News Club, to meet on school campuses or distribute religious materials. In those instances where these privileges have been afforded nonreligious groups, they have been successful in their efforts. For example, the Montgomery County (Maryland) Public Schools regularly distributed to families materials for children's groups such as the Boy Scouts and 4-H. However, when asked to distribute materials to promote the after-school Good News Club, they refused, citing establishment clause concerns. The Fourth Circuit disagreed noting that the Good News Club would be receiving no benefit other than those afforded other organizations and ordered the district to allow the distribution of the materials (*Child Evangelism Fellowship of Maryland v. Montgomery County Public Schools,* 2004).

In cases that involve individual student attempts to distribute materials, the courts have also applied the equal access rationale but have acknowledged the authority of school officials to impose the same time, place, and manner restrictions as apply to other forms of student expression. For example, the court upheld the actions of schools in stopping a first grader from distributing candy canes with an attached religious message during a class holiday party. Parents had been instructed that the party was to be "as generic as possible" and the student was the only one to bring a nongeneric gift. The court ruled that the parties were part of the curriculum and not an appropriate forum for religious advocacy (*Walz v. Egg Harbor Township Board of Education,* 2003).

Religious Access to School Buildings.   Partially in response to public sentiment that prayer and other devotional activities should not be banned from the school grounds, in 1984 Congress passed the Equal Access Act (EAA) (20 U.S.C., sections 4071–73). The act specified that if a federally assisted public secondary school provides a **limited open forum** to non-curriculum-related student groups to meet on school premises during the lunch hour, before or after school, or during other noninstructional time, "equal access" to that forum cannot be denied because of the "religious, political, philosophical, or other content of the speech at such meetings." Access can be denied only if the ideas that the group wishes to express are likely to lead to a material and substantial disruption of the functioning of the school.

Although the EAA did not define a non-curriculum-related group, in 1990 the U.S. Supreme Court in *Board of Education of Westside Community Schools v. Mergens* said a student group was curriculum related if

> the subject matter of the group is actually taught, or will soon be taught, in a regularly offered course; if the subject matter of the group concerns the body of courses as a whole; if participation in the group is required for a particular course; or if participation in the group results in academic credit. (p. 239)

The Court went on to say that the direct relation to the curriculum does not mean "anything related to abstract educational goals" and that schools cannot evade the intent of the act by "strategically describing existing groups" (*Bd. of Educ. of Westside Community Schools v. Mergens*, 1990, p. 244). Subsequent courts have clarified that "access" means not simply to the school building but to fund-raising activities, bulletin boards, and any other resources made available to other student groups (*Prince v. Jacoby*, 2002).

Use of school facilities by community groups, for which there is no school sponsorship or supervision, although very different from use by student-initiated groups under the EAA, has also been the subject of ongoing controversy. Following *Mergens*, access to school facilities was expanded even further by the U.S. Supreme Court in *Lamb's Chapel v. Center Moriches School District* (1993), which said that school districts that allow community groups to use school facilities for civic or social purposes have created a limited open forum and cannot, therefore, bar religious groups from using the facilities on the same terms. And, in *Good News Club v. Milford Central School* (2001) the U.S. Supreme Court said that to refuse access to a community group simply "because it is religious" if it is not engaged in strictly "religious activities" would constitute viewpoint discrimination in violation of the First Amendment. However, the court did not clarify what constitutes "religious activities" as opposed to, for example, in this case, teaching moral and character development from a religious perspective.

In recent years, compliance with the EAA has created a dilemma for a number of school districts. At the same time, the very words in the EAA that grant access and the right to free expression to religious groups like the Good News Clubs also grant access to same-sex sexual orientation support groups, atheist clubs, or various "fringe" or unpopular groups (Broberg, 1999). Schools attempting to deny access to such groups have been successful in excluding hate groups such as the Aryan Nation, but not lifestyle organizations such as Gay Straight Alliance Clubs. The one exception has been where the high school had previously adopted a formal abstinence policy and had excluded any discussion of sexual activity on its campus (*Caudillo v. Lubbock Independent School District*, 2004).

Released Time for Religious Instruction. Historically, a not uncommon practice in American public schools was the releasing of children during the school day for religious instruction. In the first case to reach the Supreme Court, *McCollum v. Board of Education of School District No. 71* (1948), students had been excused from regular classes to attend private religious instruction in another part of the building. The court ruled that the program violated the establishment clause of the First Amendment. Four years later the Court upheld a program in which children were permitted to leave the public school to receive religious instruction (*Zorach v. Clauson*, 1952). The distinction made by the court between *Zorach* and *McCollum* was that public school facilities were not involved in *Zorach*.

The case law that has evolved since *Zorach* has clarified that the schools "have the discretion to dismiss students to receive off campus religious instruction so long as they do not encourage or discourage participation, expend funds in soliciting students to attend religious instruction, or penalize those who do not attend (see, e.g., *Pierce v. Sullivan West Central School District*, 2004).

Challenges to the Curriculum

First Amendment challenges to the curriculum generally have been brought by parents attempting to eliminate specific courses, activities, or materials thought to be advancing religion. While many people claim that the schools are hostile to religion and that all mention of religion is forbidden in the schools, in fact, public school curricula may include teaching about religion or may use religious material. The Supreme Court has specifically said that the study of the Bible or of religion, when presented objectively as part of a secular program of education, is not a violation of the First Amendment (*School District of Abington Township v. Schempp*, 1963). But of course, the curriculum may neither endorse nor inculcate religion.

Teachers, like all citizens, have the right of free exercise of religion. However, in exercising their free exercise, they cannot make their religious beliefs part of classroom instruction. Schools have a constitutional duty under the establishment clause to prevent teachers from promoting religion or being hostile to it. For example, teachers cannot require students to modify, include, or exclude religious views in their assignments. Teachers can control students' assignments for legitimate pedagogical reasons, or if it may give the appearance of endorsement of religion, but student work that includes religious expression, should be assessed under ordinary academic standards including the criteria established for the assignment. For example, in *DeNoyer v. Livonia Public Schools* (1992), the court concluded that a second grader had no right to show a videotape of her singing a proselytizing religious song. The court upheld the teacher's rationale that the presentation wasn't in line with the assignment (developing self-esteem by giving an oral presentation), was longer than assigned, and would encourage other students to bring in long videos. And, in *Settle v. Dickson County School Board* (1995), the court held that the teacher could give a student a zero on a research paper without violating the student's free exercise rights. The student's choice of topic was the life of Jesus Christ, but the student did not meet the teacher's requirements of using at least four sources to research a topic.

In recent years a growing number of parents have contended that certain courses, materials, and practices in the curriculum promote nontheistic or antitheistic beliefs, referred to as **secular humanism.** These parents demand that the influences of these "religions" be removed from the curriculum or that Christian doctrine be inserted in the curriculum to bring balance. In the cases to date, the courts have rejected the argument that the challenged courses or materials advanced any nontheistic or antitheistic creed and have reaffirmed the position taken by the Supreme Court in 1968 in *Epperson v. Arkansas*. In this case, the Court struck down an Arkansas law forbidding instruction in evolution, stating: "The state has no legitimate interest in protecting any or all religions from views distasteful to them." For example, the courts have not been convinced that the teaching of sex education promotes an antitheistic faith. The courts consistently have found that sex education courses present public health information that promotes legitimate educational objectives, and that the establishment clause prevents the state from barring such instruction merely to suit the religious beliefs of some parents (Cambron-McCabe et al., 2004).

The courts generally are satisfied in these and other areas where statutes or policies allow the student to be exempted from the challenged course or exposure to the objectionable content. However, the exemption will not be given unless the material or activity actually violates the student's religion, or if the state can show a compelling interest in educating regarding a particular topic. For example, in *Ware v. Valley Stream High School District* (1989), the Court ruled that the states' compelling interest in requiring all primary and secondary students to receive instruction regarding AIDS prevention and the dangers of alcohol and drug abuse did not violate the First Amendment rights of parents who believed that such education was "evil."

The teaching of evolution is one area that has been targeted as advancing secular humanism. Following the ruling in *Epperson* that evolution is a science, not a secular religion, and that states cannot restrict student access to such information to satisfy religious preferences, attempts were made in several states to secure "balanced treatment" or "equal time" for the teaching of creationism. However, these statutes have also been invalidated. In

VIDEO INSIGHT

Religion Versus Science

In this ABC News video segment, you will be confronted with a multitude of opinions and views regarding the teaching of intelligent design in public schools.

1. One of the major positions presented in the video is that regardless of whether you consider the intelligent design theory, creationism, or any other theory of evolution, there is no place for religious beliefs in the science classroom. According to those who espouse this position, to co-mingle religion and science in the classroom not only threatens the separation of church and state required by the First Amendment but threatens the quality of education in public schools. Present arguments for and against this position.

2. Consider the following statement: "Students should be challenged with controversial questions and issues, including the theories of intelligent design and evolution in the classroom." If we considered this statement as philosophical in nature, then as teachers we should not accept or reject the responses to the above statement uncritically. How might a critical theorist respond to the teaching of evolution in the classroom?

To submit your answers online, go to the *Video Insight* module for this chapter of the Companion Website at **http://www.prenhall.com/webb**.

Edwards v. Aguillard (1987), the U.S. Supreme Court ruled that creation science is a religious doctrine and to require it be taught would violate the establishment clause. Similarly, the courts have declared unconstitutional a requirement that teachers read a disclaimer immediately before the teaching of evolution stating that the teaching of evolution was "not intended to influence or dissuade the Biblical version of creation" and that it is "the basic right and privilege of each student to form his or her own opinion or maintain beliefs taught by parents" (*Freiler v. Tangipahoa Parish Board of Education*, 1999). School districts have also been successful in requiring teachers to follow the prescribed curriculum, which includes teaching evolution, and to stop teaching creationism as if it were also a legitimate scientific theory (*Peloza v. Capistrano Unified School District*, 1994).

In addition to challenges to curricular programs, another set of challenges has focused on the use of specific curriculum materials or methods, the wearing of particular clothing in physical education classes, and coeducational dancing in physical education classes. In deciding these cases, the courts applied the same analysis used in considering religious objections to secular courses and have said that the particular method or material does not violate the establishment clause, but that the free exercise clause may give the students the right to be excused from exposure to the objectionable material or practice (Sendor, 1997). Parents in a number of cases have claimed that the required use of a specific reading series violated their rights by exposing their children to beliefs that were offensive to their religious beliefs. For example, the *Impressions* reading series has been the focus of a number of challenges in recent years. The series uses the whole-language approach to teach reading, and among its readings are selections dealing with the supernatural and witchcraft. Both the Seventh and Ninth Circuit Courts have held that merely reading about these practices, or even creating poetic chants, did not constitute the practice or advancement of these practices (*Fleischfresser v. Directors of School District 200*, 1994; *Brown v. Woodland Joint Unified School District*, 1994). In fact, echoing what seems to be the sentiment of most courts in reviewing this type of case, the court quoted from the U.S. Supreme Court's 1948 decision in *McCollum*: "If we are to eliminate everything that is objectionable to any [religious group] or inconsistent with any of their doctrines, we will leave public education in shreds" (p. 235).

Few areas of the curriculum have not been challenged as advancing secular humanism. Popular targets have been AIDS and drug awareness and drug prevention curricula, global education, values clarification, and outcomes-based education. Yet another, multicultural education, is faulted for threatening traditional values and cultural heritage. This vast body of litigation has not resulted in a concrete list of what can be included and what must be excluded from the school curriculum. However, some conclusions can be drawn:

> On the one hand, schools may not tailor their programs in accordance with religious beliefs, offer religious instruction or theistic moral training, or endorse the Bible as the only true source of knowledge. On the other hand, schools may not systematically purge the curriculum of all mention of religion or ideas that are consistent with religious belief, endorse atheism, or declare that science is the only source of knowledge or that the Bible is not true. (Imber & van Geel, 2000, p. 88)

Public Aid to Private Schools

About 11.5% of K–12 students attend private schools. In recognition of the financial burden placed on parents who pay property taxes to support the public schools as well as tuition at private schools, legislatures have regularly attempted to provide some type of public support to these parents or to the schools their children attend. The legal issue involved in these attempts is whether the assistance violates the First Amendment prohibition against governmental actions that promote the establishment of religion.

Although most state constitutions forbid state aid to religious schools, the courts have relied on the **child benefit theory** to provide several types of assistance whose primary benefit is to the child rather than the private school itself. This theory was first articulated by the U.S. Supreme Court in *Cochran v. Louisiana State Board of Education* (1930), in which the Court upheld a Louisiana law that provided for the loan of textbooks to children attending nonpublic schools. The same rationale was applied in another Supreme Court decision, *Everson v. Board of Education* (1947), which supported a New Jersey law reimbursing parents for the cost of bus transportation for children attending both public and nonpublic schools. However, the fact that the U.S. Supreme Court has said that transportation, textbooks, or the provision of other services is permissible under the federal Constitution does not mean that the states are required to provide this assistance, or that such assistance may not be prohibited by state laws or constitutions. As previously stated, the constitutions of 30 states expressly forbid the use of public funds for the support of religious schools.

Since the 1970s, the courts have applied the *Lemon* test in determining the constitutionality of various state aid programs. Because no two cases presented the same set of facts, and because the answer to whether the "primary effect" is considered aid to religion as opposed to aid to education or to the student varied depending on the facts, the decisions of the courts differed for different forms of government aid. Such aid as the costs of testing and the purchase of secular textbooks were allowed, while maintenance and repair of school facilities and salary reimbursements for parochial school teachers were disallowed.

In recent years, the courts have abandoned a strict interpretation of the *Lemon* test and have shown a greater receptivity to various types of aid directed at providing services to students. In *Zobrest v. Catalina Foothills School District* (1993), the Court did not rely on the *Lemon* test but more on the child benefit theory, or neutrality principle, in ruling in favor of a deaf student's request that the school district provide him with a sign language interpreter in the Catholic school he attended. The Court stated:

> When the government offers a neutral service on the premises of a sectarian school as part of a general program that is in no way skewed towards religion, it follows that provision of service does not offend the Establishment Clause. (p. 2462)

Adopting this reasoning in an even more far-reaching decision in 1997, *Agostini v. Felton,* the U.S. Supreme Court modified the *Lemon* test and overturned two of its earlier decisions and ruled that public school employees could provide Title I remedial services in the parochial school. According to the Court, although it will continue to ask if the *purpose* of the aid is to advance or inhibit religion, it has changed its stand on the criteria used to assess whether the aid has an impermissible *effect.* Rather than acting on the presumption that the mere presence of public school employees in parochial schools created an impermissible "symbolic link" between government and religion, the Court held that aid that is allocated on the basis of neutral, nonsectarian criteria is not invalid under the establishment clause.

Three years later, in *Mitchell v. Helms* (2000), the Supreme Court effectively negated the effect criterion of *Lemon*. In its decision that Title II permits the loaning of computers, library books, and other instructional equipment to sectarian schools, the Supreme Court said that the effect test basically becomes one of satisfying a neutrality standard. According to the Court, if aid is offered to the "religious, irreligious, and unreligious" alike, then its allocation is neutral and thus any indoctrination that the recipient conducts cannot be attributed to governmental action. Also important to the court's rationale was that the decision as to what schools receive aid was the result of the private choice of the recipient to apply for funds, rather than the "unmediated will of the government."

According to many legal experts, after the *Agostini* and *Helms* decisions, "the *Lemon* limitations restraining government aid to religious schools appear to be largely nullified and the separation precedents of earlier Supreme Court decisions, in most relevant parts, rescinded" (Alexander & Alexander, 2001, p. 164). At this point in history, it appears that if any wall is to separate church and state it will come from state institutions.

Vouchers.   **Vouchers** are seen as a means of providing all parents greater choice in the school their child attends. In particular, vouchers are seen as a way to extend private school options to disadvantaged students in urban areas and students attending failing public schools. The last decade has seen increasing support for the voucher concept. Various voucher bills have been introduced in more than half of the states. And, until the 2002 decision of the U.S. Supreme Court in *Zelman v. Simmons-Harris,* all attempts to provide vouchers for students to attend parochial schools had been overturned by the courts. The Cleveland voucher plan in the *Zelman* case was unique in that it applied only to districts that were under court order requiring supervision by the state superintendent. The vouchers were based on financial need and were sent directly to the parents not the schools. Given the *Zelman* decision, there appears to be no doubt that other states and school districts will continue in their efforts to fashion voucher plans that will pass state and federal constitutional muster.

Tax Relief.   Various tax deduction and tax credit proposals have been introduced in the U.S. Congress, as well as in almost every state legislature. They have invariably invoked challenges on establishment clause grounds. Two such cases have reached the U.S. Supreme Court. In *Committee for Public Education and Religious Liberty v. Nyquist* (1973), the Court overturned a New York statute that allowed state income tax credits for parents of nonpublic school students. Although the plan aided parents rather than the schools, the court said it was nonetheless an aid to religion in violation of the establishment clause.

In the decade after *Nyquist,* various other tax relief measures were struck down by the courts. Then, in *Mueller v. Allen* (1983), the Supreme Court upheld a Minnesota statute that permitted a state income tax deduction to parents of both public and nonpublic school students for expenses for tuition, books, and transportation. In upholding the statute, the Court distinguished this case from *Nyquist* in that the New York statute provided the **tax benefits** only to parents of nonpublic school students. Here, the Court said, a secular purpose was served in providing financial assistance to a "broad spectrum" of citizens. The Supreme Court has also let stand a decision of the Supreme Court of Arizona which held that state tax credits for donations to public schools for extracurricular programs ($200) and to private school tuition organizations ($500) did not violate the establishment clause (*Kotterman v. Killian,* 1999). According to the Arizona court, the primary beneficiaries of the tax credits were the taxpayers, not the nonpublic schools.

Compulsory Attendance

Each of the 50 states has legislation requiring school attendance by children of a certain age range residing within the state. The age range is normally from 7 to 16 years. Parents may satisfy this requirement by sending their children to a public or private school, or by homeschooling. In addition, although attendance is compulsory, attendance in a specific district or at a particular school within the district may legally be restricted to those residing within the district or within a certain attendance zone or by voluntary or court-ordered desegregation remedies.

For Your Reflection and Analysis

If income tax collections are reduced as a result of providing tax benefits, how should replacement revenues be generated?
*To submit your response online, go to http://www.
prenhall.com/webb.*

CW

The residency requirement is not the same as a citizenship requirement. The U.S. Supreme Court, in *Plyler v. Doe* (1982), upheld the right of children of illegal aliens to attend school in the district of their residence. According to the Court, the state's interest in deterring illegal entry was insufficient to justify the creation and perpetuation of a subclass of illiterates within the nation's borders. On a similar note, the courts have ruled that school districts also must educate homeless youth who have no address but are living within their boundaries.

The number of homeschoolers continues to grow.

Private and Homeschooling

The states' right to mandate school attendance does not extend to requiring that schooling take place in the public schools. In 1925, in *Pierce v. Society of Sisters,* the Supreme Court recognized the right of parents to educate their children in private schools. However, the decision also recognized the right of the state to regulate private

CONTROVERSIAL ISSUE

Homeschooling

The number of students being homeschooled has grown 29% since 1999. There are an estimated 1.5 million homeschooled children in the United States. While the movement continues to grow at an estimated 8% to 10% per year, the major educational organizations as well as the National Parent Teacher Association oppose homeschooling. Among the pros and cons most often cited are the following:

Pros

1. Homeschooling allows the tailoring of the curriculum to each individual student's interest and learning styles.
2. Parents are free to incorporate religious and spiritual beliefs into the homeschool curriculum.
3. Homeschooling sponsors closer family relationships.
4. Students are freed from peer pressure and competition and therefore develop greater self-esteem and confidence.
5. Greater flexibility in learning times is provided; learning need no longer revolve around a school calendar.
6. Education takes place in a safe and drug-free environment.

Cons

1. A heavy time commitment is required of parents.
2. Homeschoolers have limited opportunities to interact with diverse populations.
3. Students have limited opportunities to compete in team sports.
4. Parents are with their children all day, every day.
5. Expenditures for education are increased.
6. Homeschools are not required to meet the "quality" teacher requirements under the No Child Left Behind Act.

If the homeschooling movement continues to grow, what possible impacts might it have on local school districts? What standards should the state require homeschools to meet?

 To answer these questions online, go to the *Controversial Issue* module for this chapter of the *Companion Website* at **http://www.prenhall.com/webb**.

schools, including requiring that their teachers be certified and that their curricula comply with established state guidelines.

Homeschooling as a form of private schooling is another alternative to attendance in the public schools. Homeschooling is allowed in all states either by express statutes or judicial interpretations (Mawdsley, 2000). The interest in homeschooling has increased dramatically in the last two decades as more and more parents have become concerned about instruction or safety in the public schools. The number of homeschoolers increased from 600,000 in 1994 to close to 1.1 million in 2003 (U.S. Department of Education, 2005b). As the number of homeschoolers grows, so does the debate about the practice (see the Controversial Issue on page 294). A number of state and national homeschooling associations support the efforts of homeschoolers, and a vast array of commercial curriculum materials are directed at the homeschooling market. In some states and school districts, homeschooled children can enroll in independent study programs

through a public school or participate in some form of part-time school attendance. In fact, 18% of homeschoolers are enrolled in public schools part time and about 6% participate in extracurricular activities (Toppo, 2001). However, where state funding is not provided for part-time students or where state athletic associations deny eligibility to part-time students, homeschoolers may be denied attendance or participation.

State statutes providing for homeschooling range from those that are very strict to those that simply treat homeschooling the same as any other form of nonpublic education. Thirty-nine states require that parents notify the local school district of their intent to homeschool, but only six require advance approval in addition to the notification (Mawdsley, 2000). Generally, state statutes or regulations require that (1) instruction be essentially equivalent to that taught in the public schools and include the subjects required by state law, (2) the parent or other adult providing the instruction be qualified (not necessarily certified) to teach, (3) systematic reporting be made to local school authorities, and (4) a minimum number of hours of instruction per day be provided.

In about two-thirds of the states, students in homeschools must be periodically assessed for academic progress. In fact, a federal court has upheld a state statute making ineligible for homeschooling those students whose scores fall below the 40th percentile and do not improve after home remediation (*Null v. Board of Education of the County of Jackson,* 1993). The courts have also upheld the right of school officials to visit the home and to observe

For Your Reflection and Analysis

Should parents who homeschool receive state aid?

To submit your response online, go to http://www. prenhall.com/webb.

CW

PROFESSIONAL REFLECTION

Court decisions have very favorably impacted the practice of teaching. Without decisions that promoted diversity, we would still have shamefully segregated schools where bias and racism are allowed to thrive. Without decisions that promoted gender equity, we would still have half of our population subject to fewer choices and offerings in their lives. Without decisions that promoted mainstreaming of learners with disabilities, we would still have a dim understanding of the necessity for accommodations and coping skills in life. Without decisions that promoted separation of religion from public education, we would still have bias against world views and a progressive loss in our ability to learn from our differences. Without decisions that allowed for formation of unions, we would still have overworked, underpaid teachers who are not respected for their professionalism. Without decisions that promoted the search for evidence from measurable observations, we would still have pseudoscience limiting our ability to develop scientific innovations. Without decisions that promoted healthy working environments, we would still have asbestos-filled schools and dangerous chemical use and storage practices. Without decisions that promoted rigor in our curriculum along with the development of optimal learning environments, we would still have unmotivated, uninspired educators who lack in professional development opportunities and the success-for-all that comes from sharing among colleagues.

Cathy Bockenstedt
National Board Certified Teacher, Minnesota

To analyze this reflection, go to the *Professional Reflection* module for this chapter of the Companion Website at **http://www. prenhall.com/webb.**

the teaching and to examine student work. However, where states have attempted to impose requirements on homeschools that were not required of the public schools, or were unreasonable, the courts have overturned the requirements (e.g., *Clonlara, Inc. v. State Board of Education*, 1993, 180-day minimum school year requirement for homeschools but not for public schools).

Summary

The legal foundation of education derives from state and federal constitutional provisions, the laws of state and federal legislatures, the enactments of state and federal agencies, and court decisions. Every state constitution includes a provision for education, and the wording of the provision has proved important in determining the obligation of the state in providing for education and the constitutionality of legislative action. Although the federal Constitution does not mention education, a number of its provisions affect education and afford protection to school personnel, pupils, and patrons.

The interaction of the institutions of religion and education has become the source of increasing legal controversy in recent years. A tension exists between the efforts of the schools to accommodate religion and yet maintain the wall of separation between church and state required by the First Amendment. Thus far, the courts generally have been consistent in their decisions that keep religious practices and proselytizing efforts out of the schools. However, the decisions of the U.S. Supreme Court in *Mergens* (1990), *Agostini* (1997), and *Helms* (2000) represent not only a potential crack in the wall of separation between church and state, but also the growing conservative thrust of the Court. In the next chapter, other constitutional rights of teachers and students are explored.

Key Terms

Administrative law, 278	Ex post facto law, 275	Secular humanism, 290
Case (common) law, 278	Homeschooling, 295	*Stare decisis*, 278
Child benefit theory, 292	*Lemon* test, 284	Statutory law, 277
Constitution, 274	Limited open forum, 288	Tax benefits, 293
Eminent domain, 276	Plenary, 278	Voucher, 293

PROFESSIONAL DEVELOPMENT WORKSHOP

Prepare for the Praxis™ Examination

Mr. Reid is a sixth-grade teacher at Fairview Middle School. Fairview has been labeled "Performing" on the state performance assessment. Mr. Reid's class is a heterogeneous class of 27 that includes 3 students with disabilities. Mr. Reid participated in the development of the IEP for each of these students. One student, Samuel, has been diagnosed as learning disabled and also suffers from ADHD. He often gets out of his seat and walks around the class disturbing other students. Mr. Reid has moved him to the back of the class, hoping to limit his span of activity. Samuel rarely turns in any homework assignments and has trouble following directions for class assignments and activities. The work he does do is often incomplete and performed carelessly.

Mr. Reid is teaching a lesson on the Constitution and the Bill of Rights. He tells the students that it is important that they take notes because some of the information is not in the textbook. As he delivers his lecture he tries to speak slowly and clearly enough for Samuel and all students to take notes. Nonetheless, on several occasions students interrupt his lecture to ask him to clarify or repeat some comment. As he talks, he walks around the class to see how students are doing. When he gets to Samuel's desk he sees that he has not written any notes. Rather, he has drawn a picture of various action figures. Several other students also seem to have rather "sketchy" notes. Mr. Reid completes the lecture but senses that the lesson has not gone as he planned. After some reflection he decides to seek the advice of the designated master teacher for his grade level in designing cooperative learning activities or other instructional strategies that would involve students more.

1. Explain the least restrictive environment requirement of the IDEA and what must be included on the IEP.
2. Describe three behavioral management strategies the master teacher might suggest Mr. Reid use to manage Samuel's behavior.
3. What instructional strategies might the master teacher suggest Mr. Reid use as an alternative to lecture and note-taking? Explain the advantages of each.

CW To submit your responses online, go to the *Prepare for the Praxis™ Examination* module for this chapter of the Companion Website at **http://www.prenhall.com/webb.**

Build Your Knowledge Base

1. Given the situation described in the vignette at the beginning of this chapter, how might Mr. Kindrick accommodate Mrs. Collins's desire to wear the cross and students' desires not to be exposed to this symbol of Christianity?
2. What are the provisions of your state constitution regarding education?
3. Describe the levels and types of state courts in your state.
4. What is your school (or school system) policy on silent meditation? Is there support for prayer or Bible reading? On what grounds?
5. What is meant by the *Lemon* test? How effective has it been in distinguishing permissible and impermissible aid to nonpublic school students?
6. How does the child benefit theory serve to justify educational vouchers? How does it operate in the school systems in your area? Are textbooks or bus transportation provided?
7. What First Amendment issues are currently being debated in the schools in your area?

Develop Your Portfolio

1. As previously noted, many of the curriculum materials being objected to today have been used for decades (e.g., *Huckleberry Finn* and *Catcher in the Rye*). Interview a school librarian and a community librarian regarding their experiences in handling objections to a variety of curriculum materials. Prepare a reflection paper that describes how you would handle a situation if a parent came to you and objected to curriculum material you had selected for your class. Place your reflection paper in your portfolio under **INTASC Standard 9, Reflective Practice and Professional Growth.**
2. Review Table 11.1, Summary of Major Civil Rights Statutes Affecting Education, on page 279. Using an Internet website such as http://web.lexisnexis.com/universe, select one legal case from your state that exemplifies a lawsuit pertaining to a major civil rights statute. Prepare a brief (one-page) paper that summarizes the case. Include a discussion of how the outcome of the case has impacted education in your state. Place your paper in your portfolio under **INTASC Standard 1, Knowledge of Subject.**

CW To complete these activities online, go to the *Develop Your Portfolio* module for the chapter of the Companion Website at **http://www.prenhall.com/webb.**

Explore Teaching and Learning: Field Experiences

1. Contact the central office of a nearby local school district and arrange to review the district's policies and procedures concerning (a) access of religious groups to school buildings, (b) distribution of religious material, and (c) absence for religious holidays. Outline the key procedures that must be followed.

2. Search the Internet for your state government's website or for the National Conference of State Legislatures' website and determine if your state's school finance system has been challenged in the courts. Review the materials to determine the constitutional arguments of the plaintiffs. Write a short synopsis of the issue(s) involved.

Professional Development Online

Visit this text's Companion Website at **http://www.prenhall.com/webb** to gain access to a variety of questions, activities, and exercises to help build your knowledge of this chapter's content. Below are just a few items available at this text's Companion Website:

- Classroom Video—To see actual classroom footage and work through activities and questions to analyze the content of the video, click on the *Classroom Video* module for this chapter.
- Teaching Tolerance—To go to this organization's website and complete activities to explore issues and topics dealing with how to teach tolerance to students, click on the *Teaching Tolerance* module for this chapter.
- Self-Test—To review terms and concepts presented in this chapter, click on the *Self-Test* module for this chapter.
- Internet Resources—To link to websites related to topics in this chapter, go to the *Internet Resources* module for this chapter of the Companion Website.

If there is any principle of the Constitution that more imperatively calls for attachment than any other it is the principle of free thought—not free thought for those who agree with us but freedom for the thought that we hate.
—Justice Oliver Wendell Holmes, Jr. (1841–1935)

TEACHERS, STUDENTS, AND THE LAW

Helen Tye is a high school English teacher. Maria Collins is in Ms. Tye's third period class. Ralph Tyler, the pitcher on the school baseball team, is also in this class. Soon after the class begins, Ralph appears to be trying to get Maria's attention but she ignores him. He then gives a folded piece of paper to Andrew, another student in class, and motions for Andrew to pass it to Maria. However, Ms. Tye intercepts the note before Andrew can give it to Maria. She puts the note in her pocket and continues with the class discussion of Shakespeare's sonnets.

At home later that afternoon as she is changing clothes, Ms. Tye retrieves the forgotten note from her pocket and is shocked when she reads its contents. Ralph has described in graphic sexual terms what he would like to do to Maria. As she remembers the incident in class, Ms. Tye is afraid that Maria's attempt to ignore Ralph suggests that this is not the first time Ralph has made offensive remarks to Maria.

Is this a case of sexual harassment? What action should Ms. Tye take now? What should be done to protect both Maria's rights and Ralph's rights?

Like Ms. Tye, teachers must make decisions every day that affect the rights of students, their own rights, and their professional lives. Therefore, it is imperative that teachers be knowledgeable about applicable state and federal legislation, school board policies, and court decisions. After completing this chapter, you will be able to:

- Identify the personal and professional requirements for employment of prospective teachers.
- Describe teachers' employment rights as derived from the employment contract and tenure status.
- Outline the legal requirements for dismissing a teacher.
- Provide an overview of teachers' rights, inside and outside the classroom.
- Discuss the teacher's responsibility in reporting child abuse and using copyrighted materials.
- Define the elements of negligence.
- Compare equal opportunity and affirmative action.
- Contrast the procedural requirements for suspension, expulsion, and corporal punishment.
- Trace the development of student rights in the area of search and seizure.
- Explain the restraints that may be placed on student expression and personal appearance.
- Distinguish between quid pro quo and hostile environment harassment as the concepts apply to employees and students.
- Discuss how the Family Educational Rights and Privacy Act has expanded parental and student rights.

Teacher Rights and Responsibilities

Although school personnel are not expected to be legal experts, it is imperative that they understand their rights and obligations under the law and that these rights and obligations be translated into everyday practices in the schools. In this chapter, the basic concepts of law are presented as they relate to terms and conditions of employment; teacher dismissal; teacher rights inside and outside the classroom; tort liability; discrimination, equal opportunity and affirmative action; and certain legal responsibilities of teachers. Although there is some variation in the application of these legal concepts from one state or locality to another, certain topics and issues are of sufficient importance and similarity to warrant consideration. Some of these topics are also discussed in other chapters of this text. Here, attention is given to the legal considerations of these topics.

Terms and Conditions of Employment

As emphasized in Chapter 11, within the framework provided by state and federal constitutional and statutory protections, the state has complete power to conduct and regulate public education. Through its legislature, state board of education, state department of education, and local school boards, the state promulgates the rules and regulations for the operation of the schools. Among these rules and regulations are those establishing the terms and conditions of employment. The areas most often covered by state statutory and regulatory provisions are those dealing with certification, citizenship and residency requirements, health and physical requirements, contracts, and tenure.

Certification.   As noted in Chapter 1, to qualify for most professional teaching, administrative, and other positions in the public schools, an individual must acquire a valid certificate or license. The certificate does not constitute a contract or guarantee of employment; it only makes the holder eligible for employment.

All states have established certification requirements for prospective teachers. These requirements may include a college degree with minimum credit hours in specific curricular areas, evidence of specific job experience, "good moral character," a specified age, U.S. citizenship, the signing of a loyalty oath, good health, and, as discussed in Chapter 1, a minimum score on a test of basic skills such as the Praxis™ examination (39 states require a test of basic skills of teacher education candidates). Where specified certification requirements exist, failure to meet the requirements can result in dismissal.

Citizenship and Residency Requirements.   The courts have upheld both citizenship and residency requirements for certification and/or as a condition of employment. With regard to the citizenship requirement, the U.S. Supreme Court has held that education is among those governmental functions that is "so bound up with the operation of the state as a governmental entity as to permit the exclusion from those functions of all persons who have not become part of the process of self-government" (*Ambach v. Norwick,* 1979, pp. 73–74).

Requirements that teachers reside within the district where they are employed also have been upheld if it can be shown that there is a rational basis for the requirements. For example, the Arkansas Supreme Court determined that a school district requirement that teachers reside within the district or within 10 miles of town was "rationally related to community involvement and district identity as it related to tax base in support of district tax levies, and (the) 10 mile limit was reasonable commuting distance and was not arbitrary" (*McClelland v. Paris Public Schools,* 1988, p. 908). Note, however, that although residency requirements have been upheld in many jurisdictions, a number of states have statutory provisions prohibiting school districts from imposing such requirements (Cambron-McCabe, McCarthy, & Thomas, 2004).

Health and Physical Requirements.   Most states and school boards have adopted health and physical requirements for teachers. The courts have recognized that such requirements are necessary to protect the health and welfare of students and other employees. Accordingly, the courts have upheld the release or reassignment of employees in instances where their failed eyesight, hearing, or other physical or mental condition made it impossible for them to meet their contractual duties. The courts have also upheld school districts in requiring medical examinations to determine employees' fitness to perform their duties. For example, a Michigan court upheld a school board that suspended a teacher for 3 years and required that she undergo physical and mental examinations before returning to work. The court determined that the district had a legitimate concern, following several instances of misconduct and insubordination, that she might be experiencing a breakdown (*Sullivan v. River Valley School District*, 1998).

Although the courts have upheld school districts' imposition of health and physical requirements, they are concerned that such requirements not be arbitrarily applied, be specific to the position, and not violate state and federal laws intended to protect the rights of people with disabilities. For example, Section 504 of the Rehabilitation Act of 1973, which protects otherwise qualified individuals with handicaps from discrimination, served as the basis for a 1987 U.S. Supreme Court ruling that overturned the dismissal of an Arkansas teacher with tuberculosis (*School Board of Nassau County v. Arline*, 1987). According to the Court, discrimination based solely on fear of contamination is to be considered discrimination against people with disabilities. The Supreme Court instructed the lower court to determine if the teacher posed a "significant risk" that would preclude her from being "otherwise qualified" and if her condition could reasonably be accommodated by the district. Ultimately, the court found the teacher posed little risk and was otherwise qualified, and she was reinstated with back pay.

The significant risk standard and the provisions of Section 504 have been relied on by plaintiff teachers in cases involving AIDS. In the lead case, *Chalk v. U.S. District Court Central District of California* (1988), the U.S. District Court relied heavily on the significant risk standard articulated in *Arline* to determine when a contagious disease would prevent an individual from being "otherwise qualified." In applying the "significant risk of communicating" standard in this instance, the court found that the overwhelming consensus of medical and scientific opinion regarding the nature and transmission of AIDS did not support a conclusion that Chalk posed a significant risk of communicating the disease to children or others through casual social contact.

A major federal statute impacting on health and physical requirements for school district employees is the Americans With Disabilities Act of 1990, which prohibits employment discrimination against "qualified individuals with a disability." Such a person is defined as one who "satisfies the requisite skill, experience, education, and other job-related requirements of the (position). . . and who, with or without reasonable accommodation, can perform the essential functions" of the position. Although the law does not require the hiring or retention of unqualified persons, it does prohibit specific actions of employers that adversely affect the employment opportunities of people with disabilities (e.g., inquiring into a disability or requiring a medical examination before an offer is made, writing job descriptions that include nonessential job functions), and it does require employers to make "reasonable accommodation" for a known mental or physical disability.

An area of current dispute in regard to health and physical requirements for school employees involves mandatory testing for alcohol or drug use. As explained later in this chapter, employees have challenged such testing as violating their rights of privacy and constituting an unreasonable search under the Fourth Amendment.

The Employment Contract.   The general principles of contract law apply to the teacher employment contract; that is, in order for the contract to be valid, it must contain the basic elements of (1) offer and acceptance, (2) legally competent parties, (3) consideration (compensation), (4) legal subject matter, and (5) agreement in the form required by law. In addition, the employment contract must meet the specific requirements of applicable state law.

To be valid, a contract must contain an offer by one party and an acceptance by another. Typically the offer of employment specifies that the acceptance must be made within a certain period of time of the offer. Until the prospective employee to whom the offer is made accepts the offer (i.e., acceptance can not be made by a spouse or relative), the contract is not in force.

The authority to contract lies exclusively with the school board. Although the superintendent or other officials may screen candidates and recommend employment, only the

Playground duty is among those non-classroom duties that teachers may be required to perform.

school board is authorized to enter into contracts, and only when it is a legally constituted body; for instance, contracts issued when a quorum of the board is not present or at an illegally called meeting of the board (e.g., adequate notice is not given) are not valid.

To be enforceable, a contract must pertain to a legal subject matter (i.e., a contract for the commission of a crime is not enforceable). Nor can the terms of the contract violate state or federal statutes or regulations or public policy (e.g., pay less than the federal minimum wage). Last, the contract must be in the proper form required by law. In most states, this means the contract must be in writing and signed.

The employee's rights and obligations of employment are derived from the contract. The courts have held that all valid rules and regulations of the school board, as well as all applicable state statutes, are part of the contract, even if not specifically included. Accordingly, employees may be required to perform certain tasks incidental to classroom activities, regardless of whether the contract specifically mentions them. These have included such activities as field trips; playground, study hall, bus, and cafeteria duty; supervision of extracurricular activities; and club sponsorship. Teachers cannot, however, be required to drive a bus, perform janitorial duties, or perform duties unrelated to the school program (compare this with the duties required of teachers in Colonial America presented in the Historical Note on page 305). If an employee refuses to perform reasonable extracurricular duties required as a condition of employment, the courts may construe such a refusal as insubordination justifying removal.

Tenure.   **Tenure** is "the status conferred upon teachers who have served a probationary period . . . which then guarantees them continual employment until retirement, subject to the requirements of good behavior, financial necessity, and in some instances good periodic evaluations" (Sperry, Daniel, Huefner, & Gee, 1998, p. 1041). Tenure is a creation of statute designed to maintain permanent and qualified instructional personnel. Most state statutes specify the requirements and procedures for obtaining tenure, which normally include the satisfactory completion of a probationary period of 3 years of regular and continuous teaching service. During the probationary period, the teacher is usually issued a 1-year contract that, subject to satisfactory service and district finances, is renewable at the end of each of the probationary years. If the district decides not to renew a probationary contract, in about half the states school districts are not required to give the reasons for the nonrenewal or to even provide a hearing on the decision. However, most states do require that the probationary teacher be given timely notice of intent to nonrenew (usually no later than April 1). And, in all cases, if the district attempts to break the contract of a probationary teacher during the term of the contract, the teacher must be given, at a minimum, a notice of dismissal and a hearing on the causes.

Satisfactory completion of the probationary period does not guarantee tenure. In some states, tenure is automatically awarded at the end of the probationary period unless the school board notifies teachers that they will not be rehired, whereas in other states official action of the school board is required for the awarding of tenure. In cases where the school district fails to follow applicable state laws, the courts will attempt to balance the public policy interests of employing competent and qualified teachers against the rights of the individual teacher.

The granting of tenure does not guarantee the right to teach in a particular school, grade level, or subject area. Subject to due process requirements, teachers may be reassigned to any position for which they are certified. The awarding of tenure also does not guarantee permanent employment. As discussed in the following sections, the teacher may be dis-

HISTORICAL NOTE

Duties of a Colonial Schoolmaster

"First. That the schoolmaster shall diligently attend his school and do his utmost endeavor for benefiting his scholars according to his best discretion.

"Second. That from the beginning of the first month until the end of the seventh, he shall every day begin to teach at seven of the clock in the morning and dismiss his school at five in the afternoon. And for the other five months, that is, from the beginning of the eighth to the end of the twelfth month he shall every day begin at eight of the clock in the morning and end at four in the afternoon.

"Thirdly. Every day in the year the usual time of dismissing at noon shall be at eleven and to begin again at one, except that

"Fourthly. Every second day in the week he shall call his scholars together between twelve and one of the clock to examine them what they have learned on the sabbath day preceding, at which time he shall take notice of any misdemeanor or outrage that any of his scholars shall have committed on the sabbath to the end that at some convenient time due admonition and correction may be administered.

"Fifthly. He shall equally and impartially receive and instruct such as shall be sent and committed to him for that end whether their parents be poor or rich, not refusing any who have right and interest in the school.

"Sixthly. Such as shall be committed to him he shall diligently instruct, as they shall be able to learn, both in humane learning and good literature, and likewise in point of good manners and dutiful behaviour towards all, especially their superiors as they shall have occasion to be in their presence whether by meeting them in the street or otherwise.

"Seventhly. Every sixth day in the week at two of the clock in the afternoon he shall catechise his scholars in the principles of Christian religion, either in some Catechism which the wardens shall provide and present, or in defect thereof in some other.

"Eighthly. And because all man's endeavors without the blessing of God needs be fruitless and unsuccessful, therefore it is a chief part of the schoolmaster's religious care to commend his scholars and his labors amongst them unto God by prayer morning and evening, taking care that his scholars do reverently attend during the same.

"Ninthly. And because the rod of correction is an ordinance of God necessary sometimes to be dispensed unto children, but such as may easily be abused by overmuch severity and rigor on one hand, or by overmuch indulgence and lenity on the other, it is therefore ordered and agreed that the schoolmaster for the time being shall have full power to administer correction to all or any of his scholars without respect of persons, according as the nature and quality of the offence shall require." The rule further requires that the parents "shall not hinder the master therein" but if aggrieved they can complain to the wardens "who shall hear and impartially decide between them."

To research and explore this topic further, go to the *Historical Note* module for this chapter of the Companion Website at **http://www.prenhall.com/webb**.

missed for disciplinary reasons (for cause) or because declining enrollments, financial exigencies, or other circumstances necessitate a reduction in force. Tenure statutes normally specify the grounds for dismissal of a tenured teacher as well as the procedures that must be followed in the dismissal. The dismissal protection afforded tenured teachers, compared with that of nontenured teachers, is perhaps the major benefit of obtaining tenure. Tenure status gives teachers the security of practicing their profession without threat of removal for arbitrary, capricious, or political motivations. In fact, the courts have said that the granting of tenure in effect awards the teacher with a **property right** to continued employment that cannot be taken away without due process of law.

Teacher Dismissal

Grounds for Dismissal. *Dismissal* is defined as the termination of employment during the term of the contract. The statutory provisions regarding teacher dismissal "for cause" vary among the states in terms of the specified grounds for dismissal as well as the legal requirements for dismissal. The behaviors that would justify dismissal apply equally

VIDEO INSIGHT

Transgender Teacher

In the ABC News video segment, a gifted teacher named David Warfield has been undergoing a medical transformation from male to female (Dana Warfield). After viewing the video segment, consider several important legal and educational issues that were raised.

1. Should David Warfield, who left his teaching post in June as a male, be allowed to return to the classroom as a female teacher in September? Why or why not? Was the $150,000 settlement for his agreeing to resign the best resolution for this case? What other possible personnel options might the school board have considered? Should Dana Warfield be allowed to keep her California teaching license? What do you believe will be the outcome if Dana Warfield files a discrimination suit against the school board?

2. As discussed in Chapter 10, "Students at Risk," gay, lesbian, bisexual, and transgender youth are at risk for a variety of problems: alienation from family and peer group, violence, sexual abuse, depression, and suicide. Recognizing this reality, what are the advantages and disadvantages to having a transgender teacher like Dana Warfield in the classroom?

CW To submit your answers online, go to the *Video Insight* module for this chapter of the Companion Website at **http://www.prenhall.com/webb**.

---

to tenured and nontenured teachers. The reasons for dismissal most frequently cited in statutes are immorality, incompetency, and insubordination. Among the other commonly mentioned reasons are neglect of duty, unprofessional conduct, unfitness to teach, and the catch-all phrase, "other good and just cause." Most challenges to dismissals center around two primary issues: (1) whether the conduct in question fits the statutory grounds for dismissal, and (2) if so, whether the school board presented the facts necessary to sustain the charge. The burden of proof in justifying a dismissal lies with the school board and must be supported by sufficient evidence to justify the dismissal. In addition, as will be discussed in the next section, in any dismissal the school board must provide the teacher with all the due process required by state statute, school board policy, or negotiated agreement.

Immorality. Although **immorality** is the most frequently cited ground for dismissal in state statutes, they normally do not define the term or discuss its application to specific conduct. Consequently, these tasks have been left to the courts. A review of cases challenging dismissals related to immorality shows that they generally have been based on one or more of the following categories of conduct: (1) sexual conduct with students; (2) same-sex sexual orientation; (3) making sexually explicit remarks or talking about sexually related topics unrelated to the curriculum; (4) distribution of sexually explicit materials to classes; (5) use of obscene, profane, or abusive language; (6) public lewdness; (7) possession and use of controlled substances; (8) other criminal misconduct; and (9) dishonesty.

While the concept of immorality "is subject to ranging interpretations based on shifting social attitudes (and therefore) must be resolved on the facts and circumstances of each case" (*Ficus v. Board of School Trustees of Central School District,* 1987, p. 1,140), some standards have evolved from the cases in this area that are often applied to other cases involving dismissal for immorality. The first is the exemplar standard. The majority of the public believes that teachers should be good role models for students, both in and out of the school (Imber & van Geel, 2000). The courts also recognize that there are "legitimate standards to be expected of those who teach in the public schools" (*Reitmeyer v. Unemployment Compensation Board of Review,* 1992, p. 508). Second, in most jurisdictions there must be a nexus, or connection, between the out-of-school conduct of the teacher and the teacher's ability to teach, or the conduct must have an adverse effect on the school relationship or be the subject of public notoriety. For example, in a Pennsylvania case the court upheld the dismissal of a teacher after her third driving under the influence conviction after ruling that her conduct set a bad example for her students and offended the community's morals (*Zelno v. Lincoln Intermediate Unit No. 12 Board of Directors,* 2001) The exceptions to the principle that the behavior must affect teaching performance or become the subject of notoriety have been made most often in regard to notoriously illegal or immoral behavior, including sexual conduct with minors, where no such nexus is required.

Because the facts of no two cases are exactly the same, the connection may exist in one case involving a particular conduct but not in another. For example, the courts have held that conviction for a felony or misdemeanor, including possession of illegal drugs, does not necessarily, in and of itself, serve as grounds for dismissal. Again, the circumstances of each case are important, especially regarding the effect on the school, students, and coworkers. Thus, the courts might not uphold the dismissal of a teacher solely because the teacher once was indicted for possession of a small amount of marijuana, but they probably would support a firing based on evidence of a widely publicized conviction, combined with testimony that the teacher's criminal behavior would undermine the teacher's effectiveness in the classroom (Fischer, Schimmel, & Kelly, 2003). Similarly, most courts have overturned the dismissal of homosexual and bisexual teachers based only on their private conduct, when no conviction of breaking the law had taken place (see, e.g., *Glover v. Williamsburg Local School District Board of Education,* 1998). However, dismissal has been upheld in cases where public sexual conduct was involved (see, e.g., *C. F. S. v. Mahan,* 1996).

Although cases involving alleged immoral conduct must be settled on a case-by-case basis, the courts have agreed on the factors to be considered in determining if the alleged conduct renders a teacher unfit to teach. These factors include (1) the age and maturity of the teacher's students, (2) the likelihood that the teacher's conduct will have an adverse effect on students or other teachers, (3) the degree of anticipated adversity, (4) the proximity of the conduct, (5) any extenuating or aggravating circumstances surrounding the conduct, (6) the likelihood that the conduct would be repeated, (7) any underlying motives, and (8) the chilling effect on the rights of teachers (*In re Thomas,* 1996).

Incompetency.   Courts typically describe **incompetence** as lack of ability, legal qualifications, or fitness to discharge the required duties. Those conditions or behaviors that have been sustained most successfully as constituting incompetence fall into six general categories: (1) inadequate teaching, (2) lack of knowledge of the subject matter, (3) unreasonable discipline or failure to maintain classroom discipline, (4) failure to work effectively with colleagues, supervisors, or parents, (5) physical or mental incapacity, and (6) willful neglect of duty.

As with dismissals for alleged immorality, in dismissals for incompetence the courts require that there be an established relationship between the employee's conduct and the operation of the school. Additionally, the standard against which the teacher is measured must be one used for other teachers in a similar position, not some hypothetical standard of perfection, and the conduct must not be an isolated incident but a demonstrated pattern of incompetence. Most jurisdictions also require that before termination a determination be made as to whether the behavior in question is remedial, a notice of deficiency be given, and a reasonable opportunity to remediate be provided.

Insubordination.   Regardless of whether it is specified in a statute, insubordination is an acceptable cause for dismissal in all states. **Insubordination** involves the persistent, willful, and deliberate violation of a reasonable rule or direct order from a recognized authority. The rule not only must be reasonable but it must be clearly communicated, and it cannot be an infringement on the teacher's constitutional rights. For example, rules that limit what teachers can say or write may, in some cases, violate their First Amendment right to free speech. Normally, unless the insubordinate act is severe, a single action is not sufficient grounds for dismissal. Dismissal may also not be supported if the teacher tried, although unsuccessfully, to obey the rule or no harm resulted from the violation (Alexander & Alexander, 2001).

In cases involving insubordination, it is not necessary to establish a relationship between the insubordinate action(s) and teaching effectiveness. In a case in point, an industrial arts teacher was terminated for repeated refusal to submit lesson plans even though he had received positive performance evaluations (*Vukadinovich v. Board of School Trustees of North Newton School Corporation,* 2002). Among the actions that have been held to constitute insubordination are refusal to obey the direct and lawful orders of school administrators or school boards, unauthorized absence from duty, abuse of sick leave, refusal to follow established policies and procedures, inappropriate use of corporal punishment, refusal to meet or cooperate with superiors, encouraging students to disobey school authority, refusal to perform assigned teaching or nonteaching duties, and failure to acquire required approval for use of instructional materials.

Constitutional Rights of Teachers

School boards in this country have historically considered it their right, indeed their responsibility, to control the personal as well as the professional conduct of teachers. School boards have sought to regulate teachers' dress, speech, religion, and association. However, in the last quarter of the 20th century, teacher activism, court decisions, and enlightened legislators and school boards have greatly expanded the rights of teachers.

Procedural Due Process.   In keeping with the Fourteenth Amendment, if the dismissal of a teacher involves either a property or liberty right, **procedural due process** must be provided. As previously noted, teachers who are tenured have a "property right" to continued employment. On the other hand, nontenured teachers do not have such a claim to due process unless they are dismissed during the contract year or unless the dismissal action impairs a fundamental constitutional right, creates a stigma, or damages the employee's reputation to the extent that it forecloses other employment opportunities. Nontenured teachers may also establish a **liberty interest** claim if the nonrenewal decision was made to retaliate for the teacher's exercise of a fundamental liberty.

Once it has been established that a school district action requires procedural due process, the central issue becomes what process is due. In arriving at its decision, the court will look to the procedural due process requirements in state statutes, state agency or school board regulations, or employment contracts to determine both their propriety and the extent to which they were followed.

Generally, the courts have held that an employee facing a severe loss such as termination of employment must be ensured the following procedural elements:

1. Notice of charges;
2. The opportunity for a hearing;
3. Adequate time to prepare a rebuttal to the charges;
4. The names of witnesses and access to evidence;
5. A hearing before an impartial tribunal (which can be the school board);
6. The right to representation by legal counsel;
7. The opportunity to introduce evidence and cross-examine witnesses;
8. A decision based solely on the evidence presented and the findings of the hearing;
9. A transcript or record of the hearing; and
10. The opportunity to appeal. (Cambron-McCabe et al., 2004)

Notice must not merely be given, it must be timely (on or before an established date) and in sufficient specificity to enable the employee to attempt to remediate or to prepare an adequate defense. The hearing requirements will typically be specified in state statutes, school district policies, or the employment contract. A formal hearing as in a court may not be required, but the hearing must provide the employee a full and fair opportunity to rebut all charges. Table 12.1 lists some Supreme Court cases affecting teachers' rights, many of which are discussed in the sections that follow.

Freedom of Expression.   In the landmark U.S. Supreme Court decision regarding freedom of expression in the public schools, *Tinker v. Des Moines Independent Community School District* (1969), the Court ruled that neither teachers nor students shed their constitutional rights to freedom of speech or expression when they enter the schoolhouse

Table 12.1 — Selected U.S. Supreme Court Cases Affecting Teachers' Rights

Case	Decision
Indiana ex rel. Anderson v. Brand (1938)	Tenure statutes provide qualifying teachers with contractual rights that cannot be altered by the state without good cause.
Keyishian v. Board of Regents (1967)	Loyalty oaths that make mere membership in a subversive organization grounds for dismissal are unconstitutionally overboard.
Pickering v. Board of Education (1968)	Absent proof of false statements knowingly or recklessly made, teachers may not be dismissed for exercising the freedom to speak on matters of public interest.
Board of Regents v. Roth (1972)	A nontenured teacher does not have a property right to continued employment and can be dismissed without a statement of cause or a hearing as long as the employee's reputation or future employment have not been impaired.
Perry v. Sindermann (1972)	Teachers may not be dismissed for public criticism of superiors on matters of public concern.
Cleveland Board of Ed. v. Le Fleur (1974)	School board policy requiring that all pregnant teachers take mandatory leave is unconstitutional.
Hortonville Joint School District No. 1 v. Hortonville Education Association (1976)	A school board may serve as the impartial hearing body in a due process hearing.
Washington v. Davis (1976)	To sustain a claim of discrimination, an employee must show that the employer's action was a deliberate attempt to discriminate, not just that the action resulted in a disproportionate impact.
Mount Healthy City School District v. Doyle (1977)	To prevail in a First Amendment dismissal case, school district employees must show that the conduct was protected and was a substantial and motivating factor in the decision not to renew, and the school board must prove that it would have reached the same decision in the absence of the protected conduct.
United States v. South Carolina (1978)	Use of the National Teachers Examinations both as a requirement for certification and as a factor in salary determination serves a legitimate state purpose and is not unconstitutional despite its disparate racial impact.
Connick v. Myers (1983)	The First Amendment guarantee of freedom of expression does not extend to teachers' public comments on matters of personal interest (as opposed to matters of public concern).
Cleveland Board of Education v. Laudermill (1985)	A teacher dismissed for cause is entitled to an oral or written notice of charges, a statement of the evidence against him or her, and the opportunity to present his or her side prior to termination.
Garland Independent School District v. Texas State Teachers Association (1986)	Teachers can use the interschool mail system and school mailboxes to distribute union material.
Wygant v. Jackson Board of Education (1986)	Absent evidence that the school board has engaged in discrimination or that the preferred employees have been victims of discrimination, school board policies may not give preferential treatment based on race or ethnicity in layoff decisions.
School Board of Nassau County v. Arline (1987)	People suffering from diseases are considered to have a disability, and discrimination against them based solely on fear of contamination is considered unconstitutional discrimination against people with disabilities.

gate. However, this does not mean that teachers or students are free to say or write anything they wish or express themselves through dress or other symbolic expression in anyway they choose. Rather, in reviewing cases involving expression, the courts attempt to balance the rights of the individual against the harm caused to the schools.

In the lead case involving teachers' freedom of expression, Marvin Pickering, a high school teacher, was terminated after writing a letter to the newspaper severely criticizing the superintendent and school board for their handling of school funds. The U.S. Supreme Court (*Pickering v. Board of Education,* 1968) overturned his dismissal and ruled that teachers, as citizens, do have the right to make critical public comments on matters of public concern. The Court further held that unless the public expression undermines the effectiveness of the working relationship between the teacher and the teacher's superior or coworkers, the employee's ability to perform assigned duties, or the orderly operation of the schools, such expression may not furnish grounds for reprisal. Finding that the issue of school board spending is an issue of legitimate public concern, that Pickering's statements were not directed at people he normally worked with, nor that there was any disruption of the operation of the schools (in fact, the letter had been greeted with apathy by everyone but the board), the Supreme Court overturned Pickering's dismissal.

If, however, the public comment is not related to matters of public concern, then it is not protected. The U.S. Supreme Court ruled in *Connick v. Myers* (1983) that free expression is not protected when a public employee "speaks not as a citizen upon matters of public concern, but instead as an employee upon matters only of personal interest" (p. 147). Thus, comments related to political advocacy, general issues of administrative management, instructional methods, or the curriculum have been found to be matters of public concern, whereas comments or complaints related to personnel actions or relations with superiors have been found to be matters of personal concern and are not protected speech.

Even if expression does involve a matter of public concern, it still is not protected if the impact of the expression undermines the effectiveness of working relationships or is disruptive to the normal operation of the schools. For example, the Fourth Circuit upheld the dismissal of a teacher who wrote and circulated a letter to fellow teachers objecting to a delay in receiving summer pay, complaining about budgetary management, and encouraging teachers to stage a "sick-out" during final examination week. The court ruled that any First Amendment interest inherent in the letter was outweighed by the public interest in having public education provided by teachers loyal to that service (i.e., not causing a disruption of exams by a sick-out that was both in violation of district policy and the teachers' contract and represented professionally questionable behavior), and by the employer interest "in having its employees abide by reasonable policies adopted to control sick leave and maintain morale and effective operation of the schools" (*Stroman v. Colleton County School District,* 1992, p. 159).

The exact definition of what constitutes disruptive speech was not defined by the *Pickering* court. However, a subsequent Supreme Court decision held that public employers need not prove that the speech actually caused a material disruption, only that at the time of the penalized speech the employer "reasonably believed" the speech would be disruptive (*Waters v. Churchill,* 1994). The effect of the *Waters* decision, together with *Connick,* has been to make it "more difficult for public employees to succeed in claims that adverse employment actions have impaired their First Amendment expression rights" (Cambron-McCabe et al., 2004, p. 275).

Political Activity. Teachers have the right to engage in political activities and hold public office; however, restrictions may be placed on the exercise of this right. For example, teachers may discuss political issues and candidates in a nonpartisan manner in the classroom and even wear political buttons, badges, or armbands to class. However, they may not make campaign speeches in the classroom or otherwise take advantage of their position of authority over a captive audience to promote their own political views. Political activity in the schools that would cause divisiveness among the faculty or otherwise be disruptive also may be restricted if the school can demonstrate the restriction is necessary to meet the compelling public need to protect efficiency and integrity in the school.

For Your Reflection and Analysis

If you felt strongly that a particular candidate would be in the best interest of your community or state, how would you work for that person's election? Would you consider running for office as an "education candidate" in order to improve education? *To submit your response online, go to http://www. prenhall.com/webb.*

CW

The authority of school boards to restrict teachers' political activities outside the school setting is far less than their authority to restrict activities in the schools. The courts have upheld teachers' rights to support candidates or issues of their choice, display political buttons and stickers, and participate in demonstrations. In addition, the courts generally have upheld the right of teachers to run for and hold public office. However, the courts also have indicated that if the time and activities associated with running for or holding office interfere with the performance of teaching duties, then the teacher may be required to take a leave of absence (but only if such were required for any other time-consuming activity). In addition, the courts have found the holding of certain political offices (e.g., school board member in the employing school district) to present a conflict of interest, and therefore forbid the joint occupancy of both positions.

Teachers have the right to participate in demonstrations.

Right to Associate. The courts have ruled that teachers have the right of free association, and unjustified interference with this right by school boards violates the Fourteenth Amendment. The associational rights of teachers include the right to belong to political organizations, religious or social organizations, and a union or professional association. School district actions that inhibit membership in a controversial organization can only be justified by a compelling state interest. For example, in *Melzer v. Board of Education of the City School District of N. Y.* (2003), the court upheld the school district's decision to terminate a teacher because of his membership and active participation in the North American Man-Boy Love Association, a group that advocates sexual relations between men and boys. The court found that Melzer's membership and participation in the group was potentially disruptive to the school operations and undermined his effectiveness as a teacher because students may not feel comfortable with a teacher who advocates such views.

Although teachers have a right to form or join a union or professional association, whether they have a right to engage in collective bargaining depends on state law. About 40 states have passed laws permitting school boards to engage in collective bargaining with teacher groups. The collective bargaining laws vary widely. Some states require school boards only to "meet and confer" with the teacher organization. Many specify the topics to be negotiated (typically, wages and salary, hours, fringe benefits, and other conditions of employment) and the procedures to be followed if a breakdown in negotiations occurs (Fischer et al., 2003).

Despite the recognition of the right of teachers to organize, the right to strike has not been recognized by the courts and is denied by about half the states. In those states where strikes are allowed, they usually are allowed only after the requirements for impasse resolution have been met and only after the school board has been notified of the intent to strike. When teachers strike in violation of state law or without having met the requirements of the law, the school board may seek an injunction to prohibit the strike. Violation of a court order or an injunction ordering strikers back to work may result in a contempt of court decree and fine or imprisonment. Moreover, those who engage in illegal strikes may be subject to economic sanctions, for example, withholding of salaries/wages, fines, or disciplinary actions, including dismissal (*Hortonville Joint School District No. 1 v. Hortonville Education Association,* 1979).

Academic Freedom. **Academic freedom** is not a constitutional protection in and of itself but is "the desirable end to be achieved by the enforcement of the individual rights and freedom in the classroom as guaranteed by the Bill of Rights" (Alexander &

For Your Reflection and Analysis

Should teachers be denied the right to strike? What would you do if your professional association called for a strike when state law forbids teachers to strike?

To submit your response online, go to http//www. prenhall.com/webb.

CW

Alexander, 2001, p. 708). Academic freedom refers to the teacher's freedom to discuss the subject-matter discipline and to determine the most appropriate instructional methodology. Academic freedom is not without limits. For example, teachers do not have the ultimate right to determine course content or select textbooks—that authority belongs to the school board. The school board may also require that teachers receive prior approval for the use of supplementary materials. Teachers also do not have the right to ignore prescribed content or to refuse to follow the designated scope and sequence of content or materials, even if the refusal is for religious reasons.

Although teachers have limited freedom in determining the content of the curriculum, they have greater freedom in choosing the particular strategies to teach the prescribed content. In reviewing school board attempts to restrict teachers' methodologies, the courts consider a number of factors, including:

> the adequacy of notice that use of specific teaching methodologies will result in disciplinary action, the relevance of the method to the course of study, the support for the strategy or materials by the teaching profession, and the threat of disruption posed by the method. The judiciary also has considered community standards in assessing challenges to various teaching methods. However, if a particular strategy is instructionally relevant and supported by the profession, it will probably survive judicial review even though it might offend some parents. (McCarthy, 1989, p. 260)

In a case in point, a Texas teacher was discharged for failure to obey a school board warning that she refrain from using a role-playing simulation to teach about post–Civil War American history (*Kingsville Independent School District v. Cooper,* 1980). Parents had complained that the simulation aroused strong feelings about racial issues. When the teacher refused to obey the district's directive "not to discuss Blacks in American history," her contract was not renewed. The Fifth Circuit Court of Appeals reinstated the teacher and awarded back pay and attorney's fees, finding that the district violated her constitutional rights by basing the nonrenewal on classroom discussions that were protected by the First Amendment.

If, however, the teacher is discussing, showing, or distributing material that is lewd or not relevant, or using a teaching method that is not supported by the profession, the teacher may be sanctioned. Such was the case when a teacher was dismissed for refusing to stop using a classroom management technique she had developed called "Learnball," which included a sports format, dividing the class into teams, and a system of rewards that included radio playing and shooting foam basketballs in class. The teacher not only continued to use the technique but advocated its use by others and, in connection with this advocacy, publicly criticized the school system. Although the court acknowledged the teacher's First Amendment right to advocate Learnball and to criticize school officials, it ruled that the teacher had "no constitutional right to use Learnball in the classroom" (*Bradley v. Pittsburgh Board of Education,* 1990).

Curriculum Censorship and Book Banning.

Currently, perhaps the most contested academic freedom issue involves attempts to censor the curriculum by excluding certain offerings (e.g., evolution, sex education, values clarification) or materials deemed to be vulgar or offensive or to promote secular humanism. The courts typically have supported school boards in the face of parental attempts to censor the curriculum or ban certain books from the school library (see, e.g., *Monteiro v. Tempe Union High School District,* 1998). However, when it is the school board itself that advocates censorship, judicial support is not as easily won: The courts traditionally have recognized the authority of the school board to determine the curriculum, select texts, purchase library books, approve the use of supplementary materials, and perform a host of other curriculum-related activities. Nonetheless, in a number of instances, the courts have found that specific censorship activities violated the teacher's right to academic freedom or students' First Amendment rights to have access to information. While acknowledging that the banning of books and materials on the basis of obscenity or educational unsuitability is permissible, the courts have held that censorship motivated primarily by the preferences of school board members or to suppress particular viewpoints or controversial ideas contained in a book, or for narrow partisan political or religious purposes, is not permissible.

The controversy regarding who controls instructional and curricular matters—teachers or the school board—is likely to continue, as are parental attempts to exert greater control over the curriculum. Until definitive guidance is provided by the Supreme Court, resolution will continue on a case-by-case basis, attempting to balance the teacher's interest in academic freedom against the school board's interest in promoting an appropriate educational environment.

Rights of Privacy: Employee Searches. As stated in Chapter 11, the Fourth Amendment guarantees persons the right "to be secure in their persons, houses, papers and effects against unreasonable searches and seizures." However, this right applies only to areas where the person has a reasonable expectation of privacy. Applying case law related to other public employees to education, the courts have said that school employees have reasonable expectations of privacy in regard to their lockers, personal effects, and persons. Their expectation of privacy regarding desks, filing cabinets, and storage areas depends on the extent to which these items are shared with or accessed by others. Where an expectation of privacy does exist, the employer may conduct a search only if (1) there is reasonable suspicion that the search will produce evidence of work-related misconduct, and (2) the scope of the search is reasonably related to the objectives of the search and not excessively intrusive in light of the nature of the misconduct (*O'Conner v. Ortega,* 1987). The more personally intrusive the search, the more compelling the circumstances must be to justify the search.

The heightened concerns about substance abuse and school violence have led to an increase in searches of both students and school employees. In recent years, these searches have extended beyond searches of personal belonging to searches of persons, specifically mandatory urinalysis to screen for drugs. Historically employees have successfully challenged such tests as violating their right of privacy and the Fourth Amendment prohibition against searches without an "individualized reasonable suspicion." The only exception to the individualized suspicion standard was where an employee's history or job duties implicate student safety (e.g., driving a school bus) or where employees regularly use hazardous substances or operate potentially dangerous equipment. However, in 1999 the Supreme Court let stand a decision of the Sixth Circuit that allowed mandatory urinalysis of all applicants (including teachers and principals) for positions or transfers in the district (*Knox County Education Association v. Knox County Board of Education,* 1999). The court reasoned that because educators were on the "frontline of school security," and because they occupy so-called safety-sensitive positions [i.e., positions where even a momentary lapse of attention could have serious consequences (*Skinner v. Railroad Labor Executive Association,* 1989)], the policy was justified. Also important to the court's decision was that the testing program was narrowly prescribed and not overly intrusive (it was a one-time test with advance notice), as well as the fact that educators were involved in a "heavily regulated industry," so their expectations of privacy were diminished. Despite the Supreme Court refusal to overturn this action, few districts have followed the lead of Knox County.

Teacher Rights: Freedom From Employment Discrimination and Sexual Harassment

Employment Discrimination. School districts and their employees are prohibited by the Fourteenth Amendment and numerous state and federal statutes from engaging in practices that intentionally discriminate against employees or students on the basis of race, gender, age, religion, national origin, or disability. Most cases alleging employment **discrimination** are brought under Title VII of the Civil Rights Act of 1964 (as amended) or one of the other civil rights statutes detailed in Table 11.1. Title VII covers recruitment, hiring, promotion, and compensation, as well as other terms and conditions of employment. Two types of employment discrimination claims are typically brought under Title VII: **disparate treatment,** which places the burden on the plaintiff to prove that he or she is a member of a group protected by Title VII, was qualified for the position, and was treated less favorably than others by some employment practice or policy; and **disparate impact,** which requires that the plaintiff show that an employment practice or policy had a more severe impact on a protected class than others. If the employer answers the challenge by showing the policy or practice is job related and consistent with a business necessity, the employee can still prevail by showing that the district could have accomplished its goal by less discriminatory means. For example, a female applicant for a high school biology teaching position was successful in a sex discrimination suit in showing that the district's requirement that applicants also have the ability to coach varsity softball had a disparate impact on women (*Civil Rights Division v. Amphitheater Unified School District,* 1983). The court rejected the district's business necessity defense because the district was unable to demonstrate that less discriminatory alternatives had been attempted.

Sexual Harassment. Sexual harassment is considered a form of sex discrimination prohibited under Title VII. According to Title VII, sexual harassment occurs when unwelcome advances or requests for sexual favors are made a condition of being hired, receiving a raise or promotion, or any other benefit of employment (***quid pro quo* harassment**), or where verbal or physical conduct is sufficiently severe or pervasive as to unreasonably interfere with an individual's work performance or to create an intimidating, hostile, or offensive work environment (**hostile environment harassment**).

The courts have traditionally held that under the legal principal of agency employers can be held vicariously liable for the sexual harassment committed by employees. As a result, employers were sometimes held liable in instances in which they neither condoned nor even knew of the acts of the employee. While not abandoning this position, in two cases the Supreme Court said that in cases that involved a supervisor engaging in what heretofore would have been called *quid pro quo* harassment (the court did not like these labels), the employer will still be held strictly liable. But in cases of hostile environment harassment, the employer will not be liable if it can prove (1) it had a sexual policy in place designed to prevent and effectively address allegations of sexual harassment, and (2) the harassed employee did not follow the procedures in the policy to file a complaint or to seek help (*Burlington Industries v. Ellerth,* 1998; *Faragher v. Boca Raton,* 1998).

Equal Opportunity and Affirmative Action

The legal principle of **equal opportunity,** whether equal employment opportunity or equal educational opportunity, is founded in antidiscrimination legislation. Equal opportunity requires that school districts and other agencies develop policies and procedures to ensure that the rights of employees and students are protected, and that they are given equal treatment in employment practices, access to programs, or other educational opportunities.

Affirmative action goes beyond equal opportunity. The principle of affirmative action holds that ensuring nondiscrimination is not enough; what is needed are affirmative steps to admit, recruit, hire, and retain individuals who are underrepresented in the workplace or the classroom. Beginning in the 1960s and 1970s, many school districts adopted affirmative action plans that set forth their intended goals in these areas and their intended actions to achieve diversity in the workplace and classroom and to "remedy the vestiges of past discrimination."

Although achieving diversity is a desirable goal, the U.S. Supreme Court, in *Regents of the University of California v. Bakke* (1978), ruled against the establishment of firm quotas that designate a predetermined number of "slots" only for minorities, resulting in so-called **reverse discrimination,** but said that institutions could use race as one factor to be considered in admissions. Almost 20 years later, the Court seemingly retreated from that position by ruling that universities could not use racial preferences in admissions (*Hopwood v. Texas,* 1996). And, in *Wygant v. Jackson Board of Education* (1986), the U.S. Supreme Court overturned a Michigan school district's collective bargaining agreement that provided for the release of white employees with greater seniority than black employees in order to preserve the percentage of minority teachers employed prior to the layoffs. The Court ruled that affirmative action plans must be designed to remedy location-specific past discrimination, not general societal discrimination. That is, first there must be evidence that remedial action is necessary, and second, the plan must be "narrowly tailored" to remedy the past discrimination (see also *Taxman v. Board of Education of Piscataway*, 1996, retention of an equally qualified black teacher over a white teacher to preserve racial diversity overturned by Third Circuit Court of Appeals).

Although the need for school districts to promote diversity in the ranks of their employees and student bodies has not ended, the courts have increasingly made clear that under the strict judicial review standard any program giving consideration to race, ethnicity, or gender must have a compelling state interest and be "narrowly tailored" to serve that interest. Applying that standard, the First Circuit Court overturned a school district's voluntary desegregation plan that allowed students to attend neighborhood schools and allowed transfers only if the transfer did not increase the racial imbalance at either the sending or the receiving school. The court ruled that although achieving racial and ethnic diversity in school populations was a compelling interest, the student assignment plan was not narrowly tailored to achieve this goal because it made race the decisive factor and ignored individualized consideration of transfer applications (*Comfort v. Lynn School Committee*, 2004).

Legal Responsibilities of Teachers

In addition to the terms and conditions of employment previously discussed, other requirements may be made as a condition of teacher employment as long as they do not violate teacher rights or state or federal law. Some requirements, such as those related to providing reasonable care and maintaining discipline, are discussed later in this chapter. Requirements related to two topics—reporting child abuse and neglect and use of copyrighted materials—are discussed here. These topics have become increasingly important to educators in the last decade.

Reporting Child Abuse and Neglect.   As discussed in Chapter 10, all states have enacted statutes requiring teachers to report actual or suspected child abuse and neglect immediately upon gaining knowledge or suspicion of the abuse or neglect. Most states detail the procedures that are to be followed in making the report. In all states the report may be made orally or in writing to either a law enforcement agency, child protection services, or other designated agency. State reporting statutes apply not only to suspected parental abuse but also to suspected abuse by school employees. Under most state supporting statutes, failure to report abuse may result in the teacher being found criminally liable, with penalties as high as 2 years in jail and a fine of $4,000. A civil suit claiming negligence also may be brought against the teacher for failure to report child abuse. In addition, school districts may take disciplinary measures, including dismissal, against employees for failure to follow required reporting statutes. Because of the serious consequences of failure to report child abuse—to the child, the teacher, and possibly the district (the district could be required to pay monetary damages if liability is found)—most school boards also have adopted policies affirming the responsibility of district employees to report child abuse and detailing the procedures to be followed when abuse is suspected. Such policies are also intended to protect employees against false charges of child abuse.

State statutes that require teachers to report suspected child abuse do not demand that they be absolutely sure that the child has been abused, only that there be "reasonable cause to believe" that the child is subject to abuse or neglect. Teachers and counselors are required to report suspected abuse or neglect even if to do so would violate a confidence. Under all state statutes, school employees who report suspected child abuse or neglect are immune from civil and criminal prosecution if the report was made in good faith. In many states, good faith is presumed and the person challenging the reporter would have to prove that the reporter acted in bad faith.

Observing Copyrights.   Copyright laws are designed to protect the author or originator of an original work from unauthorized or use of the work. Because of their widespread use of print and nonprint material in the classroom, it is important that teachers be knowledgeable about, and comply with, federal copyright laws. Teachers can legally use copyrighted materials under three conditions: (1) they have requested and received permission from the copyright holder to use the work, (2) the work is in the public domain (i.e., it is either more than 75 years old or has been created by a governmental agency), or

(3) it is considered fair use. The **fair use doctrine** allows the nonprofit reproduction and use of certain materials for classroom use without permission of the copyright owner if each copy bears the copyright notice and meets the tests of brevity, spontaneity, and cumulative effect outlined in the guidelines for classroom copying presented in Figure 12.1.

The increasing use of instructional technology has brought to light a number of issues related to use of copyrighted nonprint materials, namely, television programs and videotapes. In 1981, Congress issued *Guidelines for Off-the-Air Recording of Broadcast Programming for Educational Purposes.* The guidelines provide that a nonprofit educational institution may tape broadcast television programs for classroom use if requested by an individual teacher. Programs also may be taped at home by the teacher. All copies must include the copyright notice on the program and cannot be altered in any way. During the first 10 days after taping, the material may be shown once by the individual teacher and may be repeated only once for purposes of instructional reinforcement. Additional use is limited to viewing for evaluating the program for possible purchase. After 45 days, the tape must be erased or destroyed. All other off-the-air recording (except for the purpose of time shifting for personal use) is illegal unless the program is recorded from educational television. These recordings may be shown for a period of 7 days after the broadcast, but must then be erased or destroyed. The taping of television programs telecast by cable or satellite providers does not fall under these guidelines because they are not free to the public. Before taping any programs carried by cable or satellite, the particular station or network should be contacted to determine their taping guidelines.

Generally, teachers cannot duplicate audiovisual materials or convert them from one format to another (e.g., from cassette tape to CD or from 16-mm film to videotape). Use of copyrighted videotapes purchased by the district is, or course, permitted. Other videotapes for which public performance rights in a school setting have been obtained may also be shown if shown as part of a systematic program of instruction and not for entertainment or recreation. Teachers may also make a single copy of a recording of copyrighted music owned by the district or the teacher if the purpose is to construct oral exercises or examinations.

The copying of computer software and material on the Internet and World Wide Web has become a major area of copyright infringement. The high cost of software, combined with limited school budgets, has resulted in numerous cases of unauthorized copying of software. In 1980 the copyright law was amended to include software. According to the amendments, one archival or backup copy can be made of the master program; making multiple copies, even for educational purposes, would be a violation of the fair use principle. However, teachers and school districts can negotiate license agreements with a software company that would allow for multiple use of a particular program at a substantial savings over purchasing multiple copies. Teachers also have the responsibility to make sure students understand copyright restrictions and monitor compliance. Teachers who knowingly allow students to engage in illegal copying could be charged with contributing to copyright infringement. In the use of copyrighted audio, video, or software, as in the use of any copyrighted material, teachers are required to obey both the letter and the spirit of copyright laws and adhere to any relevant school board policies or guidelines.

Materials found on the Internet are also protected by copyright laws. Of particular concern to school districts is illegal file sharing. Any student or school employee who uploads a copy of a copyrighted song, video, or software with the purpose of making it available to others is violating copyright, as is any

Teachers are responsible for ensuring the ethical use of computers.

Figure 12.1 — Guidelines for Classroom Copying of Print Material

1. A single copy may be made of any of the following for your own scholarly research or use in teaching:
   A. A chapter from a book;
   B. An article from a periodical or newspaper;
   C. A short story, short essay, or short poem;
   D. A chart, graph, diagram, drawing, cartoon or picture from a book, periodical, or newspaper.

2. Multiple copies (not to exceed in any event more than one copy per pupil in a course) may be made for classroom use or discussion, provided that each copy includes a notice of copyright and that the following tests are met:
   A. Brevity Test
      (i) Poetry: (a) a complete poem of less than 250 words and if printed on not more than two pages, or (b) from a longer poem, an excerpt of not more than 250 words.
      (ii) Prose: (a) Either a complete article, story, or essay of less than 2,500 words, or (b) an excerpt from any prose work of not more than 1,000 words or 10 percent of the work, whichever is less, but in any event a minimum of 5000 words.
      (iii) Illustration: One chart, graph, diagram, drawing, cartoon or picture per book or per periodical issue.
      (iv) "Special" works in poetry, prose, or in "poetic prose" that combine language with illustrations and are less than 2,500 words in their entirety may not be reproduced in their entirety; however, an excerpt of not more than two of the published pages of such special work and containing not more than 10 percent of the words may be reproduced.
   B. Spontaneity Test
      (i) The copying is at your instance and inspiration, and
      (ii) The inspiration and decision to use the work and the moment of its use for maximum teaching effectiveness are so close in time that it would be unreasonable to expect you would receive a timely reply to a request for permission.
   C. Cumulative Effect Test
      (i) The copying of the material is for only one course in the school in which the copies are made.
      (ii) Not more than one short poem, article, story, essay or two excerpts may be copied from the same author, nor more than three from the same collective work or periodical volume during one class term.
      (iii) There cannot be more than nine instances of multiple copying for one course during one class term.
      [These limitations do not apply to current news periodicals and newspapers and current news sections of other periodicals.]

3. Copying cannot be used to create or to replace or substitute for anthologies, compilations, or collective works.
4. There can be no copying of, or from, "consumable" works (e.g., workbooks, exercises, standardized tests and test booklets and answer sheets).
5. Copying cannot substitute for the purchase of books, publishers' reprints, or periodicals.
6. Copying cannot be directed by a higher authority.
7. You cannot copy the same item from term to term.
8. No charge can be made to the student beyond the actual cost of the photocopying.

Source: Excerpt from *Report of the House Committee on the Judiciary* (House Report No. 94-1476).

person who downloads such a file. School districts have attempted to address the problem of illegal file sharing by adopting policies prohibiting the practice, blocking sites where illegal file sharing is known to take place, and disciplining offenders.

Tort Liability of School District Employees

A **tort** is defined as a civil wrong that leads to injury to another (criminal wrongs are not torts) and for which a court will provide a remedy in the form of an action for damages. To protect both school district employees and school board members against financial loss resulting from a tort suit, many school districts purchase liability insurance. Many educators also participate in liability insurance programs through their professional organizations.

The most common category of torts in education is negligence. Basically, **negligence** can be defined as a failure to do (or not do) what a reasonable and prudent person would have done under the same or similar circumstances, resulting in injury to another. Before an educator can be found guilty of negligence, four elements must be proved:

1. The educator had a duty to provide an appropriate standard of care to another individual (student, coworker, the public).
2. The educator failed in his or her duty to provide the reasonable standard of care.
3. A causal relationship exists between the negligent action and the resultant injury (i.e., the action was the proximate cause of the injury).
4. A physical or mental injury occurred, resulting in actual loss.

Standard of Care and Duty.   Although teachers have the responsibility of providing an appropriate standard of care for their students, the standard of care expected is not the same for all teachers and all students. Teachers of younger children are held to a higher standard of care than are teachers of more mature students. A higher standard of care also is required of teachers of students with physical or mental disabilities, as well as of physical education and vocational and industrial arts teachers because of the inherent dangers in the activities involved.

Reasonableness Doctrine.   In determining whether the educator failed to provide the appropriate standard of care, the courts compare the teacher's actions with those of the hypothetical "reasonable and prudent" teacher—one with average intelligence and physical attributes, normal perception and memory, and possessing the same special knowledge and skills as others with the same training and experience—not some "ideal" or "super" teacher.

Foreseeable Doctrine.   A related element is whether the hypothetical reasonable teacher could have foreseen, and thus prevented, the injury. The actions of the teacher are compared with those of the reasonable teacher to determine negligence.

Proximate Cause.   Even in situations in which the teacher has failed in a recognized duty to provide a reasonable standard of care, liability will not be assessed unless it can be shown that the teacher's action was the **proximate cause** of the injury, that is, that the injury would not have occurred had it not been for the teacher's conduct. In some cases an intervening event, such as the negligent act of a third party, may relieve the teacher of liability. Because each case brings with it a set of circumstances distinct from all others, the determination of proximate cause must be made on a case-by-case basis.

Educational and Professional Malpractice.   Historically, most educational liability litigation has involved student injuries. However, in recent years, a new topic of negligence litigation, **educational malpractice,** has emerged and become the focus of concerned discussion in both the educational and legal communities. As in medical malpractice, the term is concerned with some negligence on the part of the professional. In general, there are two kinds of educational malpractice suits: (1) *instructional malpractice* suits concerned with students who have received certificates or diplomas and have actually failed to learn (see, e.g., *Peter W. v. San Francisco Unified School District,* 1976, a student was awarded a high school diploma even though functionally illiterate) and (2) *professional malpractice* suits involving misdiagnosis, improper educational placement (see, e.g., *Hoffman v. Board of Education of the City of New York,* 1979, a kindergarten student of normal intelligence but with severe speech impediment was placed in class for mentally retarded based on an intelligence test that, in part, requires verbal responses and, although a psychologist recommended retesting in 2 years, the student was not retested for 13 years), or improper advising.

Although there have been a number of instructional malpractice suits, none have been successful in the courts. However, students have been successful in a limited number of cases based on the theory of professional malpractice. These claims differ from educational malpractice claims in that they do not challenge academic or curriculum decisions or educational standards. Rather, they claim that specific individuals have negli-

For Your Reflection and Analysis

What impact does the potential for negligence suits have on you as a prospective or practicing teacher?
To submit your response online, go to http://www. prenhall.com/webb.

CW

gently performed their professional duties. In the first successful suit of its kind in education, *Eisel v. Board of Education of Montgomery County* (1991), two school counselors were found negligent in failing to communicate to a parent a student's suicidal statements made to other students and told to them. The counselors had questioned the student about the statements, but when she denied them, they did nothing further. The court ruled that the counselors had "a duty to use reasonable means to prevent a suicide when they are on notice" of a student's suicidal intent.

In two cases dealing with similar facts but very dissimilar results, the courts addressed the issue of improper advising. In the first case, *Stain v. Cedar Rapids Community School District* (2001), the law related to negligent misrepresentation, which applies to accountants, attorneys, and other professionals who are in the business of supplying information to others who might forseeably rely on it, was extended to the incorrect advice given by a high school counselor. The counselor told a basketball player that a particular English course would be approved by the NCAA toward its core course requirement when, in fact, the course had not been submitted by the school for approval. After graduation, the student was notified by the NCAA that he was one-third of a credit short of what was needed to participate in Division I basketball. As a result, he lost his college scholarship. In finding for the student, the court concluded that it was appropriate to extend the tort of negligent misrepresentation to the duty of a guidance counselor "to use reasonable care in providing specific information to a student when (1) the counselor has knowledge of the specific need for the information and provides the information to the student in the course of a counselor–student relationship, and (2) a student reasonably relies upon the information under circumstances in which the counselor knows or should know of the student's reliance" (*Stain v. Cedar Rapids Community School District*, 2001, p. 125). A different conclusion was reached by the Wisconsin Supreme Court in *Scott v. Savers Property and Casualty Insurance Co.* (2003) when it ruled that the district was not liable when a guidance counselor's faulty advice also resulted in a student losing a college athletic scholarship.

Student Rights and Responsibilities

Traditionally, it was accepted that school officials had considerable authority in controlling student conduct. Operating under the doctrine of ***in loco parentis*** (in place of a parent), school authorities exercised almost unlimited, and usually unchallenged, discretion in restricting the rights of students and in disciplining students. However, beginning in the late 1960s students increasingly challenged the authority and actions of school officials. Subsequent court decisions have broadened the scope of student rights and, at the same time, have attempted to maintain a balance between the rights of students and the rights and responsibilities of school officials (see Figure 12.2 and the Controversial Issue discussion of service learning on p. 321).

Student Discipline

Although the *in loco parentis* doctrine has been weakened in recent years, school officials do have the authority—and in fact the duty—to establish reasonable rules of student conduct designed to protect students and employees, as well as rules necessary to establish and maintain a climate conducive to learning. The authority and responsibility to establish rules of conduct carries with it the authority to discipline students for violations of these rules. The severity of the violation will determine the nature of the discipline and the due process required. Because state compulsory attendance laws give students a property right to attend school, if a disciplinary action involves exclusion from school or the removal of the student from the classroom for even a minimal period of time, some due process is required, even if in the latter instance it is only informally providing the student the opportunity to give his or her side of the story. Moreover, academic sanctions and the withholding of diplomas should only reflect academic performance and should not be used as a form of discipline for nonacademic conduct.

   Suspensions and Expulsions.   Short-term **suspensions** usually are defined as exclusions from school for periods of time of 10 days or less; long-term suspensions and **expulsions** are for periods of time in excess of 10 days. Although a teacher or

For Your Reflection and Analysis

What effect, if any, does the weakening of the doctrine of *in loco parentis* and the apparent expansion of student rights have on the willingness of educators to discipline disobedient or disruptive students?

To submit your response online, go to http://www. prenhall.com/webb.

CW

Figure 12.2 — Balancing the Rights of Students and the Responsibilities of School Officials

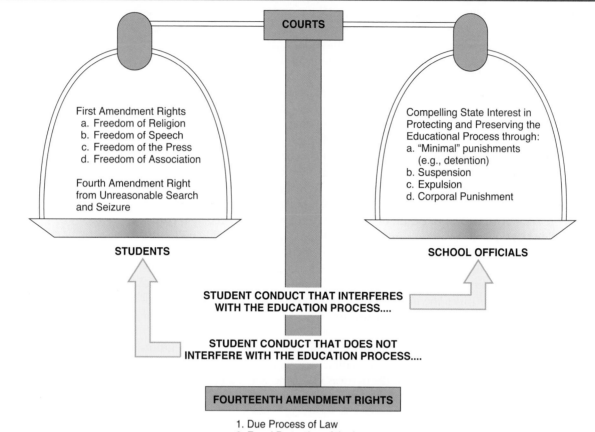

Adapted from *The Schools, the Courts and the Public Interest* by J. C. Hogan. Copyright © 1974, by Lexington Books, an imprint of Macmillan, Inc.

administrator may initiate an expulsion proceeding, normally only the school board can expel the student. Because of the severity of expulsions, state statutes and school board regulations usually detail the grounds for expulsion, as well as the procedures that must be followed. Grounds for expulsion typically include theft or vandalism of school property, possession of weapons (may be mandated by "zero tolerance" policies), possession or use of alcohol or drugs, causing or attempting to cause injury to another, and engaging in any behavior forbidden by law. In addition, the Gun Free Schools Act of 1994 requires any school receiving federal funds to expel for 1 year any student who brings a firearm to school. (This can be mitigated on a case-by-case basis by the local superintendent.)

The procedures that must be followed in an expulsion usually include the right to:

1. A written notice specifying the charges, the time and place of the hearing, and the procedures to be followed at the hearing;
2. Sufficient time between the notice and the hearing to allow the student to prepare a defense;
3. A hearing before an impartial tribunal;
4. A cross-examination of witnesses and a presentation of witnesses and evidence to refute adverse evidence;
5. Representation by legal counsel or other adult;
6. A written statement of the findings/recommendations of the hearing body that demonstrate the decision was based on the evidence presented;
7. A written or taped record of the hearing, if appeal is to be made; and
8. A clear statement of the right to appeal.

CONTROVERSIAL ISSUE

Service Learning

National leaders as well as national organizations have called on all citizens to become, as one initiative is called, "Volunteers in Service to America." The National and Community Service Act, which was passed in 1993, encouraged the schools to become involved in school-based community service/service learning programs. Since that time, numerous schools and school districts have moved to establish voluntary service learning programs, while a number of others have made community service a requirement for high school graduation. Although there is little opposition to the schools establishing volunteer service learning programs, mandatory community service has been the subject of considerable debate.

Arguments For

1. It helps prepare students for responsible citizenship.
2. It reduces students' feeling of alienation and builds self-esteem.
3. It has a positive effect on students' grades, attendance, and motivation.
4. It promotes a feeling of social responsibility and capacity to empathize.
5. It provides students the opportunity to explore career interests or abilities.
6. It provides scarce resources to community service projects and organizations.
7. It promotes community and parent involvement in the school.

Arguments Against

1. It takes students' time away from much-needed academic programs.
2. It exposes the school to unnecessary liability for students' injury or harm.
3. It requires considerable staff resources to administer and monitor the program.
4. It violates the Thirteenth Amendment's prohibition against involuntary servitude.
5. It interferes with parents' right to direct the moral education of their children.
6. In some students it will create resentment and destroy their spirit of volunteerism.

What kinds of community service are appropriate for high school students to perform? What protections should be established to ensure that both students and the district are protected from liability?

 To answer these questions online, go to the *Controversial Issue* module for this chapter of the Companion Website at **http://www.prenhall.com/webb**.

In contrast to the detailed statutory guidelines pertaining to expulsions, in *Goss v. Lopez* (1975), the U.S. Supreme Court ruled that for short-term suspensions of less than 10 days the student need only be given oral or written notice of the charges, an explanation of the evidence, and the opportunity to rebut the charges before an objective decision maker. However, the Court did recognize that there might be situations that would require more detailed procedures, such as situations in which the facts are disputed and not easily resolved, as well as emergency situations in which the safety of persons or property is threatened, where no due process is required prior to disciplinary action. However, even in these situations due process must be followed as soon as possible after the danger of harm has passed. Although *Goss* specified only the basics of due process that must be followed for short-term suspensions, state statutes may, and often do, require additional procedures.

Students may be disciplined for conduct off-campus that has a direct and immediate effect on school discipline or the safety and welfare of students the same as they would for on-campus conduct and are entitled to the same due process protections. However, students are not entitled to due process protections when suspended or expelled from extracurricular activities since students have no property right to participate in those activities.

Special considerations are involved in the suspension or expulsion of children with disabilities. According to the 2004 revisions of the IDEA, disruptive students with disabilities can be suspended or relocated to an "interim alternative educational setting" for up to 10 days while awaiting an expulsion hearing, but they cannot be summarily suspended. Expulsion or long-term suspension is considered a change in placement and cannot take place until the IEP team has undertaken an inquiry to determine if the misconduct is a "manifestation of the disability." If it is found to be a manifestation of the disability, then change-of-placement procedures must be followed before any relocation or expulsion can take place. If it is not a manifestation of the disability, then the student is subject to the same disciplinary actions as students without disabilities.

Corporal Punishment.   As noted in Chapter 11, the U.S. Supreme Court has said that corporal punishment is not prohibited by the Eighth Amendment. However, corporal punishment that is arbitrary, capricious, or unrelated to a reasonable educational purpose may be a violation of the student's right to privacy and personal security, as well as due process rights under the Fourteenth Amendment. In addition, if the punishment is cruel or excessive, a student may have an assault and battery claim, and the administrator or teacher administering the corporal punishment may be found liable under tort law for the injuries sustained. However, punishment administered in a "privileged manner" is not a tort. Punishment is said to be privileged when it serves a reasonable educational purpose and is reasonable in its method and degree of force. The determination of reasonableness includes a consideration of the nature of the infraction; the past record of the student; the age, gender, and physical and mental condition of the student; and the force and instrument employed (Valente & Valente, 2001).

More than half the states prohibit corporal punishment by state law (see Figure 12.3). In a number of others, corporal punishment is prohibited by school board policy. In the states and school districts where corporal punishment is permitted, school board policies

Figure 12.3 — The State of Corporal Punishment

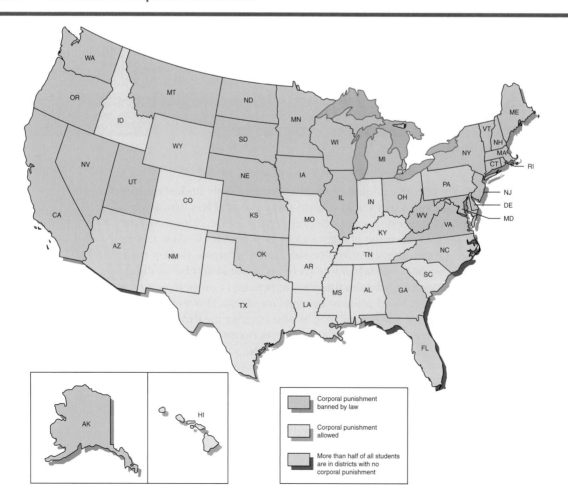

will normally dictate the conditions under which corporal punishment can be administered. Most such policies require that the principal rather than the teacher administer the punishment and that another adult be present.

Search and Seizure

The issues surrounding student search and seizure have increased in recent years, along with the concern about the presence of drugs and weapons in the schools. Historically, the Fourth Amendment protection against unreasonable search and seizure has been interpreted as requiring law enforcement officials to have "probable cause" that a crime has been committed and to obtain a search warrant before conducting a search. Prior to 1985, some courts held school officials to the same standard. However, in *New Jersey v. T.L.O.* (1985), the Supreme Court ruled that school officials' interest in maintaining discipline in the schools was sufficient to justify their being held to a lesser standard than probable cause. Rather, school officials may conduct a warrantless search if it passes the two-pronged "reasonableness test": (1) There is reasonable cause or individualized suspicion that a search of that particular person will reveal evidence of a violation of the law or school rules, and (2) the scope of the search is reasonably related to the objective of the search and is not "excessively intrusive" in light of the age and gender of the child and the nature of the alleged infraction.

The court in *T.L.O.* did not say that an individualized suspicion is an absolute requirement for a reasonable search. Exceptions may exist where the privacy interests are minimal or the object of the search is very serious: Imminent danger may justify an intrusive search based on reasonable suspicion. For example, in *Thompson v. Carthage School District* (1996), the Eighth Circuit Court upheld a search of all male students in grades 6 through 12 based on a report that a weapon was being concealed by a student. The court ruled that the search was minimally intrusive and justified in light of the need to uncover a dangerous weapon. On the other hand, a search of all students in an art class for a pair of allegedly stolen sneakers was not upheld by the court. The court said that deviation from the individualized suspicion requirement is justified only in special circumstances, such as protecting students from weapons or drugs (*DesRoches ex rel. DesRoches v. Caprio,* 1997).

In determining whether a particular search is reasonable, some courts have distinguished between school property (e.g., lockers) and personal property (e.g., a book bag, wallet, or purse) and that individualized suspicion is required to search the locker the same as it would be to search a book bag. These courts have held that although a student may have exclusive use of a locker in regard to other students, since the possession is not exclusive in regard to school officials who retain control of the lockers, the student has a limited expectation of privacy. Other courts have said that students have the same expectation of privacy regarding a locker as they do a wallet or purse. Many schools or school districts minimize the expectation of privacy by notifying students in the student handbook that lockers are subject to inspection.

A number of districts have turned to the use of drug-sniffing dogs in their efforts to combat drugs and violence. The Supreme Court has held that the use of dogs to sniff objects is not a search since it is not a violation of someone's reasonable expectation of privacy. The dogs merely sniff the air surrounding the object, that is, they only explore that which is within "plain smell" (*United States v. Place,* 1983). This holds true in schools as well, but there are limitations. Schools may use dogs to sniff lockers, possessions, and book bags. However, canine searches of students has been more limited, and since the dogs may touch the children and individually sniff them, a greater expectation of privacy is involved. Thus, most schools limit canine searches to unpopulated areas. Some schools employ private companies or local law enforcement with dogs to regularly sniff hallways and parking lots.

Strip searches, because of their intrusive nature, have been prohibited by law in a number of states (California, Iowa, New Jersey, Oregon, Washington, and Wisconsin), and in all areas are carefully scrutinized and most often disallowed by the courts. However, such searches have been allowed if they meet the *T.L.O.* reasonableness standard, particularly in regard to the scope of the search. In a case in point, the Court upheld the partial strip

For Your Reflection and Analysis

What would be examples of student conduct that would constitute "reasonable suspicion" for you to institute a search for drugs?

To submit your response online, go to http://www.prenhall.com/webb.

CW

search of a student suspected of being under the influence of marijuana. The student was "giggling and acting in an unruly fashion" and had dilated pupils and bloodshot eyes. A school nurse conducted a cursory medical assessment of the student as well as a search that required the student to remove his underjersey, shoes, and socks, and empty his pockets. The court held that there was a reasonable basis for the search given the student's behavior and that the search was not excessively intrusive (*Bridgman v. New Trier High School District*, 1997). Pat-down searches are also considered relatively unobtrusive and are also generally upheld by the courts.

Perhaps the most controversial issue in the area of student searches is drug testing of students. Thus far, the courts have invalidated blanket drug testing of the general student population on the basis of the individualized suspicion standard. However, the question of "suspicionless" random drug testing of students who wish to participate in extracurricular activities has yielded mixed conclusions. In *Vernonia School District v. Acton* (1995), the Supreme Court found a school district's policy requiring student athletes to submit to a random urinalysis not unreasonable under the Fourth Amendment. The Court not only agreed with the district's contention that the policy was justified based on its interest in preventing injuries and deterring drug use (some of the athletes were leaders in the drug culture) but also noted that the testing procedure used was no more intrusive than the students' daily undressing in the locker room. A similar conclusion was reached by the U.S. Supreme Court in *Board of Education of Independent School District No. 92 of Pottawatomie County v. Earls* (2002), where drug testing was required of all middle and high school students who participated in "competitive" extracurricular activities. Once again the court found the required urinalysis to be only a negligible intrusion on the student's privacy, a privacy that is limited in the school environment where the school district is responsible for maintaining a safe and orderly environment. Also important to the court's decision was the fact that the results were not turned over to law enforcement or used to discipline the students.

In a case not involving athletics or "competitive" extracurricular activities, a different conclusion was reached by the Colorado Supreme Court. The court blocked the mandatory drug testing of members of a school marching band (*Trinidad School District No. 1 v. Lopez*, 1998) based, in part, on the court's holding that these students have a higher expectation of privacy than student athletes.

The *Vernonia* "special needs" argument has been used in subsequent decisions to support random searches with metal detectors. Table 12.2 lists some Supreme Court decisions affecting students' rights.

Freedom of Expression

The First Amendment protects all forms of expression, not only verbal communication, but written and symbolic communication (e.g., dance, art, dress) as well. In 1965, several students in Des Moines, Iowa, were suspended after wearing black armbands to school to protest the Vietnam War. The wearing of armbands was prohibited by a school district policy that had been adopted to prevent possible disturbances after it was learned that students planned to wear the armbands. The suspended students filed suit, and the decision by the Supreme Court (*Tinker v. Des Moines*, 1969) has become a landmark case, not only in student expression but also in the broader area of student rights. In finding for the students, the Court said that students have the freedom to express their views by speech or other forms of expression, so long as the exercise of this freedom does not cause "material disruption," "substantial disorder," or invade the rights of others. According to the Court:

> In order for the State in the person of school officials to justify prohibition of a particular expression of opinion, it must be able to show that its action was caused by something more than a mere desire to avoid the discomfort and unpleasantness that always accompany an unpopular viewpoint . . . undifferentiated fear or apprehension of disturbance is not enough to overcome the right to freedom of expression. (pp. 508–509)

The "material and substantive disruption" standard articulated in *Tinker* has been applied to the numerous student expression cases that have followed. Subsequent rulings

Table 12.2 — Selected U.S. Supreme Court Cases Affecting Students' Rights

Case	Decision
Tinker v. Des Moines (1969)	School officials cannot limit students' rights to free expression unless there is evidence of a material disruption or substantial disorder.
Goss v. Lopez (1975)	For suspensions of less than 10 days, the student must be given an oral or written notice of charges, an explanation of the evidence against him or her, and the opportunity to rebut the charges before an objective decision maker.
Wood v. Strickland (1975)	Students may sue school board members for monetary damages under the Civil Rights Act of 1871.
Ingraham v. Wright (1977)	Corporal punishment does not constitute cruel and unusual punishment under the Eighth Amendment and does not require due process prior to administration.
Board of Education, Island Trees Union Free School District v. Pico (1982)	Censorship by the school board acting in a narrowly partisan or political manner violates the First Amendment rights of students.
Bethel School District v. Fraser (1986)	School boards have the authority to determine what speech is inappropriate and need not tolerate speech that is lewd or offensive.
New Jersey v. T.L.O. (1985)	School officials are not required to obtain a search warrant or show probable cause to search a student, only reasonable suspicion that the search will turn up evidence of a violation of law or school rules.
Hazelwood School District v. Kuhlmeier (1988)	School officials may limit school-sponsored student speech as long as their actions are related to a legitimate pedagogical concern.
Honig v. Doe (1988)	Disruptive students with disabilities may be expelled but must be kept in their current placement until an official hearing is held.
Franklin v. Gwinnett (1992)	The sexual harassment of a student may be a violation of Title IX for which monetary damages can be sought.
Vernonia School District v. Acton (1995)	Special needs can justify "suspicionless" random searching of students.
Board of Education of Independent School District No. 92 v. Earls (2002)	Drug testing of students in extracurricular activities does not violate the Fourth Amendment's prohibition against unreasonable searches.

have clarified that although the fear of disruption must be based on fact, not intuition, school officials need not wait until a disruption has occurred to take action. If they possess sufficient evidence on which to base a "reasonable forecast" of disruption, action to restrict student expression is justified.

Freedom of expression does not include the right to use vulgar and offensive speech, even if it does not cause disruption. At a high school assembly, Matthew Fraser nominated a classmate for a student council office using what the Court described as "an elaborate, graphic, and explicit sexual metaphor." Fraser was suspended for 2 days. Lower courts found his suspension to be a violation of his right to free speech and that his speech was not disruptive under the *Tinker* guidelines. The Supreme Court, however, went beyond *Tinker*'s concern with the effect of the student's speech to the content of the speech, and concluded that the school board has the authority to prohibit vulgar or offensive speech or conduct that is inconsistent with the educational mission of the school. In fact, the court said that schools must teach by example the "shared values of a civilized social order" (*Bethel School District No. 403 v. Fraser,* 1986).

Student Publications.   Although students have the right to free expression and the right to publish and distribute literature published both on and off campus, school officials can enact time, place, and manner restrictions to ensure that the student expression or distribution of student publications does not interfere with the learning environment or endanger the safety of students and employees. However, the restrictions must be reasonable, must not treat speech differently based on viewpoint, and must be consistently applied to all expression. In cases in which school policies require faculty or administrative approval prior to publication, censorship is justified only if the material is libelous,

Student publications may be censored for legitimate educational concerns.

obscene, or likely to cause material and substantial disruption. In addition, the procedures and standards for review must be clearly articulated. Unpopular or controversial content, or content critical of school officials, has been considered insufficient justification for restricting student expression. This standard was applied to school-sponsored as well as to non-sponsored publications.

In a 1988 case, however, the U.S. Supreme Court awarded significant discretion to school authorities in censoring school-sponsored publications. In this case, *Hazelwood School District v. Kuhlmeier,* a school principal deleted two articles from a school newspaper. According to the principal, he was not concerned with the content of the articles, but felt that they were not well written by journalistic standards (e.g., did not maintain the anonymity of pregnant students or give a father a chance to defend himself against condemning remarks made by a student relative to the impact of divorce on students). Believing that there was not enough time before the publication deadline to make the needed changes in the articles, he deleted the two articles.

The Supreme Court decision in the case said that school officials "do not offend the First Amendment by exercising editorial control over the style and content of student speech in school-sponsored expressive activities so long as their actions are reasonably related to legitimate pedagogical concerns." Thus, the Court made a distinction between personal expressions by students and those activities that students, parents, and the public might reasonably assume bear the "imprimatur of the school." In the latter category, the Court included not only school-sponsored publications but "theatrical productions and other expressive activities." The effect of the *Hazelwood* decision has been to allow school officials greater discretion in determining what is inappropriate student speech and expression. When read together, the *Tinker, Bethel,* and *Hazelwood* decisions present three principles for assessing the First Amendment rights of students:

> First, vulgar or plainly offensive speech (Fraser-type speech) may be prohibited without a showing of disruption or substantial interference with the school's work. Second, school sponsored speech (*Hazelwood*-type speech) may be restricted when the limitation is reasonably related to legitimate educational concerns. Third, (personal) speech that is neither vulgar nor school-sponsored (*Tinker*-type speech) may only be prohibited if it causes a substantial and material disruption of the school's operation. (*Pyle v. South Hadley School Community,* 1994, p. 166)

These principles apply not only to print publications but to expression on school-sponsored websites.

Student Appearance.   Thus far the U.S. Supreme Court has refused to accept a case that deals directly with student appearance and the circuit courts are split as to whether dress is considered a form of expressive activity. In those jurisdictions where dress is considered protected speech, the courts will not uphold appearance regulations unless the district can show a compelling interest in having such a regulation, such as the disruptive effects of the appearance on the educational process or for health and safety reasons. For example, in *Botoff v. Van Wert City Board of Education* (2000), the court agreed that the school could prohibit a student from wearing a Marilyn Manson t-shirt it considered offensive based on the band's promotion of values contrary to the school's educational mission. But in *Doe v. Brockton School Committee* (2000) the court ruled in favor of a student's cross-dressing because the school did not show any disruption.

In jurisdictions where dress is not considered protected speech, it can be restricted for legitimate reasons. For example, schools have been successful in prohibiting dirty, scant, or revealing clothing; excessively tight skirts or pants; baggy pants; clothing displaying obscene pictures, sexually provocative slogans, or vulgar and offensive language;

For Your Reflection and Analysis

Did the elementary and secondary schools you attended have dress codes or regulations regulating student appearance? How did you respond to them at the time? Do you feel they served any educational purpose?

To submit your response online, go to http://www.prenhall.com/webb.

CW

loose clothing in shop areas; or other dress deemed inconsistent with the mission of the school.

Gang-related Apparel.   The response of many schools to the increase of gang-related activity on campus has been to enact dress codes that seek to restrict the wearing of clothing, jewelry, or other symbols reputed to be associated with gang membership. The response of the courts to challenges to these dress codes is to say that schools may prohibit students from wearing specific clothing or other symbols of gang membership if it can be shown that a gang problem exists and that, in fact, a relationship exists between the particular item(s) prohibited and the public policy goal of curbing gang activity on campus. However, if no gang problem exists or if a relationship between the items and gang activity cannot be established, then the school district policy will not be upheld. The dress code of one California school district prohibited the wearing of clothing identifying any college or professional sports teams. However, testimony showed that gang members were, in fact, wearing Pendleton shirts; Nike shoes; white T-shirts; and baggy, dickie, or black pants; that there was negligible gang activity at the middle school; and no gang activity at the elementary level. Absent a rational relationship between the dress code and the activity it aimed to curtail, the dress code was not upheld (*Jeglin v. San Jacinto Unified School District*, 1993).

Student dress codes also will not be upheld if they do not provide sufficient clarity so that students know what expression is prohibited. In *Stephenson v. Davenport Community School District* (1997), a student, under threat of expulsion, underwent laser surgery to remove a tattoo of a cross from between her thumb and index finger. She later sued for damages because the procedure left a scar. The court ruled in her favor and held that the school district's policy which prohibited "gang-related activities such as display of colors, symbols, signals, signs, etc." was too vague to put the student on notice that the tattoo would fall within the scope of the policy. (See also *Chalifoux v. New Caney Independent School District*, 1999, school district policy too vague as to prohibit wearing of rosary beads as "gang-related apparel.")

School Uniforms.   School uniforms are seen as one way to reduce gang activity and school violence. They are also thought to improve discipline, academic performance, and self-esteem, while reducing social stratification and overall clothing costs (Lumsden, 2001). As a result, a growing number of schools and school districts have adopted mandatory school uniform policies. In several of these school districts, students have challenged the policies, alleging a violation of their First Amendment rights to self-expression. Also alleged in some cases is a violation of the right of free exercise of religion. To date, the courts have been unanimous in holding that uniform policies do not violate the First Amendment speech rights of students, that the policies are content neutral in regard to religion, and that the policies furthered a compelling state interest. Important to the court's decision in these cases is that the policy contained an "opt-out" provision whereby students, with parental permission, could request an exemption from the requirement.

Sexual Harassment of Students

As noted in Chapter 10, as many as 80% of the students in the public schools have been victims of some form of sexual harassment. As with employees, students can be victims of *quid pro quo* harassment if the condition of some benefit is on the granting of sexual favors. More often, however, students are the victims of hostile environment harassment. In *Franklin v. Gwinnett* (1992), which involved the sexual harassment of a student by a teacher, the Supreme Court recognized that sexual harassment, if sufficiently severe, persistent, or pervasive, can create a hostile environment for the victim that limits the student's ability to benefit from, or participate in, an educational program or activity in violation of Title IX. Sexual harassment is not limited to harassment of a member of one gender or a member of the opposite gender. The harassed and the victim can be of the same gender. Sexual harassment based on sexual orientation may also be a violation of Title IX if it is sufficiently serious to limit a gay or lesbian student's ability to participate in or benefit from the school program. Under Title IX a student victim of sexual harassment can sue for damages. However, the Supreme Court has ruled that the school district is

For Your Reflection and Analysis

As a K–12 student, were you ever sexually harassed by a peer? How did it make you feel? Did a teacher or other school officer take any action?
To submit your response online, go to http://www.prenhall.com/webb.

CW

liable for damages only if a school official with authority to address the harassment and take corrective action had actual knowledge of the harassment and was deliberately indifferent to it (*Gebster v. Lago Vista Independent School District*, 1998).

The overwhelming majority of the student sexual harassment that occurs in the schools is student-to-student sexual harassment. The Supreme Court addressed this issue in its 1999 decision in *Davis v. Monroe.* Applying the "deliberate indifference" standard of *Gebster,* the court ruled that schools may be liable for student-to-student sexual harassment that "is so severe, pervasive, and objectively offensive, and that so undermines and distracts from the victims' educational experience, that the victims are effectively denied equal access to an institution's resources and opportunities" (p. 1664) and to which the school responded with deliberate indifference. The court in *Davis* did recognize that not all unwelcome physical harassment nor all offensive comments are sexual, and that students often engage in "insults, banter, teasing, shoving, pushing, and gender specific conduct that is upsetting to the students subjected to it" but which do not rise to the level of conduct to impose liability. Guidance in determining what sexual harassment is, and what it is not, are provided by the U.S. Department of Education in its 1997 guidelines, *Sexual Harassment Guidance: Harassment of Students by School Employees, Other Students, or Third Parties.*

Student Records and Privacy

For every student who attends the public schools, various records are kept by school authorities. Questions about the contents of these records, and who has access to them, are addressed by a federal statute, the Family Educational Rights and Privacy Act (FERPA) of 1974. FERPA provides protection to parents and students against unauthorized access to students' educational records while guaranteeing their right to access. FERPA requires that school districts establish procedures for providing parents, guardians, and eligible students (over age 18 years) access to student records. Such procedures are to identify staff members with access to the records and to include a log of those who access the records. The act also stipulates that personally identifiable information from the records is not to be released without written permission from the parent or eligible student. However, FERPA does allow personally identifiable information to be released without permission to the following persons or under the following circumstances: (1) parents of a dependent student or educators or officials in the school district who have a legitimate educational interest; (2) officials of a school in which the student is enrolling; (3) persons who have obtained a court order; (4) persons for whom the information is necessary to protect the health or safety of the student or other individuals in case of an emer-

PROFESSIONAL REFLECTION

Teachers should have complete academic freedom, as long as they are good teachers and as long as they constantly assess student learning. There are always 10 ways to teach to meet a standard, but how do you know through the method of instruction that you have student success? Feeding sentences to fourth graders when they are learning about Newton's laws of motion and expecting them to understand is like giving them a piece of candy right before lunch and telling them not to eat it. It doesn't happen. But having them do several experiments that bring them around to seeing the terms *force, inertia, mass, acceleration, equal,* and *opposite* will then allow students to make the necessary connections between knowledge and thinking about what they have learned. The next step is easy. Relating concepts to their world—once students are already thinking—can be as simple as designing a poster project finding examples of the laws of motion in the sports section of the paper. Academic freedom of curriculum is not a good idea, but academic freedom of instruction for teachers is the one and only way to get to the bottom line—student success is not negotiable.

Teri Cosentino
National Board Certified
Teacher, New Jersey

To analyze this reflection, go to the *Professional Reflection* module for this chapter of the Companion Website at **http://www.prenhall.com/webb.**

gency; (5) in connection with financial aid for which the student has applied; (6) accrediting organizations in order to carry out their accrediting function; or (7) to state and federal agencies for research or statistical purposes. When students reach 18 years of age or enroll in a postsecondary institution, they must be allowed to see the record if they so desire.

Although the FERPA guarantees parents and eligible students access to records, this does not mean that records must be produced anytime or anywhere on demand. School officials can adopt rules that specify reasonable time, place, and notice requirements for reviewing. Neither does this law give parents the right to review the personal notes of teachers and administrators if these records are in their sole possession and not shared with anyone except a substitute teacher.

After reviewing the record, if the parents or the eligible student believes that information contained in the record is inaccurate, misleading, or in violation of the rights of the student, the parents or student can request that the information be amended. If school officials refuse, the parents or eligible student must be advised of the student's right to a hearing. If the hearing officer also agrees that the record should not be amended, the parents or student is entitled to place a statement of explanation or objection in the record.

> **For Your Reflection and Analysis**
>
> What kind of information would you record in your personal notes that you would not record in a student's official record?
>
> *To submit your response online, go to http://www.prenhall.com/webb.*
>
> CW

Summary

The educational process takes place in an environment in which the rights of teachers and students are constantly being balanced against the rights and responsibilities of school officials to maintain a safe and orderly environment conducive to learning. Although the rights of both teachers and students have been greatly expanded in the past quarter century, they do not include the right to say, publish, or teach whatever they feel or believe. The courts continue to uphold the rights and responsibilities of school districts to limit teacher conduct that has a negative impact on performance in the classroom, that is unrelated to the course of study, or that is materially or substantially disruptive. Teachers also have the responsibility to comply with various statutory requirements related to terms of employment, copyright, and so on, and to provide a reasonable standard of care for their students. When they do not comply with these statutory requirements or when they breach the standard of care, they can be subjected to a variety of disciplinary actions both within and outside the school system. Although every situation is unique, certain legal principles have been established that can provide direction in many situations. It is imperative that teachers not only be knowledgeable about these principles, many of which are broadly discussed in this chapter, but that they become familiar with applicable laws and school board policy in their state and district.

In the next chapter, we will discuss a topic that sometimes is not given sufficient attention in teacher preparation programs—the governance structure of the public schools. Yet, as you will see, the way schools are organized, administered, and financed has a vital impact on the teacher and the educational program.

Key Terms

Academic freedom, 311
Affirmative action, 314
Discrimination, 313
Disparate impact, 313
Disparate treatment, 313
Educational malpractice, 318
Equal opportunity, 314
Expulsion, 319
Fair use doctrine, 316

Hostile environment
    harassment, 314
Immorality, 306
In loco parentis, 319
Incompetence, 307
Insubordination, 307
Liberty interest, 308
Negligence, 318

Procedural due process, 308
Property right, 305
Proximate cause, 318
Quid pro quo harassment, 314
Reverse discrimination, 314
Suspension, 319
Tenure, 304
Tort, 317

PROFESSIONAL DEVELOPMENT WORKSHOP

Prepare for the Praxis™ Examination

Mrs. Angelina Jimenez is a sixth-grade teacher at Hiawatha Elementary School. It is the first week of the school year. After giving a writing assignment, she walks around the room. The children are bent over their desks busily writing "What I Did on My Summer Vacation." Stopping at Tommy Rhodes's desk, she notices deep scratch marks on his neck. When asked how he got the marks, Tommy says his cat scratched him. After school, however, Marty Robinson, who was sitting near Tommy when Mrs. Jimenez asked the question and heard Tommy's reply, comes to her and volunteers that "Tommy has marks all over his back. I saw them during gym."

The next day Mrs. Jimenez asks Tommy about the marks and also asks him if he has any marks on his back and if she can see them. Tommy continues to say that the marks came from his cat, but refuses to let Mrs. Jimenez see his back.

Mrs. Jimenez worried about this all weekend and tried to call Juanita Ruiz, the school principal, at home but was not able to reach her. She arrived at school 30 minutes earlier than usual hoping to meet with Mrs. Ruiz before her first class began. She was relieved to find Mrs. Ruiz already at her desk busily returning telephone calls from last Friday. Mrs. Jimenez briefly shared her concerns about Tommy and asked Mrs. Ruiz's guidance relative to whether she should report the scratch marks as suspected abuse. Mrs. Ruiz told Mrs. Jimenez that she made the right decision to come in and discuss the matter. She complimented Mrs. Jimenez about taking the appropriate steps relative to this potential serious matter.

Mrs. Jimenez got right to the point. She said, "I am truly worried about Tommy but at the same time I must admit I am worried about the fallout that may follow if I do report suspected child abuse. What if I am wrong? Can I be sued? Having never been confronted with such an issue, I have no idea what comes next. Over the weekend I surfed the Internet and came across a legal case that literally brought on an anxiety attack. I learned that in one state, after a thorough review of the alleged possible abuse, which by the way was dismissed, the superintendent of a particular school district actually sent the parents a letter which included the name of the teacher who reported the alleged abuse. I have not slept since Friday just worrying about this whole matter."

Mrs. Ruiz interrupted Mrs. Jimenez by responding, "Hold on—you are putting the cart before the horse. Let's take this issue and break it down into some manageable parts. First of all each state has passed legislation relative to protecting the confidentiality of those who report allegations of child abuse. We are fortunate to live in a state that has passed a statute that clearly protects the confidentiality of the individual(s) who make the report. Second, before you leave my office, I will arrange for you, Joan Shephard, our school nurse, and I to meet with Tommy and assess the scratch marks and see if they really do look like cat scratch marks; maybe he does have a very mean cat at home who jumped on his back. Then we will decide on whether to make a report of child abuse. But remember, when in doubt, it is always better to err on the side of protecting the student."

1. What are some of the visible signs of child abuse or neglect?
2. What are the teacher's responsibilities regarding the reporting of child abuse or neglect?
3. Enumerate some of the consequences of failing to report suspicion of child abuse.

To submit your response online, go to the *Prepare for the Praxis™ Examination* module for this chapter of the Companion Website at **http://www.prenhall.com/webb.**

Build Your Knowledge Base

1. What limits can be placed on teachers expressing themselves on political issues in the classroom? Outside the classroom?
2. Describe the "reasonable teacher" guideline as it relates to tort liability.

3. What should be the role of the schools in confronting the AIDS epidemic?
4. To what extent should teachers, administrators, and school board members be held liable for the education, or lack of education, received by the students under their control?
5. What are the statutory requirements in your state regarding student expulsions? Student suspensions?
6. How does the doctrine of *in loco parentis* serve to give students expectations about the care given them in the schools? How does the doctrine serve to define the teacher's right to control and supervise students?

Develop Your Portfolio

1. One of the important responsibilities of the teaching profession is to understand teacher rights and obligations under the law. Select one of the following issues relative to teacher rights and responsibilities: (1) conditions of employment; (2) teacher dismissal; (3) teacher rights inside and outside the classroom; (4) tort liability; and (5) discrimination, equal opportunity, and affirmative action. After researching a particular right and responsibility, prepare a reflection paper that summarizes your thinking about the legal protections and risks associated with being a teacher. Place your reflection paper in your portfolio under **INTASC Standard 9, Reflective Practice and Professional Growth.**
2. Review the U.S. Supreme Court cases affecting students' rights as shown in Table 12.2 on page 325. With the assistance of the Internet resources at the Companion Website, select one of the more controversial issues related to students' rights (e.g. freedom of expression, student appearance as symbolic speech, search and seizure). Prepare a reflection paper that summarizes your views relative to the legal decisions pertaining to certain students' rights. Place your reflection paper in your portfolio under **INTASC Standard 9, Reflective Practice and Professional Growth.**

To complete these activities online, go to the *Develop Your Portfolio* module for this chapter of the Companion Website at **http://www.prenhall.com/webb.**

Explore Teaching and Learning: Field Experiences

1. Contact the central office of a local school district to determine the due process procedures for dismissing school personnel. What specific steps are required to dismiss a teacher?
2. Contact the state department of education or its website to secure information about alternative routes to licensure for teachers in the K–12 public schools. How do these requirements differ from regular certification requirements in your state? In your opinion, what are the advantages and disadvantages of a state providing alternative routes to securing a license to teach, or a student using an alternative route?

Professional Development Online

Visit this text's Companion Website at **http://www.prenhall.com/webb** to gain access to a variety of questions, activities, and exercises to help build your knowledge of this chapter's content. Below are just a few items available at this text's Companion Website:

- Classroom Video—To see actual classroom footage and work through activities and questions to analyze the content of the video, click on the *Classroom Video* module for this chapter.
- Teaching Tolerance—To go to this organization's website and complete activities to explore issues and topics dealing with how to teach tolerance to students, click on the *Teaching Tolerance* module for this chapter.
- Self-Test—To review terms and concepts presented in this chapter, click on the *Self-Test* module for this chapter.
- Internet Resources—To link to websites related to topics in this chapter, go to the *Internet Resources* module for this chapter.

CHAPTER 13

We may have reached the time when the public will not grant us more money for public instruction unless we can show greater efficiency in spending the dollars which have already been voted for school use.
—NASSP Fifth Yearbook, 1921

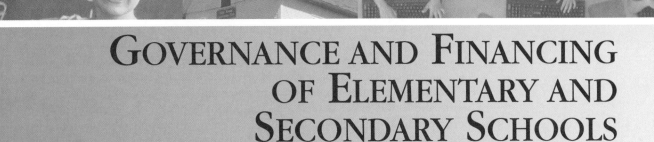

GOVERNANCE AND FINANCING OF ELEMENTARY AND SECONDARY SCHOOLS

A school board election is scheduled in a few months in the school district in which Mr. Rodriguez lives and works as a teacher; he has spent his entire life in the school district. At a parent–teacher meeting at the school, a parent asks about the functions and desirable qualities of school board members in the community. As a senior teacher in the district, Mr. Rodriguez is asked to be a panelist at a public forum on school board selection. His assignment is to indicate why he decided to work in the district, what he thinks are some needs of the district, and what he thinks would be desirable qualities of school board members.

What level of education should be required of school board members? How active should teachers be in school board elections? Should the teachers' association endorse specific candidates? What are some possible implications of teachers endorsing candidates for the school board? What information does Mr. Rodriguez need about the district to prepare for the meeting?

After 85 years, the quotation from the previous page may be even more relevant for the first quarter of the 21st century than the first quarter of the 20th century. Throughout your career as an educator you will be asked to justify educational funding and to explain how schools are governed and funds are expended. Because education is the nation's largest industry consuming a large public expenditure, a high level of public interest is to be expected and justified.

In the following overview of the governance and financing structure for public elementary and secondary education in the United States, initial attention is given to the overall governance structure of public education. This is followed by a discussion of state school finance programs and revenues for the support of schools. The chapter concludes with a discussion of private education and current issues related to the governance and financing of public schools. After reading the chapter, you should be able to:

- Describe the roles of the school board and the superintendent of schools.
- Determine the number and different types of school districts in your state.
- Discuss the impact that site-based management decision making might have on the roles and responsibilities of the classroom teacher.
- Discuss the growth of charter schools and the possible impact on public schools.
- Differentiate between the responsibilities of the state board of education and that of the chief state school officer.
- Describe the three public policy goals of school finance programs.
- Compare the major types of the state school finance programs.
- Identify the major local, state, and federal revenue sources.
- Discuss the role of private education in America.
- Discuss the changing role of the federal government in financing elementary and secondary education.
- Identify ways in which the accountability and student assessment movements will affect the classroom teacher, building principal, schools, and school boards.

The Context of the Public Schools

The complexity of the educational enterprise in the United States is awesome: One person in five either attends or is employed in the nation's public elementary and secondary schools. Consistent with the checks and balances inherent in the American governmental system, the governance system for public elementary and secondary education also has its checks and balances. Public elementary and secondary education has been referred to as a state responsibility, a local function, and a federal concern. Among the nations of the world, the United States is unique in the emphasis placed on decentralization and local participation in the conduct of public elementary and secondary education.

As noted in Chapter 11, even though education is not referred to in the federal Constitution, an education clause can be found in each state constitution. Within the guidelines of the constitution, each state establishes the governance system for its schools, provides for the funding of the schools, and establishes various minimum standards for school operation. While no two states have exactly the same organizational structure, finance system, or educational tax support system, in many ways state provisions for education are similar. For example, the grade structure of kindergarten through grade 12 is found in all states. Statutes and regulations for teacher licenses also do not vary greatly among the states; usually, only limited additional study is required to receive a license in another state. Textbooks are published for a national market, creating a commonality in academic content among the states. National curriculum standards provide another example of the similarities, rather than the differences, in public elementary and secondary schools among the states.

Organization for Education

Rather than a single monolithic system of schools resembling a large corporation, the American education system operates through 50 separate state educational agencies with instruction being provided by more than 15,200 school districts in about 90,000 schools staffed by 3.0 million teachers (National Education Association [NEA], 2005a).

Policies for the operation of the schools are set by governors, state legislatures, state boards of education, and local school boards. Governors and legislators not only face the public policy challenge of determining the funding system for the schools but also are expected to provide adequate and equitable financing for this system of schools.

Elementary and secondary education is the largest single item in the budgets of many state and local governments. In the 2004–05 school year, total expenditures for public elementary and secondary schools reached almost $500 billion. Although funds come from a combination of local, state, and federal sources, the majority of the money comes from state and local taxes. Federal funding is targeted for special programs or conditions and provided about 8.8% of the expenditures for public elementary and secondary schools in 2004–05. Figure 13.1 shows the national average of funding sources for education from each of the three levels of government.

Unlike governmental functions such as national defense, interstate commerce, and international relations, which have a heavy federal orientation, the governmental structure for the public schools has evolved as a combination of state and local powers and responsibilities. Rather than being the source of centralized educational policies and decisions about the operation of public elementary and secondary schools, the federal government has had a very limited role, primarily concerned with funding for the educational needs of special populations, national re-

Figure 13.1 — Sources of Funds for Public Elementary and Secondary Schools, 2004–05.

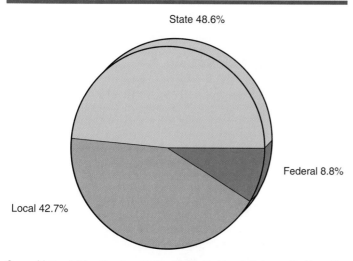

State 48.6%
Federal 8.8%
Local 42.7%

Source: National Education Association. (2005). *Rankings & Estimates: Rankings of the States 2004 and Estimates of School Statistics 2005.*

search priorities, and data gathering and reporting. However, the federal role appears to be changing, as illustrated by the mandated assessment and reporting requirements of the No Child Left Behind Act.

Education at the Local Level

Public education in the United States is a highly decentralized endeavor. States have provided for the creation of local school districts that are responsible for the actual operation of schools. The sole purpose of the school district is to operate elementary and secondary schools. Even though state and federal requirements exist, school districts and individual schools have great freedom in organizing their programs and the teaching/learning environment. The primary functions of local school districts are as follows:

- Adopt policies and regulations for the operation of schools.
- Within the context of state guidelines, adopt the curriculum for the schools.
- Serve as links between community patrons and the schools and provide periodic reports about the schools.
- Provide the human and material resources needed to operate schools.
- Take the necessary steps to provide and maintain adequate facilities for instruction.
- Provide the state department of education and other agencies with required information about the schools.

School Boards.   The governing body for the operation of a school district is the **school board.** State statutes provide for the selection of lay citizens to serve on school boards. The role of lay citizens in the governance of public education through a system of local school boards is a unique feature of the American educational system. In principle, school boards represent all the people; members are chosen as stewards with a public trust.

School boards can be either appointed or elected. In most cases, there are no educational requirements for school board membership. Members come from all walks of life. The only prerequisite may be that the board member be a resident of the school district.

The primary function of the school board is to set the **policies** under which the schools will operate. Before making decisions, the board has a responsibility to consider the beliefs, values, and traditions of the community. However, boards typically rely on the counsel and recommendations of the superintendent. As they serve, board members must function as a group, for they have power and authority only when the board is in session.

Other functions of the school board include budget adoption, approval of expenditures, approval of the schools' organizational pattern, employment of personnel, and issuance of contracts. These legal functions are in addition to the role of the school board in informing the community. Community support is especially critical because of the role of the local property tax in financing schools in many states and the importance of maintaining a strong base of citizen support for the public schools. The typical administrative organization of a school district is illustrated in Figure 13.2.

Superintendent of Schools.   Each school district has a chief administrator, usually referred to as the **superintendent of schools.** As the role and responsibilities of the superintendent have evolved, the job has become that of a chief executive officer of the school district. Typically, the educational program and related responsibilities of the superintendent include planning, staffing, coordinating, budgeting, administering, evaluating, and reporting. Basically, the superintendent's primary responsibility is to work with the school board and the school district's staff to improve educational programs in the district. In many ways the school board functions like the board of directors of a corporation while the superintendent of schools, the counterpart of the chief executive officer of the corporation, is responsible for the day-to-day operation of the enterprise, the schools.

In contrast to an earlier time when the superintendent on occasion was a part-time teacher, today's superintendent has a full-time position and may view the job as a career. School superintendents typically come from the ranks of teachers. Specialized training in educational administration beyond the master's degree is typically required for licensing or certification. Among large school districts, there appears to be some interest in persons

For Your Reflection and Analysis

What should be the qualifications of school board members?
To submit your response online, go to http://www. prenhall.com/webb.

CW

For Your Reflection and Analysis

What kinds of experience and educational preparation should a superintendent of schools have?
To submit your response online, go to http://www. prenhall.com/webb.

CW

Figure 13.2 — Local Education Governance

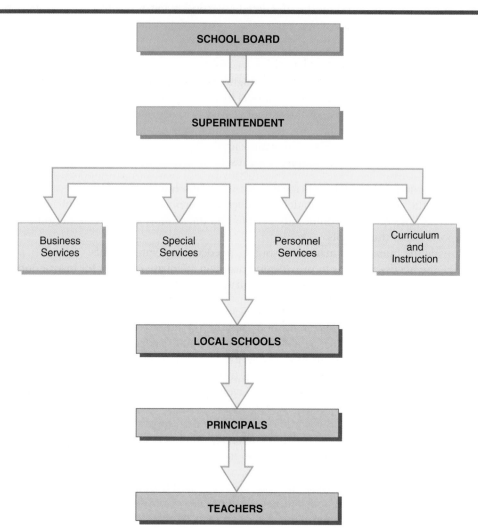

who have demonstrated in fields outside of education that they possess the management and leadership skills required to be a successful superintendent of schools. Some of these school districts have looked to private-sector executives and retired military officers to assume the superintendency. Examples of this practice may be found in Minneapolis, New Orleans, San Diego, Seattle, and Washington, DC.

Building Principal.   The individual with the primary responsibility for the success or failure of the educational program in each school is the **building principal.** The school principal's responsibilities are multidimensional. Not only is the principal responsible for the day-to-day administration of the school and implementation of the school district's regulations and policies, but the principal also leads the staff in establishing the vision and climate of the school. What principals understand, believe, say, and do has a profound consequence on those around them; they set the climate of the school (Spark, 2004).

The effective principal is an advocate in the district and the community for securing the materials that the staff needs in the classroom. The effective principal also serves as a buffer to protect teachers from intrusions so that they may work with students. Skillful principals make data-driven decisions by using various sources of information to support change, establish plans, monitor progress, and document results of efforts to achieve goals. Effective principals lead staff in the development of visions of the student learning and teaching desired in their schools. The success of all students becomes the highest priority; this leads to the development of an environment that nurtures continuous improvement in teaching and creates interdependent relationships among all staff members.

Principals are responsible for the induction and professional growth of the school staff. This requires that they give attention to the development of the knowledge, skills, and attitudes of the individuals and the group that comprises the professional learning community.

Traditionally, principals have been teachers and may have served as an assistant principal before becoming a principal. Some have viewed the principalship as a career and others have considered the job to be a stepping stone to assistant superintendent or superintendent.

Pattern of School Districts and Enrollments in the States.   Since 1950, the number of school districts in the nation has been reduced from approximately 100,000 to about 15,325. Among the states, the number of school districts varies. The number of school districts and the enrollment in each state are shown in Table 13.1. Excluding Hawaii, the number of school districts in the states ranges from as few as 17 in Nevada and 24 in Maryland to over 700 in states such as California, Illinois, Michigan, Ohio, and Texas. As the data in Table 13.1 suggest, the number of school districts in a state is not related to either the enrollment or geographic size of the state.

Among the 50 states, the estimated number of enrolled pupils in 2004–05 ranged from about 6.3 million in California and 4.4 million in Texas to less than 84,000 in Wyoming and about 95,000 in Vermont. The 14 states with more than 1 million pupils accounted for 64% of the almost 48.5 million public school pupils nationwide.

As each state organized school districts, it created different types of school districts. The most common school district organization is the unit school district, which provides educational programs for students in kindergarten through grade 12. However, a few states (e.g., Arizona, California, Illinois, Montana, New Jersey, and Vermont) permit the operation of separate high school districts serving grades 9 through 12 and elementary districts serving students in kindergarten through grade 8.

School District Budgeting.   Public elementary and secondary schools are labor-intensive endeavors. Personnel costs represent the majority of expenditures in school district budgets. More than 60% of a typical school district's current expenditures budget goes for instructional services, including teachers' salaries. Figure 13.3 shows

For Your Reflection and Analysis

What kinds of experience and educational preparation should a school principal have?
To submit your response online, go to http://www.prenhall.com/webb.

CW

Figure 13.3 — Percent of Total Current Expenditures by Function, 2001–02

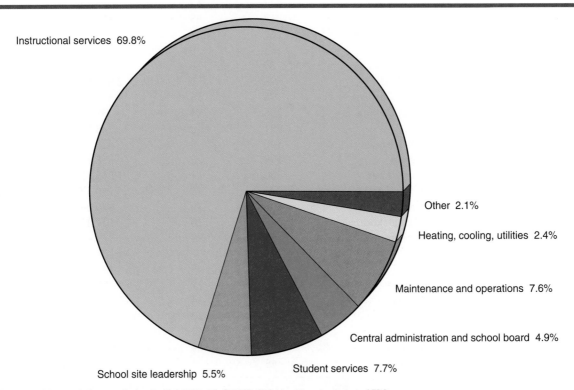

- Instructional services 69.8%
- Other 2.1%
- Heating, cooling, utilities 2.4%
- Maintenance and operations 7.6%
- Central administration and school board 4.9%
- Student services 7.7%
- School site leadership 5.5%

Source: Educational Research Service, *Budget Profiles 2001–02.* © 2002, ERS. Used by permission of ERS.

Table 13.1 — Estimated Number of Operating Districts and Fall Enrollment for Public Schools, 2004–05

	Districts	Rank	Fall Enrollment	Rank
United States	15,325		48,458,742	
Alabama	131	35	727,829	23
Alaska	53	43	132,970	45
Arizona	628	7	986,221	15
Arkansas	254	22	452,057	34
California	1059	2	6,322,142	1
Colorado	178	28	766,707	22
Connecticut	189	26	576,474	28
Delaware	33	47	119,109	47
Florida	67	41	2,628,429	4
Georgia	184	27	1,553,437	9
Hawaii	1	50	183,361	42
Idaho	114	37	249,984	39
Illinois	877	4	2,086,053	5
Indiana	317	18	1,019,410	14
Iowa	367	16	478,318	32
Kansas	301	19	468,512	33
Kentucky	176	29	631,989	26
Louisiana	85	40	724,002	24
Maine	231	23	200,649	41
Maryland	24	48	865,836	20
Massachusetts	387	15	976,674	16
Michigan	752	5	1,730,897	8
Minnesota	339	17	838,673	21
Mississippi	152	32	485,094	31
Missouri	524	10	892,194	18
Montana	437	13	146,705	44
Nebraska	477	12	284,559	37
Nevada	17	49	400,671	35
New Hampshire	162	31	206,852	40
New Jersey	593	8	1,420,374	10
New Mexico	89	38	322,800	36
New York	698	6	2,822,000	3
North Carolina	115	36	1,420,375	11
North Dakota	206	24	99,324	48
Ohio	891	3	1,843,555	6
Oklahoma	540	9	629,134	27
Oregon	198	25	558,956	29
Pennsylvania	500	11	1,815,170	7
Rhode Island	36	46	160,574	43
South Carolina	87	39	670,080	25
South Dakota	165	30	121,327	46
Tennessee	135	33	929,428	17
Texas	1,227	1	4,383,871	2
Utah	40	45	494,100	30
Vermont	286	21	95,187	49
Virginia	132	34	1,204,808	12
Washington	296	20	1,024,495	13
West Virginia	55	42	279,457	38
Wisconsin	426	14	881,480	19
Wyoming	48	44	83,633	50

Source: Data from *Rankings of the States 2004 and Estimates of School Statistics 2005.* Used with permission of the National Education Association © 2005. All rights reserved.

the percentage of the budget allocated to the major budget categories in the typical school district.

Site-Based Management.   As the smallest management unit of the school district, the local school is the most critical unit in the educational delivery system. **Site-based management (SBM)** is the shifting of decision making from the central administration to site-based councils composed of parents and teachers. SBM has been promoted as a way to increase teacher morale, improve the management of schools, raise student performance, and increase the involvement of school faculties, parents, and community leaders in education decision making. SBM is mandated for every school in five states and is practiced in hundreds of other school districts throughout the nation (Brown, 2001).

An underlying assumption of SBM is that teachers should be involved in planning, discussing, and making decisions and that parents should be involved in critical aspects of school-site decision making. In addition, research suggests that schools are more successful when teachers have a voice in decisions about their working conditions and the operation of the local school.

In practice, SBM operates along a spectrum in terms of the control and authority given to the site council and the extent to which the council operates in a policy-making or advisory capacity. In no case, however, is complete decentralization in decision making possible because local schools, as part of a school district within a state system of education, are subject to statutes, policies, and regulations from the district and the state.

Although the new assessment and accountability measures have taken away much of the site council's power in terms of guiding the school curriculum and student assessment, the practice of SBM is projected to increase: "psychologically, teachers can not give up their involvement in the decision making process of the schools; (and the SBM) process costs policy makers nothing and they gain praise for providing teachers this opportunity" (Brown, 2001, p. 5).

Charter Schools.   The most recent development in the organization of the public schools has been the **charter school** movement. The movement began in the 1990s to provide parents and students with a choice between the traditional public school and an alternative public school that is under the control of the parents or other individual(s) holding the school's charter. The first charter school was opened in 1991. Currently, legislatures in 40 states have enacted statutes providing for the operation of charter schools. As of the 2004–05 school year, more than 3,400 charter schools were serving about 800,000 students (see Figure 13.4). The states with the largest number of charter schools are Arizona, California, Michigan, and Texas.

The growth in the charter school movement can be attributed to several factors:

1. Students and/or their parents exercising choice by enrolling students in a charter school rather than enrolling them in the school to which they were assigned on the basis of their residence;
2. Public school staff seeking exemption from local and state rules and regulations so that they can provide innovative programs and services to at-risk youth;
3. Community interest in special schools to provide support for programs not being adequately provided in the regular schools, for example, performing arts, technology, or one of the sciences; and
4. School patrons seeking relief from regulations so that the schools can explore nontraditional approaches to instruction.

Rather than charter schools having a common reason for being, similar goals or programs, or sponsors with similar interests, the common characteristic of charter schools is seen in their diversity. Sponsors include parents, teachers, community nonprofit agencies, and a diverse group of entrepreneurial interests. Some charter schools are individually autonomous and others are owned and operated by a for-profit firm or a service agency.

The procedures for approving an application to open a charter school vary by state. Statutes in some states give school boards the authority to approve applications for charter schools; in others, the state board of education has the authority; and, in others, a state

For Your Reflection and Analysis

What kinds of decisions should be made at the school site, and who should make them?
To submit your response online, go to http://www. prenhall.com/webb.

CW

Figure 13.4 — Number of Charter Schools, 1992–93 to 2004–05

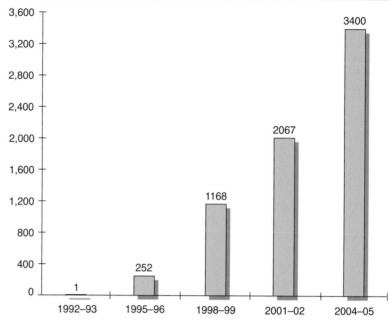

Source: Center for Education Reform. (2005). *Charter schools*. Retrieved January 25, 2005, from http://www.edreform.com/index.cfm?fuseAction=stateStats&pSectionID=&cSectionID=44

Charter schools grow in numbers and continue to be the most popular choice option.

charter school board has the authority. Arizona has all three options and if an application is denied by one board, the applicant may submit the application to one of the other boards. Responsibility for monitoring charter schools varies by state, but the local school board often has this responsibility if the charter school is located in its district.

Considerable controversy has focused on the characteristics of the student body of charter schools and the achievement of those students. According to some advocates, the allegation that charter schools would attract the most able students has been proven false; instead, charter schools also tend to attract poor and minority students and students with poor academic records (Finn, 2005). Somewhat different conclusions came from the Economic Policy Institute's analysis of state-level studies of charter schools and their students (Carnoy, Jacobsen, Mishel, & Rothstein, 2005). They concluded the following:

1. Charter schools have not enrolled the most disadvantaged youth; their minority students are no more likely to be low income than those in the public schools.
2. Students in charter schools did not outperform those in regular public schools.
3. Charter schools have not improved the educational performance of low-income minority youth.
4. The achievement of charter school students suffers because these students tend to have a higher mobility rate.
5. The introduction of competition through the opening of a charter school does not appear to have resulted in the public schools making efforts to do better.

CONTROVERSIAL ISSUE

Charter Schools

One of the most obvious outcomes of the school reform movement has been the emergence of charter schools. These schools are public schools in which state and school district controls typically have been relaxed. Parents and teachers have a greater voice in school decisions. After a somewhat modest beginning, the number of charter schools is increasing rapidly. Impetus for the state legislation authorizing charter schools has come from a variety of sources: parents seeking a particular curricular emphasis in the schools, teachers wanting relief from state and district requirements so that they can address the educational needs of at-risk students, parents desiring a specific type of school environment, and entrepreneurial firms seeking an entrée into the education market.

Opinions about charter schools are divided; some people view these schools as the panacea for all of the wrongs in education, whereas others view them as being divisive and leading to separatism based on personal values and philosophies of parents. Consider these pros and cons for charter schools:

Pros

1. Provides parents and students with a choice in the public school system.
2. Permits each school to determine its philosophy and curricular emphasis with a coherent academic mission and high standards.
3. Increases the heterogeneity of students in schools by attracting private school students into the charter schools.
4. Have an image of being smaller and safer than the typical public school.
5. Gives teachers greater freedom and the challenge of starting and designing a program for a new school.
6. Have been given operational and programmatic freedom in return for results-based accountability.

Cons

1. Can ignore the national education goals and state goals and content standards in developing their programs.
2. May be controlled by for-profit firms that impose standardized programs with limited local school choice.
3. Fail to provide teachers with the same salaries and fringe benefits they would receive in the public schools.
4. Have encountered fiscal accountability and management problems in the use of public funds.
5. Do not have the perceived independence because they are still a part of the public education system and thus are subject to changes in local and state requirements.

To what extent have charter schools been effective or not effective in your state? Give reasons why or why not. Would you consider teaching in a charter school? Give reasons why or why not.

 To answer these questions online, go to the *Controversial Issue* module for this chapter of the Companion Website at **http://www.prenhall.com/webb.**

The charter school movement is only 15 years old, and the growth in charter school enrollments is impressive. However, these numbers must be considered in the context of 94,000 public schools that enrolled over 48 million students as of the fall of 2004.

Education at the State Level

The state-level governance structure for the education system typically includes a **state board of education** as the policy-making body, a state administrative agency referred to as the **state department of education,** and a **chief state school officer,** who serves as executive officer of the state board of education and administers the state department of education. Figure 13.5 reflects the state-level administrative organization in many states.

Figure 13.5 — State Education Governance

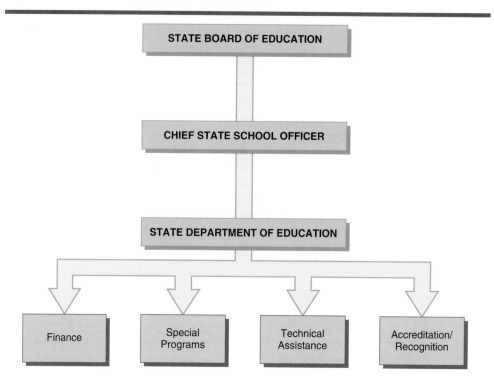

State Department of Education.   The legal principle of education being a state responsibility has resulted in the creation of state educational agencies that have a key role in the development of the structure and delivery system for public elementary and secondary education. Each state has a state-level administrative agency whose primary functions include the following:

- Implementing the state board of education's broad policies for the operation of the state's public elementary and secondary schools;
- Monitoring schools to ensure implementation of legislative mandates;
- Disbursing state funds to operate local school districts;
- Providing the state legislature and citizens with information about the schools, including student performance and related accountability indicators;
- Providing technical assistance to the schools;
- Collecting and reporting data about the schools; and
- Being an advocate for public education.

State Boards of Education.   Most state boards of education are not responsible for the direct operation of educational institutions or schools; rather, their concern is with the overall direction of the state's schools. State boards of education have various responsibilities. These boards usually are charged with adopting regulations to ensure implementation of the constitutional and statutory mandates related to the operation of the state system of schools. Their directives and mandates become policy and are enforced within the context of the state's statutory provisions. Examples include graduation requirements for high school students and mandated curricular offerings in schools. Among the important state board functions are providing the state legislature with timely reports about the schools, proposing changes in statutes, proposing new initiatives and programs, and presenting and serving as an advocate for the budget for state support of schools.

Chief State School Officer.   Each state has either constitutional or statutory provisions for a chief state school officer. This person often is referred to as the superintendent of public instruction or the commissioner of education. In most instances, responsibilities are limited to elementary and secondary education, but in a few states the person also has responsibilities for postsecondary education.

The professional status of the state superintendent is improving, but in several states qualifications are unstated or very broad. This is especially true in states where the chief state school officer is elected. In states where the chief state school officer is appointed, the tendency is to select a person with professional training and experience as an educational administrator. Of the 50 chief state school officers, 25 are appointed by the state board of education and 10 are appointed by the governor or some other official body. The remaining 15 were elected on a popular basis statewide (Council of Chief State School Officers, 2002).

State Secretaries of Education.   Recently, several states have adopted the federal cabinet system with a **secretary of education** who is responsible to the governor. Usually, the statutory provisions related to the chief state school officer and the state board of education have not been greatly altered by the creation of this cabinet position, and the state department of education has remained in place. The primary duties of the secretary of education have been related to long-range planning and budgeting rather than to administering the state department of education or monitoring schools. In a few instances, the secretary of education also functions as the chief state school officer.

The Federal Government and Public Education

As noted in Chapter 6, the absence of mention of education in the federal Constitution and the reservation of this function to the states should not be interpreted as indicating a lack of interest in education by the nation's founders. When the federal Constitution was being written, several states already had provided for education in their state constitutions and leaders in those states did not want the federal government to interfere with those provisions. In addition, private and church-related schools were numerous in some states and some persons may have supported this option for providing education.

Federal Role and Involvement.   The emphases of current federal education programs have been fourfold. First, since 1965, the major portion of federal funds have gone to programs and services for special populations, including funding for programs to serve students with disabilities, educationally disadvantaged youth, financially needy college students, and vocational education students.

The second emphasis area is educational statistics and research. Since the creation of the first Department of Education in 1867, the one continuing role of the federal education agency has been data gathering and reporting. Rather than each state gathering and reporting data independently, it has been more cost effective for the function to be performed by a federal education agency, the National Center for Education Statistics. The centralization also facilitates the reporting of consistent and comparable data that can be use for a variety of purposes, including international comparisons.

A third emphasis of the federal government has been research and demonstration projects. The rationales for federal support of educational research and demonstration projects are similar to those for data gathering and reporting. Cost effectiveness is improved by central funding of national research priorities and dissemination of this information for better informed educational decision making.

The fourth and most recent emphasis of the federal government in education has been on student performance and assessment. As has been discussed, the No Child Left Behind Act of 2001 requires that *all* students in grades 3–8 be assessed annually in reading and math as a condition of participation in federal programs for elementary and secondary school youth. The FY 2006 budget includes a proposal that the assessment be extended to high school youth.

U.S. Department of Education.   Beginning in 1867 with the creation of a Department of Education without cabinet status, some type of federal education agency has been in existence. In 1869 the title was changed to Office of Education, in 1870 to Bureau of Education, and in 1929 back to Office of Education. The latter designation was retained until the creation of the Department of Education in 1980, when education was given cabinet status. Until the creation of the Department of Education headed by a secretary of education, the federal education agency had been administered by a commissioner of education.

For Your Reflection and Analysis

How much control should the federal government exercise over education?

To submit your response online, go to http://www. prenhall.com/webb.

CW

U.S. Secretary of Education. The secretary of education is a member of the president's cabinet and is responsible for the operation of the U.S. Department of Education. Since 1980 when the Department of Education was established with cabinet status, secretaries have come from a variety of backgrounds including being a federal judge, college professor, university president, governor, chief state school officer, local school district superintendent, and domestic policy adviser. The one common element is that, in contrast to the historical pattern for some other cabinet officers, they have been involved in education in some manner prior to becoming secretary. As secretary of education, they have been an advocate for the president's educational initiatives.

Financing of Education

In addition to establishing the governance structure for education, state legislatures also establish the basic structure for financing public elementary and secondary schools. The state enacts the funding system for schools and sets the taxing and spending powers of local school districts, including the state's method for funding schools, the types of taxes that may be used to support education, and the tax rate that may be levied.

Methods of financing public elementary and secondary schools as well as expenditures per pupil differ in a variety of ways both within and among states. However, two basic legal principles guide the financing of the public schools in the United States. First, education is a responsibility of the state, and, second, in the design and implementation of the state school finance program, the state has an equal responsibility to each pupil within its jurisdiction. Adhering to these principles has often been difficult because the states have chosen to let the school districts, with their wide differences in enrollment, taxable wealth, and citizen aspirations, administer and deliver education.

Public Policy Goals in State School Finance

Public policy decisions about how schools should be financed are made with three goals in mind: equity, adequacy, and choice. The three school finance goals are not independent, but are interactive. One can have equity without adequacy, for equity has been interpreted merely as equal treatment of students in different school districts in a state. Adequacy implies that the level of funding is sufficient, but does not assume either equal treatment or choice. To some extent, there is agreement in the school finance community about definitions for equity and adequacy, but that is not the case for choice. Originally, choice referred to the power of a local school district to choose its level of spending, which may or may not be either equitable or adequate. Choice currently has been extended to the power of the parent to choose the school that the child attends.

Equity. The concept of **equity** refers to the equal treatment of persons in equal circumstances. For students, this means funds used to address student needs should ensure that all students have an equal opportunity for education. For taxpayers, this means equal tax rates on similar property regardless of the wealth of the district (the wealth of the district is expressed in terms of the assessed value of property per pupil). The problem with achieving this goal is that even if equity is achieved it may not result in adequate or sufficient funds for schools; it may only result in equal treatment.

Adequacy. **Adequacy** refers to the extent to which educational funding is sufficient to provide the programs and services needed by all students. Factors affecting adequacy include quality of staff, sufficient materials, and skill levels of teachers. The applicable standard for adequate funding has not been established, but one can argue that the student should have access to the human and material resources required to demonstrate attainment of the applicable academic standards and pass proficiency examinations.

Choice. Since the 1990s, the term **choice** has been used to refer to two different goals. One goal is local control of funding decisions. Traditionally, school boards were permitted to choose the level of funding for the schools. In some cases, equity and choice have come into conflict because a district's freedom to choose the level of funding has resulted in inequitable treatment of taxpayers and students. Currently, choice also is being used to refer to the power of parents to select the school that their child will attend. Many states and school districts have adopted *open enrollment* policies that allow students to attend any school in the state or district, under certain provisions. In addition, the provisions of the federal No Child Left Behind Act give parents the option of transfering their child out of a low-performing school.

State School Finance Programs

The history of state school finance programs can be traced to the early 1900s, when Ellwood Cubberley (1905) contended that the state had a responsibility to address the unfairness of a school finance system that relied almost exclusively on the local property tax to finance schools. As a result of his efforts, state school finance equalization models were developed in the early decades of the 20th century; prior to that time, state funds were limited and typically were distributed on a flat-grant basis irrespective of differences in local wealth or educational need.

Of the four major models or funding approaches, three are considered equalization models: equalized foundation grants, equalized reward for tax effort, and full state funding. The other model is the flat grant. **Equalization models** compensate for the differences in taxable wealth among school districts. More than two-thirds of the states use a school finance formula that can be classified as an equalized foundation grant. The major state school finance programs are illustrated in Table 13.2.

Equalized Foundation Grants.   Under the equalized foundation plan, the state provides the difference between a fixed expenditure level per pupil set by the state and the amount the district can collect locally through a uniform tax rate. A pupil-based foundation program is used to fund schools in 36 states; a teacher unit-based foundation is used in 6 additional states. While **foundation grants** are the most common method used to finance education among the states, they have often been criticized because the funding level set by the state may be at a minimum level and not be sufficient to support an adequate educational program.

Equalized Effort-Oriented Programs.   Under equalized effort-oriented programs, or **power equalization,** local school districts officials choose the level of funding they desire for their schools. Revenues raised by the taxes in the district are then "equalized" by back-filling with state funds so that low wealth districts will receive the same funds for a certain tax rate as a high-wealth district making the same effort. This differs from the foundation plan in which the state sets the target amount per pupil or per teacher. Effort-oriented programs are used in eight states.

Full State Funding.   **Full state funding** for public schools occurs when no local tax revenues are collected for the support of schools; all funds for schools come from state-level taxes. This model is used only in Hawaii, which has one school district for administrative management of all state schools. Under full state funding, students and taxpayers are treated equally, but attainment of adequacy will be solely dependent on the funding level determined by the state. No opportunity for local district choice is available.

Flat Grants.   As previously stated, historically, **flat grants** were the most common form of state aid to school districts. Under the flat grant program the state paid a uniform amount, usually on a per pupil basis, to each district irrespective of local wealth. No state currently uses the flat grant as the primary funding method; they have been replaced by equalized foundation programs. However, several states still include a low-level flat-grant program as a part of the equalization program to ensure that high-wealth districts receive some state funds.

Categorical Grants.   As a supplement to the basic funding approach, states often target funds for a specific educational purpose (e.g., bilingual education, education of students with disabilities, gifted education, student transportation, technology, textbooks, and instructional materials). These targeted grants often are referred to as **categorical funding.** While widely used to fund specific programs, this is not the principal method for funding schools in any state.

State Spending Differences.   In 2004–05, among the 50 states, current per pupil expenditures ranged from $12,879 in New York to $5,474 in Arizona. The national average was $8,554 per pupil. At the same time, the average teacher salary ranged from $58,688 in Connecticut to $34,040 in South Dakota with a national average of $47,750. Per pupil expenditures and average teachers' salaries provide an indicator of a state's effort. Per capita

For Your Reflection and Analysis

Of the three school finance policy goals, which is most important?
To submit your response online, go to http://www.prenhall.com/webb.

CW

For Your Reflection and Analysis

Which school finance formula is used to fund schools in your state?
To submit your response online, go to http://www.prenhall.com/webb.

CW

Table 13.2 — Current Funding Approaches

Description	Who Uses It?	Problems
Strayer-Haig Equalization Funding Model (foundation plan)		
Developed in 1920s by George D. Strayer and Robert M. Haig at Columbia University.	Used in some form in three-fourths of the states.	Keeps funding at a minimum level; insufficient to support an adequate educational program.
Provides difference between district's need and amount collectible locally.		State does not participate in efforts to provide funds beyond minimum.
Uniform tax rate applied to assessed value of property in school district.		
Entitlement based on funds required to ensure a minimum per pupil or per teacher; minimum determined by legislature.		
Adjusted to recognize additional funds needed for concentration of pupils with special needs.		
Equalized Effort-Oriented Programs (power equalization)		
Developed in 1922 by Harlan Updegraff at University of Pennsylvania.	About one-sixth of states used it in some form in the late 1990s.	No assurance of funding at an adequate level.
Local school officials choose level of funding.		
Tax revenues in district "equalized" by state allocations.		
Any excess raised in a district sent to state treasury.		
Full State Funding		
No local taxes collected.	Used only in Hawaii.	No local choice permitted.
Flat Grants		
State provides uniform amount per student; funds available for any legal educational purpose.	Originally most common form of state support. May be used with an equalization program to ensure that wealthy school districts receive some funds.	Funds do not generally go to area of greatest need.
Categorical Funding		
State funds are allocated for specific purpose (e.g., bilingual education, in-service programs for teachers, instructional materials).	Often used to encourage specific programs that are not mandated by state law.	Typically allocated irrespective of district's wealth.

personal income, a commonly used measure of a state's wealth or ability to provide for education, ranged from $45,398 in Connecticut to $24,650 in Mississippi. These amounts have not been adjusted for interstate cost differences (NEA, 2005a).

As the data in Table 13.3 show, there often is not a relationship between the wealth of the state and its support for education as measured by per pupil expenditures or average

Table 13.3 — Current Per Pupil Expenditures (PPE), Per Capita Personal Income (PCPI), 2002, Average Teacher Salary (ATS), 2004–05

	PPE	Rank	PCPI	Rank	ATS	Rank
U.S. Average	8,554		49,429		47,750	
Alabama	$ 6,993	42	$27,795	40	38,863	34
Alaska	10,042	11	34,454	13	52,424	10
Arizona	5,474	49	28,442	38	42,905	27
Arkansas	6,202	48	25,725	49	40,495	35
California	7,815	29	35,019	12	57,876	2
Colorado	8,095	25	36,063	7	44,161	22
Connecticut	11,893	2	45,398	1	58,688	1
Delaware	10,329	9	35,861	8	50,869	12
Florida	7,040	39	31,455	23	41,081	31
Georgia	8,500	22	30,051	34	46,526	17
Hawaii	8,356	23	32,160	20	44,273	21
Idaho	6,743	44	27,098	44	42,122	29
Illinois	10,439	8	34,351	14	55,629	6
Indiana	8,734	21	30,094	33	46,851	16
Iowa	7,477	35	30,560	31	40,347	37
Kansas	7,558	33	30,811	28	39,190	41
Kentucky	7,719	30	27,709	41	41,002	32
Louisiana	7,552	34	27,581	42	38,880	43
Maine	10,736	6	30,566	30	40,940	38
Maryland	9,762	13	39,247	4	52,331	11
Massachusetts	11,322	5	41,801	2	54,596	7
Michigan	8,909	19	31,954	22	55,693	5
Minnesota	9,239	18	35,861	9	46,906	15
Mississippi	6,452	46	24,650	50	36,590	48
Missouri	7,452	36	30,608	29	38,971	42
Montana	8,025	26	26,857	45	38,485	45
Nebraska	7,617	32	31,339	25	39,456	39
Nevada	7,098	40	33,405	17	43,394	25
New Hampshire	9,566	16	37,040	6	43,941	23
New Jersey	11,502	4	41,332	3	56,600	3
New Mexico	7,227	37	26,191	47	39,328	40
New York	12,879	1	38,228	5	56,200	4
North Carolina	6,958	43	29,246	37	43,313	26
North Dakota	7,033	41	31,398	24	36,449	49
Ohio	9,573	15	31,322	26	48,692	14
Oklahoma	6,269	47	28,089	39	37,141	47
Oregon	7,913	27	29,971	36	50,790	13
Pennsylvania	9,638	14	33,348	18	52,700	9
Rhode Island	10,641	7	33,733	16	53,473	8
South Carolina	8,161	24	27,172	43	42,207	28
South Dakota	7,636	31	30,856	27	34,040	50
Tennessee	6,725	38	30,005	35	41,527	30
Texas	7,140	45	30,222	32	41,009	33
Utah	5,245	20	26,606	46	39,965	38
Vermont	11,641	3	32,770	19	44,535	20
Virginia	8,847	20	35,477	10	44,763	19
Washington	7,858	28	35,299	11	45,712	18
West Virginia	9,448	17	25,872	48	38,360	46
Wisconsin	9,881	12	32,157	21	43,466	24
Wyoming	10,198	10	34,306	15	40,392	36

Source: Data from *Rankings of the States 2004 and Estimates of School Statistics 2005*, used with permission of the National Education Association © 2005. All rights reserved.

teacher salaries. For example, Colorado ranks 25th in per pupil expenditure, but 7th in per capita personal income, while West Virginia ranks 17th per pupil expenditures and 48th in per capita personal income. On the other hand, the pattern for Connecticut, Delaware, Massachusetts, New Jersey, and New York is quite different; the data for these states show a favorable balance between ability and effort. Each state ranks in the top 10 states on each of these ability and effort measures.

Sources of Revenue for Schools

Funds for public elementary and secondary schools come from various taxes levied by local, state, and federal governments. As discussed previously, and as shown in Table 13.4, the proportion of revenues from each source varies among and within states. The principal source of local revenue for schools is the *ad valorem* tax on real property, commonly referred to as the **local property tax.** This tax is levied on the value of land, residences, apartment buildings, commercial buildings, railroads, and utilities. On average, more than 90% of all local tax revenues for schools come from the property tax.

State sales and income taxes are the principal sources of the state revenues that go the schools. All states have either a sales tax or personal income tax, and most have both. Other state tax revenues come from corporate income taxes and excise taxes on tobacco, alcohol, and motor vehicles. In addition, 40 states operate state lotteries. (See the Historical Note on lotteries on page 349.)

Table 13.4 — Estimated Percent of Revenues for Public Schools From Local, State, and Federal Sources, 2004–05

	State	Local	Federal		State	Local	Federal
U.S.	48.6%	42.7%	8.8%				
Alabama	57.1%	31.5%	11.4%	Montana	47.1%	40.7%	12.2%
Alaska	63.5	23.9	12.5	Nebraska	40.4	52.5	7.1
Arizona	51.2	41.0	7.7	Nevada	31.6	60.8	7.6
Arkansas	51.8	36.9	11.3	New Hampshire	52.4	41.6	6.0
California	63.7	25.5	10.8	New Jersey	38.3	58.9	2.8
Colorado	43.1	50.3	6.6	New Mexico	72.5	12.0	15.4
Connecticut	39.2	54.8	6.0	New York	45.3	48.1	6.6
Delaware	64.1	29.2	6.7	N Carolina	63.4	24.4	12.1
Florida	42.7	46.6	10.8	North Dakota	35.7	50.0	14.2
Georgia	45.1	46.1	8.8	Ohio	46.0	47.8	6.3
Hawaii	90.3	1.5	8.2	Oklahoma	53.6	33.2	13.1
Idaho	60.1	30.4	9.6	Oregon	53.9	35.1	11.0
Illinois	30.3	61.9	7.8	Pennsylvania	35.6	56.1	8.3
Indiana	50.3	42.9	6.8	Rhode Island	36.7	59.9	3.4
Iowa	46.2	46.4	7.3	S Carolina	44.8	43.7	11.5
Kansas	52.8	39.2	8.1	South Dakota	34.4	49.2	16.4
Kentucky	58.4	29.7	11.9	Tennessee	45.3	42.8	11.9
Louisiana	48.6	37.8	13.5	Texas	37.3	51.1	11.6
Maine	41.8	48.7	9.5	Utah	57.7	32.9	9.5
Maryland	37.3	55.5	7.2	Vermont	85.9	6.1	8.0
Massachusetts	38.5	54.9	6.6	Virginia	41.5	51.7	6.8
Michigan	66.9	27.4	5.7	Washington	61.6	28.1	10.3
Minnesota	69.5	23.7	6.8	West Virginia	59.3	28.8	11.9
Mississippi	54.2	30.7	15.1	Wisconsin	54.3	40.0	5.7
Missouri	32.4	58.5	9.1	Wyoming	51.4	39.0	9.5

Source: Data from *Rankings of the States 2004 and Estimates of School Statistics 2005,* used with permission of the National Education Association © 2005. All rights reserved.

HISTORICAL NOTE

The Lotteries and Education

The use of lotteries, both for settling disputes and as games of chance, has been traced to 3500 B.C. When the English colonists came to the New World, they brought with them a tradition of private and public lotteries. Colonial churches and governments made use of the lottery. Benjamin Franklin and other leading citizens of Philadelphia sponsored a lottery to raise money to buy a battery of cannons for the city. The Continental Congress used a lottery to generate funds to support the troops. In the 1790s, lotteries were used to help finance the construction and improvement of Washington, D.C.

Lotteries were also used by various educational institutions. Dartmouth, Harvard, Kings College (now Columbia University), Pennsylvania, Princeton, and William and Mary are among the colonial colleges that benefited from lotteries. From the signing of the Constitution to the Civil War, some 300 elementary and secondary schools and 47 colleges were beneficiaries of lotteries (Ezell, 1960).

Unfortunately, as the use of lotteries grew, so did the abuses and irregularities associated with them. In the second and third quarters of the 19th century, state after state passed regulatory bills, and by 1878 all states except Louisiana prohibited lotteries. By the end of the century, Louisiana's "Golden Octopus" lotteries, so called because they reached into every state and large city in the nation, had also died out.

The first modern government-operated lottery in the United States was instituted in 1964 by the state of New Hampshire as a means of generating revenues for education. In 1967, New York started a lottery, and within the next decade, a dozen other states joined the list of those operating lotteries. In 2004, 40 states and the District of Columbia operated lotteries, and in 20 states, education was the beneficiary of part or all of the lottery proceeds.

To research and explore this topic further, go to the *Historical Note* module for this chapter of the Companion Website at **http://www.prenhall.com/webb**.

The principal source of federal revenue for education is the federal income tax. A major advantage of the federal income tax is that it relies on the taxable income of the entire nation as the taxpaying base.

Differences Among States in Sources of Tax Revenues. In the 2004–05 school year, excluding Hawaii, the percentage of the revenues for schools from state tax sources ranged from 85.9% in Vermont to 30.3% in Illinois. The percent of funds from local tax sources ranged from 61.9% in Illinois to 6.1% in Vermont, and the percentage from the federal government ranged from 16.4% in South Dakota to 2.8% in New Jersey. The national average was 42.7% from local sources, 48.6% from state sources, and 8.8% from federal sources. Data for each state are presented in Table 13.4.

The states with the largest percentage of federal revenues tend to be those in the southeast. They are also the states with the highest percentage of children in poverty (thus the

Many poor communities whose students have complex educational needs do not have sufficient funds for their schools because of the heavy reliance on the property tax as a major source of school funding.

recipients of Title I funds) as well as having heavy concentrations of military bases (thus receiving federal impact aid). Other states with large amounts of federal property (e.g., national parks and forests, Indian reservations, or military bases) also receive higher proportions of federal funds.

Sources for Nontax Revenues.   As a result of state restrictions on local school spending, local budgetary shortages, and court actions seeking greater equity in funding for public education, many schools have been forced to curtail or eliminate programs and services (e.g., art and music). As a result, local schools and their supporters have sought to find other sources of funding for schools, including charging participation or user fees for school activities, formation of nonprofit educational foundations at the school or district level, and profit-making activities.

Fees for participation in elective or extracurricular activities (e.g., driver education, athletics, school clubs) are becoming a significant source of revenue in many school districts. However, the charging of these fees is in conflict with court cases that have sought to bring about greater equity in funding and equality of access to educational programs and services. The basic question may be whether the activity is considered a necessary part of the school program or a truly extracurricular activity being provided under the sponsorship of the school. If the activity is a basic part of the school program, then charging a participation fee might be considered discriminatory because a student from a low-income family may be denied access to the program. To address this concern, many school districts provide waivers to children from low-income families.

Another source of nontax revenues for schools is donor activities, including booster clubs and educational foundations. Some school districts have created these nonprofit foundations to secure funds for programs and services that cannot be supported from tax funds. These foundations, which are allowed to receive tax-deductible gifts from parents, interested citizens, and businesses, provide a means for districts to provide programs and services that are important components of a quality education for their constituents.

Enterprise activities include such things as leasing school facilities and services (e.g., food services or the roof of a building for a telephone tower) and the sale of school access. The latter is generally through advertising on school property (e.g., buses or athletic fields) or in school publications (e.g., school yearbooks or newspapers). A growing and more controversial practice is commercialism in the schools. The main form of in-school commercialism is in the form of ads. Schools have traditionally allowed, even courted, advertisements in school yearbooks or newspapers to offset the cost of the publication, or at athletic events to support extracurricular activities. However, most of the advertising in schools today has not been solicited by the school and it is everywhere: It is on "bulletin boards and wallboards in corridors and lavatories. It's on telephone kiosks and book covers. It's on radio programs piped into school corridors and lunchrooms. In addition, hundreds of thousands of product coupons and samples are distributed through schools each year. The list goes on and on" (Consumers Union, 2005, p. 2).

There are hundreds, possibly thousands of companies trying to get their messages to students. Some of the larger companies have their own marketing operations that design and operate marketing programs targeted to schools (Consumers Union, 2005). One of the major outlets for many companies is the Channel One daily news program. Channel One provides schools equipment in return for showing a 12-minute news program that also contains at least two commercials targeted to the school-age population.

Commercialism in the form of ads is increasing in the schools.

The Courts and School Finance

Since the early 1970s when the first wave of school finance litigation began, state programs for financing the public schools have been challenged in more than 45 states. The contention in most of these cases has been that the state has failed to provide an "equal protection" for students because the state system for financing education relies too heavily on the local property tax as a major source of revenue for the schools, and, as a consequence, the disparities in taxable wealth among the districts create fiscal and educational inequalities. As a result of the disparities in taxable wealth, taxpayers in different districts must be taxed at different rates to provide the same level of support. Students in low-wealth districts are at a disadvantage relative to students in other districts with greater wealth or higher tax rates. Plaintiffs contend that the result is unfair to both taxpayers and students in the low-spending districts who often receive an inadequate or inferior education.

In the landmark federal school finance case, *San Antonio v. Rodriguez* (1973), the U.S. Supreme Court rejected the argument that education is a constitutionally protected right and that equal treatment is required in providing education under the U.S. Constitution. Since the *Rodriguez* decision effectively closed the door to challenges in the federal courts, challenges to existing state school finance programs have been based on the education clause in a state constitution discussed in Chapter 11 rather than on provisions in the U.S. Constitution.

Plaintiffs in the more recent school finance cases have expanded their interests to include not only equity but the extent to which the funding level is adequate and takes into consideration intrastate geographical and programmatic cost differences. The concern with adequacy has been that even if every district were to receive equal funding per pupil, because of such things as geographic and cost differences and concentrations of students with special needs in some districts, they would still need additional funds if they are to provide the same adequate education to each student. Consider, for example, the differences in the cost of the land for a school building or hiring a school social worker in New York City compared to rural New York State. Plaintiffs have prevailed in more than two-thirds of these cases.

Federal Aid for Elementary and Secondary Schools

The No Child Left Behind (NCLB) Act of 2001 has become the cornerstone of the federal education program. However, many educators have expressed concerns about the impact of various features of the statute. In a comprehensive national study of the impact of the NCLB act, the Center on Education Policy (2005) identified several problems. For example, small rural schools in which teachers must teach different subjects have had problems hiring teachers who meet the highly qualified teacher requirements of the NCLB act. Concerns also were expressed about the narrowing of the curriculum to prepare students for the tests in reading and mathematics. The statute also indicates that in underperforming schools parents are to be provided with the opportunity to enroll their child in another school and that supplemental services are to be provided for the children who remain in the school. However, the study found that only about 15% of the schools provided the school choice option and that only 1% of the eligible children had exercised the choice to transfer to another school. In addition, supplemental services were being provided in only about 10% of the districts, and 10% of the eligible students were participating in supplemental services. Concern has also been expressed about determining a school's status on the basis of one test and limiting the test to reading and mathematics (Rose & Gallup, 2004). Whatever concerns may exist, it is clear that the NCLB act is having an impact on the schools that receive federal funds and that it is affecting the ways used to educate youth.

Despite the requirements imposed by the NCLB act, revenue projections suggest that the federal government will continue to play a somewhat limited role in the financing of elementary and secondary education. Although the 2004-05 federal share of the financing of education, 8.8%, represented a 1.3% increase over the 2002 pre-NCLB funding level of 7.5%, the federal share remains below its 1980 peak of 9.8%.

Support for the major federal programs such as Title I and the Individuals with Disabilities Education Act (IDEA) has been maintained for 40 years, and has increased under the NCLB act, but other programs have been more dependent on the preferences of Congress and the executive branch. As a result, specific programs initiated by one administration may be terminated or consolidated by a subsequent administration because of different priorities. However, even though funding is limited, the federal government's involvement in education continues to be influential in providing programs for youth with special needs, and this involvement likely will increase as the student assessment programs are implemented.

Education of Special Needs Youth.   Of the federally funded elementary and secondary education programs, the largest is for the Title I program for the education of disadvantaged pupils. As indicated on Table 13.5, the proposed 2006 federal education budget included $13.3 billion for Title I. An additional $34.3 million was proposed for migrant education. Another major program for disadvantaged youth, the Head Start program for low-income preschool children, typically is not operated by public school districts, but is an important component of the educational system. Funding for this program in 2006 is budgeted at $6.9 billion.

Table 13.5 — Federal Budget for Major Federal Education Programs (in billions), 2002–2006

Program	FY 2002	FY 2003	FY 2004	FY 2005	FY 2006
K–12 Programs					
Title I	$10.4	$11.7	$12.3	$12.7	$13.3
Special education grants	7.9	8.9	10.5	11.9	11.5
Impact aid	1.1	1.2	1.2	1.2	1.2
Vocational-education state grants	1.3	1.2	1.3	1.3	—
Teacher quality grants	2.9	2.9	2.9	2.9	2.9
21st Century learning centers	1.0	1.0	1.0	1.0	1.0
State assessment	0.4	0.4	0.4	0.4	0.4
High school assessment	—	—	—	—	0.3
Educational technology	0.7	0.7	0.7	0.5	—
High school intervention	—	—	—	1.2	1.2
Reading First state grants	0.9	1.0	1.0	1.0	1.0
School reform	0.2	0.2	0.2	0.2	—
Title V block grants	0.4	0.3	0.3	0.2	0.2
English language acquisition	0.7	0.7	0.7	0.7	0.7
Work study grants	1.0	1.0	1.0	1.0	1.0
Adult & literacy education	0.5	0.5	0.5	0.5	0.1
Even Start	0.3	0.3	0.2	0.2	—
Safe & drug free schools	0.4	0.4	0.4	0.4	—
TOTAL	**$30.1**	**$32.4**	**$34.6**	**$37.3**	**$34.8**
Higher Education Programs					
Direct student loans	$11.2	$12.0	$12.0	$13.9	$15.2
Pell grants	11.9	12.7	13.1	12.9	13.5
TOTAL	**$23.1**	**$24.7**	**$25.1**	**$26.8**	**$28.7**
Major Outside Programs					
Head Start	$6.5	$6.7	$6.8	$6.8	$6.9
School lunch program	6.9	7.2	7.6	8.1	8.5
TOTAL	**$13.4**	**$13.9**	**$14.4**	**$14.9**	**$15.4**

Source: U.S. Department of Education (2005). *Fiscal Year 2001–2006 State Tables for the U.S. Department of Education.* Washington, DC: Author.

The second largest federally funded K–12 education program is special education grants. The 2006 federal budget proposal included $11.5 billion for special education programs. This program has been in existence since the late 1970s, but the level of federal funding has never reached the commitment in the original legislation: 40% of the average per pupil expenditure. However, no modification has been made in program requirements or regulations because of the failure to fully fund the program.

Another long-standing federal program is impact aid to school districts for the education of youth residing with parents who live or work on federal property, Indian reservations, or are active-duty uniformed military personnel. Proposed funding for this program in 2006 was $1.2 billion.

Educational Research and Assessment.   While the federal government has provided more funds for elementary and secondary education programs, interest in federal funds for a national research program has not kept pace with the growth in other areas. Currently, about $200 million in federal research and dissemination funds for education are administered through the Institute for Education Sciences. Other federal funding for educational research efforts is provided by a variety of federal agencies, including the National Science Foundation, Department of Energy, Department of Defense, and Department of Labor.

Private Education

In contrast to public education which is provided through a range of school districts with multiple schools, private education typically is provided by independent schools. As individually controlled schools, they have been created for a variety of reasons, including college preparation, religious instruction, or military training.

The private school option is not new; it has provided an alternative to public education in the United States since the colonial period. More recently, in response to the rising level of concern about a variety of educational issues, interest in the private school alternative has been expressed by parents across a wide socioeconomic and political spectrum. Private schools take different forms in response to parents who want broader educational opportunities for their children, who seek a more rigorous or more restrictive environment for their children, or who desire a more permissive environment than the public schools can provide. This pattern of diverse aspirations has contributed to the development of a variety of private schools that are noted more for their differences than their similarities. Such schools include church-related schools, private traditional day schools, and "free" schools in which students can pursue individual interests. Some of these interest groups may select the charter school option if they do not think that state requirements for charter schools are too restrictive.

Proprietary schools, schools operated for profit, comprise a growing sector of the private school market. Their popularity has been attributed to parents being attracted to the high standards that many such schools espouse, the extras (e.g., before- and after-school remediation and counseling and a wide variety of extracurricular activities), in-depth education, and smaller class size. However, proprietary schools represent only 1% of all elementary and secondary schools.

Some concerns have been expressed related to the lack of accountability for private schools and to the fact that they are not subject to the same regulations as the public schools. If these schools increase in popularity, the impact on the composition of the student body in the public schools could be

For Your Reflection and Analysis

In the current era of accountability, what kinds of controls should the state exercise over private schools?
To submit your response online, go to http://www. prenhall.com/webb.

The number of students attending private schools could increase if vouchers are provided by the state or federal governments.

VIDEO INSIGHT

Vouchers

This ABC News video consists of interviews about vouchers to pay tuition for students in grades K–12 to attend church-related and secular nonpublic schools. Advocates for vouchers have been heartened by the recent decision of the U.S. Supreme Court [*Zelman v. Simmons-Harris,* 122. S. Ct. 2460 (2002)] that approved the voucher program for disadvantaged youth in the Cleveland Public Schools. The Court ruled that the Cleveland program did not violate the establishment clause of the U.S. Constitution calling for separation of church and state as long as parents have a choice from a range of church-related and secular schools. With your classmates and/or other students, research and discuss the following topics:

1. Form a study group of fellow students to review the wording of the establishment clause in the U.S. Constitution and the related subsequent decisions, and have the study group give a background report and lead a class discussion on the topic.
2. Have another study group review and summarize the literature about the public's attitude toward vouchers.
3. Using the information above, have class debate on vouchers.

To submit your answers online, go to the *Video Insight* module for this chapter of the Companion Website at **http://www.prenhall.com/webb.**

---

significant. Financial support for the public schools could also be impacted if more and more students opt out of the public schools. The attention of educators and policy makers to these issues likely will increase, particularly if the number of proprietary schools continues to grow.

Private School Enrollments

The number of students attending the 27,000 private schools in the United States totaled about 6.3 million students in 2003–04. The proportion of elementary and secondary school students in private schools has changed little during the past 20 years: 11.5% of all students were enrolled in private schools both in 1980 and in the 2003–04 school year. Of the 6.3 million students attending private schools, over 80% attend church-related schools, or **parochial schools,** with about 3.0 million of these students attending Roman Catholic schools (Council for American Private Education, 2005).

Despite the recent growth in private school enrollment growth in some sectors, projections suggest that the overall percentage of American students enrolled in private elementary and secondary schools will remain stable for the next several years. However, if states or the federal government provide **vouchers** to students or direct funding for the general operation of nonpublic schools, then the percentage of students enrolled in these schools might increase dramatically. This possibility does not seem imminent given that citizen support for using public money to fund attendance at private or church-related schools continues to remain low (Rose & Gallup, 2004).

Current Issues in the Governance and Financing of Education

The new century has brought old problems as well as new challenges. The most dramatic is a more active federal interest in the progress students in each school are making on state assessment tests. The new federal requirements placed on the receipt of federal funds have created additional burdens on state education agencies and local school districts. In response to the requirements of the NCLB act, states have increased their assessment and accountability requirements. Separate from these concerns is the continuing school finance litigation in which the plaintiffs have broadened their complaints from a quest for greater equity in state school finance programs to also include the adequacy of the funding level. Supporters of sufficient funds for public education also are confronted with increased school enrollments and increased competition for funds from other governmental functions.

The New Federal Role

The No Child Left Behind Act marked a major expansion and change in the direction of federal involvement in education. The expanded role and new direction for the federal government in education created by the NCLB act is evident in several areas (Jennings, 2002). First, unlike previous federal legislation, which was limited to specific purposes or directed to children with special needs, the NCLB act is directed at *every* student and *every* teacher in *every* public school in the country: *All* children in grades 3–8 will be tested, *all* students will be grade-level proficient, and *all* teachers must be "highly qualified."

Second, the NCLB act made a change in the very underlying purpose of the federal government's involvement in education. Historically, the federal government's involvement was based on the premise that an educated citizenry would contribute to the national political and economic welfare. The NCLB act, however, made clear that the principal reason for the federal government's involvement in public education is to raise student achievement (Jennings, 2002).

Another way in which the role of the federal government has changed, and in a monumentally important way, is that for the first time in our nation's history the federal government has become involved in determining the qualifications of instructional personnel. States still issue teaching certificates, but what it means to be a "qualified teacher" has not only been defined by the federal government, but, *de facto,* imposed on the states.

The response to the NCLB act has been understandably mixed. Yet, whatever the disagreements on the merits of the law, on one thing there has been no disagreement: it "involve(d) the federal government in local education in a way it never had before" (Hardy, 2002, p. 21).

For Your Reflection and Analysis

Why is the NCLB act referred to as an unfunded mandate?
To submit your response online, go to http://www. prenhall.com/webb.

CW

Expanded State and Local Responsibilities

For more than two decades, states have become more and more involved in issues that traditionally had been the responsibility of local school boards. In part, this was perhaps a natural result of the state assuming greater financial responsibility. It was also a result of the school reform movement and the standards, testing, and accountability measures that accompanied the 1994 Elementary and Secondary Education Act. The NCLB act expanded the state role even further. Under the NCLB act, states must develop and expand existing student assessment systems and provide technical assistance to schools identified as being "in need of improvement." Sanctions imposed on schools who continue to fail to make adequate yearly progress include state takeover of the operation of the schools.

The NCLB act also gives states the primary responsibility for ensuring that by 2005–06 all teachers are "highly qualified" and for making annual reports on their progress in achieving this goal. And, perhaps most important, since it is the state, not the local school district or the federal government, that has the legal responsibility to provide for education, it is ultimately the state's responsibility to meet the goal that all children in the state will be achieving at the proficient level by 2014.

Accountability

As discussed previously in this chapter, as well as in Chapter 7, the education reform and **accountability** movements have resulted in state legislatures and state boards of education imposing a variety of requirements on local school districts. Examples include graduation requirements, entrance examinations for teachers, school and school district report cards, content standards for disciplines, standardized tests, and "no pass, no play" requirements for participants in interscholastic activities. The federal government has also enacted accountability reporting requirements and assurances under the No Child Left Behind Act. Each state is required to annually submit a detailed state plan to the U.S. Department of Education.

By 2005 all 50 states had established standardized testing programs, were rating schools, and were requiring schools to publish report cards to inform policy makers and the public about student/school performance. To further promote accountability, some observers have advocated that funding for schools be based on student performance. However, opponents to such plans have cautioned that reducing state aid to under-achieving schools would mean that the school would have less to spend on programs even though its need for such aid would be greater.

Funding an Adequate Education

As previously discussed, in the 1990s the focus of school finance policy and legislation began to shift from the pursuit of equity in funding to the attainment of adequacy, from an emphasis on ensuring equal inputs to ensuring that sufficient resources are provided to produce the level of student performance deemed to constitute an adequate education. Policy makers in a number of states initiated reform of their state finance programs in an effort to provide a sufficient level of funding to deliver an adequate education to every child in the state.

Despite the growing interest in adequacy, the financial crisis and large budget deficit faced by many states resulted in a number of states actually cutting their K–12 budgets at the same time the NCLB act was initiated, thereby undermining efforts to create state finance systems that would provide the support needed by those schools and students who were not making adequately yearly progress under the NCLB act. An estimate by the National Education Association suggested that $41.8 billion would be needed in 2004 to reach all the students eligible for services and schools eligible for interventions under NCLB (Hoff, 2004). Yet federal funding provides only about half of the 20% to 30% increase in educational expenditures estimated as necessary to meet NCLB mandates.

PROFESSIONAL REFLECTION

As with all large issues in education, the answer to whether "money matters" depends on what areas need improvement. Money will certainly purchase updated curriculum materials, computers, software, furniture, and building repairs and will lower staff-to-student ratios. All of these things are helpful and can lead to increased student achievement. However, money alone cannot change the fact that students have different abilities and disabilities, different family situations, and different economic situations. Money also cannot buy a motivated, positive staff with the belief that all children and families are valuable. It takes a mix of money and good administrative leadership to truly create effective school improvement.

Cara Convery
National Board Certified
Teacher, Colorado

To analyze this reflection, go to the *Professional Reflection* module for this chapter of the Companion Website at **http://www.prenhall.com/webb**.

Enrollment Increases

Public school enrollments reached an all-time high of 48.5 million in 2002 and are projected to reach 50 million in 2014 (Hussar, 2005). The impact of this growth has been to exacerbate the need for (1) additional classroom space to cope with enrollment increases and replace educationally obsolete facilities that were constructed to meet enrollment increases in the 1960s and 1970s, and (2) more teachers to cope with the enrollment increases and replace the large number of teachers and other professional staff members who are projected to retire in the next decade (Skinner, 2005). Securing the funding to meet these needs presents a major financial challenge to states and school districts.

Summary

The annual revenues for public elementary and secondary education reached $472 billion by 2004–05 (National Education Association, 2005a). This outlay is viewed as an investment because education contributes trained workers who support the economy through their production and purchase of consumer goods and because it is believed that an educated populace is necessary to sustain a democracy.

State governmental and organizational structures for schools differ in some ways, but the general pattern is consistent. Greater differences can be found in the patterns of school finance and the range in the proportion of funds that comes from state and local revenue sources. An ongoing challenge for all states is to provide for an acceptable balance between the conflicting goals of equity, adequacy, and choice. A second challenge will be to raise the revenues for the programs in a fair and equitable manner to ensure that all students have access to an appropriate educational program and that all taxpayers are treated fairly.

Under President George W. Bush, the federal government has assumed a more active role related to elementary and secondary education. Federal funds have not increased dramatically, but the focus has been on accountability, including each school's performance and annual progress on achievement tests, school report cards, and intervention for low-performing schools. Funding levels have been maintained for major federal programs such as education of the disadvantaged and students with disabilities.

With this background on school organization, administration, and finance, you now have a context in which to place the discussion of school curriculum in the following chapter.

Key Terms

Accountability, 355

Adequacy, 344

Building principal, 336

Categorical funding, 345

Charter schools, 339

Chief state school officer, 341

Choice, 344

Equalization models, 345

Equity, 344

Flat grants, 345

Foundation grants, 345

Full state funding, 345

Local property tax, 348

Parochial school, 354

Policies, 335

Power equalization, 345

Proprietary schools, 353

School board, 335

Secretary of education, 343

Site-based management (SBM), 339

State board of education, 341

State department of education, 341

Superintendent of schools, 335

Vouchers, 354

PROFESSIONAL DEVELOPMENT WORKSHOP

Prepare for the Praxis™ Examination

Ms. Rhonda Pham has been teaching mathematics for the past 8 years at the Rainer Maria Rilke Junior High School located in the Southwest. During the past 2 years, Rhonda has also served as a part-time assistant principal assigned to work with beginning teachers on various issues, including classroom management.

Recently Ms. Pham was asked by the principal to meet with Jackson Dearborn, a first-year, seventh-grade English teacher who is having difficulty controlling the disruptive behavior of his students, especially in the library. According to Margaret Chatsworth, the librarian, Mr. Dearborn's students come into the library pushing and shoving and rush to the computers causing a great deal of commotion and noise. And, despite Mr. Dearborn's presence, they spend most of their time socializing with students

from other classes and use the computers to play games and/or send e-mail to their friends when they should be doing Internet research.

1. What are some of the major causes of disruptive behavior in classrooms?
2. Describe some of the interventions that Mr. Dearborn might use to effectively deal with the misbehavior of his students in the library.
3. Under what circumstances might coercive punishment and/or other types of penalties be used to reduce or eliminate inappropriate behavior at school?

To submit your responses online, go to the *Prepare for the Praxis™ Examination* module for this chapter of the Companion Website at **http://www.prenhall.com/webb.**   CW

Build Your Knowledge Base

1. How does education being a state function affect the powers of citizens to determine programs in local schools?
2. What qualifications should a person have to be a member of a school board, principal, superintendent, chief state schools officer, or U.S. secretary of education?
3. What kinds of responsibilities should teachers have in the administration of an individual school?
4. In what ways are private schools and their students different from public schools and their students?
5. How does the per pupil funding level for schools in your state compare with the levels in other states?
6. In what ways are public schools, charter schools, and private schools different, and how are they similar?
7. What educational programs should the federal government finance?

Develop Your Portfolio

1. To better understand how schools are financed, review the following tables: Table 13.2: Current Funding Approaches, on page 346; Table 13.3: Current Per Pupil Expenditures, Per Capita Personal Income, 2002, Average Teacher Salary, 2004–05, on page 347; and Table 13.4: Estimated Percent of Revenues for Public Schools From Local, State, and Federal Sources, 2004–05, on page 348. Interview a school business manager regarding how schools are financed in your state. Use the following questions as a guide for your interview: (1) What are the major local, state, and federal revenue sources in your state? (2) How do the state taxes compare with other states? (3) How equitable is the school finance program? (4) How adequate is the funding? (5) Explain how "choice" is being used (i.e., local control of funding decisions or the power of parents to select the school their child will attend). (6) Identify the major model or funding approach (equalized foundation grants, equalized reward for tax effort, full state funding, flat grant, or other sources of nontax revenues). (7) To what extent has your state been involved in litigation regarding the inequalities or inadequacies of school finance? Following the interview, prepare a short reflection paper that summarizes your thoughts regarding the major problems of financing public elementary and secondary schools in your state. Place your reflection paper in your portfolio under **INTASC Standard 1, Knowledge of Subject.**
2. The proposed 2006 budget for the U.S. Department of Education recommended no funding for federal vocational education programs. Interview a principal concerning the student interest in vocational education. Include his or her remarks in a position paper summarizing the pros and cons of vocational education. Include the following information in your interview: (1) When did federal funding start for vocational education? (2) How were the federal funds used? (3) Does your state provide funds for vocational education? (4) How many students are served in the program in his/her school? (5) Are vocational education teachers certified in the same manner

as public school teachers? (6) How is accountability measured? Place your position paper in your portfolio under **INTASC Standard 1, Knowledge of Subject.**

 To complete these activities online, go to the *Develop Your Portfolio* module for this chapter of the Companion Website at **http://www.prenhall.com/webb.**

Explore Teaching and Learning: Field Experiences

1. Contact the business office of a local school district and request a copy of the district's annual budget and financial report. Identify the various sources of revenue for the school district. What portions come from federal, state, and local sources? Make a pie chart that shows revenue sources similar to the one shown in this chapter. How does the pie chart for your district compare with the national one presented in the chapter?
2. Contact the business office of a local school district and request a copy of the district's annual budget and financial report. Review the document to determine the proportion of the budget allocated for teacher's salaries, utilities, classroom supplies, and salaries of central office administrators. What are their percentages of the total? Make a pie chart that shows the budget allocation for the principal functions in the budget similar to the one in this chapter. How does the pattern for your district compare with the national pattern presented in the chapter?

Professional Development Online

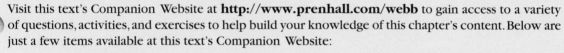 Visit this text's Companion Website at **http://www.prenhall.com/webb** to gain access to a variety of questions, activities, and exercises to help build your knowledge of this chapter's content. Below are just a few items available at this text's Companion Website:

- Classroom Video—To see actual classroom footage and work through activities and questions to analyze the content of the video, click on the *Classroom Video* module for this chapter.
- Teaching Tolerance—To go to this organization's website and complete activities to explore issues and topics dealing with how to teach tolerance to students, click on the *Teaching Tolerance* module for this chapter.
- Self-Test—To review terms and concepts presented in this chapter, click on the *Self-Test* module for this chapter.
- Internet Resources—To link to websites related to topics in this chapter, go to the *Internet Resources* module for this chapter.

PART

6

CURRICULUM AND INSTRUCTION

Chapter 14
The School Curriculum: Development and Design

Chapter 15
Instructional Practices in Effective Schools

The young man taught all he knew and more: the middle-aged man taught all he knew: the old man taught all that his students could understand.

—Anonymous

THE SCHOOL CURRICULUM: DEVELOPMENT AND DESIGN

As a new teacher, Mary Sherman has found that there is some community controversy over who should control the curriculum in the public schools. This question also is receiving considerable attention in local school board meetings and parent–teacher meetings. The community has not been able to reach consensus. Mary has read a recent Phi Delta Kappa poll of teachers that indicates teachers felt that they should have the greatest influence on what is taught in the schools. In reviewing the national content standards that have been adopted by the state for the major subject areas, Mary found that the national professional organizations had been deeply involved in the development of the standards. The state also has recently adopted a state-wide assessment program designed to determine the extent to which the students have attained the standards. Mary has also seen national polls that report that parents feel that the schools' curriculum needs to be changed to meet current needs and that they should be given a greater role in determining its direction.

What steps should the local teachers' organization take to address these apparently conflicting positions? What effects will the content standards and the statewide assessment program have on Mary's role as a teacher and what she teaches in the classroom? What are the implications for the academic freedom and academic responsibility of the public school teacher?

The curriculum in the nation's elementary and secondary schools is undergoing significant changes in part a result of the adoption of state content standards and assessment systems. In this chapter, the concept of curriculum is explored from its many perspectives, ranging from curriculum as content to curriculum as experiences. This chapter provides information to help you to:

- Review the sociopolitical and professional forces that influence curriculum policy making and design.
- Contrast the alternative approaches to curriculum development.
- Describe the curriculum mapping process.
- Compare the subject-centered and student-centered patterns of curriculum design.
- Describe the hidden curriculum and the null curriculum and their effects on schooling.

The term **curriculum** is a vague and complex notion. Curriculum theorists do not agree on any one definition. Broadly defined, curriculum is said to be all of the educational experiences of students that take place under the auspices of the school. How we perceive curriculum is important, because our perception of curriculum reflects and shapes how we think about, study, and act on the education provided to students (Sowell, 2005).

In this chapter, various views of the curriculum will be examined. First, the influence of a number of sociopolitical forces on curriculum policy making and design will be reviewed. Next, the curriculum development process will be summarized. Last, the major patterns of intended curricular organization or design will be described, followed by a discussion of the null and the unintended, or hidden, curriculum.

Forces Influencing the Curriculum

Decisions about the curriculum are not made in a vacuum by teachers, administrators, and curriculum specialists. Such decisions occur in the context of a particular community, state, and nation at a particular time. Throughout history various professional, political, social, economic, and religious groups have attempted to influence the schools' curriculum. Their relative power and influence have varied over time, as well as their motives, methods, strengths, and successes (Marsh & Willis, 2003). The process by which they attempt to influence the curriculum is political and is directed at answering four questions: (1) Who initiates the curriculum? (2) Who determines priorities? (3) Who implements the curriculum? (4) Who is responsible for what happens?

The various political, commercial, and professional groups that are influencing curriculum as the nation enters the 21st century are shown in Figure 14.1. Political forces and professional organizations have become more active as initiators because of concerns about the importance of an educated workforce if the nation is to be competitive in a global economy. This national interest may contribute to greater uniformity in curricular

For Your Reflection and Analysis

Who should determine the curriculum? Who should decide how to teach the content?

To submit your response online, go to http://www. prenhall.com/webb.

CW

Figure 14.1 — Forces and Groups Influencing Curriculum

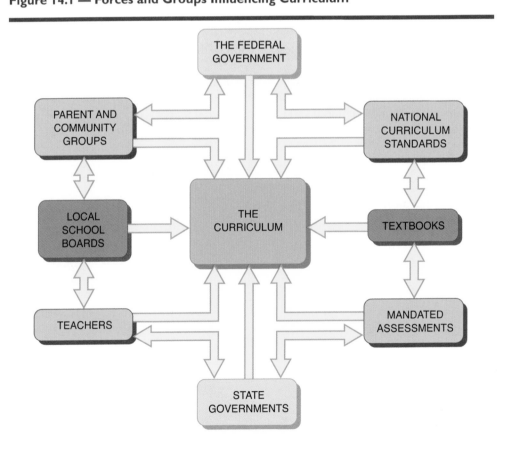

content and student assessment. The professional subject-matter organizations have identified the standards and goals that are subsequently incorporated into the textbooks and the instructional materials. The commercial testing companies then provide the standardized assessment instruments. In this scenario, teachers are ultimately responsible for results or what happens, and the individual school comes under closer scrutiny through the concern about the extent to which the students are meeting the expected performance level.

This section briefly discusses the influences of the following forces on curriculum in the schools: national curriculum standards, textbooks, mandated assessments, state governments, teachers, local school boards, parent and community groups, and the federal government. The interaction of these relationships is shown in Figure 14.1.

National Curriculum Standards

Before the mid-1980s, concerns about the curriculum were largely limited to textbook content and "what to teach when." The school reform movement and state accountability legislation changed this somewhat comfortable and isolated environment. One of the most influential developments occurred during the 1990s when the major subject-matter professional organizations received federal funds to develop curriculum content standards in the principal subject areas. This had a dramatic impact on curriculum in elementary and secondary schools, as well as on teacher preparation programs in colleges and universities. The standards identified what students should know and be able to do, called for more rigorous content, and encouraged the development of comprehensive curriculum that emphasized problem solving, integrated tasks, real-life problems, and higher order thinking skills (Wiles & Bondi, 2002). As a result of their having been developed by the major professional organizations using federal funding, the reports had instant credibility and were accorded the status of being the official sources of essential knowledge in the relevant subject area.

Questions have been raised about the extent to which national curriculum standards threaten state and local control of education. The concept of national standards appears to conflict with the traditional position that education is a local function, a state responsibility, and a national concern. However, the standards are considered to be "national" in terms of being important to the nation's citizens rather than "federal" in terms of being mandates from the federal government. In the context of the press for accountability at the state level, the curriculum standards have been used by state education agencies for the adoption of curriculum standards, and by publishers of textbooks and instructional materials for linking instructional materials and textbooks to those standards.

For Your Reflection and Analysis

What are the pros and cons of having academic professionals set standards and goals in their subject areas?
To submit your response online, go to http://www. prenhall.com/webb.

CW

Textbooks

The influence of textbooks cannot be overstated; in the course of their educational career, students may be exposed to hundreds of textbooks and spend major portions of their time in the classroom using textbooks. Teachers rely heavily on textbooks for instructional content, organization, and evaluation. Without question, textbooks and other published instructional materials influence what is taught and learned in the classroom. It is because they recognize the powerful influence of textbooks that various special interest groups have been so vocal and persistent in their attempts to influence textbook content and adoption decisions as well as the textbook industry itself.

Given the potential influence of textbooks and the unresolved concerns about their

Teachers rely heavily on textbooks for instructional content.

content, it is important that teachers be sensitive to textbook treatment of cultural diversity, gender differences, and special populations. Teachers should actively seek to participate in the textbook selection process. Ultimately, the influence that textbooks have on the curriculum is determined by the care taken in their selection and how they are used in the classroom.

Mandated Assessments

Testing has become an integral part of the American education system. Students are admitted to postsecondary institutions, private elementary and secondary schools, and specialized programs in the public schools based on their test results. By 2006 a minimum competency test must be passed before a diploma is awarded in 26 states. Many scholarships are based entirely or in part on test results. Teachers, programs, and schools are considered more or less effective based on test results. In 20 states schools considered low performing based on test results have been subject to sanction and in 18 states high-performing or improving schools are recognized (Skinner, 2005). The admission of prospective teachers and administrators into degree or certification programs, or their later certification, is determined by test results. Practicing teachers and administrators are tested in some states. Many accountability plans include test results as output indicators.

The rate of increase in the use of national standardized tests among the states in the last two decades has been significant. With the enactment of the No Child Left Behind Act of 2001, the federal government has become more active in the student assessment movement. As described in Chapter 7, this legislation requires annual testing in reading and mathematics in grades 3 through 8 and mandates state participation in the National Assessment of Educational Progress.

To a large extent, standardized tests function as "gatekeepers of knowledge" (Spring, 1998). Test developers decide what knowledge most merits testing. Although state assessments are presumed to be based on state-adopted curriculum standards, test makers exercise considerable influence. And, although they may not necessarily advocate "teaching to the test," school boards, administrators, and teachers seek to ensure that they prepare students to do well on the test. If test scores are down in a particular school or certain curriculum area, district resources and instruction may be redirected to that area. Increasingly, individual students and their families invest in tutorial books, computer software, and seminars in an attempt to raise test scores.

Standardized tests can play an important role in providing the data needed for assessing curriculum and measuring student progress, but their limits must be recog-

 ## VIDEO INSIGHT

Cheating 101: Pressures to Boost Standardized Test Scores

This ABC News video includes a series of interviews about questionable practices related to the administration of standardized tests that are a part of the state accountability program. With your classmates or other students, reflect on the following questions:

1. In your different schooling experiences, what types of unethical testing behavior have you witnessed?
2. What appropriate actions can teachers take to help students raise their scores on standardized tests?
3. What ethical responsibilities do you have when you are instructed by the principal to provide students with the answers to test questions?

 To submit your answers online, go to the *Video Insight* module for this chapter of the Companion Website at http://.www.prenhall.com/webb.

nized. Educators, policy makers, and parents should keep in mind that much of what most tests measure is achievement; they do not measure other desired outputs of the learning experience.

State Governments

As the level of government with legal responsibility for education, the state's influence over the curriculum is exercised in several ways. One important way the state influences the curriculum is through the adoption of content standards for different subject areas. By 2005, 49 states had adopted content standards in the core academic subjects, and each of these states had formal assessments to measure student progress toward attaining these standards (Skinner, 2005).

Another example of the influence of the state on the curriculum is through state statutes that mandate that students receive a passing grade in certain courses or pass a proficiency test in order to graduate from high school. As of 2001, in only 6 states was the decision regarding the number of credits required for graduation left to the discretion of local school boards (Skinner, 2005). In those states where the number of Carnegie units required for high school graduation was mandated by the state, the number of units required ranged from 13 to 24, with the median being 21 units.

The influence of the state on the curriculum has been particularly evident in the aftermath of the reform reports of the 1980s. A major recommendation of many of these reports was that students be required to take an increased number of basic courses in English, social studies, mathematics, and science. In response, between 1980 and 2001, the average number of Carnegie units required by states for graduation from high school increased by 1.2 units in English, 1.6 units in social studies, 2.2 units in mathematics, and 2.0 units in the sciences (Skinner, 2005). Figure 14.2 provides a comparison of the average number of Carnegie units in major subject-area state requirements for graduation required in 1980 and 2001.

In addition to statutory requirements, the state influences the curriculum through the state board of education, which, in many states, is authorized to determine curriculum requirements and promulgate curriculum guidelines. The state department of education also influences the curriculum through the textbook adoption process, support for professional development activities, and the provision of instructional resources and curriculum guides. State curriculum guides detail the goals and objectives, competencies, and instructional activities for every subject at every grade level. (See Chapter 13 for a discussion of the roles and responsibilities of state boards and departments of education.)

Teachers

Historically, teachers have had a significant impact on their school's curriculum. Teachers once were considered the primary source of knowledge in the classroom and were perceived to have the knowledge and skills to determine what was to be taught, what materials to use, and how student mastery was to be measured. They participated in the development of curriculum guides and related materials.

With the enactment of state accountability and assessment programs and the adoption of content standards, teachers now have less control over what is to be taught and when. Teachers retain the academic freedom to determine how to teach, but their freedom to

Figure 14.2 — Average Number of Carnegie Units in Major Subject Areas Required by the States for Graduation from High School in 1980 and 2001

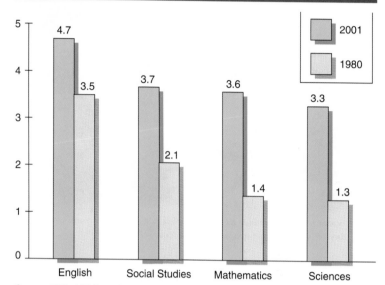

Sources: Table 152. State Requirements for High School Graduation in Carnegie Units, 2001, *Digests of Education Statistics 2004 and 2001*. Washington, DC: National Center for Education Statistics.

For Your Reflection and Analysis

What roles should teachers have in deciding what is to be taught and how to teach it?
To submit your response online, go to http://www. prenhall.com/webb.

CW

School board meetings provide the venue for members of the community to make public their concerns about operation of the local schools.

determine what or when to teach certain content has been restricted because of the adoption of content standards and state assessment programs (Stoddard, 2004).

Local School Boards

Local school boards make a host of curriculum decisions about the content and learning opportunities that are provided for students. Within the limits of state authority, local boards decide what electives will be offered, which textbooks and other instructional materials will be purchased, which curriculum guides are to be followed, what teachers will be hired, how the budget will be spent, and how to respond to innumerable other issues that directly or indirectly influence the curriculum. It is the local school board that most often feels the pressure of parents and special interest groups, because this body decides such matters as whether a new program will be piloted, whether such courses as sex education will be offered, or whether a program for students with hearing impairments will be offered by the district or students will be provided services outside the district.

In recent years, there has been increased concern regarding the extent to which the local school board represents all constituencies in the community. One concern is that local boards are influenced too much by small but vocal groups of parents or concerned citizens. Another concern is the elitist composition of boards of education. Except for rural school boards, most school boards tend to be composed of a disproportionate number of White male professionals or businesspersons (Spring, 2005).

Parent and Community Groups

Because of their vested interest in the local schools and their proximity to local decision makers, parents and community groups have the potential for exercising tremendous influence on the curriculum. For example, in recent years parents in some African American communities have demanded an Afrocentric curriculum that presents the black perspective on history and current events as an alternative to the traditional Eurocentric curriculum. Such a curriculum, supporters argue, not only promotes a positive identity with their racial/ethnic group, it leads to improved self-esteem and academic achievement. Afrocentric public schools have been established in a number of the larger cities in the United States. In addition, in a number of areas, educators and parents have established charter schools that are Afrocentric, Chicano-centric, or Native American centric, "emphasizing what is known, valued, and respected from their own cultural roots" (Gollnick & Chinn, 2006, p. 126).

Parents also exercise their influence on the curriculum by serving on textbook adoption committees or education committees at the local, state, or national level. Parent–teacher associations, band boosters, parents of children with disabilities, parents of gifted children, and other interest groups are often active in supporting special programs or influencing legislation and supporting tax or spending referenda. Other groups bring pressure on school boards and school officials to decide whether or not to include curriculum material on sex education, substance abuse, suicide, ethnic or women's studies, and religion. Currently, various groups are bringing pressure on local school boards, state boards of education, political decision makers, and the textbook industry to rid our schools of all material and teaching that are said to promote secular humanism and ignore religion (see Chapter 11).

Parents in general also have concerns about the extent to which the curriculum needs to be changed to meet current expectations. In a 2000 Phi Delta Kappa poll, 66% of the

For Your Reflection and Analysis

How much input should parents and school patrons have in deciding what is to be taught?

To submit your response online, go to http://www.prenhall.com/webb.

parents surveyed said that they wanted more say in decisions that affect their schools (Rose & Gallup, 2000).

The Federal Government

Traditionally, the federal government's influence over the curriculum has focused on perceived national problems or programs to serve youth with special needs. Examples of these initiatives are the National Defense Education Act of 1958 discussed in Chapter 7 that was enacted in response to the launching of *Sputnik,* the Bilingual Education Act, and the Individuals with Disabilities Education Act. However, as discussed in previous chapters, the No Child Left Behind (NCLB) Act gives the federal government broader involvement and places a number of requirements on schools, school districts, and states including (1) conducting an annual assessment in reading and mathematics for students in grades 3 through 8, (2) participating in the National Assessment of Educational Progress that tests fourth- and eighth-grade students in reading and mathematics, (3) adopting and reporting yearly progress, and (4) adopting and reporting requirements related to preparation of teachers and paraprofessionals.

For Your Reflection and Analysis

Should states be permitted to ignore national standards and goals? *To submit your response online, go to http://www. prenhall.com/webb.*

CW

Curriculum Development

The curriculum development and planning literature is replete with models, paradigms, and "steps," which can basically be categorized into three primary perspectives: the prescriptive perspective, the descriptive perspective, and the critical perspective. The *prescriptive perspective* has dominated thought on curriculum planning for more than 50 years. It looks at curriculum development as a rational, objective, linear process consisting of a series of sequential steps. The *descriptive perspective* is concerned with the events and decisions of the act of curriculum development itself. In other words, it is interested in how curriculum developers actually go about doing their work in practice. Its focus is on the process for curricular decision making. The newer *critical perspective* takes issue with the very assumptions underlying the first two perspectives and advocates critical reflection on the underlying assumptions in discussions about the curriculum. This perspective asserts that curriculum development is not a linear process. This perspective holds that curriculum decisions are not value free; they are ideologically and sociopolitically based (Posner, 1998).

In his discussion of approaches to curriculum development, Wiles (2005) utilized the concept of interdependence from systems theory to explain how one part of an organization influences the other parts. Systems models typically have three phases: input, process, and output. To different degrees, the basic concepts of system theory are reflected in the description of each of the three approaches to curriculum development displayed in Table 14.1. These approaches are based on different assumptions about the inputs for curriculum development, the forces that do/should influence the process, and the desired student outcomes.

Prescriptive Perspective

The prescriptive perspective on curriculum development can be traced to Tyler's (1949) technical production perspective. This approach views curriculum planning as a rational, technical process that can be accomplished by objective decision making. Further, curriculum planning is presumed to be a production-oriented enterprise in which the planner objectively and, if possible, scientifically establishes *a priori* the means to obtain the desired educational outcomes.

Tyler's (1949) curriculum planning model is organized around four steps. In the first step, the planners *identify what educational purposes, aims, and goals to pursue.* That is, they determine which aims and objectives the school should pursue. Recognition is given to different schools of thought about the purpose of education, and these beliefs are translated into curriculum and instructional practices.

The second step is to *identify and select learning experiences* that enable the student(s) to attain the desired purposes. Once developed, possible experiences are checked

Table 14.1 — Perspectives on Curriculum Development

Perspective	Underlying Assumptions	Process
Prescriptive—technical production perspective (Tyler)	A rational model that views curriculum planning as an objective, linear process	Curriculum planning is a four-step process: • Identify purpose, aims, and goals • Identify and select learning experiences • Organize and sequence learning experiences • Evaluate
Descriptive—deliberative perspective (Walker)	A naturalistic perspective that focuses on how curriculum decision making occurs in practice	Curriculum decision making occurs in three phases: • Platform • Deliberation • Design
Critical—artistic perspective (Eisner)	A critical perspective that views curriculum decision making as embodying educational imagination and transformation (artistry)	Curriculum development is process of consensus building: • Need for deliberation in establishing priorities • Emphasis on learning events that are meaningful • Consideration of nonlinear, cross-curriculum content organization • Multiple modes of presentation

to see if they give students the opportunity to acquire the behaviors stated in the objectives and if they lead to the intended effect (Sowell, 2005).

In the third step, planners *organize learning experiences* to ensure the continuity and sequence of experiences. Consistent with Piaget's theory that a subject can be taught in some form to any student at any stage of development, **continuity** is concerned with the reiteration of major curriculum elements so that skills can be practiced and developed. Sequencing ensures that successive experiences build on preceding ones. The concepts of continuity and sequence correspond to Bruner's concept of the spiral curriculum, which treats concepts and topics at progressive grade levels in increasing complexity and detail. Effective organization of experiences also involves the integration of skills and knowledge across disciplines.

In the fourth step, the planner develops a means to *evaluate* whether the stated purposes are being attained by the selected learning experiences. (See Figure 14.3 for Tyler's curriculum planning cycle.)

Deliberative Perspective

The deliberative approach has its roots in Decker Walker's (1971, 2004) interest in what people actually do as they develop curricula. He assumed that a better curriculum results when those engaged in its delivery understand the complexity of the curriculum development process.

Walker's interest was in how decisions actually occurred as opposed to other approaches that describe in what ways the curriculum should occur. Walker's approach as-

Figure 14.3 — The Tyler Planning Cycle

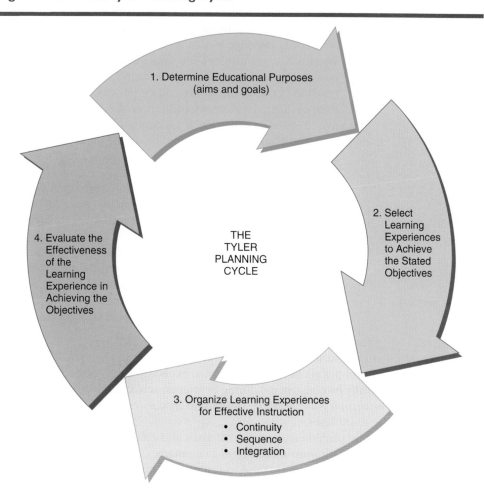

1. Determine Educational Purposes (aims and goals)

2. Select Learning Experiences to Achieve the Stated Objectives

3. Organize Learning Experiences for Effective Instruction
   - Continuity
   - Sequence
   - Integration

4. Evaluate the Effectiveness of the Learning Experience in Achieving the Objectives

THE TYLER PLANNING CYCLE

sumes that people bring their individual values and beliefs when they come together to engage in curriculum development. They have their own perceptions of the task, problems, prescriptions, and commitments (Marsh & Willis, 2003). Walker's three-step sequence for how curriculum is developed consists of platform, deliberation, and design.

In Walker's first step, *platform,* members of a working group with diverse positions are brought together to develop a consensus that delimits both the content of future discussions and the curriculum. The platform consists of conceptions about what exists and what is possible, theories about relations between entities, and aims about appropriate courses of action. The ultimate success of the approach in subsequent steps will be dependent on the clarity and comprehensiveness of the consensus-building process.

The second step, *deliberation,* goes beyond beliefs to their use in assessing the actual state of affairs and possible courses of action. Walker's model assumes that the process of deliberation includes identification of relevant facts, generating alternative courses of action, consideration of the costs and consequences of alternatives, and selection of the most desirable alternatives.

In the third step, *design,* the assumption is that the working group has reached sufficient consensus to permit the adoption of particular courses of action without consideration of other options. The culminating activity is the creation of the curriculum, which may include specific subjects, instructions, teaching materials, activities as determined by the working group, and procedures for evaluation.

Critical Perspective

In sharp contrast to the technical production perspective is the critical perspective, which rejects the notion that curriculum planning can be an objective, value-free process. Rather,

> **For Your Reflection and Analysis**
>
> In nontechnical terms, how are the approaches to curriculum different and how do the differences affect the teacher?
>
> *To submit your response online, go to http://www.prenhall.com/webb.*
>
> CW

Elliot Eisner sees curriculum development as an artistic process.

this perspective argues that curriculum decisions are essentially ideological and sociopolitical. As some critical theorists point out, the very decisions about what the objectives should be, what knowledge is of most value, and how it will be evaluated involve assumptions and values that reinforce the existing power and social structure. For example, because of the relationship between evaluators and employers, if it were known to an evaluator that the administration of a district had been active in initiating a particular curriculum and had fought to secure financial support for the program, then the evaluator would probably feel great pressure to discover results not unfavorable to the program.

One of several critical perspectives to curriculum development is the artistic approach articulated by Eisner (2002). Eisner (2002) views social reality as subjective, negotiated, and individually constructed. He sees the individuals who come together to develop curriculum as artists who choose "among an almost limitless variety of ways of representing their views of reality, in response to which students choose how to modify their own views" (Marsh & Willis, 2003, p. 82).

Eisner's (2002) concept of curriculum development is based on the following premises:

1. Attention should be given to both *explicit and vague goals and objectives.* He contends that it may not always be desirable to have explicitly stated objectives and objectives may actually be constructed during or after an actual teaching event occurs.
2. *Content can be drawn from both the individual and society,* as well as from traditional academic disciplines.
3. Emphasis should be placed on ensuring that goals and content are transformed into *learning events that are most meaningful to students.*
4. A *nonlinear approach* should be used in organizing learning opportunities to encourage diverse student outcomes that have positive educational consequences for students with differing needs.
5. The approach assumes a *cross-curriculum organization of content* in nontraditional patterns.
6. Multiple *modes of communication* are used to enhance the richness of educational opportunities for youth who may have differing interests and learning styles.
7. *Evaluation should consist of a comprehensive range of procedures* at different stages of the learning process. This perspective recognizes that learning is a complex process that cannot easily be assessed by a singular measure at one point in time.

Perspectives Compared

These three perspectives on curriculum development illustrate alternative approaches and differ in their assumptions and process. Ralph Tyler's technical production perspective is somewhat prescriptive and thus can be followed easily by curriculum workers. It sees curriculum planning as an objective, value-free process. The resulting curriculum is carefully planned, but the product may not take into account all the contingencies of the complexities of the day-to-day classroom. Walker's deliberative approach assumes the gathering and examination of alternatives, identification of possible courses of action, impact analysis of alternatives, and selection of the most desirable alternatives as the primary work of curriculum developers. In contrast, Eisner's artistic approach is a nonlinear process that assumes alternative and diverse student outcomes are to be expected and that curricula require imagination and transformation to provide students with the richness of experiences to meet their individual learning needs.

Curriculum Mapping

Although teachers work together in the same school and district, they may not have a full understanding of what other teachers in the school or building are teaching. **Curriculum mapping** is a process that allows districts, schools, and classrooms to monitor their efforts to ensure that they have reached consensus on what is to be taught, what is to be assessed, and whether there is alignment in scope, sequence, and assessment schedule. Curriculum mapping has been a component of good program planning for an extended period of time, but the importance of coordinated planning has been escalated by the widespread adoption of national and state curriculum standards with expected performance levels, mandated student assessments, and state and local accountability reports. To cope with these new developments, teachers and administrators need a sufficient understanding and agreement on what content is to be taught, how and when the content can be taught, what resources are needed, what the state standards and test objectives are, how student knowledge and progress will be assessed, when assessments will be conducted, what the acceptable performance levels are, especially for promotion and high school graduation, and how consistent the content of textbooks and instructional materials is with the curriculum standards and assessments.

The first step in the curriculum mapping process involves individual teachers or teachers at the same grade level or subject areas describing the curriculum of their class or academic subject—the concepts and topics covered, the skills and knowledge emphasized, goals and objectives, and the expected learner outcomes. These descriptions are then shared across grade levels or subjects and a curriculum map constructed that shows the entire existing curriculum. Such a map allows the identification of any gaps in the curriculum as well as any unnecessary duplication. The goal of the curriculum mapping process is to focus on articulation across subject areas and grade levels so that teachers will know what the expectations are for students to progress from one grade to the next. Uniformity in teaching methods is not the goal; the goal is to create a structure or scaffold that ensures that the scope and sequence of the educational program are consistent with post-reform accountability and assessment developments (Jacobs, 2004).

Curriculum mapping may be done at the district, school, or department levels. One such mapping framework for teachers at the classroom level developed by Jacobs (2004) has six components: (1) essential questions, (2) content, (3) skills, (4) assessments, (5) activities, and (6) resources. Delineating the specifics of these six components helps to ensure that standards, goals, and assessments are appropriately aligned. Not only can the framework be used to plan the curriculum, but it can also be used to record and track what was actually taught and assessed.

At the district level, an audit process may be developed to evaluate the actual curriculum delivery within the district. This provides information on areas for refinement, reveals potential disconnects between what is taught and what is tested, and reveals areas where targeted staff development may be of assistance to teachers in meeting students' goals and objectives.

Patterns of Curriculum Design

Decisions about how the curriculum should be organized involve choices about what content to study and how this content will be presented to the students. Although many different structures are available that reflect alternative perspectives about the nature of the curriculum, these alternatives can be classified as being either subject centered or student centered. The subject-centered perspective is the older, more traditional, and most common structure. It views the curriculum as a program of studies or collection of courses that represents what students should know. The second perspective focuses on the needs and interests of the student and the process by which learning takes place.

Table 14.2 — Perspectives on Curriculum Organization

Curriculum Design	Educational Theory	Curriculum Focus
Subject-area	Essentialism	A group of subjects or subject matter that represent the essential knowledge and values of society that have survived the test of time
Integrated		The integration of two or more subjects, both within and across disciplines, into an integrated course
Core curriculum	Perennialism	A common body of curriculum content and learning experience that should be encountered by all students; the Great Books
Student-centered	Progressivism	Learning activities centered around the interests and needs of the child, designed to motivate and interest the child in the learning process
Constructivism	Progressivism Social reconstructivism Postmodernism	Learning activities which encourage students to construct their own meaning based on current and past knowledge and experience
Social justice	Social reconstructivism Postmodernism	Critical analysis of the political, social, and economic problems facing society; future trends; social action projects designed to bring about social change

The subject-centered and student-centered perspectives represent two ends of a continuum of curricular design. In this section, six alternative curriculum designs along this continuum are examined: subject-area design, integrated design, core curriculum design, student-centered design, constructivism, and the social justice design. Various components of the different curriculum organizations are compared in Table 14.2.

The Subject-Area Curriculum Design

The **subject-area curriculum** design is the oldest and most common organization plan for the curriculum. This design views the curriculum as a group of subjects or body of subject matter. The subject matter to be included in the curriculum is that which has survived the test of time and is perceived to be of most value in the development of the intellect—said by supporters to be the primary purpose of education. The subject-area curriculum is consistent with the essentialist philosophy of education.

The subject-area design has its roots in classical Greece. In America William T. Harris, superintendent of schools in St. Louis, Missouri, in the 1870s and U.S. commissioner of education from 1886 to 1906, is credited with establishing this design, which has been the dominant curriculum organization for more than a century. Harris viewed the curriculum as the means by which students are introduced to the essential knowledge and values of society and transformed into reasoning and responsible citizens. The curriculum of the elementary school was to include the fundamentals, which Harris called the "five windows of the soul": mathematics, geography, literature and art, grammar, and history. In the high school, concentration was on the classics, languages, and mathematics (Cremin, 1962). Electives in languages, fine arts, and industrial arts were to be used to develop specific skills or to meet special interests (Ellis, Mackey, & Glenn, 1988).

Modern spokespersons for the subject-area curriculum include Arthur Bestor, Mortimer Adler, and Allan Bloom. They propose a return to fundamentals and a curriculum of basic studies. Some of the common proposals of supporters of this position are as follows:

1. Majority of the school day in elementary school spent on reading, writing, and arithmetic.
2. Heavy secondary school emphasis on English, science, mathematics, and history.
3. More authority to teachers, including the authority to use corporal punishment.
4. Instructional procedures that stress drill, homework, and frequent testing.
5. Textbooks that reflect patriotism and do not include material that challenges traditional values.

HISTORICAL NOTE

Phillips Exeter Academy Curriculum, 1818

Classical Department

First Year: Adam's Latin Grammar; Liber Primus, or a similar work; Viri Romani, or Caesar's Commentaries; Latin Prosody; Exercises in reading and making Latin; Ancient and Modern Geography; Virgil; Arithmetic.

Second Year: Virgil; Arithmetic; Exercises in reading and making Latin, continued; Valpey's Greek Grammar; Roman History; Cicero's Select Orations; Delectus; Dalzel's Collectanea Graeca Minora; Greek Testament; English Grammar and Declamation.

Third Year: The same Latin and Greek authors, in revision: English Grammar and Declamation, continued; Sallust; Algebra; Exercises in Latin and English translations, and Composition.

Fourth Year: Collectanea Graeca Majora; Q. Horatius Flaccus; Titus Livius; Parts of Terence's Comedies; Excerpta Latina, or such Latin and Greek authors as may best comport with the student's future destination; Algebra; Geometry; Elements of Ancient History; Adam's Roman Antiquities.

English Department

[For admission into this Department the candidate must be at least 12 years of age, and must have been well instructed in Reading and Spelling; familiarly acquainted with Arithmetic, through simple Proportion with the exception of Fractions, know Murray's English Grammar through Syntax, and must be able to parse simple English sentences.]

First Year: English Grammar, including exercises in Reading, Parsing, and Analyzing, in the correction of bad English; Punctuation and Prosody; Arithmetic; Geography; and Algebra, through Simple Equations.

Second Year: English Grammar; continued; Geometry; Plane Trigonometry, and its application to heights and distances; Mensuration of Sup. and Sol.; Elements of Ancient History; Logic; Rhetoric; English Composition; Declamation, and exercises of the Forensic kind.

Third Year: Surveying; Navigation; Elements of Chemistry and Natural Philosophy, with experiments; Elements of Modern History, particularly of the United States; Moral and Political Philosophy; English Composition, Forensics, and Declamation.

Source: Bell, cited in Cubberley, E. P. (1934). *Readings in public education in the United States* (pp. 223–224). New York: Houghton Mifflin.

CW To research and explore this topic further, go to the *Historical Note* module for this chapter of the Companion Website at **http://www.prenhall.com/webb.**

---

6. Elimination of electives, frills, and innovations as well as such social services as guidance, sex education, humanistic education, and peace education.
7. Promotion from grade to grade based on demonstrated proficiency on specific examinations (Sadker & Sadker, 1997).

Those who criticize the subject-area curriculum claim that it ignores the needs, interests, and experiences of students and discourages creativity on the part of both students and teachers. Another major criticism of this curriculum is that it is fragmented and compartmentalized. The subject-area curriculum is also faulted for failing to adequately consider both individual differences and contemporary social issues. The primary teaching methods of the subject-area curriculum are lecture and discussion. Rote memorization and recitation are required of students.

The subject-area curriculum has remained the most popular and dominant curriculum design for four basic reasons. First, most teachers, especially secondary school teachers, are trained in the subject areas. Secondary school teachers usually think of themselves as American history teachers, biology teachers, English teachers, and so on. Second, organizing the school by subject matter makes it easy for parents and other adults to understand a student's education because most adults attended schools that were organized by subject matter. Third, the subject-area organization makes it easy for teachers to develop curriculum and goals: The content provides the organization and focus needed in planning. Finally, textbooks and other instructional materials are usually developed for subject-area use (Ellis et al., 1988). Because the subject-area design has been so dominant in this country, it is possible to go into schools from Seattle to Key West and find much the same curriculum.

The Integrated Curriculum Design

The **integrated curriculum** design emerged as a response to the multiplication of courses resulting from the subject-area design. Emphasis remains on subjects, but in place of separate courses in history, geography, economics, political science, anthropology, and sociology, for example, an integrated course in social studies might be offered. By using this latter approach, supporters claim, knowledge is integrated in a way that makes it more meaningful to the learner. The integrated design also provides greater flexibility to the teacher in choosing subject matter.

Among the more common integrated courses are language arts, which has taken the place of separate courses in reading, writing, spelling, speaking, grammar, drama, and literature; mathematics, which integrates arithmetic, geometry, and algebra; general science, which includes botany, biology, chemistry, and geology or earth science; and the previously mentioned social studies. Although the integrated design usually combines separate subjects within the same discipline, in some instances content from two or more branches of study has been integrated into a new field of study. Futuristics, which integrates knowledge from mathematics, sociology, statistics, political science, economics, education, and a number of other fields, is one such new field of study.

The integrated curriculum has been widely accepted at the elementary level. Where once a number of separate subjects were taught for shorter periods of time, the typical elementary curriculum is now more likely to integrate these subjects into "subject areas" that are taught in longer blocks of time. Jacobs (1997) has indicated that the process of integrating curricula has matured into a workable and formidable force in high school reform. This approach is in sharp contrast with the past tendency to polarize the curriculum into separate disciplines. Jacobs contends that the question is no longer whether the curriculum should be integrated, but rather when and in what format.

The Core Curriculum Design

The definition of a **core curriculum** has changed significantly since it was first advanced in the 1930s. Originally, the core curriculum was proposed as an interdisciplinary approach of relating one subject to another in the study of everyday situations of interest and value to students. The core content was taught in an extended block of time centered around defining and solving problems of concern to all students. Attention was directed to the study of culture and fundamental social values. Typical core courses dealt with how to earn a living, social relations, or life adjustment. As described at the time, the core curriculum was said to be:

> made up of those educational experiences which are thought to be important for each citizen in our democracy. Students and teachers do not consider subject matter to be important in itself. It becomes meaningful only as it helps the group to solve the problems which have been selected for study. (MacConnell et al., cited in Goodlad, 1987, p. 10)

Different interpretations of the core concept have emerged over time. For example, the response to the national reports critical of education the 1980s was to recommend a core of subjects to be taken by all students: The National Commission on Excellence in Education (1983) recommended 13.5 units in "the Five New Basics," while Boyer (1983) proposed a "core of common learning" consisting of 14.5 units; and others wanted less specific, but still identifiable, cores. To others, the concept of a core is more reminiscent of the core curriculum espoused by the progressive educators of the 1930s, 1940s, and early 1950s. For example, although Goodlad (1983) in *A Place Called School* "deliberately and reluctantly" defined a core in conventional terms, he has since acknowledged that what is needed is not a core of subjects to be taken by all students but a core curriculum consisting of the domains of human experience and thought that should be encountered by all students. And, the Association for Supervision and Curriculum Development (ASCD) referred to a core of com-

For Your Reflection and Analysis

How is the role of the teacher different under the various curriculum types? *To submit your response online, go to http://www. prenhall.com/webb.*

CW

mon learning to help ensure that "all students are provided the curriculum content and learning experiences most appropriate to their future lives" (Cawelti, 1989, p. 33).

However, many educators are concerned that it is not possible to have a core curriculum for all students and still maintain quality. Others are concerned about the impact of a universal core requirement on the schools' ability to meet the needs of different populations, including those interested in vocational preparation. Probably all agree that the task of defining the proper core is among the most challenging professional tasks facing educators.

The Student-Centered Curriculum Design

The concept of the **student-centered curriculum** has its roots in the philosophies of Rousseau, Pestalozzi, and Froebel (see Chapter 5). In the United States, the concept was revived by the progressive education movement. There are a number of variations on the student-centered curriculum, including the experience- and activity-centered curriculum and the relevant curriculum. The emphasis of all student-centered curricula is on the student's freedom to learn and on activities and creative self-expression.

Whereas the traditional curriculum is organized around the teaching of discrete subject matter, in the student-centered curriculum, students come to the subject matter out of their own needs and interests. The student-centered curriculum focuses on the individual learner and the development of the whole student. The scope of this curriculum is as broad as all of human life and society, and its goal is to motivate and interest the student in the learning process. To achieve this goal, the curriculum encompasses a wide range of activities, including field geography, nature study, number concepts, games, drama, storytelling, music, art, handicrafts, other creative and expressive activities, physical education, and community involvement projects.

Student-centered designs are often criticized for being too broad and for being so inclusive as to be nonfunctional. They are also criticized for being too permissive and for their lack of attention to subject-matter mastery. Modern proponents (e.g., John Holt, Herbert Kohl, and Elliot

The student-centered curriculum includes a wide range of activities outside the classroom.

Eisner) counter that the student-centered curriculum enhances learning because it is based on the needs and interests of the learner. Student-centered curricula have operated in numerous districts and schools throughout this century, primarily at the elementary level. However, they have never been seriously considered at the secondary level.

The Constructivism Curriculum Design

The major theme of **constructivism** is that learning is an active process in which students construct new ideas or concepts based on their current and past knowledge and experiences (Bruner, 1960). Students select the desired information, transform those ideas into hypotheses, and make decisions based on this new knowledge. The students then adjust their understanding of reality to include this new information. The role of the teacher is to engage students in an active dialogue, translate information into the students' current sphere of understanding, and encourage students to discover the needed information and the principles. The subject-matter curriculum should be designed so that students can integrate this new knowledge with previously learned information (San Diego State University, 1996).

Building on prior knowledge, individuals construct their own view of the world through experiences within their physical and social environments. Students link their prior knowledge to the new knowledge in a continuous, active process that raises their thinking skills. In this context, constructivism and the core curriculum have similar qualities because both require the reorganization of existing knowledge to make room for new knowledge (Appalachian Rural School Initiative [ARSI], 1998).

Both constructivism and student-centered designs emphasize experiences, are activity centered, and are relevant. Students have the freedom to learn and create information; the curriculum is centered on their needs and interests. Individual students have the final responsibility for their learning (ARSI, 1998).

The Social Justice Curriculum Design

The **social justice curriculum** design is based on the belief that through the curriculum the school can and should effect social change and create a more equitable society. The social justice curriculum design had its origins in the social reconstructionism movement of the 1930s, as discussed in Chapters 4 and 7. In his book *Dare the Schools Build a New Social Order?* (1932), George Counts proposed that the schools involve students in a curriculum designed to reconstruct society. Modern reconstructionists (postmodernists) continue to advocate that the school curriculum promote social change and social justice.

The major assumption underlying the social justice curriculum is that the future is not fixed but is amenable to modification and improvement. Accordingly, the social justice curriculum seeks "to equip students with tools (skills) for dealing with changes about them. So equipped, the student can meet an unknown future with attitudes and habits of action" (Wiles & Bondi, 2002, p. 335). The primary goal of the curriculum, according to social reconstructionists and postmodernists, is to engage students in a critical analysis of society at every level so that they can improve it. Some recent applications of the social justice design have used "futurism" to justify the necessity of social intervention (Wiles & Bondi, 2002).

The social justice design combines classroom learning with application outside the school. Teachers and students join in inquiry. Instruction is often carried on in a problem-solving or inquiry format (Wiles & Bondi, 2002).

Curriculum Contrasts

In practice, most schools do not adopt a single model but use variations of one or more models in their curriculum organization. Historically, elementary schools have tended to be more student centered in their orientation and secondary schools more subject centered. Ultimately, the choice of curriculum design reflects the prevailing philosophical orientation. The major arguments in support of the subject-centered and student-centered curricula are summarized in the Controversial Issue on page 379.

The Hidden and Null Curricula

Perhaps even more important than the formal curriculum is the informal or **hidden curriculum.** This concept was briefly mentioned in Chapter 8 with regard to the socialization role of the school. Schools teach students more than is in the formal curriculum; they are influenced by the implicit aspects in the curriculum that send them messages about what they ought to be doing and thinking. Teachers help shape the hidden curriculum in the classroom by sending signals about what is considered to be important. For example, the social studies teacher may be sending an unintended message if that teacher admonishes students to read the front page of the newspaper but is observed by students to be reading only the sports pages (Armstrong, Henson, & Savage, 2005). The message may be unintended and may not be reflected in the school catalog, but a powerful message is communicated to students. Other examples may be found in student elections and contests; the informal unplanned learnings may send a variety of messages to students (Sadker & Sadker, 1997).

For Your Reflection and Analysis

How is the hidden curriculum different from the null curriculum?
To submit your response online, go to http://www. prenhall.com/webb.

CW

CONTROVERSIAL ISSUE

The Subject-Centered and Student-Centered Curricula

The debate between the essentialists and others who support the subject-centered curriculum and the postmodernists and others who support a student-centered curriculum has continued unabated for almost a decade and appears likely to continue. Among the arguments the proponents of each orientation give are the following:

Arguments for the Subject-Centered Curriculum

1. Introduces learners to the cultural heritage.
2. Gives teachers a sense of security by specifying what their responsibilities are for developing given skills and knowledge.
3. Reduces repetition or overlap between grade levels or different sections of the same class.
4. Increases the likelihood that learners will be exposed to knowledge and develop skills in an orderly manner.
5. Permits methodical assessment of pupil progress; assumes that knowledge is the only measurable outcome of learning experiences.
6. Facilitates cooperative group planning by educators in allocating the scope and sequence of learning experiences.

Arguments for the Student-Centered Curriculum

1. Releases the teacher from the pressure to follow a prescribed scope and sequence that invariably does not meet all learners' needs.
2. Has a positive influence on learners as they find that instruction is varied to meet individual needs and purposes.
3. Encourages teacher judgment in selecting the content deemed most suitable for a group of learners.
4. Increases the likelihood that content has relevance to learners.
5. Modifies instruction to accommodate developmental changes and behavioral tasks as individual differences are identified and monitored.
6. Allows much more latitude for creative planning by the individual teacher.

What other arguments can you think of for the subject-centered or student-centered curriculum?

Source: Shane, H. G., & Tabler, M. B. (1981). *Educating for a new millennium* (pp. 79–80). Bloomington, IN: Phi Delta Kappa. Reprinted with permission.

 To answer this question online, go to the *Controversial Issue* module for this chapter of the Companion Website at **http://www.prenhall.com/webb.**

The hidden curriculum includes the norms and values that underlie the formal curriculum. Even though the hidden curriculum is not taught directly or included in the objectives of the formal curriculum, it impacts both students and teachers. Evidence of the hidden curriculum may be found in textbooks and other curriculum materials and in the norms and values of the school. The hidden curriculum includes the organizational structure of the classroom and the school as well as the ways in which students and teachers interact with each other (Gollnick & Chinn, 2006).

The hidden curriculum includes the **null curriculum.** This latter term refers to the things that are consciously excluded because they are controversial, because of insufficient funds, because educators are uninformed, or because relevant materials are nonexistent (Eisner, 2002). The null curriculum, like all areas of the hidden curriculum, does not have the same impact on all students. Differences are found even within the same school or classroom in what certain students have the opportunity to learn.

In recent years, increasing attention has been focused on the hidden curriculum as more has been learned about the strength of its influence. Particular concern exists about its negative influence. For example, the lessons of the hidden curriculum tend to promote conformity and in the process may stifle creativity and independent thinking. The hidden

Figure 14.4 — Cycle of Curriculum Orientation, 1900–2005

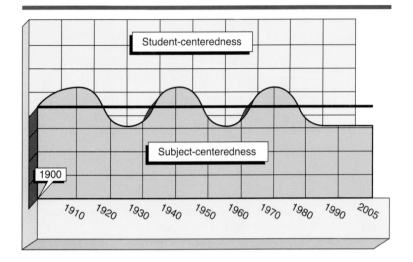

PROFESSIONAL REFLECTION

When students speak a language other than English at home, teachers need to be aware of the language acquisition process and be able to incorporate strategies that help English language learners comprehend and participate in classroom activities.

There are also a number of students who have had little or no previous education in their home countries, so they are far behind their classmates, especially if they come to the United States as teenagers. Teachers need to find ways to reach these students while still teaching to the state standards. This is a huge challenge.

Finally, teachers need to relate what they are teaching to students' lives, and allow students to learn from each other. Our students have much to share—language skills, cultural information, religious traditions, life experiences. We need to find ways to make learning student centered at the same time that we are building their academic skills. When we teach students to work together and show that we value their unique contributions, they will gain confidence and be motivated to learn.

Anne Huckins
National Board Certified Teacher, Washington

 To analyze this reflection, go to the *Professional Reflection* Module for this chapter of the Companion Website at **http://www.prenhall.com/webb**.

curriculum also teaches students to avoid conflict and change. Through the hidden curriculum, bias and stereotyping of race, gender, and social class are reproduced and reinforced (Gollnick & Chinn, 2006).

The Curriculum Cycle

Throughout the 20th century, the curriculum in America's schools shifted between a subject-centered orientation and a student-centered orientation (see Figure 14.4). The first two decades of the century were dominated by the progressive movement and its student-centeredness. In the wake of World War I came a more conservative political posture and a renewal of interest in a more orderly academic curriculum. Out of the social upheaval of the Great Depression emerged a more liberal voice that championed concern for the individual. In the 1950s, Conant's study of secondary schools, which underscored the need for greater attention to academic studies, was reinforced by the Soviet launching of *Sputnik,* and a curriculum reform movement was initiated aimed at strengthening mathematics, science, and foreign language offerings and providing greater rigor in all disciplines. The Great Society ideology of the 1960s drove the cycle in the opposite direction. The open school and alternative school movements were the most visible reflections of the increased attention being focused on students. By the early 1980s many of the curricular innovations of the previous decade had disappeared, and again a call was heard for a return to the basic academic subjects and an elimination of the frills. This mood dominated the remainder of the century.

At the turn of the 21st century, the enactment of the No Child Left Behind Act and the accompanying emphasis on standards and testing has ensured that the focus will remain on subject-matter mastery. The unknown is the degree of attention that will be given to values education, decision-making and critical thinking skills, development of self-esteem, and the individuality of students.

For those who are concerned about the direction of the curriculum cycle, the consolation is that the cycle is short and directions change (McDaniel, 1989).

Summary

The school reform movement focused its attention on the curriculum in an effort to achieve what increasing core requirements and expenditures had not been able to do—increase student performance. The increased attention on the curriculum not only highlighted the controversy about various curriculum orientations but emphasized the sociopolitical context within which curriculum decisions are made.

In the 1990s, a shift occurred in the dominant curriculum orientation. The conservative, subject-centered approach that was emphasized by the first wave of reform reports gave way to a more balanced approach that incorporated greater concern for academic performance standards. State legislatures throughout the nation enacted accountability legislation that focused attention on school and student performance and the importance of the curriculum being aligned with student assessment instruments. The implementation of the mandates of the No Child Left Behind Act intensified this focus.

A curriculum standing alone is of little value. Not until it is implemented does it take on meaning. The process by which it is implemented, known as instruction, is discussed in the following chapter, along with the emerging issues and trends in curriculum and instruction.

Key Terms

Constructivism, 377

Continuity, 370

Core curriculum, 376

Curriculum, 364

Curriculum mapping, 373

Hidden curriculum, 378

Integrated curriculum, 376

Null curriculum, 379

Social justice curriculum, 378

Student-centered
curriculum, 377

Subject-area curriculum, 374

PROFESSIONAL DEVELOPMENT WORKSHOP

Prepare for the Praxis™ Examination

Amy is starting her seventh year of teaching at Mountain Springs School District High School and is the new chair of the science department. Amy completed her master's degree in curriculum and instruction at the local teachers' college. Her principal, Dr. Carolyn Fielding, has selected Amy to review the school's science curriculum to evaluate its efficacy in light of the school's failure to make adequate yearly progress (AYP) as defined by the No Child Left Behind Act. The committee includes teachers from each of the science areas, the district science curriculum coordinator, the principal, and two parents from the site council. Before the committee begins meeting, Amy copies a number of research articles on school effectiveness and distributes them to each member of the committee.

As the committee begins its meetings, it becomes clear that a major concern is that the standards, scope, and sequence of the curriculum are not in alignment with state standards. It is also clear that the administrators, teachers, and parents disagree as to how the committee should function and what steps should be taken to improve academic performance. By the third meeting, each group is blaming the other for the poor test scores.

1. What are the major provisions of the No Child Left Behind Act?
2. What actions can Amy take to facilitate positive working relationships between the teachers and the administrators? Between the parents and the teachers?

3. Describe the best approach for the committee to take to ensure the science curriculum is aligned with state standards.

To submit your responses online, go to the *Prepare for the Praxis™ Examination* module for this chapter of the Companion Website at **http://www.prenhall.com/webb.**

Build Your Knowledge Base

1. As a new teacher like Mary Sherman in the opening vignette, how would you respond to a parent who is critical of the school's curriculum?
2. How would you define the terms *curriculum* and *hidden curriculum?* Should the lessons of the hidden curriculum be incorporated into the formal curriculum? If not, how can they be dealt with by the teacher? Should they be dealt with?
3. Which of the agencies or groups discussed in this chapter has had the most influence on the curriculum in your district in the last 5 years?
4. How have the national standards and accountability movements impacted the professional life of the individual teacher?
5. Who should have the most input on textbook content? The author? The publisher? The user?
6. Which of the curriculum designs discussed in this chapter is most consistent with your philosophy of education as identified in Chapters 3 and 4?
7. Describe the curriculum that would best prepare students for the 21st century.

Develop Your Portfolio

1. Review INTASC Standard 7: "The teacher plans instruction based upon knowledge of subject matter, students, the community, and curriculum goals." Many educators believe that with the enactment of state accountability and assessment programs as well as the adoption of state and national content standards, teachers tend to have less control over curriculum and instruction. Prepare a position paper that either agrees or disagrees with the idea that the enactment of state accountability and assessment programs, as well as the adoption of state and national content standards, has led to less control by teachers over curriculum and instruction. Place your position paper in your portfolio under **INTASC Standard 7, Planning Instruction.**
2. Review Table 14.2, Perspectives on Curriculum Organization, on page 374. Using "Constructivism" as the curriculum design, select three different learning activities from your particular field of study that encourage students to construct their own meaning based on current and past knowledge and experience. Place your learning activities in your portfolio under **INTASC Standard 1, Knowledge of Subject.**

To complete these activities online, go to the *Develop Your Portfolio* module for this chapter of the Companion Website at **http://www.prenhall.com/webb.**

Explore Teaching and Learning: Field Experiences

1. Contact the director of curriculum in a local school district and arrange for an interview or a review of available documents to determine the curriculum process used in the district to develop new components of a curriculum, that is, the process for planning, design, pilot testing, implementation, and evaluation. Who has input into this process: teachers, administrators, students, parents, community leaders, outside experts?
2. Arrange for an interview with a central office administrator in a local school district to determine the process used in adopting textbooks. Who has input into this process: teachers, administrators, students, parents, community leaders, consultants?

Professional Development Online

Visit this text's Companion Website at **http://www.prenhall.com/webb** to gain access to a variety of questions, activities, and exercises to help build your knowledge of this chapter's content. Below are just a few items available at this text's Companion Website:

- Classroom Video—To see actual classroom footage and work through activities and questions to analyze the content of the video, click on the *Classroom Video* module for this chapter.
- Teaching Tolerance—To go to this organization's website and complete activities to explore issues and topics dealing with how to teach tolerance to students, click on the *Teaching Tolerance* module for this chapter.
- Self-Test—To review terms and concepts presented in this chapter, click on the *Self-Test* module for this chapter.
- Internet Resources—To link to websites related to topics in this chapter, go to the *Internet Resources* module for this chapter.

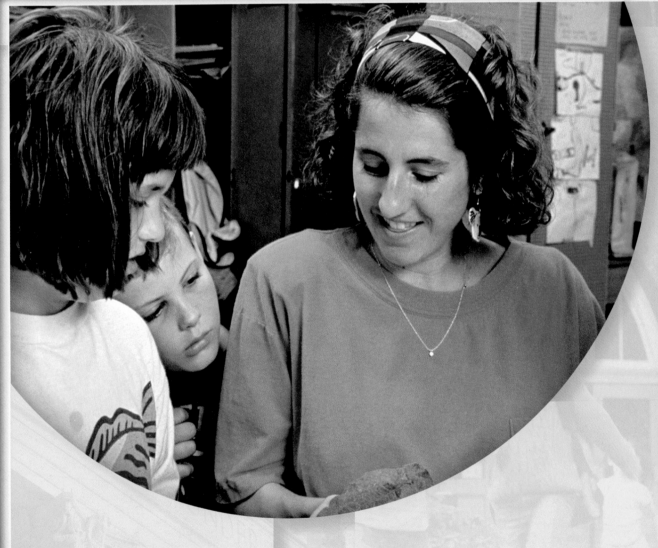

CHAPTER 15

*All education is a continuous dialogue—questions and answers
that pursue every problem to the horizon.*
—William O. Douglas, *Wisdom* (October 1956)

INSTRUCTIONAL PRACTICES IN EFFECTIVE SCHOOLS

David Crowley is a beginning teacher in a school that has had a high percentage of students who receive free or reduced-priced lunches, large numbers of students from single-parent households, low parental participation in school functions, high teacher turnover, low student attendance, and low levels of student performance on standardized tests for more than a decade. The school has been identified as a "target for improvement" by the accountability unit in the state department of education. This designation makes the school eligible to receive a $100,000 grant for school reform. The principal has appointed David to a committee comprised of staff members and parents. The charge is to recommend a whole-school reform model that might be used to "reinvent" the school.

Where would you secure information about the different whole-school reform models? What criteria would you use to guide the selection of the model for the school? Of the different approaches for improving instruction, which approach do you think should be used in this school? What additional information would the committee need to make a recommendation?

Instructional practices differ among schools and teachers. Ongoing and exciting discussions are under way about the goals and objectives of education and the ways in which teachers and students interact. Increasing attention is being focused on ways to improve schools and student performance and on the characteristics of effective schools. As you study, observe, and analyze the practices found in today's classrooms and schools, this chapter should provide you with information that will help you to:

- Describe the difference between educational goals and educational objectives.
- List the eight intelligences included in Gardner's theory of multiple intelligences.
- Identify the models of instruction that have been classified as belonging to the information processing family of models, and the behavioral systems family of models.
- Explain the relationship between teaching and learning.
- Discuss the primary goals of the different models for whole-school reform.

This chapter reviews various instructional practices associated with effective teaching and the characteristics of different school reform models. Rather than advocating a particular approach, the focus is on different models and strategies that teachers and schools have used for different purposes with different groups of students. First, attention is given to the importance of instructional goals and objectives in schools. The next section provides an overview of some of the more commonly employed models of instruction. The chapter concludes with a discussion of school reform models.

Instructional Goals and Objectives

An overarching goal of American public education, and thus of states, school districts, and individual schools, has been to provide free public instruction for all citizens. This goal, along with more specific educational and instructional goals, has served as a guide for school districts and schools as they select educational and instructional objectives. The interaction between educational goals and objectives is discussed in the following paragraphs.

Educational Goals

In making decisions about education, the first issue is to decide what to teach. To make that decision, educators and policy makers need clearly defined goals and objectives for instruction and information about the roles and responsibilities of learners in relation to specific goals and objectives. **Educational goals** are general statements about directions toward which we want learning outcomes to lead. Educational goals are ideals one intends to reach or one's accomplishment targets. Rather than identifying specific skills, educational goals describe the attributes that should be found in an educated person. They may be goals for you as a teacher, goals for your students, or joint goals (Kellough & Kellough, 2003). Examples of goal statements are as follows:

- The learner will develop basic math skills.
- The learner will develop an appreciation of poetry.
- The learner will develop an understanding of the events leading to and outcomes of World War II.

Goals are achieved through the cumulative effect of a series of learnings. As defined, goals designate the desired outcome of instruction but lack the specificity to actually implement an instructional sequence (Kellough & Kellough, 2003). That is where educational objectives come into play.

Educational Objectives

An **educational objective** is a clearly defined, observable, and measurable student outcome that indicates learner progress toward the achievement of a particular educational goal. Educational objectives provide both the teacher and the student direction regarding where they should be going and lets them know when they have arrived. The specification of objectives is necessary to ensure the alignment of the goals curriculum and is required before the design of any assessments.

Reference is often made to a more specific term, *behavioral objectives*. Unlike other educational objectives, behavioral objectives force the teacher to describe the learning outcomes in terms of observable student behaviors. Behavioral objectives answer these questions: "How do you know the learner has learned?" and "What must the learner to do to prove that the knowledge has been learned?" (Jacobsen, Eggen, & Kauchak, 1999; Mager, 1997). Examples of behavioral objectives include these:

- The student will list five reasons for the fall of the Roman Empire.
- The student will place 50% or more of the arrows within 6 inches of the target.
- The student will be present for all rehearsals and is error free in the recital.
- The student will prepare a 10-page report with five or fewer grammatical errors.

For Your Reflection and Analysis

What is the difference between goals, objectives, and outcomes?
To submit your response online, go to http://www. prenhall.com/webb.

Figure 15.1 — Taxonomy of Teaching, Learning, and Assessing

The Knowledge Dimension	The Cognitive Process Dimension					
	1 Remember	2 Understand	3 Apply	4 Analyze	5 Evaluate	6 Create
A. Factual Knowledge						
B. Conceptual Knowledge						
C. Procedural Knowledge						
D. Metacognitive Knowledge						

Source: Anderson, L. W., & Krathwohl, D. R. (Eds.). (2001). *A taxonomy for learning, teaching, and assessing.* Published by Allyn and Bacon, Boston, MA. Copyright © 2001 by Pearson Education. Reprinted by permission of the publisher.

Taxonomies of Educational Objectives

Educational outcomes vary in their complexity and in terms of the types of knowledge being addressed. In the development of educational objectives, a taxonomy or classification system is needed. One of the oldest and most widely used has been the hierarchy of intellectual behaviors developed by Benjamin S. Bloom in 1956 and referred to in the literature as **Bloom's *Taxonomy of Educational Objectives.*** A recent revision of the taxonomy by some of Bloom's students reflects the research and our increased understanding of teaching and learning in the 50 years since the original taxonomy was developed. Expanding on the one-dimensional original taxonomy, the revised taxonomy presents two dimensions: a knowledge dimension and a cognitive dimension. The knowledge dimension describes four categories of knowledge (factual, conceptual, procedural, and metacognitive) along a continuum from concrete to abstract. For example, knowing technical vocabulary (factual knowledge) is less complex than actually knowing how to do something (procedural knowledge).

The cognitive process dimension contains six ways of thinking (remember, understand, apply, analyze, evaluate, and create) along a continuum of cognitive complexity. For example, analyzing something is more complex than simply remembering it. As illustrated in Figure 15.1, the revised taxonomy can be depicted as a matrix of 24 cells representing the intersections of the two dimensions.

It is important when planning instruction to incorporate activities from the full range of levels into students' learning experiences to stimulate and develop their intellectual skills. This helps students master what is popularly referred to as higher order thinking skills. The higher order thinking skills in the revised taxonomy of educational objectives are analyze, evaluate, and create.

Goals and objectives become the structure that schools and teachers use in making decisions about models of instruction. As described in the following section, several models may be used to achieve these educational goals and objectives.

Models of Instruction

Historically, teachers have used different strategies, tactics, or methods of instruction depending on their personal talents, the content to be taught, and the interests and abilities of the students. As discussed in Chapter 1, teaching is often described as an art. This does not imply that teachers operate without design or planning; rather, it underscores the need for teachers to understand and be able to use a variety of strategies as they work with students of different abilities, learning styles, and intelligences.

The growing recognition in recent years that intelligence is not a single construct and that students have multiple intelligences and can have differing levels of ability depending on the category of intelligence can be traced to the research of Howard Gardner (1999). Gardner has identified eight categories of intelligence that provide a wider and more universal set of competencies that encompass the realm of human cognition. Here are Gardner's eight intelligences:

- Verbal-linguistic intelligence (V) refers to the use of words orally and in writing and in the manipulation of language structure. People who have strengths in verbal-linguistic intelligence have highly developed auditory skills and like to use words to express themselves. They excel in the academic environment and learn best when they can speak, listen, read, or write.
- Logical-mathematical intelligence (L) is the basis for the hard sciences and all fields of mathematics. People who have strength in logical-mathematical intelligence use numbers and reasoning in logical patterns and relationships. They think in terms of concepts and questions and enjoy mathematical problems and strategy games.
- Spatial intelligence (S) refers to the use of pictures and images with a sensitivity to color, line, shape, and form and their interrelationships. People who have strengths in spatial intelligence are keenly perceptive of visual details; they tend to think in images and have a good sense of location and direction.
- Bodily-kinesthetic intelligence (B) is the expression of ideas and feelings through the use of one's body. Using physical skills such as coordination, balance, and dexterity, people who have strengths in bodily-kinesthetic intelligence like to move around, act things out, and touch people during the discussion. They learn best when doing, moving, or acting things out.
- Musical intelligence (M) uses musical forms as a means of expression, perception, and transformation of thoughts. People with strengths in musical intelligence are sensitive to environmental and musical sounds and often hum or sing while they work.
- Interpersonal intelligence (P) refers to perceiving and making distinctions in the words, intentions, motivations, and feelings of others. People with strengths in interpersonal intelligence like to work in groups and serve as mentors; they learn best when interacting with other people.
- Intrapersonal intelligence (I) is the ability to gain access to one's feelings and emotional state. People with strengths in intrapersonal intelligence tend to be independent and self-directed; they are intuitive and often introverted.
- Naturalist intelligence (N) refers to being attuned to the world of plants and animals, geography, and natural objects such as rocks. People with strengths in naturalist intelligence prefer to be outdoors and have an appreciation for and an understanding of the environment (Silver, Strong, & Perini, 2000).

The assumption undergirding the **multiple intelligences theory** is that each person possesses all eight intelligences to varying degrees and can develop all to a specified level of competency. Each is interwoven into the complex fabric of an individual. Thus, there is no single expression of intelligence (Gardner, 1999).

Musical intelligence is one of Gardner's eight multiple intelligences.

The theory of multiple intelligences has direct implications for teachers and emphasizes the importance of teachers respecting and nurturing each student's special interests and talents. It also implies that each classroom should have a series of learning centers in which students have access to equipment and supplies that will enable them to use their particular intelligence in solving problems (Silver et al., 2000). Still another implication is that teachers will need to employ multiple models of instruction as they interact with their students.

Over the years many different models of instruction have been developed. Joyce, Weil, and Calhoun (2004) have categorized various models of instruction into four primary families: the information processing family, the social family, the personal family, and the behavioral systems family (see Table 15.1). Rather than selecting a single model of instruction, the effective teacher is familiar with and understands how to use various models within the four families in response to different teaching/learning goals and objectives used with different students. It is not realistic for the beginning teacher to be familiar with the more than 20 models described by Joyce et al. What we have chosen for discussion in the following sections are the models in most common use in the schools today.

The Information Processing Family of Models

Models of instruction under the information processing family represent a distinct philosophy about how people think and how teachers can affect the way in which students receive, process, and utilize information. The models are linked to concepts and principles of information processing developed by cognitive psychologists such as Piaget and Vygotsky. Information processing models are also associated with constructivist education.

The models vary in the structure of their views about information handling and in the depth of their approach from a narrow focus on memorization to specific types of inductive thinking. Three models of instruction that have been classified as members of the information processing family of models—inquiry instruction, critical thinking instruction, and synectics—are described in the following sections.

Inquiry Instruction.   As described in Chapter 7, **inquiry instruction** was made popular in America by John Dewey at the beginning of the 20th century. This student-centered method of instruction is also referred to as problem solving, the inductive method, creative thinking, the scientific method, or conceptual learning. The underlying presumption of inquiry instruction is that students would prefer seeking knowledge rather than having it provided to them through demonstrations and textbook readings. As the concept has developed, the ultimate form of inquiry instruction occurs when students recognize and identify the problem as well as decide the process and reach the conclusion (Hlebowitsh, 2005; Kellough & Kellough, 2003). Students use the inquiry process to develop a better understanding of current knowledge and to create new knowledge.

Table 15.1 — Models of Instruction

Models	Orientation	Examples
Information processing family	Student-centered Constructivism	• Inquiry instruction • Critical thinking instruction • Synectics
Social family	Student-centered Progressivism	• Cooperative learning • Problem-based instruction
Personal family	Student-centered Rogerian Counseling	• Nondirective instruction
Behavioral systems family	Teacher-centered Behaviorism	• Direct instruction • Mastery learning

Source: Based on *Models of Teaching* (7th ed.), by B. Joyce, M. Weil, & E. Calhoun, 2004, Boston: Pearson/Allyn & Bacon.

In inquiry instruction, the assumption is that students construct their knowledge. The teacher, the classroom, the school, and the community provide the setting and support that will encourage students through the process. Because of differences among students, knowledge is constructed through different processes and patterns of thinking. Through engagement in the learning process, the learner becomes active and assumes responsibility for acquiring and applying knowledge (Orlich, Harder, Callahan, & Gibson, 1998).

Inquiry instruction takes place when a person is faced with a problem or forced choice and he or she actively seeks out an answer to the dilemma. Students generate ideas and then identify ways to test the ideas. The five phases of the inquiry cycle are (1) identification or recognition of the problem, (2) application of thought or exploration of the problem, (3) organization and analysis of the data, (4) identification of a tentative conclusion, and (5) testing of the conclusion (Hlebowitsh, 2005; Kellough & Kellough, 2003). The sequence of the inquiry process is illustrated in Figure 15.2.

Successful inquiry instruction depends on the effective interaction of sophisticated students and teachers in a supportive learning environment. Students and teachers must be comfortable with the challenges and the freedoms associated with the student-centered dimensions of the inquiry process. Successful inquiry instruction in today's educational environment requires that students have easy access to research tools and educational technology and be free to use them at their own pace.

Critical Thinking Instruction.   When the development of **critical thinking** is the instructional goal, the student becomes more active and responsible and the teacher becomes less dominant. The teacher organizes and provides direction for student learning, but the student is an active, rather than passive, participant. The teacher is no longer the center of activity. In both the critical thinking and the inquiry models, the teacher is a guide, facilitator, motivator, stimulator, even a cheerleader who challenges learners. In essence, the teacher abdicates the central position and empowers students. However, the teacher often assumes the role of the devil's advocate and forces students to defend and explain their positions.

Figure 15.2 — The Inquiry Cycle

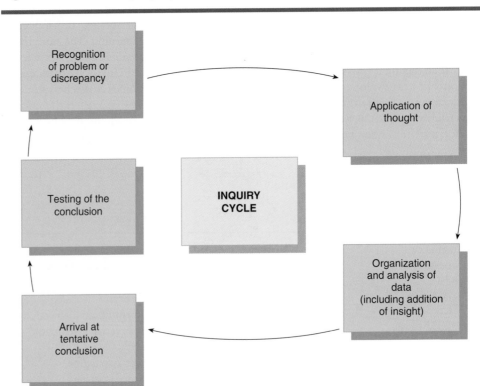

Source: Adapted from *Secondary School Teaching: A Guide to Methods and Resources* by R. D. Kellough & N. G. Kellough, 1999, Upper Saddle River, NJ: Prentice Hall. Reprinted by permission of Pearson Education, Inc.

Analytical or higher order thinking skills are the central elements in the process of critical thinking. Students who become critical thinkers can view problems in different dimensions and consider problems in a larger context. They seek maximum information before deciding on a course of action. Rather than finding quick and simple solutions to complex problems, critical thinkers not only examine the particular problem as an individual issue but also consider it in the larger dimension of related issues (Ellis, Mackey, & Glenn, 1988). Teachers and students become active in identifying and seeking solutions to problems. This model evolved from the research of Hilda Taba (1966) and is used in a wide variety of curriculum areas with students of all ages. The process of critical thinking is illustrated in Figure 15.3.

The problems associated with this mode of instruction are primarily an outgrowth of teachers' experiences as students; teachers tend to teach as they were taught. For this reason, teachers often have difficulty adapting to change. Most teachers were taught by direct instruction; to change roles and focus on teaching and helping students learn differently requires a new orientation.

Synectics.   **Synectics** is a model that engages all students in creative thinking; the focus is on coming to an understanding together by looking at things in unique and different ways. The approach, which is often used by groups, can help students develop creative responses to problem solving, retain new information, assist in generating writing, and explore social and disciplinary problems. It helps users break existing mind-sets and internalize abstract concepts (Gordon, 1961).

Synectics is based on two simple concepts for problem solving and creative thinking: (1) the need to generate ideas and (2) the need to evaluate ideas. Through brainstorming, the learners can consider a new idea without fear and gain new insights into otherwise mundane or uncomfortable topics. Synectics can be used with all ages and works well with those who withdraw from traditional methods (Couch, 1993).

According to Joyce et al. (2004) there are two models of instruction based on synectics procedures: (1) the *creating something new model,* which is "designed to make the familiar strange, to help students see old problems, ideas, or products in a new, more creative light" and (2) the *making the strange familiar model,* which "is designed to make new, unfamiliar more meaningful" (p. 167). Although both strategies use analogy or metaphor as a primary tool, as shown in Table 15.2, their syntaxes differ in other important regards.

Models of teaching based on synectics require a great deal of skill and creativity on the part of the teacher. However, synectics can be a powerful model to assist the teacher in breaking through entrenched thinking so that students examine and reflect on things and ideas from new and different perspectives.

The Social Family of Models

The social family models combine a belief about learning and a belief about society. Learning is viewed as a socially and intellectually stimulating cooperative behavior; thus, tasks that require social interaction will stimulate learning. A further assumption underlying these models, one that can be traced to John Dewey, is that a central role of education is to prepare citizens to perpetuate a democratic social order.

Social family models can be used to enhance individual teaching repertoires and also to design entire school environments. The models envision the school as a productive literate society rather than as a collection of individuals acquiring knowledge independently. The models may be used with models from other families to acquire the knowledge and skills for which these models were developed (Joyce et al., 2004). The following discussion contains brief descriptions of cooperative learning and problem-based learning. These two models of instruction have been classified as members of the social family of models.

Figure 15.3 — The Process of Critical Thinking

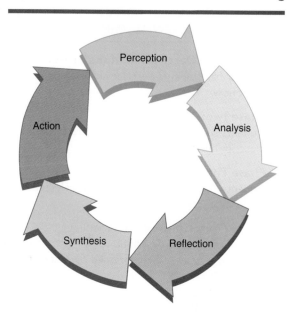

For Your Reflection and Analysis

Which model information processing would you feel most comfortable using? *To submit your response online, go to http://www.prenhall.com/webb.*

CW

Table 15.2 — Synectics Models of Instruction

Strategy One: Creating Something New	Strategy Two: Making the Strange Familiar
Phase One: Description of the Present Condition Teacher has students describe situation or topic as they see it now.	**Phase One: Substantive Input** Teacher provides information on new topic.
Phase Two: Direct Analogy Students suggest direct analogies, select one, and explore (describe) it further.	**Phase Two: Direct Analogy** Teacher suggests direct analogy and asks students to describe the analogy.
Phase Three: Personal Analogy Students "become" the analogy they selected in phase two.	**Phase Three: Personal Analogy** Teacher has students "become" the direct analogy.
Phase Four: Compressed Conflict Students take their descriptions from phases two and three, suggest several compressed conflicts, and choose one.	**Phase Four: Comparing Analogies** Students identify and explain the points of similarity between the new material and the direct analogy.
Phase Five: Direct Analogy Students generate and select another direct analogy, based on the compressed conflict.	**Phase Five: Differences** Students explain where the analogy does not fit.
Phase Six: Reexamination of the Original Task Teacher has students move back to original task or problem and use the last analogy and/or the entire synectics experience.	**Phase Six: Exploration** Students reexplore the original topic on its own terms.
	Phase Seven: Generating Analogy Students provide their own direct analogy and explore the similarities and differences.

Source: Based on *Models of Teaching* (7th ed., pp. 185–186), by B. Joyce, M. Weil, & E. Calhoun, 2004, Boston: Pearson/Allyn & Bacon.

Cooperative Learning.   In **cooperative learning,** students work in small groups (usually three to four) to complete an assignment or task. The teacher still has responsibility for setting the stage and working with students, but students work in groups rather than as individuals. Typically the groups are composed of students of varying abilities and are heterogeneous in terms of race, ethnicity, and gender. Because the group often is the unit that is evaluated, students are rewarded for helping one another. Rather than being in competition with each other, the likelihood of failure is reduced and the probability of success is enhanced because of the combined resources of the group.

Although there is no one model of cooperative learning, the steps or phases common to most models would include these:

1. The teacher goes over the goals of the lesson and gets students motivated to learn.
2. Information is presented, often in the form of text rather than lecture.
3. Students are organized into study teams.
4. Students, assisted by the teacher, work together to accomplish interdependent tasks.
5. Presentation of the group's end product or testing on what students have learned
6. Recognition of group and individual efforts (Arends, 2004).

Cooperative learning is one of the most researched teaching models (Arends, 2004). Research suggests that the positive effects of cooperative learning in elementary and secondary schools appear to be primarily associated with two types of learner outcomes: social development and academic achievement (Slavin, 1989). By working together, students not only develop more cooperative behavior, they have the opportunity to exercise leadership. At the same time they tend to be less competitive and demonstrate more cross ethnic/racial cooperation (Arends, 2004). Cooperative learning allows students to reap the benefits of group success while remaining individually responsible for their own personal performance and achievement.

Problem-based Learning. Problem-based learning (PBL) is a student-centered, student-directed model in which the teacher serves as a facilitator and tutor. The goals of PBL are to provide students with the opportunity to identify and explore a real-life problem that is relevant to the student and to acquire an extensive, integrated knowledge base and set of research and human relations skills that can be readily recalled and applied to the analysis and solution of subsequent problems. The model's purpose is for students to develop effective and efficient problem-solving skills, self-directed learning skills, and team skills. PBL models provide an equal opportunity for all students and work well with students who traditionally have not done well in conventional educational settings. These include students who had difficulty reasoning, could not acquire and apply knowledge and skills, and exhibited classic signs of boredom (distractive classroom behavior and absences).

Cooperative learning is one of the most commonly used instructional strategies at both the elementary and secondary levels.

Under PBL, students are responsible for their own learning. They identify what they feel they need to learn and what resources they are going to use to accomplish that learning. Under faculty guidance, students design their learning to meet individual needs and career aspirations. This experience prepares them to become effective and efficient lifelong learners. The students learn how to decide what they need to learn and seek out appropriate learning resources, using the faculty as resource consultants as well as books, journals, online resources, and other experts. The teacher serves as a somewhat passive resource person.

PBL problems must be loosely structured learning situations, with just the initial presenting situation to stimulate learners to generate multiple hypotheses about the problems. Students gain contextual information through observations, interviews, and review of records or documents. Learning should be integrated from a wide range of disciplines or subjects; PBL should not occur within a single discipline or subject.

Collaboration is an essential component of PBL; it occurs naturally during the group's discussions with the tutor. Students must be encouraged to collaborate during their self-directed study; they will need this skill to work as a member of a team.

Outcomes from the self-directed learning must be applied back to the problem with reanalysis and resolution. Through this process, the student will develop a deeper understanding of the problem and will recall that information when faced with similar problems in the future. This step helps convert procedural knowledge gained through problem solving into declarative knowledge for use and recall with other problems in the future.

Self and peer assessment should be carried out at the completion of each PBL project. Students must become proficient at assessing their individual learning progress and that of their peers. The ability to accurately monitor the adequacy of personal performance is essential to developing lifelong self-directed study skills. The ability to provide colleagues with accurate feedback is an important skill in life and career.

The activities carried out in PBL must be those valued in the real world, and PBL students must go through the same activities as experts and professionals go through in their problem work. The problems must be relevant and important. This ensures that the activities and the skills and knowledge acquired are relevant to their future careers.

Student examinations must measure student progress toward the goals of PBL. A major component of the assessment of students' progress comes from self and peer assessments

For Your Reflection and Analysis

In what ways is PBL different from the traditional classroom?
To submit your response online, go to http://www. prenhall.com/webb.

CW

that occur at the end of every PBL activity, but additional formal assessments must assess the students' problem-solving and self-directed learning skills.

The Personal Family of Models

A major thesis of the personal family of models is that the better developed, more affirmative, self-actualizing learners have increased learning capabilities. The assumption underlying the personal family models is that academic achievement can be increased by tending to the needs of individual learners.

Personal family models can be used to moderate the entire learning environment, enhance the personal qualities and feelings of students, and provide opportunities to make students partners in the teaching/learning process. Personal family models are designed to lead the student toward greater mental and emotional health by developing self-confidence and a realistic sense of self and empathy for others (Joyce et al., 2004). In the following discussion, the focus is on one of the personal family models—nondirective instruction.

Nondirective Instruction. **Nondirective instruction** models bring the student and teacher together in a cooperative effort in deciding what and how the student will learn. The nondirective instruction model is student centered. The role of the teacher is as a guide and facilitator of student learning who helps students identify personal or academic problems or goals and explore how they might be resolved or attained. The nondirective teaching model is based on the work of Carl Rogers (1961) and other advocates of nondirective counseling. He proposed that positive human relationships enabled people to grow and that instruction should be based on concepts of human relationships in contrast to concepts of subject matter (Joyce et al., 2004).

Despite what might appear to be lack of structure, the nondirective instruction model does have structure. Joyce et al. (2004) describe these as consisting of five phases:

- *Phase One:* Defining the Helping Situation
  Teacher encourages free expression of feelings.
- *Phase Two:* Exploring the Problem
  Student is encouraged to define problem.

  Teacher accepts and clarifies feelings.
- *Phase Three:* Developing Insight
  Student discusses problem.

  Teacher supports student.
- *Phase Four:* Planning and Decision Making
  Student plans initial decision making.

  Teacher clarifies possible decisions.
- *Phase Five:* Integration
  Student gains further insight and develops more positive actions.

  Teacher is supportive.

The nondirective model has a variety of potential applications and can be used in conjunction with other models to ensure that the teacher maintains contact as a guide for the student. The model creates an environment in which students and teachers are partners in learning, share ideas openly, and communicate honestly with one another. The model is particularly useful when students are planning independent or cooperative learning.

The Behavioral Systems Family of Models

Models of instruction under the behavior systems family umbrella focus on observable skills and behaviors. These models are teacher centered, are typically highly organized, and emphasize knowledge acquisition and skill development.

The intellectual roots of the behavioral systems model can be traced to the use of Pavlovian principles (Pavlov, 1927) to address the psychological disorders of school-age youth. The efforts were successful with some learners who had been making virtually no progress in language development or development of social skills. Progress also was made with milder forms of learning problems as well as with youth who had severe learning problems. These models of instruction have not only been quite effective with students with disabilities, but with other students as well. Two of the models of instruction classified as belonging to the behavioral systems family are direct instruction and mastery learning.

Direct Instruction. **Direct instruction** is a teacher-centered method that is used to convey information. The most common forms of direct instruction are formal lecture, informal lecture, and teacher-led discussion. Direct instruction is considered appropriate when (1) all students need to know an essential body of knowledge, and (2) the students are relatively homogeneous in their ability and knowledge of the topic.

In direct instruction, the teacher controls and directs the learning process. The teacher also determines the methods of presentation, the pace of instruction, the quantity of supervised practice or reinforcement, and the form of student evaluation. Students are expected to listen, read, and answer questions as the teacher directs.

For direct instruction to be effective, the teacher must recognize that students differ in their levels of competence and that direct instruction requires more extensive and detailed daily lesson planning, for example, possibly the scripting of lectures. The structure and direction of the lecture or discussion should be obvious to the learner. Further, even with extensive preparation and a quality presentation, the teacher must realize that portions of the information contained in a lecture will have to be repeated or retaught (Hlebowitsh, 2005).

Mastery Learning. **Mastery learning** is based on a set of assumptions about both the content and the process of learning. Mastery learning assumes that all students will master a uniform set of predetermined expected outcomes and also assumes that learning is a sequential, linear process. The basic assumptions of mastery learning are as follows: (1) Mastery learning of any subject is possible for all students if the learning units are small enough; (2) for quality learning to occur, the instruction rather than the students must be modified and adapted; (3) some students will take longer to attain mastery than others; (4) most learning outcomes can be observed or measured; (5) most learning units are sequential and logical; and (6) students can experience success at each phase of the instructional process. Thus, the concepts from one unit are built on and extended by the next unit. Mastery learning is generally taught through **group instruction** and, therefore, is primarily teacher centered (Kellough & Kellough, 2003).

The mastery learning instructional format assumes that the teacher presents the learning unit and then administers what is called the first formative test. The purpose of the test is to check learning progress and provide the students with feedback and suggestions to help them overcome any difficulties they are experiencing. Following the test, students who have not mastered the material are provided corrective work for a few class periods. Then a second parallel test is administered to ensure that the students have achieved mastery before the class moves on to the next learning unit. Students who demonstrated mastery on the first formative test are given enrichment activities during the corrective phase of instruction. Figure 15.4 illustrates the mastery learning instructional process.

Mastery learning enables the teacher to address the special needs of students in multicultural environments. However, critics assert that the process has been oversimplified, that mastery of the individual units does not necessarily transfer to future learning, and that students cannot be expected to learn and achieve at the mastery level indefinitely.

Relationship Between Teaching and Learning

Various proposals to reform, reinvent, restructure, and renew schools as ways to improve education have come from both public and private sources. Many of the recommendations have focused on the mandates and admonitions designed to change school operations or programs as a means to improve student performance. Significant emphasis has been placed on modifying the structure or the decision-making process. However, one of the problems with the various education improvement models is that the simplistic prescriptions are not consistent with what educational research says about teaching and

Figure 15.4 — The Mastery Learning Instructional Process: (a) Instructional Sequence and (b) Achievement Distribution Curve in a Mastery Learning Classroom

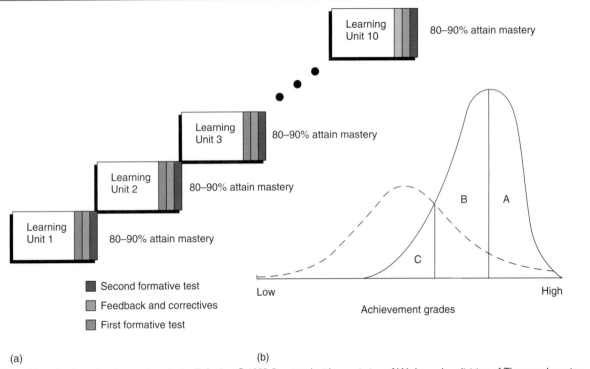

(a)   (b)

learning. After two decades of school reform recommendations, the question remains as to whether sufficient attention is being given to the most critical consideration—the relationship between how teachers teach and how children learn.

As discussed in Chapter 9, students vary greatly in their learning styles, that is, in the composite of cognitive, affective, and physiological behaviors that indicate how a learner perceives, interacts with, and responds to educational experiences and the educational environment (Parkay & Stanford, 1995). Each student's learning style is determined by the interaction of hereditary and environmental influences. Some students learn best through seeing (visual), others learn best by hearing (auditory), while yet others learn best by

Learning styles differ: some students learn better by hearing, others by seeing.

CONTROVERSIAL ISSUE

Whole-School Reform Programs

As a result of the enactment of the No Child Left Behind Act, states have adopted accountability programs that identify schools not making adequate yearly progress in student achievement. In response, a new education industry whose purpose is to work with low-performing schools in the development and implementation of school improvement plans has emerged. As the pros and cons listed below illustrate, the adoption of whole-school reform programs has been the topic of heated debate in some schools.

Pros	**Cons**
1. Whole-school reform programs have been based on different philosophies; schools should be able to find a program that is compatible with their interests.	1. Prescriptive features in packaged whole-school reform programs may inhibit the creativity and ingenuity of individual teachers.
2. Costs vary significantly; the quantity of external support from consultants appears to be a key factor.	2. Program costs in some reform programs for consultants, materials, and released time for staff will be extensive and may be viewed as excessive.
3. Benefits appear to increase over time; schools cannot expect progress from a quick fix.	3. The combination of start-up costs and continued support and participation may be excessive.
4. Schools that have selected a particular school reform often form leagues for sharing information or securing a quick response from someone who has been successful in dealing with a specific problem.	4. The philosophy of the school reform may not be consistent with the philosophy of the school.

As a prospective teacher, would you support participation in one of the school reform programs, or would you prefer to rely on school district staff? Which reforms appear interesting to you?

 To answer these questions online, go to the *Controversial Issue* module for this chapter of the Companion Website at **http://www.prenhall.com/webb**.

touching (tactile). Some need structure and directions; others need independence and freedom. Some need total silence; others can function in a noisy environment. The critical point is that there is no one correct view of learning styles to guide teachers in their decision making (Parkay & Stanford, 1995). The Historical Note on page 398 describes the work of Polingaysi Qöyawayma with Hopi students, which emphasized the importance of adapting teaching to the learning styles and experiences of the students.

Not only do students vary in their skills and preferences in how they receive information, but they also vary in how they mentally process the information once it has been received. Kellough and Kellough (2003) have identified four types of learners: imaginative, analytic, common sense, and dynamic. They are described as follows:

- The **imaginative learner** receives information, concretely processes it reflectively, and learns well by listening and sharing with others and integrating the ideas of others with their own experiences. Imaginative learners have difficulty with traditional instruction and may be at-risk students.
- The **analytic learner** receives information abstractly and processes it reflectively; these learners prefer sequential thinking, need details, value expert thinking, and do well in traditional classrooms.
- The **commonsense learner** receives information abstractly and processes it actively. These learners may find schooling frustrating unless they can see an immediate application; this type of learner is likely to be at risk for dropping out.
- The **dynamic learner** receives information concretely and processes it actively. These learners prefer hands-on activities, are risk-takers, and also may be at risk in traditional classrooms (pp. 29–30).

HISTORICAL NOTE

Polingaysi Qöyawayma

Polingaysi Qöyawayma (1892–1990), whose English name is Elizabeth White, was an innovator in shaping American Indian education in the United States and preserving the cultural traditions of the Hopi Indians. As one of nine children in a traditional Hopi family, she was educated by missionaries and taught in schools operated by the Bureau of Indian Affairs (BIA). She was influential in Indian education because of her emphasis on the importance of basing education on the content and examples from the lives of students.

After having first been hidden by her mother to avoid attending the BIA school, in which the Hopi language could not be spoken and students were given English names, Polingaysi became curious and followed her sister to school. When she heard about an opportunity to attend school in "the land of the oranges," she persevered until her parents reluctantly gave their permission. She rode in a wagon to Winslow, Arizona, and took the train to the Sherman Indian Institute in Riverside, California. She was there for 4 years without returning home. On her return, she attempted to become a missionary to the Hopis, but found neither success nor fulfillment because of the conflict with traditional Hopi beliefs.

Polingaysi then became a teacher in the BIA schools. Very soon, she became concerned because the teaching

materials, illustrations, and photographs were not within the life experiences of Indian students. To provide a more realistic educational environment, she took the students into the natural surroundings and used Hopi legends, songs, and stories. Students translated these stories into English. Polingaysi's goal was to blend the best of the Hopi culture with the best of white culture and to retain the essence of good from this blend. After initial skepticism, her supervisors began to support her teaching efforts. With the appointment of John Collier as commissioner of Indian affairs, Polingaysi found unexpected support for her teaching methods. She was chosen to demonstrate her teaching methods at a summer institute for BIA teachers. The focus was on starting the teaching/learning process by basing teachings on what students already know, rather than utilizing a totally new set of experiences. When teachers and students met on mutual ground, students tended to come out of their shells and become active learners. In her life as a teacher, Polingaysi learned to meet criticism with serenity and to appreciate the good in both the Hopi and non-Hopi ways of life.

Source: Reyhner, J. (1994). Polingaysi Qöyawayma. In M. S. Seller (Ed.), *Women educators in the United States, 1820–1993* (pp. 397–402). Westport, CT: Greenwood.

To research and explore this topic further, go to the *Historical Note* module for this chapter of the Companion Website at **http://www.prenhall.com/webb.**

The determination of a student's learning characteristics requires a consideration of not only the student's preferred learning style, but the student's *developmental stage* and *learning history.* Observations of visual perceptions, language pronunciation, and cognitive thinking provide indications that the student is developmentally ready to learn. Teachers need to have a sufficient understanding of developmental indicators so that they can respond to the indicators.

Learning history refers to the prior learning that a student brings to the learning opportunity. To maximize learning, teachers need to be sensitive to and knowledgeable about each student's learning characteristics (Keefe & Jenkins, 2002).

These differences in learning and teaching styles and experiences of students and teachers provide a rich topic of discussion for the following topic: models of school improvement.

Whole-School Reform Models

Beginning in the last quarter of the 20th century considerable research was devoted to identifying the conditions that contribute to differences in effectiveness among schools (see, e.g., Clark, Lotto, & Astuto, 1984; Edmonds, 1979, 1982; Taylor, 2002; Westbrook,

Figure 15.5 — Characteristics of an Effective School

Strong administrative leadership

- Principal has a clear vision about the desired direction of the school.
- Principal has a commitment to improvement of instruction.
- Principal encourages participative decision making.
- Principal serves as a buffer for teachers so that they can devote maximum time to working with students.

Safe and orderly environment

- Working conditions support the efforts of teachers to address specific problems of their students.
- Environment is conducive to teaching and learning.

Emphasis on instruction in the basic skills

- The school has a commitment to the basic skills as instructional goals.
- Basic skills are the foundation for higher order thinking skills.

High teacher expectations of students

- Teachers set high performance standards for students.
- Teachers provide specific instructions and are sensitive to individual differences.
- Teachers use clear and appropriate rewards to recognize student work.

Monitoring and reporting student performance

- Systematic methods are used to assess student progress.
- Curriculum is aligned across subject areas and grades.
- Curriculum, desired outcomes, and assessment activities all match.

Necessary resources to meet objectives

- Sufficient personnel and materials are available in the school.
- Sufficient time is provided for instructional planning, staff development, and adapting new innovations.
- Opportunities are provided for professional growth.

Culture of the school

- Positive human interactions exist among students and teachers.
- Continuous growth and development of students and teachers is encouraged.
- State-of-the-art instructional practices and strategies are provided for teaching and learning.

1982). The typical characteristics of effective schools as identified by the research are summarized in Figure 15.5. Subsequent research on the conditions that contribute to student success in high-improving or high-performing schools has identified those conditions depicted in Figure 15.6.

Following the publication of the initial research on effective schools, various educational researchers began to design and develop alternative school improvement models. At the same time, state legislatures began to enact legislation that called for improvement in school and student performance, greater accountability in the public schools, and for underperforming schools to choose a research-based school reform model from an approved list. Federal legislation also provided support for low-performing schools to develop comprehensive school reform programs and disseminated information about 17 comprehensive models that were endorsed by the U.S. Department of Education. In their school reform efforts, schools were not restricted to these 17 models; they could develop their own program or use another program, provided it was based on rigorous research and met predetermined criteria.

The federal role in the dissemination of school reform models and research has continued, and by 2005, in conjunction with the Center for Comprehensive School Reform

Figure 15.6 — Key Elements for Student Success

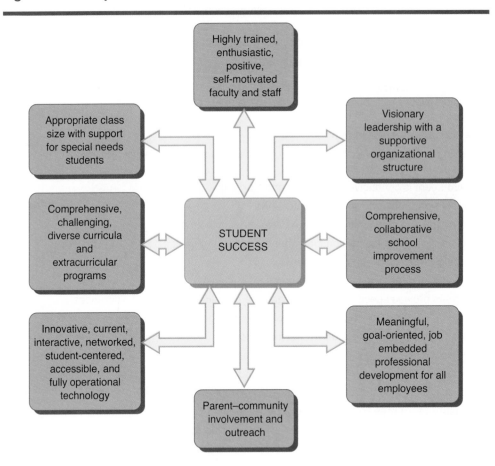

and Improvement, the Northwest Regional Educational Laboratory was maintaining *The Catalog of School Reform Models.* Criteria for inclusion on the list of school reform models included (1) effectiveness in improving academic achievement, (2) extent of replication, (3) training and support provided schools in implementation, and (4) comprehensiveness (Northwest Regional Educational Laboratory, 2005). The school reform models included in the catalog vary in their approach; some provide very specific curricula and

School reform requires the collaborative effort of the entire school staff.

instructional strategies. They also have a variety of emphases and organize classroom practice, school structure, and school culture around a specific vision of teaching and learning (Northwest Regional Educational Laboratory, 2005). They offer varying strategies for the use of technology, increased parent involvement, community outreach, and coordination with other social service agencies. The most widely adopted of the school reform models listed in the catalog are those summarized in Table 15.3.

The various whole-school reform models are based on different beliefs about the best process for school reform. The focus of the different reform models is also somewhat different: Some focus on providing an enriched accelerated curriculum for disadvantaged students, others emphasize the importance of school climate, and still others stress cognitive processes that increase learning. There are, however, some recurring themes among the models: empowerment of the individual school, staff collaboration, parent involvement, and high expectations of students. The various whole-school reform models assume that implementation requires a change in the ways that schools operate; however, there also seems to be some agreement that standardized innovation will not lead to universal school reform. To increase the possibilities of success, schools may need to adapt a model to local conditions.

Table 15.3 — Whole-School Reform Models

Reform Model	Primary Goal	Main Features
Accelerated Schools *Level:* K–12 *Founder:* Henry Levin, Stanford University, now at Columbia University	Provide all students with enriched instruction based on entire school community's vision of learning.	■ Gifted-and-talented instruction for all students through "powerful learning" ■ Participatory process for whole-school transformation ■ Three guiding principles (unity of purpose, empowerment plus responsibility, and building on strengths)
America's Choice *Level:* K–12 *Founder:* National Center on Education and the Economy	Enable all students to reach internationally benchmarked standards.	■ Standards and assessments ■ Aligned instructional systems ■ Focus on literacy and mathematics ■ High performance leadership, management, and organization ■ Professional learning communities
Atlas Communities *Level:* PreK–12 *Founders:* Coalition of Essential Schools, Education Development Center, Project Zero, School Development Center	Align the efforts of a school district, K–12 feeder patterns of schools, individual faculties, and parents to promote student success.	■ PreK–12 pathways ■ Development of coherent K–12 educational programs for every student ■ Authentic curriculum, instruction, and assessment ■ Whole-faculty study groups ■ School/pathway planning and management teams
Coalition of Essential Schools *Level:* K–12 *Founder:* Theodore Sizer	Improve teacher quality and student achievement.	■ Personalized instruction to address individual needs and interests ■ Classrooms and other learning environments where teachers and students know each other well and work in an atmosphere of trust and high expectations ■ Multiple assessments based on performance of authentic tasks ■ The achievement of equitable outcomes for students ■ Democratic governance practices ■ Close partnerships with the school's community

(continued)

Table 15.3 — Continued

Reform Model	Primary Goal	Main Features
Community for Learning *Level:* K–12 *Founder:* Margaret Wang, Temple University	Achieve social and academic success for students by linking schools with community institutions.	■ Collaboration with homes, libraries, museums, and other places where students learn ■ Coordinated health and human services delivery ■ Site-specific implementation design ■ Adaptive Learning Environments Model of instruction
Co-nect *Level:* K–12 *Founder:* BBN Corporation	Improve achievement in core subjects.	■ Design-based assistance for comprehensive K–12 school reform ■ Customized online/on-site training and personal support ■ Project-based learning ■ Peer and progress review programs ■ Leadership processes for whole-school technology integration
Core Knowledge *Level:* K–8 *Founder:* E. D. Hirsch, Jr.	Help students establish a strong foundation of vocabulary and skills to build knowledge and understanding.	■ Sequential program of specific topics for each grade in all subjects ■ Structured program to build vocabulary and skills to improve literacy
Different Ways of Knowing *Level:* PreK–8 *Founder:* Galef Institute	Raise students' academic achievement and improve their attitudes toward school.	■ Standards-based interdisciplinary arts-infused curriculum ■ Development of multiple intelligences ■ Promotion of collaborative learning and higher order thinking ■ Increase in independent research and engaged learning time
Direct Instruction Model *Level:* K–8 *Founder:* Siegfried Engelmann	Significantly improve academic performance over current performance levels.	■ Field-tested reading, language arts, and math curricula ■ Scripted instructional strategies ■ Extensive training ■ School-wide analysis of student performance data
Expeditionary Learning: Outward Bound *Level:* K–12 *Founder:* Outward Bound, USA	Attain high achievement for all students.	■ Challenging standards-based learning expeditions that involve research, fieldwork, and high-quality products and performances ■ Instructional and assessment strategies in the content areas ■ Intensive on-site and off-site professional development ■ Regular review of classroom- and school-level implementation linked to student outcomes
First Things First *Level:* K–12 *Founder:* Institute for Research and Reform in Education (IRRE), James P. Connell, President	Raise the academic performance of all students to levels required for postsecondary education and for high-quality employment without remediation.	■ Seven research-based critical elements ■ Small learning communities at all levels, with themes at middle and high school levels ■ Family advocate system ■ Instructional improvement focus on active engagement of students, alignment of what is taught with standards, and high-stakes assessments and rigor

Reform Model	Primary Goal	Main Features
High Schools That Work *Level:* 9–12 *Founder:* Southern Regional Education Board, Atlanta, GA	Increase the achievement of all students with special emphasis on career-bound students by blending the content of traditional college prep studies with quality vocational and technical studies.	■ Upgraded academic core ■ Common planning time for teachers to integrate instruction ■ Higher standards/expectations
High/Scope Primary Grades Approach to Education *Level:* K–3 *Founder:* David P. Weikert	Provide children with effective, developmentally sound learning experiences in all curriculum areas and be sensitive to their backgrounds, strengths, and interests.	■ Active learning ■ Use of hands-on materials ■ Focus on student interests ■ Classroom organized into learning stations ■ Observational and portfolio assessment ■ Reflective review and self-study
Middle Start *Level:* 5–9 *Founder:* Academy for Educational Development (AED) with sponsorship of W. K. Kellogg & Foundation for the MidSouth	Improve student academic performance, positive development, and equitable access to opportunities and results for all students.	■ Small learning communities ■ Rigorous curriculum, instruction, and assessment ■ Distributed leadership and sustainable partnerships
Modern Red Schoolhouse *Level:* K–12 *Founder:* Hudson Institute	High achievement for all students through development of a coherent instructional program aligned with state standards and implementation of school governance practices that support school reform.	■ Differentiated instruction ■ Data-based school-wide planning process ■ Alignment with state standards and assessments ■ Participatory governance structure (leadership team and task forces) ■ Integration of instructional technology ■ Parent and community partnerships
More Effective Schools *Level:* K–12 *Founder:* Robert E. Sudlow, Ron Edmonds, Lawrence Lezotte, Beverly Bancroft, and Ben Birdsell	Improve academic achievement for all students.	■ Aligns and maps curriculum (written, taught, and tested) with state standards ■ Enables positive changes in school culture ■ Provides leadership training for teachers and administrators to improve and sustain school results ■ Provides technology solutions to support instruction and instructional program
Onward to Excellence *Level:* K–12 *Founder:* Northwest Regional Educational Laboratory	Help schools build capacity through shared leadership for continuous improvement.	■ School leadership teams ■ Two-year improvement process ■ School profiles (data on student achievement) ■ Effective practices research ■ Curriculum mapping
Quantum Learning *Level:* K–12 *Founder:* Quantum Learning, Bobbi DePorter, President, Atlas Curriculum Mapping, Rose Davis, Partner	Create an optimum school-wide environment for learning.	■ Integrating best practices into a unified whole ■ Learning and life skills curriculum ■ Planning and collaborative software

(continued)

Table 15.3 — Continued

Reform Model	Primary Goal	Main Features
QuESt *Level:* K–12 *Founder:* Diane Rivers, Quality Educational Systems, Inc.	Increase student achievement at all grade levels for all students in all content areas through quality process improvements and systemic applications.	■ Aligned to Baldrige Criteria for Performance Excellence in Education ■ Standards-based processes ■ Educational auditing of research-based practices ■ Curriculum alignment processes ■ Curriculum and instructional mapping based on state standards ■ Systemic assessment model
School Development Program *Level:* K–12 *Founder:* James Comer, Yale University	Mobilize entire community of adult caretakers to support students' holistic development to bring about academic success.	■ Three teams (school planning and management team, student and staff support team, parent team) ■ Three operations (comprehensive school plan, staff development plan, assessment and modification) ■ Three guiding principles (no-fault, consensus, collaboration) ■ Understanding and application of principles of child and adolescent development ■ Establishment of healthy relationships among all stakeholders
School Renaissance *Level:* K–12 *Founder:* Renaissance Learning, Inc.	Help educators use data to meet the needs of all learners and ensure success for every child.	■ Ongoing, formative, student-level information ■ Information technology to monitor activities and differentiate instruction ■ Ongoing professional development and implementation support
Success for All/Roots and Wings *Level:* PreK–6 *Founder:* Robert Slavin, Nancy Madden, and others at Johns Hopkins University	Ensure that all children learn to read, acquire basic skills in other subject areas, and build problem-solving and critical thinking skills.	■ Research-based curricula in four subjects ■ Integrated science and social studies program ■ Cooperative learning ■ One-to-one tutoring ■ Family support team
Talent Development High School with Career Academies *Level:* 9–12 *Founder:* Center for Research on the Education of Students Placed At Risk, Johns Hopkins University, and Howard University	Improve achievement and other outcomes for at-risk students in large high schools.	■ Ninth-grade success academy ■ Career academies for grades 10–12 ■ Core curriculum in a four-period day ■ Transition courses in math and reading, freshman seminar ■ Alternative after-hours program
Talent Development Middle School *Level:* 4–9 *Founder:* Johns Hopkins University	Create high-performing schools by providing all teachers with training, support, and materials and all students with standards-based learning opportunities and supportive learning environments.	■ Focused and sustained professional development ■ Standards-based instructional programs in each subject ■ Frequent extra help ■ Restructuring of school organization and staffing

Reform Model	Primary Goal	Main Features
Turning Points *Level:* 6–8 *Founder:* Center for Collaborative Education	Improve teaching, learning, and achievement for all students in middle schools, including those with special needs.	■ Building leadership capacity and a professional collaborative culture ■ Using data-based inquiry and decision making ■ Creating a school culture to support high achievement and personal development ■ Networking with other schools ■ Developing district capacity to support school change
Urban Learning Centers *Level:* PreK–12 *Founder:* Los Angeles Unified School District, United Teachers of Los Angeles, Los Angeles Educational Partnership	Build learning environments where high-quality instruction is supported by a well-organized school that is strongly connected to its community.	■ Thematic, interdisciplinary curriculum ■ Transitions from school to work and postsecondary education ■ Integrated health and human services on school site ■ Collaborative governance model

Source: From Whole School Models, 2005, *The catalog of school reform models.* Portland: Northwest Regional Educational Library.

Among the general conclusions from the site observations and research on school reform models are the following:

- Disadvantaged children are capable of achieving levels of performance that meet and exceed the national average.
- Implementation of school reform models can best be achieved when the strengths of the selected program match the school's needs and assets.
- In choosing a program for a particular school, careful consideration should be given to whether the selected program is likely to work with the school's teachers and administrators. Each program needs a supportive and accepting environment to be successful.
- A school's ability to obtain and maintain sufficient fiscal support is critical to the implementation of any new program.
- Ongoing access to program-specific technical support is a critical element to long-term success.
- Programs that concentrate on the lower grades tend to be more successful than those that are spread evenly over all elementary grades or in secondary schools.
- Whole-school programs appear to be more successful than pullout programs.
- Externally designed programs appear to achieve more consistent implementation than locally developed programs.

PROFESSIONAL REFLECTION

The way I determine the most effective teaching strategy to use with a certain group of students is to first determine what kind of learners my students are. At the beginning of the school year, I give them an assessment that determines whether they are audio, visual, or kinesthetic learners. Based on this assessment, when the majority are, say, a visual learning group, I make sure lesson plans address that learning style. However, being engaged with students on a daily basis also provides a glimpse of their likes and dislikes, attention span, developmental level, and background knowledge. A teacher cannot engage students in the learning process if they have difficulty sitting in their seats! Therefore, I use strategies that incorporate song and movement to address those needs of students. Finally, it has become increasingly apparent that students need to be entertained. Incorporating strategies that include the use of games is invaluable.

    Denise Fandhess
    National Board Certified Teacher, Ohio

 To analyze this reflection, go to the *Professional Reflection* module for this chapter of the Companion Website at **http://www.prenhall.com/webb.**

Summary

Teachers entering the profession in the 21st century are confronted with an increasingly complex set of expectations. Traditional goals and objectives for the public schools remain in place with the addition of periodic assessment-based state standards. Mandated assessments and proficiency examinations in consort with school and district report cards are focusing attention on the performance of individual schools.

Research indicates that effective instruction will be dependent on the extent to which the teacher (1) recognizes and adapts to the learning styles of the students in the classroom and (2) recognizes the attributes of the students in the selection of models of instruction.

The various whole-school reform models provide an additional resource for underperforming schools. The challenges are to select the model most appropriate for your school and to make the necessary adaptations without betraying the intent and philosophy of the model. Professional learning communities can be a valuable resource in the implementation of reform models.

Key Terms

Analytic learner, 397
Bloom's *Taxonomy of Educational Objectives,* 387
Coalition of Essential Schools, 401
Commonsense learner, 397
Cooperative learning, 392
Critical thinking, 390

Direct instruction, 395
Dynamic learner, 397
Educational goals, 386
Educational objectives, 386
Group instruction, 395
Imaginative learner, 397
Inquiry instruction, 389
Mastery learning, 395

Multiple intelligences theory, 388
Nondirective instruction, 394
School Development Program, 404
Success for All, 404
Synectics, 391

PROFESSIONAL DEVELOPMENT WORKSHOP

Prepare for the Praxis™ Examination

Levi Morgan, a fourth-grade teacher, is a 5-year veteran working in an elementary school with an enrollment of 380 students. The school population has 90% free or reduced lunch and the majority of the students come from single-parent homes. The teaching faculty is almost evenly split between novice teachers (less than 2 years in the classroom) and experienced teachers nearing retirement. The school is on the watch-list in terms of annual yearly progress under the No Child Left Behind Act. Some progress has been made in improving scores, but overall improvement goals have not been achieved.

Dr. Carolyn Bright is starting her second year as principal at the school having replaced an administrator who had been at the school since it was constructed 27 years ago. This is Dr. Bright's first administrative position; she has just completed her dissertation. Her topic was related identification of gifted students, and her experience has been in upper income suburban communities.

At the beginning of the school year, Dr. Bright called Levi to her office to discuss Levi's opinion of the characteristics of effective schools. After their conversation Dr. Bright stated that "if students see meaning in their lessons and connections between classroom experiences and their lives, they will become active learners and build on their own strengths." Using this quote as a starting point for school reform she asked Levi to investigate ways to "reinvent" the school with the primary focus of school improvement. To help frame the task, Dr. Bright asked Levi to review the organization of the school's instructional goals and objectives, individual teacher's teaching strategies, and finally the learning styles of the students.

1. How do goals and the implementation of instructional objectives impact the education of the students?
2. Why do teachers need to understand the relationship between learning styles and instructional strategies?
3. What are the "characteristics of an effective school" and what evidence in the case study illustrates that this elementary school is "effective"?

To submit your responses online, go to the *Prepare for the Praxis™ Examination* module for this chapter of the Companion Website at **http://www.prenhall.com/webb**.

Build Your Knowledge Base

1. In what ways should goal statements differ from objectives?
2. Do you think that you would be a better teacher if you only used one mode of instruction?
3. As a teacher, how do you know when a student has achieved mastery learning?
4. How is teaching different from learning?
5. Which whole-school reform model would be appropriate for a school identified as in need of improvement? Which would be more appropriate for a high-performing school?
6. How can teachers best determine the learning styles of their students?

Develop Your Portfolio

1. Review the whole-school reform models presented in Table 15.3, select one model that you think best reflects the essence of INTASC Standard 5: "The teacher uses an understanding of individual and group motivation and behavior to create a learning environment that encourages positive social interaction, active engagement in learning, and self-motivation." Collect examples of instructional strategies (artifacts) in your particular field that reflect the essence of Standard 5. Place the artifacts in your portfolio under **INTASC Standard 5, Motivation and Classroom Management.**
2. Review the process of critical thinking illustrated in Figure 15.3 on page 391 and collect examples of how each step in the process can be applied to curriculum and instruction in your field of study. Place the artifacts in your portfolio under **INTASC Standard 7, Planning Instruction.**

To complete these activities online, go to the *Develop Your Portfolio* module for this chapter of the Companion Website at **http://www.prenhall.com/webb**.

Explore Teaching and Learning: Field Experiences

1. Contact a local school district to determine if the district is using any of the school improvement strategies discussed in this chapter. Arrange to observe a school implementing one of these strategies. Interview the principal and a teacher to determine how the school improvement strategy was implemented in the school, including barriers to implementation, costs of implementing the new strategy, and required professional development.
2. Contact the principal of a nearby school and make an appointment to observe a classroom lesson that utilizes cooperative learning strategies. Write a brief observation report that

includes the objective of the lesson, a description of how children had to cooperate to complete assignments, your assessment of the percentage of time that students were on task and not "goofing off," and the roles that students with different talents played in cooperatively completing the lesson.

Professional Development Online

Visit this text's Companion Website at **http://www.prenhall.com/webb** to gain access to a variety of questions, activities, and exercises to help build your knowledge of this chapter's content. Below are just a few items available at this text's Companion Website: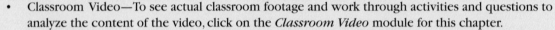

- Classroom Video—To see actual classroom footage and work through activities and questions to analyze the content of the video, click on the *Classroom Video* module for this chapter.
- Teaching Tolerance—To go to this organization's website and complete activities to explore issues and topics dealing with how to teach tolerance to students, click on the *Teaching Tolerance* module for this chapter.
- Self-Test—To review terms and concepts presented in this chapter, click on the *Self-Test* module for this chapter.
- Internet Resources—To link to websites related to topics in this chapter, go to the *Internet Resources* module for this chapter.

PART

7

PROJECTIONS FOR THE FUTURE

Chapter 16
Trends in Education

SCHOOL

For the future to be bright, it must be lit by the lamp of learning—the true Olympic torch.
—William A. Henry, III (1992)

TRENDS IN EDUCATION

It was midday on July 23, 2025. Cheryl Woo sat down at her networking console (home/work/school station) and started her interactive video system. Instantaneously, she was connected with the Tate Gallery in London, the Louvre in Paris, and the online libraries at Oxford and the University of Michigan. She retrieved a printout of the works of Rodin from the Louvre, a series of holograms from the Tate Gallery, and background narrative from the library at Oxford. Now she could put the finishing touches on the multimedia project she was completing for summer session credit from Cambridge University. Next, she accessed the Worldwide Electronic Bulletin Board and sent a message to her classmate Donna, who was finishing her summer term at the Sorbonne.

Cheryl's younger brother Todd was downstairs working with his keyboard emulator. Physically disabled since birth, Todd had very limited mobility but was able to control his computer by merely gazing at the terminal screen.

A red light flashed across the center wall accompanied by a subliminal sound. It was their mother, Dr. Audrey Woo, who was calling while en route home from Singapore, where she had con- sulted with the World Congress of Biomedical Scientists the previous day. She was calling from Concorde II to tell Cheryl and Todd that she expected to arrive home by the dinner hour. Cheryl's father is returning this evening from an anthropological dig in Manchuria; her grandparents will be coming for dinner so that they can catch up on the family events. She also reminded Cheryl to reprogram SRV3, their household robot, so that dinner would be ready when she arrived.

Cheryl is the recipient of a lifetime scholarship because she scored in the top decile of 18-year-olds on the International Assessment of Academic Potential (IAAP). She has unrestricted electronic access to depositories throughout the world. The IAAP scholars meet annually for an international conference; in addition to online access to scholars throughout the world, Cheryl can apply for an all-expenses-paid period of study at one of the research institutes throughout the world.

What will pre-K–12 schooling be like at mid-century? What type of individual would be most suited for teaching in the year 2025? Do you anticipate that you will still be teaching in the year 2030? Why or why not?

This chapter contains a discussion of projected educational, social, and technological trends for the 21st century. If students are to maximize their potential they will need to develop a vision of an emerging world that is much different from the one they are now experiencing. The information in the chapter and the class discussion should enable you to:

- Identify and discuss the projected demographic changes in the U.S. population and their impact on schools and the larger society.
- Discuss the ways in which changing governmental roles with respect to education have impacted school districts.
- Identify the dimensions of choice and their potential for reforming education.
- Speculate on the impact of technology on teaching and learning.
- Describe the educational system that would best prepare students for participation in an increasingly globalized society.

We live in a global society that continues to experience unprecedented change. What will the world of 2050 be like? What will America's educational system look like? Numerous hypotheses attempt to answer these questions. The Historical Note below discusses an early futurist's attempt to answer similar questions. As students become discriminating and responsible consumers and citizens, they will look for links between yesterday and today.

One way to glimpse education in the 21st century is to study projected societal trends. For America, a number of significant social changes are forecast for the 21st century. The current challenges facing the public schools will be made even more complex by the projected demographic changes. The population 65 years of age and older will outnumber the population 18 years and under, and the nation will have no dominant single racial or ethnic group the by mid-21st century. Governmental roles and responsibilities in education will continue to evolve as will the choice options available to parents and students. Social and economic capital will become the primary economic value, and pressures on the schools will increase as dramatically more knowledge will be needed to function in an increasingly globalized society. Advances in technology will continue at a rate that may exceed the rate of the education system to adopt or adapt to change.

In this chapter a number of the most important trends impacting education as the nation nears the end of the first decade of the 21st century are identified (see Figure 16.1), and questions are raised about the future of the schools in the context of these trends. Initial attention is given to the demographic changes that will influence education in the 21st century. Next, attention focuses on the changing intergovernmental relationships in elementary and secondary education. The multiple dimensions of choice are addressed as a third trend. The fourth trend addresses the potential presented by technology. A final trend discusses increased globalization. Our discussion closes by calling attention to the interactive challenges confronting teachers who face the continuing need to become active learners and discriminating consumers of information throughout their lives.

HISTORICAL NOTE

Nostradamus—Astrologer, Physician, and Futurist

Nostradamus (Michel de Nostredame) was born in 1503 at St. Remy in Provence and died in 1566. An astrologer, physician, and adviser to Henry II, Charles IX, and Catherine de Medici, Nostradamus was well known for his predictions of the future. In 1555 and in subsequent years, he published 10 "Centuries" or books, each containing 100 rhymed quatrains of predictions of the future. For example, he predicted with accuracy the death of Henry II, the decline of the Catholic Church, and the details of the French Revolution and the Napoleonic period.

During Nostradamus's lifetime, futuristic prophecy was considered taboo and was condemned. As a result, he was forced to disguise his prophecies by using symbolism, hidden meanings, and terminology from several languages, including French, Spanish, Portuguese, Italian, Latin, Greek, and Hebrew.

The fame of Nostradamus has continued beyond his lifetime. Generations of followers have regarded his quatrains as serious prophetic messages. For example, several contemporary commentators have alleged that he foresaw World War II in great detail. Now that we have entered a new millennium, Nostradamus enthusiasts will no doubt be particularly interested in his predictions and visions for the years ahead.

Source: Cavendish, R. (Ed.). (1983). *Man, myth and magic.* New York: Marshall Cavendish.

To research and explore this topic further, go to the *Historical Note* module for this chapter of the Companion Website at **http://www.prenhall.com/webb.**

Figure 16.1 — Trends in Public Education

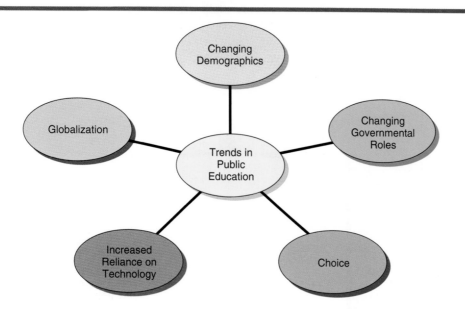

Changing Demographics

The changing demographics in the United States have implications for the full range of social services including education. Overall, the population of the United States is projected to increase by 46.6% between 2000 and 2050, and by 107.4% between 2000 and 2100. The proportion of the population 65 years and older was about 12% in 2004 and is projected to increase because of improved health care and medical advances. The proportion of the population in the traditional wage-earning years (20–64), which was 60% in 2004, is expected to decline to just over 50% by 2050, whereas the proportion under 20 years is projected to decrease from about 28% in 2004 to about 22% in 2050 (see Figure 16.2). As the proportion of the population over 65 increases and the proportion of the population from 20 to 64 years of age decreases, the demand for social services will be increasing at the same time that the proportion of persons in their productive years will be decreasing.

Population projections by race suggest a growth in all racial ethnic groups except for the white, non-Hispanic group (See figure 16.3). The Hispanic population is projected to be the fastest growing segment of the U.S. population. Projections suggest that this group will double its 2000 number by 2050 and triple it by 2100. As the percentage of the population that is white, non-Hispanic declines from 71% in 2000 to 53% in 2050 and 40% in 2100, the percentage of the population that is of Hispanic origin is projected to increase from 12% in 2000 to 24% in 2050 and 33% in 2100. The black, non-Hispanic sector of the population is projected to remain relatively stable: from 12% in 2000 to 13% in 2050 and 13% in 2100 (U.S. Census Bureau, 2006). The most notable change in the racial makeup of the population has been in the West, which became the first region in which the minority enrollment exceeded the white population (U.S. Department of Education, 2005b).

Poverty rates are disproportionately high for some racial/ethnic groups. As noted in Chapter 8, poverty rates in 2003 varied from 8% for non-Hispanic whites, to 23% for Hispanics, 24% for blacks, and 12% for Asians. Poverty rates are also disproportionately high for some age groups. As shown in Figure 16.4, the incidence of poverty appears to be higher among the young. The percentage

Figure 16.2 — Percent of Population by Age Group, 2004

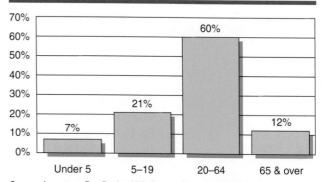

Source: American FactFinder. U.S. Census Bureau. (2005). Retrieved December 21, 2005, from http://factfinder.census.gov/servlet/ADPTable?_bm=y&-qr_name=ACS_2004_EST_2004

Figure 16.3 — Growth/Decline in Percent of Population by Race

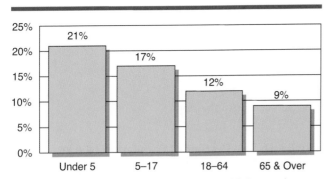

Source: U.S. Census Bureau, (2004). "U.S. interim projections by age, sex, race, and Hispanic origin." <http://www. census.gov/ipc/www/usinterimproj/> Interim Release Date, March 18, 2004. Table 1a.

Figure 16.4 — Percent in Poverty by Age, 2004

Source: American FactFinder. U.S. Census Bureau. (2005). Retrieved December 21, 2005, from http://factfinder.census.gov/servlet/ADPTable_ bm=y&-geo_id=01000 US&_qr_name=ACS_2004_ES

of children under the age of 5 living in poverty was 21%, for children ages 5 to 17 years the rate was 17%, for adults 18 to 64 years 12%, and for adults 65 years of age and older 9%.

The data related to the poverty rates for school-age youth become of special interest in light of the research and discussion in Chapter 8 related to the importance of preschool experiences to the success of children in school. The poverty research is especially important for single-parent families. In 2004, 38% of families with a single female householder and with related children under the age of 18 had incomes below the poverty level (American FactFinder, 2005). Unfortunately, of the 19 million children under age 5, only 1.5 million were in state-financed pre-K programs or in Head Start programs. Of the eligible children, only 12% were receiving federal child care subsidies (Quality counts, 2002).

Educational Implications of Changing Demographics

The changing demographics of the U.S. population have multiple consequences. Pressures for public service programs for the elderly and for school-age children will increase. Both the young and the elderly will need educational programs, medical services, recreational programs, and other social services. Public schools will find themselves competing with the elderly for limited resources. Rather than creating divisions and reinforcing barriers between programs for the youth and for the elderly, creative educators will need to find ways to integrate the interests of both groups.

The proportion of the U.S. population over 65 is increasing at the same time the proportion under 18 is decreasing.

The increased funding required to meet the various services and medical needs of the growing elderly population will probably have a negative effect on the financing of education. Not only will there be competition for limited resources, but an aged population that does not have children enrolled in school may be less supportive of public education. The challenge for the community will be to renew the interest and support that this group has for education. On a more positive note, a significant number of these senior citizens may take advantage of occupational and postsecondary educational opportunities to prepare for second careers or enhance avocational opportunities. They will be an entirely new group of students, the septuagenarians.

The need for day-care programs will increase with the increasing number of children with working parents. Schools or private providers will be asked to develop or expand before-school and after-school programs. The need for safe, affordable, and quality care for infants and children whose parents are working will continue to plague families, in particular poor families. Recognizing the importance of preschool experiences, state and federal legislators must continue to work toward the development and implementation of comprehensive child care policies. The efforts of Head Start programs to prepare all students for schooling will become increasingly important. In 2005, the federal government provided $6.8 billion for Head Start (Davis, 2005). In 22 states, the legislature provided additional funds to supplement the federal funds and serve additional children through Head Start, and 30 states were underwriting one or more programs for infants and toddlers. At the kindergarten level, every state was subsidizing some districts or providing funds for a portion of the school day.

Changing Governmental Roles

As discussed in Chapter 13, state governments have become increasingly involved in issues that have traditionally been considered the responsibility of local school boards. The increasing state influence is illustrated by the adoption of state standards and assessment programs in 48 states and provisions for sanctions for underperforming schools, including state takeover, in 20 states (Skinner, 2005). (In fact, the state has taken over the operation of schools in several states.)

Increasing state influence has also come with additional state funding. During the past 30 years, the percent of public school funds from state sources has increased in more than 30 states. State reporting and **accountability** mandates have also served to expand the role of the state. And, perhaps most important, the No Child Left Behind Act places the responsibility for ensuring that *all* children in the state will be achieving at the proficiency level by 2014 on the state, not on local school districts.

For Your Reflection and Analysis

What actions can teachers take to maintain public support for education in the growing elderly population?
To submit your response online, go to http://www.prenhall.com/webb.
CW

For Your Reflection and Analysis

What are the pros and cons of schools providing extended day-care programs for one-parent families and families in which both parents work?
To submit your response online, go to http://www.prenhall.com/webb.
CW

Not only has the state role been expanded, but so has the role of the federal government, in large part as a result of the provisions of the No Child Left Behind (NCLB) Act. As discussed in Chapter 13, for the first time in its history the federal government has become involved in development and implementation of standards and assessments for the general education program and in determining the qualifications of educational personnel. As previously discussed, the focus of the NCLB act is on reports of average annual yearly progress of individual schools. These reports are forwarded annually to the state department of education and eventually to the U.S. Department of Education.

Changes in state and federal roles, including mandatory assessments and accountability, have brought major changes in the discretionary powers and responsibilities of local school boards. In the post–No Child Left Behind era, it has become the responsibility of school boards to address the problems of underperforming schools without corresponding adjustments in state statutes or regulations. At the same time, the focus on the test performance of individual schools has contributed to an increased interest in increasing the budgetary authority of school sites. And, in some of the nation's largest cities, the accountability movement, community unrest, low student test scores, and fiscal management problems have resulted in mayors and the state governors taking a more active interest in the operation of the schools. Unfortunately, in some instances the school board

CONTROVERSIAL ISSUE

Federally Mandated Assessments

The role of the federal government in K–12 education has changed with enactment of the assessment requirements in the No Child Left Behind Act. Experiences with federal guidelines, regulations, and state interpretations, and local efforts to implement the NCLB act with separate, but related, state accountability programs have resulted in achievement tests in the elementary grades and high school proficiency examinations. Reports refer to the performance of the school, not to the students attending the school. Pros and cons about the legislation range from strong support to outright opposition:

Pros

1. Focus on the performance of students and schools rather than districts and states.
2. Disclosure of test performance information to the community, state agencies, and federal government.
3. Support for the federal interest in a well-trained workforce.
4. Continued interest in federal funds to provide programs and services for youth with special needs.
5. Assurances of students being accorded due process and access to programs.

Cons

1. Insufficient funds to pay for purchase and administration of the tests.
2. Excessive school time used for testing.
3. Possible narrowing of the curriculum as emphasis is placed on teaching for the test.
4. Questions about the capacity of any national assessment instrument to measure achievement in view of the cultural and ethnic differences of the students.
5. Federal action of this magnitude contrary to traditional governance of education in the United States.

As a prospective teacher, do you endorse the federal government becoming more active in governance of education? Should student achievement test data be used in evaluating teachers and determining their continued employment?

To answer these questions online, go to the *Controversial Issue* module for this chapter of the Companion Website at **http://www.prenhall.com/webb.**

is considered part of the problem: Some school boards tend to micro-manage, fractional-ize along ethnic and political lines, and use their jobs for patronage (Glover, 2004). As a re-sult, a number of school boards have come under increased scrutiny, and in Baltimore, Boston, Chicago, Detroit, New York, and Philadelphia the school board has been ap-pointed by the mayor or governor or has been stripped of some of its powers.

Educational Implications of Changing Governmental Roles

State laws that promote magnet schools, charter schools, and public and private school choice have changed the direction of accountability from the traditional model in which teachers and principals are responsible to the central office and school board to a model that extends responsibility to the state and federal governments. These devel-opments, in combination with the various requirements of the No Child Left Behind Act, illustrate the manner in which local school boards are being subjected to a wide range of regulations from local, state, and federal agencies (Howell, 2005). One possible positive result that could evolve from these structural changes would be that the state's share of the financing of education would increase, bringing more equity to the state finance program.

Individual schools no longer operate in anonymity as a part of a larger bureaucracy; the focus is on each school's average annual progress as a result of statewide assessment programs and federal requirements. Various authors have expressed concerns about the transfer of power from local boards to state and federal agencies (Howell, 2005; Stoddard, 2004). Major concerns are related to the decline in the authority of the teacher to focus on the needs of individual students. Increasingly, decisions about what content to teach and when to teach that content are externally influenced by the assessment schedule and state content standards. With or without dramatic changes in governance, the roles and responsibilities of school-level personnel will change even if it is merely to implement, without modification, one of the whole-school reform models mentioned in Chapter 15.

For Your Reflection and Analysis

In an era where the educational goal is that no child be left behind, what actions can you take to reduce the possibility that no teacher is left behind?
To submit your response online, go to http://www.prenhall.com/webb.

CW

Choice

In discussions related to American education, the concept of **choice** has become multi-dimensional. First, there is the traditional school finance dimension of choice in which lo-cal school boards have the leeway to choose their tax rate or spending level. However, many state school finance systems no longer permit that dimension of choice because of the constraints resulting from the school finance litigation that began in the 1970s. As dis-cussed in Chapter 13, these school finance cases focused on the fiscal equity in state school finance systems; if districts have the power to exercise the right to choose their level of spending, inequities in funding per pupil likely will occur.

A second dimension of choice is related to the power of the parent to choose where the education of their children will occur. Advocates for choice contend that school im-provement will occur when parents can choose schools for their children from a vari-ety of options. Rather than the single option of the public school, parents and children will have a variety of options including the choice to attend another public school on a space-available basis, enroll in a charter school, receive public funds for home school-ing, enroll in a virtual school website by going online, or use a public voucher to attend a private or parochial school. Some of the more prominent choice options are shown in Figure 16.5.

Many voucher supporters had predicted that after the U.S. Supreme Court upheld the use of vouchers to attend public or private schools in *Zelman v. Simmons-Harris* (2002) the concept would be widely adopted. However, it has not happened. In fact, public sup-port for vouchers has decreased since *Zelman* (Rose & Gallup, 2004). Only a few interest groups are speaking in favor of vouchers. Much of the active and visible support comes from low-income parents and child advocates who are concerned about underperform-ing schools. For example, a proposal has been made to expand the Cleveland voucher pro-gram to permit students to transfer to a secular or church-related school if they are

Figure 16.5 — Choice Options

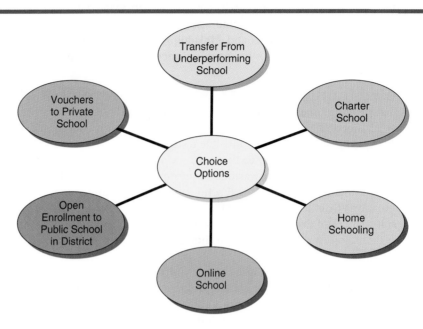

For Your Reflection and Analysis

Should state accountability and assessment requirements also apply to nonpublic schools?

To submit your response online, go to http://www. prenhall.com/webb.

CW

attending any school in the district with the designation of "academic watch" or "academic emergency" (Richard & Samuels, 2005). Some parochial and private schools have also supported the concepts of vouchers. Still, advocates for choice have been encouraged by legislation in Arizona and Florida and the 2005 legislative proposals in Minnesota, Ohio, South Carolina, and Texas. These initiatives have included a variety of voucher proposals as well as corporate and individual income tax credit proposals (Richard & Samuels, 2005)

The opposition to vouchers has a broader social and political base, including the American Civil Liberties Union, some protestant faiths, and the National School Boards Association. Both of the major national teachers' associations have opposed vouchers for decades. The National Education Association (NEA) reports that teachers, parents, and the general public have long opposed vouchers especially when funds for private schools compete with funds for public schools (NEA, 2005c). The American Federation of Teachers (AFT) notes that private and religious schools can exercise choice in admitting students—a privilege that public schools do not have (AFT, 2005).

Another element in the second dimension of choice, charter schools, provides parents with the opportunity to exercise choice within the public system. Charter schools are concentrated in Arizona, California, Michigan, and Texas (Center for Education Reform, 2005). In addition to contracting for the operation of public schools, private providers also manage some of the charter schools. Arsen, Plank, and Sykes (2001) reported that about 70% of Michigan's charter schools in 2001 were operated by education management organizations such as Edison and the National Heritage Academies.

Educational Implications of Choice

For Your Reflection and Analysis

Why do parents choose the charter school option for their children?

To submit your response online, go to http://www. prenhall.com/webb.

CW

If court decisions and state statutes permit parents and students to exercise unconstrained choice by transferring their child to another public or private school, not only will there be greater in-year mobility as parents and pupils change schools without being required to justify their actions, but schools are also likely to become more racially, ethnically, or economically divided. The use of quotas, or active recruitment of underrepresented students, is one possible response, but both concepts seem to be a vestige of the previous century. A significant issue in these transfers is whether the *dollars will follow the child* whenever the child changes schools. If this should be the case, in schools that have a significant number of students transferring out, a fiscal crisis may develop as the school is forced to make cost savings within the budget year or from year to year.

Increased Reliance on Technology

From the simple to the complex, technological developments in the schools have both empowered teachers and students and increased the expectations that are held of them. Technology is firmly established as important to the performance of a variety of functions in the educational process (see Figure 16.6). In a 2005 nationwide survey, teachers indicated that technology is pervasive and growing in all aspects of the educational enterprise: administrative functions, communications, research and planning, and classroom instruction (CDW-Government, 2005). More than three-quarters of the teachers surveyed indicated that technology was an effective tool for teaching the subject that they personally taught, and more than two-thirds believed technology was an effective tool for improving academic performance. However, 58% were skeptical about how technology could improve performance on standardized tests. Middle and high school teachers were more likely than elementary teachers to consider computers important for administrative functions such as attendance and grading, while elementary teachers were more likely than middle or high school teachers to rate computers as important teaching tools for students.

An important trend highlighted in a *Teachers Talk Tech* survey (CDW-Government, 2005) was the increasing use of technology to meet the mounting administrative requirements of K–12 educators, sometimes at the expense of instruction. According to some reports:

> The No Child Left Behind Act is driving the shift in priorities from instructional computing to data management for reporting purposes. And, as schools scramble to meet accountability standards and qualify for government funding, the rush to build complex data networks and huge databases may be leaving instructional computing behind. (Rother, 2005, p. 34)

The focus of the No Child Left Behind Act and the accountability movement is on the individual school as the unit of analysis, and accountability reports contain detailed information about the school. In response, states and school districts are spending millions of dollars to build data repositories that will provide teachers with information that they can use to improve teaching and student performance (Electronic transfer, 2005) and to better inform data-driven decision making. Data-driven decision making (D3M), the new buzz phrase of the 21st century, involves data-centered dialogue that is focused on improving student achievement (Mercurius, 2005). The availability of these data repositories likely will contribute to an increased interest in reviewing how districts and schools allocate their funds and the relationship of those allocations to student outcomes.

For Your Reflection and Analysis

How can technology be used to expedite communication in a school?
To submit your response online, go to http://www. prenhall.com/webb.

CW

Figure 16.6 — Impact of Technology

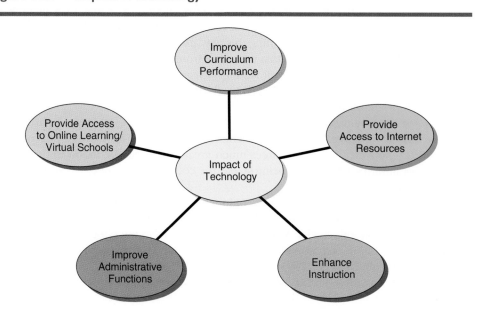

The Florida virtual school provides web-based learning for grades K–12.

Another area of technology that has shown tremendous growth is online learning. Some form of online learning is offered by about half of the nation's K–12 schools. The most expanded form of e-learning is the virtual school; 23 states have established virtual schools (Electronic transfer, 2005). Virtual schools, also referred to as online schools, cyber schools, and Internet schools, are different from regular schools in that (1) they are not limited by school district or even state boundaries or daily schedules, (2) they can serve students who live in remote areas or have lifestyles that make it difficult to attend a regular school, and (3) parents are expected to monitor and provide instructional support (Long, 2004). As an alternative to traditional schooling with its classrooms and the teacher as the source of knowledge, the virtual school has great potential as an efficient way to make courses accessible to students who reside in isolated rural areas, have a health problem that prevents school attendance, or who, for other reasons, need an alternative to traditional schooling. These online, web-based programs can offer single courses as well as the entire curriculum. Convenience and flexibility are the most often cited factors contributing to the growth of e-learning (Podoll & Randle, 2005).

One of the most recent developments in the use of technology is blogging. In 2005 more than 32 million web users read blogs (web logs) regularly, with the number growing exponentially (Harper, 2005). With this growth some educators have begun to use blogging for classroom purposes. Blogs, they have found, extend the learning experience beyond the classroom, creating a more complete learning experience. Some teachers have also found that blogs provide an avenue for interpersonal relationships and student self-disclosure that was previously inaccessible. This is important they say because self-disclosure between teachers and students can improve learning outcomes and is currently "an underutilized tool in the repertoire of most educators" (Harper, 2005, p. 30).

Educational Implications of the Increased Reliance on Technology

The technology changes taking place in education will require teachers to have a broader set of skills and knowledge if they are to take advantage of the potential of technology to improve teaching and learning in their classrooms and improve the management of schools. One of the most beneficial results of technology integration will be increased access to information. Rather than retaining this new power for personal use, the task of the teacher is to recognize the benefits that can come from empowering others. The efficient use of technology not only will permit students throughout the nation to complete their schooling, but also has the capability of giving all students access to the nation's best scholars to enrich programs in any school throughout the nation.

Technology is a valuable resource in those activities that are an integral part of the process of **lifelong learning** for both teachers and students. Through the Internet, students and teachers can access resources much greater than can be found in the collections of most libraries. Rather than being stable, the collection continues to grow with the introduction of new information.

New technologies have brought an age of inexpensive, effortless, and universal web access to the classroom. Wireless technology has progressively "moved downstream and down the socioeconomic ladder. With this incredible availability, educators and learners are brought together in common effective, intellectual, and pedagogical planes that have never existed before" (Harper, 2005, p. 30). The challenge confronting educators will be to maintain their own technology skills and to find ways to most effectively utilize new technologies.

For Your Reflection and Analysis

What are the advantages and disadvantages of taking courses online?
To submit your response online, go to http://www.prenhall.com/webb.

CW

For Your Reflection and Analysis

What are the different ways in which technology is affecting you as a student?
To submit your response online, go to http://www.prenhall.com/webb.

CW

The No Child Left Behind Act has brought not only dedicated technology funds from the federal government but a refocusing of technology programs in schools. Previously most federal, and many state and local, programs focused on increasing access to technology—getting more hardware in the schools. The NCLB act focuses on the integration of technology into curriculum and instruction. By the beginning of 2007 states must show how technology will be integrated throughout all of the curriculum and instruction. Technology is increasingly seen (and the research supports this view) as important in closing the achievement gap, ensuring the development of highly qualified teachers for all students, and facilitating the use of the data schools need to meet the adequately yearly progress requirements. Increasingly educators recognize that, like any other tool, technology will improve the quality of education only to the extent they adopt new ways of applying this tool to teaching and learning.

For Your Reflection and Analysis

What additional technical skills do you need to make effective use of technology as a teacher?

To submit your response online, go to http://www. prenhall.com/webb.

CW

Globalization

Globalization has been alternatively defined as the growth in international exchange and interdependence resulting in the abolition of barriers between nations or as the flow of capital, populations, ideas, production, and systems (e.g., capitalism) all over the planet. However defined, the interactive effect of advancements in transportation with the opening of markets through trade agreements among nations has contributed to the breakdown of international trade barriers, created employment opportunities in developing nations, and brought unprecedented challenges and opportunities to the American economy and educational system. Globalization is an important reality of today's world: "From one continent to another, information, lifestyles, and commodities traverse the planet. What happens in one nation affects life in others" (Kagan & Stewart, 2005, p. 185). Not only has

Globalization has brought new challenges and opportunities to the U.S. educational system.

globalization contributed to a de-localization of education (e.g., the provision of education is no longer confined to a specific local school), it has, as Thomas Friedman (2005) maintains, "flattened the world."

If the United States is to maintain or improve its political leadership and competitive position in the global economy, concerted efforts must be devoted to developing an understanding of, and respect for, the values, traditions, cultures, and languages of not only the developed nations in Europe, Latin America, and Japan, but also the older nations in the Far East such as China and India. These mega-economies offer tremendous opportunities as a market for goods and services as well as sources of labor for the production of goods and services.

Globalization is impacting the American economy in a variety of ways. The combined effect of shifting jobs offshore to other nations and the worldwide availability of technology has been a depression of the wages and standard of living of the American workforce. Perhaps more important, some would contend, is the potential for the globalization of finance, production, and trade to contribute to a more socially responsive form of government that values social justice and seeks a better quality of life for all citizens (Danaher, 2005). Other impacts of globalization are depicted in Figure 16.7.

For Your Reflection and Analysis

What changes should be made in a school's curriculum to recognize the social and economic changes related to the development of a global economy?

To submit your response online, go to http://www. prenhall.com/webb.

CW

Educational Implications of Globalization

The increased globalization of the world economy, the restructuring of the world political and economic system, and the requirements for knowledge and information within

Figure 16.7 — Impact of Globalization

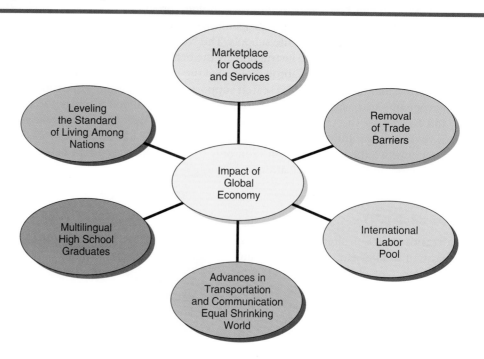

that system have created new educational needs in terms of structure, function, curriculum, and approaches to education at all levels (Cogburn, 2005). It has been suggested that an educational system that would meet these needs and would best prepare students for the increasingly diverse and complex "flattened" world of the 21st century is one that:

1. Focuses on abstract concepts;
2. Uses a holistic, as opposed to linear, approach;
3. Enhances the student's ability to manipulate symbols;
4. Enhances the student's ability to acquire and utilize knowledge;
5. Produces an increased quantity of scientifically and technically trained persons;
6. Blurs the distinction between mental and physical labor;
7. Encourages students to work in teams;
8. Uses virtual teams around the world;
9. Is an agile and flexible system; and
10. Breaks the boundaries of space and time (Cogburn, 2005).

Increased globalization holds significant import for the exchange of educational ideas and research. As was described in earlier chapters, historically American education borrowed from and was deeply influenced by ideas originating outside this country. Similarly, other nations have adopted or adapted educational ideas from the U.S. In an era of increased globalization, "educational ideas germinated in one setting. . . can yield helpful adaptations as nations strive to prepare their children for a world in which shared science and technology and increased communication across the boundaries of languages and cultures become the norm" (Kagan & Stewart, 2005, p. 185).

"Globalization will increasingly affect how students experience national identity and cultural belonging, which are complicated by the increasingly fluid political and cultural borders that once separated nation-states and the people within them" (Suárez-Orozco, 2005, p. 211). In response, U.S. schools must break down what many refer to as the egocentrism of the American perspective. No longer can American schools ignore the historical and cultural roots of nations in the Far East, Middle East, Africa, and Latin America. If these nations are to be treated as economic neighbors that provide a market for goods and services, the content and emphasis of the school's curriculum need to be expanded so that students not only develop an appreciation for the United States and its heritage, but also a better understanding of the different values, traditions, cultures, languages, and current conditions in the community of nations that are affected by the different dimensions of globalization. Whether this is done by incorporating the study of other countries and cultures into the curriculum, requiring students to study foreign languages, or in other ways attempting to prepare students for "global competence and global citizenship" (Stewart, 2005, p. 230) will vary by state and from school district to school district. Regardless of the approach chosen, the imperative is for U.S. schools to create classrooms where students and faculty can "pursue global learning as a means to global understanding" (Kagan & Stewart, 2005).

Coping With the Future

In this era of ongoing school reform teachers must function in an educational environment that is in constant flux as state and federal legislators continue to enact legislation related to performance standards, accountability, and assessment. These reforms are being introduced during a period when the economic and political interactions among nations demonstrate that the world is shrinking. The increasingly rapid pace of advancements in basic knowledge, transportation, and communication makes it impossible to teach the concepts and facts that will influence the characteristics of the world that your students will experience during their adult lives. For this reason it is important that teachers and students develop the skills needed for lifelong learning.

Because of the rapid rate of change and the rapid development of technology, teachers must continue to teach in a world that cannot be projected with a high degree of certainty. However, teachers can attempt to recognize the relationships between different events and search for ways to anticipate events. To do so, teachers need to develop the skills needed to identify problems and probe for underlying cause-and-effect relationships. These approaches emphasize the power of the individual or group to alter the environment. The challenge for teachers is to utilize these approaches in the current climate which emphasizes an adherence to state content standards and assessment of student performance.

PROFESSIONAL REFLECTION

My role as a teacher in an information technology–centered world is more important than ever before. Technology is everywhere, and it is not going away. It is imperative to develop a broad collection of pedagogical strategies to ensure that I can provide the learning skills necessary for my students in the Information Age. I have the responsibility to involve my students in learning activities that are meaningful. I need to provide an atmosphere for student-centered learning through the structure and stability in my classroom while being a facilitator for my students' learning.

Because I believe that engaged learning is the key to educational success, I integrate technology on a daily basis. Using technology allows my students to showcase their creativity. My lessons contain a wide variety of strategies in an attempt to reach all learning styles. The ability to use word processing skills is incorporated early on, because the expertise demonstrated will carry over to proficiency in other technology areas as well. Multimedia presentations have become an important part not only of my teaching, but also as a means for my students to present their learning to a wider audience.

Allowing students to utilize the Internet for research has provided increased motivation. Students have had to develop expertise in analyzing quality websites for their use, another skill that I have added to my teaching repertoire. The Internet has also been a valuable assistant for finding answers during some of the "teachable moments" that often arise in the classroom. A wealth of information is constantly at my fingertips.

The classroom environment is important in allowing children the freedom to learn. Students need to be in an environment where they feel safe taking chances while knowing it is a learning community that cultivates respect for themselves and others. Through all this, developing a love for lifelong learning is my ultimate goal.

Brenda McKone

National Board Certified Teacher, Iowa

To analyze this reflection, go to the *Professional Reflection* module for this chapter of the Companion Website at **http://www.prenhall.com/webb.**

For Your Reflection and Analysis

Why has the concept of lifelong learning become so critical to today's teachers?

To submit your response online, go to http://www.prenhall.com/webb.

CW

One challenge teachers face in coping with the future is to develop an optimistic perspective by focusing on the positive and empowering capabilities of new developments. Rather than merely disseminating facts and information, instruction could involve inquiries into hypothetical simulations or scenarios and the development of alternative solutions. The application of an open-ended, inquiry-based methodology might include an analysis of student performance data, the development of strategies to address problems, and the development of exploratory predictions of the future through attitude surveys and open-ended brainstorming techniques. The goal is to develop creative thinking skills so that both students and teachers can cope with the ever-changing world.

Another major challenge for teachers is to prepare themselves and their students to cope with the complexity of change. Despite the uncertainty of the future, much can be done to aid students in preparing for it by helping them develop the skills needed to analyze, clarify, generalize, and make critical judgments. In addition, the study of the future offers numerous creative opportunities for imagining and designing the best possible alternatives and visions for tomorrow.

Summary

From different perspectives, trends potentially can have an immediate impact on the day-to-day operations of schools or the impact may not be experienced for a decade or two. Projecting trends is never without its risks. The trends discussed in this chapter will affect education in significant ways. Two demographic trends that will affect education the most are the growing minority student body and the aging population. Both have the potential of placing a heavy financial burden on the economy, which in turn may have a negative effect on the financing of education. The great debate of the 21st century may be centered around the competition for resources to meet the needs of youth and those of the aging population.

The interaction of the accountability movement and governance changes may contribute to dramatic changes in the decision-making options in individual schools. In an era when some policy makers stress the importance of staff empowerment and individualization, considerable support is also being given to the use of standardized approaches in addressing problems and issues related to student performance.

The educational implications of both increased technology and globalization are limitless. Both present tremendous challenges and opportunities. It is important for educators to recognize that despite its potential technology is not the panacea for all of the ills of education. Extensive use of technology may call for the redesign of the entire educational enterprise. The challenge for the teacher will be to develop an efficient data management and reporting system while simultaneously addressing the student performance issues associated with the accountability movement.

Key Terms

Accountability, 415

Choice, 417

Globalization, 421

Lifelong Learning, 420

PROFESSIONAL DEVELOPMENT WORKSHOP

Prepare for the Praxis™ Examination

Joel Abraham has been teaching science for the past decade at Evergreen Preparatory Academy, a non-sectarian high school in suburban Chicago. What is unique about Joel is that he has integrated both art and science in his classes. He has also been able to enhance his teaching by incorporating a wide variety of teaching strategies including the use of CD-ROMs, simulations, and virtual websites. Each of his students is required to create his or her own electronic portfolio on a science project of his or her choice. And, for Joel the "medium" is equally as important as the "method."

This semester the students in each of his advanced classes are required to integrate a variety of mixed media in their science projects including photography, video, CDs, and music that features some of the world's greatest artists. Last year Joel completed all the requirements for national board certification in both art and science. He was also awarded the Outstanding Teacher of the Year by his peers from the science community. In addition, one of the major electronic companies in his community awarded him $10,000 worth of electronic equipment for his classroom.

When asked by the science editor of the *Evergreen Gazette* why it was so important to teach science via the arts, Joel replied, "Because science is 'Truth,' and art is the soul."

1. How effective would Joel's teaching strategy be with students who are concrete operational thinkers? Students for whom English is not their first language? Students who have visual and perceptual difficulties? Give reasons for each of your responses.
2. Describe the type(s) of assessment that Joel might use in evaluating his students' electronic portfolios.
3. Give examples of instructional strategies that Joel could have used that were not computer technologically driven that would also have been effective for enhancing student learning.

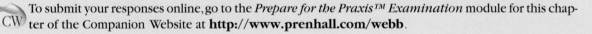

To submit your responses online, go to the *Prepare for the Praxis™ Examination* module for this chapter of the Companion Website at **http://www.prenhall.com/webb**.

Build Your Knowledge Base

1. How will the increased federal role—through assessment, school report cards, and state accountability—affect the development of teaching as a profession and the daily life of a teacher?
2. As the face of the nation changes with an increase in minority students to the point where one of the current minority groups becomes the majority group, what does this mean for you as a teacher and for the processes of teaching and learning?
3. If you were asked to write an essay predicting the changes facing elementary and secondary schools in 2050, what would be your principal points relative to developments in the educational program, student–teacher interactions, types of instruction, school calendar, length of the school day, and use of technology?
4. The concept of parental choice is becoming an integral part of America's elementary and secondary schools. How will expansive choice options affect regular schools? What actions can be taken to increase the likelihood that parents will be making informed choices as they select the school for their child?
5. How can teachers reconcile the tension between state standards, state assessment, and proficiency exams and (1) the importance of the growth of students as individuals and (2) the need to develop the skills and interests that lead to an understanding of the importance of lifelong learning?
6. Design a home/work/school station of the future that integrates the use of advanced technology in your subject-matter discipline.

Develop Your Portfolio

1. One of the major challenges facing educators for the new millennium is to retain a focus on students as individuals in an era of accountability when the focus is on labeling the progress of the school. Review INTASC Standard 3: "The teacher understands how students differ in their approaches to learning and creates instructional opportunities that are adapted to diverse learners." Prepare a thought paper that identifies the social and technological changes you believe will be necessary for tomorrow's educators to effectively implement Standard 3. Place your thought paper in your portfolio under **INTASC Standard 3, Adapting Instruction for Diverse Learners.**

2. Imagine that today is December 26, 2037. You are making plans to celebrate the arrival of the year 2038. For the past three decades, you have prepared a New Year's resolution. As you ponder the arrival of 2038, consider the following questions: Will you still be involved in some form of instruction or education? If the answer is "no," what do you anticipate you will be doing instead? If you anticipate that you will continue to be an educator or instructor, prepare a New Year's resolution that enumerates what you plan to do to improve your ability to help your students cope with the uncertainty of the future, while achieving a satisfying and fulfilling life. Place your New Year's resolution plan in your portfolio under **INTASC Standard 9, Reflective Practice and Professional Growth.**

To complete these activities online, go to the *Develop Your Portfolio* module for this chapter of the Companion Website at **http://www.prenhall.com/webb**.

Explore Teaching and Learning: Field Experiences

1. Search the Internet for virtual high schools that provide courses through online instruction. How many schools did you locate, and what different courses were offered? Who was operating or sponsoring the schools—a public school district, state agency, university, community college, or private entity? What are the requirements for enrollment and graduation? Does your local school district accept courses taken from a virtual high school for credit toward graduation requirements?

2. Search the Internet website for your state department of education to determine the student assessment and accountability requirements in your state. What reporting requirements must schools follow? Secure a school report card and compare its content with the state requirements. Do you think that the report card clearly communicates the quality of education to the school patrons?

Professional Development Online

Visit this text's Companion Website at **http://www.prenhall.com/webb** to gain access to a variety of questions, activities, and exercises to help build your knowledge of this chapter's content. Below are just a few items available at this text's Companion Website:

- Classroom Video—To see actual classroom footage and work through activities and questions to analyze the content of the video, click on the *Classroom Video* module for this chapter.
- Teaching Tolerance—To go to this organization's website and complete activities to explore issues and topics dealing with how to teach tolerance to students, click on the *Teaching Tolerance* module for this chapter.
- Self-Test—To review terms and concepts presented in this chapter, click on the *Self-Test* module for this chapter.
- Internet Resources—To link to websites related to topics in this chapter, go to the *Internet Resources* module for this chapter.

GLOSSARY

A

Academic freedom. The teacher's freedom to determine the most appropriate instructional materials and the most appropriate teaching strategies without censorship, interference, or fear of reprisal.

Academy. A type of private secondary school operating in the 1800s, designed to teach subjects useful in trade and commerce.

Accountability. A concept in which the schools and teachers are held responsible for the accomplishment of expressed educational goals.

Acquired immunodeficiency syndrome (AIDS). A serious health condition caused by a virus that destroys the immune system and leaves the body incapable of fighting disease.

Activity curriculum. A curriculum that is determined to a large extent by student interest and that emphasizes self-expression through games, singing, or other creative and spontaneous activities.

Adequacy. The extent to which funding for programs and learning opportunities is sufficient.

Administrative law. The formal regulations and decisions of state or federal agencies.

Aesthetics. The branch of philosophy concerned with values in beauty, especially in the fine arts.

Affirmative action. Affirmative steps to recruit and hire, or recruit and retain, individuals from groups who are underrepresented in the workplace or the classroom.

Alternative teacher certification. State provisions or regulations for awarding a teaching license to a person who has not followed the traditional teacher education program; exceptions typically are related to completion of a concen-

trated professional education sequence, teaching internships or prior experience, or credits for work experience.

Alternative schools. Schools that offer specialized programs and learning experiences not normally found in the public schools, or that provide greater individual attention for students who are not making normal progress.

Amalgamation. A form of diversity that supports the "melting pot" notion and envisions American culture as emerging from the best elements of many cultures.

Analytic learner. A person who perceives information in an abstract form and processes that information in a reflective manner.

Analytic philosophy. A philosophy that incorporates an analysis of languages and assumes that the words we use must be empirically verified and tested to be meaningful.

Apparent reality. The reality made up of day-to-day experiences and life events.

Assimilation. A response to population diversity that requires conformity to a single model, which is largely defined by traditional British political, social, cultural, and religious institutions.

At risk. A term used to describe students who are achieving below grade-level expectations or are likely to experience educational problems in the future, as well as students who are likely to experience physical and mental health problems.

Authentic assessment. A form of evaluation based on the cooperation between the student and teacher, student and student, teacher and administrator or supervisor, and community and teacher.

Axiology. The branch of philosophy concerned with the nature of values.

B

Back-to-basics movement.   A revival of essentialism begun in the 1970s and echoed in education reform reports of the 1980s that emphasizes the three Rs, a core curriculum, and more rigorous academic program requirements.

Behavioral objectives.   Action-oriented statements that indicate specific behaviors or knowledge that students are expected to learn or demonstrate upon completion of an instructional sequence.

Behaviorism.   An educational theory predicated on the belief that human behavior can be explained in terms of responses to external stimuli. The basic principle underlying behaviorism in education is that behaviors can be modified in a socially acceptable manner through the arrangement of the conditions for learning.

Bibliotherapy.   The use of books as a therapeutic intervention.

Bilingual education.   Instruction to non–English-speaking students in their native language while teaching them English.

Bloom's *Taxonomy of Educational Objectives*.   List and organizing scheme containing expected learnings for students.

Board certified.   Certification awarded by the assessment board of a profession acknowledging the recipient's qualifications in specified areas.

Building principal.   The person responsible for the administration and management of a school.

C

Career ladder.   A career development plan that provides differential recognition and rewards for teachers at steps of the plan, which coincide with increased experience and expertise.

Carnegie unit.   A measure of clock time associated with a high school course used to award credit toward high school graduation.

Case (common) law.   That body of law originating from historical usages and customs.

Cartesian method.   A process proposed by Descartes that involves the derivation of axioms on which theories can be based by the purposeful and progressive elimination of all interpretations of experience except those that are absolutely certain.

Categorical funding.   The practice of state funding of specific educational programs or activities (e.g., bilingual education, education of pupils with disabilities, pupil transportation, or in-service programs).

Categorical imperatives.   Universal moral laws that guide our actions and behaviors.

Certification.   The authorization of an individual by the state to teach in an area where the state has determined that the individual has met established state standards.

Charity (pauper) schools.   Schools in colonial New England designed for children who could not afford to attend other fee-charging schools.

Charter schools.   Publicly supported schools established upon the issuance of a charter from the state, local school board, or other entity and designed to provide greater autonomy to individual schools and greater choice in educational programs to parents and students.

Chief state school officer.   The elected or appointed executive officer of the state department of education, responsible for elementary and secondary education, and sometimes for higher education; often referred to as the superintendent of public instruction or the commissioner of education.

Child abuse.   The repeated mistreatment or neglect of a child, which can result in physical, emotional, verbal, or sexual injury or harm.

Child benefit theory.   The legal theory that supports providing state aid to private education when the aid benefits the private school child rather than the private school itself.

Child neglect.   Child abuse that includes an unwillingness to provide for the basic needs of the child.

Child (student)-centered curriculum.   Curriculum designed with the child's interest and needs at the center of the learning process; learning takes place through experience and problem solving.

***Chlamydia* infection.**   One of the most prevalent sexually transmitted infections that affects both males and females.

Choice.   Power or authority of (1) a local school board to select the instructional program and level of funding to be provided students in the school district, or (2) parents to select the school that their child attends.

Classical conditioning.   A type of behaviorism that demonstrates that a natural stimulus that produces a certain type of response can be replaced by a conditioned stimulus.

Clinical field experiences.   Those opportunities provided teacher education students to observe, assist, tutor, instruct, or conduct applied research in the classroom.

Clinical practice.   Student teaching and internships that provide candidates with experiences that allow for full immersion in the learning community so that candidates are able to demonstrate proficiencies in the professional roles for which they are preparing

Coalition of Essential Schools (CES).   Developed by Professor Ted Sizer of Brown University, the Coalition of Essential Schools is based on the concept of a triangle of learning between teacher, student, and subject matter. The model assumes that effective school reform requires fundamental changes in the school as an institution.

Code of ethics.   A set of professional standards for behavior of members of a profession.

Cognitive styles.   The alternative processes by which learners acquire knowledge.

Common schools.   Publicly supported schools started during the mid-1800s attended in common by all children.

Commonsense learner.   One of four learning styles related to the perceiving and processing of information. The commonsense learner perceives information abstractly and processes it actively.

Compensatory education. Special educational programs designed to overcome the educational deficiencies associated with the socioeconomic, cultural, or minority group disadvantages of youth.

Competency testing. Testing designed to assess basic skills and knowledge.

Competency-based pay. Compensation given to employees as they acquire new knowledge or skills or demonstrate higher level competence for their existing abilities.

Comprehensive high school. A public secondary school that offers curricula in vocational education, general education, and college preparation.

Constitution. A written contract for the establishment of a government; the highest level of law.

Constructivism. (See Postmodern constructivism.)

Continuity. The repetition of major curriculum elements to ensure that skills can be practiced and developed.

Cooperative learning. Instructional system that assumes that students will study and work together in a supportive relationship rather than competitively.

Core curriculum. A curriculum design that emphasizes the required minimum subjects and topics within subjects that all students are expected to learn.

Cosmology. The branch of philosophy concerned about the nature of the universe or cosmos.

Crisis intervention team. Volunteer teachers, counselors, administrators, social workers, school nurses, and school psychologists who network with each other and identify the student who appears to be overwhelmed by stress, or displays suicidal gestures or suicidal threats.

Critical literacy. A type of curriculum that challenges all unequal power relationships and denounces any form of exclusion.

Critical theory. A set of principles that focuses on the political nature of education, including social control and power.

Critical thinking. The process of thinking and problem solving that involves the examination and validation of assumptions and evidence and the application of logic to the formulation of conclusions.

Cultural literacy. An assumed body of knowledge about which persons should be able to demonstrate mastery if they are to function at an optimal level in society.

Cultural pluralism. A form of diversity that emphasizes the multiple cultures in the larger society.

Culturally relevant teaching. Instruction that seeks to integrate the cultural context of the learner in shaping an effective learning environment and strategies.

Culture. The behavioral patterns, ideas, values, religions and moral beliefs, customs, laws, language, institutions, art, and all other material things and artifacts characteristic of a given people at a given period of time.

Curriculum. All the educational experiences of students that take place in the school.

Curriculum mapping. Process designed to ensure that teachers take the necessary actions required to ensure a logical sequence in the schedule in terms of the availability of instructional materials, introduction of concepts in classroom instruction, sequence embedded in the state standards, and content of formal assessments.

D

Dame school. The elementary school in the New England colonies, usually held in a kitchen or living room and taught by women with minimal education.

de facto **segregation.** Segregation existing as a matter of fact, regardless of the law.

de jure **segregation.** Segregation sanctioned by law.

Deductive logic. Reasoning from a general statement or principle to a specific point or example.

Desegregation. The abolition of racial, ethnic, or gender segregation.

Direct instruction. Teacher-dominated mode of instruction in which smaller learnings are integrated into meaningful wholes; basic or simpler skills (parts) are not taught in isolation from meaningful contexts (e.g., activities, problems). The teacher tells, demonstrates, restates, and helps students to state and restate rules and cognitive strategies. Knowledge is made explicit and overt, and students are taught to use this knowledge (e.g., how to figure a total cost) in their activities. With practice, this knowledge becomes covert (internalized).

Discrimination. Showing bias or prejudice in the treatment of individuals because of their race, ethnicity, gender, disability, or sexual orientation.

Disparate impact. The situation that exists when a policy or practice has a differential impact on individuals in a protected class.

Disparate treatment. The less favorable treatment of an individual protected by Title VII by an employment policy or practice.

Dropout. A pupil who leaves school for any reason except death, before graduation or completion of a program of studies and without transferring to another school or institution.

Dynamic learner. One of four learning styles related to the perceiving and processing of information. The dynamic learner perceives information concretely and processes it actively.

E

Educational foundations. Charitable or not-for-profit entities established to receive or distribute funds that can be used to enrich the educational opportunities for students.

Educational goals. Broad general statements of desired learning outcomes.

Educational malpractice. Failure on the part of an education professional to render a reasonable amount of care in the exercise of assigned duties with resultant injury or loss to another.

Educational objective. A clearly defined, observable, and measurable student behavior that indicates learner progress toward the achievement of a particular educational goal.

Emergency (temporary) certificate. A certificate issued to a person who does not meet the specified degree, course, or other requirements for regular certification; issued with the presumption that the recipient teacher will obtain the necessary credentials for regular certification.

Eminent domain. The right of the government to take private property for public use.

Emotional abuse. Nonphysical abuse such as blaming, rejecting, or withholding security and affection.

Employee services. A benefit designed to help the employee to enjoy an improved lifestyle or meet certain obligations at a free or reduced cost (e.g., credit unions, employee assistance programs, child care).

Enculturation. The process of learning about one's culture.

English as a second language (ESL). A form of bilingual education in which standard English is taught to students with limited proficiency in English.

Epistemology. The branch of philosophy concerned with the investigation of the nature of knowledge.

Equal opportunity. A legal principle that, when applied to education, requires school districts and other agencies to develop policies and procedures to ensure that the rights of employees and students are protected and that they are given equal treatment in employment practices, access to programs, or other educational opportunities.

Equalization model. A model for the distribution of financial aid to education in inverse proportion to school district wealth.

Equity. The equal treatment of persons/students in equal circumstances.

Essentialism. An educational theory that focuses on an essential set of learnings that prepare individuals for life by concentration on the culture and traditions of the past.

Ethics. The branch of philosophy concerned with the study of the human conduct and what is right and wrong or good and bad.

Ethnic group. A subgroup of the population distinguished by having a common heritage (language, customs, history, etc.).

ex post facto **law.** A law passed after the fact or after the event.

Existentialism. A philosophical belief that focuses on personal and subjective existence; the world of choice and responsibility is primary.

Expository instruction. A teacher-centered instructional method designed to convey information through formal lecture, informal lecture, and teacher-led discussion.

Expulsion. Exclusion of students from school for periods of time in excess of 10 days.

F

Fair use doctrine. The rules that govern the reproduction and use of copyrighted materials.

Flat grants. A method for allocation of educational funds based on the allocation of a uniform amount per student, per teacher, per classroom, or other unit.

Formative evaluation. Form of evaluation designed to provide feedback while an activity is underway to improve the manner in which the activity is conducted.

Foundation grant. State school finance system that provides a base amount per pupil to local school districts from a combination of state and local tax sources with the amount of state funds per pupil received by a local school district being in inverse relation to the fiscal capacity per pupil of the local school district.

Full state funding. A school finance system whereby all funds for the support of the public schools come from the state and from state-level taxes.

G

Gender bias. The biased behavior that results from believing in gender role stereotypes.

Gender equity. In education, this term refers to the concepts of equal treatment and equal opportunity for all students, regardless of their gender.

Gender role stereotyping. The attribution of specific behaviors, abilities, personality characteristics, and interests to a given gender.

Globalization. The development of multidimensional relationships and interdependent relationships among nations and cultures throughout the world.

Grammar school. A secondary school, originating in ancient Rome and continuing into the nineteenth century, which emphasized a classical education; forerunner of the high school; in current usage, an elementary school.

Great Books. The great works of the past, including literature, philosophy, history, and science, which represent absolute truth according to perennialist theory.

Group instruction. An instructional system in which teachers divide the class into groups of students (often five to eight students) and structure instruction and learning activities for this smaller number of students.

H

Hermeneutics. The art or science of the interpretation of lived experience.

Hidden curriculum. The unexpressed perpetuation of the dominant Western culture through its rules, regulations, and rituals.

High-stakes testing. Testing, the results of which determine such important "stakes" as promotion or high school graduation.

Homeschooling. The education of children in the home; a form of private education.

Hornbook. A wooden board on which a sheet of parchment was placed and covered with a thin sheath of cow's horn; used in colonial New England primary schools.

Hostile environment harassment. Verbal or physical conduct of a sexual nature that interferes with an individual's work performance.

Human immunodeficiency virus (HIV). Any of several retroviruses that cause AIDS.

Humanism. The dominant philosophy of the Renaissance that emphasized the importance of human beings and promoted the literature and art of classical Rome and Greece.

Humanistic education. An educational program reflecting the philosophy of humanism.

I

Idealism. The oldest philosophic belief which views the world of the mind and ideas as fundamental.

Imaginative learner. One of four learning styles related to the perceiving and processing of information. The imaginative learner perceives information concretely and processes it reflectively.

in loco parentis. In the place of a parent.

Incentive pay. Paying teachers more for different kinds or amounts of work (e.g., master teacher plans or career ladder plans).

Inclusion. Serving students with a variety of abilities and disabilities in the regular classroom with appropriate support services.

Incompetence. Lack of legal qualification, inability or capacity to discharge the required duty. In regard to teachers, incompetence falls into four general categories: (1) inadequate teaching, (2) poor discipline, (3) physical or mental incapacity, and (4) counterproductive personality traits.

Indirect compensation. Payments or fringe benefits that employees receive in addition to payments in the form of money; classified as either employee benefits or employee services, such as health and life insurance, long-term disability protection, or leaves with pay.

Individualized education program (IEP). A program designed by a team of educators, parents, and at times the student to meet the unique needs of the child for whom it is developed.

Individualized instruction. Instructional system in which teachers work with students on a one-on-one basis and structure instruction and learning activities for each student.

Inductive logic. Reasoning from a specific fact or facts to a generalization.

Infant school. A type of public elementary school introduced in the United States in the 19th century to prepare children aged 4 to 7 years for elementary school.

Inquiry instruction. A problem-oriented instructional system in which students assume major responsibility for designing and structuring their learning activities and teachers serve as resource persons and facilitators.

Insubordination. The persistent and willful violation of a reasonable rule or direct order from a recognized authority.

Integrated curriculum. A curriculum design that combines separate subjects from within the same discipline, and in some instances content from two or more branches of study.

Integrated studies. A component of the teacher education program that includes on- and off-campus clinical, laboratory, and practicum experiences.

Integration. The coordination of skills and knowledge across disciplines in the curriculum.

Intelligence quotient (IQ). A number intended to indicate an individual's level of mental development or intelligence.

Interstate reciprocity. A mutual agreement between states that allows teachers who are certified in one state to be eligible for certification in another.

Intervention programs. Programs or strategies directed at providing assistance to at-risk children and adolescents.

J

Junior college. An educational institution that offers courses for 2 years beyond high school. These courses may transfer to a 4-year institution or may be complete career or vocational programs.

Junior high school. An intermediate school between elementary and high school that includes grades 7 and 8 or 7, 8, and 9.

L

Language minority. An individual whose native language is not English and who may have limited proficiency in the English language.

Learning disability. A disorder or delayed development in one or more of the processes of thinking, speaking, reading, writing, listening, or doing arithmetic operations.

Least restrictive environment (LRE). The educational setting that enables children with disabilities to have an educational experience most like that of children without disabilities.

Lemon test. A tripartite test used by the courts to evaluate claims under the establishment clause. Asks three questions: Does the action or policy (1) have a primarily secular purpose, (2) have the primary effect of advancing or inhibiting religion, or (3) foster an excessive entanglement between the state and religion?

Liberty interest. The right to a fundamental constitutional liberty (speech, press, etc.).

Life-adjustment education. An educational program, popular in the mid-twentieth century, which focused on youth who did not attend college, rejected traditional academic studies, and stressed functional objectives such as vocation and health.

Lifelong learning. Formal or informal program through which an individual is engaged in planned and sequential activities designed to provide the person with the opportunity to acquire developing knowledge and skills on a continuous basis.

Limited open forum. The condition said to exist when schools provide noncurriculum student groups the opportunity to meet on school premises during noninstructional time.

Local property tax. A tax on real property (land and buildings) levied by a local governmental unit such as a school district.

Logic. A method of knowing that is concerned with making inferences, reasoning, or arguing in a rational manner.

Logical positivism. The view that no proposition can be considered valid unless it can be verified on logical or empirical grounds.

Lyceum. A voluntary organization sponsoring programs, demonstrations, and lectures for the education and information of its members.

M

Magnet school. A school offering specialized and unique programs designed to attract students from throughout the district, thereby promoting racial integration.

Mainstreaming. The placing of children with disabilities, to the maximum extent possible, into the regular classroom where they have contact with children without disabilities.

Major depression. An emotional state with persistent symptoms of sadness and hopelessness warranting referral to a mental health professional.

Mass media. Television, popular music, movie, music video, radio, newspaper, and magazine industries.

Master teacher. A teacher who is given special status, pay, and recognition, but remains in the classroom as a role model for other teachers, or is released from a portion of the regular classroom assignment to work with other teachers in a supportive, nonsupervisory role.

Mastery learning. An instructional system in which the desired learning and performance levels are identified and teachers work with students until they attain the desired level of performance.

Mentoring. Formal and informal relationships between a beginning teacher and an experienced teacher(s) that are sources of information and support for the beginning teacher.

Metaphysics. The branch of philosophy concerned with the nature of reality and existence.

Monitorial school. A school where one teacher taught a lesson to a group of older students, called monitors, who then each taught the lesson to a larger group of younger students.

Multicultural education. An educational strategy that provides for students whose cultural and linguistic backgrounds may prevent them from succeeding in the traditional school setting, which historically reflects the dominant Anglo-Saxon culture.

Multiple intelligences theory. Developed by Howard Gardner at Harvard University, the concept of multiple intelligences assumes that human cognitive competence is pluralistic rather than unitary.

municipal overburden. A burden caused by the need for a greater range of social services in urban areas that must be paid for by the same taxpayers who support the schools.

N

National Assessment of Educational Progress (NAEP). A series of tests mandated by Congress and administered nationally in reading, mathematics, and science.

National Board Certification. National program through which a person is awarded a nationally recognized certificate that signifies successful completion of a series of activities designed to indicate excellence as a teacher. An individualized portfolio is a key component of the process. In some districts or states, these teachers receive a stipend upon successful completion of the program.

Naturalism. A philosophic or educational philosophy that emphasizes the natural world, the freedom of the individual, and the development of that which is natural in humans.

Negligence. A failure to do (or not to do) what a reasonable and prudent person would do under the same or similar circumstances, the result of which is injury to another.

Neo-Thomism. A traditional philosophy that bridges the dualism of idealism and realism and emphasizes the existence of God, which can be known by both faith and reason.

New basics. A curriculum composed of English, mathematics, science, social studies, computer sciences, and foreign languages for those aspiring to college.

Nondirective instruction. Student-dominated mode of instruction that incorporates the concepts of problem-based learning in which students and/or the teacher identify problems related to current experiences or problems experienced by students and proceed to solve the problems. The teacher serves as a resource person for students throughout the process.

Nongraded school. A school in which grade divisions are eliminated for a sequence of 2 or more years.

Normal school. Institutions established in the 1800s for the purpose of training teachers.

Null curriculum. Those things that are not included in the formal curriculum because of their controversial nature, because they represent different values, or because of the lack of resources or information.

O

Object lesson. An instructional activity that centers on concrete materials within the child's experience and involves discussion and oral presentation.

Ontology. The branch of metaphysics that is concerned about the nature of existence and what it means for anything "to be."

Open classroom. An architectural design for elementary schools popular during the 1960s that consisted of large, open instructional spaces not divided into traditional walled classrooms.

Operant conditioning. A type of behaviorism in which any response to any stimulus can be conditioned by immediate reinforcement or reward.

P

Paideia. The general body of knowledge that all educated individuals should possess.

Parochial school. A private elementary or secondary school supported or affiliated with a church or religious organization.

Perennialism. An educational theory that focuses on the past, namely the universal truths and such absolutes as reason and faith. Perennialists believe the purpose of the school is to cultivate the rational intellect and search for the truth.

Performance-based pay. Compensation given to an employee or group of employees based on the attainment of certain prescribed standards or outcomes (e.g., increased student achievement or lower dropout rates).

Phenomenology. The study of the consciousness and experiencing of phenomena in philosophy.

Philosophical analysis. The process of systematic questioning of assumptions, values, theories, procedures, and methods designed to help formulate and clarify beliefs about teaching and learning.

Philosophy of education. The theory of philosophic thought that defines our views about the learner, the teacher, and the school.

Plenary. Absolute, as the power of the state legislature to enact any legislation controlling the schools that is not contrary to the federal Constitution or the state constitution.

Policies. Guidelines or principles for action adopted by a local school board to provide direction for administrative rules and regulations used in administering a local school district.

Postmodern constructivism. A theory of learning which states that learners construct their own knowledge and meaning based on their prior experiences within a social context.

Postmodernism. A philosophy, ideology, movement, and process that incorporates the philosophies of pragmatism, existentialism, social reconstructionism, and critical pedagogy.

Postvention programs. Strategies or programs designed to help the school return to normal in the aftermath of a crisis, which include grief counseling, support groups, interacting with the media, and follow-up care.

Power equalization. A state school finance system in which the governing board of each local school district determines its spending level per pupil. For each unit of local tax rate, the state will provide sufficient funds to ensure a guaranteed amount; state funds will be in inverse relation to the fiscal capacity per pupil of the local school district.

Pragmatism. A philosophy that focuses on the things that work; the world of experience is central.

Praxis™. Series of national content and pedagogical tests used to determine if a prospective or intern teacher demonstrates the level of knowledge expected of new teachers.

Premack principle. States that because organisms freely choose to engage in certain behaviors rather than others, providing access to the preferred activities will serve as a reinforcement for engaging in nonpreferred activities.

Prevention strategies. Strategies including programs, activities, and services designed to reduce the occurrence of at-risk behaviors in children and adolescents.

Procedural due process. The process by which individuals are provided fair and equitable procedures in a matter affecting their welfare (procedural due process) and are protected from unfair deprivation of their property.

Profession. An occupation involving relatively long and specialized preparation on the level of higher education and governed by its own code of ethics.

Professional development. Activities designed to build the personal strengths and creative talents of individuals, and thus create human resources necessary for organizational productivity.

Programmed instruction. A teaching method that enables individual students to answer questions about a unit of study at their own rate, checking their own answers and advancing only after answering correctly.

Progressivism. A theory of education that is concerned with "learning by doing" and purports that children learn best when pursuing their own interests and satisfying their own needs.

Project method. An instructional methodology that attempts to make education as "life-like" as possible through the use of educative activities that are consistent with the child's own goals.

Property right. The right to specific real or personal property, tangible and intangible, e.g., the right to continued employment or the use of one's name.

Proprietary school. A school operated by an individual, group, or corporation for profit to serve the educational needs of a particular clientele.

Protective factors. Personal attributes, family factors, and community factors that guard against maladaptive behavior.

Proximate cause. The primary act or mission that produces an injury and without which the injury would not have occurred. A standard used to determine a teacher's liability in the cause of an injury.

Q

Quid pro quo harassment. Making a benefit of employment conditional upon the receipt of sexual favors.

R

Rate bill. A tuition fee based on the number of children paid by the parents during the mid-1800s.

Real reality. A form of reality that includes the realm of ideas, eternal truths, and perfect order in the philosophy of idealism.

Realism. A philosophy in which the world of nature and physical matter is superior to the world of ideas. Matter exists whether the mind perceives it or not.

Religious realism. The interface of the secular ideas of Aristotle and Christian teachings of St. Augustine. Neo-Thomism is also called religious realism.

Resegregation. A return to a segregate status following a period of integration.

Resiliency. Having developed the necessary coping mechanisms despite overwhelming hardships and obstacles.

Restructuring. A buzzword of the 1990s, connoting a number of prescriptions for education: parental choice, year-round schools, longer school days and years, recast modes of governance, alternative funding patterns, and all-out commitments to technology.

Reverse discrimination. Discrimination or bias against members of one class in an attempt to correct past discrimination against members of another class.

S

Scholasticism. The philosophy of Thomas Aquinas that serves as the foundation for Catholic education and holds that man is a rational being who possesses both a spiritual nature and a physical nature, that truth can be arrived at through the deductive process, and that when reason fails, man must rely on faith.

School board. As created by the state, the governing body for a local school district, with members generally selected by popular vote.

School culture. Social interactions of the students and adults in the school environment and the ways in which their behavior is influenced by the official rules and established mores of the school.

School Development Program. Developed by James Comer and his colleagues at the Yale Child Study Center, the School Development Program is a schoolwide restructuring project to address the needs of the whole child, including school-based health services, parent involvement, and teacher participation in restructuring the school's programs. A central component of the model is a school management and governance team composed of the principal, teachers, parents, a mental health specialist, and support personnel who are responsible for development of the school's master plan.

School effectiveness. The level at which students are performing in the basic skills.

Scientific method. The systematic reporting and analysis of what is observed and retesting of hypotheses formulated from the observations.

Secondary school. A program of study that follows elementary school, such as junior high school, middle school, or high school.

Secretary of education. The executive officer of the U.S. Department of Education; a member of the president's cabinet.

Secular humanism. Allegedly a faith that denies God, deifies man, and glorifies reason.

Self-renewal. Personal program of professional development designed to help a person improve teaching competencies by updating specified skill and their knowledge base.

Sense realism. The belief that learning must come through the senses.

Separatism. A form of diversity that suggests that by maintaining a separatist position, minority groups can build strength, maintain their identity, and gain power.

Sequence. The arrangement of learning experiences in a curriculum to ensure that successive experiences build upon preceding ones.

Seven liberal arts. The curriculum that includes the trivium (grammar, rhetoric, and logic) and the quadrivium (arithmetic, geometry, music, and astronomy).

Sex discrimination. Any action that denies opportunities, privileges, or rewards to a person or persons because of their gender, in violation of the law.

Sexism. Discrimination against an individual on the basis of gender, in particular, discrimination and prejudicial stereotyping of females.

Sexual abuse. Contact or interaction between a child and an adult when the child is being used for the sexual stimulation of the perpetrator or another person.

Sexually transmitted infections (STIs). Infections such as gonorrhea or *Chlamydia* that are transmitted through sexual activity.

Single salary schedule. A salary schedule for teachers that provides equivalent salaries for equivalent preparation and experience.

Site-based management (SBM). Delegation by a school board of certain decision-making responsibilities about educational programs and school operations to individual schools. Usually provides that teachers, parents, and the principal serve as the decision-making group.

Social class. A social stratum in which the members share similar characteristics, such as income, occupation, status, education, etc.

Socialization. The process by which persons are conditioned to the customs or patterns of a particular culture.

Social justice curriculum. A curriculum design that aims to engage students in a critical analysis of society and prepare them to effect change and create a more equitable society.

Social mobility. The movement upward or downward among social classes.

Social reconstructionism. An educational theory that advocates change, improvement, and the reforming of the school and society.

Social selection. A position that suggests that schools serve the wealthy and powerful at the expense of the poor.

Society. A group of persons who share a common culture, government, institutions, land, or set of social relationships.

Socioeconomic status. The social and economic standing of an individual or group.

Socratic method. A dialectical teaching method employed by Socrates using a questioning process based on the student's experiences and analyzing the consequences of responses, leading the student to a better understanding of the problem.

Spiral curriculum. Curriculum in which a subject matter is presented over a number of grades with increasing complexity and abstraction.

Stare decisis. Let the decision stand; a legal rule that states that once a court has laid down a principle of law as applicable to a certain set of facts, it will apply it to all future cases in which the facts are substantially the same and that other courts of equal or lesser rank will similarly apply the principle.

State board of education. A state agency charged with adopting regulations and monitoring local school districts to ensure implementation of the constitutional and statutory mandates related to the operation of the state system of schools.

State department of education. The operating arm for the administration of state education activities and functions.

Statutory law. The body of law consisting of the written enactments of a legislative body.

Strategic planning. A planning process that involves the establishment of a mission statement, the specification of goals and objectives, and the linking of funding priorities to the accomplishment of program priorities.

Student-centered curriculum. Learning activities centered around the interests and needs of the students that are designed to motivate and interest the student in the learning processes.

Student-to-student sexual harassment. A form of sexual abuse that includes being verbally harassed or touched, pinched, or grabbed in a sexual gesture by a classmate or peer.

Subject-area curriculum. A curriculum design that views the curriculum as a group of subjects or a body of that subject matter which has survived the test of time.

Subject-centered curriculum. Curriculum designed with the acquisition of certain knowledge as the primary goal. The learning process usually involves rote memorization, and learning is measured using objective test scores.

Success for All. Developed by Professor Robert Slavin at Johns Hopkins University, this program assumes a research-based preschool program; full-day kindergarten; beginning reading programs with the integration of phonics and whole language; homogenous reading groups; one-on-one tutoring with an integration of the regular curriculum in grades 1–3; cooperative learning in intermediate reading, writing/language arts, and mathematics; family support services; and a facilitator to coordinate the program and provide training and technical assistance.

Suicide gesture. A behavior that suggests a willingness to commit suicide.

Sunday schools. Educational programs of the later 1700s and early 1800s offering the rudiments of reading and writing on Sunday to children who worked during the week.

Superintendent of schools. The chief executive officer of the local school district whose educational program and related responsibilities include planning, staffing, coordinating, budgeting, administering, evaluating, and reporting. This person informs and works with the local school board.

Suspension. Exclusion of students from school for a period of time of 10 days or less.

Synectics. An approach to creative thinking that depends on looking at what initially appears on the surface to be unrelated phenomena and drawing relevant connections. With its main tools, analogies or metaphors, the approach, often used in groupwork, can help students develop creative responses to problem solving, retain new information, assist in generating writing, and explore social and disciplinary problems. Synectics works well with all ages, as well as those who withdraw from traditional methods.

T

Tabula rasa. Literally, blank slate; applied to the concept of the human mind which says that children come into the world with their minds a blank slate.

Tax benefits. Tax deductions and tax credits designed to benefit patrons and nonpublic schools.

Teacher institute. A teacher training activity begun in the nineteenth century, lasting from a few days to several weeks, where teachers met to be instructed in new techniques, informed of modern materials, and inspired by noted educators.

Teacher-leader. Teacher who assumes a leadership role in the school on specific activities or on a continuing basis but does not serve in a formal capacity.

Tenure. The status conferred on teachers who have served a specific period that guarantees them continuation of employment, subject to the requirements of good behavior and financial necessity.

Theory. A hypothesis or set of hypotheses that have been verified by observation or experiment, or a general synonym for systematic thinking or a set of coherent thoughts.

Theory of education. Systematic thinking or generalization about schooling.

Tort. A civil wrong that leads to injury to another and for which a court will provide a remedy in the form of an action for damages.

Transgender. An individual who appears as, desires to be considered as, or has undergone surgery to become a member of the opposite sex.

V

Vernacular schools. Elementary schools originating in Germany in the 16th century that offered instruction in the mother tongue or vernacular, and a basic curriculum of reading, writing, mathematics, and religion.

Voucher. A grant or payment made to a parent or child to be used to pay the cost of the child's education in a private or public school.

W

White flight. The exodus of middle and upper class White families from urban school districts to avoid desegregation.

Whole-child movement. An educational movement emphasizing totality of the child as the composite of the social, emotional, physical, and mental dimensions.

Adler, M. (1982). *The Paideia proposal: An educational manifesto*. New York: Macmillan.

Adler, M. J. (1984). *The Paideia program: An educational syllabus*. New York: Macmillan.

Adler v. Duval County School Board, 206 F.3d 1070 (11th Cir. 2000), *cert. denied*, 122 S. Ct. 664 (2001).

Agostini v. Felton, 521 U.S. 203 (1997).

Alexander, K., & Alexander M. D. (2001). *American public school law* (5th ed.). Belmont, CA: West/Thomson Learning

Ambach v. Norwick, 441 U.S. 68 (1979).

American Association for Employment in Education. (2005). *2005 Education supply and demand*. Columbus, OH: Author.

American Association of University Women. (1998). *Gender gaps: Where schools still fail our children*. Washington, DC: AAUW Educational Foundation.

American Association of University Women. (2001). *Beyond the gender wars: A conversation about girls, boys, and education*. Washington, DC: AAUW Educational Foundation.

American FactFinder. (2005). *Profile of demographic characteristics*. Washington, DC: U.S. Census Bureau.

American Federation of Teachers. (2000). *Building a profession: Strengthening teacher preparation and induction*. Washington, DC: Author.

American Federation of Teachers. (2005). *Who we are*. Washington, DC: Author.

American Psychiatric Association. (2000). *Diagnostic and statistical manual of mental disorders* (4th ed.). Washington, DC: Author.

American Psychological Association. (2005). Warning signs of youth violence. Retrieved April 28, 2005, from http://helping.apa.org/featurededtopics/feature.php.id=38

Anderson, C. A. (2004). An update on the effects of violent video games. *Journal of Adolescence, 27,* 113-120.

Anderson, J. D. (1978). The Hampton model of normal school industrial education, 1868-1900. In V. P. Franklin & J. D. Anderson (Eds.), *New perspectives on black educational history*. Boston: Hall.

Anderson, J. D. (1997). Supporting the invisible minority. *Educational Leadership, 54*(7), 65-68.

Anderson, L. W., & Krathwohl, D. R. (Eds.). (2001). *A taxonomy for learning, teaching, and assessing: A revision of Bloom's Taxonomy of Educational Objectives* (p. 28). New York: Longman.

Anderson, R. N., & Smith, B. L. (2003). *Deaths: Leading causes for 2001. National vital statistics report, 52*(9), 1-86.

Annie E. Casey Foundation. (2001). *Kids count 2001*. Retrieved January 31, 2001, from http://www.kidscount.org

Annie E. Casey Foundation. (2005). *Kids count 2005*. Retrieved July 31, 2005, from http://www.kidscount.org

Appalachian Rural School Initiative. (1998). *Constructivism key points*. McConnelsville, OH: Todd Spence.

Arends, R. I. (2004). *Learning to teach* (6th ed.) Boston: McGraw-Hill.

Armstrong, D., Henson, K., & Savage, T. (2005). *Teaching today: An introduction to education* (7th ed.) Upper Saddle River, NJ: Merrill/Prentice Hall.

Aronowitz, S. A., & Giroux, H. A. (1991). *Postmodern education: Politics, culture, and social criticism*. Minneapolis, MN: University of Minnesota Press.

Arsen, D., Plank, D., & Sykes, D. (2001). *A work in progress*. Stanford, CA: Hoover Institution.

Augus, D. L., & Mirel, J. (2000). *Professionalism and the public good: A brief history of teacher certification*. Washington, DC: Thomas B. Fordham Foundation.

Avicenna. (1997). In *The new encyclopedia Britannica* (Vol. 1, pp. 739-740). Chicago: Encyclopedia Britannica.

Bae, S., Choy, C., Geddes, J., Sable, J., & Snyder, T. (2000, Summer). *Educational Statistics Quarterly*, pp. 1-9.

Bagley, W. C. (1938). An essentialist platform for the advancement of American education. *Educational Administration and Supervision, 24*, 241-256.

Ballentine, J. H., & Spade, J. Z. (Eds.). (2004). *Schools and society: A sociological approach* (2nd ed.). Belmont, CA: Thomson Learning.

Banks, J. A. (2002). *An introduction to multicultural education* (3rd ed.). Boston: Allyn & Bacon.

Barton, P. E. (2004). Why does the gap persist? *Educational Leadership, 62*(3), 8-13.

Bates, J. A. (1987). Reinforcement. In M. J. Dunkin (Ed.), *The international encyclopedia of teaching and teacher education* (pp. 349-358). New York: Pergamon.

Bayles, E. E. (1966). *Pragmatism in education*. New York: Harper & Row.

Beaulieu, D. L. (2000). Comprehensive reform and American Indian education. *Journal of American Indian Education, 39*(2), 29-58.

Beck, A. G. (1964). *Greek education 450-350 B.C.* London: Methuen.

Beilan v. Board of Public Education of Philadelphia, 357 U.S. 399 (1958).

Bell, T. H. (1993). Reflections one decade after *A Nation at Risk*. *Phi Delta Kappan, 74*, 592-597.

Benard, B. (1997). Drawing forth resilience in all our youth. *Reclaiming Children and Youth, 6*(1), 29-32.

Bennett, C. I. (2002). *Comprehensive multicultural education: Theory and practice* (5th ed.). Boston: Allyn & Bacon.

Bennett, W. J. (1987). *James Madison High School: A curriculum for American students.* Washington, DC: U.S. Department of Education.

Bennett, W. J. (1988). *James Madison Elementary School: A curriculum for American students.* Washington, DC: U.S. Department of Education.

Bennett, W. J. (1993). *The book of virtues: A treasury of great moral stories*. New York: Simon & Schuster.

Bethel School District No. 403 v. Fraser, 106 S. Ct. 3159 (1986).

Biesta, G. J. (2001). Preparing for the incalculable: Deconstruction, justice, and the question of education. In G. J. Biesta & D. Egea-Kuehne (Eds.). *Derrida & education* (pp. 32-54). London: Routledge.

Biglan, A., Brennan, P., Foster, S., & Holder, H. (2004). *Helping adolescents at risk: Prevention of multiple problem behaviors.* New York: Guilford Press.

Binder, F. M. (1974). *The age of the common school, 1830-1865*. New York: Wiley & Sons.

Binderman, A. (1976). *Three early champions of education: Benjamin Franklin, Benjamin Rush, and Noah Webster.* Bloomington, IN: The Phi Delta Kappa Foundation.

Black, H. C. (1990). *Black's law dictionary*. St. Paul, MN: West.

Blair, J. (2004, February 25). State of the Union. *Education Week*, p. 1.

Blake, N., & Masschalein, J. (2003) Critical theory and critical pedagogy. In N. Blake, P. Smeyers, R. Smith, & P. Standish (Eds.). *The Blackwell guide to the philosophy of education* (pp. 38-56). Malden, MA: Blackwell Publishing.

Bloom, A. (1987). *The closing of the American mind*. New York: Simon and Schuster.

Bloom, B. (1956). *Taxonomy of educational objectives 1: Cognitive domain.* New York: McKay.

Board of Education of Independent School District No. 92 of Pottowatomie County v. Earls, 122 S. Ct. 2559 (2002).

Board of Education of Westside Community Schools v. Mergens, 496 U.S. 226 (1990).

Board of Education v. Rowley, 458 U.S. 175 (1982).

Bohen, D. (2001). Strengthening teaching through national certification. *Educational Leadership, 58*(8), 50-54.

Bonjean, L. M., & Rittenmeyer, D. C. (1987). *Teenage parenthood: The school's response.* Bloomington, IN: Phi Delta Kappa Foundation.

Bonner, T. N. (1963). *Our recent past: American civilization in the twentieth century*. Englewood Cliffs, NJ: Prentice Hall.

Borja, R. (2001, December 5). Black state lawmakers target "Gap." *Education Week*, pp. 1, 27.

Botoff v. Van Wert City Board of Education, 220 F.3d 465 (6th Cir. 2000).

Bowen, J. (1972). *A history of Western education* (Vol. 1). London: Methuen.

Boyer, E. (1983). *High school: Report on secondary education in America.* New York: Harper & Row.

Bradley v. Pittsburgh Board of Education, 913 F.2d 1064 (3d Cir. 1990).

Branch, A. J. (2001). Increasing the number of teachers of color in K-12 public schools. *The Educational Forum, 65*, 254-261.

Bridgman v. New Trier High School District, 128 F.3d 1146 (7th Cir. 1997).

Broberg, S. (1999, Summer). Gay/straight alliance and other controversial student groups: A test for the Equal Access Act. *Brigham Young University Education and Law Journal*, 87-116.

Brosio, R. S. (2000). *Philosophical scaffolding for the construction of critical democratic education*. New York: Peter Lang.

Brown, F. (2001). Site-based management: Is it still central to the school reform movement? *School Business Affairs, 67*(4), 5-10.

Brown v. Board of Education of Topeka, 347 U.S. 483 (1954).

Brown v. Gilmore, 258 F.3d 265 (4th Cir. 2001), *cert. denied*, 122 S. Ct. 465 (2001).

Brown v. Woodland Joint Unified School District, 27 F.3d 1373 (9th Cir. 1994).

Bruner, J. (1960). *The process of education*. Cambridge, MA: Harvard University Press.

Bruner, J. (1966). *Toward a theory of instruction*. Cambridge, MA: Harvard University Press.

Brunetti, G. J. (2001). Why do they teach? A study of job satisfaction among long-term high school teachers. *Teacher Education Quarterly, 28*, 49-74.

Burlington Industries v. Ellerth, No. 97-569 S. Ct. (1998).

Burns, R. (1999). Curriculum mapping and interdisciplinary teaching. *ITI Review, 1*(2), 33-48.

Butler, J. D. (1966). *Idealism in education*. New York: Harper & Row.

Butts, R. F. (1978). *Public education in the United States*. New York: Holt, Rinehart and Winston.

C. F. S. v. Mahan, 934 S. W. 2d 615 (Mo. Ct. App. 1996).

Cain, M. (2001). Ten qualities of the renewed teacher. *Phi Delta Kappan, 82*(9), 702-705.

California Safe Schools Coalition and the 4-H Center for Youth Development, University of California Davis. (2004). *Safe place to learn*. Sacramento, CA: Author.

Callahan, C. M., & McIntire, J. A. (1994). *Identifying outstanding talent in American Indian and Alaska Native students*. Washington, DC: U.S. Department of Education, Office of Educational Research and Improvement.

Cambron-McCabe, N. B., McCarthy, M. M., & Thomas, S. B. (2004). *Public school law: Teacher's and student's rights* (5th ed.). Boston: Allyn & Bacon.

Campbell, D. E. (2000). *Choosing democracy: A practical guide to multicultural education*. Upper Saddle River, NJ: Merrill/Prentice Hall.

Carnoy, M., Jacobsen, R., Mishel, L., & Rothstein, R. (2005). *The charter school dust-up: Examining the evidence on enrollment and achievement*. Washington, DC: Economic Policy Institute.

Carpio v. Tucson High School District No. 1 of Pima County, 517 P.2d 1288 (1974).

Carroll, J. (2004, March 2). *American public opinion about religion*. Gallup Tuesday Morning Briefing, retrieved October 13, 2005, from http://www.gallup.com

Castle, E. B. (1967). *Ancient education and today*. Baltimore, MD: Penguin.

Caudillo v. Lubbock Independent School District, 311 F. Supp. 2d 550 (N.D. Tex. 2004).

Cawelti, G. (1989). Designing high schools for the future. *Educational Leadership, 47*(1), 30-35.

CDW-Government (2005). *Teachers talk tech 2005*. Retrieved October 25, 2005, from http://www.cdwg.com

Center for Education Reform. (2005*). About charter schools*. Washington, DC: Author.

Center on Education Policy. (2005). *Charter Schools*. Washington, DC: Author.

Chalifoux v. New Caney Independent School District, 976 F. Supp. 659 (S.D. Tex. 1999).

Chalk v. U.S. District Court Central District of California, 840 F.2d 701 (9th Cir. 1988).

Chavers, D. (2000, April). *Deconstructing the myths: A research agenda for American Indian education*. Paper presented at the Summit Meeting on Indian Education Research, Albuquerque, NM.

Chavkin, N., & Gonzalez, J. (2000). *Mexican immigrant youth and resiliency: Research and promising programs*. Charleston, WV: Clearinghouse on Rural Education and Small Schools.

Cheema v. Thompson, 67 F.3d 883 (9th Cir. 1995).

Chiang, L. (2000, October). *Teaching Asian American students: Classroom implications*. Paper presented at the annual meeting of the Midwestern Educational Research Association, Chicago, IL.

Child Evangelism Fellowship of Maryland v. Montgomery County Public Schools, 370 F.3d 589 (4th Cir. 2004).

Children's Safety Network. (2000). Fact sheets: Youth suicide prevention plans. Newton, MA: Education Development Center.

Christle, C., Jolivette, K., & Nelson, M. (2000). *Youth aggression and violence risk, resilience, and prevention* (pp. 1-4). Arlington, VA: ERIC Clearinghouse on Disabilities and Gifted Education.

Church, R. L., & Sedlak, M. W. (1976). *Education in the United States*. New York: The Free Press.

Civil Rights Division of the Arizona Department of Law v. Amphitheater Unified School District No. 10, 680 P. 2d 517 (Ariz. 1983).

Clark, D., Lotto, L., & Astuto, T. (1984). Effective schools and school improvement. *Educational Administration Quarterly, 20*(3), 41-86.

Clonlara, Inc. v. State Board of Education, 501 NW.2d 88 (Mich. 1993).

Cloud, J. (2001, March 19). The legacy of Columbine. *Time, 157*(11), 32-35.

Coalition of Essential Schools. (2005). About CES. Retrieved August 19, 2005, from http://www.essential schools.org/1pt/ces_docs/22

Cochran v. Louisiana State Board of Education, 281 U.S. 370 (1930).

Cogburn, D. L. (2005). *Globalization, knowledge, education and training in the information age*. Retrieved December 20, 2005, from http://www.unesco.org/webworld/infoethics_2/eng/papers/paper_23.htm

Cohen, S. S. (1974). *A history of colonial education, 1607-1776*. New York: Wiley & Sons.

Collins, G. J. (1969). Constitutional and legal basis for state action. In L. S. Fuller & J. B. Pearson (Eds.), *Education in the states: Nationwide development since 1900*. Washington, DC: National Education Association.

Comfort v. Lynn School Committee, No. 03-24 (October 20, 2004).

Committee for Public Education and Religious Liberty v. Nyquist, 413 U.S. 756 (1973).

Conant, J.B. (1959). *The American high school today.* New York: McGraw-Hill.

Connell, W. F. (1980). *A history of education in the twentieth century.* New York: Teachers College Press, Columbia University.

Connick v. Myers, 461 U.S. 138 (1983).

Consumers Union. (2005). *Captive kids: A report on commercial pressures on kids at school.* Retrieved October 4, 2005, from http//www.consumersunion.org/other/captivekids/pressures. htm

Couch, Richard (1993). Synectics and imagery: Developing creative thinking through images. In *Art, science & visual literacy: Selected readings from the 24th annual conference of the International Visual Literacy Association,* Pittsburgh, PA, September 30–October 4, 1992. (ERIC Document Reproduction Service No. ED363330)

Council for American Private Education. (2004). *Facts and studies.* Germantown, PA: Author.

Council of Chief State School Officers. (2002). *Handbook.* Washington, DC: Author.

Council of Chief State School Officers. (2005). *ECS governance notes.* Denver, CO: Education Commission of the States.

Council of State Directors of Programs for the Gifted. (2000). *The 1999-2000 state of the states gifted and talented education report.* Longmont, CO: Author.

Counts, G. S. (1932). *Dare the schools build a new social order?* Carbondale, IL: Southern Illinois Press.

Counts, G. S. (1933). *A call to the teachers of America.* New York: John Day.

Court won't stop graduation prayers. (2001, December 11). *Arizona Republic,* p. A4.

Cremin, L. A. (1962). *The transformation of the school.* New York: Knopf.

Cremin, L. A. (1970). *American education: The colonial experience, 1607-1783.* New York: Harper & Row.

Cremin, L. A. (1982). *American education: The national experience, 1783-1876.* New York: Harper & Row.

Cremin, L. A. (1988). *American education: The metropolitan experience, 1876-1980.* New York: Harper & Row.

Cubberley, E. P. (1905). *School funds and their apportionment.* New York: Teachers College Press, Columbia University.

Cubberley, E. P. (1934). *Readings in public education.* Cambridge, MA: Riverside.

Curry, T., Jiobu, R., & Schwirian, K. (2005). *Sociology for the twenty-first century.* Upper Saddle River, NJ: Pearson/Prentice Hall.

Cushner, K., McClelland, A., & Safford, P. (2000). *Human diversity in education—An integrative approach.* Boston: McGraw-Hill.

Danaher, K. (2005). *Globalization and the downsizing of the American dream.* San Francisco: Global Exchange.

Danielson, C. (2001). New trends in teacher evaluation. *Educational Leadership, 58*(5), 12-15.

Darling-Hammond, L. (2000). *Solving the dilemma of teacher supply, demand, and quality.* New York: Columbia University, National Commission of Teaching and America's Future.

Darling-Hammond, L. (2001). Teacher testing and the improvement of practice. *Teaching Education, 12*(1), 11-40.

Darling-Hammond, L., Chung, R., & Frelow, F. (2002). Variations in teacher preparation: How well do different pathways prepare teachers to teach? *Journal of Teacher Education, 53,* 286-302.

Darroch, J. E., Frost, J., & Singh, S. (2001). *Teenage sexual and reproductive behavior in developed countries: Can more progress be made?* New York: The Alan Guttmacher Institute.

Davis, M. (2005, May 4). Tensions ease at Head Start reauthorization. *Education Week,* p. 33.

Davis v. Monroe, 119 S. Ct. 1661 (1999).

DeAngelis, T. (2000). Punishment of innocents: Children of parents behind bars. *Monitor on Psychology, 32*(5), 56-59.

DeJong, D. H. (1993). *Promises of the past: A history of Indian education in the United States.* Golden, CO: North American Press.

Derrida, J. (1976). *Of grammatology* (G. C. Spivak, Trans.). Baltimore, MD: The Johns Hopkins University Press.

DeNoyer v. Livonia Public Schools, 799 F. Supp. 744 (E.D. Mich. 1992).

DesRoches ex rel. DesRoches v. Caprio, 974 F. Supp. 542 (E.D. Va. 1997).

Devoe, J. F., Peter, K., Kaufman, P., Miller, A., Noonan, M., Snyder, T. D., & Baum, K. (2004). *Indicators of school crime and safety: 2004.* Washington, DC: U.S. Departments of Education and Justice.

Dewey, J. (1916). *Democracy and education: An introduction to the philosophy of education.* New York: Macmillan.

Dewey, J. (1938). *Experience and education.* New York: Macmillan.

Dewey, J. (1956). *The child and the curriculum and the school and society.* Chicago: University of Chicago Press.

Dewey, J. (1963). *Experience and education.* New York: Collier.

Doe v. Brockton School Committee, 2000 WL 33342399 (Mass. App. 2000).

Doe v. Duncanville Independent School District, 70 F.3d 402 (5th Cir. 1995).

Doll, B., Song, S., & Siemers, E. (2004). Classroom ecologies that support or discourage bullying. In D. L. Espelage & S. M. Swearer (Eds.), *Bullying in American schools: A socio-ecological perspective on prevention and intervention* (pp. 161-183). Mahwah, NJ: Lawrence Erlbaum.

Downing v. West Haven Board of Education, 161 F. Supp. 2d 19 (D. Conn. 2001).

Draper, J. W. (1970). Cultural developments in Spain. In H. J. Siceluff (Ed.), *Readings in the history of education* (pp. 47–51). Berkeley, CA: McCutchan.

Duhon-Hayes, G., Augustus, M., Duhon-Sells, R., & Duhon-Ross, A. (1996). Post-baccalaureate teacher certification programs: Strategies for enhancement, improvement, and peaceful co-existence with traditional teacher certification programs. (ERIC Document Reproduction Service No. ED404334).

Duncan, G. J., & Brooks-Gunn, J. (2001). Poverty, welfare reform, and children's achievement. In B. J. Biddle (Ed.), *Social class, poverty, and education* (pp. 49–65). New York: Routledge Falmer.

Dunn, S. G. (2005). *Philosophical foundations of education: Connecting philosophy to theory and practice.* Upper Saddle River, NJ: Merrill/Prentice Hall.

Dwyer, K., Osher, D., & Warger, C. (1998). *Early warning, timely response: A guide to safe schools.* Bethesda, MD: National Association of School Psychologists. (ERIC Document Reproduction Service No. ED418372).

Edmonds, R. (1979). Some schools work and more can. *Social Policy, 9*(5), 28–32.

Edmonds, R. (1989). The "at-risk" label and the problem of school reform. *Educational Leadership, 40*(3), 5–11.

Education Commission of the States. (2005). *Alternative certification.* Denver, CO: Author.

Education Policies Commission. (1942). *A war policy for American schools.* Washington, DC: National Education Association.

Edwards v. Aguillard, 107 S. Ct. 2573 (1987).

Eisel v. Board of Education of Montgomery County, 597 A.2d 447 (Md. 1991).

Eisner, E. (Ed.). (1985). *Learning and teaching the ways of knowing: The eighty-fourth yearbook of the National Society for the Study of Education.* Chicago: University of Chicago Press.

Eisner, E. W. (2002). *The educational imagination* (4th ed.). Upper Saddle River, NJ: Merrill/Prentice Hall.

Electronic transfer. (2005, May 5). *Education Week,* pp. 8–9.

Elliott, S., & Umberson, D. (2004). Recent demographic trends in the U.S. and implications for well being. In J. Scott, J. Treas, and M. Richards (Eds.), *The Blackwell companion to the sociology of families* (pp. 34–41). Maldon, MA: Blackwell Publishing.

Ellis, A. K., Mackey, J. A., & Glenn, A. D. (1988). *The school curriculum.* Boston: Allyn & Bacon.

Emmer, E. T. (1987). Classroom management. In M. J. Dunkin (Ed.), *The international encyclopedia of teaching and teacher education* (pp. 437–446). New York: Pergamon.

Engel v. Vitale, 370 U.S. 421 (1962).

Epperson v. Arkansas, 393 U.S. 97 (1968).

Evans, R. (2005). Reframing the achievement gap. *Phi Delta Kappan, 86*(8), 582–590.

Everson v. Board of Education, 330 U.S. 1 (1947).

Ezell, J. S. (1960). *Fortune's merry wheel: The lottery in America.* Cambridge, MA: Harvard University Press.

Faragher v. Boca Raton, No. 97-282 S. Ct. (1998).

Feinberg, W., & Soltis, J. F. (2004). *School and society.* New York: Teachers College Press, Columbia University.

Feistritzer, E., & Chester, D. (2001). *Alternative teacher certification: An overview 2001.* Retrieved January 1, 2002, from http://www.ncei.com/2001_Alt_Teacher_Cert.htm

Feistritzer, E. (2005). *Alternative teacher certification: An overview 2005.* Retrieved May 24, 2005, from http://www.ncei.com/2001_Alt_Teacher_Cert.htm

Feller, B. (August 22, 2005). States' measures of qualified teachers vary widely. *San Luis Obispo Tribune,* p. A10.

Ficus v. Board of School Trustees of Central School District of Green County, 509 N.E. 2d 1137 (Ind. App. 1 Dist. 1987).

Finn, C. E., Jr. (2005, March 30). Judging charter schools. *Hoover Institution Essays.* Retrieved June 13, 2005, from http://www.hoover.stanford.edu/publicaffairs/we/2005/finn03.html

Fischer, L., Schimmel, D., & Kelly, C. (2003). *Teachers and the law* (6th ed.). New York: Longman.

Fleischfresser v. Directors of School District 200, 15 F.3d 680 (7th Cir. 1994).

Florey v. Sioux Falls School District 49-5, 619 F.2d 1311 (8th Cir. 1980), cert. denied, 449 U.S. 987 (1980).

Ford, P. L. (Ed.). (1962). *The New England primer.* New York: Columbia University Teachers College.

Frankfurt, K. (1999, May/June). Countering a climate hostile to gay students. *High School Magazine,* pp. 25–29.

Franklin v. Gwinnett, 503 U.S. 60 (1992).

Freiler v. Tangipahoa Parish Board of Education, 185 F.3d 337 (5th Cir. 1999).

Freier, P. (1973). *Pedagogy of the oppressed.* New York: Seabury.

Friedman, T. L. (2005). *The world is flat: A brief history of the twenty-first century.* New York: Farrar, Straus and Giroux.

Frieman, B. (2001). *What teachers need to know about children at risk.* Boston: McGraw-Hill.

Friend, M. (2005). *Special education: Contemporary perspectives for school professionals.* Boston: Allyn & Bacon.

Gabriel, J. (2005). *How to thrive as a teacher leader.* Alexandria, VA: Association for Supervision and Curriculum Development.

Galezewski, J. (2005). Bullying and aggression among youth. In K. Sexton-Radek (Ed.). *Violence in schools: Issues, consequences, and expressions.* Westport, CT: Prager.

Gardner, H. (1999). *Intelligence reframed: Multiple intelligences for the 21st century.* New York: Basic Books.

Garrison, J. (1994). Realism, Pragmatism, and educational research. *Educational Researcher, 23*(1), 5–14.

Garrison, J., & Neiman, A. (2003). Pragmatism and education. In N. Blake, P. Smeyers, R. Smith, & P. Standish (Eds.), *The Blackwell guide to the philosophy of education* (pp. 21–37). Malden, MA: Blackwell.

Gebster v. Lago Vista Independent School District, 118 S. Ct. 1989 (1998).

Gentile, D. A., & Gentile, J. R. (2005). *Violent video games as exemplary teachers.* Paper presented at the Biennial Meeting of the Society for Research on Child Development. April 9, 2005, Atlanta, GA.

Gentile, D. A., & Walsh, D. A. (2002). A normative study of family media habits. *Journal of Applied Developmental Psychology, 23,* 157–178.

Gilbert, W. S. (2000). Bridging the gap between high school and college. *Journal of American Indian Education, 39,* 36–58.

Gillett, M. (1966). *A history of education: Thought and practice.* Toronto: McGraw-Hill.

Gillett, M. (Ed.). (1969). *Readings in the history of education.* Toronto: McGraw-Hill.

Glazer, N. (1997). *We are all multiculturalists now.* Cambridge, MA: Harvard University Press.

Glover, S. (2004, Summer). Steering a true course. In *Education Next.* Palto Alto, CA: Hoover Institute, Stanford University.

Glover v. Williamsburg Local School District Board of Education, 20 F. Supp. 1160 (S.D. Ohio 1998).

Goertz, M. E. (2001). Redefining government roles in an era of standards-based reform. *Phi Delta Kappan, 83,* 62–66.

Goldhaber, D., Perry, D., & Anthony, A. (2004). National Board for Professional Teaching Standards (NBPTS) process: Who applies and what factors are associated with NBPTS certification? *Educational Evaluation and Policy Analysis, 26*(4), 259–280.

Gollnick, D. M., & Chinn, P. C. (2006). *Multicultural education in a pluralistic society* (7th ed.). Upper Saddle River, NJ: Merrill/Prentice Hall.

Good, C. V. (Ed.). (1973). *The dictionary of education.* New York: McGraw-Hill.

Good, H. G., & Teller, J. D. (1969). *A history of Western education.* Toronto: Collier-Macmillan.

Good News Club v. Milford Central School, 121 S. Ct. 2093 (2001).

Goodlad, J. (1983). *A place called school.* New York: McGraw-Hill.

Goodlad, J. (1987). A new look at an old idea: Core curriculum. *Educational Leadership, 44*(4), 8–16.

Goodlad, J. (2004). Fulfilling the public purpose of schooling. *School Administrator, 61*(5), 14–18.

Gordon, W. (1961). *Synectics.* New York: Harper & Row.

Goss v. Lopez, 419 U.S. 565 (1975).

Graham, P. A. (1974). *Community & class in American education.* New York: Wiley & Sons.

Gray, R., & Peterson, J. M. (1974). *Economic development of the United States.* Homewood, IL: Irwin.

Grier, T. B. (2000). Staying in school. *American School Board Journal, 187*(5), 55–57.

Gullatt, D. E., & Stockton, C. E. (2000). Recognizing and reporting suspected child abuse. *American Secondary Education, 29*(1), 19–26.

Gurian, M., & Henley, P. (2001). *Boys and girls learn differently: A guide for teachers and parents.* San Francisco: Jossey-Bass.

Gurian, M., & Stevens, K. (2004). With boys and girls in mind. *Educational Leadership, 62*(3), 21–26.

Gutek, G. L. (1988). *Education and schooling in America.* Upper Saddle River, NJ: Prentice Hall.

Gutek, G. L. (1991). *Education in the United States: An historical perspective.* Upper Saddle River, NJ: Prentice Hall.

Gutek, G. L. (2001). *Historical and philosophical foundations of education* (2nd ed.). Upper Saddle River, NJ: Merrill/Prentice Hall.

Gutek, G. L. (2004). *Philosophical and ideological voices in education.* New York: Allyn & Bacon.

Hale, L. (2002). *Native American handbook: A reference handbook.* Santa Barbara, CA: ABC-CLIO.

Hamilton, B. E., Martin, J. A., & Sutton, P. D. (2005). *Births: Preliminary data for 2003.* Retrieved April 10, 2005, from http://www.cdc.gov/mmwr/preview/mmwrhtml/mm5404a6.htm

Hardy, L. (2002). The new federal role. *American School Board Journal, 189*(9), 20–24.

Hare, N., & Swift, D. W. (1976). Black education. In D. W. Swift (Ed.), *American education: A sociological view.* Boston: Houghton Mifflin.

Harper, V. B., Jr. (2005). The new student–teacher channel. *T.H.E. Journal, 33*(3), 30–32.

Harris, L., & Associates, Inc. (1996). *The Metropolitan Life survey of the American teacher 1996: Part II. Students voice their opinions on their education, teachers, and schools.* New York: Metropolitan Life Insurance Co.

Haynes, C. C. (2001). *Religious liberty and the public schools.* Bloomington, IN: Phi Delta Kappa Educational Foundation.

Hazelwood School District v. Kuhlmeier, 108 S. Ct. 562 (1988).

Heffernan, H. (1968). The school curriculum in American education. In *Education in the states: Nationwide development.* Washington, DC: Council of Chief State School Officials.

Henderson, J. G. (2001). *Reflective teaching: Professional artistry through inquiry.* Upper Saddle River, NJ: Merrill/Prentice Hall.

Henniger, M. L. (2004). *The teaching experience.* Upper Saddle River, NJ: Merrill/Prentice Hall.

Henriques, D. B. (2003, September 2). Rising demands for testing push limits of its accuracy. *New York Times,* p. A-1.

Henry J. Kaiser Family Foundation, National Public Radio, & Kennedy School of Government. (2004). *Sex education in America.* Washington, DC. Retrieved March 25, 2005, from http://www.siecus.org/pubs/fact/fact0017.html

Herbst, J. (1996). *The once and future school: Three hundred and fifty years of American secondary education.* New York: Routledge.

Hirsch, E. D., Jr. (1987). *Cultural literacy: What every American needs to know.* Boston: Houghton Mifflin.

Hlebowitsh, P. (2005). *Designing the school curriculum.* Boston: Pearson/Allyn & Bacon.

Hoff, D. (2004, February 4). Debate grows on true cost of school law. *Education Week,* pp. 1, 22.

Hoff, D. (2005, March 30). Online tools for sizing up schools debut. *Education Week,* pp. 1, 22.

Hoffman v. Board of Education of the City of New York, 400 N.E. 2d 317 (1979).

Hogan, P., & Smith, R. (2003). The activity of philosophy and the practice of education. In N. Blake, P. Smeyers, R. Smith, & P. Standish (Eds.), *The Blackwell guide to the philosophy of education.* Malden, MA: Blackwell Publishers.

Holland, H. M. (1995). Thurgood Marshall. *Encyclopedia Americana* (Vol. 18, p. 367). Danbury, CT: Grolier.

Holt, J. (1981). *Teach your own.* New York: Delacorte.

Holt, M. (2001). Performance pay for teachers: The standards movement's last stand. *Phi Delta Kappan, 83*(4), 312–317.

Hopwood v. Texas, 518 U.S. 1033 (1996).

Horn, A. M., Opinas, P., Newman-Carlson, D., & Bartolomucci, C. L. (2004). Elementary school bully busters programs: Understanding why children bully and what to do about it. In D. L. Espelage and S. M. Swearer (Eds.), *Bullying in American schools: A social-ecological perspective on prevention and intervention* (pp. 297–325). Mahwah, NJ: Lawrence Erlbaum.

Horn, R. A., Jr. (2002). *Understanding educational reform: A reference handbook.* Santa Barbara, CA: ABC-CLIO.

Horn, R. A., Jr. (2004). Empowerment of teachers and students. In J. L. Kincheloe & D. Weil (Eds.), *Critical thinking and learning, an encyclopedia for parents and teachers* (pp. 211–216). Westport, CT: Greenwood Press.

Hortonville Joint School District No. 1 v. Hortonville Education Association, 225 N.W. 2d 658 (Wis. 1975), *rev'd* on other grounds and remained, 426 U.S. 482 (1976), *aff'd,* 274 N.W. 2d 697 (Wis. 1979).

Howe, K. (1997). Understanding equal educational opportunity. New York: Teachers College Press.

Howell, W. (2005, March 9). School boards besieged. *Education Week,* pp. 32–33.

Hoyert, D. L., Kung, H., & Smith, B. L. (2005). *Deaths: Preliminary data for 2003: National Vital Statistics Reports.* Washington, DC: U.S. Department of Health and Human Services.

Human Rights Watch. (2005). Hatred in the hallways. Retrieved August 9, 2005, from http://www.hrw.org/reports/usigbt/final-04.htm

Hussar, W. (2005). *Projections of education statistics to 2014* (Report NCES 2005-074). Washington, DC: U.S. Department of Education, Institute of Education Sciences.

Hutchins, R. M. (1936). *The higher learning in America.* New Haven, CT: Yale University Press.

Illich, I. (1974). *Deschooling society.* New York: Harper & Row.

Illinois ex rel. McCollum v. Board of Education, 333 U.S. 203 (1948).

Imber, M., & van Geel, T. (2000). *Education law.* New York: McGraw-Hill.

Improving teaching quality. (2002, January 10). *Education Week,* pp. 79–80.

In re Thomas, 926 S.W. 2d 163 (Mo. App. 1996).

Ingersoll, R. M. (2004). The status of teaching as a profession. In J. H. Ballantine and J. Z. Spade (Eds.), *Schools and society: A sociological approach to education* (2nd ed., pp. 102–115). Belmont, CA: Wadsworth/Thomson Learning.

Ingraham v. Wright, 430 U.S. 651 (1977).

Jacobs, H. (1997). Designing with rigor: Crafting interdisciplinary high school curricula. The *High School Magazine, 4*(3), 32–37.

Jacobs, H. (2004). *Getting results with curriculum mapping.* Alexandria, VA: Association for Curriculum Development.

Jacobsen, D. (2003). *Philosophy in classroom teaching: Bridging the gap* (2nd ed.). Upper Saddle River, NJ: Merrill/Prentice Hall.

Jacobsen, D., Eggen, P., & Kauchak, D. (1999). *Methods of teaching: Promoting student learning* (5th ed.). Upper Saddle River, NJ: Merrill/Prentice Hall.

Jeglin v. San Jacinto Unified School District, 827 F. Supp. 1459 (C.D. Cal. 1993).

Jennings, J. (2002). Knocking on your door. *American School Board Journal, 189*(9), 25–27.

Johnson, J. G., Cohen, P., Smailes, E. M., Kasen, S., & Brook, J. S. (2002). Television viewing and aggressive behavior during adolescence and adulthood. Retrieved July 31, 2005, from http://www.sciencemag.org/cgi/content/abstract/295/5564.

Jones v. Clear Creek Independent School District, 977 F.2d 963 (5th Cir. 1992).

Joyce, B., Weil, M., & Calhoun, E. (2004). *Models of teaching* (7th ed.) Boston: Pearson/Allyn & Bacon.

Kaestle, C. F. (1983). *Pillars of the republic: Common schools and American society, 1780–1860.* New York: Hill and Wang.

Kagan, S. L., & Stewart, V. (2005). Introduction: A new world view: Education in a global era. *Phi Delta Kappan, 87,* 185–187.

Kamman, J. (2005, June 9). 1 in 2 Americans since 2000 is Hispanic. *Arizona Republic,* pp. A1, A13.

Kandel, L. L. (1948). *The impact of the war upon American education.* Chapel Hill: University of North Carolina Press.

Kaplan, G. (1990). Pushing and shoving in videoland U.S.A.: TV's version of education (and what to do about it). *Phi Delta Kappan, 71,* K11–K12.

Katz, L. G., & Chard, S. C. (2000). *Engaging children's minds: The project approach* (2nd ed.). Stamford, CT: Ablex.

Kauchak, D., & Eggen, P. (2005). *Introduction to teaching: Becoming a professional* (2nd ed.). Upper Saddle River, NJ: Merrill/Prentice Hall.

Kauffman, J. M., McGee, K., & Brigham, M. (2004). Enabling or disabling? Observations on changes in the purpose and outcomes of special education. *Phi Delta Kappan, 25,* 613-620.

Keefe, J., & Jenkins, J. (2002). Personalized instruction. *Phi Delta Kappan, 83*(6), 440-448.

Kellough, R., & Kellough, N. (2003). *Secondary school teaching: A guide to methods and resources* (2nd ed.). Upper Saddle River, NJ: Merrill/Prentice Hall.

Kerr, C. (1963). *The uses of the University.* New York: Harper & Row.

Keyes v. School District No. 1 of Denver, Colorado, 413 U. S. 189 (1973).

Kidwell, C. S., & Swift, D. W. (1976). Indian education. In D. W. Swift (Ed.), *American education: A sociological view.* Boston: Houghton Mifflin.

Kincheloe, J. (2004). *Twelve ways of looking at school.* Menlo Park, CA: Sunset Publishing.

Kincheloe, J. L., Slattery, P., & Steinberg, S. R. (2000). *Contextualizing teaching: Introduction to education and educational foundations.* New York: Longman.

King, J. (2004). Paige calls NEA "terrorist organization." Washington, DC: Cable News Network.

Kingsville Independent School District v. Cooper, 611 F.2d 1109 (5th Cir. 1980).

Kirkland, E. C. (1969*). A history of American economic life* (4th ed.). New York: Appleton-Century-Crofts.

Kliebard, H. M. (1995). *The struggle for the American curriculum, 1893-1958* (2nd ed.). New York: Routledge.

Kneller, G. F. (1971). *Introduction to the philosophy of education.* New York: Wiley & Sons.

Knight, E. W. (1952). *Fifty years of American education.* New York: The Ronald Press.

Knox County Education Association v. Knox County Board of Education, 158 F.3d (6th Cir. 1998), *cert. denied,* 120 S. Ct. 46 (1999).

Koenick v. Felton, WL 635622 (4th Cir. 1999).

Kohl, H. R. (1976). *On teaching.* New York: Schocken.

Kosciw, J. G. (2004). *The 2003 national school climate survey: The school related experiences of our nation's lesbian, gay, bisexual, and transgender youth.* New York: Gay, Lesbian, Straight Education Network.

Kotterman *v. Killian,* 972 P.2d 606 (1999).

Kozol, J. (1972). *Free schools.* Boston: Houghton Mifflin.

Kozol, J. (1991). *Savage inequalities.* New York: Crown.

Labaree, D. F. (2000). Resisting educational standards. *Phi Delta Kappan, 82*(1), 28-33.

Lamb's Chapel v. Center Moriches School District, 959 F.2d 381 (2d Cir. 1992), *rev'd,* 113 S. Ct. 2141 (1993).

LeCapitaine, J. (2000). Role of the school psychologist in the treatment of high-risk students. *The School Psychologist, 121*(1), 73-79.

Lee v. Weisman, 505 U.S. 577 (1992).

Lemon v. Kurtzman, 93 S. Ct. 1463 (1971).

Lerner, M. (1962). *Education and radical humanism.* Columbus, OH: Ohio State University Press.

Levine, D. U., & Levine, R. (1996). *Society and education.* Boston: Allyn & Bacon.

Lewis, A. C. (2002). New ESEA extends choice to school officals. *Phi Delta Kappan, 83,* 423-425.

Long, A. (2004), Cyber schools. *State notes.* Denver, CO: Education Commission of the States.

Lumsden, L. (2001). ERIC Digest: Uniform and dress code policies. Eugene, OR: ERIC Clearinghouse on Educational Management.

Lunenburg, F. C. (2000). *High school dropouts: Issues and solutions.* U.S. Department of Education. (ERIC Document Reproduction Service No. ED448239)

Lyotard, J. (1985). *The postmodern condition: A report on knowledge.* Minneapolis: University of Minnesota Press.

Madsen, D. L. (1974). *Early national education, 1776-1830.* New York: Wiley & Sons.

Magee, J. B. (1971). *Philosophical analysis in education.* New York: Harper & Row.

Mager, R. (1997). Preparing instructional objectives: *A critical tool in the development of effective instruction* (3rd ed.). Atlanta, GA: Center for Performance.

Maritain, J. (1941). *Scholasticism and politics.* New York: Macmillan.

Maritain, J. (1943). *Education at the crossroads.* New Haven, CT: Yale University Press.

Markow, D., & Martin, S. (2005). *The Metlife survey of the American teacher: Transitions and the role of supportive relationships.* Washington, DC: Harris Interactive.

Marsh, C., & Willis, G. (2003). *Curriculum: Alternative approaches, ongoing issues* (3rd ed.). Upper Saddle River, NJ: Merrill/Prentice Hall.

Martusewicz, R. A. (2001). *Seeking passage: Post-structuralism, pedagogy, ethics.* New York: Teachers College Press.

Mawdsley, R. D. (2000). Homeschools and the law. *ELA Notes, 35*(2), 4-5.

Mayer, F. (1973). *A history of educational thought.* Upper Saddle River, NJ: Merrill/Prentice Hall.

McCarthy, M. (1989). Legal rights and responsibilities of public school teachers. In M. C. Reynolds (Ed.), *Knowledge base for the beginning teacher* (pp. 255-266). New York: Pergamon.

McClelland v. Paris Public Schools, 742 S. W. 2d 907 (Ark. 1988).

McCollum v. Board of Education of School District No. 71, 333 U.S. 203 (1948).

McDaniel, T. R. (1989). Demilitarizing public education: School reform in the era of George Bush. *Phi Delta Kappan, 71*, 15-18.

McLaren, P. (2003). *Life in schools: An introduction to critical pedagogy in the foundations of education.* Boston: Pearson/ Allyn & Bacon.

McLaren, P., & Torres, C. A. (1998). Voicing from the margins: The politics and passion of pluralism in the work of Maxine Greene. In W. Ayers and J. L. Miller (Eds.), *A light in dark times: Maxine Greene and the unfinished conversation* (pp. 190-203). New York: Teachers College Press.

McManis, J. T. (1916). *Ella Flagg Young and a half century of the Chicago public schools.* Chicago: McClurg.

McNergney, R. F., & McNergney, J. M. (2004). *Foundations of education: The challenge of professional practice.* Boston: Pearson/ Allyn & Bacon.

Melzer v. Board of Education of the City School District of New York (2003). 336 F.3d 185 (2nd Cir. 2003).

Mendez et al. v. Westminister School District of Orange County, 64 F. Supp. 544 (S.D. Cal. 1946), *aff'd* 161 F.2d 774 (1947).

Mercurius, N. (2005). Scrubbing data for IBM. *T. H. E. Journal, 33*(3), 15-16, 18.

Metcalf, K. K., & Legan, N. A. (2002). Educational vouchers: A primer. *Clearinghouse, 76*(1), 25-26.

Metzl v. Leininger, 850 F. Supp. 740 (Ill. 1995).

Meyer, A. E. (1972). *An educational history of the Western world.* New York: McGraw-Hill.

Miller, P. C., & Endo, H. (2004). Understanding and meeting the needs of ESL students. *Phi Delta Kappan, 85*, 786-791.

Mills v. Board of Education of the District of Columbia, 348 F. Supp. 866 (D.D.C. 1972).

Minard, S. (1993). The school counselor's role in confronting child abuse. *The School Counselor, 41*, 9-15.

Mitchell v. Helms, 120 S. Ct. 2530 (2000).

Monroe, P. (1939). *Source book of the history of education for the Greek and Roman period.* New York: Macmillan.

Monteiro v. Tempe Union High School Dist., 158 F.3d 1022 (9th Cir. 1998).

Morris, V. C., & Pai, Y. (1976). *Philosophy in the American school.* Boston: Houghton Mifflin.

Morrow, R. D. (1991). The challenges of Southeast-Asian parental involvement. *Principal, 70*, 20-22.

Mueller v. Allen, 103 S. Ct. 3062 (1983).

Nabozny v. Podlesny, 92 F.3d 446 (7th Cir. 1996).

National Board for Professional Teaching Standards. (2000). *National Board for Professional Teaching Standards.* Retrieved April 7, 2005, from http://www.nbpts.org

National Board for Professional Teaching Standards. (2001). *National board certification.* Arlington, VA: Author.

National Board for Professional Teaching Standards. (2002). *What teachers should know and be able to do.* Arlington, VA: Author.

National Board for Professional Teaching Standards. (2005). *About NBPTS.* Retrieved August 28, 2005, from http://www. nbpts.org/aboutus/newscenter.2005

National Center for Alternative Certification. (2005). Reciprocity and acceptance of teaching certification across state lines. Retrieved June 30, 2005, from http://www.teach-now.org/frm. ReciprocityAndAceptance.asp

National Center for Education Information. (2005). *Profile of teachers in the U.S. 2005.* Washington, DC: Author.

National Clearinghouse for Alcohol and Drug Information. (1998). *Youth oriented prevention initiatives.* Retrieved March 10, 1998, from http://www.health.org/ndcs98/iv-.html

National Commission on Excellence in Education. (1983). *A nation at risk: The imperative for educational reform.* Washington, DC: U.S. Government Printing Office.

National Commission on the States. (2005). Negative sanctions: Dropouts don't drive. Telephone interview August 2, 2005.

National Conference of State Legislatures. (2005, February 23). *State legislators offer formula for improving No Child Left Behind.* Retrieved April 6, 2005, from http://www.ncsl.org/ programs/press/2005/pr050223.htm

National Council for the Accreditation of Teacher Education. (2002). *Professional standards for the accreditation of schools, colleges, and departments of education.* Washington, DC: Author.

National Education Association. (1933). *Current conditions in our nation's schools.* Washington, DC: Author.

National Education Association. (2001a, November 9). *American Indian education on the upswing.* Retrieved January 23, 2002, from http://www.nea.org

National Education Association, Health Information Network. (2001a). *National youth anti-drug media campaign.* Washington, DC: Author.

National Education Association, Health Information Network. (2001b). *School-based HIV, STD, and pregnancy prevention education: What Works?* Washington, DC: Author.

National Education Association. (2005a). *Rankings & estimates: Rankings of the states 2004 and estimates of school statistics 2005.* Washington, DC: Author.

National Education Association. (2005b). *NEAFT partnership.* Washington, DC: Author. Retrieved July 14, 2005, from https:// www.nea.org/aboutnea/NEAFTPartnership.html

National Education Association. (2005c). Vouchers. In *Issues in Education.* Washington, DC: Author.

National Institute on Drug Abuse. (1997). *Facts supporting NIDA's drug abuse and AIDS prevention campaign for teens* (Capsule Series C-90-01). Washington, DC: Author.

National Institute on Drug Abuse. (2005a). *Consequences of the abuse of anabolic steroids.* Retrieved April 8, 2005, from http://www.drugabuse.gov/about/welcome/messagesteroids305.html

National Institute on Drug Abuse. (2005b). *Ecstasy/MDMA.* Retrieved April 8, 2005, from http://nida/hih.gov/DrugPages/MDMA.html

National Institute on Drug Abuse. (2005c). *Inhalant abuse is an emerging public health problem.* Retrieved April 8, 2005, from http://www.nida.hih.gov/about/welcome/messageInhalants105.html

National Institute on Drug Abuse. (2005d). *Teen drug use declines 2003-2004, but concerns remain about inhalants and painkillers.* Retrieved April 8, 2005, from http://www.drugabuse.gov/Newsroom/04/NR12-21.html

National Institute on Drug Abuse. (2005e). *Preventing drug abuse among children and adolescents.* Retrieved December 13, 2005, from http://www.nida.nih.gov/Prevention/principles.html

National Policies Commission. (1941). *The Civilian Conservation Corps, the National Youth Administration, and the public schools.* Washington, DC: National Education Association.

Neill, A. S. (1960). *Summerhill: A radical approach to child rearing.* New York: Hart.

New Jersey, Petitioner v. T.L.O., 105 S. Ct. 733 (1985).

Newcomer, M. (1959). *A century of higher education for women.* New York: Harper & Brothers.

Newman, J. W. (1998). *America's teachers.* New York: Longman.

NMSA. (2005). New Mexico Revised Statutes, Sec. 22-10A-7-12.

No Child Left Behind Act. (2001). P.L. 107-102, Title I, Section 1111(2)(A).

Noddings, N. (1992). *The challenge to care in schools: An alternative approach to education.* New York: Teachers College Press.

Noddings, N. (1995). *Philosophy of education.* Boulder, CO: Westview Press.

Northwest Regional Educational Laboratory. (2005). *The catalog of school reform models.* Portland, OR: Author.

Null v. Board of Education of the County of Jackson, 815 F. Supp. 937 (S.D. W. Va. 1993).

Oakes, J., & Lipton, M. (2004). Forward. In J. J. Romo, P. Bradfield, & R. Serrano (Eds.), *Reclaiming democracy: A multicultural educators' journey toward transformative teaching* (pp. vii–ix). Upper Saddle River, NJ: Merrill/Prentice Hall.

O'Conner v. Ortega, 480 U.S. 709 (1987).

Odden, A. (2000). Paying teachers for performance. *School Business Affairs, 66*(6), 28–31.

Olson, L. (2003, January 9). The great divide. *Education Week,* pp. 9–16.

Orfield, G. (2001). *Schools more separate: Consequences of a decade of resegregation.* Cambridge, MA: Harvard University, The Civil Rights Project..

Orlich, D., Harder, R., Callahan, R., & Gibson, H. (1998). *Teaching strategies: A guide to better instruction.* Boston: Houghton Mifflin.

Ozmon, H. A., & Craver, S. M. (2003). *Philosophical foundations.* Upper Saddle River, NJ: Merrill/Prentice Hall.

Painter, B. (2001). Using teaching portfolios. *Educational Leadership, 58*(5), 31–34.

Pang, V. O. (2005). *Multicultural education: A caring-centered, reflective approach.* New York: McGraw-Hill.

Parkay, F. W., & Stanford, B. H. (1995). *Becoming a teacher* (3rd ed.). Boston: Allyn & Bacon.

Partelli, J. P. (1987). Analytic philosophy of education: Development and misconceptions. *Journal of Educational Thought, 21*(1), 20–24.

Pavlov, I. (1927). *Conditional reflexes: An investigation of the physiological activity of the cerebral cortex* (G. V. Anrep, Trans.). London: Oxford University Press.

Peloza v. Capistrano Unified School District, 37 F.3d 517 (9th Cir. 1994), *cert. denied,* 115 S. Ct. 2640 (1995).

Pennsylvania Association of Retarded Citizens v. Commonwealth of Pennsylvania, 343 F. Supp. 179 (E.D. Pa. 1972).

Perkinson, H. J. (1977). *The imperfect panacea: American faith in education, 1965–1976* (2nd ed.). New York: Random House.

Peter, K., & Hern, L. (2005). *Gender differences in participation and completion of undergraduate education and how they have changed over time.* Retrieved April 5, 2005, from http://nces.ed.gov/das/epubs/2005169/gender_2asp

Peter W. v. San Francisco Unified School District, 131 Cal. Rptr. 854 (Cal. App. 1976).

Piaget, J. (1951). *The child's conception of the world.* New York: The Humanties Press.

Pickering v. Board of Education, 391 U.S. 563 (1968).

Pierce v. Society of Sisters, 268 U.S. 510 (1925).

Pierce v. Sullivan West Central School District, 2004 WL 1789894 (2nd Cir 2004).

Pifer, A. (1973). *The higher education of blacks in the United States.* New York: Carnegie.

Planeaux, C. (1999). *Christopher's Plato: The academy.* Retrieved August 1, 2005, from http://php.iupui.edu/~cplaneau/Plato%20and%20His%20World.Plato%20Academy%Introduction.html

Plato. (1958). *The Republic* (F. Carnford, Trans.). New York: Oxford University Press. (Original work 360 B.C.)

Plato. (360 B.C.). Laws, VII, p. 805.

Plessy v. Ferguson, 163 U.S. 537, 16 S. Ct. 1138 (1896).

Plyler v. Doe, 457 U.S. 202 (1982).

Podoll, S., & Randle, D. (2005). Building a virtual high school click by click. *T.H.E. Journal, 33*(2), 14–15, 17–19.

Poland, S., & McCormick, J. S. (1999). *Coping with crisis: Lessons learned*. Longmont, CO: Sopris West.

Posner, G. (1998). Models of curriculum planning. In L. Beyer & M. Apple (Eds.), *The curriculum: Problems, politics and possibilities* (pp. 79–100). Albany: State University of New York Press.

Power, E. J. (1982). *Philosophy of education: Studies in philosophies, schooling and educational policies*. Upper Saddle River, NJ: Prentice Hall.

President's Advisory Commission on Educational Excellence for Hispanic Americans. (2000). *Creating the will: Hispanics achieving educational excellence*. Washington, DC: Author. (ERIC Document Reproduction Service No. ED446195)

Prince v. Jacoby, 303 F 3d. 1074 (9th Cir. 2002).

Progressive Education. (1924). pp. 1, 2.

Provasnik, S., & Dorfman, S. (2005). *Mobility in the teacher workforce* (Report NCES 2005-114). Washington, DC: U.S. Department of Education, National Center for Education Statistics.

Pugh, M. J., & Hart, D. (1999). Identity development and peer group participation. *New Directions for Child and Adolescent Development, 84*, 55-70.

Pulliam, J. D., & Van Patten, J. (2003). *History of education in America* (8th ed.). Upper Saddle River, NJ: Merrill/Prentice Hall.

Pyle v. South Hadley School Community, 861 F. Supp. 157 (D. Mass. 1994), *vacated*, 55 F.3d 20 (1st Cir. 1996).

Quality counts. (2002, Jaunuary 9). *Education Week*, pp. 3-34.

Random House Webster's College Dictionary. (2001). New York: Random House.

Ravitch, D. (1983). *The troubled crusade—American education, 1945-1980*. New York: Basic Books.

Ravitch, D. (2000). *Left back: A century of failed school reforms*. New York: Simon & Schuster.

Ravitch, D., & Finn, C. E. (1987). *What do our 17 year olds know? A report on the first national assessment of history and literature*. New York: Harper & Row.

Regents of the University of California v. Alan Bakke, 438 U.S. 265 (1978).

Reitmeyer v. Unemployment Compensation Board of Review, 602 A. 2d 505 (Pa. Commw. 1992).

Richard, A., & Samuels, C. (2005, February 23). Legislatures hit with a surge of school choice plans. *Education Week*, p. 8.

Rickover, H. G. (1963). *Education and freedom*. New York: New American Library.

Riordan, C. (1990). *Girls and boys in school: Together or separate?* New York: Teachers College Press.

Rippa, S. A. (1997). *Education in a free society: An American history* (8th ed.). New York: Longman.

Roberts v. City of Boston, 59 Mass. (5 Cush.) 198 (1850).

Rogers, C. R. (1961). *On becoming a person: A therapist's view of psychotheraphy*. Boston: Houghton Mifflin.

Rorty, R. (1998). *Philosophers of education: Historical perspectives*. London: Routledge.

Rose, L. C., & Gallup, A. (2000). The 32nd annual Gallup Poll of the public's attitudes toward the public schools. *Phi Delta Kappan, 82*(1), 41-58.

Rose, L. C., & Gallup, A. M. (2004). The 36th Annual Phi Delta Kappa poll of the public's attitudes toward the public schools. *Phi Delta Kappan, 86*(1), 41-58.

Rose, L. C., & Gallup, A. (2005). The 37th annual Phi Delta Kappa poll of the public's attitude toward the public schools. *Phi Delta Kappan, 87*(1), 41-57.

Rose, S. J. (2000). *Social stratification in the United States*. New York: New Press.

Rother, C. (2005). Is technology changing how you teach? *T.H.E. Journal 33*(3), 34-36.

Rothstein, R. (2004). A wider lens on the black-white achievement gap. *Phi Delta Kappan, 86*, 105-110.

Sadker, D. (2001). Gender equity: Still knocking at the classroom door. *Equity & Excellence in Education, 33*(1), 80-83.

Sadker, M., & Sadker, D. (1997). *Teachers, schools and society*. New York: McGraw-Hill.

Sadovnik, A. R. (2004). Theories in the sociology of education. In J. H. Ballantine & J. Z. Spade (Eds.), *Schools and society: A sociological approach to education* (pp. 7-26). Belmont, CA: Wadsworth/Thomson Learning.

Salend, S. J. (2005). *Creating inclusive classrooms: Effective and reflective practices* (5th ed.). Upper Saddle River, NJ: Merrill/Prentice Hall.

San Antonio Independent School District v. Rodriguez. 411 U.S. 1 (1973).

San Diego State University. (1996). *Constructivism*. Retrieved May 18, 1998, from http:// edweb.sdsu.edu/courses/edtec540

Sandler, B. R. (2004). The chilly climate: Subtle ways in which women are often treated differently at work and in classrooms. In J. Z. Spade and C. G. Vallentine (Eds.), *The kaleidoscope of gender: Prism, patterns, and possibilities* (pp. 187-191). Belmont, CA: Wadsworth/Thomson Learning.

Santa Fe Independent School District v. Doe, 120 S. Ct. 2266 (2000).

Santelli, J. D., Abma, J., Ventura, S, Lindberg, L, Morrow, B., Anderson, J. E., et al. (2004). Can changes in behaviors among high school students explain the decline in teen pregnancy rates in the 1990s? *Journal of Adolescent Health, 35*, 80-90.

Sappenfield, M. (2002). Mounting evidence links TV viewing to violence. Retrieved July 31, 2005, from http://www.csmonitor.com

Sartre, J. P. (1956). *Being and nothingness* (H. Barnes, Trans.). New York: Philosophical Library.

Scheffler, I. (1960). *The language of education*. Springfield, IL: Thomas.

Schmid, C. (2001). Educational achievement, language-minority students, and the new second generation. *Sociology of Education, 74* (extra issue), 71–87.

School Board of Nassau County v. Arline, 107 S.Ct. 1129 (1987).

School District of Abington Township v. Schempp, 374 U.S. 203 (1963).

Scott v. Savers Property and Casualty Insurance Co. (2003), No. 01-2953 (Wis. June 19, 2000).

Sendor, B. B. (1997). *A legal guide to religion and public education* (2nd ed.). Dayton, OH: Education Law Association.

Serrano v. Priest, 487 P. 2d 1241 (1971).

Settle v. Dickson County School Board, 53 F.3d 152 (6th Cir. 1995).

Shafritz, J. M., Koeppe, R. P., & Soper, E. E. (1988). *The Facts on File dictionary of education.* New York: Facts on File.

Sherman v. Consolidated District 21 of Wheeling Township, 980 F.2d 437 (7th Cir. 1992), *cert. denied,* 508 U.S. 950 (1993).

Silberman, C. (1970). *Crisis in the classroom.* New York: Random House.

Silver, H., Strong, R., & Perini, M. (2000). *So each may learn.* Alexandria, VA: Association for Supervision and Curriculum Development.

Skinner, R. (2005, January 6). State of the states. *Education Week,* p. 80.

Skinner v. Railroad Labor Executive Association, 489 U. S. 602 (1989).

Slavin, R. (1989). Research on cooperative learning: Consensus and controversy. *Educational Leadership, 47*(4), 52–54.

Sleeter, C. E., & Grant, C. A. (2002). *Making choices for multicultural education: Five approaches to race, class, and gender* (4th ed.). New York: John Wiley & Sons.

Smith, B. O. (1987). Definitions of teaching. In M. J. Durkin (Ed.), *The international encyclopedia of teacher education.* New York: Pergamon.

Soltis, J. F. (1978). *An introduction to the analysis of educational concepts.* Reading, MA: Addison-Wesley.

Sommers, C. H. (2000). *The war against boys: How misguided feminism is harming our young men.* New York: Simon & Schuster.

Sowell, E. (2005). *Curriculum: An integrative introduction* (3rd ed.). Upper Saddle River, NJ: Merrill/Prentice Hall.

Sowell, T. (1984). *Civil rights: Rhetoric or reality.* New York: William Morrow.

Spade, J. Z. (2004). Gender and education in the United States. In J. H. Ballentine and J. Z. Spade (Eds.), *Schools and society: A sociological approach* (2nd ed.). Belmont, CA: Thomson Learning.

Spark, D. (2004, September). *Principals as leaders of learning. Results.* Oxford, OH: National Staff Development Council.

Sperry, D. J., Daniel, P. T. K., Huefner, D. S., & Gee, E. G. (1998). *Education law and the public schools: A compendium* (2nd ed.). Norwood, MA: Christopher-Gordon.

Spring, J. (1976). *The sorting machine: National educational policy since 1945.* New York: McKay.

Spring, J. (1998). *American education: An introduction to social and political aspects.* Upper Saddle River, NJ: Merrill/Prentice Hall.

Spring, J. (2004). *American education* (11th ed). New York: McGraw-Hill.

Spring, J. (2005). *The American school, 1642–2004* (6th ed.). New York: McGraw-Hill.

St. Charles, J., & Costantino, M. (2000). *Reading and the Native American learner: Research report.* Olympia, WA: Office of the State Superintendent of Public Instruction, Office of Indian Education.

Stain v. Cedar Rapids Community School District, 626 N.W. 2d 115 (Iowa 2001).

Stein, C. B., Jr. (1986). *Sink or swim: The politics of bilingual education.* New York: Praeger.

Stephens, J. E., & Harris, J. J., III. (2000). Teacher shortage: Implications for educators of color. *School Business Affairs, 66*(6), 44–47, 53.

Stephenson v. Davenport Community School District, 110 F.3d 1303 (8th Cir. 1997).

Stewart, V. (2005). A world transformed: How other countries are preparing students for the interconnected world of the 21st century. *Phi Delta Kappan, 87,* 209–212.

Stewart, V., & Kagan, S. L. (2005). Conclusion: A new world view: Education in a global era. *Phi Delta Kappan, 87,* 241–245.

Stoddard, L. (2004, March 3). The best thing we can do for children? Let teachers act as professionals. *Education Week,* pp. 37–38.

Stone v. Graham, 449 U.S. 39 (1980).

Stroman v. Colleton County School District, 981 F.2d 152 (4th Cir. 1992).

Suárez-Orozco, M. M. (2005). Conclusion: A new world view: Education in a global era. *Phi Delta Kappan, 87,* 209–212.

Sullivan v. River Valley School District, 20 F. Supp. 2d 1120 (W.D. Mich. 1998).

Sutton, T. (2003). *Dropouts: An abiding educational issue.* Retrieved April 5, 2005, from http://www.mssutton.com/portfolio/drop_out_rates_page.htm

Swann v. Charolotte-Mecklenburg Board of Education, 403 U.S. 1 (1971).

Swartz, J. (2005, March 7). Schoolyard bullies get nastier online: Hurtful messages can hit kids anytime, anywhere. *USA Today,* pp. 1–2A.

Sweatt v. Painter, 339 U. S. 629 (1950).

Szasz, M. C. (1999). *Education and the American Indian: The road to self-determination since 1928* (3rd ed.). Albuquerque, NM: University of New Mexico Press.

Szasz, M. C. (1988). *Indian education in the American colonies: 1607–1783.* Albuquerque, NM: University of New Mexico Press.

Taba, H. (1966). *Teaching strategies and cognitive functioning in elementary school children.* San Francisco: San Francisco State University.

Tape v. Hurley, 66 Cal. 473 (1885).

Taxman v. Board of Education of Township of Piscataway, 91 F.3d 1547 (3d Cir. 1996).

Taylor, B. (2002). The effective schools process: Alive and well. *Phi Delta Kappan, 83*(5), 375–378.

Thompson v. Carthage School District, 87 F.3d 979 (8th Cir. 1996).

Tinker v. Des Moines Independent Community School District, 393 U.S. 503 (1969).

Tollett, K. S. (1983). *The right to education: Reaganism, Reaganomics, or human capital?* (p. 47). Washington, DC: Institute for the Study of Educational Policy, Howard University.

Toppo, G. (2001, August 6). 850,000 kids are being taught at home, study finds. *USA Today,* p. 5D.

Torres, J., Santos, J, Peck, N. L., & Cortes, L. (2004). *Minority teacher recruitment, development, and retention.* Providence, RI: The Education Alliance at Brown University.

Totah, K. A. (1926). The contribution of the Arabs to education. New York: Bureau of Publications, Teachers College, Columbia University.

Trinidad School District No. 1 v. Lopez, 963 P.2d 1095 (Col. 1998).

Trustees of Dartmouth College v. Woodward, 17 U.S. (4 Wheat) 518 (1819).

Tucker, M. S., & Toch, T. (2004). The secret to making No Child Left Behind work? More bureaucrats? *Phi Delta Kappan, 86,* 28–33.

Tyler, R. W. (1949). *Basic principles of curriculum and instruction.* Chicago: University of Chicago Press.

UCLA Asian American Studies Center. (2005). *2005 statistical portrait of the nation's Asian and Pacific Islander populations.* Retrieved August 10, 2005, from http://www.sscnet.ucla.edu?aasc/change/data2005.html

Ulich, R. (Ed.). (1971). *Three thousand years of educational wisdom* (2nd ed.). Cambridge, MA: Harvard University Press.

United States v. Board of Education for the School District of Philadelphia, 911 F.2d 882 (3d Cir. 1990).

United States v. Place, 462 U.S. 696 (1983).

Updegraff, H. (1922). *Rural school survey in New York state: Financial support.* Ithaca, NY: Author.

U.S. Census Bureau (1975). *Historical statistics of the United States, colonial times to 1970* (Series H 316-326). Washington, DC: U.S. Government Printing Office.

U.S. Census Bureau. (2005a). *College degree nearly doubles annual earnings.* Retrieved July 31, 2005, from http://census.gov/Press-Release/www/releases/archives/education/004214.html

U.S. Census Bureau. (2005b). *Facts for features: African-American history month: February 2005.* Retrieved July 31, 2005, from http://www.census.gov/Press-Release/www/releases/archives/facts_for_specialeditions

U.S. Census Bureau. (2005c).). *Facts for features: Hispanic Heritage Month 2005.* Retrieved July 31, 2005, from http://www.census.gov/Press-Release/www/releases/archives/facts_for_specialeditions

U.S. Census Bureau. (2005d). *Facts for features: Women's history month: March 2005.* Retrieved July 31, 2005, from http://www.census.gov/Press-Release/www/releases/archives/facts_for_specialeditions

U.S. Census Bureau. (2005e). *U.S. interim projections by age, sex, race, and Hispanic origin.* Retrieved July 31, 2005, from http://www.census.gov/ipc/www/usinteriumproj

U.S. Department of Education, National Center for Education Statistics. (1989). *The condition of education, 1989.* Washington, DC: U.S. Government Printing Office.

U.S. Department of Education, National Center for Education Statistics. (1991). *The condition of education, 1991.* Washington, DC: U.S. Government Printing Office.

U.S. Department of Education. (1993). *National excellence: A case for developing America's talent.* Retrieved August 12, 2005, from http://www.ed.gov/pubs/DevTalent/intro.html

U.S. Department of Education, National Center for Education Statistics. (1994). *The condition of education, 1994.* Washington, DC: U.S. Government Printing Office.

U.S. Department of Education, National Center for Education Statistics. (1997). *Job satisfaction among teachers: Effects of workplace conditions, background characteristics, and teacher compensation.* Washington, DC: U.S. Government Printing Office.

U.S. Department of Education, National Center for Education Statistics. (2004a). *Digest of education statistics, 2003.* Washington, DC: U.S. Government Printing Office.

U.S. Department of Education, Office of Safe and Drug Free Schools. (2004b). *Report on the implementation of the Gun Free Schools Act in the states and outlying areas, school year 2001–2002.* Retrieved July 10, 2005, from http://www.ed.gov/abouts/annual/gfsa/gfsarpt04.doc

U.S. Department of Education, National Center for Education Statistics. (2004c). *The condition of education, 2004.* Washington, DC: U.S. Government Printing Office.

U.S. Department of Education. (2005a). *Biennial evaluation: Report to Congress on the implementation of the state formula grant program.* Washington, DC: U.S. Government Printing Office.

U.S. Department of Education, National Center for Education Statistics. (2005b). *The condition of education, 2005.* Washington, DC: U.S. Government Printing Office.

U.S. Department of Education, National Center for Education Statistics. (2005c). *Digest of education statistics, 2004.* Washington, DC: U.S. Government Printing Office.

U.S. Department of Education, National Center for Education Statistics. (2005d). *Dropout rates of 16-to-24-year olds, by race/ethnicity: 1972-2003.* Washington, DC: U.S. Government Printing Office.

U.S. Department of Education, National Center for Education Statistics. (2005e). *The nation's report card: 2005.* Washington, DC: U.S. Government Printing Office.

U.S. Department of Education, National Center for Education Statistics. (2005f). *Status and trends in the education of American Indians and Alaska Natives.* Washington, DC: U.S. Government Printing Office.

U.S. Department of Education, National Center for Education Statistics. (2005g). *Trends in educational equity of girls and women: 2004.* Washington, DC: U.S. Government Printing Office.

U.S. Department of Health and Human Services, Centers for Disease Control and Prevention. (2004a). *Cigarette smoking among high school students—United States, 1991-2003.* Retrieved January 26, 2005, from http://www.cdc.gov/tobacco/research_data/youth/mm5323_highlights.htm

U.S. Department of Health and Human Services, Centers for Disease Control and Prevention. (2004b). *Smokeless tobacco.* Retrieved February 1, 2005, from http://www.cdc.gov/tobacco/factsheets/smokelesstobacco.htm

U.S. Department of Health and Human Services, Centers for Disease Control and Prevention. (2004c). *Trends in reportable sexually transmitted diseases in the United States, 2003.* Washington, DC: Author.

U.S. Department of Health and Human Services, Centers for Disease Control and Prevention. (2004d). Youth risk behavior surveillance—United States 2003. *Morbidity and Mortality Weekly Report, 53*(SS-2). Washington, DC: Author.

U.S. Department of Health and Human Services, Administration on Children, Youth, and Families. (2005a). *Child Maltreatment 2003.* Washington, DC: U.S. Government Printing Office.

U.S. Department of Health and Human Services, Centers for Disease Control and Prevention. (2005b). *HIV/AIDS Surveillance in Adolescents 2003.* Retrieved August 17, 2005, from http://www.cdc.gov/hiv/graphics/images/1265/1265-htm

Valente, W. D., & Valente, C. M. (2001). *Law in the schools* (5th ed.). Upper Saddle River, NJ: Merrill/Prentice Hall.

Ventura, S. J., Abma, J. C., Mosher, W. D., & Henshaw, S., (2005). *QuickStats: Pregnancy, birth, and abortion rates for teenagers aged 15-17 years—United States, 1976-2003.* Retrieved April 10, 2005, from http://www.cdc.gov/mmwr/preview/mmwrhtml/mm5404a6.htm

Vernonia School District v. Acton, 115 S. Ct. 2386 (1995).

Villegas, A. M., & Clewell, B. C. (1998). Increasing teacher diversity by tapping the paraprofessional pool. *Theory Into Practice, 37,* 121-125.

Vukadinovich v. Board of School Trustees of North Newton School Corporation, 47 Fed. App. 417 2000, WL 31159318 (7th Cir. 2002).

Wadsworth, D. (2000). A sense of calling. *American School Board Journal, 187*(10), 33-34.

Walker, D. F. (1971). A naturalistic model for curriculum development. *School Review, 80*(1), 51-65.

Walker, D. F., & Soltis, J. F. (2004). *Curriculum and aims* (4th ed). New York: Teachers College Press.

Walker, T. (2004). Something is wrong here. *Teaching tolerance, 26,* 40-43.

Wallace, J. M., Forman, T. A., Celdwell, C. H., & Willis, D. S. (2003). Religion and U.S. secondary school students: Current patterns, recent trends, and sociodemographic correlates. *Youth & Society, 35,* 98-105.

Wallace v. Jaffree, 105 S. Ct. 2479 (1985).

Walz v. Egg Harbor Township Board of Education, WL22038715 (3d Cir. 2003).

Ware v. Valley Stream High School District, 545 N.Y.S. 2d 316 (N.Y. App. Div.), *appeal denied,* 545 N.Y.S. 2d 539 (N.Y. 1989).

Washegesic v. Bloomington Public Schools, 33 F.3d 679 (6th Cir. 1994), *cert. denied,* 115 S. Ct. 1822 (1995).

Waters v. Churchill, 511 U.S. 661 (1994).

Waxman, H. C., Padron, Y. N., & Gray, J. P. (Eds.).(2004). *Educational resiliency: Student, teacher, and school perspectives.* Greenwich, CO: Information Age Publishing.

Webb, L. D., & McCarthy, M. M. (1998). Ella Flagg Young: Pioneer of democratic school administration. *Educational Administration Quarterly, 34,* 224-242.

Webb, L. D., McCarthy, M. M., & Thomas, S. (1988). *Financing elementary and secondary education.* Columbus, OH: Merrill.

Webb, R. B., & Sherman, R. R. (1989). *Schooling and society* (2nd ed.). Upper Saddle River, NJ: Merrill/Prentice Hall.

Weinberg, M. (1997). *Asian-American education: Historical backgrounds and current realities.* Mahwah, NJ: Lawrence Erlbaum.

Weinstock, H., Berman, S., & Cates, W. (2004). Sexually transmitted diseases among American youth: Incidence and prevalence estimates, 2000. *Perspectives on Sexual and Reproductive Health, 35*(1), 11-19.

West, E. (1972). *The black American and education.* Upper Saddle River, NJ: Merrill/Prentice Hall.

West Virginia State Board of Education v. Barnette, 319 U.S. 624 (1943).

Westbrook, J. (1982). *Considering the research: What makes an effective school?* Austin, TX: Southwest Educational Development Laboratory.

Westheimer, J., & Kahne, J. (1993). Building school communities: An experience-based model. *Phi Delta Kappan, 75*(4), 324-328.

White, J. & White, P. (2001). An analytic perspective on education and children's rights. In F. Heyting, D. Lenzen, & White, J. (Eds.), *Methods in philosophy of education* (pp. 13–29). London: Routledge.

Wiles, J. (2005). *Curriculum, essentials: A resource for educators* (2nd ed.) Boston: Pearson/Allyn & Bacon.

Wiles, J., & Bondi, J. (2002). *Curriculum development* (5th ed.). Upper Saddle River, NJ: Merrill/Prentice Hall.

Wilkins, A. S. (1914). *Roman education.* Cambridge, UK: Cambridge University Press.

Wingo, G. M. (1974). *Philosophies of education: An introduction.* Lexington, MA: Heath.

Wink, J. (2005). *Critical pedagogy: Notes from the real works.* Boston: Allyn & Bacon.

Winn, C., & Jacks, M. (1967). *Aristotle.* London: Methuen.

Wittgenstein, L. (1953). *Philosophical investigations.* New York: Macmillan.

Wittrock, M. C. (1987). Models of heuristic teaching. In M. J. Dunkin (Ed.), *The international encyclopedia of teaching and teacher education* (pp. 68–76). New York: Pergamon.

Woodward, W. H. (1906). *Studies in education during the age of the Renaissance, 1400–1600.* Cambridge, UK: Cambridge University Press.

World book special census edition. (2002). Chicago, IL: World Book.

Wraga, W. G. (2000). *The comprehensive high school in the United States: A historical perspective.* Paper presented at the annual meeting of the American Educational Research Association, April 2000, New Orleans, LA.

Wu, P., Hoven, C. W., Liu, X., Cohen, P., Fuller, C., & Shaffer, D. (2004). Substance use, suicide ideation, and attempts in children and adolescents. *Suicide and Life-Threatening Behavior, 34,* 408–420.

Wygant v. Jackson Board of Education, 106 S. Ct. 1842 (1986).

Zehr, M. A. (2001, November 7). GAO: Student achievement lagging at Bureau of Indian Affairs schools. *Education Week,* p. 12.

Zelman v. Simmons-Harris, 122 S. Ct. 2460 (2002).

Zelno v. Lincoln Intermediate Unit No. 12 Board of Directors, 786 A.2d 1022 (Pa. Commw. 2001).

Zigler, E., & Valentine, J. (Eds.). (1979). *Project Head Start: A legacy of the War on Poverty.* New York: The Free Press.

Zimmerman, F. J., Glew, G. M., Christakis, D. A., & Katon, W. (2005). Early cognitive stimulation, emotional support, and television watching as predictors of subsequent bullying among grade school children. *Archives of Pediatric & Adolescent Medicine, 159,* 384–388.

Zirpoli, T. J. (2005). *Behavior management: Applications for teachers* (4th ed.). Upper Saddle River, NJ: Merrill/Prentice Hall.

Zirpoli, T. J., & Melloy, K. J. (2001). *Behavior management: Applications for teachers.* Upper Saddle River, NJ: Merrill/Prentice Hall.

Zobrest v. Catalina Foothills School District, 113 S. Ct. 2462 (1993).

Zorach v. Clauson, 72 S. Ct. 679 (1952).

AUTHOR INDEX

Page numbers followed by "*n*" (such as 20*n*) indicate notes.

SUBJECT INDEX